BEHAVIOR IN ORGANIZATIONS
An Experiential Approach

Sixth Edition

A. B. (RAMI) SHANI, PhD
Professor of Organizational Behavior and Management

JAMES B. LAU, PhD
Professor Emeritus

*Both of California Polytechnic State University
San Luis Obispo*

IRWIN

Chicago • Bogotá • Boston • Buenos Aires • Caracas
London • Madrid • Mexico City • Sydney • Toronto

Irwin Book Team

Sponsoring editor: John E. Biernat
Editorial Assistant: Kimberly Kanakes
Marketing manager: Michael Campbell
Project editor: Ethel Shiell
Production supervisor: Pat Frederickson
Assistant manager, graphics: Charlene R. Breeden
Designer: Keith McPherson
Cover designer: Margaret Armour
Cover illustrator: Earl Keleny
Art studio: David Corona Design
Compositor: TCSystems, Inc.
Typeface: 10/12 Times Roman
Printer: Malloy Lithographing, Inc.

Times Mirror
Higher Education Group

Library of Congress Cataloging-in-Publication Data

Shani, Abraham B.
Behavior in organizations: an experiential approach / A.B. (Rami) Shani, James B. Lau.—6th ed.
p. cm.
Rev. ed. of: Behavior in organizations / James B. Lau. 5th ed., 1992.
Includes index.
ISBN 0-256-14115-0
1. Organizational behavior. 2. Group relations training. I. Lau, James Brownlee, 1916- Behavior in organizations. II. Title.
HD58.7.L37 1996
302.3′5—dc20 95-14431

Printed in the United States of America
1 2 3 4 5 6 7 8 9 0 ML 2 1 0 9 8 7 6 5

Acknowledgments

The sixth edition of this book is the outcome of ongoing dialogues with colleagues, students, and managers, all of whom share the fascination with fostering adult learning and discovery. We wish to acknowledge the many scholars, managers, and researchers who contributed to the text. We are indebted to all those individuals who granted permission for the use of figures, tables, cases, simulations, and activities. The rich input from many of the adopters of the book on how to continuously improve this product is appreciated. Their support gave us the vote of confidence to carry out this revision.

The book was shaped significantly by three colleagues: David Peach, Michael Stebbins, and Roger Conway at CalPoly State University. They have shared and put into practice a common belief that experiential learning is a synergistic and exhilarating way to teach and learn about organizational behavior and management. Rebecca Ellis, James Sena, Allan Bird, and Ram Krishnan at CalPoly; Robert Grant at Georgetown University; Torbjorn Stjernberg, Bengt Stymne, Jan Lowstedt, and Peter Docherty at the Stockholm School of Economics; Dov Eden at Tel-Aviv University; David Kolb and William Pasmore at Case Western Reserve University; Mary Ann Hazen at the University of Detroit; Thom Sepic at Pacific Lutheran University; Gervase Bushe at Simon Fraser University; Harvey Kolodny at the University of Toronto; and Yoram Mitki at Ruppin Institute have exchanged ideas, materials, and views with the authors over the years, many of which are reflected in the book.

As with the previous editions, our primary indebtedness is to our students who were involved in the origination, testing, and evaluation of most of the educational aspects of this text. We personally thank the following students—some of whom are now faculty members—for their direct contributions and suggestions that have been integrated into the text: James Craig, Anna Cunningham, Jennifer Fashing, Ian Keoki Ikemori, Maria-Elena (Mar) Radriguez, Martin Rogberg, Chris Roth, Anjali Saraf, Carol Sexton, James Sundali, and Jeff Trailer.

We would like to thank the following colleagues for the many suggestions they provided in reviewing the book.

Sixth Edition Reviewers

James W. Carr, *West Georgia College*

Jane Humble, *Arizona State University*

Esther Long, *The University of West Florida*

Chris Poulson, *California State Poly U-Pomona*

Charles Smith, *University of Southern Maine*

David Turnipseed, *Indiana University-Purdue University at Fort Wayne*

Fifth Edition Reviewers

John R. Aiello, Rutgers, *The State University*

Gerald L. Arffa, *Indiana University-Purdue University at Indianapolis*

Jane Burman-Holtom, *University of Florida*

Christine Clements, *North Dakota State University*

Elaine D. Guertler, *Augustana College*

Finally, our thanks to our families—Elaine, Talia, Liat, Leora, and Arlene—who have listened, watched, and continuously supported us as we tried to bring this project to completion.

A. B. (Rami) Shani
James B. Lau

Contents in Brief

Contents

List of Activities

List of Case Studies

Introduction

The first edition of this book was originated in the early 1970s, when there were few textbooks in organizational behavior (OB), and only a handful of educators recognized the need to teach OB experientially. Twenty years later, as we complete the sixth edition of this book, the Organizational Behavior Division is the Academy of Management's largest division, the Organizational Behavior Teaching Society has 500 active members, some scholarly journals have incorporated the term *organizational behavior* into their titles, and many basic textbooks are available on this subject. The original textbook launched what has become a continuing enterprise, the essence of which was to learn about organizational behavior in an experiential way and to go beyond trying to summarize the existing and growing body of knowledge.

We have used the OB approach in this text by focusing first on design and second on classroom management practices. A current OB emphasis is to influence behavior and outcome through use of design (the subject of Module 13), whether it be architectural, organization, work, or job design. In our case, we have designed a management workshop for this OB course to achieve our learning objectives. We have selected certain learning methods and sequences to implement the design. And we provide guidance for classroom management practices that creates a learning community in which behavioral and intellectual change occurs. In this sense, the instructors are managers of the educational design, the learning processes, the classroom, and the learning community, using the OB methods in which they are instructing the students. As managers, instructors are models of their own OB instruction.

As with the five preceding editions, this sixth edition of *Behavior in Organization* is designed first and foremost to meet needs we have not found satisfied in other texts. There are many continuities with prior editions, but there are some important changes to freshen and update the text. We revised the overall design of the book to include 18 stand-alone modules, such that the instructor can have more freedom in the design of the course to fit desire, knowledge base, and style. We strived to improve the balance between experiential activities, cases, and theoretical knowledge for each part and module; we reduced the number of modules to 18; we merged or deleted five modules; we added four modules to cover the important topics of diversity, dynamics between teams, technology and information technology, and quality management; we emphasized the international dimension of organizational behavior by more relevant discussion in the appropriate modules and by adding five new cases that focus on organizational behavior issues in other countries; and we increased considerably the number of activities (28 new activities) and case studies (nine new cases) by adding some fine original contributions from colleagues.

Major continuities with previous editions include our basic approach, aims, and emphasis. As before, the text is intended for use in an experiential learning course for undergraduate or graduate business administration students in a required organizational behavior core course. Thus, we provide basic coverage of essential OB topics. These topics are often taught solely by lectures and readings, a cognitive approach primarily emphasizing content. Content-based approaches do not deal adequately with the need for student involvement, nor do they help students acquire behavioral skills. In contrast, *Behavior in Organizations* emphasizes involvement exercises to help students quickly and effectively enter the process of thinking about behavior, applying concepts, and developing their own expertise. Lectures and readings are intended to bolster this process orientation. At the graduate level, we usually supplement our book with a book of readings.

Experiential methods provide a powerful stimulus for learning, growth, and change by helping participants focus on their own behaviors and reactions as data. For this very reason, some students may at first be uncomfortable about encountering experiential methods in a required course. (In contrast, students who have elected such courses are often eager and excited by experiential learning—or, if they find it threatening, they can quickly drop the course.) To help students deal with this problem, we begin with more structured, less personal exercises that are readily recognized as relevant to human effectiveness in organizational settings. Personal growth and self-understanding activities are introduced later in the text, after students have had enough experience to become more comfortable and ready for them.

This edition also retains its emphasis on bringing to the university classroom the type of training that supervisors, managers, and executives experience in management development programs. It includes methods of adult education such as team activities, role playing, case studies, in-baskets, and other simulation exercises. Managers generally will not sit through many lectures, nor do they find time for long reading assignments. But action-oriented exercises that provide a new conceptual input and permit them to apply their experience and share it with others are undertaken with great energy and involvement. Most of the activities in this text (or others similar to them) have been used successfully with supervisors, managers, and executives in education programs in our major industries and government agencies.

Since one of our objectives is to bring what is being done in management education into the college classroom in a basic course, there has been no attempt to be highly original in content or activities. Many activities have been written by the authors but are similar to others already in use. In this edition we have been fortunate to be able to include fresh activities and case studies written by creative colleagues. The theoretical and conceptual writings that integrate the activities are basic organizational behavior theory. Both theory and activities are intended to present an eclectic approach, and no attempt is made to take a position of advocacy, except for the experiential approach.

Alternative Plans for Using the Text

The design of the text allows instructors to adapt the course to the conditions under which they are teaching and the type of students with whom they work. It can be used in classes with time blocks of one, one and a half, two, three, or four hours by planning the activities and readings accordingly. The workload can also be adjusted for desired depth of coverage by following one of the three plans suggested in Figure A.

Figure A
Alternative Course Designs for Using This Text

Plan A: Complete selected activities and readings with classroom discussion.

Plan B: Complete Plan A and add the outside-of-class team task project described in Appendix A.

Plan C: Complete Plan A and add the in-class and outside-of-class team tasks described in Appendix B.

Plan A can be used when no homework is required other than the modules, activities, and case studies in the text. A basic supervisory or management course is frequently conducted in this manner. Plan B can provide the richest and most challenging approach. The teams complete an outside-of-class task project lasting throughout the course, which allows for the skills development and the application of course concepts to team members' own behavior. Plan C has the same objectives, but no task project; team activities are limited to classroom exercises and several outside preparatory meetings. The time requirements of plan B make it more appropriate for a semester course, while plan C can be readily completed in a quarter course.

The Course Topics

The sequence of the topics in this text is depicted in Figure B. The modules have been arranged to utilize the appropriate learning methods and to provide a generally logical development of the theory and concepts. Several considerations were important in the design.

Involvement learning proceeds best when it starts with the first class session and continues with growing intensity, particularly early in the course. Because students

Figure B
Sequence of Learning in the Course

	Levels of Focus				Areas of Focus				
Text Modules	Individual	Team	Interteam	Organizational	Diversity	Communication	Motivation	Perception	International
1.	Defining organizational behavior				X	X	X	X	X
2.	Learning styles	Team boundaries		Organizational dialoguing	X	X	X	X	
3.	Leadership style	Team skills		Organizational style	X	X	X		X
4.	The organization: systems, formal, and human				X				X
5.	Personality Personal growth				X	X	X	X	X
6.	Motivation	Group influence on motivation		Motivation and the human organization	X		X		X
7.	Perception				X	X	X	X	X
8.	Communication	Interpersonal communication	Intergroup communication		X	X	X	X	X
9.		Group problem solving and decision making		Organizational skills	X		X		X
10.		Small group dynamics			X	X	X		
11.	Manager effectiveness	Team building			X	X	X	X	
12.	Individual conflict	Team conflict	Interteam dynamics		X	X	X	X	
13.	Job design	Group work design	Organizational design		X	X	X	X	X
14.	Total quality management: system approach at all levels				X	X	X	X	X
15.	Creativity	Group creativity		Innovation	X	X	X	X	X
16.	Technology and IT: system approach at all levels					X	X	X	
17.	Organizational change and development: all levels					X	X	X	X
18.	Career planning and development			Organizational career management	X	X	X	X	X

come with the expectation that the classroom is a lecturer–listener, chairs-in-a-row environment, they will quickly lapse into that mode if the course structure does not avoid it. Thus there are class activities in the introductory modules. Students use their own experience to define organizational behavior (Module 1), and the classroom climate is established through dialoguing (Module 2).

Reinforcement and opportunities to apply learning are provided for by introducing major concepts early and studying their various aspects throughout the course. Thus the small group, a primary focus of the text, is introduced at the end of Module 2 and returned to at intervals throughout the course. Group processes and group skills are integrated throughout the duration of the course with a specific module (Module 9) on team problem solving and decision making halfway through the course: Module 10 on group dynamics and Module 11 on team building. In courses that adopt plans B or C, which require group projects, student groups can apply new theory and concepts to their own project teams throughout the course. Five pervasive core concepts—diversity, communication, motivation, perception, and international (see the right-hand columns of Figure B)—are discussed throughout the text in conjunction with other topics as the course progresses. This learning is integrated when the topics are addressed directly in later modules (Module 1 and 4 for diversity, Module 6 for motivation, Module 7 for perception, and Module 8 for communication).

The general logical sequence of material—progression from the micro to the macro—after the introduction proceeds through increasingly inclusive organizational levels, from individual behavior (leadership style, Module 3), to small-group and intergroup behavior in the middle of the course (for example, group problem solving and decision making, Module 9) to key organizational processes (for example, work and organization design, Module 13) to the effectiveness of the organization as a whole (Module 17).

The text has been divided into five parts. Statements at the beginning of each part provide previews of the coming modules and, in Parts 2 through 5, a review of material already covered. A more complete understanding of the subject areas and the learning method of the entire text can be achieved by reading through these statements at the beginning of Parts 1 through 5.

Human behavior in organizations is both fascinating and important to understand. It surrounds and concerns us all, and affects every aspect of our lives. Moreover, it is the heart of effective management. Students respond with great eagerness to organizational behavior concepts in a properly designed course. Their enthusiasm offers the quickest route to the working skills they will find essential in the organizational world. This text's main aim is to help them succeed.

Note to Participants

Please do not read ahead in this book unless the assignment at the end of the module or the instructor specifically instructs you to do so. The format of this book is to start many modules with an activity, and then to develop the concepts and theories using your experience as data. If you look at the activities ahead of time, some of the spontaneity of participation will be lost. You will miss out on the enjoyment and on an important part of the learning as well.

BEHAVIOR IN ORGANIZATIONS
An Experiential Approach

PART 1 THE ORGANIZATIONAL BEHAVIOR CONTEXT: MANAGING DIVERSITY, THE LEARNING COMMUNITY, THE MANAGER, AND THE ORGANIZATION

The exploration of behavioral issues in the context of the work organization is the focus of this course. The dual objectives set forth are individual and organizational learning. As such we are concerned with *how* you learn as well as *what* you learn about human behavior in organizations. The how and the what are closely connected in this course because so much of what you will learn is a process: a different way of looking at your own experience, a deeper way of understanding the power of attitudes or expectations, or a new awareness of how people experience work organizations. Management education strives to provide viewpoints and learn-by-doing methods that help participants ''walk through'' new learning. We use experience in this way. Your own experiences in this course will be the basic data to build your understanding. The activities of this course are structured to help you understand the behavior of people in organizations.

Management and executive workshops often spend the first hours or days developing a sense of community and deciding how to use experience and the interactions of participants for maximum learning. The workshop becomes a *learning community*—a community in this sense refers to a group of people with common interests, values, and purposes who meet regularly; it suggests supportiveness; it implies exchange of information as a primary process of community integration. Workshop participants find out about one another and about faculty, they become part of a team, and they learn more effective ways of interacting.

The climate that best promotes learning is one in which participants support one another, are open with one another about their responses, and are willing to confront or compare different responses, insights, and experiences. Learning to learn is important enough (and difficult enough) for managers to spend time building such a climate systematically. We too will spend time learning to learn and creating an appropriate climate. A key aspect of this sort of learning environment involves learning how to effectively utilize our own experiences and those of others.

Part 1 of this book is designed to accomplish these ends. Allocating the limited classroom time available for lectures and exercises is a continuous struggle for instructors using the experiential learning approach. The assumption in this ''workshop model'' is that class time will be used primarily for examining more intently a limited number of theories and concepts at the sacrifice of extensive content coverage in lectures and readings. However, many students feel the need for more complete cognitive learning. The modules lay the foundation for content learning. The references and endnotes provide a window into the extensive material available to enhance knowledge and understanding of the different topics covered in the organizational behavior area.

Preview of Part 1

The learning climate of the classroom is developed in the first two modules. In Module 1 and Activity 1–1, class members participate in a triad exercise in which each tells of an experience from his or her work. A number of participants then relate their experiences to the entire class. From these experiences, the topic areas of organizational behavior are constructed for the class by the professor to demonstrate that the behavioral study of the course has immediate relevance to everyone. Activity 1–2 provides an opportunity to explore the experience of individual differences at the workplace. A brief discussion of diversity and the management of diversity at the workplace is followed by a historical review of the evolution of the organizational behavior field.

In Module 2 and Activity 2–1, an open communication dialogue is practiced to examine the assumptions of the students and the professor that are relevant to the course and its learning goals. Content and process learning are discussed, and the first two activities are used as illustrations to enhance understanding of process (experiential) learning. Special emphasis is given to the role of the participant as a coach and contributor to the learning of others. A review of expectations and learning theories is followed by a discussion of the adult learner and experiential learning. The values of the learning community model are also discussed. Activity 2–2 provides an opportunity for the learner (1) to articulate individual learning objectives, performance goals, potential obstacles, and specific action statements in a contract and (2) to have the contract cosigned with the instructor.

Once the classroom learning climate is established, participants are assigned to working teams. Activity 2–3 is designed to foster team dialogue around the development of the team's name and the creation of the team's logo. The next substantive area focuses on management and leadership. We start Module 3 with Activities 3–1 or 3–2, which explore the meaning of leadership and management based on your own experiences. From these experiences, the topic areas of leadership and management are developed by the instructor. The multifaceted definition of leadership is followed by a synopsis of the debate on the differences between leadership and management. Next, we review different schools of leadership thoughts. Last, current themes and challenges are discussed. Activities 3–3, 3–4, and 3–5 provide alternative leadership diagnostic instruments, each of which is based in a different theory of leadership. The first case study, ''The Santa Theresa Family Services,'' is introduced as an important learning tool for facilitating the exploration of the organizational behavior topic—leadership and managerial challenges at the workplace.

Module 4 concludes this section by providing a conceptual framework and analytical tools to begin the investigation of the organizational context in which human behavior takes place. The organization is viewed as an open system. Activity 4–1 provides an opportunity to compare two different types of organizations and explore some key elements of organizations. Next we discuss characteristics of human and formal organizations. Two conceptual tools—the ''Operational Blueprint'' (Figure 4–1) and ''Actors Playing Their Roles'' (Figure 4–2)—are provided for the analysis of the work organization. The systems view of organizations is introduced as an alternative cognitive roadmap. The ''Transcal Petroleum Company'' case provides an opportunity to further explore the nature of organizations and their management.

The establishment of the learning method and climate through interaction exercises and the introduction of the framework of the content areas to be studied should satisfactorily prepare course participants for Part 2, which deals with the core concepts in understanding and managing individual behavior.

1 Organizational Behavior, Diversity, and the Manager

Learning Objectives

After completing this module you should be able to

1. Define the field of organizational behavior.
2. Explain why it is important to study organizational behavior.
3. Identify the relevant course topics.
4. Explain the importance of diversity, cultural diversity, and the management of diversity.
5. Summarize the historical evolution of the field.
6. Briefly describe the systems approach to understanding, managing, and directing people in organizations.
7. State the four levels of improving organizational effectiveness.
8. Explain some of the issues associated with rationality and irrationality in management.
9. Describe the objectives of the course.

List of Key Concepts

Administrative school
Behavioral science school
Classical era
Contingency school
Diversity
Effectiveness
Human relations school
Management
Management science school
Managing diversity
Modern era
Neoclassical era
Operational research school
Organizational behavior
Prescientific era
Rationality
Scientific management school
Sociotechnical school
Structuralist school
System
Systems school

Module Outline

Premodule Preparation

Activity 1–1: Defining Organizational Behavior

Objectives:

a. To identify course topic areas from your own work experiences.
b. To introduce involvement learning and to begin building the learning environment.
c. To introduce the communication skills of sharing, listening, and paraphrasing.

Task 1:

Your past work experiences often make interesting case studies. The worksheet for Activity 1–1 that follows presents three alternatives for selecting your case study. Your professor will assign one of these to the entire class or divide the class into three groups, one for each alternative. Use the worksheet for Activity 1–1 to make notes on your case study. (Time: Individuals have five minutes to think about their experiences and jot down notes.)

Task 2:

Participants form triads. Member A tells his or her case study and what it illustrates to Member B. Member B listens carefully and paraphrases back to A the story and what it illustrates. Member B must do this to Member A's satisfaction that B has understood fully what A was trying to communicate. Member C is the observer and remains silent during the process (a role many find difficult). Member B tells an experience to Member C, while A observes. Member C tells an experience to Member A, while B observes. (Time: Each member will have five minutes to relate a case study and have it paraphrased back by the listener. The instructor will call out the time at the end of each five-minute interval to allow for equal "air time" among participants. Total time: 15 minutes.)

Task 3:

Each group selects one of its members to relate his or her case study to the class. The instructor briefly analyzes for the class how the incident fits in with some topic to be studied in the course, such as motivation or leadership style. Topic areas are listed on the blackboard.

Task 4:

Questions for discussion: What are the general character and tone of the stories you have heard? What are the implications of these findings for managers who have the responsibility for persons similar to those in this class?

Worksheet for Activity 1–1

Make notes below on your case study for the alternative you were assigned for Task 1.

Alternative 1: Describe an experience in a past work situation that you think illustrates something about human relations in organizations. What does it illustrate?

Alternative 2: Describe a difficult problem you encountered while working. What caused the problem? What was done or could have been done to reduce or overcome the problem?

Alternative 3: Describe a work experience that illustrated good management. What happened? Why was it good? How did it affect you?

Introduction

Organizations in Transition

The economic, social, and political global trends coupled with the changing nature of the workplace present new challenges to individuals in organizations. The accelerated rate of technological development fosters the emergence of new behavioral patterns at every level of the organization. One of the many emerging trends is the increasing emphasis on teams and teamwork. Creating teams at work fosters the need to manage diversity or differences. Putting people in teams also means that we need to understand better (1) the sources of human diversity, (2) the dynamics between diverse individuals, and (3) the effects of diversity on individual motivation, communication, perception, competence, career development, work design, leadership, performance, team productivity, organizational development, and competitiveness.

Diversity

As a participant in a management course, you should find it of interest to speculate on the type of people with whom you will be working in your career. Look around you on campus and in this classroom. Note the ethnic, racial, gender, age, economic, regional, and cultural mixes. Are they representative of the country or your state? Are they representative of your fellow workers of the future? Of course, this will vary depending on your location; however, it is certain that your people mix will be different from that of the generation who preceded you. This is most obvious in gender ratios. How many women are there in this classroom? Probably about 50 percent. Twenty years ago, women in management courses accounted for nearer to 10 percent.

Managing Diversity

We open our textbook with the focus on diversity on the assumption that industry and business of the future will employ a more nearly representative mix of the population. Until the present, in most organizations, the white male culture has predominated. But numerous pressures are bringing about a natural transition just as recession and a tight economy have brought downsizing and restructuring to manufacturers. Marketing is a primary force. International competition is the keynote to our quality of life and financial success. This requires a continuous concern for accommodating our products to the need of a great range of nations abroad. And on the home front, businesses are ever more aware of the need to earn the goodwill of all to whom they are providing goods and services. More direct pressures, population pressures, will arise from the availability of professional and technical talent: There will be highly qualified personnel in all diverse groups, with no one element having enough to dominate the others.[1] This does not mean there will not be biases and prejudices to be reckoned with—there always will be. Legislation and regulations can alleviate this, but that is not a topic to be dealt with in our limited venture into organizational behavior.[2]

We choose an initial theme of diversity because it is timely; it is an issue that most individuals, managers, and organizations alike are struggling with. Much of what we have to say about the concepts of organizational behavior is related or can be illustrated in the context of this subject area. But at this point, let us step back and be more definitive about our course of study.

Behavior in Organizations

Behavior in organizations refers generally to different types of interactions: people interacting with people; people interacting with managers; people interacting with technology and information technology; people interacting with organizations; and people interacting with the culture created by themselves and management as they perform the tasks needed to achieve a variety of goals. Whenever a collection of people is brought together by managers to start up a business, they are creating a community. Not only must the ''citizens'' be trained for their roles and coordinated into work teams, but their needs must be provided for in a nurturing, inspiring climate. As the community takes form, it develops a social character unique to the organization. The manager in a sense is the mayor, the educator, and the trainer who makes it all happen. The process by which a collection of newly hired people is developed into a community of hard-working, productive, enthusiastic, comfortable citizens is difficult and complex. Coordinating and integrating diverse talents, educations, belief systems, and backgrounds into smoothly functioning interactions is a great challenge. Here the discipline of organizational behavior makes its contribution to commercial, educational, and other institutions.

Why Organizational Behavior?

Why is organizational behavior as a discipline for studying these interactions offered in a management course? First, the greater your awareness and understanding of how and why people react in work settings, the more comfortable you will be and the less stress you will feel. Second, understanding helps you predict what people will do under different circumstances. Third, understanding permits people and management to influence and guide behavior so that goals can be achieved more efficiently and, above all, more effectively.

The Systems Approach to Organizational Behavior

The Experience of Work

The work experiences described by participants in Activity 1–1 illustrate numerous topics to be discussed in this book. They include behavior of bosses, relationships with fellow workers, what makes people want to and not want to perform well, and communication problems. We can organize these subjects into a conceptual framework that will make organizational behavior easier to study in a systematic way by using the idea of effectiveness. **Effectiveness** as we will use it means the ability to achieve goals. Organizations and all groupings of people within them perform tasks to achieve goals. Organizational behavior provides guidelines for defining goals and methods for augmenting the process of attaining them. To organize the learning process, we use a systems approach to understanding, predicting, and managing people in organizations. Later we devote a complete module to the development of the systems analytical view of work and organizations. For this stage we define a **system** as an arrangement of interrelated parts.

Initial Framework

As an initial framework, we use the systems approach to study the collection of people making up an organization. The total unit is a system and the interacting groupings and individuals within are subsystems. We can create a systems approach to effectiveness as follows:

1. *Total organizational effectiveness:* This will include a definition of the overall purposes and goals of the organization. Thus business organizations must continuously determine whether they are in the right business to avoid becoming obsolete in a changing environment. Smalltown newspapers, for example, recently finding they could not survive solely as a press, have redefined their role to be that of distributor of advertising brochures. Management practices to divide up the responsibilities of all subunits may include managing by output. Practices that focus on continuous improvements and the improvement of service and product quality—Total Quality Management—are discussed in terms of total system effectiveness. Integrating people of diverse professions, skills, and cultural backgrounds into a harmoniously operating company may require leadership skills similar to those of a symphony conductor. Climate building provides a supportive environment for workers. Designing procedures for use of technology as well as providing education and training, particularly for managers, are other examples.

2. *Intergroup effectiveness:* Groups coordinating their processes to achieve company objectives must have well-developed methods of communication. Procedures for conflict prevention and resolution need to be understood and paracticed by interacting subsystems.

3. *Team effectiveness:* Small group skills related to teamwork design, goal setting, problem solving and creativity, communication, decision making, and conflict resolution must be used. Self-managed teams are currently emerging as a specific organized form of teams. Regardless of the specific team form, team skills require education and practice by both leaders and teams.

4. *Individual effectiveness:* Models of leadership styles appropriate for a specific organization are an important ingredient of managerial education and practice. The ability to perform well is the obvious focus for individual employees. But to go beyond that we must be concerned with the personal growth and development of all personnel. Skills in goal setting and interpersonal communication as well as attitudes toward failure and success are of prime relevance for the individual who must ever face a turbulent work world, a world always undergoing restructuring. Motivation to work is the driving force around which all other aspects of individual effectiveness can be viewed.

Understanding behavior in organizations can start with the total system and delve down into the subsystems or with the individual and work out into groups, on up to the whole. The specific order of the learning journey can vary from individual to individual and from situation to situation.

Rationality in Managing

In attempting to define our area of study, a special comment should be made about rationality. Typically, managers look at employee behavior from the viewpoint of how people ought to behave. People should make sense, they should do what they are supposed to do, and they should do what is good for the organization. After all, the basic definition of an organization is a rational model: people gathered together to achieve a purpose. Only logic, rationality, and objectivity—what makes common sense—can achieve that purpose. Specialty areas of business management, such as finance, engineering, marketing, accounting, and law, all are based on rational, logical models. Thus, **rationality** is a process that is based on logic and reason. When executives and managers participate in workshops and when students come to courses in organizational behavior, someone almost always makes the comment that understanding behavior is just a matter of common sense.

If rationality were our only concern in this field, there would be no study of behavior. Managers would simply plan, organize, direct, and control. But as shown in Figure 1–1, rationality is just the tip of the iceberg. Below the water line are forces that are potent generators of behavior: emotions, feelings, needs, stress reactions, impulsiveness, energy, creativity, conformity forces, loyalties, and groupthink, just to mention a few. Are we saying that managers do not know what is below that water level? Not at all. The problem is that managers are so involved in the rational model they often fail to take into account, or understand, the less rational forces. They are so involved with tasks, purposes, goals, deadlines, and balance sheets that they can become blinded to the realities below the surface until some eruption occurs.

An outstanding example is the *Challenger* space shuttle disaster. The blue-ribbon commission investigating the explosion came to this conclusion: "If the decision makers had known all of the facts, it is highly unlikely they would have decided to launch." Thus, management broke one of the oldest rules in the management book. Why? Many newspaper articles at the time reported that the entire management staff had become mesmerized by past successes. Information and dissent did not flow up the ladder to give input to the final decision makers. The objections to the launch by engineers who were aware of the shuttle's weaknesses were overruled and top management did not get the message. When we study groupthink later in the course we will have more to say about this, but for now our point is that the so-called mesmerizing factor does not belong to the world of rationality; it is below the water line in Figure 1–1.

Unions would probably not arise if managers were more fully aware and responsive to the behaviors at the bottom of the iceberg. Astronauts experienced a disastrous

Figure 1–1
Rational Behavior Is Only the Tip of the Iceberg

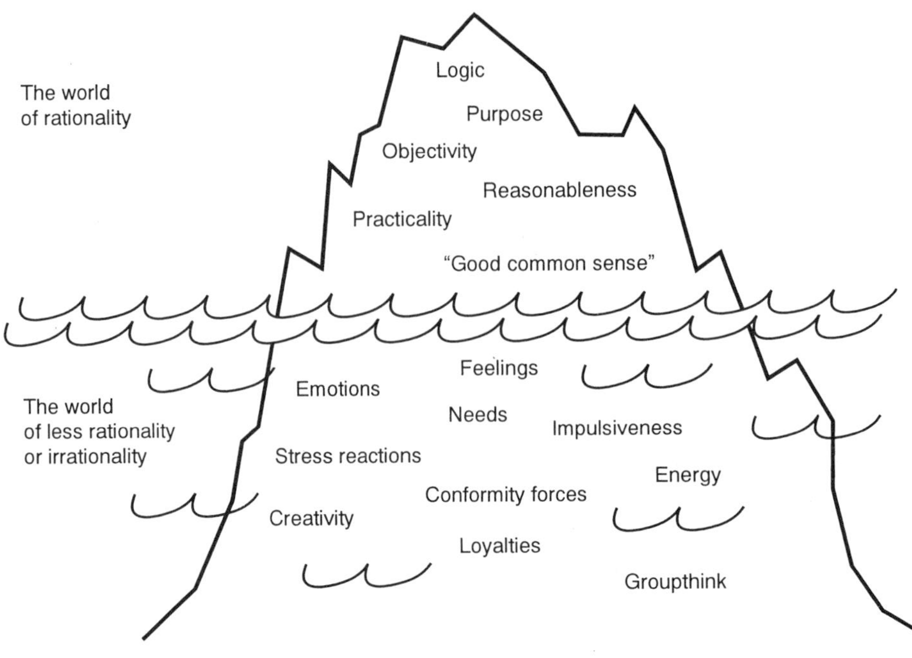

The study of organizational behavior focuses heavily upon the less rational aspects of human action and interactions in order to understand why people do not always behave according to the rational model of organizations.

shock to their trust in their organization when they learned that management had not informed them of the long-standing problem with the O-rings in the shuttle's boosters, which turned out to be a factor in the blowup of the *Challenger.* When this was revealed, the astronauts' representative made a number of protest speeches on their behalf.

It is fascinating to watch students in these courses switch perceptions from employee to management viewpoints and in the process completely forget or ignore what is below the water line. When students are engaged in task 1 from Activity 1–1 on defining human relations in business, over 90 percent of their examples are negative experiences that illustrate how little concern managers have for the factors below the water line. Yet by the time they assume the role of managers taking remedial action at a later stage in the course, they most always design solutions that take only the rational factors into consideration; they assume workers should respond rationally to management direction.

Our hope, an improbable one, is that managers will develop viewpoints that (1) maximize the human assets of employees for purposes of economic gain and (2) humanistically focus on quality. This presumes a more integrated awareness of the rational and irrational forces. In turn, we hope that employees develop more trust and understanding of the rational model, which is essential to help our industries become productive and competitive.

Organizational Behavior: Historical Evolution

Although discussions about management, administration, organization, and organizing can be traced to ancient Greek, Egyptian, and Biblical times, the study of management and organizational behavior as a distinct and separate field has largely been confined to the beginning of the 20th century. Today's theories are an integral part of the logical and natural evolution in management thought and practice. The systematic theorizing of the field has been clustered in many ways. For our purpose we follow the sociology of knowledge perspective that proposed four clusters: prescientific (pre-1880s), classi-

Figure 1–2

Historical Evolution of Management Thought: A Brief Roadmap

	Period			
	Prescientific pre-1880s	**Classical 1880–1930s**	**Neoclassical 1930–1960s**	**Modern 1960–present**
Emerging schools of thought		• Scientific management • Administrative school • Structuralist school	• Human relations school • Behavior schools: - Group dynamics - Leadership - Decision making	• Systems school • Sociotechnical system school • Management science school • Contingency school
Focus/emphasis	• Basic principles for nature and society • The position of authority and order in society • Economic rationale • Division of labor (early development)	• Basic principles of organizing and managing the most effective firm • The basic functions of managers • Characteristics of "the ideal type of an organization"	• Organizations are cooperative systems • Informal roles and norms influence individual performance • Work group dynamics influence individual and group performance • Leadership styles affect individual and group behavior • Decision making styles influence performance	• Organization is a system composed of subsystems • Organization as an open system composed of social, technological, and environmental subsystems • The use of quantitative methods to solve organization and managing issues • Exploration of alternative organization design configurations and managerial actions for changing situations
Representative scholars	• Jethro (Moses's father-in-law) • Sun Tzu • Socrates, Aristotle • Xenophon • Machiavelli • Adam Smith	• Taylor • Fayol • Gulick • Weber	• Berbard • Roethlisberger • Lewin • McGregor • Maslow	• Bertalanffy • Katz and Kahn • Emery and Trist • Thompson • Lorsch and Lawrence • Galbraith

cal (1880s–1930s), neoclassical (1930s–1960s) and modern (1960s–present).[3] Figure 1–2 captures the essence of each era.

The Prescientific Era (pre-1880s)

The **prescientific era** is characterized by little systematic theorizing about management and organizations. Yet we find Jethro's advice to Moses to delegate authority over the tribes of Israel along hierarchical lines around 1491 BC. Sun Tzu's *The Art of War* (written in 500 BC) recognizes the need for hierarchical organizations, interorganizational communications, and staff planning. Socrates's work, around 44 BC, argues for the universality of management as an art unto itself. Aristotle, around 360 BC, asserts that the nature and power of executive functions must reflect a specific cultural environment. Xenophon, around 370 BC, records and describes the Greek shoe factory focus on the advantages of the division of labor. Machiavelli's *The Discourses* (1513) and *The Prince* (1532) focus on both the principles of unity of command and how to succeed as a leader. Adam Smith's *The Wealth of Nations* (1776) describes the optimal organization of a pin factory and focuses on the economic rationale for the division of labor and the factory system.[4] The ruling class in the pre-industrial societies perceived work, trade, and commerce as being beneath their dignity, something to be accomplished by slaves and ''low-level'' classes.[5] The sources of authority were based on long-standing institutions and procedures that were perceived as legitimate by the citizens of these societies. Most individuals obeyed the ruling elite in accordance with traditional customs.[6]

The Classical Era (1880s–1930s)

The **classical era** of management thought evolved between the end of the 19th century and into the beginning of the 20th. The transition from agrarian to industrial society coupled with the changing economic, social, and technological environment established the condition to begin the systematic study of management and organizations. The focus of the early studies centered on the search for alternative ways to organize and structure the industrial organization; the way to organize, delegate, and coordinate work; and the ways to motivate people who work within the emerging organizational structures. Three dominant schools can be identified in this era:

The **scientific management school** led by Frederick Taylor focused on the measurement of work. It followed four basic principles of organization and management with the aim of creating the most effective way to carry out work tasks. The four basic principles included finding the one best way to do each job, the scientific selection of individuals for the position, the development of financial incentives that will ensure that the work be carried out as required, and the establishment of functional foremanship.[7]

The **administrative school** led by Henry Fayol focused on the functions of management. Five basic functions of management were identified: planning, organizing, commanding, coordinating, and controlling.[8]

The **structuralist school** led by Max Weber focused on the basic tenets of the ideal type of organization, the bureaucratic model, as the most effective way to organize and manage organizations. The model emphasized order via a system of rules and procedures, rational-legal authority, division of labor based on functional specialization, a well-defined hierarchy, differentiation between organizational functions, rationality, uniformity, and administrative consistency.

The Neoclassical Era (1930s–1960s)

The **neoclassical era** is characterized by direct challenges to the classical schools, their assumptions, and their implications. The neoclassical theories focused on the dimension of human interaction, which the classical schools neglected. During this era behavioral science theories were introduced and integrated with management thought. The theories are anchored in two major sources: social psychologists and sociologists who focused on human interactions and human relations within groups (the human relations or the group dynamics schools), and psychologists who focused on individual behavior in different settings (the behavioral science school).

The **human relations school** argued that organizations are cooperative systems and not the product of mechanical engineering.[9] The first large-scale empirical studies that focused on the relations between productivity and social interaction were conducted at the Hawthorne plant of the Western Electric Company. They illustrated the importance of workers' attitudes and feelings and argued that informal roles and norms influence individual performance.[10]

The **behavioral science schools** include three clusters of theories that were an outgrowth of the human relations school and focused on individual behavior within work groups:

Group dynamics focused on the effect of work group dynamics on individual and group performance.

Leadership stressed the importance of groups having both task and social leaders, differentiated between Theory X and Theory Y management, and identified different theories of leadership and leadership styles.

Decision making focused on the degree of individual involvement in decision making and its influence on performance. The contributions of these schools to our understanding of human behavior will be discussed in depth in the appropriate modules throughout this book.

The Modern Era (1960s–Present)

The **modern era**—or what some call contemporary management and organization era—is characterized by increased emphasis on integration of some key elements of the classical and neoclassical eras. The underlying assumption is that organizations are systems composed of interrelated and interdependent components that function within an environmental context. Throughout this course we explore in depth many key elements of the modern era schools of thoughts. Four clusters of schools can be delineated: systems, sociotechnical systems, management science, and contingency.

The **systems school** is anchored in general systems theory. The organization is viewed as a system composed of subsystems or subunits that are mutually dependent on one another and that continuously interact. General systems theory concepts such as holism, equifinality, equilibrium, input, transformation, output, and feedback provide the foundation for this school of thought (to be discussed in a later module).[11]

The **sociotechnical systems school** at the most basic level considers every organization to be made up of a social subsystem (the people) using tools, techniques, and knowledge (the technical subsystem) to produce a product or a service valued by the environmental subsystem. This school further argues that the degree to which the technical subsystem and the social subsystem are designed with respect to each other and the environmental subsystem determines how successful and competitive the organization will be.[12]

The **management science and operational research schools** of thought's orientation is to apply quantitative techniques, methods, and technologies to organization and management issues. The emphasis of this problem-solving approach is relatively narrow; it centers on merging strategic concern for planning and forecasting with the administrative concern for organizational objectives and goal accomplishment. Recently, the field of management science expanded its focus to include advanced technologies such as computer-integrated manufacturing, flexible manufacturing systems, and new manufacturing and integrated orientations such as just-in-time, total quality management, and reengineering.[13]

The **contingency school** seeks (1) to understand the relationships within and among subsystems as well as between the organization and its environment and (2) to define patterns of relationships or configurations of variables. The essence of this orientation is that there is ''no one best way'' and that there is a middle ground between ''universal principles'' and ''it all depends.'' Furthermore, the emphasis is on the degree of fit between organizational processes and characteristics of the situation. Contingency views are ultimately directed toward suggesting organizational designs and managerial actions most appropriate for specific situations.[14]

Core Concepts of the Course

Organizational behavior, to define it most broadly, is the utilization of theory and methods of multiple academic disciplines (such as anthropology, biology, economics, political science, psychology, social psychology, and psychology) for understanding and influencing behavior of people in organizations. Definitions of organizational behavior vary widely because the field has evolved with parallel developments in the social sciences, the behavioral sciences, and management and human relations courses in schools of business. One large frame of reference focuses on the differences between ''organizations without people'' and ''people without organizations.'' The former, the realm of organizational sociology, relates to organizations as systems interacting with their environment; the latter, the realm of psychology, relates to human relations in work situations. More recent approaches have emphasized the need for integrating these two realms to account for the great variability among people, tasks, and environment. Another point of focus is the macro–micro perspective. In the *macro view* the big picture is emphasized, such as the entire organization and its relationships to the environment. The *micro view* considers smaller units, such as the individual, work groups, or work systems. This text works with the micro initially and moves on to the macro as the course progresses.

There are four basic concepts that we will be applying as we go through all phases of the course: motivation and frustration; perception and perceptual distortion;

communication and misinformation; and diversity. These are dynamically interrelated in that they are continuously influencing one another. How individuals perceive their tasks determines how they communicate about them and their willingness to perform.

Motivation: The concept pertains to an individual's psychological energy to achieve goals. This is one of the most researched subjects in organizational behavior. Understanding what makes a person work diligently, be productive, and become creative is a primary concern of management. Theories abound. Probably you have heard of Maslow's hierarchy of needs as well as Herzberg's satisfiers and dissatisfiers. Helping individuals achieve their personal goals while attaining organizational goals is the thrust of motivation to work. Most important are the methods developed by behavioral scientists such as goal setting, work design and redesign, team skills development, self-managed teams, and management processes that provide employees with maximum opportunity for self-direction, creativity, and innovation.

Frustration: Equally important as knowledge of what turns people on is knowing what turns people off. You saw evidence of this in Activity 1–1—the majority of participants' stories about human relations at work were about dissatisfactions on the job. Workers have a tremendous capacity for resistance to a management they disrespect or dislike. Considerable creativity can go into lowering productivity or sabotaging on the job.

Perception: How the individuals perceive the company activities, management, and fellow workers determines how they will respond. At the company level, behavioral specialists often use questionnaires to survey employees' attitudes and opinions toward policies, practices, problems, and functioning activities. The assumption is that employees and management need to be perceiving them in a similar manner. Any significant discrepancies have implications: Worker productivity may be affected; changes may be needed; and, above all, additional communication is essential. Goal-setting programs have the advantage of bosses dialoguing with employees not only to increase motivation but also to ensure that the two groups are seeing things the same way.

Perceptual Distortion: One of the most frequently found facts of surveys is that serious misperceptions exist between different functional departments. Finance, marketing, engineering design, and production assume they are all working on the same set of company goals and implementations, but great discrepancies are often revealed. Poor productivity and progress, accompanied by considerable resentment, are consequences.

Communication: Open, two-way communications between management and all elements of an organization can enhance motivation, reduce or prevent frustration, clarify perceptions, and alleviate distortion. Information technology and organizational behavior technology have developed numerous methods of dialoguing that are applied to process the difficulties discussed in these three core concept areas.

Misinformation: Frustration and inadequate information dissemination can lead to rumors, speculation, and inappropriate activities. Disinformation (intentionally planted false information) is sometimes generated by hostile employees.

Diversity: Returning to our theme of diversity, corporate engineers engaging in international trade must know a good deal about the needs of the foreign nations where they sell their products. They must know how other countries perceive the product, the United States, and interacting with Americans. Production, policies, and practices must be molded to these factors.

The composition of the U.S. work force is continuing to change. Here are a few examples based on data and projected data published by the Bureau of Labor Statistics (BLS).[15] The median age of workers will rise from 36.6 years in 1990 to 40.6 years by the year 2005; the number of workers 45 years of age and older has risen from 21 million in 1950 to 36 million in 1995 and is projected to reach 58 million by the year 2005; women have gone from 42.5 percent of the total work force in 1980 to 45.3 percent in 1990 and are projected to rise to 47.4 percent in 2005; white males are projected to decrease from 43 percent of the total work force in 1990 to 38.2 percent in 2005; the Hispanic-American portion of the work force is projected to increase from

7.7 percent in 1990 to 11.1 percent in 2005; the African-American portion is projected to increase from 10.7 percent in 1990 to 11.6 percent in 2005; the portion of Asian-Americans and others (including Pacific Islanders, American Indians, and other Alaskan natives) is projected to increase from 3.1 percent in 1990 to 3.3 percent in 2005. Between 1990 and 2005, most new workers will be nonwhite or Hispanic-American. Hispanic-American men and women will make up the fastest-growing group of entrants, increasing their number by 75.3 percent. Activity 1–2 was designed to begin the systematic exploration of diversity based on your own experience.

For a U.S. company, diversity can be regarded as a garden of varied talents and viewpoints. The greater the range of knowledge, competence, abilities, educational background, and ethnicity, the greater the reservoir for creativity.[16] This is the potential and hope. Management is viewed as the ability to orchestrate and harmonize the interactions between diverse individuals and tasks in order to attain maximum effectiveness and productivity. More than ever, management needs to understand workers' culture heritages, how they perceive each other (stereotypes abound), how they perceive management and the work, and what kind of nurturing organizational climate they need to be productive and innovative.[17] Knowing sensitivities (understanding what offends and what turns people off) is ever more important, the greater diversity becomes.

Objectives of the Course

Our aims for the course are high. To the extent possible in a one-quarter or one-semester experience, we'd like you to achieve the following:

- Knowledge of behavioral science theory and concepts useful in organizations, with special emphasis on small group theory.
- Knowledge of methods and techniques that are helpful in developing effectiveness in individuals, teams, and organizations.
- Appreciation of diversity, its dynamics, and its impact on individual, team, and organizational effectiveness.
- Understanding of how perceptual distortion affects communication, motivation, and frustration in human organizations.
- Understanding of the potential cause-and-effect relationships among motivation, perception, communication, and the management processes of work design and flexibility, quality, creativity, innovation, technology, and information technology.
- Ability to effectively use team skills, such as group problem solving and decision making.
- Ability to analyze diverse management situations and your own experience while utilizing course concepts.
- Improved skills in personal goal setting and interpersonal communications.
- Better awareness of your own motivation and responses to frustration; how to enhance motivation and cope with stress.
- Understanding of the process of change and the management of change in organizations.

Our overall intent is to emphasize skills development, understanding, and knowledge that you can use.

Summary

We started our textbook with the focus on diversity based on the assumption that industry and business of the future will employ an increasingly representative mix of the population. We have introduced the course by examining your own experience with human behavior in organizations. We have suggested that the diversity of people's experiences in organizations typically includes many problems that affect individual, group, and organizational performance and the sense of satisfaction or dissatisfaction felt. Both task and human dimensions are important for understanding organizational effectiveness. Such topics as fair treatment, good supervision, effective communication, and motivation are closely interwoven. This implies that an effective theoretical framework must deal with both task and human dimensions of effectiveness and must include all four levels of behavior: individual, group, intergroup, and organizational. This is known as the systems approach to organizational behavior, which will serve as an overall framework for the learning process of this book. Objectives of the course are drawn from this theoretical approach but emphasize improving effectiveness in real organizations, not just academic knowledge. In addition, we stressed that our studies will include the ''irrational'' as well as the rational factors in behavior (see Figure 1–1), the latter being the perceptual window through which management typically views employee conduct.

Organizational behavior is viewed as an interdisciplinary field of study. While the study of organizational behavior is relatively ''young,'' issues of human behavior in the context of work, organization, and management can be traced to ancient Greek, Egyptian, and Biblical thought. We have provided a brief review of the historical evolution of management thought. Following the sociology of knowledge perspective, we identified four clusters of thoughts: the prescientific, classical, neoclassical, and modern eras. In each era we briefly discussed the major schools of organization and management thought with their focus and emphases.

Since our approach to learning stresses involvement, the first activity was designed to help integrate your experience with organizational behavior ideas. Your experience, perceptions, and reactions will continue to be a key part of this course. In Activity 1–1, we saw that individuals' experiences offer important data that we can draw upon to increase our understanding. We saw that many common experiences and perceptions were widely shared among participants and that, even so, effective communication can be difficult. The communications skills of listening, paraphrasing, and sharing were explicitly related to participants' attitudes and responses to one another. We saw that differences can be either useful or troublesome, depending on how they are handled. Finally, we began the process of applying organizational behavior knowledge directly to your own experience. We will build on these experiences throughout the course. Activity 1–2 that follows provides another opportunity to illustrate how individual experiences can be used as an important data base for understanding and discovery. This activity is designed to begin the systematic exploration of human diversity and the implications of diversity in the context of organizational behavior.

Study Questions

1. What is meant by ''managing diversity''?
2. What is meant by a ''learning community''? In what way did Activity1–1 (''Defining Organizational Behavior'') contribute to the development of the classroom learning community?
3. What is meant by the ''systems approach'' to studying organizational behavior?
4. Why do we emphasize ''irrational'' as well as rational aspects of behavior?
5. Review the historical evolution of organizational behavior. Select any two schools of thought that you feel influenced our understanding of individual behavior the most. Provide the reasoning for your choice.
6. Review the goals of the course. Select the two that you feel have the greatest potential for improving your learning at this time. Name the two and give the reasons.

Endnotes

1. See, for example, L. Gardenswartz and A. Rowe, *Managing Diversity* (Homewood, Ill.: Richard D. Irwin, 1993); and G. N. Powell, *Gender and Diversity in the Workplace* (Thousand Oaks, Calif.: Sage, 1994).

2. J. H. Coil and C. M. Rice, ''Managing Work-Force Diversity in the Nineties: The Impact of the Civil Rights Act of 1991,'' *Employee Relations* 18, no. 4 (1993), pp. 547–65.

3. Many scholars examined the evolution of management thought in the context of the evolution of the society. Among them we find R. Miles, *Theories of Management* (New York: McGraw-Hill, 1975); T. Parsons and N. Smelser, *Economy & Society* (London: Routledge & Kegan, 1956); C. Perrow, ''The Short & Glorious History of Organizational Theory,'' *Organizational Dynamics* (Summer 1973), pp. 2–15; M. Weber, *The Theory of Social & Economic Organization* (New York: Free Press, 1947); D. Wern, *The Evolution of Management Thought* (New York: Wiley, 1979).

4. A nice summary of the chronology of organization theory is found in J. M. Shafritz and J. S. Ott, *Classics of Organization Theory* (Chicago: Dorsey, 1987).

5. See, for example, Parsons and Smelser, *Economy & Society.*

6. See, for example, J. Bowditch and A. Buono, *A Primer on Organizational Behavior* (New York: Wiley, 1994).

7. F. Taylor, *The Principles of Scientific Management* (New York: Harper & Brothers, 1911).

8. H. Fayol, *General and Industrial Management* (London: Pitman, 1916).

9. C. I. Barnard, *The Function of the Executive* (Cambridge, Mass.: Harvard Press, 1938).

10. F. J. Roethlisberger and W. Dickson, *Management and the Worker* (Cambridge, Mass.: Harvard Press, 1938).

11. L. Bertalanffy, *General Systems Theory: Foundations, Development, and Applications* (New York: Braziller, 1967).

12. For a full description of the sociotechnical systems school of thought, see F. E. Emery, *Some Characteristics of Sociotechnical Systems* (London: Tavistock, 1959); W. A. Pasmore, *Designing Effective Organizations: Sociotechnical System Perspective* (New York: Wiley, 1988); and E. L. Trist, ''Sociotechnical System Perspective,'' in A. H. Van de Ven and W. F. Joyce (eds.), *Perspectives on Organization Design & Behavior* (New York: Wiley, 1982), pp. 19–75.

13. See, for example, C. W. Churchman, R. L. Ackoff, and E. L. Arnoff, *Introduction to Operations Research* (New York: Wiley, 1961).

14. For a detailed description of this orientation, see, for example, F. E. Kast and J. E. Rosenzweig, *Contingency Views of Organizations and Management,* (Palo Alto, Calif.: Science Research Associates, 1973).

15. *Monthly Labor Review,* November 1991.

16. J. P. Fernandez, *The Diversity Advantage* (New York: Lexington Books, 1993).

17. See, for example, S. E. Jackson, *Diversity in the Workplace* (New York: Guilford Press, 1992).

Activity 1–2: Initial Exploration of Diversity

Objectives:

a. To identify individual differences.

b. To introduce the range and basic sources of diversity.

c. To explore issues associated with the management of diversity.

Task 1:

We all feel that in some way we are different from others. The worksheet for Activity 1–2 asks you to explore the differences. Use the worksheet to take notes. (Time: Five minutes for individuals to think about their experience and jot down notes.)

Task 2:

Each participant shares these thoughts with a small group. After each has done so, discuss what common elements seem to emerge. Have a spokesperson make a list.

Task 3:

The spokesperson reports findings to the class.

Worksheet for Activity 1–2

1. Drawing upon your cumulative experiences, identify and describe one important way in which you feel different from most of the people that you work with or most of the people on your team or most of the people in this class or most of the people in your family or most of your friends.

2. How do you feel about this difference?

3. What might be the source or sources of the difference?

4. What are the positive and negative consequences of this difference?

5. Are there any managerial implications for managing the difference?

2 The Management of Expectations and Learning

Learning Objectives

After completing this module you should be able to

1. Explain the importance of managing expectations.
2. Understand the process of communication dialoguing as a managerial tool.
3. Describe the role of expectations, expectations discrepancies, and self-fulfilling prophecies in organizational settings.
4. Appreciate the process and the importance of developing a "psychological contract."
5. Explain the relationship between expectation, learning, experiential learning, and self-learning competency.
6. Discuss the differences between the organismic and the mechanistic theories of learning.
7. Explain the basic assumptions about the adult as learner.
8. Appreciate the roles of the participant and the instructor in an involvement learning course.
9. Describe the design of the course.

List of Key Concepts

Adult learner
Classical conditioning
Cognitive theories
Communication dialoguing
Content learning
Expectations
Experiential learning
Fair conditioning system
Involvement learning
Learning
Learning community
Operant conditioning
Process learning
Psychological contract
Self-efficacy
Self-fulfilling prophecy (Pygmalion)
Self-learning competency
Social learning
Social learning theories

Module Outline

Premodule Preparation

Activity 2–1: Organizational Dialoguing about Learning and Expectations

Objectives:

a. To help you understand the learning goals and methods of the course, the instructor's viewpoints about the course, and other participants' learning needs and attitudes in several areas.

b. To help the instructor understand your viewpoints, attitudes, and needs.

c. To build the classroom learning climate by involvement learning and dialoguing.

Task 1:

Individuals, while reflecting on their learning goals and this specific course, should write a few notes in response to the following three questions:

1. What things would you like to learn, study, or have emphasized in this course on human behavior in organizations?

2. What doubts or concerns do you have about this course? What are some things you would *not* like to study or have happen in the course?

3. What are your viewpoints toward college life, college education, or your major course of study that might influence your attitudes toward this course?

In general, these questions are to bring out any factors that may account for your expectations, hopes, or doubts for the course. These may be directly related to the subject of study, but they may also be related to the life you are experiencing on campus or in the greater environment. Feel free to express any views. Your representative does not have to identify who said what. (Time: 15 to 20 minutes)

Task 2 (to be completed in class):

Participants will form work groups of five to seven members (no larger). Individuals are to share their responses to Task 1's three questions. Each group will elect a representative and keep notes of the discussion. Each group is to prepare its answer to the three questions. (Time: 15 to 20 minutes)

Task 3:

Representatives from the groups will meet in a fishbowl circle in the center of the room to report and discuss their groups' viewpoints. The instructor will raise issues for clarity and understanding after they have completed their discussion but will not respond at this point. (Time: 10 to 15 minutes)

Task 4:

Work groups will choose a second representative for this task. Groups will prepare a list of questions you would like to have the instructor answer to help you understand his or her expectations and attitudes about the course (such as learning approach, education, background, satisfactions or frustrations gained from teaching, or what the instructor hopes to see participants gain from the course). Any questions that will help you get to know the instructor or understand the course and how it is to be conducted are appropriate. The instructor's expectations of students should be probed here. See if you can prepare confrontational questions such as those a good television interviewer would use. (Time: 10 minutes)

Task 5:

"Put the instructor on the hot seat." Representatives will meet in a circle with the instructor. Each poses one question at a time until all have been answered. (Time: 15 to 20 minutes)

Introduction

The increasing diversity of the workplace brings to the forefront one of the basic and most persistent problems of organizational life. Individuals see situations, issues, or goals differently, depending on their particular perspectives, experiences, educational and cultural backgrounds, personality traits, competencies and skills, and biases—yet everyone typically assumes that everyone else sees things as they do. We fail to take into account that what seems ''obvious'' and ''common sense'' to us may appear bizarre and inexplicable to others. Or, lacking some key piece of information to interpret the situation, someone may come to a resoundingly different conclusion about data that others agree upon. Neither the problem nor its recognition is new. One classic study in 1966 showed relatively low agreement between bosses and subordinates on what subordinates' job duties were, and very low agreement on what obstacles were faced in accomplishing these duties.[1] In another study, carried out over 30 years ago, 80 percent of supervisors said they ''very often'' praised good performance, but only 14 percent of their employees said this was true.[2] Similar results are found widely both in formal research and in studies of contemporary organizations by consultants.

Diversity and Expectations

The difficulties described above, seem typical of human interactions and interpersonal relations at work, at school, in social settings, and even in the family. Yet we seldom discuss the assumptions and beliefs on which we base our behavior, so it's often difficult to identify the causes of the failures, let alone to deal effectively with them. But whether they're discussed or ignored, underlying assumptions and beliefs have a powerful effect on our behavior. Two people with contradictory expectations of one another are likely doomed to ongoing conflict. Such conflict can result in low productivity, alienation, absenteeism, dissatisfaction with work in the organization, or even divorce in marriage.

As the work force becomes more diverse, are there some things that have to be done differently to more fully utilize human potential? We think yes. Are we trapped in our own assumptions and beliefs, forever separated from others? We think not. Methods exist to improve understanding and communication within a diverse work force by creating shared assumptions, thus enabling common interpretations. **Communication dialoguing** is one way to overcome diversity and contradictory expectations by bringing similarities and differences in perspective out into the open. They can then be discussed, modified by other data or new interpretations, and shared. The premodule activity uses a form of dialoguing to develop an effective learning climate in the classroom. Figure 2–1 diagrams this dialoguing process as it might exist between a boss and employees, or between professor and students. Somewhat different methods might be used in business, but the shared exchange of perspectives and expectations would be visible there as well. For instance, an employee might explicitly inquire about the boss's expectations for a project or report, about the extent of his or her discretion, or the flexibility possible in time schedules. Such exchange is the foundation for understanding, trust, and, thus, effective working relations. Successful managers and employees use this exchange frequently.

Figure 2–1
Dialoguing to Overcome Differences in Expectations in Business or the Classroom

In Business

My expectations of what subordinates should, ought, and must do. My managerial philosophy. Etc.

Our expectations of what bosses and organizations should, ought, and must do. Our goals—what we want out of our jobs. Etc.

In the Classroom

My expectations of what students should, ought, and must do. My educational philosophy. What I hope students will get out of this course. What I want from this course. Etc.

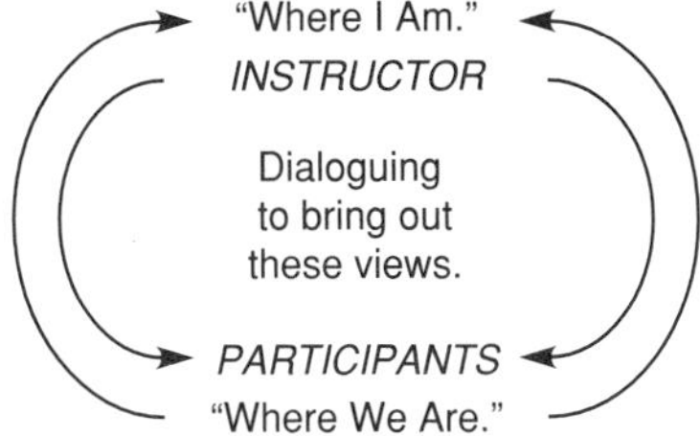

Our expectations of what instructors should, ought, and must do. Our attitudes toward education, professors, college life. What we want out of this course. Etc.

The Psychological Contract

The premodule activity initiates a set of understandings between you and the instructor on (a) the educational program for this course and (b) the conduct and attitudes of those who will take part in it. In a sense it is a **psychological contract** we hope to follow. Activity 2–2 (''Personal Learning Statements'') at the end of the module was designed to make the learning contract more explicit. Edgar Schein applies this idea to an agreement between the individual and an organization when he says

> The notion of a psychological contract implies that the individuals have a variety of expectations of the organization and that the organization has a variety of expectations of them. These expectations not only cover how much work is to be performed for how much pay, but also involve the whole pattern of rights, privileges, and obligations between worker and organization.[3]

The clearer these expectations are to both sides, the more coordination and cooperation are possible. The psychological contract is a dynamic, living process in that it needs to be adjusted to trends and ongoing activities. In Activity 2–1's model, a continuous flow of communication between worker and management is possible. This means that a value system that includes some degree of openness and trust must exist as part of the organizational culture. We might say that organizations need a **fair conditioning system,** meaning a continuous and open flow of communication in which fairness—fair treatment—is an essential ingredient. Activity 2–2 in this module was created both as a learning tool and an experiential mechanism to help you develop a psychological contract between you and your instructor.

Expectations and Self-Fulfilling Prophecy

Expectations Discrepancies

Recent research indicates that many organizational problems can be traced to expectations discrepancies. Interpersonal dialoguing is seen as a managerial tool to bridge the discrepancy gap. Raising managerial expectations about employees' abilities and performances can improve performance and boost productivity. Hence, productivity as a self-fulfilling prophecy presents a variety of unique possibilities for crafting desired behavior and outcomes in the workplace.

Based on the experience of working with several organizations, Livingston concluded that (1) what a manager expects of his subordinates and the way he treats them largely determine their performances and career progress, (2) a unique characteristic of superior managers is their ability to create high-performance expectations that subordinates fulfill, (3) less effective managers fail to develop similar expectations and, as a consequence, the productivity of their subordinates suffers, and (4) subordinates, more often than not, appear to do what they believe they are expected to do.[4]

The **self-fulfilling prophecy (Pygmalion)** has been attracting growing interest in the past decade. Self-fulfilling prophecy (SFP) is described as a three-stage process beginning with a person's belief that a certain event will occur. In the second stage, this expectation or "prophecy" leads to some new behavior that the person would not have performed were it not for the expectation. In the third stage, the expected event occurs and the prophecy is fulfilled.[5] The phenomenon of self-fulfilling prophecies has become widely recognized in the behavioral, social, educational, and organizational sciences. Recent empirical studies shed light on the multiple dimensions of the phenomenon and its important role in the context of work. For example, a set of studies carried out by Eden and his colleagues demonstrated empirically that high expectations resulted in improved performance, raised self-expectancy, increased overall satisfaction, and improved leadership, which in turn augmented subordinates' productivities. Furthermore, Eden envisions managers as prophets. He argues that managers as prophets expect certain things to happen and then act in ways to fulfill their expectations.[6] The relationship between expectancy and learning, leadership, group behavior, motivation, perception, and performance is addressed in the succeeding modules.

At this point we will continue to clarify expectations and to build the psychological contract by discussing our view about learning, the adult learner, learning competencies, the management of learning, the learning methods, and designs we are to use in the course. Your awareness of these is important not only for understanding the course but also for learning techniques and competencies that you can acquire and apply later when you are supervising people.

Expectations and Learning

Learning

The rapid and continuing changes of the workplace foster the preoccupation of most human beings with learning and the need to learn—just to survive. The expectations that individuals are willing to learn are increasing. **Learning** is defined as the process whereby new skills, knowledge, ability, and attitudes are created through the transformation of experience.[7] At the most basic level, organizations expect individuals to learn productive work behaviors. Furthermore, individuals and organizations alike must learn to adapt to the new rules of the game and the ever changing and increasingly diverse global business environment. The major challenge that organizations face has to do with providing learning experiences in an environment that will promote employee behaviors desired by the organization.

Learning seems to have been a preoccupation for centuries. The many scientific theories of learning developed since 1885 are clustered in the literature in a few ways. Two general families of theories seem to be the most popular clustering: theories based on a *mechanistic model* and theories based on an *organismic model.*

The Mechanistic Approach

The mechanistic model represents the universe as a machine composed of discrete pieces in a spatio-temporal field. These pieces—elementary particles in motion—and their relations form the basic reality to which all other more complex phenomena are ultimately reduced.[8] Thorndike, in the first systematic study of learning in the United States, conceived learners to be empty organisms who responded to stimuli more or less randomly and automatically.

Classical Conditioning

A specific response is connected to a specific stimulus when it is rewarded.[9] Soon after Thorndike started his work, a Russian physiologist, Pavlov, inaugurated his experiments with dogs which resulted in what is today called **classical conditioning**—the process by which individuals learn reflex behavior. Pavlov's famous dog experiments were described by Hilgard as follows:

> When meat powder is placed in a dog's mouth, salivation takes place; the food is the *unconditioned* stimuli and salivation is the *unconditioned* reflex. Then some arbitrary stimulus, such as a light, is combined with the presentation of the food. Eventually, after repetition and if time relationships are right, the light will evoke salivation independent of the food; the light is the *conditioned stimulus* and the response to it is the *conditioned reflex.* (Emphasis added.)[10]

Operant Conditioning

Operant conditioning—a term coined by B. F. Skinner[11]—extends classical conditioning to focus on a process by which individuals learn voluntary behavior. While stimulus still cues a response behavior, the desired or undesired consequences that follow the behavior determine whether the behavior will occur. Learning occurs due to the consequences that follow the behavior. Examples of operant behaviors and their consequences include (1) the worker learns new skills and as a consequence receives more pay and (2) a supervisor gives a worker a task (stimulus), the worker completes the assignment (behavior), and the supervisor praises the worker (consequence).

The Organismic Approach

The organismic theories of learning represent a universe that is a unitary, interactive, developing organism. Accordingly, an individual is viewed as an active organism rather than a reactive organism, and as a source of acts rather than a collection of acts initiated by external forces. The cognitive theories and the social learning theories represent two examples of theories in this family of theories.

Cognitive Theories: The **cognitive theories** emphasize the internal mental processes involved in gaining new insights. Learning occurs as a result of the interplay between various cues from the environment that form a mental map.

Social Learning Theories: The **social learning theories** demonstrated that individuals can learn new behavior by watching others in social situations and then imitating their behavior. As such, social learning theories integrate the behaviorist and cognitive approaches with the idea of imitating behaviors. Learning occurs when an individual tries the observed behavior and experiences a favorable result.[12] Two central concepts of social learning theory are self-efficacy and response–outcome expectations. **Self-efficacy** is a judgment of one's capability to accomplish a certain level of performance in a situation, whereas an outcome expectation is a judgment of the likely consequence such behavior will produce. Self-efficacy influences individual choices of tasks and how long they will try to reach their goals.[13] Individuals with high self-efficacy believe that they have the ability needed, that they are capable of the effort required to achieve the goal, and that no outside events will prevent them from obtaining a desired level of performance.[14] The manager's expectations about a subordinate's behavior affect the person's self-efficacy. The manager's role in raising expectations and in increasing work motivations is explored in detail in the modules on leadership and motivation. Recent research suggests that while managers play a role in fostering individuals' expectations, individual learning competencies are a set of skills that individuals must develop to survive in the 1990s.[15]

Self-Learning Competency

The most critical skill that an individual must acquire is **self-learning competency.** Self-learning competency enables people to learn actively in a variety of situations. This means, for example, that people have the skills to apply knowledge gained in one situation to other situations.

> This competency makes people aware of, and open to, learning opportunities in their day to day experiences. A workforce possessing this competency sees learning as an everyday natural occurrence. This kind of workforce is able to exploit learning opportunities which arise "on the job," as well as make effective use of formal structured learning experiences, open learning and multi-media delivery systems.[16]

Self refers to the fact that the learner must take primary responsibility for his or her own learning, and that learning is an inner activity. *Competency* is meant to focus on the development of independent self-learners as a goal of training as distinct from the narrower use of the term *self-learning,* which refers to "individualized delivery systems," often using computer-based packages. As we can see, self-learning is related to self-motivation, self-awareness, and self-control. It presupposes that the learners are interested in learning. Further, knowing oneself and having the ability for planning and a sense of commitment seem critical.

Skills that the adult learner must master to develop self-learning competency include the ability to engage in divergent thinking and the ability to be in touch with curiosities; the ability to perceive one's self objectively and accept feedback about one's performance nondefensively; the ability to diagnose one's learning needs in the light of models of competencies required for performing life roles; the ability to formulate learning objectives in terms that describe performance outcomes; the ability to identify human, material, and experiential resources for accomplishing various kinds of learning objectives; the ability to design a plan of strategies and carry out the plan systematically while utilizing the appropriate learning resources effectively; and the ability to collect evidence of the accomplishment of learning objectives and have it validated through performance.[17]

The Adult Learner and Experiential Learning

Basic Assumptions about Adult Learners

This book and the learning that it attempts to foster is based on a few assumptions about adults as learners:[18] (1) Adults have a need to be self-directed in establishing and implementing their learning goals. (2) Adults desire to integrate their past experiences with new learning. (3) Adults have a dominant and a preferred learning style. (4) Adults can modify their learning processes to suit changing needs and conditions. (5) Learning is a continuous lifelong process that is grounded in experience.

Experiential Learning Process

As can be seen from the set of assumptions listed above, the guiding approach to this book is **experiential learning.**[19] That is,

> Learning, growth, and change are facilitated by an integrated process that begins with here-and-now experience followed by collection of data and observation about the experience. These observations are assimilated with previous knowledge into a "theory" from which new implications for actions can be deduced. These implications then serve as guides in acting to create new experiences.[20]

The design of most of the modules and topic areas covered in this book follow this experiential learning cycle. Thus your involvement as a learner is critical.

Rationale for Learning by Involvement

So far, the course has been developed almost entirely by interaction exercises. Involvement methods (developed widely in business and government workshops for training managers, supervisors, and executives) are designed for adult education. The basis for learning is not simply the instructor or a textbook. Instead, the course is built around using the participants' own experiences, both before and during the course. Participants are involved in sharing with one another what they have learned in the process of working with others. Exercises or experiences are emphasized to allow participants to apply the insights of theory in practice, to try alternative methods, and to experience first-hand the situations and issues they are studying. In essence, the participants use their own experiences as a laboratory for exploring how people behave in organizations. Team interactions examine different perspectives; solutions naturally arise out of different backgrounds and experiences. Even more important, teams provide a rich resource for participants to draw upon; team members learn from one another just as they learn from the instructor and text. This approach to learning is participant-centered rather than instructor-centered. The instructor's role is that of facilitator of learning as well as specialist or expert.

Most large companies—such as IBM, Ford, Intel, Digital Equipment, General Motors, AT&T, and General Electric—regularly use these workshop methods for management education and training. So do federal government agencies such as the IRS, National Park Service, Forest Service, CIA, and Office of Personnel Management. The methods are widely used by consultants and management institutes that specialize in education of executives and managers. We have used all of the activities in this book (or variants of them) with various levels of management in business and government as well as with undergraduate, MBA, and executive MBA students.

After completing Activity 2–1, participants often express their hopes that the course will provide them with understanding and skills that will be useful in the real world of work and, more important, in their personal and university life at present. The fact that managers and executives testify that they get practical, useful learning from workshops conducted within their corporations indicates that the involvement method is on target.

Involvement Learning Methods

Involvement-process learning, the central approach in this course, places primary emphasis on the process of interaction and thinking, rather than on rote memory of factual content of the area being studied. In contrast, **content learning** is learning based on knowledge, facts, and theory only, which serve as the data base for analysis and reasoning. Application of ideas, experience in the subject, and attention to participants' responses are crucial in process learning. We chose this approach because we believe it is more effective for three reasons. First, content or subject matter is proliferating so rapidly that knowledge soon becomes outdated. Keeping current will be a lifelong process for any manager. Second, changes in attitudes and behavior (that is, real learning) come about by doing and understanding, not just by knowing intellectually. Third, the most effective learning is learning in which the student participates knowledgeably. Since the effective manager will have to continue to learn in a self-directed manner, learning how to learn from his or her own experience acquires a special importance. For each of these issues, involvement learning has proven superior to content-oriented approaches.

Your experience is important because ultimately *you* must apply and interpret whatever you learn. So we start here. There's no substitute for experience in this as in other matters. You cannot really understand what honey tastes like until you have tasted it, and you cannot comprehend group problem solving until you have been involved and seen it work. You may read a book on skiing or tennis that is very helpful, but you won't really develop skill in your sport until you've practiced it. The same thing could be said about sex—no amount of intellectualizing or theoretical knowledge will substitute for actual experience. So it is with the knowledge of people and interactions that are our subjects. Some differences between involvement learning and content learning are shown in Figure 2–2.

Figure 2–2
Some Differences between Types of Learning and Methods Used in Process-Involvement and Content Courses

Process-Involvement Learning	Content Learning
Ways of thinking	Theories and concepts
Inductive reasoning	Knowledge
Deductive reasoning	Facts
Viewpoints (e.g., change as a way of life)	Database for reasoning
Models	
Application of theories and concepts	
Skills	
Interaction	
Communications	
Working with feelings and emotions	
Learning-to-learn skills	
Methods of instruction	*Methods of instruction*
Involvement exercises	Reading
Group exercises	Lecturing
Application case studies	Discussion
Role playing	
Discussion	

The Special Role of the Participant

In an involvement learning course, ''students'' are participants as well. This implies a dual role—that of learning from others and that of contributing to the learning of others. Your views, your interactions, your reactions to others, and your ideas are the essential database from which others gain knowledge and develop skills and viewpoints. We assume the classroom activities are where the primary learning takes place, and the textbook only reinforces that process. Therefore, if you are interacting and sharing your views with others, you are providing them with an opportunity to learn. In a sense you are a coach for your fellow participants, just as you will coach your employees in your future role as a manager.

Developing a Climate to Encourage Learning

This text advocates and uses the classroom as a dynamic learning community. **Learning community** refers to classroom interactions shaped to create norms, values, and roles conducive to a supportive and stimulating learning climate. In the first two sessions of this course, our efforts were aimed at developing the interaction and communications atmosphere conducive to learning. In involvement learning, the interactions between participants are as important as those between instructor and participants. Some special requirements of a learning climate are:

1. Two-way communication and influence.
2. Openness in expressing views, feelings, and emotions. Tell it like it is, but do so with a respect for others, whose views may differ.
3. Supportiveness. When you are in agreement with others, give them your support. But also learn to express differences without offending. Often two people in conflict are 90 percent in agreement but focus only on their differences. Acknowledging areas of agreement can help provide the basis for a satisfactory resolution, making each person more inclined to consider the validity of the other's view.
4. Recognition that conflict can be creative when differences are expressed appropriately. Differences can lead to new and better perspectives and new bases for acceptable solutions.
5. Appreciation for individual differences, what they represent in different backgrounds or experiences, and how they can contribute to effective group relations and problem solving.
6. Effective confrontation:
   a. Have you the courage to express your own convictions?
   b. Can you take feedback as well as give it usefully?

c. Are you overconcerned about disagreement or disapproval?
d. Are you willing to risk learning and change?
e. Are you using your share of the air time, not too much nor too little?

7. Tolerance for ambiguity, the willingness to explore uncertain issues (which includes most important issues), rather than leaping to what H. L. Mencken called the simple, obvious—and wrong—solution that typically presents itself for every complex problem.

Caution: How much openness is desirable? How much confrontation? How can you effectively protect yourself and others from undue intrusion?

Ground Rules for the Course

Management workshops in industry are often scheduled in one-week, full-time blocks and are frequently held at locations away from the office. The reason is that learning can be much greater if it is continuous, intensive, and undisturbed by daily crises or the interruptions of mundane details. Learning points are developed and reinforced as the participants "live through" each session. Intense, continuous interaction allows participants to build a rich repertoire of experience quickly. In the university setting, weekly classroom sessions may consist of different arrangements, such as three or four one-hour meetings, two two-hour meetings, or one three-hour meeting every week for 10 weeks (quarter plan) or 16 weeks (semester plan). Results can nevertheless be excellent for those who attend all sessions. Those who miss sessions find they lose out in continuity, in understanding, and, most important, in their experience with the group. Participation, as well as attendance, is what makes the difference. For these reasons, attendence at all sessions is required. The entire experience can be meaningful only if you are there.

It is difficult to design examinations to determine what learning has taken place in involvement situations. But evaluation is a fact of life, so some written responses from the participants must be obtained upon which a grade can be awarded in a college setting. The written work will not be an adequate or complete measure of what you have learned in any session since there is no way of testing that except through experience. Instead, written work will test the cognitive portion of your learning, which will depend very much on your thoughtful interpretation of classroom experiences and readings.

Design of the Course

Team Project Assignment (Appendixes A and B)

Two of the three plans for conducting this course recommended in the Introduction to the text are detailed in the first appendixes following the last module. Appendix A proposes a team task assignment to develop understanding of team action. This is the recommended route to follow when class size and time availability are right. Participants will be assigned to a work group of six members who will complete selected activities from the text in the classroom and meet outside of class to carry out the group task. Teams will be responsible for writing two papers: one on the task and one on the group's interaction and effectiveness. Members working individually will also keep journals (see Appendix "C") and write term papers (see Appendix "D") on their observations of the group. Because of the time needed for outside meetings, the text and project assignments will constitute most of the homework for the course. This approach is best suited for a class of no more than 36 members (that is, up to five or six teams). It has been used successfully with university undergraduates and with master's programs in business administration.

Individual Term Paper on Understanding Team Dynamics (Described in Appendix B)

When time or class size does not permit completing the Appendix A project, a good alternative is the team activity outlined in Appendix B. Participants will complete the classroom exercises in six-member teams, keep a journal on their observations of the group as it develops in the classroom, and write a term paper on that data at the end of the course. Since this requires only a few outside meetings, additional homework of readings and/or case studies may be assigned by the instructor. Guidance for preparing the individual term paper on team dynamics and skills—required in both alternative plans—is given in Appendix C and D.

Team Term Paper on Understanding Team Dynamics (Described in Appendix B)

This is similar to the option described above (the individual term paper on understanding team dynamics) with one major difference—the paper is written by the team, not by individual team members (see Appendix D for guidance).

How Team Assignments Are Made

You will have noted that students are assigned to teams by the instructor. There is a very definite reason for this practice, which is followed in management workshops. Learning about behavior has been found to be accomplished best when individuals are with strangers or with those they do not know well. Frequently students take courses with acquaintances and friends, and the already established patterns of interaction interfere with the learning process. Further, a certain amount of heterogeneity of background can be a positive contribution to the team process, while too much homogeneity can be a problem. The instructor will tell you what method of assignment will be used.

Summary

Differences in perception and expectations among individuals, groups, or levels of the hierarchy of an organization can be sources of conflict and frustration for all concerned. Organizational dialoguing is a method used to explore differences and similarities in expectations in these interface situations and to develop a ''psychological contract.'' In Activity 2–1 dialoguing focuses on instructor–participant expectations relevant to the goals and methods of the course, an additional purpose being to develop the classroom climate and interaction patterns that will facilitate learning. Activity 2–2 that follow takes the psychological contract one step further: Individuals refine and articulate their learning objectives, goals, potential roadblocks, and desired outcome. The instructor reviews and co-signs the student learning contract. Activity 2–3 takes expectations from the individual level to the team level. Each team is asked to create a name and logo that capture its essence. This activity sets in motion the formation of team identity. Overall the first five activities of the course are illustrations of the advantage of employing involvement methods for attitudinal and behavioral learning, with primary emphasis on the process of interaction and thinking rather than on the pure factual content of the area being studied.

Assignment

1. Reread the module to make sure that you understand the basic orientation of the course.
2. Complete Activity 2–2 (''Personal Learning Statements'') and provide the instructor with two copies of it at the beginning of the next class session.
3. The newly formed teams are to complete Activity 2–3 (''Group Dialoguing and the Development of Name and Logo''). A group's spokesperson should be ready to share the name, logo, and process with the rest of the learning community.

Study Questions

1. What is meant by ''managing expectations''?
2. What is a psychological contract? What is its relationship to Activities 2–1, 2–2, and 2–3?

3. In what way did Activities 2–1 and 2–3 contribute to the development of the learning community?
4. Describe the roles of expectations, expectations discrepancies, and self-fulfilling prophecy in organizational settings.
5. Explain the relationship between expectation, self-efficacy, learning, experiential learning, and self-learning competency.
6. Discuss the differences between the organismic and mechanistic theories of learning.
7. What is the difference between process and content learning? Why do we emphasize this distinction?
8. Explain the basic assumptions about the adult as learner.
9. What are the roles of participants and instructors in an involvement learning course?
10. What is the learning sequence used in this course? What advantages does using this approach offer the student? What are the disadvantages?

Endnotes

1. Arnold S. Tannenbaum, *Social Psychology of the Work Organization* (Belmont, Calif.: Wadsworth, 1966), p. 47.

2. Rensis Likert, *New Patterns of Management* (New York: McGraw-Hill, 1961), p. 91.

3. Edgar H. Schein, *Organizational Psychology* (Englewood Cliffs, N.J.: Prentice-Hall, 1970), p. 12

4. J. S. Livingston, "Pygmalion in Management," *Harvard Business Review* 47, no. 4 (1969), pp. 81–89; and J. S. Livingston, "Retrospective Commentary," *Harvard Business Review,* September-October 1988, p. 125.

5. The original scientific work on SFP was conducted by Robert K. Merton and reported in R. K. Merton, "The Self-Fulfilling Prophecy," *Antioch Review* 8 (1948), pp. 193–210. Dov Eden's research provides a holistic understanding of the phenomenon, part of which is published in D. Eden, *Pygmalion in Management* (Lexington, Mass.: Lexington Books, 1990). A recent study demonstrated the effect of self-fulfilling prophecy on seasickness and performance. See D. Eden and Y. Zuk, "Seasickness as a Self-Fulfilling Prophecy: A Field Experiment on Self-Efficacy and Performance at Sea," paper presented at the Ninth Annual Meeting of the Society of Industrial and Organizational Psychology, Nashville, Tenn., April 8–10, 1994.

6. See, for example, D. Eden and G. Ravid, "Pygmalion vs. Self-Expectancy: Effects of Instructor- and Self-Expectancy on Trainee Performance," *Organizational Behavior and Human Performance* 30 (1982), pp. 351–64; D. Eden and A. B. Shani, "Pygmalion Goes to Boot Camp: Expectancy, Leadership, and Trainee Performance," *Journal of Applied Psychology* 67 (1982), pp. 194–99.

7. While many definitions of learning can be found in the literature, for our purpose we have modified Kolb's definition that can be found in D. A. Kolb, *Experiential Learning* (Englewood Cliffs, N.J.; Prentice Hall, 1984), p. 38.

8. M. Knowles, *The Adult Learner: A Neglected Species* (Houston: Gulf Publishing, 1990).

9. E. L. Thorndike, *Adult Learning* (New York: Macmillan, 1928).

10. E. R. Hilgard and G. H. Bower, *Theories of Learning* (New York: Appleton-Century-Crofts, 1966).

11. B. F. Skinner, *About Behaviorism* (New York: Knopf, 1974).

12. A. Bandura, *Social Learning Theory* (Englewood Cliffs, N.J.: Prentice-Hall, 1977).

13. As of late, the topic of self-efficacy has been getting increased attention. See, for example, A. Bandura, *Social Foundations of Thought and Action: A Social Cognitive View* (Englewood Cliffs, N.J.: Prentice Hall, 1984); D. Eden and A. Aviram, "Self-Efficacy Training to Speed Reemployment: Helping People to Help Themselves," *Journal of Applied Psychology* 78 (1993), pp. 352–60; D. Eden and J. Kinnar, "Modeling Galatea: Boosting Self-Efficacy to Increase Volunteering,'' *Journal of Applied Psychology,* 76 (1991), pp. 770–80; and C. Frayne and G. P. Latham, ''Application of Social Learning Theory to Employee Self-Management of Attendance,'' *Journal of Applied Psychology* 72 (1987), pp. 387–92.

14. M. E. Gist, ''Self-Efficacy: Implications in Organizational Behavior and Human Resource Management,'' *Academy of Management Review* 12 (1987), pp. 472–85; and Frayne and Latham, ''Application of Social Learning Theory.

15. See, for example, *Modeling Learning and the Learning Organization,* Technical Report no. 66740 (Hovik, Norway: Det Norske Veritas Research As, 1994).

16. B. Nahan, *Developing People's Ability to Learn* (Brussels' European Interuniversity Press, 1991), p. 16.

17. Adapted from Knowles, *The Adult Learner: A Neglected Species.*

18. For in-depth discussion on adults as learners, see M. Knowles, *Self-Directed Learning: A Guide for Learners and Teachers* (Chicago: Association Press, 1975); and M. Knowles, *The Modern Practice of Adult Education: From Pedagogy to Andragogy* (Chicago: Association Press, 1980).

19. The theoretical foundation for experiential learning theory can be found in the works of K. Lewin, *Field Theory in Social Science* (New York: Harper & Row, 1951); J. Dewey, *Experience and Education* (New York: G. P. Putnam Books, 1938); J. Piaget, *Play, Dreams and Imitation in Childhood* (New York: W. W. Norton, 1951); C. Argyris and D. Schon, *Organizational Learning: A Theory of Action* (Reading, Mass: Addison-Wesley, 1978) and Kolb, *Experiential Learning.*

20. Kolb, *Experiential Learning,* p. 26.

Activity 2–2: Personal Learning Statement[1]

Objectives:

a. To identify individual learning objectives for the course.

b. To develop a realistic set of expectations.

c. To establish a roadmap for individual progress assessment.

Task 1:

The following are some thoughts on how to complete and write the attached learning contract:

- The purpose of this learning contract is to set attainable objectives that you can then work toward. It is a way of setting reasonable expectations of yourself and then sticking to them.
- Before you begin to respond to the attached guided areas, please review the course syllabus, scan this textbook and consider what they mean for you.
- Be as realistic as you can be in putting your objectives on paper. At the end of the course, you will want to see how well you have done at attaining them.
- Please make two copies of the contract and return them to the instructor at the beginning of the third class session. The instructor will review it and return one copy to you.
- You may revise your contract during the course if you wish by submitting a revision to the instructor.
- The instructor will keep one copy of your contract until the end of the course, at which time it will be returned to you. Your contract is a confidential agreement between you and your instructor.

[1] This activity was inspired and initially developed by Professor Christian F. Poulson, California State Polytechnic University, Pomona, California. We are grateful to Professor Poulson for his contribution.

Name: ______________________________ Section: ______________

Personal Learning Statement

Based on personal reflection, my review of the course syllabus, initial scanning of Shani and Lau's *Behavior in Organization,* and the class discussion thus far, my learning objectives in this course are (include things that you would like to learn about yourself as well as specific course content):

My performance objectives for the course (the grade I want to work toward) are:

The following obstacles (e.g., conflicting pressures, personal limitations) may get in the way of meeting my objectives:

I want to work on improving in the following areas (e.g., listening skills, writing skills, speaking in class):

Specifically, I will do the following to meet my objectives (identify specific actions of your choice):

I understand that this statement is for my personal guidance and will not be graded. It is a contract between you and me. I may change it by submitting a new contract at any time. In signing this contract, I am committing myself to full participation in the course and to adherence to the norms outlined in the syllabus.

Signature: ______________________________

Date: ______________________________

Accepted: ______________________________
(Instructor's name)

Date: ______________________________

Activity 2–3: Group Dialoguing: The Development of a Team Name and Logo

Objective:

To help the newly formed teams begin to develop a distinct identity.

Task 1:

The newly assigned team is to get together and brainstorm about a name for it. The name that the group agrees on is going to be the team's name throughout the entire course. You might want to choose a name that reflects who you are, that you can be pround of, and that reflects what you would like to become as a team.

Task 2:

Working together as a group, your assignment is to create a team logo, on a regular-size page, that captures creatively who you are. Your team logo is due at the beginning of the next class session.

Task 3:

A group spokesperson will be asked to share with the rest of the learning community your team's name, its logo, and how they were developed or created.

3 Management and Leadership*

Learning Objectives

After completing this module you should be able to

1. Explain what leadership is and what role it plays in organizational life.
2. Identify the different leadership schools of thought and their contribution to our understanding of leadership.
3. Appreciate the complexity of the leadership process.
4. Gain insights into your own leadership style, its effect on others, and its effectiveness.
5. Set up leadership-skill goals for self-improvements.
6. Explain some of the issues associated with the role of the future leader as a transformational leader.
7. Appreciate the role that culture and globalization play in leadership effectiveness.

List of Key Concepts

Achievement-oriented leadership
Behavioral leadership theory
Charismatic leader
Consideration
Directive leadership
Employee involvement
High LPC
Initiating structure
Leadership
Leadership style
Least preferred co-worker (LPC)
Low LPC
Management involvement
Managerial role
Participative leadership
Path–goal theory
Relationship behavior
Role behavior
Situational leadership
Supportive leadership
Task behavior
Traits and skills theory
Transformational leadership
360-degree leadership feedback

* Our colleague, Roger Conway, Department of Management, California Polytechnic State University, took the lead on the revision of this module. We are grateful to Professor Conway.

Module Outline

Premodule Preparation

The instructor may assign any one of the following activities as a premodule assignment: Task 1 of Activity 3–1 (''What Is Leadership?'') or Task 1 of Activity 3–2 (''Creating a Dialogue with a Leader'') or Activity 3–6 (''Santa Theresa Family Services'').

Activity 3–1: What Is Leadership?

Objective:

To examine your perceptions of leadership prior to discussing methods of studying the subject and some research results.

Task 1:

Write down the following:

a. Your favorite fictional hero or leader—for example, from a book (Tom Clancy's Jack Ryan), a movie (*Forrest Gump*), or TV show ("Murphy Brown").
b. Your favorite real-life leader.
c. Your personal definition of leadership.

(Time: 5 minutes)

Task 2:

Each participant shares these impressions with team members. After each has done so, what common elements seem to emerge? Have a spokesperson make a list of these. (Time: 15 minutes)

Task 3:

Spokespersons report findings to the class. List on the board all of the fictional leaders and real-life leaders discussed in your group. (Time: 15 minutes)

Discussion Questions:

1. Was it easier to pick a fictional leader than a real-life example of a leader?
2. What professions do the leaders, both fictional and real-life, come from? Are any examples from business? Do military, political, or church leaders dominate the listings?
3. Is it easier to write a definition of leadership than it is to find worthy examples?

Activity 3–2: Creating a Dialogue with a Leader*

Objectives:

a. To provide you with an opportunity to be aware of aspects of leadership that are important to you.
b. To enable you to learn from your own past experiences with a person who has acted as a leader.
c. To integrate what you have learned about leadership theory with what you know about leadership based on your own experience.

Task 1 (Homework):

Choose a person whom you admire as a leader. Choose someone you respect for his or her positive qualities and actions. It is best if the individual is someone you know personally, such as your supervisor at work, a leader of an organization at school or at church, or someone in your family. If you cannot think of any such person, you might choose someone of national or international importance whom you know through the news media; or you might choose a historical person about whom you have read, such as Gandhi, Clara Barton, or Abraham Lincoln. Be sure, however, that this is a person you have some knowledge of and from whom you want to learn.

Task 2 (Classroom):

Follow your instructor's guidance through the steps of this exercise, which is based on a journal writing technique developed by Ira Progroff and described in *At a Journal Workshop* (New York: Dialogue House, 1973). There are nine steps to the exercise. In the first step, you will have a few minutes to relax so that you will be less distracted by everyday tension and more able to enter into your imagination. In the next step, you will remember the leader you have chosen and write a brief statement about your relationship with him or her. Then you will imagine the person as clearly and in as much detail as possible and recall and list some of the important times in this person's life. The next step in the exercise is to imagine having a dialogue with this person about leadership and to record the results of this imagined conversation. After reflecting on the dialogue, you will read what you have written, add what you wish, then record your feelings. Then you will return from your imagination to your classroom. While you will not be required to share what you have written, you will be given the opportunity to share what you wish and to discuss what you have learned about leadership from this experience.

1. Discuss what you choose about this experience with a small group or in the class. Your instructor will provide you with questions to focus your discussion.

Suggestions for Discussion Questions:

1. What was this exercise like for you? Was it difficult or easy for you to choose a leader with whom to dialogue? Why?
2. Were you surprised by anything that occurred during the exercise? What? What did you learn about this leader or about leadership from this surprise?
3. What one thing about leadership emerged as most important to you?
4. How is your personal, experienced-based understanding of leadership, as articulated through this exercise, like what you have learned about leadership from the readings and lectures? How is it different?
5. If the person you chose for this dialogue is someone with whom you have regular contact, will you relate differently to him or her the next time you meet? If so, how? Do you think you would like to have a real-life conversation with this person about leadership? How might you go about doing this?

Introduction

Leadership and management are very much on everyone's mind today. Institutions and organizations are struggling as they face increasingly turbulent times. Leading and managing occurs at the federal government level in Washington, D.C., at the corporate level as foreign competition increases, and in religious institutions, schools, courts, museums, hospitals, computer-integrated manufacturing facilities, and other institutions that all seem to be in the midst of change and an uncertain future. As the challenges of managing and leading increase, so does our need to understand the unique features of leaders, the leadership process, and managers and leadership dynamics in the context of behavior in organizations.

Module 2 opened the discussion of organizational behavior with exercises demonstrating key aspects of the involvement learning process. We began with a discussion of what organizational behavior was, drawn from participants' own experiences. We then moved to creating a climate for learning, based on communication and trust building. In this module, we turn to a key contextual dimension of organizational behavior—leadership. Leadership is most comprehensible as an aspect of individual effectiveness. The leader's own effectiveness is individual; in exercising leadership, interpersonal effectiveness is involved. However, contemporary leadership includes encouragement of employees to look beyond their self-interests to larger concerns.

Leaders have new visions of organizational success and they influence others to bring about change. The Premodule Activity focuses on the exploration of some of the tenets of leadership in the context of individual and interpersonal effectiveness.

Leadership: An Overview

Leadership Defined

Group discussions of leadership are fascinating, whether the participants are business executives, college students, or academics. Many executives believe strongly that when it comes to leadership, ''you've either got it or you haven't.'' But when it comes to defining what it is you've got or haven't got, they can't agree. In contrast, academic views of leadership range from the benign ''we don't really know what it is'' to rigorous definitions based on very narrow research. In 1974, Stogdill concluded that ''there are almost as many definitions of leadership as there are persons who have attempted to define the concept.''[1] Three massive reviews by Bass[2] and Yukl[3,4] provide excellent surveys of the leadership literature and help to clear the air. Yukl notes that while conceptual disagreements are deep, most definitions emphasize leadership as an *influence process.* Beyond this common theme, researchers disagree on many other aspects, including how leaders are identified, who exerts influence, how leaders differ from followers, and which elements in the work situation influence leader behavior. Sample definitions of **leadership** include

1. Leadership is the behavior of an individual when he is directing the activities of a group toward a shared goal.[5]
2. Leadership is interpersonal influence, exercised in a situation, and directed, through the communication process, toward the attainment of a specified goal or goals.[6]
3. Leadership is the influential increment over and above mechanical compliance with the routine directives of the organization.[7]
4. Leadership appears to be the art of getting others to want to do something that you are convinced should be done.[8]
5. Leadership is broadly defined as influence processes affecting the interpretation of events for followers, the choice of objectives for the group or organization, the organization of work activities to accomplish the objectives, the motivation of followers to achieve the objectives, the maintenance of cooperative relationships and teamwork, and the enlistment of support and cooperation from people outside the group or organization.[9]
6. Leadership is an activity or set of activities, observable to others, that occurs in a group, organization, or institution involving a leader and followers who willingly subscribe to common purposes and work together to achieve them.[10]

The Leadership-versus-Management Debate

One debate raging in popular management literature concerns the differences between leadership and management. Certainly, if a leader is loosely defined as a person who influences others in any manner, then the person can be a leader without being a manager. Also, a person can be manager but can fail to lead. Managers have numerous roles and activities to carry out, and leadership activities only relate to a subset of the larger managerial functions and activities.[11] These distinctions are well accepted and have not been part of the debate. The controversy concerns the notion that leading and managing are qualitatively different or mutually exclusive.

The first writer to take a hard line on this issue was Abraham Zaleznik, when his landmark article was published in *Harvard Business Review* in 1977.[12] Zaleznik argues that managers carry out responsibilities, exercise authority, and worry about how things get done, whereas leaders are concerned with understanding people's beliefs and gaining their commitment. Managers and leaders differ in what they attend to and in how they think, work, and interact. Zaleznik believes that these differences stem from unequal developmental paths, from childhood to adulthood. Essentially, leaders have encountered major hardships or events, in stark contrast to the orderly upbringing of the typical manager. Leaders have achieved separateness; this enables them to dream up ideas and to stimulate others to work hard to bring these dreams into reality. In contrast, managers are process-oriented and believe that good systems and processes produce good results.[13] In a related argument, Kotter states that leadership is about coping with change, whereas management is about coping with complexity.[14] Warren Bennis believes that the difference between leaders and managers is the ability to master the context rather than surrender to it: ''The manager does things right; the leader does the right thing.''[15] Figure 3–1 summarizes the unique features of both management and leadership.

Figure 3–1
A Comparative Summary of Leadership and Management Features

Management

Carry out traditional management functions:
Planning, budgeting, organizing, staffing, problem solving, and control.
Assume roles as required:*
Interpersonal roles of symbolic figurehead, liaison with key people, supervisor of employees.
Informational roles of information monitor, information disseminator, and spokesperson.
Decision-making roles of innovator within the unit, disturbance handler, resource allocator, and negotiator.

Leadership

Challenging the status quo.
Developing vision and setting direction.
Developing strategies for producing changes toward the new vision.
Communicating the new direction and getting people involved.
Motivating and inspiring others.

* From Henry Mintzberg, ''The Manager's Job: Folklore and Fact,'' *Harvard Business Review,* July-August 1975.

The response to the writers who claim there is a distinction between leadership and management was immediate and strong. Many executives and academicians see considerable overlap between leadership and management activities and preoccupations, and they believe that it is wrong to assume that a person cannot be good at both. Certainly, there is little or no research to support the notion that selected people can be classified as leaders rather than managers, or that managers cannot adopt visionary behaviors when they are required for success. We maintain that it is important for all managers and supervisors to establish themselves as leaders. Further, team-based organization designs are extending leadership functions to work groups and cross-department teams in most modern organizations. There is opportunity for more innovation and critical thinking at all levels of the organization.

We will not argue that leadership and management are mutually exclusive, but they are distinct. We will draw from Clark and Clark[16] that choosing to lead is an intentional act—not everyone is willing to fully accept the responsibilities and burdens of leadership or perceive themselves as leaders. Leadership skills can be developed and enhanced at any developmental stage of one's career—the earlier this decision is made, the more likely that those skills will develop to their potential.

Large numbers of people choose not to lead but to ''boss''; they view their group members as inferior, undisciplined, untrainable, and requiring ''management.'' We surmise that there may be as much tyranny today as the world has ever seen. However, it is widely condoned as the necessary tyranny of the foreman getting the job done, the enforcement of rules by the bureaucrat preventing disorder, the control of thugs by the police protecting the populace, or the right of the ''big people'' dominating ''little people.'' Our comics and cartoonists find this form of tyranny a dependable source for plying their trade.[17]

Role Behaviors

Behavioral science investigations of leadership now cover more than 50 years. Personality, traits, attitudes, role behaviors, and situational factors (among others) have been used as the basis for leadership studies. What emerges from all of this is, frankly, less than one might hope. It is difficult to identify traits or characteristics an individual must possess to be a successful leader. Little progress has been made in identifying future leaders on the basis of personality, traits, or attitudes, even though these factors are apparently important. In leadership, as in other aspects of human behavior, complexity dictates that there is no single "one best way," however much we might wish it. Instead, contingent approaches, depending on circumstances, seem more likely. Current research is aimed at identifying the circumstances. One of the more meaningful ways of understanding and studying leadership is in terms of **role behaviors,** which we emphasize in this text.

Roles are patterns of behavior an individual learns in order to perform tasks and relate to people while fulfilling the responsibilities of a given position. Thus a manager must learn the skills and acquire the knowledge necessary to accomplish duties and relate to superiors, peers, and subordinates. Focusing upon role behaviors has several advantages.

First, it is possible to study what more competent managers do to get results and to involve people in the performance of their work. The patterns of these behaviors and the assumptions upon which they are based are frequently referred to as managerial style. There are different styles of management; one may be successful under one set of conditions, while another may work better under other circumstances. What works in the electronics industry may not work in the steel industry. What works in the military may not work in NASA, and what works in NASA may not work at a university. Different styles are needed to achieve results in different work environments.

Second, while it is difficult to change personality or traits, it is assumed that most people, to some degree, can learn the role behaviors of different leadership styles. Role behaviors are determined in part by attitudes, assumptions, knowledge, and skills, all of which can be learned. Research knowledge has provided the substance for leadership training and management development programs and for courses such as this one.

Third, role behaviors are part of a systems approach to understanding effectiveness at the four levels of behavior targeted by this course. The **managerial role** is related to those of superiors, subordinates, and peers, and to those of the small group or team. The small-group behaviors are in turn a subsystem of activities related to other teams or subsystems, and these are integrated into the total system of organization. Understanding leadership styles calls for an understanding of team style and organization style—concepts that will be developed in future chapters.

Leadership Style

We have chosen role behaviors as our focus of the study of leadership, but when we turn to a definition of leadership style, it will be in terms of attitudes and beliefs. The reason is that our expectations and assumptions about people are based upon our belief systems. Role behaviors may be what we see people actually do, but what people actually do is based upon what they believe or assume should be done when acting out their roles in a particular set of circumstances.

Leadership style, as we shall use it here, refers to a pattern of philosophy, beliefs, attitudes, feelings, and assumptions about leadership that affect the individual's behavior when managing people. More specifically, style refers to the individual's expectations about how to use a leadership position both to participate and to involve other people in the achievement of results. This will become clearer with some examples. If you believe that people are basically "no damned good" and that they'll do as little as possible if you let them get away with it, then as a supervisor you'll seek to control people closely. You may have the image of yourself as "the boss" who spends much time checking up on what people are doing. A contrary set of assumptions holds that people are responsible, if given the opportunity for self-direction, and that they work as naturally as they play. If you hold these beliefs, your image of yourself as a supervisor may emphasize helping or coordinating people's efforts—you may concentrate on planning so that employees can act autonomously within the guidelines you set down. The main point is that your attitudes, expectations, and assumptions about yourself, your position, and the appropriate behavior for dealing with your employees will have a major impact on how you behave as a manager. In our sense, you have role behavior models in your head that determine how you behave.

Manager and Employee Responsibility for the Job

Serious attention to leadership in management began about 100 years ago with the scientific management movement. This rather mechanistic approach sought to rationalize division of labor and definition of tasks, so that the "one best way" could be found, recorded, and passed on to others. As part of the scientific management approach, the management tasks of planning, organizing, controlling, and directing were distinguished and separated from the employee tasks of performing the work.

Frederick Winslow Taylor is most closely associated with this view, but it was widely held by others as well. It seemed a logical extension of the idea of division of labor, and, in an era when education was often minimal, it seemed to make sense. The idea also coincided with social norms that held that the fittest people would rise to the top of the social scale, and that those who did not succeed were demonstrably less fit. Such views are no longer acceptable in American society. But the issues of control and participation are very much with us, as suggested by accounts of industrial democracy and Quality of Work Life (QWL) movements as well as attention paid to union board members at Chrysler. Social developments such as the human potential movement, stressing individual autonomy and responsibility, also testify to changed times. The issue of management control is at the heart of the difficult task of managing a highly educated work force, often in highly technical tasks.

Leadership Style and Life-Style

Styles of managing cannot be separated from the general culture in which they occur. The style of management would be expected to be consistent with the national character of a country. The autocratic style, with its highly directive involvement by management and a strongly conforming involvement by employees, is apparently more acceptable in societies more structured than the United States. Generally, family style also can be fitted into the models used here. For instance, parents can take the disciplinary role of the autocratic style with their children, or they can place major emphasis upon conforming to the community, which parallels the emphasis upon system in the corporate style. They can overindulge their young as the permissive style does employees; they can neglect them and assume little responsibility, like the retired-on-the-job type; or they can produce a supportive, problem-solving environment so the offspring can assume the responsibility for their own self-direction as they gain competence, as in the professional-transformational manager style.

Most managers believe that they must adapt their style of leadership to the culture of the employees; that is, they believe that leadership is culturally contingent.[18] The interrelationship between life-styles and the culture or subcultures of a country is also similar to the interrelationship between leadership style and organizational style. They tend to be consistent with and reinforce one another. The study of leadership and its unique dynamics have attracted scholars from a variety of disciplines. Each school of thought contributed insight into this complex phenomenon. In the next section we examine some of these perspectives.

Leadership: Multiple Schools of Thought

The study of leadership in the behavioral sciences now covers over five decades. Personality, physical appearance, attitudes, behavior, and other factors have been studied as the basis for leadership and leadership success. A few distinct schools of thought have emerged. Figure 3–2 provides a skeleton of dimensions to the different schools of thought.

Researchers initially thought that personal traits would identify leaders and explain different levels of success. Later, studies focused on the leader's behavior as viewed by subordinates and they related different behavior with effectiveness of work units. More

Figure 3–2
Overview of Leadership

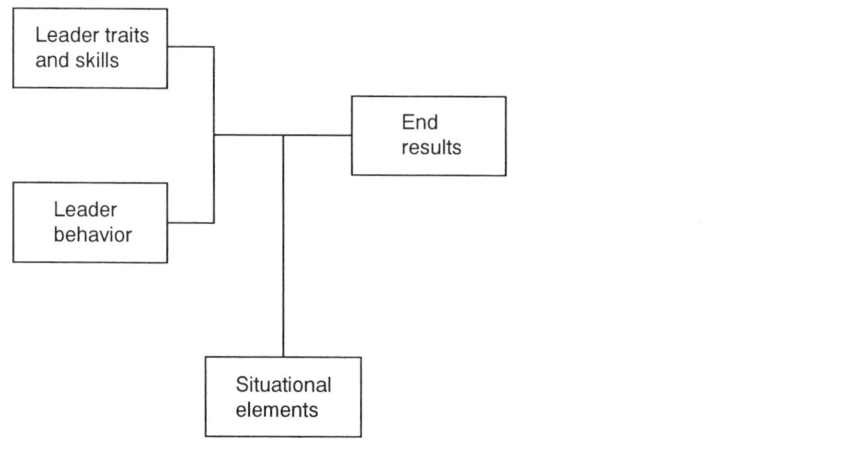

recently, some researchers have studied elements in the situations that influence the traits, behavior, and end results. Simply put, they believe that some people function better in certain situations, or that leader behavior must adjust to reflect the peculiar demands of each situation. Next we explore the different schools of thought on leadership.

Leadership Traits and Skills

Between 1920 and 1950, researchers hoped to discover how individual traits are connected to leadership effectiveness. The ''natural born leader'' concept seemed a logical basis for investigation. According to the **leadership trait** concept, leaders naturally possess traits that set them apart from other people. Thus height, appearance, personality, intelligence, race, sex, and other traits were used to explain the emergence of leaders and leadership effectiveness. This line of thinking produced few significant results. The trait theories were dealt a significant blow by leadership scholar Ralph Stogdill, who—after a thorough review of the research literature—concluded, ''A person does not become a leader by virtues of the possession of some combination of traits.''[19] Since Stogdill's pronouncement, much more research has been conducted. Kirkpatrick and Locke now assert that traits do matter.[20] They have identified six traits:

1. Drive: achievement, ambition, energy, tenacity, and initiative.
2. Leadership motivation (personalized versus socialized).
3. Honesty and integrity.
4. Self-confidence (including emotional stability).
5. Cognitive ability: intelligence and the perception of intelligence.
6. Knowledge of the business.

Skills have also been found to be predictors of leadership effectiveness. Depending on the organizational level, different mixes of technical skills, conceptual skills, and interpersonal skills are needed for success. At the lowest organizational levels, technical and interpersonal skills are very important, while at the highest levels, conceptual and administrative knowledge and skills are most required. Skills such as analytical ability, persuasiveness, memory for details, tact, and empathy are helpful in all leadership positions.

Charismatic Leadership

Charismatic leaders are those individuals who, by the sheer strength of their personality, effect strong influence over others. The charismatic leader may work from within or outside formal power structures; their intentions and outcomes can be beneficial or harmful. Conger and Kanungo describe seven characteristics of charismatic leaders: (1) self-confidence, (2) vision, (3) ability to communicate that vision, (4) strong convictions about that vision, (5) behavior that is out of the ordinary, (6) other people's perception of them as being change agents, and (7) environmental sensitivity.[21]

The arguments around the development of charismatic leaders vary, but there is some acknowledgment that these skills or attributes can be taught in much the same way that an actor learns a part.[22] Charismatic leadership appears to be most common among founders of organizations, who persist with bringing a vision to reality and may also become a liability to that organization as it approaches maturity. It is possibile for charismatic leaders' overwhelming self-confidence to become a barrier to effective communication; they simply may not listen or accept ideas that differ from their own.

Leadership Behavior

The identification of successful leadership behavior has had a more fruitful history than the trait approach. One of the earliest research programs, the Ohio State Leadership Studies, identified 1,800 specific examples of leadership behavior resulting in 150 questionaire items of important leadership functions.[23] The approach was to ask subordinates to describe their immediate supervisor using the survey items. Two factors emerged as important general dimensions of leadership: consideration and initiating structure. Consideration covers a wide variety of behaviors related to the treatment of people, including showing concern for subordinates, acting in a friendly and supportive manner, and looking out for their welfare. Finding time to listen to subordinates' problems and consulting with subordinates on important issues before making decisions are good examples of consideration. Initiating structure is a task-related dimension. It also covers a wide variety of behaviors, including defining roles and guiding subordinates toward attainment of work-group goals. Assignment of work, attention to standards of performance, and emphasis on deadlines are examples of initiating structure. In brief, the differences in the two dimensions can be reduced to concern for people and concern for task completion. This distinction has survived over the years as a major element in leadership models and studies.

In roughly the same time period (the 1950s), a second major program was launched at the University of Michigan. The research methods of that program included interviews and questionnaires; its objective was to determine if leaders of high-production units behaved differently from those of low-production units. The essence of the findings was that effective leaders performed different work than their subordinates, concentrating on planning and scheduling of work, coordinating projects, and offering various types of support. Effective supervisors were also relationship-oriented, showing trust and confidence, trying to understand subordinates' problems, and helping to develop subordinates' potential.[24] The early Michigan studies identified task- and people-oriented behaviors that were surprisingly similar to those found in the Ohio State studies. They also concluded that successful leaders emphasize participation in decision making and rely on group discussions in place of one-on-one supervision. An extension of these findings was that most leadership functions can be carried out by the subordinates as well as the manager.

By the 1960s, the University of Michigan model had been advanced to include five leadership dimensions, and the leadership questionnaire had been used in hundreds of organization climate studies in both the public and private sectors.[25] Activity 3–4 at the end of this module provides an insight and demonstrates the practical use of the Michigan model.

Case Example of the Michigan Behavioral Approach

During a recent management conference, the CEO of a large private gerontological institue asked the program directors for feedback on his performance as boss. He felt comfortable making the request because he had a history of good rapport with all of the directors. The directors managed legal, psychosocial (therapy), community program, research, and educational services for senior citizens at a central facility within a large metropolitan area.

The consultant proposed the Michigan leadership model as an initial basis for discussion. Each director was asked to anonymously rate the CEO on a continum from two stars (high score), one star, one flag, and two flags (low score) for each of the five

Michigan leadership dimensions. The directors complied. The tally of the scores appears below.

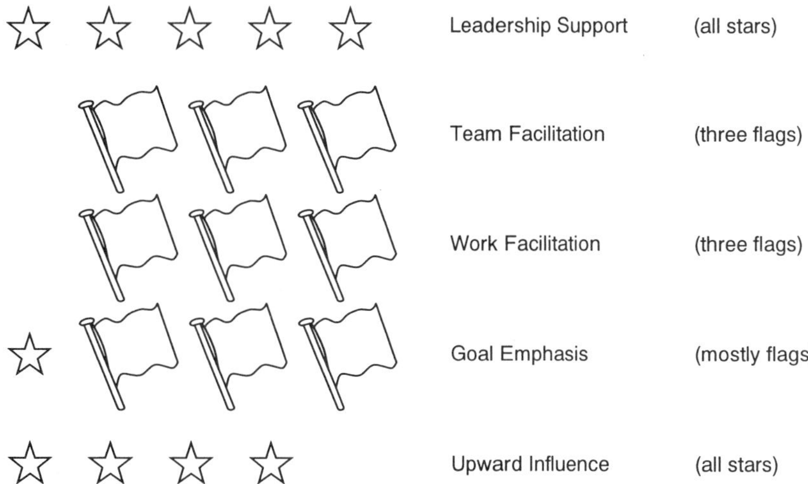

"That's awful!" exclaimed the CEO. "The profile is so unbalanced. It appears that I don't promote teamwork and I'm bad at helping with the work."

The ensuing discussion helped clarify the CEO's scores. One director mentioned that the CEO seldom called staff meetings, and the management conference was the first team-oriented activity in years. It was noted that the CEO spent little time advising the directors on day-to-day work matters, and he left the program goals up to each division. In contrast, the CEO spent most of his time representing the institute to the outside community, corporate sponsors, and other national gerontological organizations. Still, the CEO was available on a personal basis to meet with each director. An excellent communicator, the CEO was in high demand as a conference speaker and was highly involved with professional societies.

As the team discussed work demands, it became clear that the CEO's skills and behavior matched the requirements of the top-executive position. The directors valued his openness and personal support, but they believed he was not qualified to give technical advice regarding many of their respective functions. In fact, his help in facilitating their work was not needed or welcomed. The directors thought the CEO functioned best as a generalist, and they were delighted with his successful fund-raising activities. His outside focus produced a steady stream of donations to the institute, providing a measure of security to its employees. While they appreciated his contributions, the directors felt some changes were in order regarding goals and teamwork. The exercise ended with agreement on action steps for setting more institutewide goals and planning additional managerial meetings. In brief, the exercise affirmed the CEO's strengths and resulted in a few action steps to strengthen the team.

Situational Theories of Leadership

So far, although we have discussed the possibility that leadership behavior depends on the situation, we have not identified the factors in the situation that might influence the leader. The situational approach emphasizes that leaders may not have the required authority and discretion to make decisions, may not possess technical expertise in the unit managed, may be new to the subordinates in the work group, and may face other factors that make it easy or tough to manage. Do leaders behave differently in very unfavorable circumstances than they do in "normal" assignments? Situational theories attempt to discover aspects of the situation that influence behavior and explain how differently leaders respond. To illustrate the factors to consider in understanding the situational approach, we turn to Fred Fiedler's contingency theory.[26]

Fiedler's Contingency Model

Fiedler's work has been widely discussed and disputed over the years, but his theory provides some insight into certain aspects of directive and nondirective styles of leadership. The focus is upon designing the managerial position to match the motivational and personality characteristics of the manager, or what he calls engineering the job to fit the leadership style. Fiedler's work is meaningful for two other reasons: Interesting managerial implications can be drawn from the theory, and it provides an opportunity to examine important research questions, such as those on the questionnaire in Activity 3–4, "Least Preferred Co-Worker (LPC) Scale" on page M3-29.

An individual's managerial style is defined with reference to his score on the "Least Preferred Co-Worker (LPC) Scale," an exercise consisting of 18 pairs of bipolar adjectives. The manager is asked to choose the adjectives that most accurately describe the individual with whom he has worked least well. Those who receive a "high," score on the scale are defined as relationship-motivated: The score indicates they obtain satisfaction from working with others. Individuals whose scores fall at the other extreme are said to be task-motivated, obtaining their satisfaction primarily from accomplishing tasks and generally enjoying achievement for its own sake.

The second part of the contingency model—situational control—has three components. In descending order of importance they are: (1) leader-member relations—the support and loyalty obtained from the work group, (2) task structure—the clarity with which critical task components (goals, methods, and standards of performance) are defined; and (3) position power—the degree of power bestowed by the organization to reward and punish subordinates.

Fiedler posits that task-motivated **(low LPC)** leaders perform best in situations where they have either very much or very little situational control; relationship-motivated **(high LPC)** leaders perform best in situations allowing them moderate control and influence. In leader-match training, the individual's leadership style and situational control are identified, and the individual is offered strategies for changing critical components of his situation rather than suggestions for modifying his personality. This approach differs from that of the traditional leadership program, in which leadership is defined in absolute terms thought to be universally applicable or in which managers are instructed to change their leadership behavior to fit different situations.

The contingency model assumes that the manager's behaviors and personal characteristics are more difficult to change than is the work situation.[27]

Research Design and Results: The design of Fiedler's research was to form work groups, each of which had some combination of the three job situation variables. Eight different combinations were used. (See Figure 3–3.) Thus the first would have a work group that made good leader-member relations possible, had a structured task, and was one in which the leader had strong position power. Numerous relationship-motivated (high-LPC) leaders and task-motivated (low LPC) leaders were used to manage all eight variations to see if the style of leadership made a difference in the group performance.

Needless to say, the results from a research project with such an extensive design were complicated and difficult to interpret. Figure 3–4 provides a broad summary of the findings. The high-control situation represents regions 1 and 2 of the eight categories in Figure 3–3, the low-control situation represents regions 7 and 8, while the moderate-control regions are near the center.

Figure 3–3

Types of Job Situations for Leaders

	1	2	3	4	5	6	7	8
Leader–member relations	Good	Good	Good	Good	Poor	Poor	Poor	Poor
Task structure	High	High	Low	Low	High	High	Low	Low
Leader position power	Strong	Weak	Strong	Weak	Strong	Weak	Strong	Weak

Adapted from Fred E. Fiedler, "The Leadership Game: Matching the Man to the Situation," *Organizational Dynamics,* Winter 1976.

Figure 3–4

Summary of Leadership Style, Behavior, and Performance in Varying Situations

Leader Type	Situational Control: High Control	Moderate Control	Low Control
High-LPC (relationship-motivated)	Behavior: Somewhat autocratic, aloof, and self-centered. Seemingly concerned with task Performance: Poor	Behavior: Considerate, open, and participative Performance: Good	Behavior: Anxious, tentative, overly concerned with interpersonal relations Performance: Poor
Low-LPC (task-motivated)	Behavior: Considerate and supportive Performance: Good	Behavior: Tense and task-focused Performance: Poor	Behavior: Directive, task-focused, and serious Performance: Relatively good

Reprinted from Fred E. Fiedler and Martin M. Chemers with Linda Mahar, *Improving Leadership Effectiveness: The Leader Match Concept* (New York: John Wiley & Sons, 1976), p. 136.

Hersey and Blanchard's Situational Leadership

The situational leadership model developed by Hersey and Blanchard is one of the more widely used in corporate training, the military, and other government agencies in the United States. "It has been a major factor in training and development programs for more than 400 of the *Fortune* 500 companies, such as Bank of America, Caterpillar, IBM, Mobil Oil, Union 76, and Xerox."[28] This model owes its origins to the Ohio State studies and uses concepts similar to initiating structure (task behavior) and consideration (relationship behavior). The model emphasizes behavior that is observable as opposed to attitudes.

Situational leadership asserts that there is no one correct style of leadership with a single set of accompanying behaviors. They contend that the leader must respond to the environmental stimulus with appropriate sets of task and relationship behaviors based on followers' behavior and environmental context. They propose four possible sets of behaviors:

S1: high-task and low-relationship behaviors in response to followers who are unable and unwilling or insecure.

S2: high-task and high-relationship behaviors in response to followers who are unable and willing or confident.

S3: high-relationship and low-task behaviors in response to followers who are able but unwilling or insecure.

S4: low-relationship and low-task behaviors in response to followers who are able and willing or confident.

"**Task behavior** is defined as the extent to which the leader engages in spelling out duties and responsibilities of an individual or group."[29]

"**Relationship behavior** is defined as the extent to which the leader engages in two-way or multiway communication." The behaviors include listening, facilitating, and supportive behaviors.[30] Figure 3–5 respresents the range of leader behavior in response to follower readiness.

The most recent evolution of the Hersey and Blanchard model is their *tridimensional leader effeciveness model.* This model takes situational leadership into a third dimension, effectiveness. The model asserts that with each response to a set of stimuli, there is a corresponding leader behavior that is either ineffective, neutral, or effective. Effective is defined as when the leader's behavior is appropriate to a given situation. Appropriate behavior requires the leader to select the correct set of behaviors given the follower's readiness. The accompanying illustration builds on the previous illustration by providing ineffective styles (−4 to −1), neutral behaviors, and effective behaviors (+1 to +4). These models have a highly intuitive appeal to them—but, to date, only a limited amount of research supports their effectiveness (limited to situational leadership and not the tri-dimensional model). One study conducted by Gumpert and Hambleton at Xerox concluded that, of the 65 managers in their study, those who were considered highly effective indicated a greater knowledge and use of situational leadership than the less effective managers.[31] Figure 3–6 captures the essence of the tri-dimensional model.

Figure 3–5

Hersey and Blanchard's Situational Leadership Model

Task Behavior—
The extent to which the leader engages in defining roles—i.e., telling what, how, when, where, and, if more than one person, who is to do what in:

- Goal-setting
- Organizing
- Establishing time lines
- Directing
- Controlling

Relationship Behavior—
The extent to which a leader engages in two-way (multi-way) communication, listening, facilitating behaviors, socioemotional support:

- Giving support
- Communicating
- Facilitating interactions
- Active listening
- Providing feedback

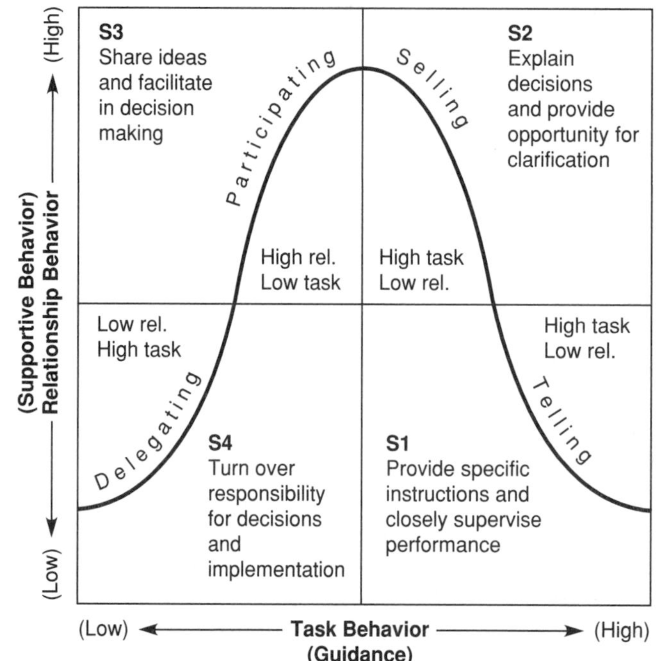

Decision Styles

1
Leader-made decision

2
Leader-made decision with dialogue and/or explanation

3
Leader/follower-made decision or follower-made decision with encouragement from leader

4
Follower-made decision

Follower Readiness

High	Moderate		Low
R4	**R3**	**R2**	**R1**
Able and willing or confident	Able but unwilling or insecure	Unable but willing or confident	Unable and unwilling or insecure
Follower directed		Leader directed	

Ability: has the necessary knowledge, experience, and skill

Willingness: has the necessary confidence, commitment, motivation

When a leader behavior is used appropriately with its corresponding level of readiness, it is termed a *high-probability match.* The following are descriptors that can be useful when using situational leadership for specific applications:

S1	**S2**	**S3**	**S4**
Telling	Selling	Participating	Delegating
Guiding	Explaining	Encouraging	Observing
Directing	Clarifying	Collaborating	Monitoring
Establishing	Persuading	Committing	Fulfilling

Source: Paul Hersey and Kenneth Blanchard, *Management of Organizational Behavior: Utilizing Human Behavior,* 6th ed. (Escondido, Calif.: The Center for Leadership Studies, 1988), p. 207. Reprinted with permission. All rights reserved.

Path–Goal Theory

A third situational approach that has generated considerable interest is **path–goal theory.**[32] This approach is unique because it combines leadership with motivation theory. (See Module 6.) Path–goal theory suggests that leaders motivate subordinates to achieve high performance by showing them the path to reach valued goals or results. When the tasks along the way have been performed and the goals reached, rewards follow. The leader's role is to show a clear path and to help eliminate barriers to achievement of the goals.

Path–goal theory starts with this simple scenario, but it becomes increasingly complex when leadership style enters the picture. Leadership style was defined earlier in this module as a pattern of philosophy, beliefs, and assumptions about leadership that affects the individual's behavior when managing people. Path–goal theory includes

Figure 3–6
Hersey–Blanchard Tri-Dimensional Leader Effectiveness Model

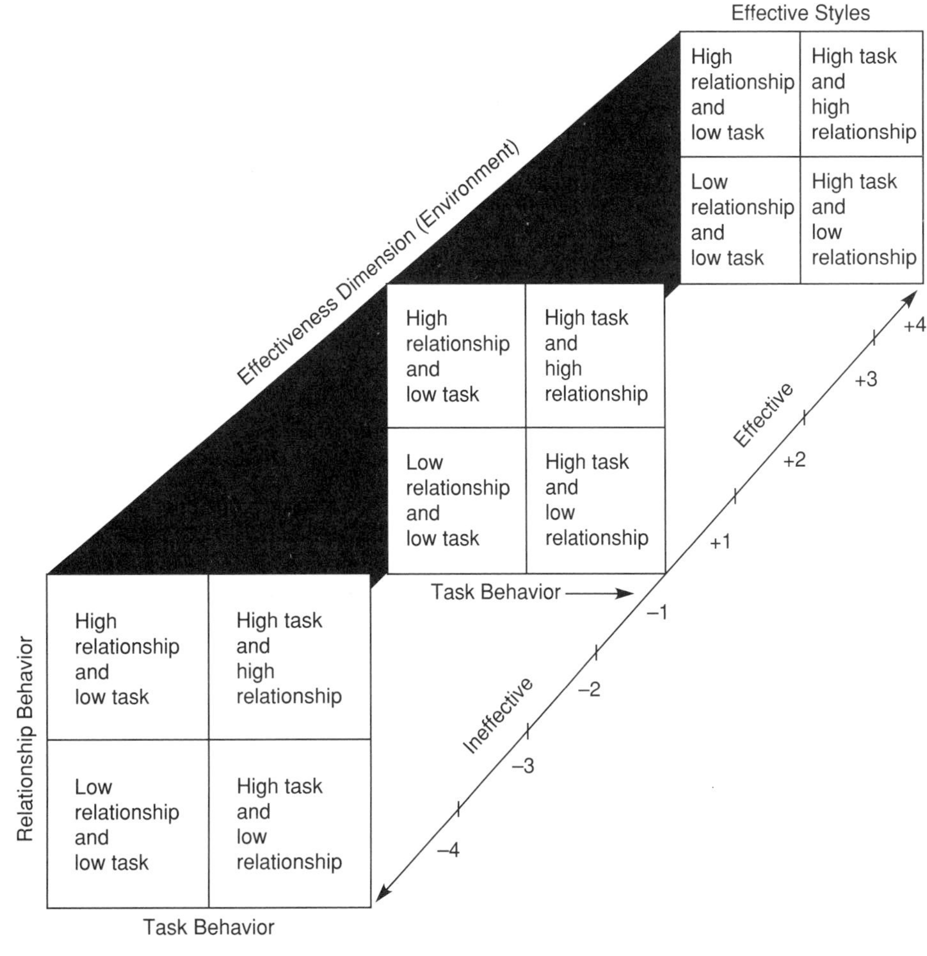

Source: Paul Hersey and Kenneth Blanchard, *Management of Organization Behavior: Utilizing Human Behavior,* 6th ed. (Escondido, Calif.: The Center for Leadership Studies, 1988), p. 131. Reprinted with permission. All rights reserved.

four different leadership styles: **directive leadership,** which is similar to the Ohio State concept of initiating structure; **supportive leadership,** which is similar to the concept of consideration; **participative leadership,** which emphasizes consultation with subordinates before decisions are made; and **achievement-oriented leadership,** where the leader is preoccupied with setting challenging goals for the work group. Leader style and behavior interact with several contingency factors to determine the employee's job performance and satisfaction. Figure 3–7 summarizes the contingency and outcome factors involved.

Path–goal theory is difficult to summarize given the number of contingency factors involved. Three subordinate characteristics are covered by the model, including ability, attitude toward authoritarianism, and preference for self-control or internal control (in contrast to control by others). These characteristics influence how subordinates perceive the leader's behavior. For example, people who have an internal locus of control prefer participative leaders; those who are high in authoritarianism react positively to directive leadership. Background factors such as the nature of the task and rewards also come into play. If subordinates know how to do the job and the task is routine, then the path to the goal is clear and the best style may be supportive. When tasks are uncertain, a more directive style of leadership may be welcomed by subordinates. The leader's task is to reduce uncertainty by clarifying either the desired results or the tasks to accomplish them. Also, the leader must remove barriers to performance and attempt to influence attitudes about tasks, goals, and rewards.

Path–goal theory is complex and difficult to study. Most researchers have focused on a few aspects of the complete theory, and the results have been mixed.[33] The princi-

Figure 3–7
Path–Goal View of Leadership Dynamics

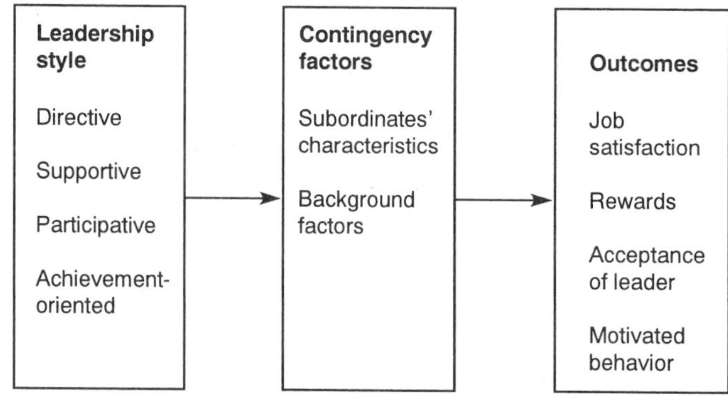

pal contributions of this approach have been an expanded search for relevant contingency factors and clarification of ways that managers can influence employee motivation and performance. It suggests that managers can determine the best mix of behavior to apply in guiding subordinates toward improved effort, performance, and satisfaction. This is a dramatic shift away from Fiedler's contingency theory, where leadership style is considered to be relatively fixed and the solution may be to change leaders or aspects of the work situation.

Personality Assessment Theory

The best way to forecast leadership is to use a combination of measurements of cognitive ability, personality, simulations, role play, and multi-rater instruments and techniques according to Hogan, Curphy, and Hogan.[34] It is generally acknowledged that personality assessments alone cannot be used to forecast leadership, but these authors assert that they can play a very useful role in predicting leaders' behavior. They specifically advance the ''big five dimensions of personality'' as a substantial enhancement of personality research. The components of the big five dimensions of personality are surgency, emotional stability, conscientiousness, agreeableness, and intellectance.

''Surgency measures the degree to which an individual is sociable, gregarious, assertive, and leaderlike versus quiet, reserved, mannerly, and withdrawn.''[35]

Emotional stability is concerned with ''the extent to which individuals are calm, steady, cool, and self confident versus anxious, insecure, worried, and emotional.''[36]

Conscientiousness ''differentiates individuals who are hard working, persevering, organized and responsible from those who are impulsive, irresponsible, undependable, and lazy.''[37]

''Agreeableness measures the degree to which individuals are sympathetic, cooperative, good-natured, and warm versus grumpy, unpleasant, disagreeable, and cold.''[38]

Intellectance ''concerns the extent to which an individual is imaginative, cultured, broad minded, and curious versus concrete minded, practical, and has narrow interests.''[39]

We will explore the big five theory in more depth in Module 5 that focuses on individual personality. In the context of leadership, utilizing the basic definitions of the five factors, the authors revisit the work of Stogdill, Bent, Bray, and Howard to find support for their assertion of personality determinants of leadership.[40] The above dimensions form a continuum with each definition starting with the most positive attributes and ending with negative attributes. It is the researchers' assertion that the dimensions' positive end of the continuum directly correlate with managerial advancement and positive observer ratings of leaders. They argue further that these positive dimensions equate to effective group and team leadership.

Transformational Leadership

The 1980s environment brought revolutionary change to many American businesses, and the pace of change is accelerating according to political and economic developments in Europe, the Middle East, and other locations. The 1990s environment is expected to continue to emphasize the transformation and revitalization of public and private institutions. Deeply entrenched differences between management and labor, between environmentalists and businesses, and between universities and constituent organizations are being reevaluated according to the changing power of nations and increasing economic competition. In light of these unprecedented changes, transformational leadership can be viewed as vital to the survival and growth of organizations, and it is a timely topic for further discussion. Yukl refers to **transformational leadership** as the process of influencing major changes in the attitudes and assumptions of the organization's members and building commitment for the organization's mission or objectives.[41]

While the literature on transformational leadership is naturally focused on CEOs and top management, transformational leadership commonly involves the actions of leaders at all levels, not just those at the top. Bass defines transformational leaders in terms of the leader's influence on followers. Followers are motivated to do more than originally expected because of their feelings of trust, admiration, loyalty, and respect for the leader. Bass believes this motivation occurs when the leader makes subordinates more aware of the importance and values of task outcomes, helps them think beyond their own self-interest to the work team and organization, and activates higher-order needs such as creative expression and self-actualization.[42] Transformational leaders have charisma, but this is not the only factor needed to bring about change. Transformational leaders also perform the roles of coach, trainer, and mentor.

In a recent study of transformational leadership, James Kouzes and Barry Posner asked over 500 managers first to reflect on all of their leadership experiences and next to focus on one extraordinary experience. Managers were asked to get a clear mental picture of the experience (that is, to see, hear, and feel it again as intensely as possible). They were then asked to respond to a long list of open-ended questions about the situation, the project, their involvement, the leadership actions, and the outcomes. Responses to this "personal bests" study helped the authors to build a new instrument, the *Leadership Practices Inventory.*

The Leadership Practices Inventory can be regarded as a transformational leadership instrument since it was specifically developed to measure the conceptual framework developed in the case studies of managers' personal best experiences as leaders. The context was accomplishment of extraordinary things. The original interviews and questionnaire focused on five factors:[43]

1. Challenging the process. (Search for opportunities, experiment, take risks.)
2. Inspiring a shared vision. (Envision the future and enlist others.)
3. Enabling others to act. (Foster collaboration and strengthen others.)
4. Modeling the way. (Set the example, plan small wins.)
5. Encouraging the heart. (Recognize contributions, celebrate accomplishments.)

Summary of Leadership Schools of Thought

Thus far, this section has focused on the unique insights provided by scholars who have investigated leadership and its dynamics from different perspectives. Each school of thought, beyond being anchored in a specific discipline, contributed to our holistic understanding of this complex phenomenon. The traits and skills perspective focused our attention on the specific individual skills that are likely to predict leadership effectiveness. The charismatic leadership perspective focused on individuals who by the sheer strength of their personality affect others. The leadership behavior perspective highlighted the leader's behaviors and behavioral dimensions that are likely to predict effectiveness. The situational orientation focused on the contextual elements that can influence the leader's performance. Finally, the transformational perspective drew our attention to the processes and activities of influencing major changes in organizational life and direction.

Some Current Themes and Challenges

Leadership Training

If leaders are not born but rather are a product of their development with some assist from nature, then what can be done to develop our future leaders? The *Personnel Journal* reported on a 1991 survey conducted by the American Society for Training and Development (ASTD) that 60 percent of all major companies offer leadership training. Of the companies offering leadership training, 93 percent offer it to middle management, 66 percent to top management, 48 percent to executives, 79 percent to supervisors, and 33 percent to nonsupervisors.[44] While the cost of such training is not available, the data suggest that leadership training represents a growing proportion of the over $45.5 billion spent annually on training in the United States. In addition to numerous in-house programs offered by corporations, *Fortune* magazine reports that there are now over 600 firms competing in the leadership industry to provide leadership training to individuals and corporations.[45] Jay Conger asserts that leadership can be taught, ''But to be successful, training must be designed to (1) develop and refine certain of the teachable skills, (2) improve the conceptual abilities of managers, (3) tap individuals' personal needs, interests, and self-esteem, and (4) help managers see and move beyond their interpersonal blocks.[46] According to Conger, there are four categories of leadership training: *personal growth, conceptual understanding, feedback,* and *skill building.*

Personal growth experiences tap the needs and interests of the participant to build self-esteem and are linked to the leader's own motivation to lead and formulate a vision. Examples of personal growth experiences include Outward Bound, ropes courses, National Training Labs - Management Workshop, EST, and Lifespring. We address the area of personal growth in more depth in a later module.

Conceptual understanding consists of theory and research designed to give the potential leader a framework for cognitive development. Examples include the Tom Peters Group Leadership Challenge, Covey Leadership Principle-Centered Power and Leadership Seminars, and executive leadership programs at graduate business schools such as Harvard, Wharton, and Stanford.

Feedback approaches focus on a variety of data generated by psychometrics such as Meyers-Briggs Type Indicator, Firo-B (Fundamental Interpersonal Relationship Orientation), Leadership Style Indicator (a 360-degree feedback instrument), and the California Psychological Inventory. These approaches also use exercises designed to elicit behavior for videotaping and feedback by skilled observers. The Center for Creative Leadership's Leader Lab and National Training Labs' Leadership Excellence programs are examples of feedback-driven leadership development programs.

Skill building program designers identify key leadership skills that they believe can be taught. An example is the Forum Company's program, which includes interpreting the environment, shaping a vision, mobilizing employees to reach that vision.

As more corporations are investing in leadership training programs, the need to scientifically assess their effectiveness is growing. Some skepticism is echoed by Conger, who made the following statement: ''I believe that radical changes will ultimately have to occur in both content and the process of leadership training if corporations of the future are to ensure an adequate supply of leaders for themselves.''[47] The question for students contemplating their own leadership development, if leadership is a choice and leadership skills can be learned, is, What can and must I do to develop my potential?

Learning Leadership from Experience

Warren Bennis in his book *On Becoming a Leader* describes a journey toward self-discovery and understanding that comes through experience and not the classroom or workshop. Bennis's work is based on the premise that ''Leaders are people who are able to express themselves fully. They know who they are, what their strengths and weaknesses are, and how to fully deploy their strengths and compensate for their weaknesses.''[48] While Bennis arrives at his position through interviews with leaders and observation, research conducted by the Center for Creative Leadership gives strong empirical evidence to support Bennis's position. In research conducted since 1981 and through continuous refinement of that research, the center has examined key elements in the development of leaders and those factors that have led to the failure (or derailment) of similarly capable managers.[49] Results of that research appear in Figure 3–8. Note that the most significant developmental experience for both men and women came from job assignments.

Figure 3–8
Key Events in Executives' Development

	Men	Women
I. Challenging assignments	48%	32%
a. Line to staff	2.1	1
b. Projects/task forces	12.4	7
c. Scope	17	9
d. Fix-it	11	6
e. Scratch	5.6	6
II. Significant other people	17	23
a. Values playing out	9.7	14
b. Role models	7.4	9
III. Hardships	18	28
a. Failures and mistakes	4	9
b. Demotions, missed promotions, lousy job	5	5
c. Breaking a rut	4	4
d. Personal trauma	2	3
e. Employee problems	4	7
IV. Other events	17	16
a. Course work	6	1
b. First supervision	4.9	6
c. Early work	3.3	7
d. Purely personal	2.6	2

Source: Esther H. Lindsey, Virginia Homes, and Morgan W. McCall, Jr., *Key Events in Executives' Lives* (Greensboro, N.C.: Center for Creative Leadership, 1987); Morgan W. McCall, Jr., Michael M. Lombardo, and Ann M. Morrison, *The Lessons of Experience: How Successful Executives Develop on the Job* (New York: Lexington Books, 1988); Ann M. Morrison, Randal P. White, and Ellen Van Velsor, *Breaking the Glass Ceiling: Can Women Reach the Top of America's Largest Corporations?* (Menlo Park, Calif.: Addison-Wesley, 1992); and unpublished research to be released in October 1995.

The research findings raise the question for those seeking to be leaders, how do we learn the right things from experience and how do we get the right experiences? The research community has provided a whole new generation of psychometrics to measure on-the-job development called 360-degree leadership feedback. These instruments invite the individual, his or her bosses, peers, and subordinates to rate leadership skills based on a specific theory (Hersey and Blanchard's LBO-II), a model of leadership (Carlson Learning Corporation's Dimensions of Leadership Profile), or research findings (the Center for Creative Leadership's Benchmarks). All of these approaches seek to accentuate leadership strengths; some seek to mitigate potential weakness leading to derailment. The trend is to bring the work of assessment centers to the job. Current research now begins to focus on how to discover the developmental opportunities in your current job and stake out learning opportunities without ever having to leave the work site.[50] The answer to Conger's plea for further development of leadership training may be unfolding in what is euphemistically referred to as the *school of hard knocks.*

The work of the Center for Creative Leadership has focused on those factors that positively or adversely affect leadership in the work setting. These factors do not rely on innate traits, but rather on factors that can be learned from experience. These skills and perspectives really matter in a career. In the author's review of 360-degree feedback instruments, it was discovered that almost all of these psychometrics measure observable workplace behaviors. The factors described in the publication *Feedback to*

Managers in the section called Benchmarks are the basis for developmental leadership continuums.[51]

Culture and Globalization

There is a new interest in the leadership styles found in different countries, which is due to the internationalization of business. The rise of multinational corporations and the rush to acquire companies and properties is catching worldwide attention. Rapid advances in telecommunications and computers also have aided economic integration among countries. It has been noted that affluent teenagers in different countries wear the same clothes and listen to the same music. Societies are converging.

While trends toward common life-styles are unmistakable, leadership style is still influenced by cultural values and practices. Some researchers have found it useful to group countries into clusters according to common characteristics.[52] Evidence of an Anglo-American cluster, including Australia, Canada, New Zealand, South Africa, and the United States, is strong. For example, managers in this cluster value the individual and democracy and often have a British heritage. The Scandinavian cluster (Norway, Finland, Denmark, and Sweden) places even more emphasis on democracy in both government and the workplace. It is not surprising that countries in both clusters have welcomed participative management programs or that their employees resist autocratic styles. In contrast, Middle Eastern, Far Eastern, and Germanic clusters favor an autocratic style.

In some cultures, leader–follower roles and relationships are quite different. The allocation of responsibilities in the Far Eastern cluster is much less differentiated than in the Anglo-American cluster. For example, Japanese firms do not emphasize job descriptions or other mechanisms of dividing up the work. Japanese leaders are expected to provide *Amae* (love) for subordinates, and they will look to subordinates for advice. In turn, Japanese employees have high respect for their supervisors, and this respect extends beyond the workplace. The Japanese are known for participation of the work force in recommendations for worker activities, and their Quality Circles (worker suggestion and problem-solving groups) have become models of worker participation for U.S. companies. This would appear inconsistent on the surface until we understand the Japanese value of the individual denying one's own need for the good of the group and the need to contribute to the group. So the expectations of management and the employees are that the employee will contribute ideas, but at the same time be highly submissive to the will of management; in their cultural setting an autocratic style is the expectation, but a clearly defined area exists where the employee will participate. In other cultures where the autocratic style of management exists, workers may feel that management should make all decisions and therefore they do not expect to participate in any aspect of the managerial function.[53]

Leadership and Diversity

The workplace of the 1990s is consistent with the theme begun in the first module, an arena of great diversity. With the exception of the most recent research, the focus has been on the American white male. What differences might we expect if we were to expand our paradigm of leadership to an international setting with its great ethnic diversity and include women, who constitute a growing proportion of workers?

The work of Geert Hofstede includes a sample population of 116,000 employees from 40 countries. He found that managers and employees vary on four dimensions of national culture: individualism versus collectivism, power distance, uncertainty avoidance, and quality of life. Most important in our discussion of leadership is the concept of power distance. Power distance is a national cultural attribute describing the extent to which a society accepts that power in institutions and organizations is distributed unequally. In the United States and Canada, power distance is small; in Mexico and France, power distance is large, with Italy and Japan being in the middle. Missing subtleties such as power distance could adversely impact a leader's effectiveness.[54]

Since the 1970s, the number of women in leadership positions has steadily increased. In 1990, women occupied over 25 percent of the supervisory positions in U.S. industry, and women are increasingly elected to local, state, and national political positions. Another sign of this increase is the enrollment of women in schools of business. In 1990, the number of men and women enrolled in many U.S. business programs was equal. The entrepreneurial spirit is also alive. A rising number of women have started their own businesses, particularly in the service, retailing, and trade industries.[55]

As a result of these employment gains, men's attitudes toward women in the workplace are changing. Recent surveys indicate executives realize women want to be hired in positions of authority; these same executives also feel comfortable about working for women. Still, both men and women executives believe that women have to be exceptional to succeed in business. Women executives feel that they have had to struggle more to attain their positions in the business world and that they have been subjected to discrimination. It is evident that although conditions have improved, women still face disadvantages in opportunities. Some experts believe that corporate discrimination helps explain the explosive growth in small businesses owned by women.

Management has long been associated with stereotypical masculine traits and behavior such as competitiveness, willingness to take risks, and task orientation. Early studies indicated women identified with the masculine stereotypes of a successful manager as a way of overcoming the negative stereotypes of the ability of women to lead. However, recent studies indicate that women middle and top executives no longer equate management with masculine traits.

While long-held stereotypes of women and men are beginning to loosen, you might recognize stereotypes at work within your discussion group team. Research has shown that although some men are reluctant to assume leadership roles in all-male groups, they will often step forward when the group includes both men and women. Women are often viewed as better communicators and team players than men, and they are often perceived to be better at group building. These are general tendencies, which may not hold in your class group. They will be explored in a later module.

There is considerable research evidence that early trait differences disappear later in life. Differences between boys and girls, between male and female college students do not hold up as managers move into upper-level executive positions. Both men and women change with training and managerial experience. On the whole, experienced men and women managers have similar motives. Studies show both men and women executives have a high need for achievement and power, and both groups demonstrate assertiveness, self-reliance, risk taking, and other traits and behaviors associated with leadership. Women who are experienced managers show no differences in leadership ability from their experienced male counterparts. In fact, once men and women have established themselves as leaders in their organizations, women do not behave differently than men.[56]

Sally Helgesen in *The Female Advantage: Women's Ways of Leadership* studied four nationally prominent female leaders and identified their differences from their male counterparts. She characterizes their workplaces as "webs of inclusion," organizations where sharing information is key and where hierarchy is de-emphasized. While male leaders tend to champion vision, their female counterparts concentrate on developing voice. "The woman leader's voice is a means both for presenting herself and what she knows about the world, and for eliciting a response."[57] In finding one's voice, each individual leader in the study had to find her own individual strengths and weaknesses and determine how her uniqueness could contribute to her organization's success.

As global leaders, the expectation of flexibility and the ability to affect behaviors as the situation requires is critical to our success. We may also continue to learn from those who are different from us, modeling new behaviors and skills that might serve us well as the workplace continues its pace of rapid change.

Leadership and the Development of Your Class Team

If you are assigned to a permanent class team, it is an excellent opportunity to practice leadership skills. You are presumably working in a "leaderless" group since the instructor has not designated a formal leader. Leadership functions are still needed if the group is to carry out meaningful problem solving and perform various tasks. It may prove worthwhile to scan the list of roles typically assumed by members during the life of a small group. The module on small group dynamics covers these roles, indicating task- and relationship-oriented behavior needed for successful performance. Take time in your next group meeting to discuss these roles and the value of having a facilitator, recorder, and spokesperson. Some groups find it valuable to rotate these responsibilities so that all members can practice different leadership behaviors. Other groups recognize leadership skills in certain members, and the leadership positions are informally assumed early in the course.

Summary

Leadership is defined as a set of expectations for an individual to use in a leadership position to participate and to involve people in the achievement of results. The definition relates to the historical issue concerning the degree to which management and/or the employees should assume responsibility for planning, organizing, directing, and controlling organizational functions.

A review of the multiple perspectives on leadership revealed that although each school of thought is anchored in a specific discipline, taken together they contribute to our holistic understanding of leadership dynamics. The traits and skills perspective focused our attention on the specific individual skills that are likely to predict leadership effectiveness. The leadership behavior perspective highlighted the leader's behaviors and behavioral dimensions that are likely to predict effectiveness. The situational orientation focused on the contextual elements that can influence the leader's performance. Recent research on leadership training and the value of work experience on shaping or derailing leaders was explored. Finally, the transformational perspective draws our attention to the need to integrate many of the diverse factors of current society, including a highly educated and specialized work force, a vast technology, and rapid environmental change.

Study Questions

1. We have described leadership as a set of expectations. What is the advantage of focusing on expectations, attitudes, and philosophy rather than on actual behavior when defining leadership?
2. What is the best style of leadership?
3. What is the difference between leadership and management? Would you apply this to all levels of management? Give reasons for your answer.
4. Are managers born or made? The argument around this question has raged for many years. Many executives will say, "You've either got it or you haven't." What are the arguments on both sides? What do you believe?
5. In what way can leadership be regarded as a process? How does this apply to your team activities?
6. Compare and contrast between the trait approach, the behavioral approach, and the situational approach to leadership.
7. What new perspectives are offered by the situational leadership theories?

8. Discuss the relationship between leadership, expectation, learning, and diversity.
9. Describe the leadership dynamics within your team. How would you characterize the team? How effective is it? What can you experiment with to improve your team performance?

Endnotes

1. R. M. Stogdill, *Handbook of Leadership: A Survey of the Literature* (New York: Free Press, 1974).

2. Bernard M. Bass, *Bass and Stogdill's Handbook of Leadership: Theory, Research, and Managerial Implications* (New York: Free Press, 1990).

3. Gary Yukl, "Managerial Leadership: A Review of Theory and Research," *Journal of Management* 15, no. 2 (1989).

4. Gary A. Yukl, *Leaders in Organizations* (Englewood Cliffs, N.J.: Prentice-Hall, 1989).

5. J. K. Hemphill and A. E. Coons, "Development of the Leader Behavior Description Questionnaire," in *Leader Behavior: Its Description and Measurement,* eds. R. M. Stogdill and A. E. Coons (Columbus Ohio: Bureau of Business Research, Ohio State University, 1957).

6. R. Tannenbaum, I. R. Weschler, and F. Massarik, *Leadership and Organization* (New York: McGraw-Hill, 1961).

7. D. Katz and R. Kahn, *The Social Psychology of Organizations,* 2d ed. (New York: John Wiley & Sons, 1978).

8. J. M. Kouzes and B. Z. Posner, *The Leadership Challenge* (San Francisco: Jossey-Bass, 1990).

9. Gary Yukl, *Leadership in Organizations,* 3d ed. (Englewood Cliffs, N.J.: Prentice Hall, 1994), p. 5.

10. Kenneth E. Clark and Miriam B. Clark, *Choosing to Lead* (Greensboro, N.C.: The Center for Creative Leadership, 1994), p. 19.

11. Henry Mintzberg, "The Manager's Job: Folklore and Fact," *Harvard Business Review,* July-August, 1975.

12. Abraham Zaleznik, "Managers and Leaders: Are They Different?" *Harvard Business Review* 55, no. 5 (1977).

13. Abraham Zaleznik, "The Leadership Gap," *Academy of Management Review* 4, no. 1 (1990).

14. J. P. Kotter, *The Leadership Factor* (New York: Free Press, 1987).

15. Warren Bennis, *On Becoming a Leader* (Menlo Park, Calif.: Addison-Wesley, 1989), p. 45.

16. Kenneth E. Clark and Miriam B. Clark, *Choosing to Lead* (Greensboro, N.C.: Center for Creative Leadership, 1994).

17. Ibid., p. viii.

18. See, for example, N. J. Adler, *International Dimensions of Organizational Behavior* (Belmont, Calif.: Wadsworth, 1991).

19. Ralph M. Stogdill, "Personal Factors Associated with Leadership: A Survey of the Literature," *Journal of Psychology* 25 (1948), p. 64.

20. Shelley A. Kirkpatrick and Edwin A. Locke, "Leadership: Do Traits Matter," *The Executive,* May 1991, 5.2, pp. 48–60.

21. Jay A. Conger and Robert N. Kanungo, "Behavioral Dimensions of Charismatic Leadership," in *Charismatic Leadership,* Conger and Kanungo, eds. (San Francisco: Jossey-Bass, 1988), p. 91.

22. Jay A. Conger and Robert N. Kanungo, "Training Charismatic Leadership: A Risky and Critical Task," in *Charismatic Leadership,* pp. 309–23.

23. E. A. Fleishman, "The Description of Supervisory Behavior," *Personnel Psychology* 37 (1953).

24. R. Likert, *New Patterns of Management* (New York: McGraw-Hill, 1961).

25. J. Taylor and D. Bowers, *The Survey of Organizations: A Machine-Scored Standardized Questionnaire Instrument* (Ann Arbor, Mich.: Institute for Social Research, University of Michigan, 1972).

26. Fred E. Fiedler, ''Engineering the Job to Fit the Manager,'' *Harvard Business Review,* September-October 1965.

27. F. T. Sepic, L. Manar, and F. E. Fiedler, ''Match the Manager and the Milieu,'' *The Cornell HRA Quarterly,* August 1980, pp. 19–23.

28. Paul Hersey and Kenneth H. Blanchard, *Management of Organizational Behavior: Utilizing Human Resources,* 6th ed. (Englewood Cliffs, N.J.: Prentice Hall, 1993), p. 215.

29. Ibid., p. 185.

30. Ibid., p. 187.

31. Ibid., pp. 215–17.

32. R. J. House, ''A Path–Goal Theory of Leadership Effectiveness,'' *Administrative Science Quarterly* 16 (1971); and R. J. House and T. R. Mitchell, ''Path–Goal Theory of Leadership,'' *Contemporary Business* 3 (1974).

33. J. Indvik, ''Path–Goal Theory of Leadership: A Meta Analysis,'' *Proceedings of the Academy of Management Meetings,* 1986.

34. Robert Hogan, Gordon J. Curphy, and Joyce Hogan, ''What We Know about Leadership,'' *American Psychologist,* 49.6 (June 1994), p. 497.

35. Ibid., p. 503.

36. Ibid.

37. Ibid., p. 504.

38. Ibid.

39. Ibid.

40. Ibid., p. 498.

41. Gary Yukl, ''Managerial Leadership: A Review of Theory and Research,'' *Journal of Management* 15, no. 2 (1989), pp. 269, 272.

42. Bass, Ibid., p. 9.

43. Kouzes and Posner, 1990. Ibid.

44. Dawn Gunsch, ''For Your Information—Learning Leadership,'' *Personnel Journal,* 70.8 (1991), p. 17.

45. John Huey, ''The Leadership Industry,'' *Fortune,* 129.4 (1994), p. 54.

46. Jay A. Conger, *Learning to Lead: The Art of Transforming Managers into Leaders* (San Francisco: Jossey-Bass, 1992), p. 34.

47. Ibid., pp. 44–53.

48. Warren Bennis, *On Becoming a Leader* (Menlo Park, Calif.: Addison-Wesley, 1989), p. 3.

49. Esther H. Lindsey, Virginia Homes, and Morgan W. McCall, Jr., *Key Events in Executives' Lives* (Greensboro: Center for Creative Leadership, 1987); Morgan W. McCall, Jr., Michael M. Lombardo, and Ann M. Morrison, *The Lessons of Experience: How Successful Executives Develop on the Job* (New York: Lexington Books, 1988); Ann M. Morrison, Randal P. White, and Ellen Van Velsor, *Breaking the Glass Ceiling: Can Women Reach the Top of America's Largest Corporations?* (Menlo Park, Calif.: Addison-Wesley, 1992); and unpublished research to be released October 1994.

50. Cynthia D. McCauley, Marian N. Ruderman, Patricia J. Ohott, and Jane Morrow, ''Assessing the Developmental Components of Managerial Jobs,'' *Journal of Applied Psychology,* 79.4, pp. 544–60.

51. Ellen Van Velsor and J. Brittain Leslie, *Feedback to Managers, vols. 1 and 2: A Review and Comparison of Sixteen Multi-Rater Feedback Instruments* (Greensboro: Center for Creative Leadership, 1991), pp. 71–74.

52. S. Ronen and O. Shenkar, ''Clustering Countries on Attitudinal Dimensions: A Review and Synthesis,'' *Academy of Management Review* 10 (1985).

53. For additional material on leadership in other countries, see S. Ronen, *Comparative and Multinational Management* (New York: John Wiley & Sons, 1986); and Nancy J. Adler, *International Dimensions of Organization Behavior* (Boston: Kent, 1991).

54. Geert Hofstede, ''Motivation, Leadership, and Organization: Do American Theories Apply Abroad?'' *Organizational Dynamics,* Summer 1980, pp. 42–63.

55. Bass, 1990, p. 708.

56. Ibid., p. 721.

57. Sally Helgesen, *The Female Advantage: Women's Ways of Leadership* (New York: Doubleday–Currency, 1990), pp. 223–24.

Activity 3–3: Leadership Behavior

Objectives:

a. To examine a behavioral model of leadership.

b. To provide students an opportunity to evaluate a past boss's leadership behavior.

c. To demonstrate that sound leadership behavior varies with the organizational situation.

Task 1 (Homework):

a. As a homework assignment, complete the Leadership Questionnaire by rating the behavior of a past immediate supervisor.

b. Use the scoring key in Appendix E to determine high, moderate, and low ratings on each of the five University of Michigan dimensions. Be prepared to discuss the scores and their meaning to the class team.

Enter information and scores below:

Boss rated ______________________

Type of business ______________________

Description of the work situation ______________________

____

____

_______ A. *Leadership Support.* Behavior that enhances employee feelings of self-worth and importance.

_______ B. *Team Facilitation.* Behavior that encourages members of the group to develop close, mutually satisfying relationships.

_______ C. *Work Facilitation.* Activities that help achieve goal attainment by doing things such as scheduling, coordinating, planning, and providing resources such as tools, material, and technical advice and knowledge.

_______ D. *Goal Emphasis.* Behavior that stimulates an enthusiasm for meeting the group's goals, helps establish priorities, and promotes achievement of excellent performance.

_______ E. *Upward Influence.* Behaviors that advance the status of the work group and individuals (for example, acquiring resources needed by the group, securing rewards for group members, and eliminating barriers raised by other organizational units).

Task 2:

a. Meet with your class team. Let each team member describe the work situation and his/her ratings of the leader, without interruption except for clarifying questions. Move around the group until all have had their chance to participate. (Time: 20 minutes)

b. Discuss the following questions:
Do the dimensions cover all the behaviors that you believe are important for a leader in your situation? What dimensions would you add that would more fully describe the leader's actions?
What features of the situation caused the leader to behave the way she/he did? Does job success require the leader to behave in this fashion?
(Time: 10 minutes)

Name ______________________________ Date ____________________

Leadership Questionnaire*

Instructions:

This short questionnaire on leadership behaviors is based on the University of Michigan model. Identify a current or past manager who was your immediate supervisor. Circle the best choice from the options provided.

1. My supervisor is eager to recognize and reward good performance.
a. strongly disagree
b. disagree
c. not sure
d. agree
e. strongly agree

2. To what extent does your supervisor encourage you to think and act for yourself?
a. not at all
b. to a small extent
c. to some extent
d. to a great extent
e. to a very great extent

3. Generally, decisions are arrived at by my immediate supervisor with no input from people at lower levels.
a. strongly agree
b. agree
c. not sure
d. disagree
e. strongly disagree

4. My immediate supervisor is usually successful in dealing with higher levels of authority.
a. strongly agree
b. agree
c. not sure
d. disagree
e. strongly disagree

5. To what extent does your supervisor stress the importance of work goals?
a. not at all
b. to a small extent
c. to some extent
d. to a great extent
e. to a very great extent

6. My supervisor is friendly and easy to talk to.
a. strongly agree
b. agree
c. not sure
d. disagree
e. strongly disagree

7. To what extent does your supervisor offer new ideas for job-related problems?
a. not at all
b. to a small extent
c. to some extent
d. to a great extent
e. to a very great extent

8. How often does your supervisor hold group meetings for his/her employees?
a. never
b. rarely
c. sometimes
d. rather often
e. nearly all the time

9. My immediate supervisor is very successful in getting management to recognize the success of the employees he/she supervises.
a. strongly disagree
b. disagree
c. not sure
d. agree
e. strongly agree

10. My supervisor encourages people to give their best efforts.
a. strongly disagree
b. disagree
c. not sure
d. agree
e. strongly agree

* This instrument is a major modification of a survey initially developed at the Institute of Social Research, University of Michigan, Ann Arbor, Michigan, which was discussed in D. G. Bowers and S. Seashore, "Predicting Organizational Effectiveness with a Four-Factor Theory of Leadership," *Administrative Science Quarterly* 11 (1966), pp. 238–63.

11. To what extent is your supervisor attentive to what you say?

a. not at all
b. to a small extent
c. to some extent
d. to a great extent
e. to a very great extent

12. To what extent does your supervisor provide the help you need to schedule your work ahead of time?

a. not at all
b. to a small extent
c. to some extent
d. to a great extent
e. to a very great extent

13. To what extent does your supervisor encourage his/her employees to exchange ideas and opinions?

a. not at all
b. to a small extent
c. to some extent
d. to a great extent
e. to a very great extent

14. To what extent is your immediate supervisor successful in getting the best possible rewards for his/her employees (e.g., merit raises, promotions, challenging work assignments)?

a. to a very great extent
b. to a great extent
c. to some extent
d. to a small extent
e. not at all

15. To what extent does your supervisor emphasize high standards of performance?

a. to a very great extent
b. to a great extent
c. to some extent
d. to a small extent
e. not at all

16. To what extent is your supervisor willing to listen to your problems?

a. not at all
b. to a small extent
c. to some extent
d. to a great extent
e. to a very great extent

17. How would you describe the amount of responsibility delegated by your supervisor?

a. none
b. a minimum amount
c. a moderate amount
d. a considerable amount
e. a maximum amount

18. To what extent does your supervisor encourage his/her employees to work as a team?

a. not at all
b. to a small extent
c. to some extent
d. to a great extent
e. to a very great extent

19. How often does your supervisor work with you to set specific goals?

a. never
b. rarely
c. sometimes
d. rather often
e. nearly all the time

Activity 3–4: Least Preferred Co-Worker (LPC) Scale

Objectives:

a. To provide you with personal data that will increase your understanding of Fiedler's theory and research.

b. To explore the managerial and research implications of Fiedler's work.

Task 1 (Homework):

a. Complete the ratings for the "Least Preferred Co-Worker (LPC) Scale," which follows.

b. Read the summary of Fiedler's work in this chapter.

c. Compare your own LPC score with those of high and low LPC leaders described following the "Least Preferred Co-Worker (LPC) Scale" form.

d. Prepare the following questions for classroom discussion:
   (1) What do you see as possible strengths and weaknesses of Fiedler's work? What are the implications of the research for managers? For trainers?
   (2) How do you interpret your own LPC score? What cautions must you observe in making such interpretations and using the score? Would you want it used by your own manager in a business situation to make decisions about you?
   (3) Study question: You are the manager of a unit with many task groups. You have to pick supervisors for each task group. You assign a very autocratic person (the only person available at this time) to a group that is to perform a new activity of a very unstructured, ambiguous nature. The supervisor has a reputation for not getting along well with employees. In discussing the assignment, you express frankly your concern for his or her ability to handle people. You also observe that this individual is personally so well organized that he or she could find working with such an ambiguous assignment somewhat frustrating. The supervisor acts a little defensive and responds with rather exaggerated confidence, "Don't worry about me; just give me full authority and leave me alone and we'll get results." Do you think the chances of this supervisor performing successfully are high or low? Give reasons for your answer.

Task 2 (Classroom):

a. Provide your LPC scores to your instructor, if requested to do so, so the range and mean (average) for the class can be figured. (*Note: There is no need to identify yourself when providing your score.*)

b. Discuss the questions from Task 1d.

c. The instructor will provide critiquing comments on Fiedler's work.

Instructions for Least Preferred Co-Worker (LPC) Scale*

Throughout your life you will have worked in many groups with a wide variety of different people—on your job, in social groups, in church organizations, in volunteer groups, on athletic teams, and in many other situations. Some of your co-workers may have been very easy to work with in attaining the group's goals, while others were less so.

Think of all the people with whom you have ever worked, and then think of the person with whom you could work *least well.* He or she may be someone with whom you work now or with whom you have worked in the past. This does not have to be the person you liked least, but should be the person with whom you had the most difficulty getting a job done.

Describe this person on the scale that follows by placing an ''X'' in the appropriate space. The scale consists of pairs of words that are opposite in meaning, such as *Very Neat* and *Very Untidy.* Between each pair of words are eight spaces to form a scale like this:

Very Neat	___	___	___	___	___	___	___	___	Very Untidy
	8	7	6	5	4	3	2	1	

Thus, if you ordinarily think of the person with whom you work least well as being *quite neat,* you would mark an ''X'' in the space marked 7, like this:

Very Neat	___	X	___	___	___	___	___	___	Very Untidy
	8 Very Neat	7 Quite Neat	6 Somewhat Neat	5 Slightly Neat	4 Slightly Untidy	3 Somewhat Untidy	2 Quite Untidy	1 Very Untidy	

If you ordinarily think of this person as being only *slightly neat,* you would put your ''X'' in space 5. If you think of this person as being *very untidy* (not neat), put your ''X'' in space 1.

Look at the words at both ends of the line before you mark your ''X.'' *There are no right or wrong answers.* Work rapidly: your first answer is likely to be the best. Do not omit any items, and mark each item only once.

Now go to page M3-33 and describe the person with whom you can work least well.

* Instructions, LPC Scale, and Summaries of High and Low LPC Leaders reprinted from F. E. Fiedler, M. M. Chemers, and L. Mahar, *Improving Leadership Effectiveness: The Leader Match Concept,* pp. 6–11. Copyright © 1976, by John Wiley & Sons, New York, N.Y. Reprinted by permission of John Wiley & Sons.

Name ______________________ Date ______________

Least Preferred Co-Worker (LPC) Scale

										Scoring*
Pleasant	8	7	6	5	4	3	2	1	Unpleasant	____
Friendly	8	7	6	5	4	3	2	1	Unfriendly	____
Rejecting	1	2	3	4	5	6	7	8	Accepting	____
Tense	1	2	3	4	5	6	7	8	Relaxed	____
Distant	1	2	3	4	5	6	7	8	Close	____
Cold	1	2	3	4	5	6	7	8	Warm	____
Supportive	8	7	6	5	4	3	2	1	Hostile	____
Boring	1	2	3	4	5	6	7	8	Interesting	____
Quarrelsome	1	2	3	4	5	6	7	8	Harmonious	____
Gloomy	1	2	3	4	5	6	7	8	Cheerful	____
Open	8	7	6	5	4	3	2	1	Guarded	____
Backbiting	1	2	3	4	5	6	7	8	Loyal	____
Untrustworthy	1	2	3	4	5	6	7	8	Trustworthy	____
Considerate	8	7	6	5	4	3	2	1	Inconsiderate	____
Nasty	1	2	3	4	5	6	7	8	Nice	____
Agreeable	8	7	6	5	4	3	2	1	Disagreeable	____
Insincere	1	2	3	4	5	6	7	8	Sincere	____
Kind	8	7	6	5	4	3	2	1	Unkind	____
									Total	____

* Transfer your position number to the scoring column.

Summary of High-LPC Leaders

Relationship-motivated or high-LPC leaders (score of 64 or above) tend to accomplish the task through good interpersonal relations with the group in situations in which the group as a whole participates in the task performance. When their primary goal has been accomplished and things are under control, they may behave in a brusque, authoritarian manner which is seen as inconsiderate by subordinates. In a tense, anxiety-arousing situation, they may become so concerned with interpersonal relationships that they fail to accomplish the task.

Summary of Low-LPC Leaders

Task-motivated or low-LPC leaders (score of 57 and below) are strongly motivated to accomplish successfully any task to which they have committed themselves. They do this though clear and standardized work procedures and a no-nonsense attitude about getting down to work. Although they want to get the job done, they will care about the opinions and feelings of subordinates as long as everything is under control. But in low-control situations, they will tend to neglect the feelings of group members in an effort to get the job done—''business before pleasure!'' For them there is no conflict between the esteem they get from subordinates and the esteem from their boss. They use the group to do the job, and when they feel that the situation is under control, they try to do this as pleasantly as possible.

Remember that the descriptions of relationship- and task-motivated persons are useful and fit many people quite well. However, you should always keep one important point in mind: Whether you are a ''true type'' or a combination of leadership types, your effectiveness as a manager will depend on how well your individual personality and leadership style fit the requirements of your leadership situation, and not on whether you scored high or low on the LPC scale.

Activity 3–5: The Santa Theresa Family Services Case

Read the case below and answer the questions at the end of the case.

Santa Theresa Family Services*

Ed Masters, the managing director of Santa Theresa Family Services, faced a decision that might result in either conflict with his professional and clerical staff or problems with the agency's board of directors. A staff committee had developed a proposal for formalizing an experimental flextime arrangement about which he had serious reservations. Faced with different proposals from him and the committee, the agency's employees had voted to support the committee's report and asked him to submit it to the board of directors. Now he had to decide what to do at the upcoming board meeting.

Background

Santa Theresa Family Services (STFS) was a nonprofit agency supported by the United Way and by contracts with the County of Santa Theresa in central California; it provided general counseling, family counseling, and the foster care of children. STFS was governed by a 15-member board of directors; three members were selected by the city council of the City of Santa Theresa, three were selected by the county council, and the remainder were selected from the general public, who supported STFS through contributions and the purchase of annual memberships.

The board was responsible for hiring the managing director and for establishing policies that governed the programs that STFS operated. The board acted on hiring recommendations made by the managing director, and it also approved salary scales and employee benefits established within the annual budget for the agency. Some of the board's authority was delegated to the following standing committees: executive, services, personnel, finance, public relations, and nominating.

STFS employed 25 professional employees (counselors, social workers, public health workers). The professional employees were organized into three departments—general counseling, family counseling, and foster child care—each headed by a department manager, who, in turn, reported to Mr. Masters. Nine clerical employees provided office support. The clerical employees were supervised by the office manager and controller, who also reported to Mr. Masters.

Each department held regular meetings where case assignments and general concerns were discussed. A professional development committee, composed of representatives of the three departments, arranged programs and discussions throughout the year. There was also a voluntary staff association to which most employees belonged. The staff association arranged social events and brought employee concerns to the attention of Mr. Masters.

The Schedule Problem

For a number of months, Masters had been concerned with the hours being worked by professional employees. Because of the nature of the work, all client transactions could not be handled during the agency's 9 AM to 5 PM, Monday through Friday, regular work hours. (For example, during the past week, one family counselor had received an emergency call at 10 PM. It was from a client who had just entered a local spousal abuse shelter house, and the counselor spent the next three hours at the shelter with the woman. In another incident, a worker in the child care unit received a call at 11 PM from foster parents with an ultimatum that the teenager placed in their home be removed immediately.) Under existing policy, work outside of regular hours was compensated for by time off during regular work hours in the same week. However, because of the individualized case loads, most employees found it difficult to take time off, and they found themselves working increasing amounts of uncompensated overtime.

STFS had tried a work schedule in which the office was open until 9 PM on Wednesday nights, and the employees who worked late on that night took a half day off work on another day of the week. However, it had proved impossible to concentrate evening appointments on one day, and the practice had been discontinued in favor of the present policy.

In May, the professional development committee arranged a general meeting of employees to discuss the subject of a four-day workweek. There was widespread interest in the concept, and an ad hoc committee was nominated to explore the possibility of a four-day workweek and to develop a plan for adoption by the agency. The committee was composed of a representative from each of the four departments, with the managing director as ex officio.

Following the meeting, Mr. Masters summarized his thinking about a four-day workweek in a memo to all employees. He noted that such a program would

Provide clients with more opportunity for face-to-face contact with employees.

Require acceptance of a more structured workweek by professional employees.

Impose close scheduling of employee meetings.

Provide a more concentrated work period in each week, reduce ''free time'' in the middle of the week, and increase ''free time'' at weekends.

Be implemented experimentally for a minimum period of time, which would provide the basis for a realistic review.

The Committee's Work

At its first meeting, the committee defined its objectives as follows:

To make service formally available to the public before and after regular work hours, five days per week.

To rationalize the overtime being worked at present into a recognizable pattern so that

- Employees due compensatory time off would actually get it.
- Employees could anticipate when they would be off duty.
- Administrative functions such as meetings could be planned.
- The profile and logic of the workweek structure would be fair and easy to follow.

Each departmental representative was to keep his or her colleagues informed and to communicate their questions and concerns to the committee. The committee also investigated four-day workweeks at two other public service agencies. Operationally, the committee decided to christen the object of its endeavors ''ModWeek.''

By early July, the committee was ready to present its proposal to the employees. Its workweek included two 11-hour and two 7-hour days, with either Friday or Monday off. At a general meeting, employees agreed that the proposal would take effect August 1, provided that it was approved by the board.

The specifics of the proposal were

ModWeek hours will be arranged by each department.

At least half of the employees in each department will be on duty at all times.

Tuesdays, Wednesdays, and Thursdays will never be off-duty days for anyone.

The office will be open until 9 PM on Tuesdays and Wednesdays.

Only one off-duty day (Monday or Friday) may be taken in any one week.

If a holiday coincides with an off-duty day, the time will be added to the employee's vacation time.

ModWeek work schedules will be organized and altered in each department once a month. These schedules will be issued by each department no less than two working days before the beginning of the month.

Responsibility for making out the monthly schedule will rotate among all employees in a department.

The minimum workweek will be 35 hours, excluding meal breaks.

Mr. Masters submitted the proposal to the personnel committee of the board, which approved it and forwarded it to the executive committee. The ModWeek proposal was accepted on August 1 as a six-month experiment, and it would be reviewed in three months. The executive committee also approved the hiring of a part-time receptionist to help cover the extended office hours.

At this point the ad hoc committee members became the ModWeek committee, continuing to meet about twice a month. In August, the committee considered the problem of the light work load for clerical personnel who worked the evening hours. In response, it developed a system of pooling dictation tapes so that this work would be centrally available.

After a month's trial, employees at STFS seemed relatively satisfied with the ModWeek schedule. The committee considered and approved a request from some employees to work daily hours of 9 AM to 6:30 PM, with either Friday or Monday off; other variants of the basic schedule were also permitted. The committee considered complaints that the absence of certain clerical employees on either Friday or Monday impeded some agency work or resulted in an overload for other employees. The committee decided that these were problems inherent in any schedule and that everyone at STFS would just have to live with them.

However, in October, the committee decided that individually flexible work hours, such as 9 AM to 6:30 PM daily, especially among clerical employees, were causing service gaps in the office. Consequently, the rules were changed so that only three options were available to all STFS employees: (1) full ModWeek (four-day week, with two 11- and two 7-hour days), (2) half ModWeek (one 11-hour day per week), with a Friday or Monday off every other week, or (3) a regular 9 AM to 5 PM schedule. Any employee who worked a ModWeek schedule had to find a "buddy" to cover for days off. If the employee could not find a buddy to cover the job or if the job could not be adequately covered with a ModWeek schedule, the individual had to work a 9 AM to 5 PM schedule. Although all scheduling problems, other than the above-mentioned one, were in the area of clerical services, the committee decided to impose the restrictions on all employees.

The proposal was put before a meeting of all employees in late October. Some of the professional employees objected to the restrictions, saying that the new ModWeek schedule was just as rigid as the old schedule, and it was also incompatible with service demands. With the charge that the ModWeek committee attempt to find some way to provide for more personally flexible work hours, the staff approved continuing the ModWeek schedule until the end of the formal experimental period at the end of January.

Ed Masters's Dilemma

The ModWeek system continued through the end of the year. Although the ModWeek committee was unable to develop a system of personally flexible working hours, it believed that the three ModWeek options provided most employees with more flexibility than they had before. Consequently, in January the committee was preparing to propose that ModWeek become a permanent fixture at STFS.

Ed Masters had some misgivings, however. While in general the system seemed to work well, at times its operation meant that certain jobs were not completed on time. For example, the absence (on her ModWeek day off) of a key person had caused a 24-hour delay, at a critical point, in the development of the budget for the next fiscal year.

Masters believed that STFS was presently operating with an absolute minimum of clerical staff; to ensure that the agency would continue to provide full service to the public, he believed it might be necessary to require some staff to work particular hours. Because he was responsible for the operation of STFS, Masters believed he should be able to set such a requirement.

He believed that the department heads were carrying too much of a burden because of ModWeek. While none of them had complained, he was aware that they were working a full five-day week, often beyond regular hours, and, despite the "buddy" system, helping to pick up the slack on off-duty days. Masters also believed that it would be necessary to abandon the ModWeek schedule during the summer, when most employees took their vacations. At a minimum, Masters did not believe that STFS should irrevocably commit itself to an automatic year-round ModWeek schedule. In general, Masters was doubtful about making a total commitment to ModWeek, at least as it was currently practiced.

Masters was also concerned about the amount of time that had been spent on the ModWeek program. Two general staff meetings in June and October had been devoted to the subject, and another was scheduled for January. At the most recent ModWeek committee meeting, 33 person-hours had been dedicated to a decision that Masters believed he could have made in five minutes.

As a result of his misgivings, and in preparation for the six-month review of ModWeek at the general staff meeting on January 8, Masters sent the following memo to all employees:

> We have no documentation about the actual benefits of ModWeek to clients regarding face-to-face encounters after 5:30 PM. We should attempt to develop such data during the next three months, and we should provide the board with this data before making the system permanent.
>
> Most vacation time is taken during the summer, when we also have the most employee turnover; under these circumstances we cannot guarantee the absolute minimum of one-half staff coverage on any given day.
>
> Beyond the foregoing, I believe that the department heads are bearing an extra burden by covering for other professional employees on off-duty days.

At its December meeting, the ModWeek committee had prepared the following proposal to present to employees at the January 8 meeting:

> We have completed a six-month trial of ModWeek. During this period, a committee representing all departments has met regularly to discuss problems. STFS employees now propose to the board that this shortened workweek be regarded as established policy and practice in the agency. It will therefore no longer be regarded as experimental. The committee is unable to suggest ways of extending the options to include personally flexible work hours mainly because of the small number of employees, most particularly clerical employees.

Faced with different proposals from the managing director and the ModWeek committee at the January 8 meeting, employees voted overwhelmingly to support the committee's report and asked that it be submitted to the board of directors.

Now Masters wondered what he should do. Even though he believed he had the responsibility of administering STFS, and even though he had deep misgivings about ModWeek, he knew he should consider simply submitting the approved proposal to the board. He also knew he could refuse to submit the proposal, or he could present the proposal to the board along with a statement of his own concerns. The board was to meet the day after tomorrow, and he knew he had to make up his mind soon.

Discussion Questions

1. What are the likely consequences of Mr. Masters's alternative courses of action?
2. If you were Mr. Masters, what would you do? Why?
3. Other than his technical concerns with the operation of ModWeek, can you think of anything else that might be bothering Mr. Masters?
4. How well has Mr. Masters handled this situation? What might he have done differently?
5. If the situation described in the case is typical of Masters's leadership style, how would you describe that leadership style? What should he do to be more effective?

Activity 3–6: Exercising Your Leadership Skills*

Objective:

To gain some useful experience in leadership, to reflect on that experience, and to analyze your own unique behavior as a leader.

Task 1:

Persuade eight people to do some notable activity together as a group for at least two hours, an activity that they would not normally do without your intervention. You may not tell them that this is a class assignment. It can be any eight people: friends, family, roommates, club members, people at work. The activity should be something more substantial then watching TV or going to a movie or just sitting around together. Some very unusual things have occurred as a result of this activity. An elderly man's house got a much-needed paint job, a woman with a severe illness had her yard weeded and cleaned, and students participated in relief work at a local hospital during an earthquake and visited a dying patient, to name just a few examples.

Task 2:

Write a brief one-page report of your activity. Describe how you brought the group together and what forms of motivation it took to mobilize them. Develop your "vision" and how you presented it to your volunteers. Describe your accomplishments.

Task 3:

The instructor picks about five of the best examples and has students share the highlights of their leadership experience. One person can make a difference by enriching the lives of others even if just for a few hours. And for all of the frustrations and complexities of leadership, the tingling satisfaction that comes from success can be most addictive. The capacity to make things happen can become its own form of motivation.

* This activity is adapted with permission from R. Hughes, R. Ginnett, and G. Curphy: *Leadership Enhancing the Lessons of Experience* (Burr Ridge, Ill.: Richard D. Irwin, 1993), pp. 8–9.

4 The Organization

Learning Objectives

After completing this module you should be able to

1. Explain the major features of the organization.
2. Describe a cognitive map of an organization: the formal and human organizations.
3. Appreciate the background and script factors in determining the human organization.
4. Describe the major characteristics of the emergent role system.
5. Appreciate the complex dynamics between the formal organization and human organization.
6. State the key elements of open-system thinking as they apply to understanding and improving effectiveness.
7. Apply the metaphors of "script and actors" and "operational blueprint" as managerial tools.
8. Develop conceptual tools useful in diagnosing, understanding, predicting, and influencing behavior in organizations.

List of Key Concepts

Actors
Emergent role system
Equifinality
Formal organization
Human organization
Internal background factors
Negative entropy
Open system
Operational blueprint
Required role system
Required system
Script
Steady state
System boundary
Transformation process

Module Outline

Premodule Preparation

The instructor may assign either one of the following activities. If time permits, both activities might be used.

Activity 4–1: A Comparative Exploration of Two Organizations: Sandlot and Little League Baseball[1]

Objectives:

a. To identify the multiple features of an organization.
b. To learn about two types of organizations and their management.
c. To introduce alternative ways to map up an organization.

[1] This activity is a modified version of "Informal and Formal Organizations: Sandlot and Littie League Baseball" created by Professors Fremont E. Kast and James E. Rosenzweig. We appreciate the authors' permission to modify and include this activity in this textbook.

Task 1:

One of the major characteristics of a modern society is the development of numerous and more complex organizations. In this activity you are asked to draw upon your individual and shared experiences to look at the similarities and differences between two forms of athletic organizations: sandlot baseball and Little League baseball. The comparative analysis forms suggest several dimensions on which you may compare the two types of organizations. Feel free to develop any additional dimensions that you consider relevant.

a. Review the listed dimensions and add supplemental dimensions that you consider relevant.
b. Each individual should complete the individual comparison that follows.
c. Working in teams, develop a group composite of your comparative analysis on the page that follows.
d. Each group selects a spokesperson to present its analysis to the class.
e. The instructor will facilitate a class discussion.
f. Reflecting on this activity, your previous experiences, and your learning thus far, try to define below, in your own words, an organization.

An organization is ______________________________

____

____

____

Individual Comparative Analysis of Sandlot and Little League Baseball

	Sandlot Baseball	Little League
1. Who are the participants? How are members of these organizations identified?		
2. What are the goals of these organizations? Who identifies the goals?		
3. What rules govern these orgaizations? Who makes the rules?		
4. How structured are these organizations?		
5. Who performs the managerial functions of planning, decision making, and control in these organizations?		
6. How would you describe the relationships among the people in these organizations?		
7. What motivates people in these organizations?		

	Sandlot Baseball	Little League
8. What are the leadership and influence patterns in these organizations?		
9. What are some of the expectations in these organizations?		
10. How do these organizations relate to their external environments such as other groups, organizations, competitors, and resources?		
11. Who are the customers in these organizations?		
12. What is the nature of the technology used (e.g., equipment, knowledge)?		
13.		
14.		
15.		

Team Comparative Analysis of Sandlot and Little League Baseball

	Sandlot Baseball	Little League
1. Who are the participants? How are members of these organizations identified?		
2. What are the goals of these organizations? Who identifies the goals?		
3. What rules govern these organizations? Who makes the rules?		
4. How structured are these organizations?		
5. Who performs the managerial functions of planning, decision making, and control in these organizations?		
6. How would you describe the relationships among the people in these organizations?		
7. What motivates people in these organizations?		

	Sandlot Baseball	Little League
8. What are the leadership and influence patterns in these organizations?		
9. What are some of the expectations in these organizations?		
10. How do these organizations relate to their external environments such as other groups, organizations, competitors, and resources?		
11. Who are the customers in these organizations?		
12. What is the nature of the technology used (e.g., equipment, knowledge)?		
13.		
14.		
15.		

Activity 4–2: An Exploration of the Formal Organization and the Human Organization: The Transcal Petroleum Company Case

Objective:

To explore the main features of formal organizations and human organizations.

Task 1 (Homework):

Participants are to read the case "The Transcal Petroleum Company" and answer the questions at the end of the case.

Task 2 (Class):

The instructor will facilitate class discussion based on the individual answers. (See comments in instructor's manual.)

Transcal Petroleum Company*

"Who ever would think that paying people could be such a hassle?" This was one of the questions that formed in Phil Martinez's mind as he read a memo about the company's payroll process from Art McCallum, the company's director of payroll accounting. The memo outlined reasons for moving to a 100 percent direct deposit payroll system, and Martinez had agreed to discuss the matter the next day in a meeting with McCallum and Janet Bell, director of employee records.

Transcal Petroleum was an independent producer and distributor of oil and natural gas. Its production and refining operations were located near Bakersfield, California, and its headquarters office tower was located in suburban Bakersfield. In addition to distributing natural gas, the company sold oil products under its own brand in California, Nevada, and Arizona. Company personnel were concentrated in the Bakersfield area, but the nature of operations meant that personnel were located in all parts of the three states in which the company had operations. Total employment was 3,700 people.

As Martinez reflected on the issue of direct deposits, he remembered that the idea of direct payroll deposit had been in proposal form for at least 10 years in the company. One of the problems the company had experienced was that the payroll system had trouble keeping up with the growth in the number and geographic dispersion of employees. Over the past 15 years, the company had worked its way through four mainframe computers and four increasingly complex payroll systems.

The New Payroll System

The newest computer and payroll program had been installed four years ago. Employment had been stable since then and the computer and payroll system were still adequate for the company's needs. In fact, the stability of the company's operation and the acquisition of sufficient computing power had made it possible for the company to provide direct deposit of paychecks for the first time three years ago.

It hasn't been a particularly smooth ride, though, thought Martinez as he recalled all of the difficulties that accompanied the introduction of the new payroll system four years ago. The payroll system was part of an integrated human resource information system that had been designed by the company's System and Information staff, with the assistance of an outside consultant and inputs from both Accounting and Human Resources staff. The nonpayroll aspects of the system had worked reasonably well,

 We are grateful to Professor Peach.

although there were still (and probably always would be) problems with keeping data on employees complete and up-to-date.

The payroll subsystem was another story, however. Part of the problem was organizational. Technically, the Payroll Department was part of the Accounting Department, and Art McCallum, the director of payroll accounting, reported to the company's controller. However, Payroll was physically located away from the Accounting Department and was on the same floor as the Human Resources Department, which was the source of most of the data received by Payroll. Payroll had extensive daily interactions with Human Resources staff, most particularly the Salary and Benefits people and the staff of Employee Records.

Martinez could remember the first day the payroll system had been installed. It had been in early June, almost exactly four years ago. He and Art McCallum had shared an elevator upstairs after lunch, and when they reached their floor they ran into Don Hagen, the director of systems and information.

"Hi," he said, "I've been looking for you. The payroll system is loaded and ready to go."

"Fantastic," Art McCallum said. "I've got a check to run. We can give the system a tryout."

"*A single check*?" Hagen asked. "I'm not sure it can produce a single check. It's designed to run the biweekly payroll."

"What do you mean it won't produce a single check?" McCallum asked. "We have to produce checks almost every day—not just the general payroll every two weeks."

"Oh," said Hagen.

"Look, we do early checks for people going on vacation. We do pro-rated pay for people who have resigned or been discharged. Sometimes we get requests for special checks for temporary employees," McCallum said. "The system won't be of much use if I can't produce checks on a daily basis. Can I do the checks manually and adjust the general payroll to compensate?"

"I'm not sure," Hagen said. "But I don't think so. Let's see what we can do, though."

Eight hours later, they had managed to get the system to produce the check. After that things went straight downhill.

First, Systems had designed a batch system for processing payroll that could produce nonstandard checks only with great difficulty and only at the very real peril of fouling up the whole system. Second, even the batch processing didn't work well, and as the Payroll staff began to work with the system, they began to realize how many problems it had.

In 5 of the first 10 pay periods, the payroll accounts would not balance. In fact, over the first seven months of operation, the system "lost" $100,000, which never could be traced. On a total payroll of approximately $100 million, that was not a large error, but losing track of any sum of that magnitude bothered the accounting staff—and the auditors.

Over the same time span, 7,500 transactions went "floating off into space," as McCallum put it. They never reached the individual trial balance account for each employee, where wages, benefits, contributions, and various tax and other deductions were accumulated so that they could be reported to the employee and the government at year end. The amount of time required to straighten out the individual accounts had been phenomenal.

And then there were the individual errors. Employees had deductions taken from their pay for savings bond purchases when they hadn't signed up to do so. The system failed to deduct the health care plan premium for employees on an apparently random basis. These employees became concerned about whether their health care coverage had been affected and Human Resources staff and Payroll staff were kept busy answering questions and making adjustments.

The system also inexplicably produced errors in actual pay. A series of major errors involving staff in the refinery took six months to straighten out. The union had become involved and the problems with payroll became a major collective bargaining issue. None of the errors in any part of the organization were really major—the average error was about $150—but clearly Systems, Payroll, and Human Resources all lost a great deal of credibility, even though the majority of employees were not affected. Martinez recalled that at least a small measure of poetic justice occurred when a *Systems* employee received a biweekly pay check for $8.24, an amount significantly less than he should have received.

The cost of correcting the system had been enormous. Payroll personnel had to work large amounts of overtime (as late as 5 AM) for several days each pay period just to get the payroll out on time. Over 400 formal Systems Modification Requests were filed. At one time, 25 people were actively engaged in trying to "fix" the system. Finally, in September, Systems had "decomissioned" the Payroll system, which meant that although the system continued to operate, it was the official responsibility of Systems and not Payroll. The move was largely a way of stopping the flow of system modification requests and allowing Systems Department personnel to make significant changes in the computer program without receiving constant complaints from both Accounting and Human Resources personnel.

It had taken from June until the following March to get the payroll system functioning correctly in an error-free manner. Martinez had always wondered whether it had been a blessing or a curse that the Executive Payroll System had not been converted as part of the changeover of the payroll system. On one hand, if company executives had been subject to the same kind of payroll problems as other employees, the system might have been fixed faster. On the other hand, the credibility that Systems, Payroll, and Human Resources had in the organization would certainly have been worse. As it was, the credibility problems with the payroll system had filtered up to executive ranks enough to affect the decision on direct deposit when the time came for the Executive Committee to make that decision.

The payroll system had been designed to be implemented in stages. The first stage involved the processing of paychecks. Phase 2 involved the conversion of the system from one that produced paychecks to one that produced direct deposits into individual bank accounts with a "confirmation of deposit" form produced for each employee. The external consultant who had advised on the design of the system had recommended that in Phase 2, direct deposit be the mandatory method of regular wage payment at TransCal.

Preparing for Direct Deposit

In the early summer following the "debugging" of the payroll system, Art McCallum developed potential direct deposit arrangements with the company's bank, BankWest. The company would give the Automated Services Division of BankWest a direct deposit tape containing data on which employees were to be paid, the amount, and the bank where the individual employee account was located. The bank would guarantee that if the master tape was received on time, it would deposit the correct amount in any account in any bank in the United States on the date specified by the company.

Following the development of arrangements with the bank, McCallum made a presentation on the direct deposit system to the company's Executive Committee, which was composed of the chairman of the board, the president, and all the vice presidents. The presentation ended with a recommendation that direct deposit be the mandatory method of wage and salary payment for the company. At that point, one of the vice presidents said, "This system sounds almost too good to be true. Maybe it won't work as well as you think. My recommendation would be to make its use voluntary, at least for now. If it doesn't work, we won't have as many problems as we did with the payroll system."

That comment carried the day, with the Executive Committee authorizing the direct deposit system on a voluntary basis. Martinez wondered whether the fact that the executive payroll still had not been brought "on stream" into the computer system (it was still being produced manually) might have influenced the Executive Committee's decision. Certainly, if they had required all employees to use the direct deposit system, and if there had been difficulties, they could have been accused of forcing employees to go through a "payroll trauma" that they did not have to live through.

Although he was disappointed with the decision not to make direct deposit mandatory, Art McCallum set about to make direct deposit as successful as possible. Training sessions were held in June for Payroll, Human Resources, and Systems personnel. In June, the first notice went out to employees. Martinez knew that McCallum viewed the initial announcement as a mistake—one that severely influenced the sign-up rate for direct deposit. The company used an enrollment form provided by BankWest that had the bank's logo on it. McCallum believed that many employees did not read the memo carefully and thought that they needed to have an account with BankWest to participate in direct deposit. Several employees were heard to say that they didn't want to deal with BankWest.

Notices and enrollment forms were again included with paychecks in July and August, with the memo stating that the company expected to implement the direct deposit system in September.

As sign-ups came in, Payroll completed three test runs of the system. The first run produced about 100 errors. By the third run, the system was "technically flawless." The system was still subject to minor errors resulting from faulty data input from employees, which turned up even though Payroll was subjecting data provided by employees (e.g., account number) to a 100 percent audit.

By September, about 1,200 employees had signed up for direct deposit, and the new system was made operational for the September 15 pay. The system worked perfectly. Only one complaint was received. An employee who thought that she had not enrolled in the plan complained when her paycheck was deposited to her bank account. In fact, she had authorized enrollment and had provided the correct banking codes.

Over the next two years, Payroll personnel continued to promote the direct deposit system. A new enrollment form was designed with the company's logo on it. On eight occasions, promotional inserts were included in the paychecks of individuals who had not signed up for direct deposit. An advertisement was placed in the company magazine in an attempt to inform spouses of employees about the system. The Payroll Department purchased a stamp promoting direct deposit which was impressed on all paycheck envelopes that were not picked up on payday.

Last year, the executive payroll system had been automated and included in with the processing of the regular payroll; 70 percent of those on the executive payroll signed up for direct deposit. In June of this year, Martinez had agreed to have direct deposit become the required method of pay receipt for all *new* employees.

Before agreeing to this step, Martinez consulted with the union that represented employees in the Refinery and Distribution Department and also with the Clerical Employees Association. Neither group had objected to the move, nor had any of the employees involved.

McCallum's Memo

Martinez turned his attention to the recent memo from McCallum. The memo noted that 58 percent of employees had signed up for direct deposit of paychecks. (Of the various employee groups, sign-up rates ranged from 30 percent for part-time employees, to 50 percent for refinery and distribution employees, to 78 percent for managerial and professional employees. Sales and executive personnal rates were both 70 percent.) McCallum noted that the direct deposit system had operated in a totally error-free manner and that there had been no computer-related errors in payroll for three years. The memo went on to say that the company was operating two pay systems and that doing so was inefficient. McCallum estimated that 35 person-hours a month could be saved in the Payroll Department by moving to a required direct deposit system. Other than this, there were no particular *direct* cost savings to the company. Since 94 percent of paychecks cleared the company's account on payday, the loss of payroll ''float'' by moving to direct deposit was negligible.

Payroll Department efficiencies would be realized because direct deposit would simplify the bank reconciliation process. With direct deposit the department would not have to verify that checks had been properly debited to the company's account and would not have to sort checks, prepare lists of outstanding checks, or file checks. Also, the department would not have to run over 3,100 checks through the check-signing machine each month. Finally, time would be saved by eliminating lost checks and the stop-payment process such losses created, and the need to issue replacement checks as well.

The biggest benefit from direct deposit would be in ensuring that employee pay was available to them on payday. Over the years the company had some difficulty in getting paychecks delivered in a timely manner. Outside of headquarters, where checks were hand delivered to employees, a courier service was used to deliver paychecks to office and plants where employees were located. On occasion, the courier service misdirected the mail and the checks were not available for employees on payday. On other occasions, company mailroom personnel misdirected the checks. This latter error had occurred often enough so that Payroll Department personnel generally watched mailroom employees sort the paychecks, much to the latter's discomfort. On several occasions when the courier service failed to pick up the checks in a timely fashion, the company airplane was used to deliver the checks.

Apart from problems with the physical distribution system, the mobility of employees often interfered with the timely receipt of paychecks. Because of the shift work involved in that location, a number of employees were not at work at the refinery on paydays. Sales personnel were frequently away from the office on payday, as were employees who were away from their normal place of work attending meetings or training sessions.

In general, Martinez knew that Payroll personnel were frustrated because they generally worked hard to ensure that paychecks were correct and ready on time, but once the checks left the office, they lost control over them and their delivery. Recently Payroll had discovered that some employees in Arizona routinely received their checks two days late. They had come to regard the lateness as normal.

The memo from McCallum requested that Martinez approve and announce a policy of required direct deposit for all employees. The memo noted that such a move was supported by the company's auditors, by the controller, and by the vice president of finance, who had said that he did not believe there was any need for the Executive Committee to address the issue and that the decision was Martinez's to make.

Martinez thought that in many ways the move made a great deal of sense. He personally found direct deposit to be a great convenience and felt reasonably sure that once employees experienced that convenience, they would not object to the mandatory nature of the process. He wondered whether there were any reasons not to approve mandatory direct deposit of paychecks. He also wondered how such a system could best be implemented.

Discussion Questions

1. Given the information in the case, identify key dimensions of the formal organization and human organization in TransCal.
2. How does the payroll system affect both the human organization and the formal organization?
3. Describe the key actors at TransCal and their scripts.
4. If you were Phil Martinez, what decision would you make regarding mandatory direct deposit? Why?
5. If direct deposit is to become mandatory, what steps would you take to implement such a move?

Introduction

Organizational members and managers tend to develop cognitive maps that help them sort out their work experiences. A map is a graphic representation that provides a frame of reference. For geographers, a map is a means of depicting the world so that people understand where they are and where they are going.[1] In the organizational context, cognitive maps help people make sense of information and at times provide the reasoning behind actions. The broad cognitive map presented in Module 1 introduced organizations as systems composed of subsystems that interact regularly to produce and accomplish a desired goal or goals. Module 2 explored the role that expectations and learning play in organizational settings. In Module 3, management and leadership were charged with the responsibility of making organizations work as they should.

This module focuses on the exploration of the main features of the organization. We begin by inquiring into the work dynamics of two organizations: Sandlot and Little League baseball. Many models, conceptual roadmaps, frameworks, and metaphors or images of organizations and how they work can be found in the literature. In this module we focus on the metaphor of "script and actors" and open-system framework as the bases for the exploration and understanding of what organizations are and how they function. The script and actors metaphors are introduced to help understand the complex dynamics of both the human organization and formal organization. Next, we explore some unique features of systems and open systems and illustrate their use to improve results.

The Formal Organization and the Human Organization

The formal organization and the human organization provide analytical tools to examine work and organization dynamics. As we saw in Module 3 on leadership and management, the ability to predict work behavior is an important dimension of managerial performance. The difficulty in accurate predictions lies, in part, in the failure to understand the dynamics of the social system—the human organization—that workers create among themselves. The needs and emotions of the workers can be major determinants. If people like their peers and management, they may be highly productive despite poor working conditions; on the other hand, monotonous work can lead to excessive socializing, or poor management practices can lead to irritation, resulting in slowdowns or even sabotage. This statement appears obvious, but understanding the impact of needs and emotions on work group behavior is most difficult.

Another reason why the predictions are inaccurate lies in the overemphasized focus on individual, specific parts of an organization (e.g., technical tasks, information system) and not enough focus on the relationship of all the pieces as they interact together. If they don't investigate the nature of the collective interaction of people and their tasks, managers cannot hope to understand the effect of individual changes on the organization as a whole.

How can you improve your ability to predict work behavior and make your predictions the basis of improved managerial performance? Experience, of course, is primary, but learning to work with analytical tools can yield excellent insights. We will introduce some aspects of the formal organization that give the functional structure to work groups and that create the interrelated job designs and descriptions the work group members must follow to perform their required functional roles. It is while interacting to perform these required roles that the web of group dynamics begins to spin.

In this module, the analytical tools will be the models of the formal organization (the script) and the human organization (the actors) plus the open-systems theory view, which will allow us to understand the collective interaction of the use of the aforementioned models on the organization as a whole. We will be assuming managers can improve employee performance by going beyond the formal organization to acquire a working knowledge of the many aspects of the human organization. A general development of the script and actors analogy, which can be applied to the total organization or to smaller work units, follows. This is followed by a discussion of the more detailed formal and human organization models contained in the "Operational Blueprint" (Figure 4–1), "Actors Playing Their Roles" (Figure 4–2), and "Character of the Actors" (Figure 4–3).

The Script and the Actors

One of the best ways to comprehend the idea of the **formal organization** is to think of it as a **script** that has to be thoroughly understood by the director (manager) before the **actors** (employees) are given their roles to play. The script of a formal organization will include, among other things, the purpose, the functional roles that must be assigned to the actors, the coordination of the interactions between the roles, the nature of the different types of work to be performed, and the status accorded to the different work roles by the actors or the audience (the public). The background in which the play takes place must be known, as must the immediate setting. The types of people available to play the parts plus their character, attitudes, and experience are also important.

If you are a competent director, you will be able to hire the actors, train them in your particular interpretation of the script, and see that the performance of the play achieves the purposes of the script and provides satisfaction to the actors. Under these conditions, the formal organization (script) and the **human organization** (actors) are compatible and well integrated. This condition can be achieved only when the director has carefully developed, shaped, and perhaps rewritten the script and the setting so the performance can be predicted. In other terms, management can design the work, control the environment in which it takes place, and shape the human organization so that high productivity will result from the achievement of the purposes of both the organization and the people. If management does not do this, a possibly serious consequence is that the actors will spontaneously create and control their own human organization, which may not have the type of climate conducive to high productivity. It may even have an anti-organizational bias in regard to the formal system.

The area of job redesign, which is of widespread current interest in the auto industry, illustrates one aspect of script control of the formal organization. In an early study, the Volvo auto plant in Sweden (faced with annual turnover rates of up to 40 percent) experimented with processes such as job rotation, in which the employee changes jobs once or several times a day, depending on the nature of the work of the group. Jobs have also been enriched in that work teams in some cases follow the same auto body through several stations over a 20-minute period. Both strategies to control the script resulted in significant reductions in turnover and higher productivity.

In addition to job redesign, other management technologies and practices can be adopted to develop the human organization; these will be introduced later. Participation of people in the decision-making process is a subject of a later module. However, it is assumed that managers must have a good understanding of how people live and work in organizations if they are going to write and rewrite the script and direct the performance. Coming modules address the topics of small group dynamics, motivation, communications, and perception to provide you with a set of concepts and theories through which this understanding can be increased. The concepts can also be used as tools of analysis. If, for example, you know Abraham Maslow's *hierarchy of needs,*[2] you can examine any script and attempt to make predictions as to what satisfactions and frustrations employees will experience in the performance of the work. Frederick Herzberg's motivation theory is the basis of his idea of *job enrichment,* a method of redesigning work to fulfill the needs of the workers more effectively.[3]

We must now show the utility value of the formal organization and human organization models by moving on to a more detailed development, starting with the idea of the operational blueprint.

Operational Blueprint

Just as engineers follow blueprints, managers need **operational blueprints** to guide them when establishing a manufacturing organization or when attempting to understand one that is already in operation. Figure 4–1 provides an operational blueprint depicting major elements of a formal organization and the setting in which it operates. For convenience, we will focus on three areas: background factors external to the organization, background factors inside the organization, and the formal organization or script.[4]

Figure 4–1
Operational Blueprint

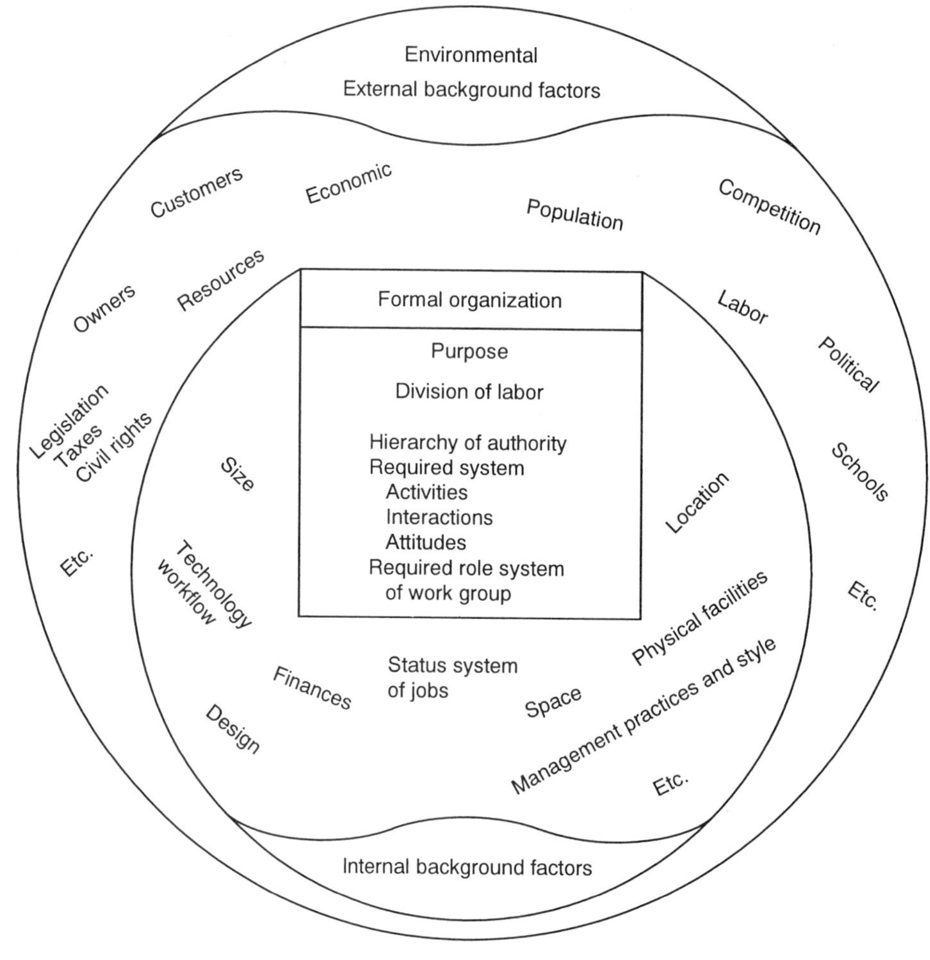

Environmental Factors External to the Organization

When designing a manufacturing company, planners must determine all the factors in the specific setting that will make the endeavor feasible or impinge upon it. These include (1) the market for the product involved, (2) potential competition, both national and international, (3) economic factors such as interest and inflation rates and the value of the dollar, (4) sources of supply, and (5) government regulations and legislation. These and many other factors related to economics, politics, social conditions, and technological development may have varying degrees of importance from case to case.

Our discussion thus far has centered on the use of Figure 4–1 as a guide for developing a new organization; however, its primary value for the reader will be in analyzing ongoing operations in case studies where only limited but essential factors are presented. Thus in the comparison of Sandlot and Little League organizations, we know only that a Little League team is likely to be sponsored by a specific business. We do not know what might be the attitudes of the players and/or public toward the sponsor. Thus the factor of public attitude permits us to make some assumptions about (1) the importance of the sponsor and how that might influence the players and (2) the relationship between the players and coach and how this might affect performance.

Internal Background Factors

Internal background factors directly relate to designing the formal organization. Examples are (1) ownership, (2) acquisition and layout of physical facilities, (3) finances, (4) technology (selection of equipment, machines, and methods), (5) work design, and (6) work flow. All plans and procedures of the manufacturing process are included here, but the required behavioral roles of the managers and employees are not.

Here is an example of how spatial arrangements can affect the work group. An insurance company was located in an old building where all insurance agents had private offices on the second floor. The clerical and support staffs were scattered in several small rooms on the first floor. A new building was built in which all personnel were located on one spacious floor. The insurance agents were located around the borders of the floor in cubicals separated by waist-high walls. In the vast center area were the desks of the clerical and support personnel. The agents initially complained about lost privacy for their clients. Six months later, they expressed satisfaction with the openness of the atmosphere, and privacy had not proved to be a problem. More important, the clerical and support personnel showed an increase in productivity of over 20 percent. Management attributed this increase to the awareness of the clerical and support personnel of their full visibility to all those agents they were supporting—it was difficult to slack off in front of people waiting for their files to be completed.

Formal Organization (the Script)

Now we move from the background setting into the functioning organization. The basic elements of the formal organization are to be found in Schein's definition:

> An organization is the rational coordination of the activities of a number of people for the achievement of some common explicit purpose or goal, through division of labor and function, and through a hierarchy of authority and responsibility.[5]

Since the behavior system is the primary interest of this text, we shall elaborate to show this definition's relevance for us.

Purpose: A statement of purposes and goals in terms of products and services is an integral element of organizational life. All roles to be performed within the organization have goals derived from the primary purposes. While these purposes change over time, they change slowly and with great difficulty.

Division of Labor and Function: Work is divided according to the specific tasks individuals are to perform. As size and complexity of a company increase, this division typically becomes more specialized.

Hierarchy of Authority: As planning, staffing, directing, and controlling processes occur, a chain of command (bosses and subordinates) of line positions is established to designate the responsibilities for activities essential to the operation of the business. Staff positions are set up to provide the support and services that help conduct these essential activities.

The Required Role System of the Work Group: Readers sometimes find the term *system* confusing, so a definition may be helpful at this point. *System* means a regularly interacting or interdependent group of elements that together make up a unified whole. The **required system** of the formal organization refers to the behavioral requirements of the role an individual plays when performing the tasks of a specific position. These consist of three elements:

1. *Required activities.* Specific sets of activities are usually an integral part of every job. Analysts in an organization, for example, are required to receive data daily from the field depots worldwide and to keep inventory sheets from these data.
2. *Required interactions.* Most positions require interaction with other positions. Thus the same analysts have to provide data to supervisors; however, little or no coordination with fellow workers might be called for in the script.
3. *Required attitudes.* The analysts may be expected to maintain attitudes of conscientiousness, carefulness, and independence in the processing of their data records.

The required role behaviors of a specific position interlock with those of one or more other roles in the basic work group, creating a required role system. It is this required role system of the work group and its relationship to other work groups as they interact in the entire system that will be our most basic focus in the formal organization.

Actors Playing Their Roles

Once an organization is in operation, how do managers and the employees make the formal organization work? As noted previously, people almost always play their roles somewhat differently than the script because it may be incomplete, may not satisfy their needs, and so on. The formal organization is therefore supplemented by the human organization—the way the system actually works rather than the way it is supposed to work. The script, with its rigidly defined purposes, chains of command, and many requirements, is elaborated into a human system with its own characteristic values, roles, and social norms as management and workers go about making the formal organization workable and livable. This differentiation of the human system occurs from two perspectives (see Figure 4–2): (1) managers adapting and changing the operational blueprint and (2) workers developing identifiable recurrent ways of acting.

Figure 4–2
Actors Playing Their Roles

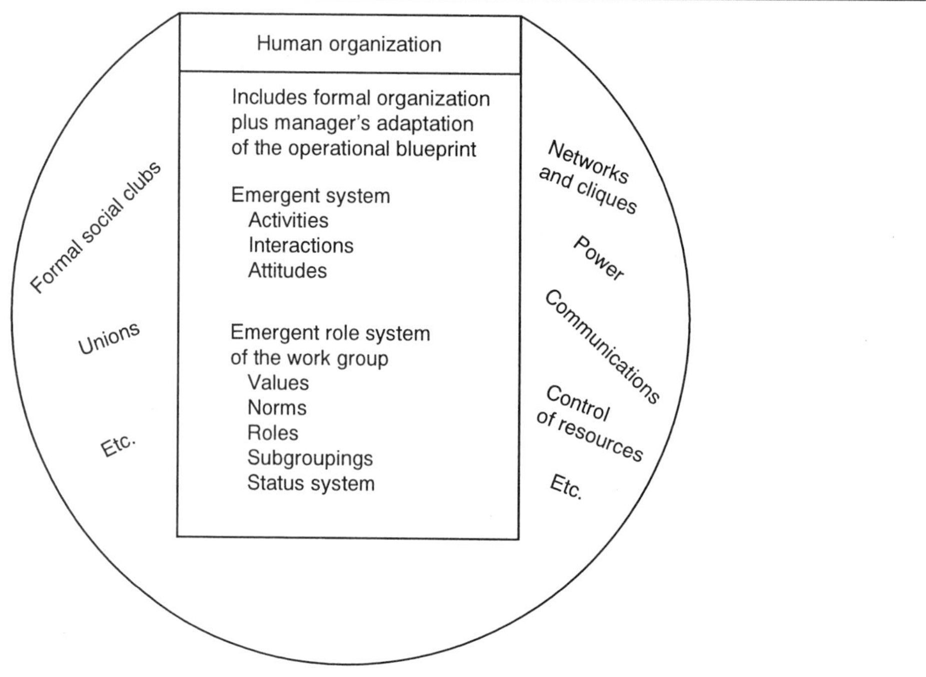

Managers' Adaptations of the Operational Blueprint

Managers often find they must innovate or adjust to the normal dynamics of the company to make plans work. Thinking of the human organization as a living, organic entity, ever adapting to the internal and external changes, provides better insight into the manager's role than limiting our view to the static, rigid positions of the formal organization.

The Emergent Role System of the Work Group

The required system of behavior of the formal organization becomes the emergent system of the human organization when the actors start playing their roles.[6] The **emergent role system** refers to those activities, interactions, and attitudes that spontaneously develop as individuals strive to follow the script but also satisfy their own needs. For example, an insurance analyst is to be at his desk working by 8 AM (a required activity). Instead, he arrives on time but goes directly to the washroom, stops off at the coffee machine on the way back to his desk (emergent activities), chats with neighboring workers along the way (emergent interactions), and starts work at 8:10. While analyzing insurance claims, he seeks his neighbor's help for a difficult case (emergent interaction) instead of his supervisor's (the required interaction) because he dislikes his supervisor (emergent attitude, since the required attitude would be favorable feelings toward the boss). He and his neighbor encounter a claim that is not covered by regulations so they improvise a solution (emergent activities and interactions) and submit it to the supervisor for approval (required interaction).

Just as the required system is adapted into the emergent system, the required role system evolves spontaneously into the emergent role system as the actors go about their work. The emergent role system of one work group is linked to the emergent role systems of one or more other work groups; the resulting total structure becomes the human organization. In this sense, a manufacturing company can be thought of as a social system or small community.

The small work group is the primary focus of the study of organizational behavior because it is here that the emergent role systems, which are major determinants of behavior, are spontaneously generated. The development of the emergent role system is the subject of small group dynamics in the next module, where group elements, processes, and attributes (such as values, norms, roles, subgroupings, status, and cohesiveness) will be discussed. At this time, however, emergent attitudes should be defined since many group elements (for example, norms) are derived from them.

Emergent Attitudes: The work group's emergent attitudes are singled out for study because they are predictors of worker behavior, just as political attitudes are often useful indicators of voter behavior. By *attitudes* we mean an individual's predisposition to respond in a given way toward situations, things, ideas, people, and issues; for example, workers frequently view management as insensitive to employee needs. Attitudes are based on general factors such as the individual's experience, knowledge, feelings, emotions, ways of thinking, needs, and goals. In a given situation they will influence how an individual perceives, acts, and reacts. In the emergent role system, attitudes may be shared initially or may develop among people as they interact and differentiate aspects of work life meaningful to their activities and well-being.

Emergent activities, attitudes, and interactions are not necessarily either helpful or harmful to company goals. However, activities, attitudes, and interactions do tend to affect one another. Some emergent behaviors and attitudes are closely related to required activities and attitudes; as we will see, others are more distant.

Networks and Cliques

In addition to the emergent behaviors closely associated with required behaviors, people form networks and cliques that do not appear in the script. Those that control scarce resources and communication (grapevines) are among the most common. For instance, formal organizational channels are often slow and give incomplete information. Managers and workers typically have a network of friendly contacts at different levels of the organization with whom they informally exchange information. Often this emergent network is closely related to the script requirements but also functions to alleviate anxieties and threats for those feeling a need to know.

Social groupings—either employee- or management-initiated (for baseball, bridge, and item collection)—are not related to the script, but members may develop acquaintances who are useful back on the job. On the other hand, a covert network running a numbers racket in a factory would not be related to the script requirements except to impact them negatively.

Diversity of the Actors

If planners responsible for starting a new company were using the operational blueprint for completing an operating plan, their concern would now turn to locating, recruiting, and hiring the work force. It would be important to know the backgrounds of the people who are going to work for the company to understand how they will work together and to predict how management might mold them into an effective human organization. For example, many industries located in the midwestern and eastern regions of the United States relocated in the southeastern region, where they could hire less expensive and more compliant workers. Some background factors to consider are listed in Figure 4–3. Questions to ask include what percentages of the employees will be

Figure 4–3
Character of the Actors

Sociological/Psychological Background Factors	Civil Rights Mix	Occupational Mix
Cultural	Ethnic	Professional and managerial
Ethnic	Male/female	Technical
Community	Handicapped	Clerical
Beliefs		Blue collar
Values		Status of above
Feelings		
Ways of thinking		

Note: These factors will be determinants of how employees perceive and react to the work situations.

managerial and professional, technical, and clerical, and unskilled? Legislative requirements will also affect the sex and race mix of the work force.

Background characteristics of the actors will influence their attitudes toward work and toward managerial policies and practices. Employers must be aware that the whole person comes to work, not just the part that does the job. Employees' immediate attitudes contain many ingredients of their backgrounds as well as their reactions to what is happening to them on the job. Currently women, ethnic minorities, and handicapped members of our society are intensely aware of equal rights legislation. Companies not heeding their rights can anticipate less than fully productive performance. Let us use status as another illustration of the relevancy of background characteristics.

Status

We define *status* as the degree of esteem, respect, or prestige an individual can command from others. This can come from a social factor such as the individual's occupation, which is evaluated higher or lower than others. Thus most people accord more respect to a physician than to a custodian. Esteem can also come from personal factors such as the way an individual behaves—good communicators command more respect than those who can't express themselves persuasively. The importance of status as a factor influencing performance showed up in a government agency a few years back where the majority of the finance and accounting personnel had a two-year–college degree from an institute specializing in their field. As consultants, we were asked to determine why this staff group was seen by all line elements of the agency as antagonistic and slow in responding to line needs. After extensive interviewing, we concluded their behavior was largely due to a status difference. All the line personnel had four-year university degrees and many held graduate degrees. The lower-status finance people had become a highly cohesive group, protective of each other and their prerogatives, who believed their excellent skills were undervalued by their longer-schooled colleagues. With some success, the agency changed its recruiting policy to one of hiring only people with four-year accounting or finance degrees. But once negative attitudes toward management are deeply formed in a cohesive group, change is difficult.

Figure 4–3 provides some basis for reflecting on the attitudes people bring to work that affect their behavior. It is of course difficult to estimate their influence. Large industries employ human resources/management specialists to assist in this area. Employee attitude surveys are often used to address the question of how the actors are perceiving their work life, usually focusing on current issues around management practices. (The role of perception in management is the topic of another module.) However, questions on employee background factors that might provide insightful data are often limited by recent legislation (for example, prohibitions against inquiry into ethnic background, marital status, and so on).

The Organization as an Open System

The basic premise of open-systems theory is that organizations have common characteristics with all other living systems—from microscopic organisms to plants to animals to humans. Understanding these characteristics allows us to work with the natural tendencies of an organization rather than struggle against them needlessly.[7] By understanding these similarities, we can apply the survival techniques of living systems to organizations and thereby increase our understanding of why certain organizations thrive while others fail.

For this discussion we shall define a *system* as an arrangement of interrelated parts. An **open system** means that the system is dependent upon open interaction with its external environment. All living systems are open systems. Likewise, all organizations are open systems; a consumer purchasing an organization's product is an example of an open interaction of the organization with its external environment. At the beginning of this chapter we discussed the operational blueprint, which included a description of an organization's environmental external background factors. (See Figure 4–1.) These factors are specific examples of interaction points between the organizational system and its environment.

All systems have a **system boundary** (border) that separates one system from another. The boundary may be physical (building), temporal (a work shift), social (a departmental grouping), or psychological (a stereotyped prejudice). Thus we should be aware that both the script (formal) and the actors (human) create boundaries. The degree to which the boundary allows interaction with the external environment or other systems is called the *permeability* of the boundary. Excessive permeability can overpower the system with external demands; too little permeability can starve the system for resources.

All systems have a *purpose* that guides their existence. In the pursuit of this purpose, systems develop internal targets or goals with which the system measures its progress. An organization's purpose and goals are often stated explicitly, and these statements are a component of the script (formal organization) that we discussed earlier.

Inputs of materials and energy from the environment to a system are required for the survival and growth of the system. The inputs received into the system are subject to a **transformation process,** which converts the inputs into an output through a variety of processes. Another function of the script (formal organization) is to formally outline the division of labor and function to make the transformation process as efficient as possible. (Figure 4–4 shows an integrative model of the formal organization, the human organization, and the open system.)

Figure 4–4
The Formal Organization, the Human Organization, and the Open System: An Integrative Model

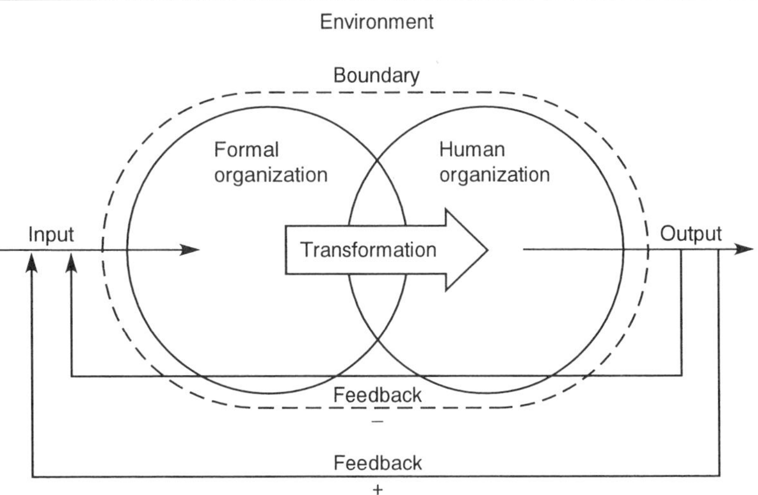

The transformation process yields *outputs* of materials and energy which are exported to the environment. The outputs are the system's attempt to fulfill its purpose. *Feedback* refers to the system's knowledge of how well it is accomplishing its purpose in terms of deviation measurements of the output from the purpose so that a correction can be made, and measurements of whether the purpose itself is appropriate in the current environment.

Everything outside the system's boundary is considered the environment. A closed system (mechanical system) does not interact with its environment. An open system (living system) interacts with its environment, but it will only interact with those segments of the environment that are relevant to its purpose. The balance between which segments are allowed to interact with the system and which are excluded (or ignored) is unique for each system. Both the script and the actors influence the balance, based on feedback, in order to pursue their purpose and internal goals. If an imbalance occurs because the script fails to address the needs of interaction with the environment, the actors will maintain the balance through the development of emergent roles through the process discussed above. If the actor's emergent role system fails to compensate, the system will starve or be overwhelmed. In either case, the purpose can no longer be pursued effectively by the system.

Using Open-Systems Thinking to Improve Results

When planning improvements to an organization, an understanding of the dynamics of open systems, as discussed above, will assist in successfully predicting the results of the planned change. To effectively use the open-systems theory, we first ask a few diagnostic questions:

- What is the apparent purpose or goal of the organization that causes activities to be coordinated into a pattern?
- What are the key outputs and their major boundary transactions?
- What are the key transformation processes, and how effectively are they balanced in achieving the purpose?
- What are the key inputs and their major boundary transactions?
- What is the reactivating feedback (both positive and negative) being delivered?

When evaluating the answers to these questions, it is important to keep in mind both the script and the actor influences at work. The effects of the script will be easier to analyze since they are in concrete terms, so care must be taken not to ignore the abstract effects of the actors. If the analysis of the diagnostic questions reveals that corrective action is appropriate, the next phase is to diagnose what happens when the system moves or exerts itself. We examine some key processes to determine if all of the parts will still function properly. The following questions can guide this diagnosis:

- **Information coding.** Does the system obtain the needed information inputs (feedback) and appropriately block out unneeded items?
- **Steady state.** Can the system maintain its operation within the limits of tolerance related to its targets?
- **Negative entropy.** Is the system able to import more than it exports by changing purpose, goals, and practices to match emerging environmental demands?
- **Equifinality.** Is there capacity, self-direction, and spontaneous self-regulation by individuals and groups to achieve the needed results?
- **Specialization.** Does the system grow and expand appropriately without becoming overspecialized?

A review of the entire analysis will create a picture or map of the organization that clarifies its strengths and weaknesses. Any planned change to improve the organization's performance should likewise be analyzed with the same criteria in mind.

This methodical approach to analyzing and understanding organizations is quite adaptable to all types and styles of organizations and has proven to be a useful tool in enhancing organizational performance.

Consequences

Our major emphasis has been on the use of behavioral science models to gain greater understanding of work behavior. But as managers we must go further, using these tools of analysis to improve your effectiveness as decision maker and leader. How can you evaluate your actions in this regard? Are improved worker performance, improved profits, and reduced costs the major criteria? They may or may not be. To answer this question, we need to return to our past view that what constitutes effective leadership depends upon the consequences of your actions. From the perspective of the human organization, we use three primary criteria for evaluating consequences:

1. *Productivity.* Are costs per unit and quality ensuring profits and meeting the competition?
2. *Worker satisfaction.* Does the worker situation maximize satisfactions and minimize frustrations?
3. *Organizational health.* Is the vitality and viability of the human organization being maintained? Does the work culture facilitate individual growth?

Managerial actions need to be evaluated in advance from both long- and short-range views. A well-recognized problem in industry is the tendency of managers to make decisions that maximize short-range profits (the overemphasized bottom line) but damage long-range effectiveness. Examples are avoiding capital reinvestment in new technology and letting working conditions deteriorate, thus stimulating employee resentment.

What are some desired characteristics of personnel where organizational health is being maintained?

- They are highly productive, results-oriented, and cost-conscious.
- They like to work in the department, identify with the organization, are cooperative with management and each other, and coordinate activities well. They do not overemphasize the goals of their section to the detriment of the department or the organization.
- They like their work, find it interesting and challenging, and are self-directing.
- They develop patterns of interaction that generate good communications, and they confront conflict meaningfully.
- They feel they have opportunities for growth and achievement of their goals.
- They have flexibility in coping with change.

You will recognize that these characteristics are similar to those of the professional-transformational manager organizational model introduced in the previous module.

In concluding, we wish to bring into balance with reality the utility value of our conceptual scheme. We have implied that managers can mold the script-and-actor systems into an effective organization. But managers have limits to their powers to change and mold people. Play directors can ask many things that managers cannot. And sometimes the ongoing organization is so rigidly locked in that change is not possible. We are hoping and assuming that there is always some wiggle room—usually more than most of us recognize.

Summary

This module attempted to provide a cognitive map or roadmap for understanding organizations and their dynamics. The purpose of this module has been to depict the formal organization as a script that tells the actors (the employees) where, what, and how to perform. The script can be broken down into certain elements that will provide the manager with insight into how the play is apt to go, where potential problems will arise, and so on. To direct the organization toward desired performance, the manager must have in mind models of how the actors are to interact and perform. Awareness that the actors will play the roles differently from how the author has intended is all-important. The human organization is always different from that called for in the formal organization; however, a manager can design and redesign the script and the environment to maximize the integration of the formal and human systems.

Figure 4–1 (''Operational Blueprint'') and Figure 4–2 (a model of ''Actors Playing Their Roles'') were provided as guides for understanding the script-and-actors approach. A third guide, ''Character of the Actors'' (Figure 4–3), focused upon cultural, educational, occupational, and other attributes of the employees and the effect these have on their attitudes toward the work situation. Finally, an integrative framework that pulls together the formal organization, the human organization, and the open-system perspective was presented.

Study Questions

1. What is the value of concepts such as the operational blueprint and actors playing their roles for managers?
2. Students frequently do not understand how to apply the operational blueprint to case studies. For instance, in Figure 4–1 a number of external background factors are given. How would you use these in analyzing a case? Could you apply them to a company that you are familiar with? Give reasons.
3. In what ways is the formal organization like the script of a play?
4. Why is there a difference between the required role system and the emergent role system of a work group?
5. Is the required role system included in the emergent role system?
6. Most managerial actions have some impact on the human organization or the emergent system. What criteria can be used in evaluating the effectiveness of management's actions?
7. How does the open-system view of organization complement the human and formal views?
8. Discuss the relationship between expectations, open-systems thinking, and organizational behavior.
9. Apply the formal organization and human organization frameworks to examine your team's effectiveness.
10. Discuss the role of diversity in the human organization.

Endnotes

1. For a good review of maps and managers, see C. M. Fiol and A. S. Huff, ''Maps for Managers: Where Are We? Where Do We Go from Here?'' *Journal of Management Studies* 29, no. 3 (1992), pp. 267–85.

2. A. H. Maslow, *Motivation and Personality* (New York: Harper & Row, 1954).

3. Frederick Herzberg, ''One More Time: How Do You Motivate Employees?'' *Harvard Business Review* 46, no. 1 (1968), pp. 53–62.

4. The discussions to follow on the required system and the emergent system and related concepts are adapted from George C. Homans, *The Human Group* (New York: Harcourt Brace Jovanovich, 1950). In constructing our diagrams in Figures 4–1 and 4–2, we have drawn upon the presentations of Arthur N. Turner in Paul R. Lawrence and John A. Seiler et al., *Organizational Behavior and Administration,* rev. ed. (Homewood, Ill.: Richard D. Irwin and the Dorsey Press, 1965), p. 158.

5. E. H. Schein, *Organizational Psychology,* 2d ed. (Englewood Cliffs, N.J.: Prentice Hall, 1970), p. 9.

6. A more complete development of the conceptual scheme described here is to be found in the book by George C. Homans *The Human Group* (New York: Harcourt Brace Jovanovich, 1950). Other adaptations of Homans's required and emergent systems are contained in the following references: A. R. Cohen, S. L. Fink, H. Gadon, and R. D. Willits, "The Work Group." In *Effective Behavior in Organizations,* chap. 5, rev. ed. (Homewood, Ill.: Richard D. Irwin, 1994).

7. A more complete development of general system theory and open-system theory and their implications to organizational dynamics can be found in the following references: P. Checkland, *Systems Thinking, Systems Practice* (New York: John Wiley & Sons, 1994); D. P. Hanna, *Designing Organizations for High Performance* (Reading, Mass.: Addison-Wesley, 1988); F. E. Kast and J. E. Rosenzweig, *Organization and Management: A Systems and Contingency Approach,* 4th ed. (New York: McGraw-Hill, 1985); W. A. Pasmore, *Designing Effective Organizations: The Sociotechnical Systems Perspective* (New York: John Wiley & Sons, 1988); W. A. Pasmore, *Creating Strategic Change: Designing the Flexible High-Performance Organization* (New York: John Wiley & Sons, 1994); P. M. Senge, *The Fifth Discipline: The Art and Practice of the Learning Organization* (New York: Doubleday, 1990).

Activity 4–3: Values in Business

Objectives:

a. To increase awareness of the importance of values as determinants of organizational behavior.

b. To increase awareness of the differences in team members' perception of values.

c. To experience some of the issues associated with group decision making.

Introduction:

The future shock era has caused continuous questioning and change of values. The Watergate crisis followed by the 1976 Bicentennial and the strong ideological orientation of the Reagan administration, and later the Newt Gingrich Congressional revolution of 1995, have been times for intensive reexamination of the values of American democracy. Particularly prominent were the negotiations involving the trade of arms for hostages between members of the National Security Council and Iranian officials; the subsequent denial by the White House set off a credibility crisis on honesty. *U.S. News & World Report* did a national survey at that time on "Lying in America." The responsibilities and roles of business in our society, in the European democracies, and in the communist countries are also constantly debated. Further, the individual American is torn as never before between the values of our past, more stable culture and those of the present world. Marriage, sex, personal commitments, trust in interpersonal relationships, religion, and material wealth are among the primary areas of value conflict.

The need for governments, organizations, and individuals to identify and live by commitment to values is currently recognized as an essential element of effectiveness in living.

The exercise that follows is to help your team evaluate the relative importance of certain values with which business organizations must be concerned. Values can be thought of as existing in a hierarchy in our thought processes, some being given higher importance or priority than others. The whole pattern of values in an organization represents the core of its operating philosophy and its organizational culture. Thus, they are major determinants of behavior of management and employees.

Values defined: Things, ideas, beliefs, and acts that are regarded as good or bad, right or wrong, desirable or undesirable, beautiful or ugly, contributing to or detrimental to human welfare, and so on. Societies, organizations, and individuals all have values with priorities of importance. For example, individuals may differ greatly in the values associated with religious beliefs, but a higher-order value that they all presumably would accept is freedom of religious beliefs.

General Exercise:

Assume you are a member of a top-management team of a large corporation. During a team development retreat, the facilitator-consultant informs the group that she has observed from individual interviews with team members that differences in perception exist as to the values by which they operate. Yet each person seems to be assuming that her or his values are shared by the other team members. As a basis for developing awareness and better consensus in values, the following tasks are undertaken.

Task 1 (Individual Rankings):

Listed in alphabetical order on the accompanying worksheet are 10 values that are among those often discussed in regard to business functioning. You are to rank these in order of the priority you would assign each in terms of importance for conducting business. Do this by writing in the first column next to the value a 1 for the value of highest importance, a 2 for the next, on down to a 10 for the value of lowest importance. In the second column, briefly note the reason for your ranking. Be sure to do this without consulting others; also, be sure your rankings are not observable to team members while completing this task. (*Note:* There is no right or wrong answer and no definite solution to this exercise. The rankings should be based on your own beliefs.)

Task 2 (Team Rankings):

Teams are to meet outside of class. Members are to compare their rankings of the values and come to a consensus as to how the team would rank the items from 1 to 10. This should be a ranking of what the team believes, not your estimate of how business people would rank them. (*Note:* Consensus does not necessarily mean that all agree with the final ranking of the team; it does mean that everyone's views were expressed and understood and that agreement was reached on how the values were to be ranked. In a real situation your personal values may differ from your colleagues', but you may decide to support the team's viewpoint for reasons such as hoping to persuade them later to your views or wanting to be open-minded to see if you could be wrong. If your values are too different, you may find, after a reasonable period, that you do not fit into the team. The main point of the exercise at this time is to increase your awareness of value issues.)

Task 3 (Classroom):

Teams are to list on the blackboard the rank ordering of their values. Discuss similarities and differences.

Name ______________________ Date ______________

Worksheet for Activity 4–3

Values	*Your Ranking*	*Reason*	*Your Team's Ranking*	*Reason*
Career growth and development of personnel				
Concern for personnel as people				
Efficiency				
Ethics (morality)				
Managerial and organizational effectiveness				
Servicing clients' needs (e.g., equipment, orders)				
Profits				
Providing products or services for society				
Quality of goods or services				
Social responsibility				

Activity 4–4: Team Development

Objectives:

a. To critique the effectiveness of your team in regard to
   (1) Achievement of results in task assignments.
   (2) Achievement of relationships among members that integrate their human resources (abilities, knowledge, views, etc.) into task solutions.

b. To suggest team goals for improved effectiveness.

Task 1:

Individuals working alone are to complete the questionnaire on team development scales on page M4-31.

Task 2:

Teams are to meet. The scale items on the questionnaire are to be discussed one at a time. Each member will report the rating he or she made prior to the meeting. The differences in ratings will be discussed to determine why members are perceiving the team's interactions differently. A group consensus rating will be made for each scale after thorough discussion. (*Note:* Avoid majority voting. Instead, seek real understanding to attain agreement.)

Task 3:

Study the comments on team goals at the end of the questionnaire. Teams are then to go back over the consensus ratings for the 15 items completed in Task 2. These ratings represent the characteristics of the team at present. Now write a *G* on each scale representing a goal the team would like to attain in its interactions by the end of the course.

Name ______________________________ Date ______________

Questionnaire on Team Development Scales

Climate Scales

1. The degree to which my team shows enthusiasm and spirit:

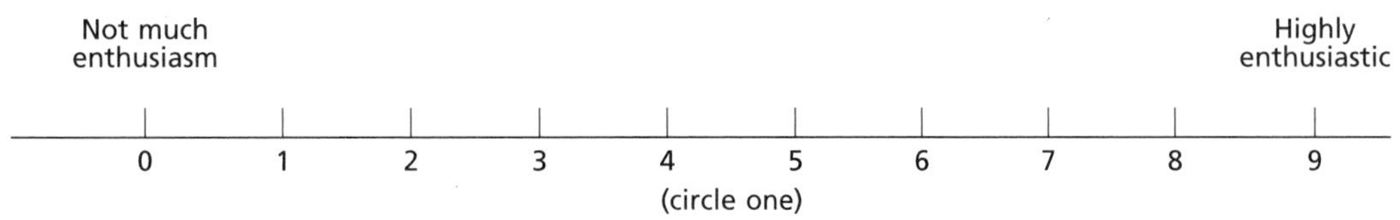

2. On humor I would rate the team:

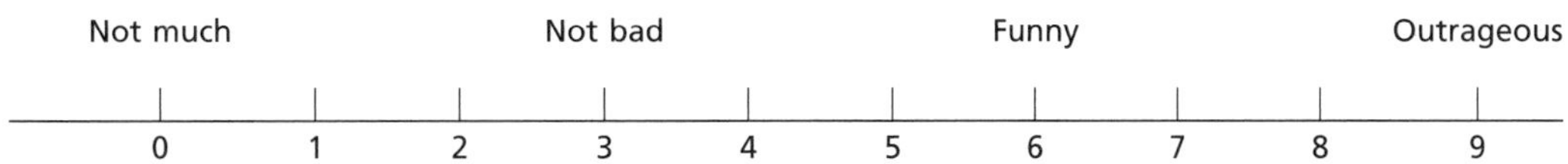

3. My team is:

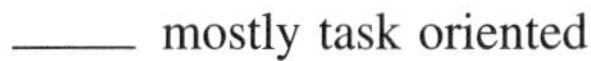

_____ mostly task oriented

_____ more task oriented than social

_____ equally task and social in orientation

_____ more social than task oriented

_____ mostly social

People Scales (How We Regard One Another as Human Beings)

4. The degree to which we are interested in one another as people is:

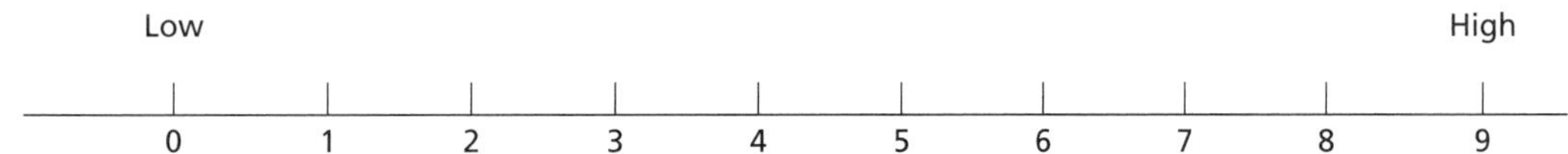

5. Our regard for each individual as a resource (knowledge, skills, abilities, viewpoints) for group goal achievement is:

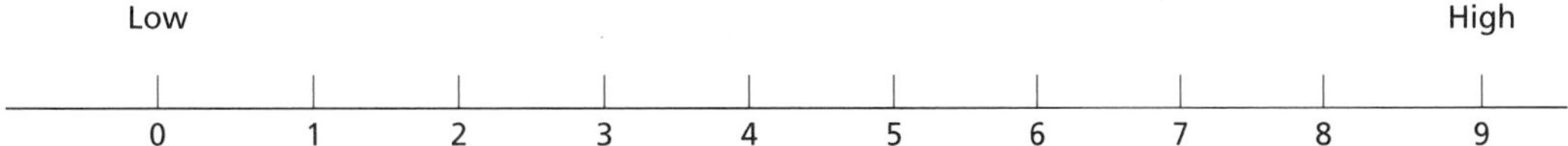

Productivity Scales (Goals, Work Accomplishment, Commitment)

6. Team's task achievement goals:

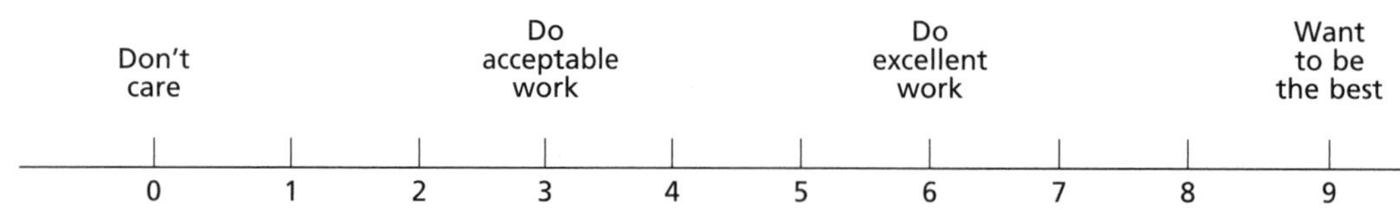

7. Actual quantity of work produced:

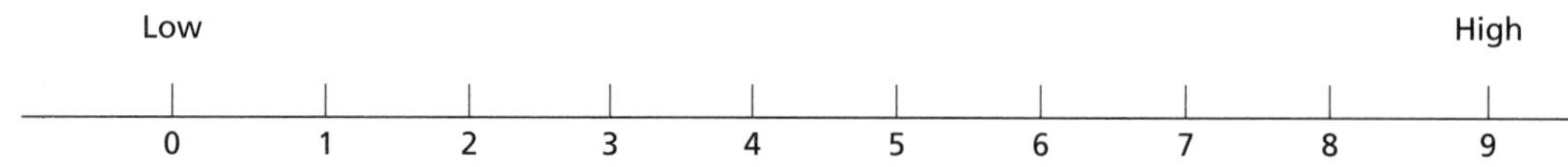

8. Quality of work produced:

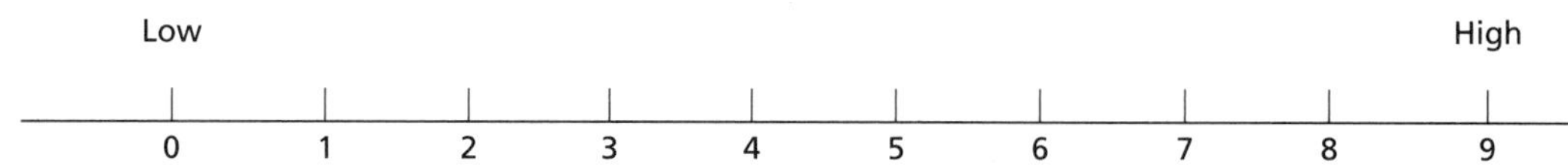

9. Interest in learning:

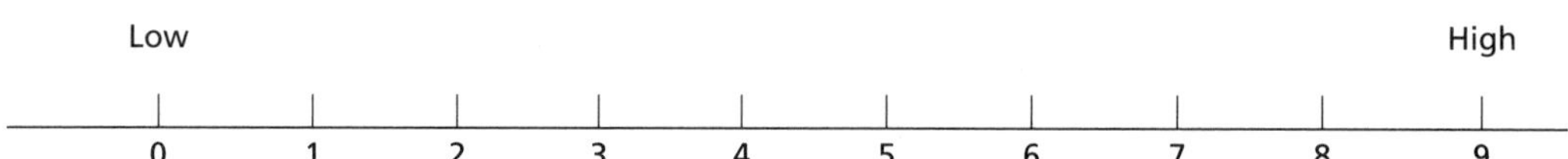

Process Scales (Participation and Communications)

10. Participation (check one):

_____ 1 to 2 members contribute the most

_____ 2 to 3 members contribute regularly

_____ 3 to 4 members contribute regularly

_____ 4 to 5 members contribute regularly

_____ all members contribute regularly

11. An input from all members is sought before decisions are made:

_____ never _____ sometimes _____ often _____ always

12. Where the team falls on the "handling conflict" scale:

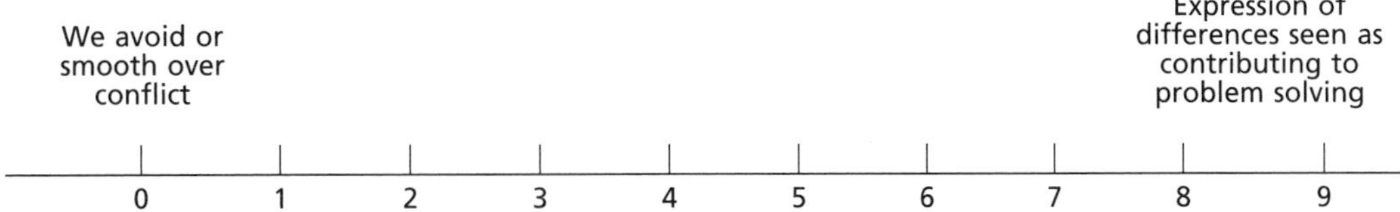

13. Openness in communications:

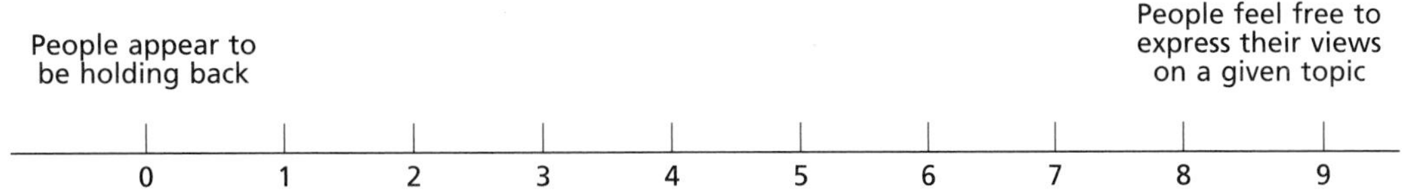

14. Expression of personal feelings:

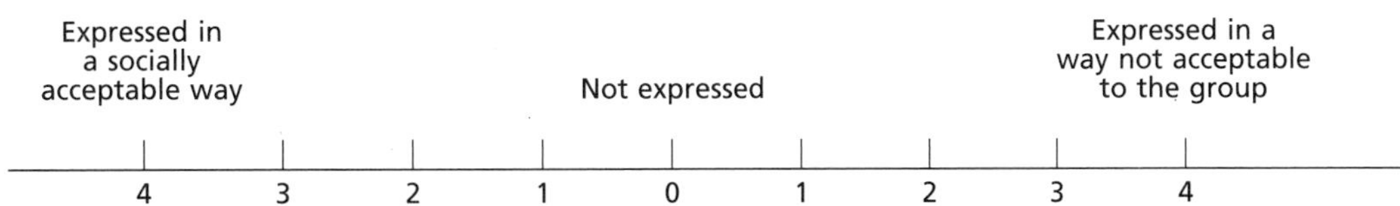

15. Degree to which we listen, and actually hear, each other's views:

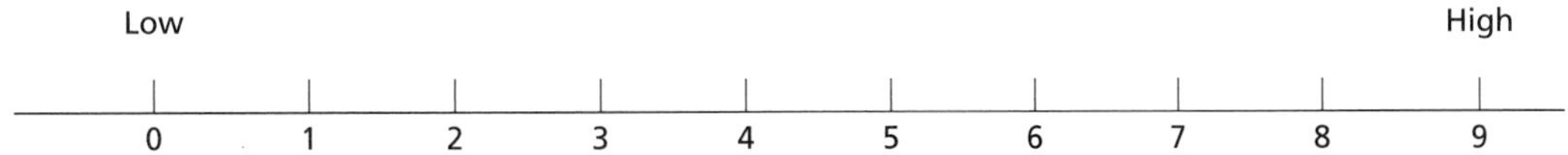

Comments: Make notes of anything you would like to feed back to the team about how members work together, or how effectiveness could be improved, that is not already suggested by the scales.

Team Goals

The scales of this questionnaire pertain to attitudes, processes, and skills that can make a team more or less effective under the conditions in which we work in this course. They thereby suggest goals for improvement of team effectiveness. *(Note: Don't assume that these attributes apply to the effectiveness of all teams under all conditions. Whether the specific goals suggested are appropriate depends on the specific conditions of the situation.)*

Scale attributes should be regarded as interacting with and reinforcing one another. The following examples illustrate this and suggest some of the consequences.

Productivity

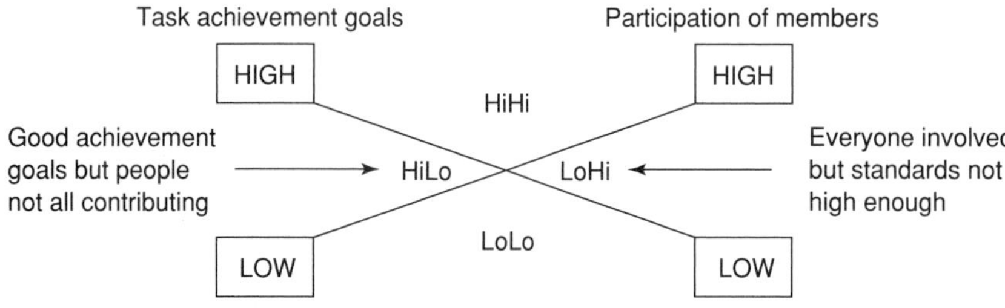

Quality of involvement

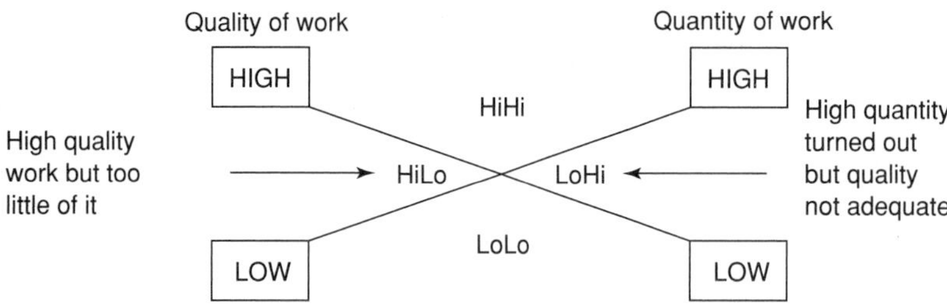

Regard for people

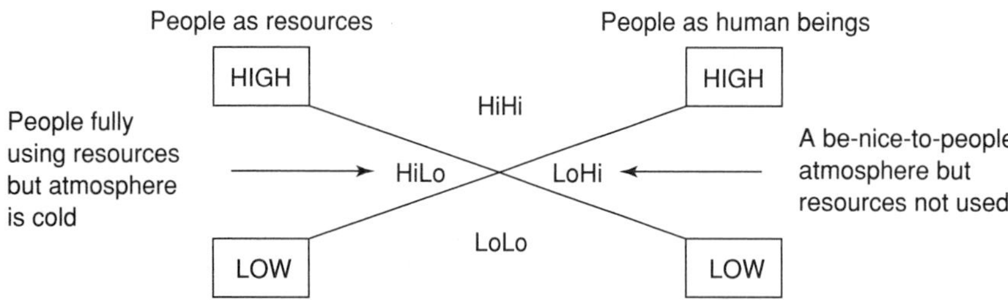

PART 2 MANAGING INDIVIDUAL BEHAVIOR: CORE CONCEPTS

Review

Thus far in the course, we have explored the context within which individuals function in organizational settings. Part 1 helped to establish the boundaries and process of the course: The field of study was defined; the learning community was established and expectations were examined; and key characteristics of the organization were discussed. Before we progress to study group behavior in organizations, we need to investigate four areas that are at the root of human behavior in organizational settings: the multiple nature of individuals, motivation, perception, and communication.

After the completion of Part 1, we need to step back and recapture some of the learning. Two distinct purposes were established for the first part: (1) to create the content and the process boundaries for the course and (2) to establish the learning community.

The Learning Community: As managers you will need to assume that your organization is an educational institution for its employees. As an educator, you need to foster the learning organization, help build the institution, and train the employees. What we did to build the learning community in the classroom can serve as a model for your work organization. We worked on five aspects:

1. *Content.* In defining organizational behavior, the topic areas were identified. The course objectives were given.
2. *Technology.* Experiential learning methods (that is, involvement learning through interaction activities) were used. A learning sequence for these methods was given that differed from a content learning approach. Skills development and learning competencies were emphasized. Through communication the bonding process emerged.
3. *Roles.* The instructor's role was defined as that of a facilitator, a coach, and a resource person. The participant's role was defined as that of learner and coach who is responsible for the learning of fellow participants.
4. *Climate.* Values of openness, sharing, full participation, and seeing conflict as creative were interwoven into the fabric.
5. *Structure.* Teams were formed and are functioning under the guidance of the facilitator.

All of these factors and more are relevant when you are building the learning organization at any work organization; they apply to any level from the basic supervision up to top management.

What did we do to create the learning community? The course started with an exercise in which you defined behavior in organizations with topics such as fair treatment, motivation to work, frustration from work, communication breakdown, relationships with supervisors, supervisory practice, and relationships with fellow workers. The text added a theoretical approach that focused on an organization as a system made up of

5 Diversity, Personality, and Personal Growth

Learning Objectives

After completing this module you should be able to

1. Identify the major elements that influence the individual's self-concept and work behavior.
2. Describe the nature and roots of individual diversity.
3. Define personality and the basic dimensions of personality differences.
4. Explain the relationship between personal growth and individual effectiveness.
5. Describe the multiple nature of humans.
6. Diagnose the Parent, Adult, and Child components of personality.
7. Appreciate the role that the learners can play in facilitating their own personal growth.
8. Explain the challenges of managing the changing workforce.

List of Key Concepts

Age diversity
Big five personality theory
Cultural diversity
Culture
Demographic diversity
Four life positions of personality development
Gender diversity
Individual diversity
Jung's theory of personality
PAC theory of personality
Personal growth
Personality
Transactional analysis

Module Outline

Premodule Preparation

The instructor may assign either one of the following activities or the last activity in this module as a presession preparation.

Activity 5–1: Learning about Self and Others: Personal Reflection via "Collage"

Objectives:

a. To identify personal life patterns.

b. To appreciate individual differences.

c. To explore the role of "relevant others" in one's own growth.

Task 1:

Working alone, you will use a heavy piece of paper (poster board is excellent) that is at least 27 inches by 33 inches to produce a collage that expresses your view of your whole life from beginning to end. Your collage—defined by Webster's Dictionary as "an art form in which bits of objects are pasted on a surface"—would correspond to your own concept of your life. It can be in any shape and form, can start at any place on the board, and can go in any direction. The project will capture your past (personal history, unique experiences, critical events/incidents, acquired skills, most influential people in your life, etc.), your present (the here and now, daily life activities and situations, joys and frustrations, current priorities, relevant friends and family, etc.), and your future (fantasies, dreams, goals, hopes and fears, daily life activities, etc.) in any creative form of expression that you can imagine.

You may want to start by going through magazines and cutting out any pictures, graphics, titles, or subtitles that seem relevant to your life. Old magazines, newspapers, yearbooks, and family picture albums usually help. Next, you might want to pull together three-dimensional items around you that seem relevant.

Once you have compiled all this memorabilia, spread it on the floor. (You being in the center might help.) The challenge that you face now is organizing this mass of items in some way that will help you express the person that you are. Move things around until the result feels right. (You will know when it feels right!)

At this point, get rubber cement, a glue stick, or a stapler, and attach the pictures/graphics/titles/items to the poster board. Colored marking pens, crayons, and pastels might be handy at this stage.

Task 2:

a. Individuals are to give three-minute synopses of their collages in small groups.

b. Each group is to identify common themes or dimensions among the different collages.

c. Each group is to choose a collage to be shared with the entire class.

Task 3:

The instructor will call upon the group's spokesperson to share her or his collage.

Task 4:

a. The instructor will call upon spokespersons to share the common themes or dimensions.

b. The instructor will facilitate a class discussion based on the themes that emerged from the activity.

Source: This activity was contributed by Professor Ken Boble, College of Business, California Polytechnic State University, San Luis Obispo, CA 93407.

Activity 5–2: Cultural Diversity: An Initial Exploration

Objectives:

a. To explore the individual's cultural profile.

b. To increase individuals' awareness of cultural diversity.

c. To explore issues associated with the management of diversity.

Task 1:

We all feel that in some way we are different from others. The worksheet for Activity 5–2 that follows asks you to explore the differences. Use the worksheet to take notes.
(Time: 10 minutes for individuals to think about their experience and jot down notes)

Task 2:

Each participant shares these thoughts with a small group. After each has done so, discuss what common elements seem to emerge. Have a spokesperson make a list.

Task 3:

Spokesperson reports findings to the class.

Source: Adapted and modified from L. Gardenswartz and A. Gowe, *Managing Diversity* (Burr Ridge, Ill.: Richard D. Irwin, 1993).

Worksheet for Activity 5–2

The following list identifies different dimensions of culture. Write down some notes about cultural differences you have encountered in each of the dimensions listed.

Dimensions of Culture	Examples of ways you are different from others.
1. Communication and language	
■ Language/dialect	______________________
■ Gestures/expressions/tones	______________________
■	______________________
2. Dress and appearance	
■ Clothing	______________________
■ Hair	______________________
■ Grooming	______________________
■	______________________
3. Values	
■ Privacy	______________________
■ Respect	______________________
■	______________________
■	______________________
4. Beliefs	
■ Social order/authority	______________________
■	______________________
■	______________________
5. Sense of self and space	
■ Distance	______________________
■ Touch	______________________
■ Formal/informal	______________________
■ Open/closed	______________________
■	______________________
6. Time and time consciousness	
■ Promptness	______________________
■ Pace	______________________
■	______________________
7. Work ethics	
■	______________________
■	______________________
■	______________________

8. ____________________

- ____________________
- ____________________
- ____________________

9. ____________________

- ____________________
- ____________________

Introduction

Any attempt to learn why people behave as they do in work settings requires some basic understanding of individual differences. When confronted with identical situations, individuals do not necessarily behave in the same way. Managers and employees alike must comprehend and appreciate individual differences in order to be effective.

One of the most dominant features of individual diversity is personality. **Personality** is a set of distinctive traits and dimensions that can be used to characterize the individual. Many of the other causes of individual diversity seem to be an integral part of the changing nature of the labor markets. Some argue that individuals who will work together in the future "will be less alike with respect to gender, cultural background, and age."[1] These differences are important because they are associated with differences in perspectives, life-styles, attitudes, values, behaviors, and thought processes and patterns. In this module we'll explore cultural diversity, demographic diversity, and personality as sources of individual differences.

The Nature of Individual Diversity

The individual is a unique set of different creatures. We are much alike in many ways yet very different in many other ways. Writers have found ready audiences for the various themes built around the many faces of human beings. The concept of "multiple nature of man" was coined long ago. One is the internal torment of the good and evil forces that appeal to the Dr. Jekyll and Mr. Hyde in all of us. Another is the idea of possession by demons that must be exorcised. A third concerns the idea that we all wear a persona or mask that helps us to conform to the world but prevents the real self from being exposed. ("No one would like me if they knew what I was really like.") Still another is the quest for identity. ("What am I really like? What is the real me?") The daily press also thrives on such stories: the quiet, conforming, nondescript man who was such a good boy but just skyjacked a Boeing 747 or was discovered to be a rapist-murderer.

Many of our behaviors are based on models long since developed and forgotten. Models on the campus include, for men, cool guy, wise guy, tough guy, Don Juan, and jock. Businessmen are sometimes analyzed in terms of a life script based on Robin Hood, Batman, Buck Rogers, Tarzan, and the Lone Ranger. Women in business are sometimes characterized as being under the influence of Cinderella, Little Red Riding Hood, Sleeping Beauty, Florence Nightingale, Queen Bee, Superwoman, or Bionic Woman models.

Effective managerial practice requires that individual behavior differences be recognized and taken into account when managing individuals, teams, and/or units. Understanding individual differences means that the manager must be able to observe and recognize the differences; understand the sources of the differences; examine the potential relationships between the different elements that influence individual behavior; and take the appropriate action that will result in improved individual and team effectiveness as well as foster personal growth. Many elements seem to have a potential influence on the individual's self-concept and work behavior: the individual's basic demographics such as gender and age; the individual's abilities and skills such as intellectual ability and physical ability; the individual's personality; cultural background; family dynamics such as marital status and number of dependents; organizational features such as leadership, structure, and policies; and work design features such as job design, tasks, and rewards. Figure 5–1 provides a partial schema of the elements that influence the individual's self-concept and work behavior. Next, we discuss in depth some of the elements. Others are discussed elsewhere in this book.

Cultural Diversity

A diverse work force typically includes individuals with a variety of cultural backgrounds. **Cultural diversity** is one of the most noted changes in the work force. As Activity 5–2 illustrated, individuals seem to have diverse cultural profiles. In the North

Figure 5–1
The Individual's Work Behavior: A Partial Schema

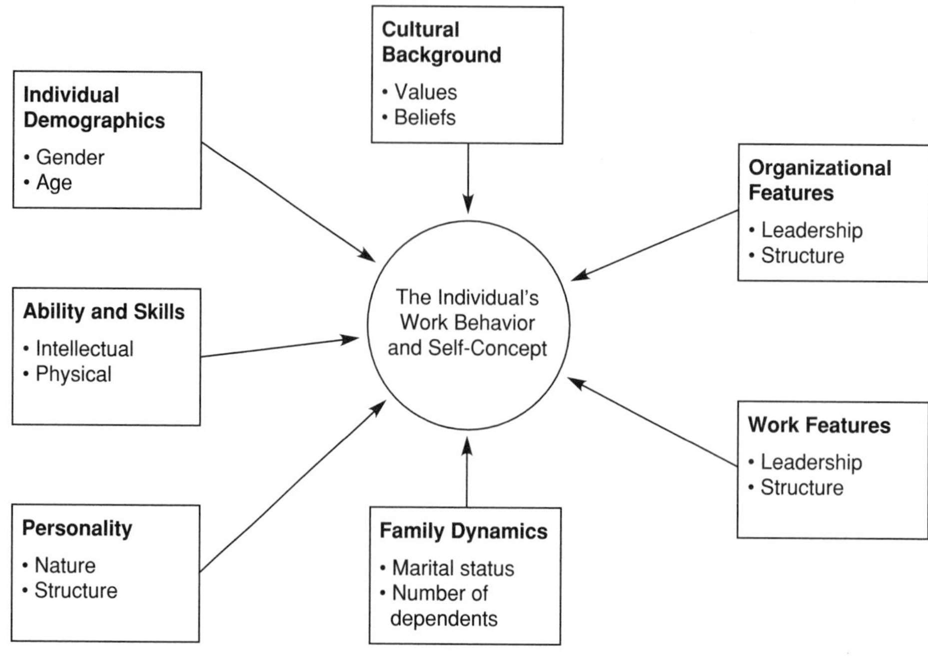

American context, *Workforce 2000* projections indicate that during this decade, only 58 percent of new entrants into the labor market will come from the majority population of white people born in the United States, with 22 percent of new entrants expected to be immigrants and the remainder being mostly African-American and Hispanic-Americans. Meanwhile, the European Community (EC) agreements are likely to change the nature of the work force throughout the European continent, as people will be able to move easily between countries and search for employment wherever they desire.

Cultures have causes that are easily experienced but more difficult to describe. At a surface level, the concept of culture invokes images of exotic customs, religions, foods, clothing, and life-style. At a deeper level, culture includes systems of values, ways of interpreting the world, social structures, and ways of interpersonal relations. By and large, the concept of culture has come to be associated with anthropological thinking. The word **culture** derives in a very roundabout way from the past participle of the Latin verb *colere* (to cultivate) and draws some of its meaning from the association with the tilling of the soil. As such, the evolutionary, integrative process within human systems through which values and belief systems are established and mental roadmaps of the environment are created are likely to have major influences on the behavior of the individual.

The growing diversity of cultural backgrounds that shapes individuals' behavior is one of the major challenges faced by today's managers and organizations. When people with different cultural backgrounds, values, and beliefs come together at the workplace, misunderstandings and conflicts inevitably occur. For example, employees who behave according to the cultural adage "the squeaky wheel gets the grease" will behave differently from employees who were taught that "the nail that sticks out gets hammered down."[2] Employees behaving according to the latter adage may be viewed as ineffective by the former group of employees.

The need for increased awareness to cultural diversity is compounded by two major factors. First, the changing nature of the workplace requires that employees interact more with each other and with different external constituencies such as suppliers and customers.[3] Second, the growing competitiveness worldwide requires understanding and sensitivity to an increasing variety of cultures, values, and belief systems in other continents.[4] Activity 5–4 ("Rough Times at Nomura") illustrates some problems that arise in a cross-cultural work environment and the relationship between cultural diversity and employee work behavior.

Demographic Diversity

The demographic composition of the work force is changing around the world. A sizable amount of research indicates that this broad category labeled *individual demographics* (including basic variables such as gender, age, marital status, number of dependents, and tenure with the firm) has significant influence on the behavior of individuals at the workplace. Of growing interest are gender and age diversity.

Gender Diversity

In the early 1960s, men were receiving about 95 percent of the MBA degrees awarded and 90 percent of the bachelor's degrees in business. Thirty years later the picture is quite different. In 1993, women received approximately 32 percent of the MBA degrees awarded as well as 48 percent of the bachelor's degrees awarded in business. The work force of the year 2000 is expected to be more balanced with respect to gender.[5]

Research suggests that there are few, if any, important differences between males and females that will affect their job performance. There are, for example, no consistent findings about male–female differences in decision-making and problem-solving abilities, analytical skills, competitiveness, motivation, or leadership.[6] Yet, while in 1990 women represented 35 percent of the population of management and administrators, they held only one-half of 1 percent of the top jobs in major corporations. A poll of 241 Fortune 1000 CEOs found that nearly 80 percent of these CEOs said that there were barriers that kept women from reaching the top. Of the 80 percent, 81 percent identified stereotypes, preconceptions, and male-dominated corporate culture as problems that women face. Yet, while gender-based segregation within organizations seems to gradually decrease, gender inequality seems to be a major managerial challenge that requires continuous improvement.[7]

Age Diversity

In 1983, about one in eight Americans was age 65 or older. In 1993, the ratio was about one in seven. It is estimated that the ratio will fall to nearly one in five in 30 years. The trend that America is aging is clear. Federal legislation has all but wiped out mandatory retirement rules. Most employees do not have to retire at 65. Furthermore, a large proportion of the work force cannot afford to retire even if they wished. Accordingly, the average age of the American work force is being pushed up. A recent comprehensive analysis of the research literature found that productivity actually increases as employees grow older.[8]

The combination of changes in the age distribution of employees and new flatter organization structures means that four generations of workers can find themselves working side by side. This potential age diversity of four generations presents a major set of managerial challenges in terms of managing four generations of value sets, belief systems, work norms, work attitudes, and physical and mental functioning, not to mention vast differences of work experiences.

Personality

Individual diversity is also rooted in the person's personality. Personality is an individual difference that lends consistency to a person's behavior. The term *personality* has two quite different meanings.[9] Sometimes it refers to the way a person is perceived by friends, family members, peers, supervisors, and subordinates. This meaning is derived from perception and judgment of the individual by others based on social interactions and reputation. The second meaning refers to the underlying, unseen structures and processes "inside" the person that explain why the individual behaves in a certain manner. The first meaning refers to a person's public reputation while the second refers to one's private inner nature.[10] In this module we are concerned primarily with the inner structures and processes that cause the individual to behave in a certain manner. *Personality* is defined as

> a relatively stable set of characteristics, tendencies, and temperaments that have been significantly formed by inheritance and by social, cultural, and environmental factors. This set of vari-

ables determines the commonalities and differences in the behavior of individuals (thoughts, feelings, and actions) that have continuity over time and that may not be easily understood as the sole result of the social and biological pressures of the moment.[11]

Personality Theories: An Overview

Psychological research and practice has produced a wide range of personality theories. It is beyond the scope of this module (and this course for that matter) to review the different theories. Here is an attempt to provide the shell and theoretical context of personality theories and an in-depth examination of two complementary theories. Four major clusters of personality theories seem to influence the study of personality in organizations:

Trait theories state that to understand individuals, we must break down behavior patterns into series of observable traits.[12]

Psychodynamics theories emphasize the unconscious determinants of behavior—for example, Sigmund Freud's theory that views personality as the interaction between three elements of personality: the id, the ego, and the superego.[13]

Humanistic theories emphasize individual growth and improvement—for example, Carl Rogers's theory that all people have the basic drive toward self-actualization, which is the quest of the individual to be all he or she can be.[14]

Integrative theories describe personality as a composite of an individual's psychological processes such as emotions, cognitions, attitudes, expectancies, and fantasies.[15]

In the context of organizational studies, many relevant personality characteristics were identified. In recent years, few conceptual frameworks for understanding individual differences have become very popular among organizational behavior educators, students, and managers. Two comparable frameworks—the Myers–Briggs model and Keirsey's temperament sorter (both rooted in the personality theory developed by Carl Jung)—have been translated into sets of concepts and tools that have practical applications.

Carl Jung's Theory of Personality Types

Carl Jung (1875–1961) is second only to Sigmund Freud among modern psychological thinkers. Jung started out as Freud's disciple and broke away to form his own unique ideas, many of which are taken for granted today. Jung's contributions to the field of psychology include his work on psychological types. He coined the terms *introversion* and *extroversion* and is the father of the work continued by Katherine Briggs, who formalized one of the first *type indicators.*

Jung believed that we have an inborn preference for how we function just as we have a preference for using one hand over the other. The preference for how we function is a characteristic, so we may be "typed" by these preferences. Although various researchers have contributed to Jung's work by refining and reorganizing the preferences in various combinations, 16 basic types have been identified from his model. David Keirsey grouped the 16 types into four temperaments, each of which consists of four types that share similar characteristics. The end result of this scholarly work is an understandable model of human personality that can be verified by simple observation of friends and family. By reading descriptions of each type, one can identify and predict both the strengths and weaknesses of themselves and others.

Four basic preferences in the way we approach life can be identified. The term *preference* means that we have an inborn tendency to behave a certain way. This does not mean that a preferred way of behaving will be the *only* way we function; it's just the most comfortably favored way. It's the same as being born with a tendency to use either our right or left hand, which results in our developing one over the other. We can only use the nondominant hand in an awkward way while the dominant hand is used without thinking. Some personality functions and behaviors come second nature to us and define our personality type.

The Four Preferences

Introversion	Extroversion
Intuition	Sensory
Thinking	Feeling
Judging	Perceiving

Introversion or Extroversion: The first preference is demonstrated when an individual is *extroverted* and attends more to the outer world of things and people or else is *introverted* and attends more to the inner world of the experience (a private world of ideas, principles, values, and feeling). As in all the personality preferences, one does not exclude the other—a person will attend to both the outer and inner world but will be most at home in one as opposed to the other. An extrovert will use more energy when attending primarily to outside events, while the introvert will use more energy in pondering his own thoughts or feelings.

Extroverts get their batteries charged by being sociable and the ''life of the party,'' while introverts seem to draw their energies from more solitary activities shared with few or no other people. There are three times as many extroverts as there are introverts, which may explain the tendency for pop psychology books to sell extroversion as the ''healthy'' preference. This, of course, is a false conclusion.

Intuition or Sensory: There are two ways to perceive information about the inner and outer world: through one's senses or through one's intuition. A preference to perceive with the senses (touch, smell, sight, hearing, and taste) is especially useful for gathering the facts of a situation. Intuition on the other hand shows meanings, relationships, and possibilities that are beyond the reach of the senses. Intuition is especially useful for perceiving what one might do about a situation. People tend to operate and become expert at one over the other.

Thinking or Feeling: People not only take in information but also make decisions based on how they think and feel about the issues and people involved. Decisions based on thinking utilize judgments that predict the logical results of any particular action in an impersonal and analytical way. Feeling-based decisions do not require logic; only personal values and the impact on others are primarily important. Those who put more confidence in decisions based on feeling typically become sympathetic and skillful in dealing with people as opposed to that part of the world that requires cold-hearted, matter-of-fact decisions.

Judging or Perceiving: As maturation takes place, one of the perceptive preferences (intuition or sensing) will become further developed and information will be received more confidentially in one of these two ways. Judgments based on this information will also be made by one of two ways (feeling or thinking) and more trust will be put in one over the other.

Not only will an individual favor one of two ways within each of these preferences, but he or she will also rely on one type of preference to deal with the world over the other. With some people, the taking in of information (perceptive) will be used more often than making decisions (judging). One type will be more comfortable in making judgments (thinking or feeling) before all the information about a situation is completely perceived. This type lives in a planned, decisive, orderly way of life. Others rely mainly on the perceptive process (intuition or sensing) and live in a flexible, spontaneous, reactive way.

The four preferences or tendencies form the basis of the 16 personality categories. If you are interested, most advisement and counseling centers in universities have access to the Myers–Briggs and/or Keirsey instruments. Use of the instruments is controlled through professionally trained people who can administer, score, and interpret the data with you.

The Big Five Personality Theory

In recent years, the views of many personality psychologists have converged regarding the structure and concepts of personality. Generally, researchers agree that there are five robust factors of personality that can serve as a meaningful taxonomy for classifying personality attributes.[16] Yet, while some differences in the specific labeling of the Big Five are debated in the literature, there is agreement about the Big Five factor structure.[17]

The Big Five factors (and prototypical characteristics for each factor) are

1. Extroversion (sociable, talkative, assertive, ambitious, and active).
2. Agreeableness (good-natured, cooperative, and trusting).
3. Conscientiousness (responsible, dependable, able to plan, organized, persistent, and achievement-oriented).
4. Emotional stability (calm, secure, and not nervous).
5. Openness to experience (imaginative, artistically sensitive, and intellectual).

Human Development and Organizational Life

Self-learning, self-learning competencies, self-management, and self-managed teams are part of personal growth. Some argue that the early 1990s can be characterized as the rebirth of the personal growth movement that was a dominant force during the 1960s and 1970s. The area of **personal growth** involves (1) understanding personality (yours and others) and its influence in the interpersonal communication process, (2) establishing personal goals that make you a winner in the sense of better fulfillment of needs and ambitions, and (3) developing ways of thinking and behavioral skills needed to achieve goals. The personal growth movement has been a part of the change in social values and the deepening interest in new educational methods that have characterized this generation. While a number of schools and methods of personal growth are appearing, in this module the intent is to examine specifically one theory of personality that can be applied in understanding many aspects of improved personal effectiveness. This system is the Parent-Adult-Child (PAC) model used in transactional analysis (TA). Thomas A. Harris's book *I'm OK—You're OK* is one of the clearest and most popular statements of the theory, and his text will be the main source used here.[18] The PAC/TA model can be used to analyze interpersonal barriers at several levels of organizational life.

Individual level. One's personal style of management may turn employees off. An employee may say, "My boss is an able guy and well intentioned, but he smothers me. He's always hovering about trying to be helpful when I just need to be left alone." Another may say, "Never write my boss a memo or give her something to read or she will get irritated. It took me awhile to learn she is a slow reader and prefers to get all her information by oral reports." In both of these cases, through application of PAC/TA the managers could learn how their personal styles are impeding effectiveness; goals for changes in these behaviors could be formed.

Interpersonal level. Basically, PAC/TA explores the dialoguing between two parties to determine barriers to a problem-solving mode, which will be demonstrated in Activity 5–3.

Organizational level. The organizational climate may encourage dysfunctional patterns of behavior. While working with managers of a bank, we found a highly critical climate where it was customary to shoot down colleagues' ideas. We traced this back to a promotion policy: To advance in the bank, one had to be a competent evaluator of loan applications, investments, and so on. The evaluator role had carried over into the personal relationships of the work force.

You will find the PAC/TA model to be applicable wherever interpersonal barriers exist in organizations. We have demonstrated in several exercises that the frustration potential of people interacting and communicating in groups can be tremendous. The organization that fails to reduce barriers to communication or to provide outlets for tension release can experience high costs. Negative feelings can be stored up and channeled into antiorganizational activities (underground networks, cliques, sabotage, absenteeism, slowdowns), which can decrease productivity. Helping employees express feelings in a manner acceptable to themselves and others has thus become a recognized function of the managerial role, as is building a supportive organizational climate. Of course, the management effort has to be directed mainly to motivation, since a goal-oriented, goal-setting group of employees presumably will not be preoccupied with resentments.

At another level the individual is confronted with a continuous bittersweet conflict between tension control and goal attainment. Excessive stress is not only a deterrent to creativity and flexibility in thinking, it also is a cause of psychosomatic illnesses such as migraine headaches, ulcers, hypertension, and heart disease. Expressing feelings appropriately is something we are all attempting. The sweet side of the conflict is attaining goal satisfaction. How we can utilize our talents to the utmost is a continuing question.

Numerous organizations and managers have turned to one or more of the personal growth and team-building methods for help in the bittersweet conflict. Transactional analysis and assertiveness training are among the many personal growth methods used. There are numerous variations with slightly unique focuses under different titles (for example, human relations laboratories, values clarification, achievement motivation, motivation management, goal setting, time management, personal power laboratories, reevaluation counseling, career planning, and psychocybernetics). Sensitivity training might be considered the predecessor of many of these. Personal growth is usually undertaken in a small group setting since interaction is essential in learning to express feelings, control defensive responses, set new goals, and try new behaviors.

Themes of Personal Growth

Several recurring themes can be found in most of the personal growth approaches, including the New Age human potential movement and the ''psychic boom'' of the late 1980s.

Theme 1: ''If I don't achieve what I want, it's my own damned fault.'' The idea is that you can achieve almost any realistic goal you set if you concentrate on changing your own behavior and do not blame lack of progress on what is ''out there.'' If your needs are not being satisfied, consider it your own fault. ''It is not your family, not your girlfriend, wife, boyfriend, or husband, not your ethnic background, not the 'establishment,' not your boss, not your teacher, etc.! You are in command! Don't let the world happen to you!'' It is essential for the individual to recognize that in all situations, a choice of actions exists if a deliberate attempt is made to think out alternatives.

Theme 2: ''I am being programmed by someone else's tape.'' The idea is that you have been programmed by your early life experience to think in specific patterns, which are not questioned by the individual. The goal is for the individual to become more aware of the nature of the programming and to rewrite it to achieve his or her own goals. Self-determination and choice are relevant.

Theme 3: ''I have tremendous potential for growth.'' Presumably most of us use only a small percentage of our potential talents and abilities. Although everyone is innately creative, few ever consider themselves to be. These forces within us need to be released and nurtured.

Theme 4: ''I will never feel good about others until I feel good about myself.'' The programming we receive in childhood includes all the things we must do, or must not do, to prevent expression of all those terrible, socially unacceptable urges such as lust. Since the urges are lurking beneath the surface, we have some feelings of rejection toward ourselves. We must learn to know, accept, respect, and love ourselves before we can be fully tolerant of and enjoy others. This is basic to improved interpersonal relations. ''I am my own best friend'' is a subtheme.

Theme 5: "What are my true values?" Being aware of and committed to a set of values is necessary for self-acceptance and goal setting.

Theme 6: "Where am I now? Where do I want to be?" The success of personal growth training is indicated solely by the individual's ability to set new goals and try new behaviors that will make achievement possible. Only by the actual behavior attempts can goals be attained. Intellectual learning alone does not usually lead to change. You must practice swinging the club if your golf score is to be lowered.

These themes will be illustrated in the following description of the Parent–Adult–Child (PAC) model of personality and the TA method. Both are used for arriving at a position of I'm OK—you're OK through personal growth. We start by discussing how certain aspects of personality are molded in infancy and childhood by receiving positive and negative strokes from parents.

Everyone Needs Strokes

Receiving strokes from others can be thought of as a need almost as essential as the basic needs for air, food, and water. One bit of evidence for this assumption is the disease marasmus, which accounted for more than half the deaths of infants in the first year of life at the turn of the century.[19] Babies receiving careful physical attention in some of the best homes and hospitals often seemed to waste away in a slow dying process, whereas many raised under less hygienic conditions in poorer homes thrived. Mother love was found to be the essential needed; the child required stroking and fondling in order to survive. When hospital authorities introduced foster mothers to care for children with the disease, it completely disappeared. Thus it is contended that interaction is essential to the survival of the child and remains an important need throughout life.

Life patterns of interaction arise from the process whereby the infant receives strokes, whether caresses or verbal approval, from the parent and learns to respond to them. It is the nature of this interaction process—that is, how and for what the parents give strokes and how these are perceived by the infant—that determines the basic life position of the infant: whether he perceives himself as OK or not OK, and whether he feels others are OK or not OK. Most typically, for reasons to be explained later, the child develops an I'm not OK—you're OK life position. The I'm not OK basic outlook, whether conscious or unconscious, is a barrier to learning new behavior or achieving personal goals.

While the parents are putting a child through the socialization process, she will learn a variety of ways of getting strokes. The child may earn positive strokes by doing what others want or, if these are not forthcoming, she may do things to earn negative strokes from others, which at least gets attention. Many of these behaviors are shaped into roles and patterned ways of interacting with others, or games people play.

This process of identifying with models, much of it at the unconscious level, is complicated. The Parent-Adult-Child concepts of transactional analysis provide tools for analyzing behavior that give us a better basis for understanding it and, most important, for becoming more aware of the processes operating and learning to control them.

The PAC Theory of Personality

For our purposes, certain aspects of the multiple nature of humans might be looked upon as three "people" who are directing our lives from inside and who are frequently in conflict as to what that direction should be. These three are the Parent, the Adult, and the Child, which are often referred to as *ego states.*

The Parent

The work of brain surgeon Wilder Penfield indicated that a considerable amount of past experience is "recorded" in the cerebral cortex.[20] Harris, having reviewed this work, describes the Parent as follows:

> The Parent is a huge collection of recordings in the brain of unquestioned or imposed external events perceived by a person in his early years, a period which we have designated roughly as

the first five years of life. . . . It is the complete record of everything the individual experienced as pronouncements of what should, ought, and must be done, or not be done, whether by verbal or nonverbal communications. The data in the Parent was taken in and recorded "straight" without editing. The situation of the little child, his dependency, and his inability to construct meanings with words made it impossible for him to modify, correct or explain. . . . The significant point is that whether these rules are good or bad in the light of a reasonable ethic, they are recorded as *truth* from the source of all security, the people who are "six feet tall" at a time when it is important to the two-foot child that he please and obey them.[21]

In addition to all the dos and don'ts, the Parent contains recordings of all the pleasures and delights that were learned during the recording process. This includes the stroking received for having performed the "right" behaviors. So the rewards of conforming are well established, as are the punishments for failing to do so.

Dependency is a vital concept in relation to the functioning of the Parent. The Parent is actually the internalization of everything that is "out there" and can include, more broadly, the parents, community, peers, television, or any external source the child is not free to question. Harris says, "Any external situation in which the little person feels dependent to the extent that he or she is not free to question or to explore produces data which is stored in the Parent."[22] Thus when there is not someone out there telling the child what to do, and pressures arise externally that do not permit it to consider all possible actions, the child is apt to fall back on instructions recorded in its Parent.

Significance of the Parent: The control and influence the recordings of the internal Parent have on the person throughout life, at the levels of both awareness and unawareness, are great. The instructions coming from the Parent, however, may not be applicable to the current situation faced by the individual. The individual needs to become aware that there are few absolutes in behavior norms and values, which are dependent on many situational factors and can be remolded by society, family, religion, and the individual. Thus they can be changed to help the individual assume problem-solving behavior that is appropriate to changing social circumstances. One goal of TA is to strengthen the Adult so that it can examine and control data coming from various sources, including the Parent, to determine its appropriateness in attempting to solve problems with which the individual is being confronted. It should be emphasized that the Parent performs the very positive and important function of providing a system of values; the main issue raised is whether they are being applied compulsively without considering the degree of applicability to a specific set of circumstances.

We had the opportunity to observe the compulsive functioning of the Parent in an executive workshop. The executives had indicated an interest in having a confrontation session with a radical youth leader. The nearby university was the only source of such a speaker, and he arrived looking like anything but an extremist. Wearing his Ivy League jacket and tie, he resembled the upper-middle-class law students on the campus. When all 60 executives were seated and he had been introduced, he burst forth with his opening thrust, shouting, "You motherf-----s have left us to die in our own s--t!" Immediately, many of the audience were on their feet: "You can't come in here and behave like that! This is un-American! Do you realize there is a woman present in this room?" And so on. Finally, one executive succeeded in silencing everyone else and said, "Let's hear what he has to say, and then we will let him have it!" There was agreement, and the speaker proceeded. Nothing else eventful happened. What he was saying was that he could come before them and talk for hours about establishing national priorities, and they would nod agreement but would feel no urgency. However, if he came in and used four-letter words they would be swept up in a riot of anger. In effect, he was asking, "Where is your true emotional investment? In the outmoded values of the past or in action to implement the realistic changes needed if we are to survive in the world we are rapidly polluting?" At the end of the talk, the executives said they really did not disagree with him.

The compulsiveness of the Parent can be most intense. The behavior of some people suggests they are a walking set of the roles society has prescribed for them and to which they must conform; there is little individuality in their makeup. Strokes from the Parent are as important, or more so, than those from others. Guilt feelings aroused by failure to follow the Parent's prescriptions add to the compulsivity of behavior for such people.

A cardiologist once told us that he often gives patients recovering from heart attacks a copy of the book *I'm OK—You're OK* in hopes of helping them cope with what appear to be problems of an overdemanding Parent. Some heart attack victims are excellent physical specimens and there appears to have been no reason they had the attack, except that they seem to be extremely tightly programmed as to what they should and must do. Trying to control ''that little guy inside that keeps telling them what to do all the time'' might prevent future attacks.

The Child

The Child is another body of recordings that consists primarily of feelings. As the Parent is recording what comes in from outside, the infant is emotionally responding to these external activities and its feelings are being recorded in the Child.

The infant has needs to gratify all impulses in the area of food, bodily functions, exploration, and so on and is frustrated by the environment and by the Parent. The results of this socialization process are negative feelings that become the basis of the feeling, I'm not OK. What is ''out there''—the parents who are doing the stroking and caring—is OK. Hence the basic position of most humans is I'm not OK—you're OK.

Significance of the Child: The recordings of the Child, which are ready for replay at any time, can influence or control behavior. Thus, at times, the individual can be completely under the control of the Child just as he or she could be under the control of the Parent. When the individual is in the grip of feelings, anger (or some other emotion) dominates reason. Fear of rejection and abandonment continues to exist at levels of awareness and unawareness. When feeling defensive, the Child is in control. The defense mechanisms of denial, projection, and others are processes operating in the Child.

A most important aspect of the Child is in its capacity for creativity. Presumably there is a vast reservoir here. An infant shows endless capacity for exploration and curiosity. It is capable of expressing great joy and spontaneity. By the time the child has become socialized, the admonitions of the Parent and the defensive feelings of the Child can have completely restrained this spontaneity. One goal of TA is to free up this potential by helping the individual burst out of the fixed role behaviors molded by society.

An excellent example of this was demonstrated in the campus streaking craze in Spring 1974. The nude student, running with great joy and spontaneity, violated and defied all the admonition forged deeply into the Parent. This was accompanied by considerable creativity in the variety of ways streaking was accomplished. In the campus toga party craze of 1978–79, we again see the Child breaking out of formal roles to vent feelings and to express creativity.

The Adult

Ten months is the time required by the infant to learn to manipulate the environment and become aware of people and needs. This self-actualization is the beginning of the Adult.

The Adult is ''principally concerned with transforming stimuli into pieces of information, and processing and filing that information on the basis of previous experience.'' It is different from the Parent, which is ''judgmental in an imitative way and seeks to enforce sets of borrowed standards, and from the Child, which tends to react more abruptly on the basis of prelogical thinking and poorly differentiated or distorted perceptions.''[23]

The Adult is a data-processing computer, which grinds out decisions after computing the information from three sources: the Parent, the Child, and the data that the Adult has gathered and is gathering. Two important functions of the Adult are (1) to examine the data in the Parent to see whether they are true and still applicable today, and then to accept or reject the data and (2) to examine the Child to see whether the feelings there are appropriate to the present or are archaic and in response to the archaic Parent data. The goal is not to do away with the Parent and Child but to be free to examine these bodies of data.[24]

The Adult can be looked upon as having a problem-solving, decision-making function in the sense of examining all data available and deciding upon alternatives. Probability estimating (that is, figuring the likelihood of something happening if certain actions are taken and what the consequences might be) is a logical, rational function the Adult performs. It also keeps emotional expression appropriate.

The ongoing work of the Adult consists, then, of checking out old data, validating or invalidating them, and refiling them for future use. If this business goes on smoothly and there is a relative absence of conflict between what has been taught and what is real, the computer is free for important new business, *creativity.* Creativity is born from curiosity in the Child, as in the Adult. The Child provides the ''want to'' and the Adult provides the ''how to.'' The essential requirement for creativity is computer time. If the computer is cluttered with old business, there is little time for new business.[25]

Significance of the Adult: When either the Parent or the Child, or both, dominates the personality, the Adult is weak and underdeveloped. This means the individual either is under the control of the Parent and will follow its directions, whether realistic or not, or is under the control of the emotions of the Child, whether or not they are appropriate. The individual may thus be spending most energy on the hang-ups of the past than on striving to achieve new goals. The individual is not free to choose a course of action. His Adult is not in command. More importantly, he is not fully aware of the I'm not OK—You're OK feelings that cause the individual to build life scripts that continuously confirm these feelings. The individual is particularly vulnerable to dependency feelings; whenever the situation impinges on freedom of choice, which most organization settings do, dependency feelings are aroused that bring the directions from the Parent and the defensiveness of the Child into full play.

The Four Life Positions

Before we discuss the ''emancipated Adult,'' we will look briefly at the **four life positions of personality development** that result from the types of strokes the infant receives from his or her parents.[26]

I'm not OK—you're OK. Most individuals arrive at the position of I'm not OK—you're OK; the next two described below can be regarded as exceptions. Harris maintains that every child makes the early decision of I'm not OK—you're OK. The reasons for this (to summarize what has been said) center on the dependency of the infant during its helpless months. The need for stroking is universal as shown by marasmus; every infant is flooded with unpleasant feelings at the time of birth. In the Freudian concept, these feelings become the model for later anxiety, and in TA they lead to the I'm not OK position.

I'm not OK—you're not OK. When the infant has a cold, nonstroking mother, and punishment becomes more frequent as the child begins to move about, the result can be the I'm not OK—you're not OK position. Withdrawal is the principal reaction; in extremes a schizoid condition results.

I'm OK—you're not OK. The infant who is abused long enough by its parents, whom the infant initially thought were OK, switches to the I'm OK—you're not OK position. This occurs during the second and third year, later than the second position. I'm OK in this case is self-stroking. The individual refuses to look inward. He or she has suffered from stroking deprivation since there are no OK people. In the extreme this is the criminal position.

I'm OK—you're OK. There is a qualitative difference between the first three positions and the desirable I'm OK—you're OK position. The first three are unconscious decisions made by the end of the third year; they are based on feelings. This fourth decision is conscious and verbal; it includes great amounts of information about the self and others.

The Transactional Analysis Method

A major goal of the Harris system is for the individual to move from the I'm not OK—you're OK position to the I'm OK—you're OK position. For Harris, the principal technique is **transactional analysis.** He uses the PAC concepts and the four positions described to analyze transactions, that is, exchanges between people.

The transaction consists of a stimulus by one person and a response by another, where the response, in turn, becomes a new stimulus for the other person to respond to. The purpose of the analysis is to discover which part of each person—Parent, Adult, or Child—is originating each stimulus and response.[27]

The goal of transactional analysis is to enable a person to have freedom of choice, the freedom to change at will, the freedom to change the responses to recurring and new stimuli. Much of this freedom is lost in early childhood, marking the onset of the neurotic process.[28]

TA for Personal Growth

If you were to go to a TA workshop, how would the method be used to help you improve your effectiveness? From the feedback of other participants and application of PAC/TA to yourself, you would become more aware of how your Parent, Adult, and Child are influencing your behavior. Is your Adult in charge of decision making or are you directed by the feelings, impulses, and defensive feelings of your Child? Are you living off the recordings of your Parent? Is an underdeveloped Parent or demanding Child preventing you from achieving goals? Are your hang-ups in your Parent and Child tying up energy that could go into goal behavior and creativity?

Most importantly, you would rewrite your life script in a way that clarified the needs of your Child and the values of your Parent; a set of goals for your strengthened Adult would be established.

Harris believes a strong Adult can be built in the following ways:

1. Learn to recognize your Child, its vulnerabilities, its fears, and its principal methods of expressing these feelings.
2. Learn to recognize your Parent and its admonitions, injunctions, fixed positions, and principal ways of expressing these admonitions and positions.
3. Be sensitive to the Child in others, talk to that Child, stroke that Child, protect that Child, and appreciate its need for creative expression as well as the not-OK burden it carries about.
4. Count to 10, if necessary, to give the Adult time to process the data coming into the computer, to sort out Parent and Child from reality.
5. When in doubt, leave it out. You can't make decisions without an ethical framework.[29]

The need for the Adult to work out a value system to which he or she is fully committed is a major aspect of TA. A TA workshop can provide you with the medium to practice new behavior and communication patterns that would accelerate goal achievements. Additional insight into what would be covered to make you the winner you are capable of becoming can be gained by restudying the themes of personal growth described at the beginning of this chapter.

TA in the Work Situation

Communication between a manager and subordinate may be characterized by Parent-to-Child, Child-to-Parent, or Child-to-Child transactions, all of which can be dysfunctional.[30] Ideally, an Adult-to-Adult, problem-solving mode would further productive relationships. PAC/TA transactions in a work situation are diagrammed for analysis in Figure 5–2.

Figure 5–2
PAC/TA Transactions in a Work Situation

Dysfunctional Parent-Child Exchange

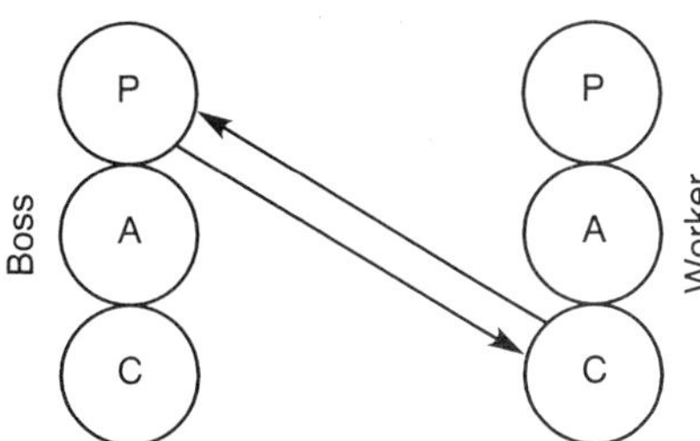

Boss: Didn't you tell me you would have the Smith estate appraisal finished yesterday?

Worker: You would have had it if I weren't getting more than my share of work around here.

Problem-Solving Adult-to-Adult Exchange

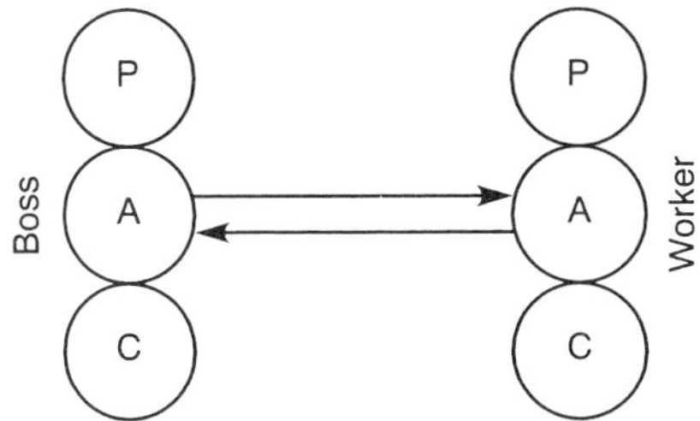

Boss: How are you doing on the Smith estate appraisal?

Worker: I'm running behind because of all the new cases that came in this week. Could we sit down and set up some priorities? You may want to reassign some of my work.

TA in Business Training and Applications

Although the use of TA in business has been decreasing in the past few years, several descriptions of unique applications of TA in business training are reported in the literature.[31] The Bank of New York incorporated TA into its formalized first-line supervisory training program, which runs a total of 40 hours. The program is designed to both increase self-awareness and teach supervisors to use the structural analysis of transaction techniques in their daily operations.[32] American Airlines, one of the first companies to use TA in its internal training and development programs, developed a TA program to teach employees how to recognize what feelings and perceptions motivate a customer's behavior and to analyze the transaction so they can correct the situation.[33] A TA program developed for women in management aimed at raising consciousness and improving managerial effectiveness.[34] Some suggest that similar programs might be developed for racial minorities or for dealing with racial conflict in organizations.[35] A further application of TA to work situations will be included in Activity 5–3.

Life Scripts

In TA the *life script* refers to a plan for interacting with others and for perceiving one's self-worth, which is developed as the child relates to its parents. These early recordings contain instructions for interpersonal style and for setting life goals. They were written so long ago that individuals are not usually aware of the guidance these instructions provide for thinking and acting. Life scripts contain scenarios originating from many sources. The four life positions are a major ingredient. For example, persons playing a script of a loser have a heavy element of not-OK–ness in their self-images, while those seeing themselves as winners have had considerable experience convincing themselves of their OK-ness. Culture, family, religion, and occupations all contribute to an individual's unique integration of the scripts and roles the individual has as models for behaving as he or she pursues a life plan. *Games* are scripts learned early to defend one's self-worth by controlling and manipulating other people.

Games People Play

One consequence of being in the I'm not OK—you're OK position is that it prevents open, authentic relationships with others and the giving and sharing of spontaneous feelings because one's behavior patterns are dictated by the forces coming from the Parent or Child. This leads to interactions with others that often are based upon rituals, pastime activities, and other conventional forms of behavior. Game playing is a way of getting and giving strokes that gives the individual a feeling of superiority over others. To use Eric Berne's definition,

A game is an ongoing series of complementary ulterior transactions progressing to a well-defined, predictable outcome. Descriptively it is a recurring set of transactions, often repetitious, superficially plausible, with a concealed motivation; or, more colloquially, a series of moves with a snare, or "gimmick." Games are clearly differentiated from procedures, rituals, and pastimes by two chief characteristics: (1) their ulterior quality and (2) the payoff. Procedures may be successful, rituals effective, and pastimes profitable, but all of them are by definition candid; they may involve contest, but not conflict, and the ending may be sensational, but it is not dramatic. Every game, on the other hand, is basically dishonest, and the outcome has a dramatic, as distinct from merely exciting, quality.[36]

Games reinforce the first position, I'm not OK—you're OK. Examples of games Berne gives are "Look How Hard I've Tried," "Let's You and Him Fight," and "Flirt."

A version of "Flirt" involved an attractive young college woman who went in for counseling because she was unhappy about her relationship with men. Men, she said, "were interested in only one thing." While the interview proceeded, she kept buttoning and unbuttoning the top button of her low-necked blouse, which covered a full bosom. The male counselor called this provocative act to her attention, and she protested and denied it. As it turned out, her problem was that she did provoke every man she dated, but she was unaware of the extent to which she did so. The result of the provocation was that the date attempted to sample the fruit, and she rejected him soundly. The young woman's Parent, handed down from her mother, told her that men were only after one thing. The game of "Flirt" she played proved to her that this was true. The ulterior transaction in this case was her unconscious effort to prove it; the payoff was to reject the suitor after he had been trapped. The strokes came from the attention accorded her beauty and from her Parent, which proved that she was right. Of course, games are played by both sexes.

A Model for Continued Growth and Effectiveness

How could you develop your own behavior change program? The most basic principle to follow is this: The way you think about yourself determines the way you feel and the way you behave. So if you want to change the way you behave, you need to change the way you think about yourself. This interrelationship can be extended to three areas: the cognitive, the communicative, and the behavioral. (See Figure 5–3.)

Cognitive. The cognitive area pertains to the way you think about yourself, the basic beliefs you have and assumptions you make about the way you are, and what you can do. Whatever the structure of this complex interrelated set of thoughts, it has devel-

Figure 5–3
A Model for Continued Growth

	Change Areas		
	Cognitive	**Communicative**	**Behavioral**
Processes	Way you think about yourself and others	Way you talk to yourself	Way you behave
Goal Activities	Imagining television scenes of self/others; changing channel to new script	Directing your new script	Trying specific behaviors from new script

oped over a long time, it is well established, and it is rigid. Changes here can lead to changes in behavior. As we will see, the reverse can also be true.

Communicative. You talk to yourself all the time. The way you talk to yourself influences your thinking and behavior. Change the way you talk to yourself and you can change your behavior. We once knew a real estate developer who carried a card in his wallet that programmed him for the day and its events. He would read it to himself when he started his day: ''I will treat every problem that arises not as a source of frustration but as a challenge for new learning or for creative solution making.'' He would read the card at lunch and critique his morning activities to see to what extent he had followed the programming. He claimed that it and other such personal ''programs'' had gained him much success.

Behavioral. The way you act determines the way you think about yourself. If you never speak up in a group, you may say to yourself you are shy or do not want to be embarrassed. Thus one behavior reinforces the other. However, if you change your behavior, you change the way you think about yourself. This interaction was dramatically observed in a young foreign service wife who found that her role required her to be a hostess to foreigners and other Americans of the diplomatic community. At first she resisted and hated the role—it was too much work, she did not have the skills, and so on. After living through this forced role for four years, she was overheard telling a new wife how she would love the role once she learned it. Having been forced to perform in the role, she found the rewards of being an excellent hostess had changed the way she thought about herself and, we presume, the way in which she communicated with herself.

Using the Model for Developing New Behavior Goals

Note that the bottom half of Figure 5–3 describes goal areas that will lead to change. In the cognitive area, it is often suggested that you can set up an imaginary television screen on which you play reruns of your present script, of the way you are behaving with important others or with people in groups, and determine what it is that you don't like or is causing you problems. Now you design a new script to show you on that screen the way you would like to be. Next you select some specific behavior you want to develop and go out and try it. For example, you may be saying, ''I see John as constantly belittling my view because he is in accounting [the ''real'' world], and I am an English literature major [the ''unreal'' world]. I would like an equal relationship so he respects my views and I respect his. Next time he belittles me, I will tell him how I feel and insist my views are realistic and that he understand what I am saying,'' and so forth. Once this is done and John has shown respect for the way you stood up for yourself, the way you think of yourself and talk to yourself will change, and it should be easier to stand up for your views.

In another example, a student who never talked in class discussions decided her future in the business world would not be advanced by never saying anything in meetings. She resolved to ask one question of the professor in each class for the new week. It did not always work, but she found herself saying to herself, ''Why didn't you do it, dummy?'' or ''What are you going to do in the next class, dummy?'' She had a number of victories in terms of asked questions, and got others in class involved in discussions. This behavior change led to more confidence and a willingness to try other things—all three areas (cognitive, communicative, and behavioral) were interacting to help achieve the goals.

In using the model, remember the following:

1. Be specific about the exact behavior you want to develop or change. Just deciding to be different does not result in success. The more specific you are, the greater your chance of success, and you will be able to adjust your behavior to change other specific behaviors.
2. Don't be too ambitious and try too much. Try a little at a time to increase the chance of positive results.

3. Be patient and tolerant with yourself. Find ways of rewarding yourself for successes.
4. Never stop trying.

Here is a good method to try: The next time you hear yourself complaining, say to yourself, ''Complaining is only a way of reducing pressure by letting off steam.'' Now, what are you going to do about it? If you're only interested in complaining, I don't want to hear about it. If you want to tell me how you feel and how it hurts, I'll listen as long as you tell me what you are going to do about it. What specific actions are you going to plan and take? Good luck!

Meism and the Now Generation

The personal growth movement has been criticized for furthering ''meism,'' for teaching selfish concern and ''doing one's own thing.'' Responsible professionals in the field have never advocated meism per se. A basic assumption of personal growth is that you can help others more, appreciate others more, and influence others more if you better understand yourself, if you overcome the hang-ups that are blocking your energies, and if you are helping yourself while helping others. In other words, feeling good about yourself and your own effectiveness enables you to feel better about others (I'm OK—you're OK).

The issue of egoism versus altruism is an eternal public issue. Surveys show that the attitudes of youth have been changing over the past decade from copping out and fighting the establishment to concern for making the establishment work. (The rising enrollment of both men and women in schools of business may be one indication of this shift.) However, as the values of youth change, we see the me–you battle flourishing on the national political and economic scene: A resurgence of the principles of rugged individualism and unshackled private enterprise is being countered by those claiming public good is suffering at the expense of private exploitation and wealth. So, within the context of public concern for egoism and altruism, it must be remembered that the personal growth movement may have been exploited by some preaching meism but that methods such as TA have a solid self–other perspective: Healthy concern for self and healthy concern for others go together.

Human Development in the 1990s and Beyond

The human potential movement of the 1960s and 1970s emphasized getting in touch with feelings as a major growth area. The movement died down in the late 1970s and early 1980s; but by the late 1980s and early 1990s, it was back in full force riding the crest of the ''creativity'' wave. The pressures of international competition forced organizations to exploit any lead that might spawn innovations and increased productivity, and the human potential movement was seen as a tool for freeing executives, managers, and professionals to think more creatively and overcome self-defeating attitudes. Personal and interpersonal effectiveness remained an important aspect of the movement.

An interesting addition to this New Age trend is the turn to the supernatural for psychic guidance. Shirley MacLaine, with her best-selling books and prime-time television account of her trip into the psychic world, followed by a 10-city tour conducting spiritual seminars, has dramatized this interesting development. As the psychic boom spread throughout the United States, managers and professionals were a high percentage of those in attendance, either listening to the wisdom of sages talking through ''channelers'' or engaging in other paranormal activities.

Summary

Many factors influence the individual's work behavior. The first part of this module provided a partial schema/roadmap of the factors that influence the individual's self-concept and work behavior. We have explored the nature of individual differences. Of the multiple sources of individual diversity, this module examined the cultural and demographic dimensions. The changing nature of organizations, coupled with the changing nature of the labor force, will likely present increasing challenges for managers. The roadmap presented can be used as a way to begin to map out the forces such that more holistic understanding of the issues will emerge.

One of the key dimensions of the individual's self-concept and work behavior is the individual's personality. The second part of the module focuses on personality theories and models. Following a short overview of personality theories, we focused on Jung's personality theory that provides the basis for two models of personality types—Myers–Briggs and Keirsey–Bates—which are widely used. We also introduced the Big-Five theory as an alternative and relatively new way to map out personality attributes that has been gaining empirical research support in recent years.

Human development is a critical area of concern in organizational life. The personal growth movement has a potential for improved communication and interpersonal effectiveness in organizational life. The PAC of transactional analysis was discussed as an example of the theoretical and conceptual models being used to analyze basic problem areas of personality and methods of developing new goals and behavior. The I'm not OK—you're OK position appears to be typical of the human condition in that it develops from infancy a dependency in which the individual is helpless (and thus not OK), while the all-powerful parents who provide for its needs are OK.

One major component of the personality, according to TA, is the Parent, which is the internal guiding force replacing the real parents. If the Parent is overdemanding, the individual is under the control of the "songs his mother has taught him" in many situations, whether or not they are relevant to present reality. The Child, on the other hand, represents the feeling component of the personality. If the Child is too strong, the individual is under the control of emotions and defensive responses, past and present, and the individual's behaviors will not be appropriate for coping with present situations. The Child also is the source of creativity, curiosity, spontaneity, and joy. The Adult is like a computer, which analyzes data from the Parent, the Child, and the past experience of the Adult itself plus data from the real world, and makes decisions for behavioral action. A major goal of TA is to develop a strong Adult so it can be in complete charge and maximize the probability that the individual will achieve the desired goals. The consequences of the Adult not being in charge are that its computer time is tied up in the old hang-ups of the Parent and Child (game playing is an example) so new business, the achievement of new goals, and the creative use of energies cannot be undertaken. When the Adult is in charge, the individual achieves that desired I'm OK—you're OK position of feeling good about the self and others.

Study Questions

1. Identify and discuss the nature of individual diversity.
2. Discuss how cultural diversity and demographic diversity influence individuals' self-concept and work behavior.
3. Identify and discuss the key dimensions of individual effectiveness.
4. How can a manager influence individual effectiveness?
5. What are some managerial skills needed to influence an employee's effectiveness?
6. What are some recurring themes in most personal growth approaches?
7. Briefly discuss the four preferences/personality types as identified by Carl Jung.
8. Briefly explain the Parent, Adult, and Child components of the personality.
9. Compare and contrast between Jung, Big Five, and PAC personality theories.
10. What are the underlying goals of transactional analysis?
11. How can PAC/TA be useful in an organizational setting? Provide specific examples.
12. How can a person build a strong Adult according to Harris?

Endnotes

1. See, for example, S. E. Jackson and E. B. Alvarez, "Working through Diversity as a Strategic Imperative," in S. E. Jackson, ed., *Diversity in the Workplace* (New York: Guilford Press, 1992); and M. McKendall, "A Course in Work-Force Diversity: Strategies and Issues," *Journal of Management Education* 18, no. 4 (1994), pp. 407–23.

2. Jackson and Alvarez, "Working through Diversity."

3. C. Gardenswartz and A. Rowe, *Managing Diversity,* (Homewood, Ill.: Richard D. Irwin, 1993).

4. See, for example, J. P. Fernandez, *The Diversity Advantage* (New York: Lexington Books, 1993).

5. G. N. Powell, *Gender and Diversity in the Workplace* (Thousand Oaks, Calif.: Sage, 1994).

6. See, for example, G. N. Powell, *Women and Men in Management* (Beverly Hills, Calif.: Sage, 1988).

7. See, for example, J. A. Jacobs, *Gender Inequality at Work* (Thousand Oaks, Calif.: Sage, 1994).

8. D. A. Waldman and B. J. Avolio, "A Meta-Analysis of Age Difference in Job Performance," *Journal of Applied Psychology* (1986), pp. 33–38.

9. See, for example, R. T. Hogan, "Personality and Personality Measurement," in M. D. Dunnette and L. M. Hough, eds., *Handbook of Industrial and Organizational Psychology* (Palo Alto, Calif.: Consulting Psychologists Press, 1991), pp. 873–919.

10. R. L. Hughes, R. C. Ginnett, and G. J. Curphy, *Leadership: Enhancing the Lessons of Experience* (Homewood, Ill.: Richard D. Irwin, 1993).

11. This definition is based on S. F. Maddi, *Personality Theories: A Comparative Analysis* (Homewood, Ill.: Dorsey, 1980), p. 10.

12. Hundreds of traits have been identified over the years. See, for example, R. R. McCrae "Why I Advocate the Five-Factor Model," in D. M. Buss and N. Cantor, eds., *Personality Psychology: Recent Trends and Emerging Directions* (New York: Springer-Verlag, 1989), pp. 237–345.

13. S. Freud, *An Outline of Pschoanalysis* (New York: Norton, 1949).

14. C. Rogers, *On Becoming a Person* (Boston: Houghton Mifflin, 1970).

15. See, for example, D. D. Clark and R. Hoyle, "A Theoretical Solution to the Problem of Personality-Situational Interaction," *Personality and Individual Differences* 9 (1988), pp. 133–38.

16. See, for example, J. M. Digman, "Personality Structure: Emergence of the Five-Factor Model," *Annual Review of Psychology* 41 (1990), pp. 417–40; and L. R. Goldberg, "The Development of Markers for the Big-Five Factor Structure," *Psychological Assessment* 4 (1992), pp. 26–42.

17. L. R. Goldberg, "The Structure of Phenotypic Personality Traits," *American Psychologist* 48, no. 1 (1993), pp. 26–34.

18. Paraphrased material and verbatim quotations from *I'm OK—You're OK* by Thomas Harris, M. D. Copyright © 1967, 1968, 1969 by Thomas A. Harris. Reprinted by permission of Harper & Row; M. James and D. Jongeward, *Born to Win: Transactional Analysis with Gestalt Experiments* (Reading, Mass.: Addison-Wesley, 1971); D. Jongeward, ed., *Everybody Wins: Transactional Analysis Applied to Organizations* (Reading, Mass.: Addison-Wesley, 1973).

19. M. A. Ribble, *The Rights of Infants* (Morningside Heights, N.Y.: Columbia University Press, 1943).

20. Wilder Penfield, "Memory Mechanisms," *A.M.A. Archives of Neurology and Psychiatry* 67 (1952), pp. 178–98.

21. Harris, *I'm OK—You're OK,* pp. 18–20.

22. Ibid., p. 24.

23. Ibid., p. 30. The quotations within the quotation are from E. Berne, *Transactional Analysis in Psychotherapy* (New York: Grove Press, 1961).

24. Harris, p. 30.

25. Ibid., p. 34.

26. Ibid., pp. 37–53.

27. Ibid., p. 65.

28. Ibid., p. 58.

29. Ibid., p. 95.

30. See, for example, O. Summerton, ''Games in Organizations,'' *Transactional Analysis Journal* 23, no. 2 (1993), pp. 87–103.

31. See, for example, R. R. Krausz ''Organizational Scripts,'' *Transactional Analysis Journal* 23, no. 2 (1993), pp. 77–86.

32. H. M. F. Rush and Phyllis S. McGrath, ''Transactional Analysis Moves into Corporate Training: A New Theory of Interpersonal Relations Becomes a Tool for Personnel Development,'' *The Conference Board Record* 10, no. 7 (July 1973), pp. 38–44.

33. D. D. Bowen and Raghu Nath, ''Transactional Analysis in Organization Development: Application within the NTL Model,'' *Academy of Management Review,* January 1978, pp. 79–89.

34. D. Scott, ''Using Transactional Analysis in Seminars for Career Women,'' in *Everybody Wins: Transactional Analysis Applied to Organizations,* ed. D. Jongeward (Reading, Mass.: Addison-Wesley Publishing, 1973), pp. 161–98.

35. J. C. Christen and Nick Nykodym, ''TA: A Training and Development Tool—The Consultant's Perspective,'' *Organization Development Journal* 4, no. 2 (Summer 1986), pp. 85–87.

36. E. Berne, *Games People Play* (New York: Grove Press, 1964), p. 48.

Activity 5–3: Transactional Analysis in the Work Situation

Objectives:

a. To develop awareness of ego states (PAC) as they operate in transactional analysis.
b. To develop awareness of the consequences of nonproductive Parent–Child, Child–Parent, and Child–Child transactions.
c. To develop awareness of the type of transactions that can lead to an Adult–Adult relationship.

Introduction:

You are about to participate in an exercise that will require an observer to use the following concepts for analyzing your interactions and communications:

a. *Ego states.* The mental frame of reference assumed by the individual in a specific communication, that is, the individual is speaking from the mode of either a Parent, Adult, or Child.
   (1) *Parent-type behaviors.* These include telling, directing, or advising another what should, ought, must, or must not be done; judging, criticizing, or implying the same by questions such as, "Don't you think you ought to . . . ?"; and speaking as an authority figure (boss, mother, father, etc.). This can, of course, be done from either the authoritarian or the kindly, helpful, supportive mode.
   (2) *Child-type behaviors.* These include emotional or feeling-directed responses such as expression of anger, attacking, or being otherwise aggressive (moving against), withdrawal, apathy, and "don't care"-type of responses (moving away from); and being overly nice or overly obedient and conforming (moving toward). These are defensive types of responses; defense mechanisms (for example, denial or rationalization) are often involved. Child responses include, of course, positive expressions of joy, happiness, creativity, and love, but these are not so apt to show up in a boss–subordinate work relationship, although feeling good about a competent, supportive boss is an emotional response of the Child.
   (3) *Adult-type behaviors.* These include problem solving, evaluation of consequences, goal setting, decision making, being open, and leveling.

b. *Complementary transactions.* These are sent from one ego state, which then receives a response from the ego state of the other person to which they were directed.

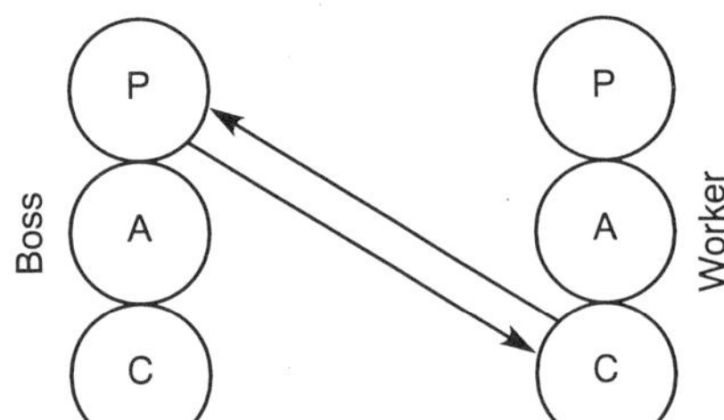

Boss: If you work particularly hard today, I'll give you time off on Friday.

Worker: Gee, I'd like that.

c. *Crossed or noncomplementary transactions.* These are transactions from one ego state that receive a response from a different ego state than was intended. These may create a communication breakdown or conflict.

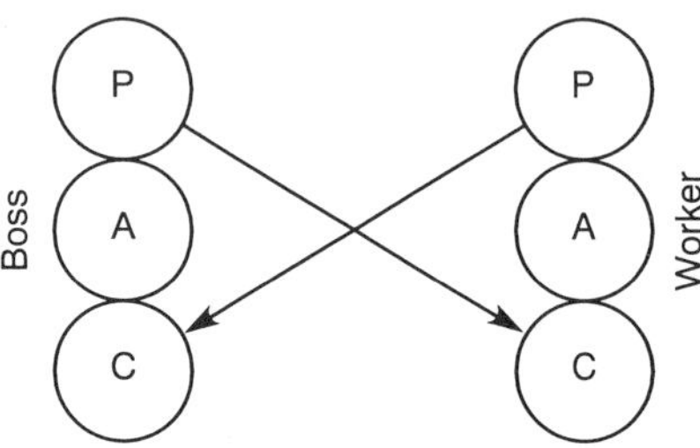

Boss: An experienced worker ought to be able to turn out more work.

Worker: I hope you are going to keep your quality standards high.

However, a crossed transaction can be constructive.

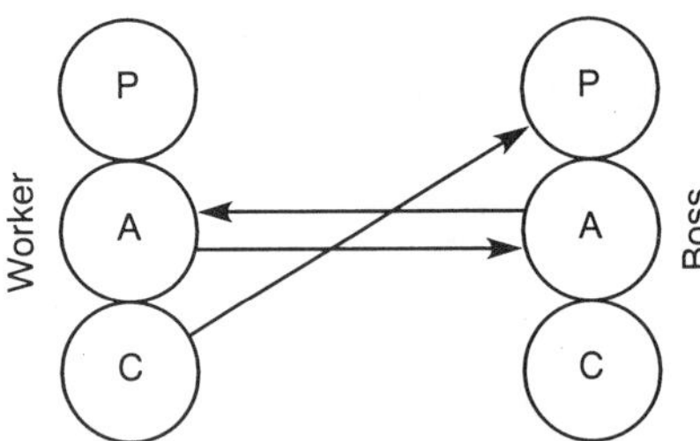

Worker: I'm so completely frustrated on this report that you're going to have to tell me what to do.

Boss: You probably have been at it too long, but I know you know what to do. For instance, if you need information on resources, where would you look?

Worker: You mean the government reports? That's a good idea. I'll check that and see where I go from there.

(*Note:* The boss's response is actually being supportive of the worker's Child at the same time the boss is making an Adult-to-Adult communication.)

d. *Ulterior Transactions.* These have a double meaning.

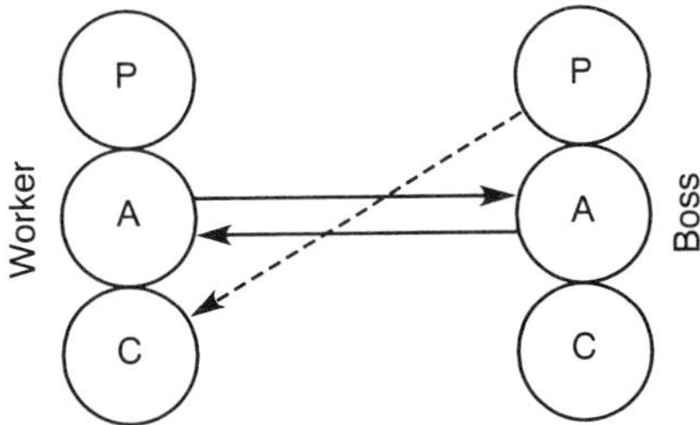

Worker: I really don't think this is the best way to approach this job.

Boss: Your opinion is valued. You do excellent work and don't have to worry about your job, but why not give this a try and come back if it does not work.

Ulterior message: "You could be fired."

The following could be the first step in a "Flirt" game. The male boss sends for a female analyst. She enters the room and says,

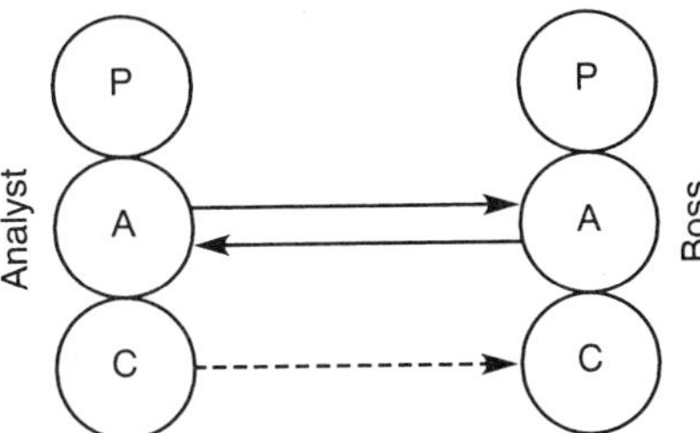

Female Analyst: Do you want to see me?

Male Boss: Yes I do.

Analyst: That will cost you extra.

Ulterior message: "I'm available."

You will recall that the definition of *games people play* given above is that they always have (1) an ulterior motive and (2) a payoff.

e. *OK—Not OK Positions.* The discussion of these in Module 5 pertained to an individual's generalized view of self–other relationships. These positions can also be used to analyze a series of transactions between a sender and receiver. Thus if an individual is communicating primarily from one ego state, it can correspond to taking one of these four positions:

Primarily		
From	**To**	**Position Being Assumed**
Parent	Child	I'm OK—you're not OK
Child	Parent	I'm not OK—you're OK
Adult	Adult	I'm OK—you're OK
Child	Child	I'm not OK—you're not OK

Alternative 1: Role Playing of a Conference between Stacy Lee (Sales Manager of an Auto Dealership) and Kris Bono (One of His Auto Sales Representatives)

Task 1:

a. Form triads with class members who are not on your regularly assigned team.

b. Triad members: Decide who is to play the roles of sales manager Stacy Lee and sales representative Kris Bono. The third member will be the observer.

c. When you have decided role assignments, the persons playing Stacy Lee and Kris Bono will turn to their role directions, which appear on page M5-30. Tear out your own without looking at the other role. Each of you is to study your role. The observer is not to read either of the roles and should continue to study the introduction to this exercise. (Also, see paragraph e for the types of observations you will be making.)

(Time: 10 minutes)

d. Role players: Kris has just entered Stacy's office for a conference Stacy requested. Stacy will begin the conversation and the roles will be played until some conclusion is reached.
(Time: 10 minutes)

e. Observer: While observing, do not interrupt the role playing. Watch for the following:
   (1) Ego states from which each is communicating.
   (2) Changes in ego states as the exercise progresses.
   (3) Complementary, crossed or noncomplementary, and ulterior transactions.
   (4) What are the primary OK—not OK positions being assumed?
   (5) Are any games being played?

f. As soon as role playing is completed, participants are to proceed immediately to Task 2.

Task 2 (Discussion in Triads):

a. Observer gives feedback on the observations made to the role players.

b. The triad members are to discuss the following:
   (1) What did each of the role players try to accomplish?
   (2) How would you characterize the final solution arrived at by the role players? Starting with the ego state of the boss, would you say the transaction was (1) Parent-to-Child, (2) Adult-to-Adult, or (3) other?
   (3) How did Stacy Lee feel about the transaction? How did Kris feel?
   (4) What would be the possible consequences of the transaction?
   (5) How could the situation have best been handled in terms of (a) types of communication, (b) specific approaches to overcome conflict, (c) solutions?
   (Time: 10 minutes)

Task 3 (Class Discussion):

a. The instructor will interview each triad as to:
   (1) Observer's report.
   (2) Kris's feelings about the transaction.
   (3) Stacy's feelings about it.

b. After hearing all the triads (if time permits), what generalizations can be reached as to the PAC/TA character of the transactions?

c. How could the situation have been best handled?
(Time: open ended)

Source: This is an adaptation of an exercise developed by M. Dale Federer, professor of psychology, California Polytechnic State University, San Luis Obispo, California. This exercise is printed here with the special permission of Dr. Federer.

Transactional Analysis in the Work Situation

On the reverse side of this page are the two role descriptions for individuals playing Stacy Lee and Kris Bono in Alternative 1 of Activity 5–3. Tear out your assigned role along the dotted line below without looking at the role description of the other role player.

Role of Stacy Lee, sales manager

(CUT ON LINE)

Role of Kris Bono, sales representative

Role of Stacy Lee, Sales Manager

You manage 10 automobile sales representatives in a very busy dealership of a leading U.S. manufacturer. Business is good, with the volume of sales the best since the 1991 recession. Kris Bono, a college dropout whom you hired two months ago, has been selling reasonably well for one so young and inexperienced, but you think Kris could do a lot better.

Kris has to learn that among the great variety of customers are two on whom you use the exact opposite approach:

> First are the customers who want a much more expensive car than they can afford. Sell them what they want! Never suggest they are wrong or they will go out the door, down the street to your competitor, and buy what you didn't want to sell them.
>
> Second are the more typical customers who have to be pushed above what they think they can afford. They come in thinking they want only the basic car without any extras. Always try to push them up to a luxury model just a little higher than they think they want. Once they buy the higher-priced car, they will learn to love the extras and they will always be back for the better models the next time they go looking for a car—which only goes to show people don't really know what they need.

Even though Kris has progressed from the tenth up to the sixth ranking in sales, Kris is still in that potentially high turnover group of salespersons whom a manager has to consider for termination if someone with a lot more experience comes along and applies for the job.

You have asked Kris, who is a bit sensitive and resistant to supervision, to come in for a conference. Plan your approach and think of some convincing reasons to use in coaching Kris to sell more cars. Kris has just sold a basic car—no extras—to a senior couple and is now coming into your office for the conference.

Role of Kris Bono, Sales Representative

You interrupted your university education for a year so you could save up some money. You sell new cars in a very busy dealership of a leading U.S. auto manufacturer, where the volume of sales is the best since the 1991 recession. This is your first selling job and you believe you have been very successful—among the 10 salespersons with whom you work, you have risen to the sixth ranking during your two-month employment.

You have developed a three-point philosophy of selling which you think will make you, in time, one of the best among salespersons. Here it is:

1. *Your personality:* You have natural enthusiasm and energy, combined with a low-key persuasiveness that customers respond to well. You love the challenge of selling—you arrive every morning looking forward to your work.
2. *The customer:* You have a sincere interest in people. You believe in approaching all customers with the idea of matching their needs to the right car. How they are going to use it and what they can afford should be the major factors to consider in helping them make a decision.
3. *The product:* A good product, presented properly, will sell itself—and yours is the best on the market. If you push people too hard, they will suspect your product and regard you as the stereotyped, devious used-car salesman.

You just sold a basic car—no extras—to an elderly couple. The woman wanted a more expensive model but the man insisted he couldn't afford it—and judging by his appearance, he probably couldn't. If you had helped the woman a little, you could have sold a higher-priced car, but you knew you would be very uncomfortable with yourself afterward.

Your manager, Stacy Lee, has just called you in for a talk. You like Stacy, who has given you some good guidance. However, you always have to be on guard because Stacy puts too much pressure on you. You must be left alone and do it your own way if you are going to sell a lot of cars.

You are about to enter Stacy's office.

Alternative 2: Role Playing Using Participants' Own Experiences

Task 1:

a. Form triads with class members who are not on your regularly assigned teams.

b. Triad members: Think of a work incident that occurred between you and your boss. Quickly relate the story to the other members. Agree on which of the three stories would make the best role-playing exercise. The individual to whom the incident occurred is designated as member A and becomes the observer. The other two are designated B and C.
(Time: 5 to 10 minutes)

c. Member B: Assume you are the boss in the situation described by member A. Start at the beginning and role play it through to conclusion. Play the role according to how you would feel and behave if you were in the situation. Make up what is consistent with the story when you need to do so.
Member C: Assume you are the worker and follow the same role-playing instructions.
(Time: 10 minutes)

d. Member A: While observing, do not interrupt the role playing.
   (1) Identify the ego states from which each is communicating.
   (2) Watch for changes in ego states as the exercise progresses.
   (3) Watch for complementary, crossed or noncomplementary, and ulterior transactions.
   (4) What are the primary OK—not OK positions being assumed?
   (5) Are any games being played?

e. As soon as role playing is completed, participants are to proceed immediately to Task 2.

Task 2 (Discussion in Triads):

a. Member A gives feedback on the observations made to the other members.

b. The triad members are to discuss the following:
   (1) What did each of the role players try to accomplish?
   (2) How would you characterize the final solution arrived at by members B and C? Starting with the ego state of the boss, would you say the transaction was (a) Parent-to-Child, (b) Child-to-Parent, (c) Adult-to-Adult, or (d) Child-to-Child?
   (3) How did the subordinate feel about the transactions?
   (4) What would appear to be possible consequences of the transactions?
   (5) How could the situation have best been handled in terms of (a) type of communication, (b) specific approaches to overcome conflict, and (c) solutions?
   (Time: 10 minutes)

c. Member A's are to report some of their observations to the class. Open-class discussion of results follows.

Task 3:

a. Have a triad volunteer report an incident they played that they think the whole class would find interesting. Have that triad's member A meet in front of the class with two volunteers from other triads and go through the same procedure, with the entire class acting as observers. Open discussion to follow.
(Time: 20 minutes)

Activity 5–4: Rough Times at Nomura

Objectives:

a. To introduce the types of problems that arise in a cross-cultural work environment.

b. To explore the relationship between cultural diversity and employees' self-concept and work behavior.

c. To examine the relationship between culture and organizational structure and process.

Task 1 (Individual):

Individuals working alone should prepare the case that follows for class discussion by reading the case and answering the questions at the end of the case.

Task 2 (Group):

Imagine you are a consulting team brought in by Nomura Securities International (NSI) to study the problems in the Japanese Equities Dept. Develop an action plan for resolving the department's immediate problem as well as a long-term plan for improving the situation at NSI's New York office.

Task 3 (Class):

Select one of the teams to present their consulting report to the class, which will serve as NSI's board of directors. Board members will be free to ask questions relating to the nature of problems and the action plans proposed to resolve them.

Source: This activity was contributed by Professor Allan Bird. We are grateful to Professor Bird.

Rough Times at Nomura

The Problem

George Rosebush sat at his desk pondering the magnitude of the decision that lay before him. He still couldn't quite believe the events that had transpired over the past year. It was July 1988, he had been with Nomura Securities International (NSI), the American subsidiary of Japanese giant Nomura Securities Company Ltd., since July 1986. During that time, George had acquired the skills necessary to be a successful stock trader; however, he now felt prevented from utilizing his skills to the fullest extent.

The management at NSI, all Japanese personnel on assignment from the home office in Tokyo, had refused to give Americans such as George the latitude to aggressively pursue business. Like his predecessors, George was experiencing great frustration at having to cope with Japanese culture and business norms. In particular, the Japanese were very slow to make either decisions or changes—primarily due to their consensus method of decision making.

Nomura was a monolithic machine where decisions emerged from the system with little need for creativity. This was a significant impediment to achieving success in the trading business, where the ability of a trader to respond quickly to customer needs was vital to success. As a pure service industry, the ability to develop strong client relationships was imperative. Here again, Nomura insisted upon doing things the Japanese way. Among the factors frequently noted as holding Nomura back were adherence to Japanese tradition; inflexibility in negotiations; lack of imagination; little expertise in critical investment banking sectors; and weak relationships with U.S. and European institutional investors. To make matters worse, the business environment in the securities industry was suffering a major recession following the stock market crash of October 1987. Despite this, since the late 1970s, NSI's staff had grown to 750, a 10-fold increase.

In the postcrash era, NSI was experiencing a larger fall in revenues and profits than other firms in the industry. This slump was particularly acute in George's department, Japanese equities, which entailed marketing Japanese stocks to U.S. institutional clients.

Despite the market's downturn, changing Japanese trading habits had accounted for much of the problem. Industry analysts noted that in actuality the Japanese had "severely misjudged the difficulty of mounting major expansion drives overseas." In numerous meetings George had made recommendations to improve business, but management remained unwilling to take the steps necessary to reverse the drop in market share and profits that the department was experiencing.

Business had slowed down so much that George and his colleagues soon found themselves doing crossword puzzles to pass the time. This was occurring in the fast-paced world of global trading.

Each day dragged slowly, and George found himself faced with a decision: He could stay at NSI and continue to develop new plans to improve business at the company, or he could leave the firm. He decided to conduct preliminary discussions about employment opportunities with some other firms. Meanwhile, some of his friends had even suggested that he quit NSI and enroll in a leading business school, to pursue an MBA.

Background

Nomura Securities, the world's largest stockbroker, continued to suffer from both host- and home-country regulatory pressures and related political risks associated with its globalization strategy. The Japanese securities industry, like that of the United States, had undergone extensive liberalization, in terms of deregulation, over the five-year period from 1986 to 1991. Within this ever-changing environment, Nomura had continued with its global expansion policy—aggressively expanding into both the London and New York Markets.

The premise governing Nomura's growth was based on its commitment to opening up international financial markets to Japanese clients and to bringing foreign investors to the Japanese market place. Being the beneficiaries of a society geared toward an unusually high savings rate, Japanese brokerage houses had allowed Japanese investors to seek out higher-yielding foreign investments. This approach was not unique to Nomura, but was pursued by a number of Japanese securities firms. The chairman of European operations for Daiwa Securities, the number 2 securities firm globally, stated, "We started off providing two-way information to U.S. and European clients interested in the Japanese markets and to Japanese clients. We knew that Japan would prove to be an economic force, and we foresaw that brokerage would be profitable."

By the mid 1980s, Japan had become the world's largest creditor nation. Capitalizing on this development, Nomura's expansion was predicated upon its desire to allow borrowers, internationally, to tap into Japan's vast pool of potential investors. Additionally, Nomura was concerned with enhancing its domestic image as a true global market player. Increasing its presence abroad not only boosted its name recognition internationally, but enhanced Nomura's reputation domestically. It generated goodwill and demonstrated the firm's commitment to international markets. In turn, such actions gave evidence of its desire to continue to strengthen its position in the growing Japanese domestic market. In short, Nomura Securities was positioning itself as the preeminent Japanese brokerage firm, able to service the large amounts of Japanese capital targeted for future U.S. investment.

Nomura expanded aggressively into the New York market throughout the early and mid-1980s. The result was an office that underwent rapid growth in terms of staffing, profits, and overall market presence.

Nomura's Growth Phase

Nomura was founded in 1878. Over the years its focus remained on high-quality research and the development of a worldwide financial network. It was the first Japanese securities firm to open an office in the United States (1927), as well as the first to become a member of the New York Stock Exchange. Its American operation suffered a major interruption as a result of World War II. Nomura did not reestablish an American presence until the 1950s. With the improvement of relations between the United States and Japan, and growth of trade between the two countries that occurred in the late 60s and 70s, Nomura sought to increase its activities in the U.S. securities markets. Nomura's expansion plans led to the formation of a wholly owned subsidiary in the 1970s, Nomura Securities International.

NSI's expansionary plans required the hiring of a large number of Americans—the intent was to rely upon talented local professionals to further market expansion. Nomura could not afford to rely on nonmanagement personnel from the parent company who were in New York for, at best, two- to three-year rotations.

Because Nomura now planned to serve American clients and compete directly with U.S. firms, it needed Americans who could build the strong client relationships necessary to achieve success in a service industry, particularly in the American securities market. Yoshihisa Tabuchi, president and chief executive of Nomura Securities Company Ltd., stated, "[t]he style and structure Nomura uses to sell securities in Japan cannot work well in the U.S. Nomura's traditional culture is as a Japanese brokerage firm, but, as it expands, it must become multicultural." It is important to develop good working relationships with other firms in the industry. Americans were hired to be on the front lines and, more importantly, to lend credibility to the firm within the U.S. market.

As a critical success factor, the internal working relationships at NSI are as important, if not more so, than its external relationships with clients—the firm cannot hope to properly service its client base, without being able to benefit from the synergies created from internal employee "harmony." Unfortunately, cultural barriers and differences still existed within the firm. All managers were Japanese, with little experience or knowledge about either the American market or, more importantly, American cultural and business values. This created a paradox. The front-line American workers knew how to serve their home market but were not allowed to make the significant and timely decisions needed for success in the American securities marketplace. These decisions were made by Japanese personnel who did not have the working knowledge necessary to properly analyze the situation.

Decisions regarding risk taking and the scope of the firm's operations usually required the consent and approval of Japanese management. However, these managers were often not qualified to make such critical decisions (being unaware of many of the nuances associated with the American market's operation and function). In particular, management was unwilling to delegate to traders the authority to commit the firm's capital. This was a major impediment to "getting a deal done." Traders could not give a quick response to client inquiries. Instead management wanted to discuss the trade under consideration. Only after much deliberation and a consensus had been reached, would the firm be willing to commit capital to a large trade. This slow response time remained unacceptable to customers in the U.S. securities markets. Due to potential rapid changes in prices and investor perceptions, clients expected and demanded quick responses to their inquiries. NSI's failure to make quick decisions severely hampered its ability to effectively compete in the U.S. securities markets. Furthermore, this lack of trust on behalf of Japanese management had a devastating effect upon the morale of the American work force.

George's Tale

In June 1986, George was looking to gain entrance into the securities business. He had just quit his job at an employee benefits consulting firm to seek work in global finance. George had previous work experience selling Individual Retirement Accounts and tax-sheltered annuities in the New England area. Much of that work involved cold calling and building a client base. While his previous jobs had helped him develop strong interpersonal skills as well as given him some familiarity with the stock market, George did not have any direct experience trading financial securities. He found it very difficult to gain entrance into the trading business without that experience. Most of the opportunities he found were for lower-level operations positions.

George had two brothers who worked in the securities industry. Both knew people who worked, or had worked, at NSI. One of their acquaintances was Mark Blanchard, whom, as it turned out, George would later succeed at Nomura. George learned that Nomura needed to hire traders to replace Mark Blanchard and Steve Montana as well as some traders from the American equities department who had also resigned. George was able to arrange an interview with Nomura to discuss trading opportunities at the firm. Before going on the interview George spoke with Mark Blanchard to get the inside story as to what life at Nomura was actually like.

Prior to the Fourth of July holiday in 1986, George had his first interview at NSI. From the interview's onset, many of the cultural differences George had been forewarned about became readily apparent. George was greeted by the head of the sales department, Mr. Yoshida, and after a few common pleasantries were exchanged, was whisked into a small conference room. The two were then joined by another Japanese manager and Mike, the head of the Japanese Equity Trading Department. Mike was also a Japanese national. However, rather than go by his last name, as was the custom in Japan, he had adopted the American nickname Mike.

George would later call the interview intense. He was bombarded by questions from each of those present. While George found many of the questions seemingly unrelated to the job at hand (e.g., questions regarding his family as well as his personal views of the work ethic and company allegiance), he nevertheless answered them.

Occasionally there were interruptions to the flow of questions when the interviewers stopped to carry on a conversation among themselves in Japanese. George found these interruptions both rude and unprofessional, but was reluctant to say anything that might ruin his prospects for the job.

After a time, other Japanese men were ushered into the room and took their turn interviewing George. Finally, several American traders from the American equities department were brought in. At this point the interview became more conventional. Specific job duties and the requisite skills were discussed. Finally, the director of personnel (another American) finished the interview. The next day George received a job offer. He started working for NSI on July 14, 1986.

George maintained no illusions of either climbing NSI's ladder of success or of making a lifelong career with Nomura. Furthermore, George held some personal reservations about working for a foreign firm, especially one from such a different culture. He viewed the position as an opportunity to learn the business. If after a few years things were not working out, he knew that he would be able to parlay his newly acquired skills to land a job elsewhere. After trading Japanese stocks for the top Japanese brokerage house, he would be very marketable to the many firms seeking to enter this area of the securities business. For George, the simple fact remained that there were few westerners with experience trading Japanese securities. Should things really go sour, George had a fallback position of returning to school for his MBA.

At the time George started at NSI, the Japanese Equity Department was in a state of disarray. Mark and Steve had been gone for two months and there were no Americans left in the department. Client relationships had deteriorated rapidly, and new traders were desperately needed. George was not the only trader to start work in the Japanese Equity Department on July 14. He was joined by François Boudreau. While growing up, François had lived in both France and the United States and had attended Columbia University in New York. He had spent a month working as a retail broker before coming to NSI, but for all intents and purposes was fresh out of college.

Neither George nor François had the experience necessary to step in and immediately start trading with clients or other firms. To make matters worse, Mike, their boss, was the only other trader in the department. George and François had no western colleagues or mentors. Mike was trying to do as much as he could to keep the business going, which meant that he had little time available to train either George or François. Moreover, Mike was introverted and did not enjoy interacting with clients. The result was that neither the clients nor George and François received much attention.

Mike had been working in the United States for five years. He had been in the New York office for the past three years; prior to that he had spent two years in Nomura's

Honolulu branch. Mike was much more westernized than his Japanese colleagues. If they had to have a Japanese boss, both George and François felt fortunate to be working for Mike. Mike was viewed by Japanese management as a renegade of sorts—willing to test the limits of the Japanese business rules and hierarchy. He had an excellent understanding of the underlying forces driving the U.S. securities industry. He, however, did not have the authority to make important policy decisions, which continued to be made by more senior Japanese managers. Senior managers were typically far removed from the daily operations of the firm. Some were even based in Tokyo, 7,000 miles away.

In Japanese corporations, new hires often spend their first year or two on the job in low-level positions that expose them to the fundamental operations of the company's business. In manufacturing firms, this typically involves working on the production line. For financial organizations, the initial period usually involves door-to-door sales solicitations. While NSI could not realistically expect American professionals to go through such a process, at the same time, it was unwilling to let Americans do too much too soon.

Both François and George were initially instructed to sit with the traders in the American Equities Department. There they were supposed to watch and listen in order to learn the fundamentals of stock trading. At first this was a worthwhile activity. However, after a few weeks, they both felt they had learned as much as they were going to learn. François and George were anxious to start trading on their own, and wanted to start assuming more responsibilities. Their superiors, however, did not feel they were ready to get directly involved in the daily trading operations. George thought this particularly odd considering how short-handed the Japanese Equity Department was.

For six months that George and François watched the traders from the U.S. Equities Department they did little else. Most of their days were spent answering the telephones and relaying information to the trading desk. George was growing restless and started asking for additional responsibilities. To appease him, Mike allowed him to start trading Japanese ADRs (American depository receipts) on NASDAQ, the over-the-counter market. ADRs represent Japanese stock held by a custodian bank in Japan. Investors cannot actually take delivery of Japanese stock outside Japan, but can take delivery of ADRs. ADRs are denominated in dollars, which further simplifies their purchase, as investors do not have to make foreign exchange arrangements.

NSI used to trade a few hundred thousand ADRs each day. However, that number had recently fallen to just a few thousand. As a market maker in ADRs and other issues, NSI used its own capital to make trades with other market makers and clients. Market makers risk their own capital in the hope of making money on the bid/ask spread. To be successful at doing this, volume is important for two reasons. First, if the spread earned is small, sizable profits can only be made through large volume. More importantly, active market makers attract more client orders because of their ability to provide more liquidity as well as their increased market presence.

Before George could rebuild the client side of the ADR business, he first had to stimulate the firm's trading activity with other market makers on the street. George gradually built good working relationships with the other major market makers of Japanese ADRs. Within a few months, he was making a modest but steady profit for the firm. He often did this by taking advantage of arbitrage opportunities between the ADRs and the underlying Japanese common stock. However, the upside potential on these activities was limited, as the size of position that George could take and the amount of time that he could hold them was restricted. Being a prominent market maker, George was able to attract additional business to NSI. However, he was capturing a larger share of a shrinking market.

After George had been with NSI for one year, he began to take on the responsibilities of a sales trader for Japanese common stocks—the position for which he had originally been hired. He also continued to function as a market maker for ADRs. Sales traders are responsible for facilitating client activity. This involves providing daily market information and late-breaking news, sending orders for execution on stock exchanges or in a third market, and negotiating prices on trades.

The job of sales trader differs from that of salesman, in that a salesman concentrates on developing investment strategies, while the sales trader is more concerned with the execution of these strategies. The sales trader is the intermediary between the position trader and the client for trades in which the firm takes the other side of the transaction. It is the trader's responsibility to negotiate the best price possible without losing the trade. The sales trader is also responsible for instructing floor brokers on the strategy to employ when executing discretionary orders.

To be a successful sales trader one must develop a good relationship with clients and be able to provide them the services they value on a timely basis. These include company research, market information and analysis, and superior trading execution. While Nomura was one of the leaders in research on Japanese companies, its advantage over other firms in the industry was narrowing as competition continued to intensify. Moreover, Nomura's analysts were stationed solely in Japan and thus weren't readily accessible to salesmen, traders, and clients in New York. Other non-Japanese firms made their analysts directly available to parties in New York via telephone and periodic visits. This gave their New York employees and clients the opportunity to go directly to the source with any questions they might have. While Nomura's research still led the industry, NSI was unable to deliver it to clients in the timely fashion they demanded.

George also found it difficult to provide clients with top-quality daily Japanese market information. This information was available in New York, but only to those who spoke Japanese. Each morning there was a conference call with the Tokyo headquarters where the most important news of the day was discussed as well as expected future market developments (i.e., which stocks were going to be rammed). The meetings were attended in New York by the salesmen (all of whom were Japanese), George's boss Mike, and a few other managers. George and François had asked several times if the meeting could be held in English. This seemed like a reasonable request to them, especially since all of the participants, in both New York and Tokyo, spoke English. However, each request was refused.

To further complicate the situation, communication between the salesmen and the traders was poor. Important information discussed during the morning meetings would inevitably not be relayed. This lack of communication between Japanese and American employees hindered the traders' ability to effectively serve their clients. Salesmen would routinely fail to tell traders which stocks clients were interested in. This precluded the sales trader from informing customers of any late-breaking information related to the recommended stock or from matching clients' buy and sell orders. Usually a trader from the buy side would telephone orders to be executed overnight in Tokyo to a sales trader. However, on occasion, the portfolio manager might also call in the same order. If the salesman then failed to notify the trading desk, duplicate orders were sometimes passed on to the Tokyo office.

Since Nomura's information pipeline was not functioning efficiently, NSI's best chance for success in the New York market lay in the firm's being able to commit its capital—taking the other side of its customers' trades. The only ingredients necessary were money and a good position trader. George's boss, Mike, who did the position trading for Japanese common stocks possessed the trading talent. In terms of available capital, Nomura had the ability to raise billions of dollars. However, management in Tokyo refused to supply NSI with any additional capital. This forced the already limited available capital to be rationed among the different departments and prevented many deals from being closed. The actual amount of money available to position trades varied from day to day, depending on the positions held by other departments. The combination of limited capital and management's aversion to risk taking made it extremely difficult to effectively position trades for clients.

George and François did their best to cope with the many internal problems at NSI. However, the decline of client interest in Japanese stocks made the situation more difficult and encouraged them to seek new ways to stimulate business. Every time they came up with a proposal that they felt would stimulate client interest they were turned down.

Following the stock market crash of October 1987, the business climate slowed drastically. The deterioration of NSI's profitability accelerated, and management decided to implement new austerity measures to help reduce costs. Cuts were made across the board, without regard for either the level of profits or expenses of individual departments. The Japanese Equities Department did not suffer any losses associated with the crash. In fact, late October was one of the most profitable periods for the department due to the temporary surge in trading volume. The department also had the lowest overhead of any of the trading areas. Despite its low cost structure and the fact that it was operating profitably while other departments were operating in the red, it was not spared from cost-cutting measures. Management canceled the department's subscriptions to *The Wall Street Journal* and *Financial Times*. The papers had been shared within the department and provided information vital to running a trading operation. George and François found it very difficult to comprehend the logic behind the cost-cutting decision.

In February 1988, Mike was transferred back to Tokyo. George and François had mixed feelings about his departure. On the one hand, they blamed Mike (as head of their department) for some of the poor decisions and operating policies that had subsequently hurt business. However, they realized that he had confronted his superiors in order to enact changes and that his efforts were a risky venture within a conservative Japanese firm such as Nomura.

Before his departure, Mike did manage to obtain greater authority for both George and François to commit the firm's capital in trading transactions. While they welcomed this change, George and François were now concerned with who would replace him.

Mike's replacement was Mr. Yamaguchi, a bond trader who had been working in Nomura's Hong Kong office for the past seven years. The Hong Kong bond market had been a profitable one for Nomura over the past couple years and, consequently, Yamaguchi had been riding on the crest of success.

Due to delays in obtaining a work permit, Yamaguchi was not expected to arrive until April. This gave George and François a two-month window with no boss. During this time, George was able to expand the firm's ADR market-making activities. François was allowed to assume some of the position trading responsibilities vacated by Mike, although major decisions still required approval of either Nomura's London or Tokyo office. François was also permitted to start making markets in Japanese stock warrants; he was soon earning sizable profits for the firm in this capacity. George and François were able to stimulate substantial new business. This boosted their morale and for the first time in a long while they were consistently busy and enjoying their work.

All of this came to a dramatic halt soon after Yamaguchi's arrival in New York. Mr. Yamaguchi had no previous experience trading stocks. Equally important, he had no familiarity with either American business or accepted cultural practices and norms. He had been placed in a position where he was supposed to manage American employees who were working in a field in which he had no related expertise.

Mr. Yamaguchi sat quietly and observed during his first few weeks on the job. Quite unexpectedly, however, he began to initiate widespread changes. First, in their role as market makers for ADRs and warrants, respectively, George and François were no longer allowed to take any positions unless specifically to fill a client's order. This eliminated almost all trading with other brokers, which effectively ended NSI's role as a market maker for these instruments.

Even more damaging to the department was Yamaguchi's assumption of position trading responsibilities for common stock. Because he had little experience in this capacity, he rapidly began to accumulate sizable trading losses—at one point totaling several hundred thousand dollars per week. Two months later, his supervisor withdrew Yamaguchi's authority to make investment decisions on his own. Instead, he was required to seek approval from the head of the sales department. In just three months, Yamaguchi had destroyed the trading operation of the Japanese Equities Department.

Because the department was unable to offer trading-related services to its clients, George and François found it very difficult to attract any business. There was little cooperation between the sales and trading departments, the result of which was to keep both the sales and trading departments in the dark as to important information regarding individual client needs and activities. Additionally, NSI was unable to effectively make bids and offers to clients upon request. The deep-rooted mistrust between American and Japanese business people growing out of these events hurt NSI's ability to build solid relationships. If NSI did not have something special to offer an American client, it remained unlikely that the firm would attract business.

As business activity in the Japanese Equities Department slowed to a virtual standstill, George and François once again became proficient at crossword puzzles; and again their morale was extremely low. To make matters worse, George and François found it nearly impossible to maintain a reasonable working relationship with their new boss. Yamaguchi liked to call frequent departmental meetings which George and François were expected to attend. However, he would announce the location of the meetings only in Japanese. Not able to understand Japanese, George and François often missed meetings. When they failed to show up, Yamaguchi would become angry and demand an explanation.

Yamaguchi also wanted to change how they interacted with clients and other employees at the company. One incident in particular led to a heated confrontation between George and Yamaguchi. George had been made responsible for covering NSI's other branch offices in the United States (Honolulu, Los Angeles, Chicago, and San Francisco). These offices were small operations consisting primarily of retail brokers, support staff, and a few institutional salespeople. In addition to executing their orders, George provided each office with a daily market analysis. Mr. Yamaguchi informed George that he must give this information directly to Mr. Honda, the sales manager of the Honolulu branch. In the past George had spoken with whichever salesperson was available, who, in turn, would pass along the information to the rest of the office. George's attempts to talk with Mr. Honda became a disaster. Honda's English was poor and he spoke with a heavy accent. Honda eventually suggested that it might be easier if George were to talk to the salespeople as before. George could not have agreed more. However, Mr. Yamaguchi continued to insist that George speak directly with Honda.

Late one Friday afternoon, Yamaguchi brought up the subject again during a meeting with George and a Japanese salesman. Once again, George tried to explain the problem. Yamaguchi replied, "You must spend more time in Chinatown so you can learn how to understand people who speak English with an Asian accent." At first, George thought this remark a joke, but soon realized Yamaguchi was serious. Yamaguchi then went on to explain to George that if he ever expected to amount to any form of true businessman, he must overcome his inability to understand people who speak with a foreign accent.

George could not believe what he was hearing. Moreover, he was exasperated by Mr. Yamaguchi's obvious failure to recognize the need for foreign nationals to respect the language and customs of their host country. George was fed up with Yamaguchi and the current state of affairs. It was time to teach Yamaguchi that business is conducted differently outside of Japan. Much to Yamaguchi's surprise, George mounted a vociferous attack on his unprofessional behavior and lack of cultural respect. Yamaguchi was stunned that a subordinate would dare raise his voice, let alone scold him, especially in front of another person.

George returned to his desk to consider what real options he had before him. He had some important and timely decisions to make.

Questions

1. Describe the nature of the formal and human organization at NSI. In what ways is it influenced by Japanese and/or American culture?
2. Describe the personality and cultural background of Mr. Rosebush and Mr. Yamaguchi. What aspects of their behavior toward each other are cultural? What aspects are due to individual personality?
3. What options are open to Mr. Rosebush in dealing with this situation? What options are open to Mr. Yamaguchi?
4. What would you do if you were Mr. Rosebush? If you were Mr. Yamaguchi?

6 Motivation

Learning Objectives

After completing this module you should be able to:

1. Gain insight into some managerial viewpoints of motivation.
2. Explain several theories of motivation.
3. Understand the process and the major factors that affect motivation.
4. Appreciate the difference between the "content" and the "process" approaches to motivation.
5. Gain insights into the role that the Pygmalion effect and self-fulfilling prophecy can play in motivation at work.
6. Describe the behavior modification motivational technique.
7. Gain insights into your own motivation patterns.
8. Identify the basic managerial actions and programs that can foster individual motivation.

List of Key Concepts

Behavior modification
Content theories of motivation
Dissatisfiers
Employee stock ownership plans
Equity
Expectancy
Frustration
Hierarchy of needs
Hygiene factors
Motivation
n achievement
n power
P–L (Porter–Lawler) model
Process theories of motivation
Profit-sharing plans
Pygmalion effect
Reinforcement theories of motivation

Module Outline

Premodule Preparation

The instructor may assign either one or a combination of the following as a presession activity: Task 1 of Activity 6–1 (''Motivation to Work''); 6–2 (''The Slade Company Case''); 6–3 (''Alternative Courses of Managerial Action in the Slade Company Case''); 6–5 (''Motivational Analysis of Organization-Behavior''); or 6–6 (''The Centurion Finance Case'').

Activity 6–1: Motivation to Work

Objectives:

a. To determine your views of what has made you most and least productive in past work situations.

b. To compare your results with some current motivational studies and theories.

Task 1:

Each individual, working alone, is to use the worksheet that follows for answers to the following:

(1) Think back on your work experience to a time when you were performing at your very best. What were the factors that accounted for your high performance? List them on the accompanying worksheet.
(Time: 5 minutes)

(2) Think back on your work experience to a time when you were performing less than your best, or poorly. What were the factors that accounted for this performance? List them on the accompanying worksheet.
(Time: 5 minutes)

Task 2:

Each team should select a spokesperson.

List the important factors agreed upon by the group for the two areas of "best" performance and "less than best." Be prepared to give an example from one member's experience for each factor listed.
(Time: 15 minutes)

The instructor will call upon spokespersons, one at a time, to give one factor from the group's "best" list to be written on the board. Examples should be given for clarification. This will be continued until all the factors from the groups have been presented.

The same procedure should be followed for "less than best" after the "best" category has been completed.

The instructor will give a short lecture.

Worksheet for Activity 6–1

Task 1: Think back on your work experience to a time when you were performing at your very best. What were the factors that accounted for your high performance? List them.
(Time: 3 minutes)

Task 2: Think back on your work experience to a time when you were performing at less than your best or poorly. What were the factors that accounted for this? List them.
(Time: 3 minutes)

Activity 6–2: Case Study—Alternative A: The Slade Company

"The Slade Company" has been one of the best-selling Intercollegiate Case Clearing House cases in the category of human aspects of administration. In spite of its 1961 setting, the problems and issues it offers are remarkably timely. It provides an excellent opportunity for applying course concepts to an industrial situation. The formal organization of Slade does not really work the way it was intended. This is due to a number of *external and internal background factors* and to an *emergent role system* of roles, status hierarchy, subgroupings, and norms the actors have developed in the process of providing for management's and their own needs.

For the purpose of gaining an understanding of what caused this emergent role system to develop and seeing how powerful it is at the time of the case study, you are to make an analysis of this case using the concepts of previous modules. When making the operational blueprint analysis (see Figure 4–1) for questions 1 and 2 of the examination that follows this introduction, assume there are no employees on the scene, but you are knowledgeable of the management and supervisory practices. In questions 3, 4, and 5 on the actors (this can be found at the end of the case), you bring the people into your analysis. The method has the advantage of showing that prediction of motivation/satisfaction outcomes from background factors and the required role system may be misleading; if management does not help shape and mold the development of the emergent role system, it will form spontaneously on its own; the emergent role system of an organization can have goals consistent or inconsistent with those of the organization; the relationship of the script and the actors' systems as they exist at present can have implications for future management practices.

Read through the examination first so you will know the type of analysis you are required to make as you read the case study.

Case Study: The Slade Company

Ralph Porter, Production Manager of The Slade Company, was concerned by reports of dishonesty among some employees in the Plating Department. From reliable sources, he had learned that a few men were punching the timecards of a number of their workmates who had left early. Mr. Porter had only recently joined the Slade organization. He judged from the conversations with the previous production manager and other fellow managers that they were, in general, pleased with the overall performance of the Plating Department.

The Slade Company was a prosperous manufacturer of metal products designed for industrial application. Its manufacturing plant, located in central Michigan, employed nearly 500 workers, who were engaged in producing a large variety of clamps, inserts, knobs, and similar items. Orders for these products were usually large and on a recurrent basis. The volume of orders fluctuated in response to business conditions in the primary industries which the company served. At the time of this case, sales volume had been high for over a year. The bases upon which The Slade Company secured orders, in rank of importance, were quality, delivery, and reasonable price.

The organization of manufacturing operations at the Slade plant is shown in Exhibit 1. The departments listed there are, from left to right, approximately in the order in which material flowed through the plant. The diemaking and setup operations required the greatest degree of skill, supplied by highly paid, long-service craftsmen. The finishing departments, divided operationally and geographically between plating and

Exhibit 1
The Slade Company:
Manufacturing organization

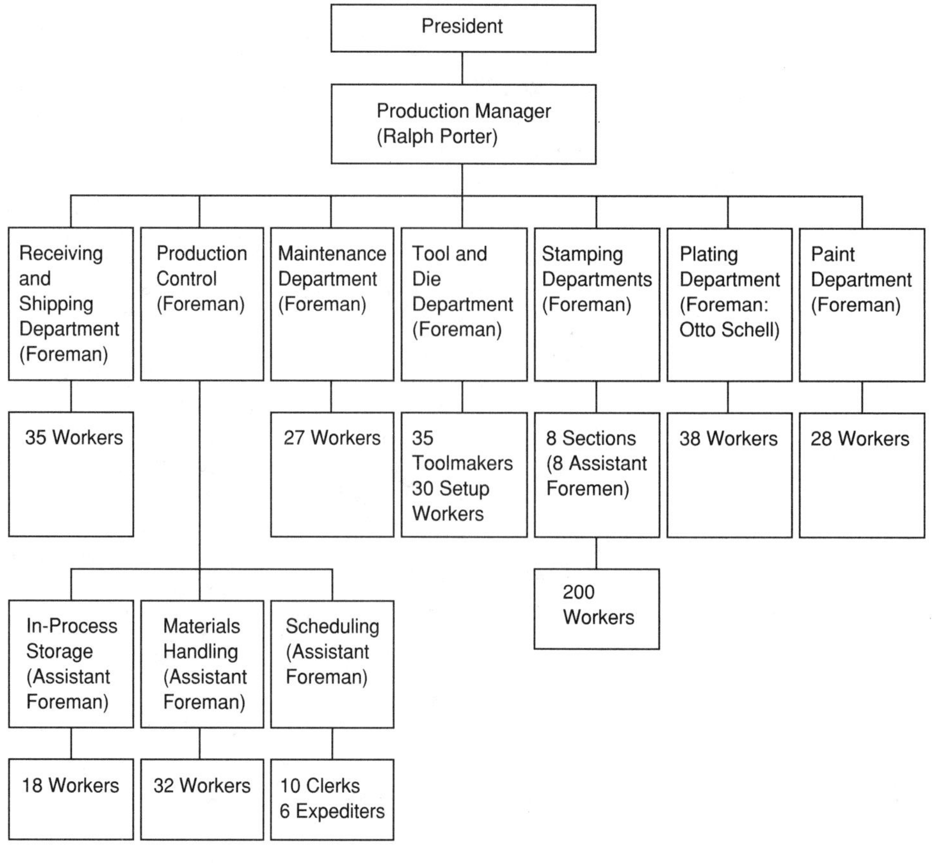

painting, attracted less highly trained but relatively skilled workers, some of whom had been employed by the company for many years. The remaining operations were largely unskilled in nature and were characterized by relatively low pay and high turnover of personnel.

The plating room was the sole occupant of the top floor of the plant. Exhibit 2 shows the floor plan, the disposition of workers, and the flow of work throughout the department. Thirty-eight men and women worked in the department, plating or oxidizing the metal parts or preparing parts for the application of paint at another location in the plant. The department's work occurred in response to orders communicated by production schedules which were revised daily. Schedule revisions, caused by last-minute order increases or rush requests from customers, resulted in short-term volume fluctuations, particularly in the plating, painting, and shipping departments. Exhibit 3 outlines the activities of the various jobs, their interrelationships, and the type of work in which each specialized. Exhibit 4 rates the various types of jobs in terms of the technical skill, physical effort, discomfort, and training time associated with their performance.

The activities which took place in the plating room were of three main types:

1. Acid dipping, in which parts were etched by being placed in baskets which were manually immersed and agitated in an acid solution.
2. Barrel tumbling, in which parts were roughened or smoothed by being loaded into machine-powered revolving drums containing abrasive, caustic, or corrosive solutions.
3. Plating—either manual, in which parts were loaded on racks and were immersed by hand through the plating sequence; or automatic, in which racks or baskets were manually loaded with parts which were then carried by a conveyor system through the plating sequence.

Within these main divisions, there were a number of variables, such as cycle times, chemical formulas, abrasive mixtures, and so forth, which distinguished particular jobs as they have been categorized in Exhibit 3.

Exhibit 2
The Slade Company:
Plating room layout

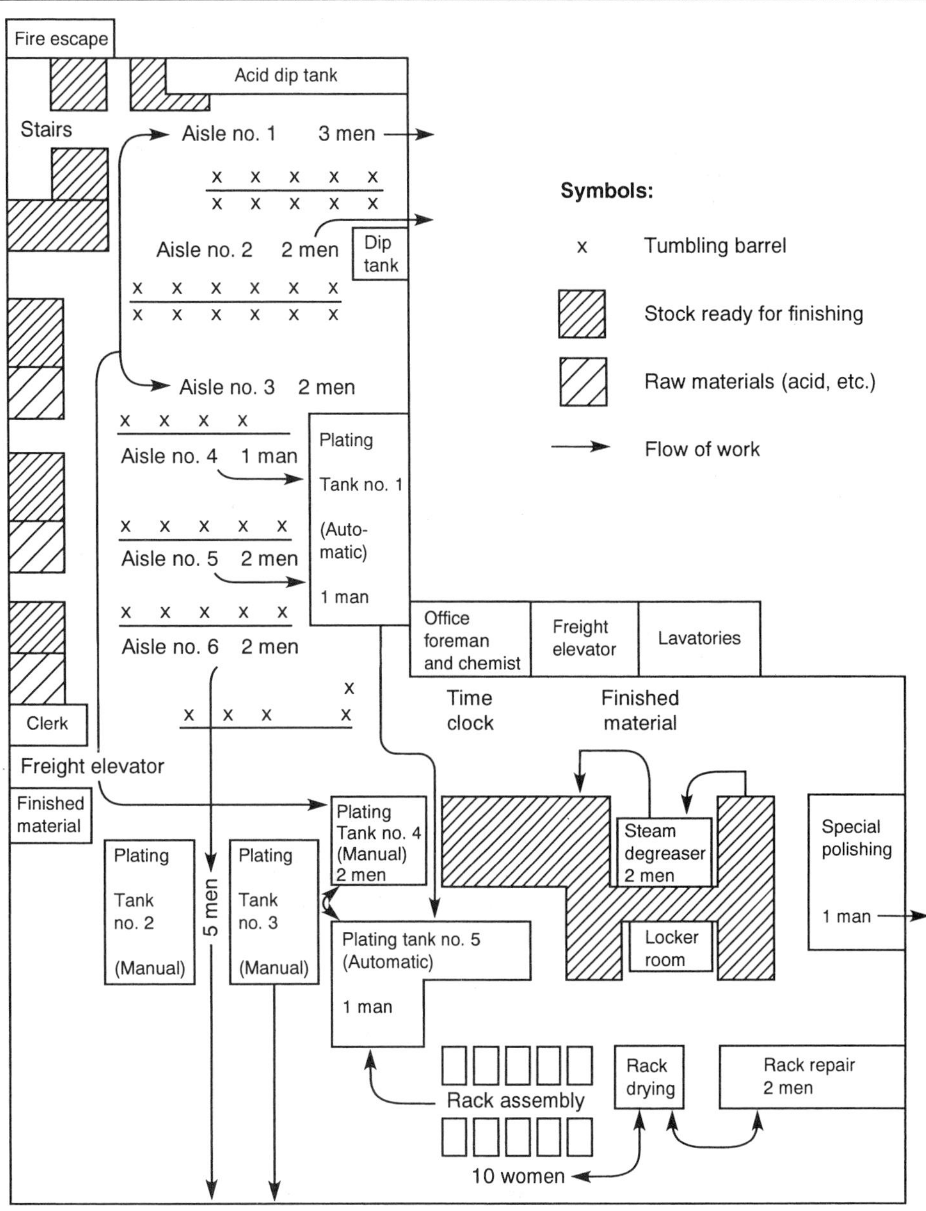

The work of the plating room was received in batch lots whose size averaged a thousand pieces. The clerk moved each batch, which was accompanied by a routing slip, to its first operation. This routing slip indicated the operations to be performed and when each major operation on the batch was scheduled to be completed, so that the finished product could be shipped on time. From the accumulation of orders before him, each man was to organize his own work schedule so as to make optimal use of equipment, materials, and time. Upon completion of an order, each man moved the lot to its next work position or to the finished material location near the freight elevator.

The plating room was under the direct supervision of the foreman, Otto Schell, who worked a regular 8:00 to 5:00 day, five days a week. The foreman spent a good deal of his working time attending to maintenance and repair of equipment, procuring supplies, handling late schedule changes, and seeing that his people were at their proper work locations.

Working conditions in the plating room varied considerably. That part of the department containing the tumbling barrels and the plating machines was constantly awash, alternately with cold water, steaming acid, or caustic soda. Men working in this part of the room wore knee boots, long rubber aprons, and high-gauntlet rubber gloves. This

Exhibit 3 **The Slade Company:** (outline of work flow, plating room)

Aisle 1:	Worked closely with Aisle 3 in preparation of parts by barrel tumbling and acid dipping for high-quality* plating in Tanks 4 and 5. Also did a considerable quantity of highly specialized, high-quality acid-etching work not required for further processing.
Aisle 2:	Tumbled items of regular quality and design in preparation for painting. Less frequently, did oxidation dipping work of regular quality, but sometimes of special design, not requiring further processing.
Aisle 3:	Worked closely with Aisle 1 on high-quality tumbling work for Tanks 4 and 5.
Aisles 4 and 5:	Produced regular tumbling work for Tank 1.
Aisle 6:	Did high-quality tumbling work for special products plated in Tanks 2 and 3.
Tank 1:	Worked on standard, automated plating of regular quality not further processed in plating room, and regular work further processed in Tank 5.
Tanks 2 and 3:	Produced special, high-quality plating work not requiring further processing.
Tank 4:	Did special, high-quality plating work further plated in Tank 5.
Tank 5:	Automated production of high- and regular-quality, special- and regular-design plated parts sent directly to shipping.
Rack Assembly:	Placed parts to be plated in Tank 5 on racks.
Rack Repair:	Performed routine replacement and repair of racks used in Tank 5.
Polishing:	Processed, by manual or semimanual methods, odd-lot special orders which were sent directly to shipping. Also, sorted and reclaimed parts rejected by inspectors in the shipping department.
Degreasing:	Took incoming raw stock, processed it through caustic solution, and placed clean stock in storage ready for processing elsewhere in the plating room.

* Definition of terms: *High or regular quality:* The quality of finishes could broadly be distinguished by the thickness of plate and/or care in preparation. *Regular or special work:* The complexity of work depended on the routine or special character of design and finish specifications.

uniform, consistent with the general atmosphere of the ''wet'' part of the room, was hot in the summer, cold in winter. In contrast, the remainder of the room was dry, was relatively odor-free, and provided reasonably stable temperature and humidity conditions for those who worked there.

The men and women employed in the plating room are listed in Exhibit 5. This exhibit provides certain personal data on each department member, including a productivity-skill rating (based on subjective and objective appraisals of potential performance), as reported by the members of the department.

The pay scale implied by Exhibit 5 was low for the central Michigan area. The average starting wage for factory work in the community was about $1.25. However, working hours for the plating room were long (from 60 hours to a possible and frequently available 76 hours per week). The first 60 hours (the normal five-day week) were paid for on straight-time rates. Saturday work was paid for at time and one-half; Sunday pay was calculated on a double-time basis.

As Exhibit 5 indicates, Philip Kirk, a worker in Aisle 2, provided the data for this case. After he had been a member of the department for several months, Kirk noted that certain members of the department tended to seek each other out during free time on and off the job. He then observed that these informal associations were enduring, built upon common activities and shared ideas about what was and what was not legitimate behavior in the department. His estimate of the pattern of these associations is diagrammed in Exhibit 6.

Exhibit 4
The Slade Company: Skill indices by job group*

Jobs	Technical Skills Required	Physical Effort Required	Degree of Discomfort Involved	Degree of Training Required†
Aisle 1	1	1	1	1
Tanks 2–4	3	2	1	2
Aisles 2–6	5	1	1	5
Tank 5	1	5	7	2
Tank 1	8	5	5	7
Degreasing	9	3	7	10
Polishing	6	9	9	7
Rack assembly and repair	10	10	10	10

* Rated on scales of 1 (the greatest) to 10 (the least) in each category.
† The amount of experience required to assume complete responsibility for the job.

Exhibit 5 **The Slade Company:** (plating room personnel)

Location	Name	Age	Marital Status	Company Seniority	Department Seniority	Pay	Education	Familial Relationships	Productivity Skill Rating*
Aisle 1	Tony Sarto	30	M	13 years	13 years	$1.50	High school	Louis Patrici, uncle Pete Facelli, cousin	1
	Pete Facelli	26	M	8 years	8 years	1.30	High school	Louis Patrici, uncle Tony Sarto, cousin	2
	Joe Lambi	31	M	5 years	5 years	1.20	2 years high school		2
Aisle 2	Herman Schell	48	S	26 years	26 years	1.45	Grade school	Otto Schell, brother	8
	Philip Kirk	23	M	1 year	1 year	0.90	College		–†
Aisle 3	Dom Pantaleoni	31	M	10 years	10 years	1.30	1 year high school		2
	Sal Maletta	32	M	12 years	12 years	1.30	3 years high school		3
Aisle 4	Bob Pearson	22	S	4 years	4 years	1.15	High school	Father in tool and die department	1
Aisle 5	Charlie Malone	44	M	22 years	8 years	1.25	Grade school		7
	John Lacey	41	S	9 years	5 years	1.20	1 year high school	Brother in paint department	7
Aisle 6	Jim Martin	30	S	7 years	7 years	1.25	High school		4
	Bill Mensch	41	M	6 years	2 years	1.10	Grade school		4
Tank 1	Henry LaForte	38	M	14 years	6 years	1.25	High school		6
Tanks 2 and 3	Ralph Parker	25	S	7 years	7 years	1.20	High school		4
	Ed Harding	27	S	8 years	8 years	1.20	High school		4
	George Flood	22	S	5 years	5 years	1.15	High school		5
	Harry Clark	29	M	8 years	8 years	1.20	High school		3
	Tom Bond	25	S	6 years	6 years	1.20	High school		3
Tank 4	Frank Bonzani	27	M	9 years	9 years	1.25	High school		2
	Al Bartolo	24	M	6 years	6 years	1.25	High school		3
Tank 5	Louis Patrici	47	S	14 years	14 years	1.45	2 years college	Tony Sarto, nephew Pete Facelli, nephew	1
Rack assembly	10 women	30–40	9M, 1S	10 years (average)	10 years (average)	1.05 (average)	Grade school (average)	6 with husbands in company	4 (average)
Rack maintenance	Will Partridge	57	M	14 years	2 years	1.20	Grade school		7
	Lloyd Swan	62	M	3 years	3 years	1.10	Grade school		7
Degreasing	Dave Susi	45	S	1 year	1 year	1.05	High school		5
	Mike Maher	41	M	4 years	4 years	1.05	Grade school		6
Polishing	Russ Perkins	49	M	12 years	2 years	1.20	High school		4
Foreman	Otto Schell	56	M	35 years	35 years	n.a.	High school	Herman Schell, brother	3
Clerk	Bill Pierce	32	M	10 years	4 years	1.15	High school		4
Chemist	Frank Rutlage	24	S	2 years	2 years	n.a.	2 years college		6

* On a potential scale of 1 (top) to 10 (bottom), as evaluated by the men in the department.

† Kirk was the source of data for this case and, as such, in a biased position to report accurately perceptions about himself.

Exhibit 6
The Slade Company:
Informal groupings in the plating room

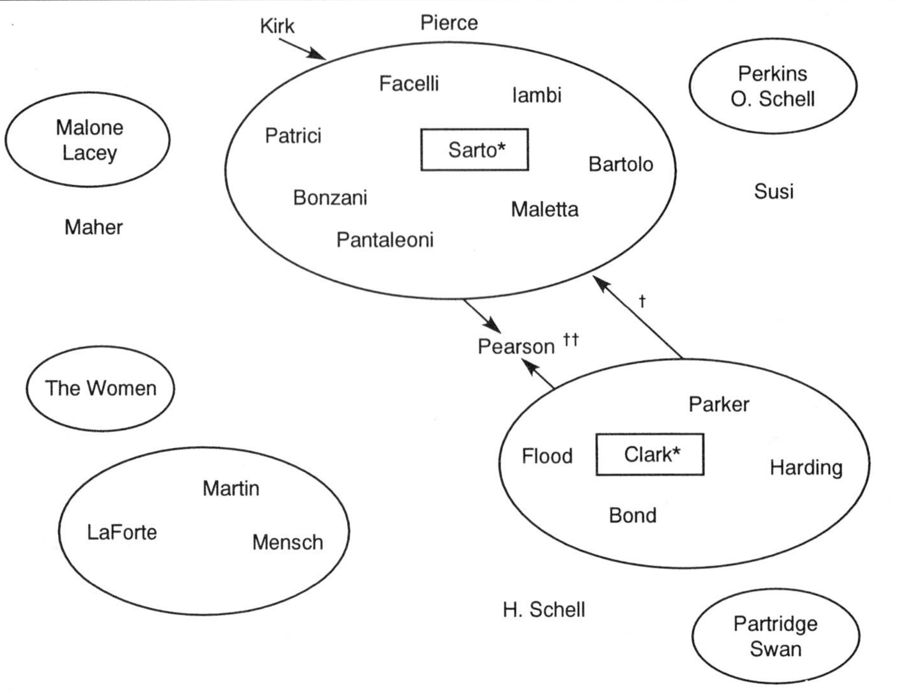

* The boxes indicate those men who clearly demonstrated leadership behavior (most closely personified the values shared by their groups, were most often sought for help and arbitration, and so forth).
† While the two- and three-man groupings had little informal contact outside their own boundaries, the five-man group did seek to join the largest group in extraplant social affairs. These were relatively infrequent.
†† Though not an active member of any group, Bob Pearson was regarded with affection by the two large groups.

The Sarto group, so named because Tony Sarto was its most respected member and the one who acted as arbiter between the other members, was the largest in the department. The group, except for Louis Patrici, Al Bartolo, and Frank Bonzani (who spelled each other during break periods), invariably ate lunch together on the fire escape near Aisle 1. On those Saturdays and Sundays when overtime work was required, the Sarto group operated as a team, regardless of weekday work assignments, to get overtime work completed as quickly as possible. (Few department members not affiliated with either the Sarto or the Clark groups worked on weekends.) Off the job, Sarto group members often joined in parties or weekend trips. Sarto's summer camp was a frequent rendezvous.

Sarto's group was also the most cohesive one in the department in terms of its organized punch-in and punch-out system. Since the men were regularly scheduled to work from 7:00 AM to 7:00 PM weekdays, and since all supervision was removed at 5:00 PM, it was possible almost every day to finish a "day's work" by 5:30 and leave the plant. What is more, if one man were to stay until 7:00 PM, he could punch the time cards of a number of men and help them gain free time without pay loss. (This system operated on weekends also, at which times members of supervision were present, if at all, only for short periods.) In Sarto's group the duty of staying late rotated, so that no man did so more than once a week. In addition, the group members would punch a man in in the morning if he were unavoidably delayed. However, such a practice never occurred without prior notice from the man who expected to be late and never if the tardiness was expected to last beyond 8:00 AM, the start of the day for the foreman.

Sarto explained the logic behind the system to Kirk:

> You know that our hourly pay rate is quite low, compared to other companies. What makes this the best place to work is the feeling of security you get. No one ever gets laid off in this department. With all the hours in the week, all the company ever has to do is shorten the work week when orders fall off. We have to tighten our belts, but we can all get along. When things are going well, as they are now, the company is only interested in getting out the work. It doesn't help to get it out faster than it's really needed—so we go home a little early whenever we can.

Of course, some guys abuse this sort of thing—like Herman—but others work even harder, and it averages out.

Whenever an extra order has to be pushed through, naturally I work until 7:00. So do a lot of the others. I believe that if I stay until my work is caught up and my equipment is in good shape, that's all the company wants of me. They leave us alone and expect us to produce—and we do.

When Kirk asked Sarto if he would not rather work shorter hours at higher pay in a union shop (Slade employees were not organized), he just laughed and said: "It wouldn't come close to an even trade."

The members of Sarto's group were explicit about what constituted a fair day's work. Customarily, they cited Herman Schell, Kirk's work partner and the foreman's brother, as a man who consistently produced below that level. Kirk received an informal orientation from Herman during his first days on the job. As Herman put it:

I've worked at this job for a good many years, and I expect to stay here a good many more years. You're just starting out, and you don't know which end is up yet. We spend a lot of time in here; and no matter how hard we work, the pile of work never goes down. There's always more to take its place. And I think you've found out by now that this isn't light work. You can wear yourself out fast if you're not smart. Look at Pearson up in Aisle 4. There's a kid who's just going to burn himself out. He won't last long. If he thinks he's going to get somewhere working like that, he's nuts. They'll give him all the work he can take. He makes it tough on everbody else and on himself, too.

Kirk reported on his observations of the department:

As nearly as I could tell, two things seemed to determine whether or not Sarto's group or any others came in for weekend work on Saturday or Sunday. It seemed usually to be caused by rush orders that were received late in the week, although I suspect it was sometimes caused by the men having spent insufficient time on the job during the previous week.

Tony and his group couldn't understand Herman. While Herman arrived late, Tony was always half an hour early. If there was a push to get out an extra amount of work, almost everyone but Herman would work that much harder. Herman never worked overtime on weekends, while Tony's group and the men on the manual tanks almost always did. When the first exploratory time study of the department was made, no one in the aisles slowed down, except Herman, with the possible exception, to a lesser degree, of Charlie Malone. I did hear that the men in the dry end of the room slowed down so much you could hardly see them move; but we had little to do with them, anyway. While the men I knew best seemed to find a rather full life in their work, Herman never really got involved. No wonder they couldn't understand each other.

There was quite a different feeling about Bobby Pearson. Without the slightest doubt, Bob worked harder than anyone else in the room. Because of the tremendous variety of work produced, it was hard to make output comparisons, but I'm sure I wouldn't be far wrong in saying that Bob put out twice as much as Herman and 50 percent more than almost anyone else in the aisles. No one but Herman and a few old-timers at the dry end ever criticized Bobby for his efforts. Tony and his group seemed to feel a distant affection for Bob, but the only contact they or anyone else had with him consisted of brief greetings.

To the men in Tony's group the most severe penalty that could be inflicted on a man was exclusion. This they did to both Pearson and Herman. Pearson, however, was tolerated; Herman was not. Evidently, Herman felt his exclusion keenly, though he answered it with derision and aggression. Herman kept up a steady stream of stories concerning his attempts to gain acceptance outside the company. He wrote popular music which was always rejected by publishers. He attempted to join several social and athletic clubs, mostly without success. His favorite pastime was fishing. He told me that fishermen were friendly, and he enjoyed meeting new people whenever he went fishing. But he was particularly quick to explain that he preferred to keep his distance from the men in the department.

Tony's group emphasized more than just quantity in judging a man's work. Among them had grown a confidence that they could master and even improve upon any known finishing technique. Tony himself symbolized this skill. Before him, Tony's father had operated Aisle 1 and had trained Tony to take his place. Tony in his turn was training his cousin Pete. When a new finishing problem arose from a change in customer specifications, the foreman, the department chemist, or any of the men directly involved would come to Tony for help, and Tony would give it willingly. For example, when a part with a special plastic embossing was designed, Tony was the only one who could discover how to treat the metal without damaging the plastic. To a lesser degree, the other members of the group were also inventive about the problems which arose in their own sections.

Herman, for his part, talked incessantly about his feats in design and finish creations. As far as I could tell during the year I worked in the department, the objects of these stories were obsolete or of minor importance. What's more, I never saw any department member seek Herman's help.

Willingness to be of help was a trait Sarto's group prized. The most valued help of all was of a personal kind, though work help was also important. The members of Sarto's group were constantly lending and borrowing money, cars, clothing, and tools among themselves and, less frequently, with other members of the department. Their daily lunch bag procedure typified the "common property" feeling among them. Everyone's lunch was opened and added to a common pile, from which each member of the group chose his meal.

On the other hand, Herman refused to help others in any way. He never left his aisle to aid those near him who were in the midst of a rush of work or a machine failure, though this was customary throughout most of the department. I can distinctly recall the picture of Herman leaning on the hot and cold water faucets which were located directly above each tumbling barrel. He would stand gazing into the tumbling pieces for hours. To the passing, casual visitor, he looked busy; and as he told me, that's just what he wanted. He, of course, expected me to act this same way, and it was this enforced boredom that I found virtually intolerable.

More than this, Herman took no responsibility for breaking in his assigned helpers as they first entered the department, or thereafter. He had had four helpers in the space of little more than a year. Each had asked for a transfer to another department, publicly citing the work as cause, privately blaming Herman. Tony was the one who taught me the ropes when I first entered the department.

The men who congregated around Harry Clark tended to talk like and copy the behavior of the Sarto group, though they never approached the degree of inventive skill or the amount of helping activities that Tony's group did. They sought outside social contact with the Sarto group; and several times a year, the two groups went "on the town" together. Clark's group did maintain a high level of performance in the volume of work they turned out.

The remainder of the people in the department stayed pretty much to themselves or associated in pairs or triplets. None of these people were as inventive, as helpful, or as productive as Sarto's or Clark's groups, but most of them gave verbal support to the same values as those groups held.

The distinction between the two organized groups and the rest of the department was clearest in the punching-out routine. The women could not work past 3:00 PM, so they were not involved. Malone and Lacey, Partridge and Swan, and Martin, La Forte, and Mensch arranged within their small groups for punch-outs, or they remained beyond 5:00 and slept or read when they finished their work. Perkins and Pierce went home when the foreman did. Herman Schell, Susi, and Maher had no punch-out organization to rely upon. Susi and Maher invariably stayed in the department until 7:00 PM. Herman was reported to have established an arrangement with Partridge whereby the latter punched Herman out for a fee. Such a practice was unthinkable from the point of view of Sarto's group. It evidently did not occur often because Herman usually went to sleep behind piles of work when his brother left or, particularly during the fishing season, punched himself out early. He constantly railed against the dishonesty of other men in the department, yet urged me to punch him out on several "emergency occasions."

Just before I left The Slade Company to return to school after 14 months on the job, I had a casual conversation with Mr. Porter, the Production Manager, in which he asked me how I had enjoyed my experience with the organization. During the conversation, I learned that he knew of the punch-out system in the Plating Department. What's more, he told me, he was wondering if he ought to "blow the lid off the whole mess."

Name ______________________________ Date ______________

Examination on "The Slade Company"

Operational Blueprint Analysis

1. What background factors are important for understanding the emergent role system that developed in the plating room? Make a list, in the space provided below, of *only* those specifically stated in this case—for example, Slade was not unionized. (You do not have to give reasons for each factor, but be prepared to do so if called upon.)

External Factors | *Internal Factors*

(Continue on the reverse side of this sheet if more space is needed.)

2. The required system can be understood from the description in Exhibit 3 in the case study and the text explaining it. Assume that all you know about the plating room operations are the important background factors listed in 1 and this required work system; make your prediction as to what satisfactions and frustrations would be experienced by the workers in the plating room. (*Note:* Include also any inferences you can draw from Exhibit 1.) Do this by commenting on each level of the hierarchy of needs in the space provided below.

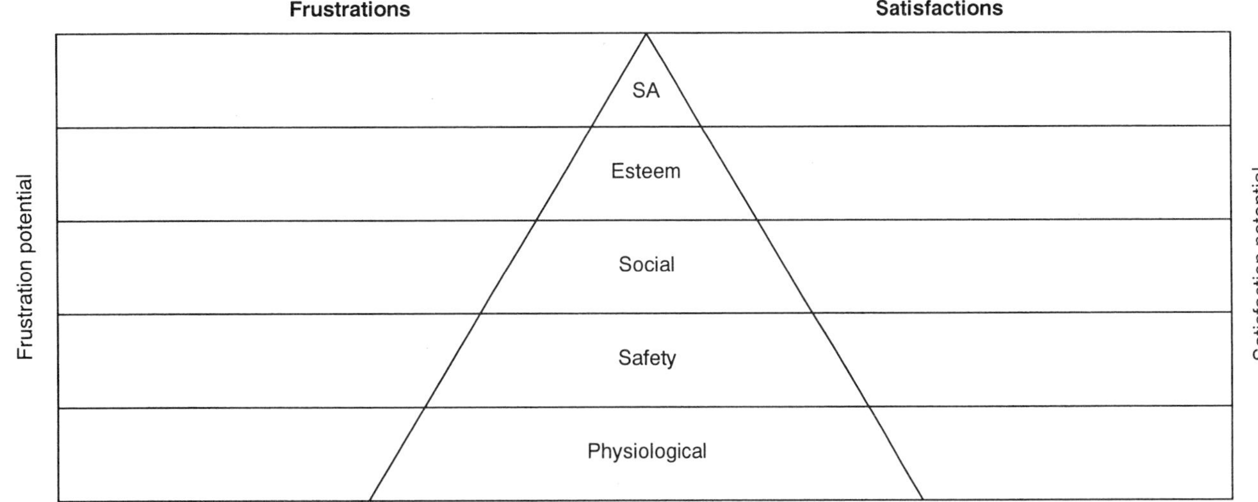

Examination on "The Slade Company"

Character of the Actors

3. In Exhibit 6 the various subgroups that developed in the plating room are shown. The Sarto and Clark subgroups are the two most important. What are some of the factors or characteristics that probably account for group membership in each subgroup? That is, there are certain similarities of the members within a group and certain differences between the two subgroups. Use Exhibits 4 and 5 as your source of data in making your analysis. Make a list of your answers in the appropriate spaces below.

Sarto Subgroup *Clark Subgroup*

Actors Playing Their Roles

4. Make a complete list of the norms of the emergent role system that developed in this case. (Use the Sarto group norms, since they seem to determine the behavior of the other subgroups.)

5. In what way did the norms of the emergent role system meet the needs of the workers? Indicate by commenting on which norms fulfilled needs at each level of the hierarchy.

Hierarchy	*Satisfaction of Need*
Self-actualization	
Esteem	
Social	
Safety	
Physiological	

Activity 6–3: Alternative Courses of Managerial Action in the Slade Company Case

Objectives:

a. To use the individual-first, team-second decision-making model to synergistically develop alternative courses of managerial action for the situation described in the Slade case.

b. To use course concepts to make the analysis.

c. To evaluate the consequences of alternative proposals.

Task 1 (Individuals Working Alone): *Alternative 1 (for one-half of the teams in the class):*

Working alone, complete the Slade case assignment immediately preceding this exercise.

Assume you are Mr. Porter, the production manager, and have become fully knowledgeable of all the data given in the case study. You are trying to decide on alternative courses of action. Complete the accompanying worksheet for Alternative 1.

Task 1 Alternative 2 (for one-half of the teams in the class):

Working alone, complete the Slade case assignment immediately preceding this exercise.

Assume you are Tony Sarto and his work group. You have heard that Mr. Porter, the production manager, has become fully knowledgeable of all the data given in the case study. You and your group have an informal meeting outside work to discuss the problem. What actions do you think management might take? How would you respond to these? How do you think management should handle this situation? Complete the accompanying Alternative 2 worksheet for the Sarto group.

Task 2 (Team Activity):

Teams are to meet outside class to analyze the questions on the worksheet for the alternative they have been assigned. A summary of your analysis (not more than one typewritten page) is to be turned in to the instructor at the next class session. (*Note:* Use a brief outline form in your paper.)

Task 3 (Classroom Activity):

Each team will have a spokesperson outline its conclusions on the blackboard and present a rationale to the class. Mr. Porter teams will all report first, followed by Sarto teams. Discussion follows.

Name ______________________________ Date ____________________

Worksheet for Activity 6–3

Alternative 1: Worksheet for Mr. Porter, Production Manager

What are all the possible alternative actions? List them below.	*What are the possible consequences that would be expected to be:*	
	Favorable	*Unfavorable*

Which of the above alternatives would you choose? Why?

Name ______________________ Date ______________

Worksheet for Activity 6–3

Alternative 2: Worksheet for Sarto's Work Group

List alternative actions management might take.	*List Sarto work group's response to each alternative.*

How would Sarto's work group think management should handle this situation? Why?

Introduction

Individual behavior is the result of many factors and motives. A major concern for managers at different levels in organizations centers around effectiveness. Motivation is one of four core concepts that must be studied as we look at the effectiveness of the individual, the small group, intergroup activities, and the organization. We will examine the subject by first giving a case study; second, by providing some philosophical viewpoints that can help managers approach motivation problems such as productivity, satisfaction, absenteeism, and turnover; third, by using a few activities and cases; and, fourth, by presenting a few well-known motivation theories.

We will open with a short case study reported by one of our students who had worked in two car washes as a teenager. The car washes were in a small city and operated by different owners. In the first, the dripping vehicle would come off the rinse line, where four teenagers waited with towels to wipe it dry. When the wipers were finished, they signaled the car owner by leaving the car door standing open. The car owner would generally walk past a pot placed in his or her path with a sign that read TIPS, THANK YOU, climb into the car, and drive away with the windows still wet and water streaming from some parts of the car. Occasionally, one of the wipers dropped a wet towel on the ground, only to pick it up and continue wiping. One customer complained to the manager that the wet towel could pick up sand from the pavement and scratch the car. Only a few small coins got into the pot. Turnover of wipers was high, and they expressed hostile attitudes toward management.

The second car wash was opened by a vigorous, enthusiastic young owner. A system was established whereby each customer paid for the service when entering the wash. A ticket was handed to the customer (a practice not followed at the first car wash), which was to be given to the final wiper when the car was dry. The car coming off the rinse line was received by four teenage wipers, three of whom would go on to another car after doing the initial work, while the fourth did the final wiping. This individual did all possible to please because the customer was not inclined to give the ticket to the wiper until the work was done to her or his satisfaction. The customers usually stood beside the wiper pointing out places where more drying was needed. While doing this, the customer was generally seen to take change out of pocket or purse and wait for the wiper to ask for the ticket. Tips were generous and customers drove away in well-dried cars. The manager often got the entire work crew together for pep talks that ran something like this:

> We're the best car wash on the coast. We do the best work, have the most satisfied customers, have the happiest workers, and hopefully make the most money of any car wash of equal size. Your tips will be good if you do a perfect job. I've set up 10 customer chairs alongside the wiping area. This is your audience. Show them how well you can do. When you finish, give your customer a guided tour of the car and ask if everything is all right. With this treatment, your customer standing there waiting to give you the ticket will develop the expectation that you should have a good tip. The "audience" on the sideline will see you get tipped. The audience will also tell other people what a great job we do here.

The owner's practices also included job rotation so workers did all jobs (all got a share of the wiper jobs so they would get tipped), flexibility in choosing work hours, and (on weekends) bonuses if a certain volume was reached. The car wash prospered.

Many basic concepts and approaches to motivation we will be discussing in this module can be applied to this simple case. We shall refer back to it.

Managerial Viewpoints on Motivation

Global competition, productivity, and *quality* have become buzzwords of this decade. *Productivity* and *quality* have many definitions. Most are related to motivation—where it is "zero defect" ratio in manufacturing, whether it is individual production averaged over a number of people, hours of work and dollar cost of labor, or individual effort and performance, the implied, ever-present question is, How do you get the individual to accomplish more and better-quality work at less cost?

Since this is a management course, we will start with some ways of thinking about motivation that can be helpful in guiding your specific managerial activities.

Ask executives and managers attending workshops what the primary problems of motivation are and they will place blame on people: Workers are not committed, they don't care if they do a good job; they are poorly trained in the school systems; parents don't bring up kids like they used to. Sometimes there is the complaint that you can't get good first-line supervisors and they won't accept full responsibility. Our answer to this is the same as for problems of personal growth and effectiveness: If you aren't achieving what you want, it's not the fault of your family, teachers, ethnic background, girlfriend, boyfriend, and so on. The only way you're going to achieve goals is to assume full responsibility for your own progress and stop blaming others.

And so it is with management. There is little to be gained by blaming the workers and much to be gained by planning, stimulating, and influencing motivation. A helpful way of focusing in on the motivation problem is to assume there are no "bad" people, just bad management practices—that is, management is causing the problem, or working conditions are poor, or the architectural, organizational, or work designs are faulty. We suggest five viewpoints that provide a philosophical base in guiding your specific managerial activities.

Horticulture Viewpoint

Think of productivity as the harvest from the nurturing of people in your organizational "hothouse." The environment in the real hothouse is planned and the climate is carefully controlled. In our car wash case study, the young owner was creating a climate—we like to use the term *organizational culture.* The important ingredients in the car wash's climate included high standards, fair treatment, satisfied customers, concern for workers, and team spirit, with management, customers, and workers being the winners. The managerial practices were all nurturing productivity.

An important aspect of the overall hothouse climate is the generalized assumptions prevailing in management about people's desire to work, to take initiative, and support management goals. Douglas McGregor's well-known theories X and Y serve as an illustration.[1]

Traditional Viewpoint

The *traditional model* (which McGregor labeled theory X) assumes that for the average worker work is inherently distasteful; that what the individual does is less important than what he or she earns for doing it; that the individual by nature is self-centered, is inclined to be lazy, and prefers to be led rather than take responsibility; and that few individuals want or can handle work that requires creativity, self-direction, or self-control. Therefore the manager's basic task is to closely supervise and control subordinates. He or she must break tasks down into simple, repetitive, easily learned operations; he or she must establish detailed work routines and resources and must enforce these firmly but fairly through rewards and punishments.

Human Relations Viewpoint

The *human relations model* (which McGregor labeled *theory Y*) assumes that people want to feel useful and important, that people desire to belong and to be recognized as individuals, and that these needs are more important than money in motivating people to work. Therefore the manager's basic task is to arrange organizational conditions so that people can achieve their goals by directing their efforts toward organizational objectives. He or she should make each worker feel useful and important, should keep subordinates informed and listen to their feedback, and should allow subordinates to exercise some self-direction and self-control on routine matters.

Going back to our hothouse analogy, if the prevailing atmosphere in an organization is that of McGregor's theory Y, it could be assumed that individuals feel the need and energy to be productive for themselves and management.

Engineering Viewpoint

In an effort to find out what management is doing wrong, the design of work is always a good place to look. In the car wash, the young owner did an incredibly good job of designing the work so the rewards to the wipers and the customers were effective in achieving company goals. The ticket the customer controlled until the work was done well, along with the rewarding tip, was about perfect here. It was similarly clever to set up chairs for the waiting customers so they could observe the wiping process and see the tipping. Rotating workers to all jobs also provided worker satisfaction and reward.

Human Resources Viewpoint

Having made our assumption about people, let us amend it. From the human resource development viewpoint, it is assumed that work is not inherently distasteful, that people want to contribute to meaningful goals that they have helped establish, and that most people can exercise far more creative, responsible self-direction and self-control than their present jobs demand. There may be no ''bad'' people, but there are those who are unsuitable or less suitable, which brings us to another assumption: People will work well if they have the abilities, aptitudes, interests, attitudes, and temperament that make them most suitable to perform the job—that is, people must be matched with jobs. Therefore the manager's basic task is to make use of ''untapped'' human resources. He or she should create an environment in which all members can contribute to the limits of their ability, and he or she should encourage full participation on important matters, continually broadening subordinates' self-direction and self-control.

Alternative Clusters of Motivational Theories

As the concerns for productivity and quality are increasing at the global level, so is the search for the ''right'' theory or the ''right'' approach to work motivation. Many models have been developed and examined over the past four decades: need models, reinforcement models, equity models, expectancy-based models, and goal-setting models. Furthermore, a variety of definitions emerged as the quest for our understanding of the phenomenon increased.

Although general agreement exists that motivated behavior consists of initiation, direction, persistence, intensity, and termination (any one or any combination of these), different managers and researchers are interested more in one aspect than in others.[2] As a result, several different attempts have been made to cluster the many theories of motivation found in the management literature: **content theories of motivation** (emphasizing reasons for motivated behavior or the specific factors that cause it) versus **process theories of motivation** (focusing on how behavioral change occurs); content theories versus process theories versus **reinforcement theories of motivation** (focusing on the elements that will increase the likelihood that described behavior will be repeated); intrinsic theories (emphasizing the drive to perform that results from a person's internalized values and beliefs that the task is rewarding in and of itself) versus extrinsic theories (focusing on the drive to perform that results from a person's expectations that a specific action will result in a desired outcome such as increase in pay); and endogenous theories (focusing on the dynamics of the motivational process) versus exogenous theories (focusing on motivationally related elements that can be changed by external agents), to mention a few.[3]

For the purpose of this chapter we have chosen to use the simplistic broad classification schema of content versus process theories. We believe that this typology not only can help you in sorting out the many different theories and models of motivation, but it can also boost understanding of the conditions and practices affecting work motivation.

Content Theories of Motivation

Content theories of motivation strive to understand and explain the elements that arouse, start, initiate, or energize behavior. These theories or models focus on causes that motivate individuals. For example, if we examine the car wash minicase at the beginning of the chapter, from a content theory point of view the focus would be on what might have motivated the workers to behave the way they did. One can argue that in the more successful car wash, the individuals' needs for money, status, and achievement were more satisfied and served as motivators for their behavior. Theories in this cluster include Herzberg's two-factor theory, Maslow's need hierarchy, Alderfer's existence relatedness growth (ERG) need theory, and McClelland's achievement/power theory.

Herzberg's Motivation-Hygiene Theory

Frederick Herzberg divides morale into two sets of factors: *dissatisfiers* and *motivators.* The **dissatisfiers** include company policy and administration, supervision, relationships with supervisor, working conditions, salary, relationships with peers, personal life, relationships with subordinates, status, and security. These are potential dissatisfiers because employees expect and hope that they will all be good. If they are not good, the employees will be unhappy; if they are good, this is what the employees, in this day, expect working conditions to be. The fact that all of these factors are favorable, however, does not make an individual happy or productive. It simply means that the individual is not unhappy. An analogy would be from garbage collection: If the garbage is collected from your home every week, you are almost unaware of it because this is what you expect. You are not unhappy since conditions are as they should be. If the garbage collector fails to pick it up, you are very much aware of your dissatisfaction and the unhygienic consequences. If all the dissatisfier factors are good in your work life, everything is hygienic.

What really makes you want to work are the motivators. These include achievement, recognition, the nature of the work itself, responsibility, and opportunities for advancement and growth. For college students, the skills and abilities they learn are part of their self-esteem; the opportunity to use these in their first job and to do good work will be a primary motivator. Using their experience and skills remains a primary force throughout their careers.

Figure 6–1 presents results of a study by Herzberg and his colleagues that shows that factors such as achievement, recognition, and the work itself are most frequently mentioned in connection with satisfying work experiences. Dissatisfying work experiences are reported most frequently as arising from company policy and administration, supervision, and other **hygiene factors.** Thus we see over 40 percent of the workers indicated achievement as a source of satisfaction while over 30 percent found company policy and administration were reasons for dissatisfaction.

Figure 6–1 also can be used to discuss Herzberg's assumption that motivation can be thought of as two entirely separate factors. Thus people may be satisfied and dissatisfied at the same time. They can, for example, appreciate the opportunity the job offers for achievement and still be most unhappy about company policy, pay, or working conditions. Figure 6–2 illustrates this by showing that the motivators may be thought of as starting at zero (or neutral) and increasing to highly satisfied as opportunities for achievement or responsibility improve. The hygiene factors can start at zero and increase to highly dissatisfied as conditions such as bad policy or salary get worse; being at zero on the hygiene scale does not mean you are satisfied. It only means that you are not dissatisfied—the garbage was picked up today so everything is hygienic.

The results college students register in Activity 6–1 generally are similar to Herzberg's findings, which provides a certain amount of apparent validity to his theory. However, some factors Herzberg lists as dissatisfiers are seen by students as motivators. For instance, students enjoy working hard for a boss they like, and they like working hard with peers who are also working hard even if the job is not exciting (possibly reflecting conformity to the social norms of the group). One reason for the basic agree-

Figure 6–1
Comparison of Satisfiers (Motivators) and Dissatisfiers

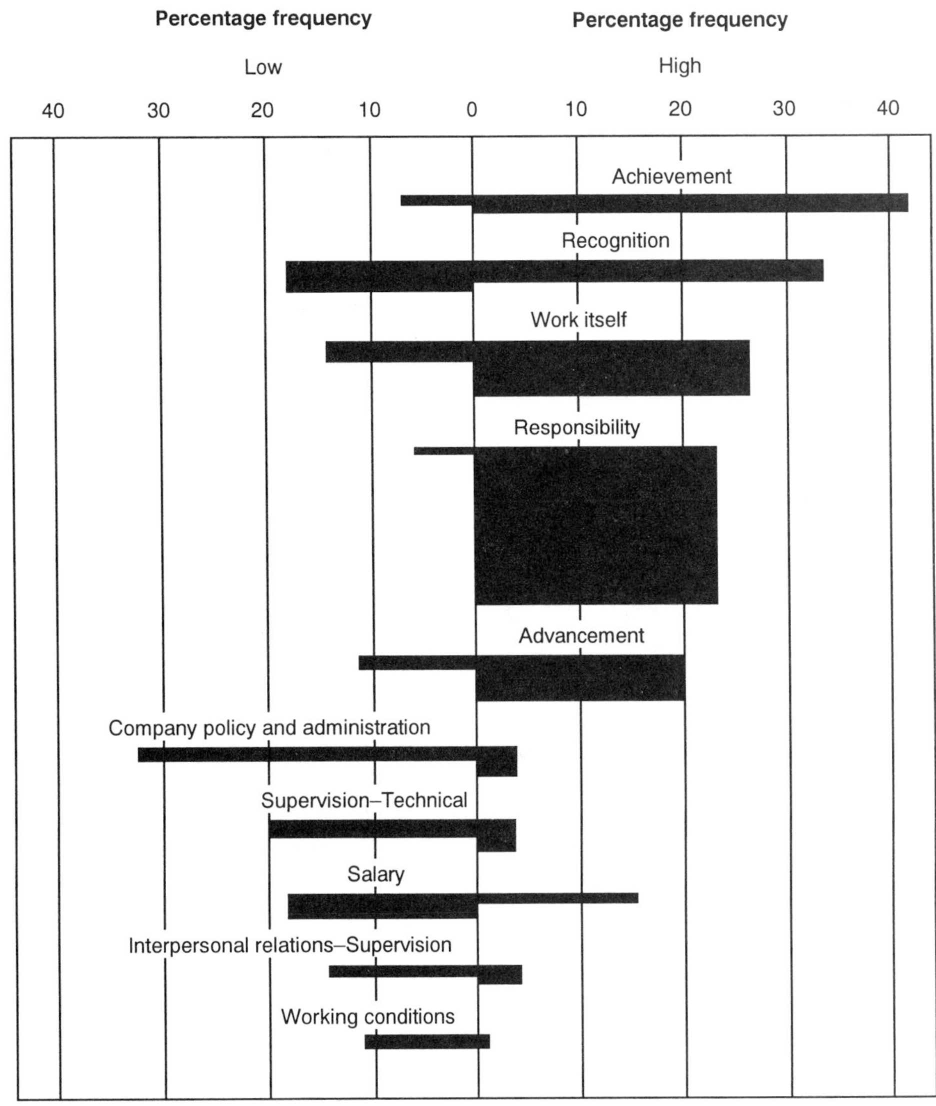

Source: Adapted from F. Herzberg, B. Mausner, and B. Snyderman, *The Motivation to Work*, 2d ed. Copyright © 1959 by John Wiley & Sons. Reprinted by permission.

Figure 6–2
Two-Factor Continua

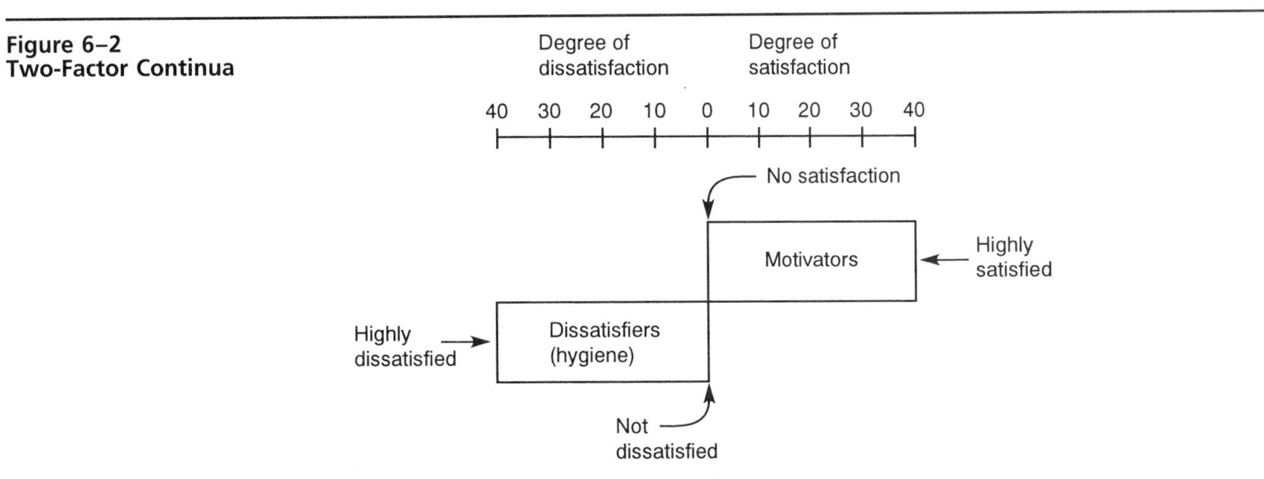

ment between Herzberg's findings and students' results may be that the data were selected by a similar method, asking people to recall past experience. This method is subject to criticism, however, because people unconsciously recall unpleasantness as due to things that are not under their control and therefore not their fault (the dissatisfiers). Pride in what they remember as having been achieved or earned (the motivators) can easily be unconsciously attributed to their own good efforts. Because of these psychological factors of recall, we cannot say that the dissatisfiers are really what turn people off; they are only what people *think* turn them off. And what turns people on or off under one set of circumstances may not so do under another; poor pay and working conditions may turn people off during prosperity but not so much during an economic depression when nothing else is available. There is also frequently a discrepancy between what young people say they want and the way they behave. Most will say they want challenge and self-direction, but many find difficulty in performing without considerable guidance and structure. The high turnover rate of young insurance salespersons during their first year provides an example of how the self-direction requirement can be overwhelming.

There has not been sufficient research to show that dissatisfiers and motivators truly account for differences in work performance.[5] Thus it cannot be said that the motivation-hygiene theory has yet provided the evidence that the motivators are what make people perform well. Whether dissatisfaction and satisfaction are two completely different factors also has not been validated. The question might be raised whether the motivators themselves are not potentially the greatest source of dissatisfaction.[6] Is it not possible for talented, educated individuals to be completely frustrated when the job does not provide opportunities for the use of their abilities and achievements? The forecast that there will be more college-educated people than there will be jobs requiring a college education means many may be dissatisfied because they cannot experience enough of the motivators even though all the dissatisfier factors offering a good life and pleasant working environment are present.

Motivation to work is so complex that it is easy to criticize any specific theory as being an oversimplification. It is important that managers be aware of the various concepts and determine if they have utility value in their own working situations. Herzberg's theory is highly important for understanding how people perceive satisfaction and dissatisfaction, realizing that this perception will vary with specific individuals. One person may be saying, "I can't work without challenge"; another may be saying, "Just let me do the routine work so I can think about what I will be doing after work." Most important is Herzberg's position that (1) it is the nature of the work itself that turns on the self-directing generators for accomplishment and (2) emphasis on human relations alone will not result in high productivity or job satisfaction. Herzberg's use of the terms *satisfaction* and *dissatisfaction* in regard to work performance suggests there is a positive relationship between satisfaction and productivity.

Maslow's Hierarchy of Needs

Another way of thinking of patterns of goals is by need categories. Under this concept, a need for achievement describes goals the individual is striving to attain in areas such as education, career, and work. Among management theorists, Abraham Maslow has proposed the best-known theory of this type in his **hierarchy of needs.**[7] Because his theory is so well known we will present only its aspect that will help you use the hierarchy as a tool for analyzing motivation in our case studies.

Our adaption of the five levels of the need hierarchy are depicted in Figure 6–3. Maslow assumed that the lower level had to be adequately satisfied before the next higher level became an important motivating force; that is, if the individual was highly concerned about physical needs, the other needs were not going to be the active basis for goal pursuance.

The three lower levels of needs are considered to be *extrinsic* in that satisfaction is initiated from factors external to the individual; the top two levels are considered to be *intrinsic* in that satisfaction is generated from within. The exception, of course, is that one's reputation, an esteem need, is dependent upon the external source. These distinc-

Figure 6–3
Maslow's Hierarchy of Needs Requiring Fulfillment in a Work Environment

Self-actualization (Self-fulfillment)* Realizing one's full potential; creativity; self-development
Esteem (Ego)* Self-esteem: use of one's skills, achievement, confidence, autonomy, independence, self-direction. Reputation: status, recognition, appreciation from others
Love (Social)* Acceptance by others; association and communication with others; being part of a group; belongingness needs
Safety needs Protection against threat of harsh supervision or unsafe working environment; getting fair treatment from management; job security; having a predictable work environment, predictable fellow workers
Physiological Good, comfortable working conditions; good pay

* Terms in parentheses are Douglas McGregor's, which are in common use.

tions become meaningful when one reexamines Herzberg's work: His dissatisfiers are the extrinsic needs, the bottom three levels of Maslow's hierarchy, while his motivators are the intrinsic needs coming from Maslow's top two levels.

Alderfer's ERG Theory

Alderfer's ERG theory[8] extends and refines Maslow's need hierarchy theory. Instead of the five categories of needs suggested by Maslow, Alderfer's ERG theory holds that the individual has three sets of basic needs: existence, relatedness, and growth. *Existence needs,* perceived as necessary for basic human existence, roughly correspond to the physiological and security needs of Maslow's hierarchy. *Relatedness needs,* involving the need to relate to others, are similar to Maslow's belongingness and esteem needs. Lastly, *growth needs* are analogous to Maslow's needs for self-esteem and self-actualization.

The ERG theory differs from Maslow's theory in one more important way. According to Maslow, individuals progress up the hierarchy as a result of the satisfaction of the lower-order needs. Alderfer's ERG theory suggests that in addition to this satisfaction-progression process, there is also a frustration-regression process. For example, if the individual is continually frustrated in his or her attempt to satisfy growth needs, relatedness needs will reemerge as a primary motivation force, and the individual is likely to redirect effort toward the lower-level needs.[9]

McClelland's *n* Achievement and *n* Power

David C. McClelland has made important contributions to need theory, focusing on the needs for achievement, power, and affiliation. He found that salespersons and small business entrepreneurs tended to be high in ***n* achievement** (*n* standing for need), and he concluded they need freedom in the working environment to exercise their strong self-direction tendencies.[10] However, *n* achievement is "a one-man game and need never involve other people." In contrast, managers are not necessarily high in *n* achievement but tend to be high in ***n* power.** The desire to influence, guide, and control others is an important aspect of a manager's motivation. D. G. Winter found, in a limited sample, that business and journalism students were significantly higher in *n* power than those from other occupational categories.[11]

McClelland distinguishes between *p* power (personalized) and *s* power (socialized) and speculates that the former precedes the latter in the development of the individual. The extreme of *p* power is raw control over others expressed in an interpersonal way, whereas *s* power is altruistic and is exercised for the benefit of others. Power fascinates executives; the topics of manipulation, win–lose situations, and Machiavellianism are of top interest when introduced into business workshops.

The concept of *n* power enhances the understanding of Maslow's hierarchy of needs. Persons having power can be assumed to have financial resources for their personal (physiological) needs; control over their environment (safety); considerable interaction with others (social); leeway for self-direction, status, and respect from their position (esteem); and opportunities to excel (self-actualization). Power thus can add considerably to the satisfaction of the person's need pattern and also is a strong reinforcer of managerial role behaviors.

In an extensive review of the research on the relationship between organization structural variables and need and job satisfaction, L. L. Cummings and C. J. Berger found excellent support for the conclusion that satisfaction increases as one moves up the organizational ladder.[12] This appears to support our analysis of *n* power.

An important aspect of McClelland's work is success in training small business people in India in *n* achievement behaviors. He reports that many of them changed dramatically after only five days of exposure to his workshop methods.[13] Psychologists have traditionally believed that an individual's basic personality structure is formed during the first five years of life and is most difficult to change. But McClelland's experience over years of work brings him more to the conclusion that leaders are not so much born as made. The emphasis in this book is that leadership types of behaviors can be learned by most people; however, we are not saying that everyone will necessarily become a leader—for one thing, *n* power is needed.

Udai Pareek further developed McClelland's work by extending the need for achievement and need for power into six needs or motives that are relevant for understanding the behavior of people in organizations:

1. *Achievement* characterized by concern for excellence, competition with the standards of excellence set by others or by oneself, the setting of challenging goals for oneself, awareness of the hurdles in the way of achieving those goals, and persistence in trying alternative paths to one's goals.
2. *Affiliation* characterized by a concern for establishing and maintaining close, personal relationships, a value on friendship, and a tendency to express one's emotions.
3. *Influence* characterized by concern with making an impact on others, a desire to make people do what one thinks is right, and an urge to change matters and develop people.
4. *Control* characterized by a concern for orderliness, a desire to be and stay informed, and an urge to monitor and take corrective action when needed.
5. *Extension* characterized by concern for others, interest in superordinate goals, and an urge to be relevant and useful to larger groups, including society.
6. *Dependence* characterized by a desire for the help of others in one's own self-development, checking with significant others (those who are more knowledgeable or have higher status, experts, close associates, etc.), submitting ideas or proposals for approval, and having an urge to maintain an "approval" relationship.[14]

Activity 6–5 provides an opportunity to diagnose individual motivation and provide the individual with a motivational profile.

Process Theories of Motivation

Process theories are used to understand and to explain the elements that would foster individual choices of behavioral patterns, the actual motivation process, its direction, and the forces that will increase the likelihood that described behaviors will be repeated over time. In this cluster of theories, the basic assumption is that individuals are capable of calculating costs and benefits and that they use the results of their calculations to choose among alternative courses of action. For example, if we examine the car wash minicase at the beginning of the chapter, from a process theory point of view the focus would be on the elements and the dynamics between them that foster individuals to put forth more effort in the one car wash than in the other. The better-known theories in this cluster include equity, expectancy, goal-setting, and reinforcement. Next we explore equity, expectancy and goal-setting theories. Reinforcement theory was discussed in Module 2 as a part of the discussion on learning.

Equity Theory

Equity theory's theoretical roots can be found in the ''cognitive dissonance'' and the ''rational economic man'' notions. The basic premise is that individuals want their efforts and performance to be judged fairly relative to others and that individuals engage in a process of evaluating their social relations much like they evaluate economic transactions in the marketplace. Thus equity theory relies heavily both on the assessment of individual inputs and outputs and on social comparison. Figure 6–4 presents a general model of equity theory.

Figure 6–4
Equity Theory of Motivation

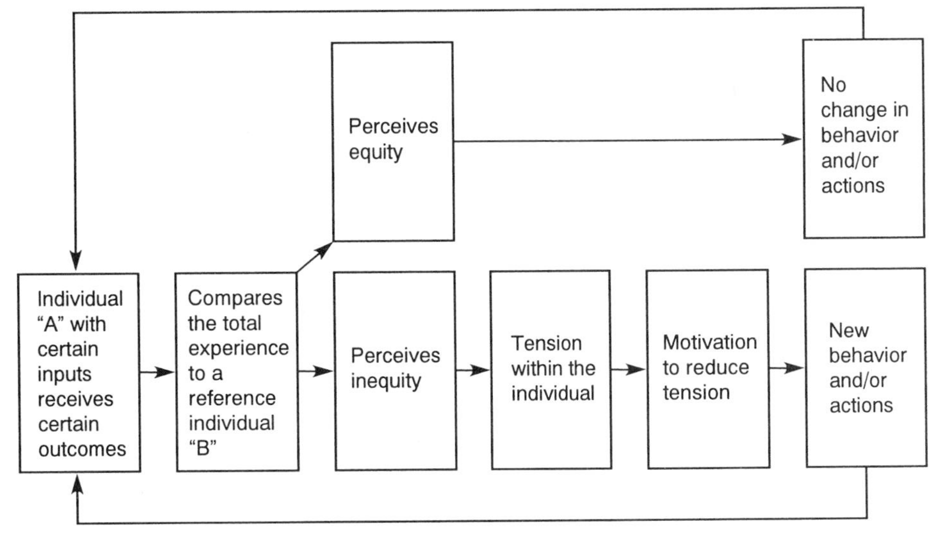

Four key elements are used to explain motivation dynamics in equity theory: input, outcomes, comparative analysis, and action. *Inputs* are what the person brings to the exchange—for example, education, past experience, skills and knowledge, and these are perceived by the person and/or by others. *Outcomes* are what the individual receives from the exchange (for example, recognition, pay, fringe benefits, promotion, and status). *Comparative analysis* is the comparison of the weights ratio attached by individuals to the perceived inputs and outcomes for themselves compared to relevant others who are in the same situation. The comparison to relevant others helps individuals determine the extent to which they feel that they have been treated equitably. Inequity causes tension both within the individual and between individuals. *Action* refers to the specific steps or behavior that the individual takes to reduce the tension that results from the feeling of inequity. The energy source for the individual's motivation is restoring equity. Equity theory further states that an individual is motivated in proportion to the perceived fairness of the rewards received for a certain amount of effort, as compared to the rewards received by relevant others.[15] Perception plays a critical role in the equity theory point of view. We will explore the phenomenon of perception in Module 7.

Expectancy Theory

Expectancy-valence motivation theory is perhaps the most researched theory of work motivation.[16] Expectancy theory suggests that individuals consider alternatives, weigh costs and benefits, and choose a course of action of maximum utility. Individuals make decisions among alternatives based on their perceptions of the degree to which a behavior can satisfy a desired want or need. At the most basic level, the expectancy that a specific level of effort will lead to a certain level of performance and the expectancy that a certain level of performance will result in a specific outcome is what facilitates an individual's motivation. Motivation is a function of expectancy, valence, and instrumentality.[17] Figure 6–5 presents a general model of expectancy theory.

Figure 6–5
A Basic Model of Expectancy Theory

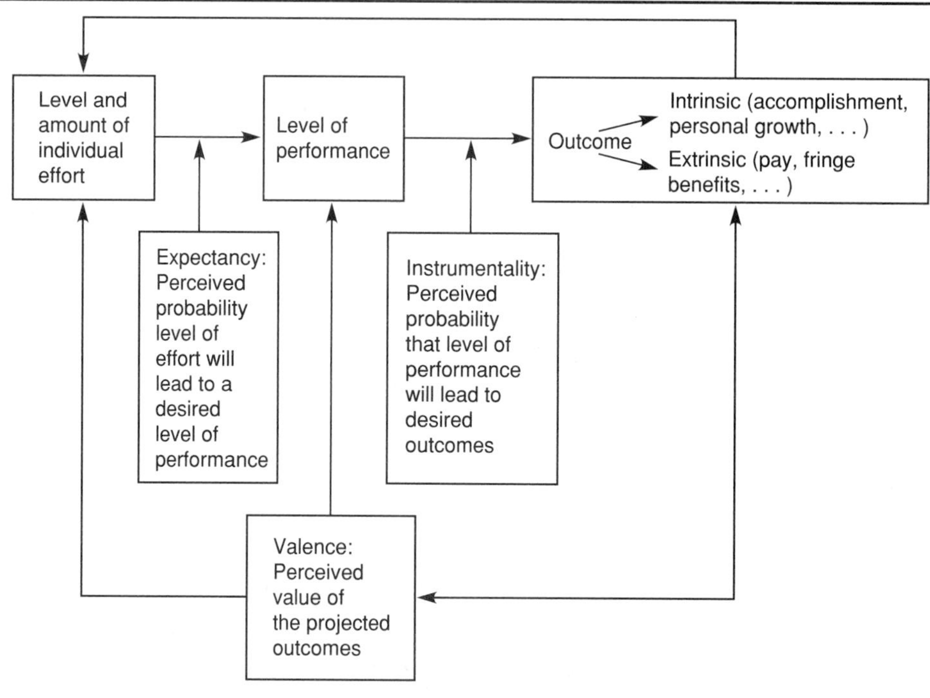

The level and the amount of effort that the individual will exert in a given situation is a result of a cumulative effect of (1) the person's perceived probability that the level of the effort will lead to a desired level of performance (*expectancy*), (2) the person's perceived probability that the level of performance will lead to a desired level of outcomes (*instrumentality*), and (3) the person's perceived value of the projected outcomes (*valence*). Although expectancy theory has dominated research in motivation since the early 1970s, due to the identification of the three useful elements to managers, its complexity has resulted in mixed empirical support.[18] Critics of the theory state that the model is too complex to measure and that the key elements are problematic in terms of definition and operationalization.[19] The comprehensiveness of the theory makes it a usable conceptual guide for understanding and fostering motivation at work.

Porter and Lawler developed expectancy theory one step further by integrating expectancy, equity, and some elements of the content theories.

Porter–Lawler Model

To help understand how people respond differently to work settings, we will turn to an individual approach to motivation, the Porter-Lawler (P–L) model (named for its developers). This model relates a number of different factors to performance and to satisfaction and it highlights how these factors interact. In simplest terms, the **P–L model** relates effort to performance. Various factors affect effort, and others affect performance. The outcome or consequences of performance are also affected by individual factors.

In Figure 6–6, we can see that (1) *reward valence,* the value an individual places on a reward, together with (2) *expectancy,* a person's estimate of how probable an out-

Figure 6–6
The Porter–Lawler Motivation Model

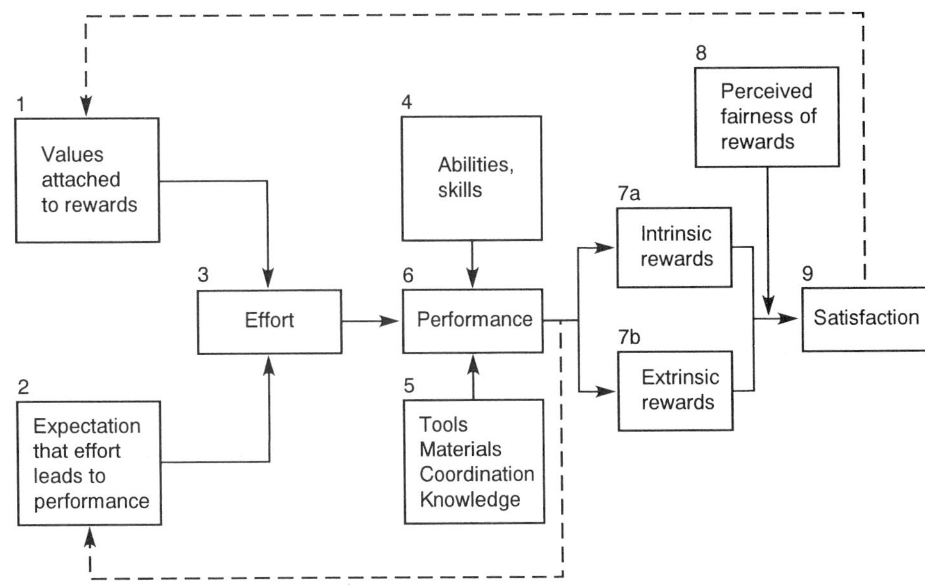

Source: Adapted from Lyman W. Porter and Edward E. Lawler, III, *Managerial Attitudes and Performance* (Homewood, Ill.: Richard D. Irwin, 1968).

come is, both affect (3) *effort.* An individual simply may not value the awards the organization is offering or may value other outcomes more. The employee who values social relationships with the work group more than potential rewards for outstanding performance will be unlikely to respond to incentives for increased production where group norms restrict performance. A person who believes that no reasonable amount of effort will produce the desired result is unlikely to try to perform. However, a challenging but possible goal is likely to be quite motivating.[20]

Expectancy is the individual's estimate of whether effort will lead to a desired reward (7a or 7b in Figure 6–6). There are several expectancy linkages. First, the individual may not believe that effort (3) will lead to performance (6). Where the job standard appears impossible to achieve, workers typically do not put in increasing effort—whether or not management shares workers' impression that the job is impossible. Similarly, if an individual believes the job is impossible for him or her, then even if others can do it, effort is unlikely.

Another sort of expectancy concerns performance and outcomes. If I do, in fact, perform, will the desired reward actually come to me? From the manager's perspective, this sort of expectancy concerns the organization's reward system. Where rewards are closely tied to performance and administered fairly, people should have high expectancy that performance will result in the specified reward. Where no such linkage exists, or where people believe the system does not operate accurately, people will have very different expectancies. Individuals' self-esteem, their past experiences in similar situations, the present situation, and communications from others (including group norms) will affect both the value they place on rewards (the reward valence) and their expectancies.[21]

In addition to people's values and expectancies, several other factors clearly affect the linkage between effort and performance. A person's abilities (4) clearly affect whether effort leads to performance; so too do the tools, material, and knowledge of when and where to apply effort (5). These factors are of special interest to managers because they seem particularly amenable to managerial change. Employees' skills can be improved by training, and their knowledge of when and where to apply effort can be improved by explicit role descriptions or directions.

The rewards actually received from performance affect both satisfaction and subsequent performance. Two sorts of outcomes can flow from performance: intrinsic rewards (7a) and extrinsic rewards (7b). (Of course, "rewards" can be negative as well as positive. Physical abuse from fellow employees attempting to restrict production or a chewing out from a supervisor are not "rewarding" but constitute "negative rewards.'') Rewards that others provide (whether positive or negative) include money, praise or recognition, censure, and promotions. These rewards from external sources (outside the individual and the work itself) are extrinsic rewards; they depend upon others' perceptions and assessments of performance. These rewards are like Herzberg's hygiene factors. These are the sorts of rewards most managers think of and most organizations at least partly control. Some of them, most notably those coming from work group members, may be not only outside management's control but also outside the manager's knowledge as well. This makes them no less real or important.

Intrinsic rewards are those that individuals get from the work itself or give to themselves. Herzberg's motivators are intrinsic. A sense of accomplishment, self-esteem, pleasure at a job well done, and the feelings of growth, triumph, and success that may come from a difficult task are all examples of intrinsic rewards. These rewards are profoundly connected both to individual needs and preferences, on the one hand, and to the design of the work, on the other. Thus challenging work creates the potential for this sort of intrinsic reward. But people looking for easy jobs that allow them to simply do the job and go home to really live will not find additional challenge rewarding. Similarly, for many college students, autonomy and self-direction are important values in general—but a part-time job that permits concentration of energies on schoolwork may be preferable.

Equity (8), the perception that rewards are fair or just, is also a factor. It's important to note that we are speaking of perception here and not necessarily fact. A reward system can be perfectly fair in actuality and still be *perceived* as biased (for instance, if employees are not told the basis for decisions about promotion). Where workers believe favoritism or unfairness is the rule, there will be dissatisfaction, especially with extrinsic rewards. (People may also be dissatisfied if they perceive someone was unfairly given a job that's high in intrinsic rewards, while they are left to contend with a less rewarding job.) Another aspect of equity is the balance between effort and reward. Either too little or too much reward will be perceived as inequitable and will be resented. Comparisons of the rewards that others receive for what appears to be equal effort are also a part of equity.

Satisfaction (9) is depicted as the outcome of valences, expectancies, effort, performance, reward, and perceived equity. Of course, this means degree of satisfaction since individuals might very well be dissatisfied. The feedback loop between satisfaction and earlier factors in the model indicates that motivation is a dynamic, ongoing process. People learn from their experiences, and their values, attitudes, and expectations are adjusted accordingly. Managers must be aware of the feedback loops for two reasons. First, individuals come to the workplace with a prior history or experience (in life if not at work). This past experience colors and affects people's values and expectations no less than their skills. Managers must deal with people as they are (at least to begin with). Second, people's new experiences in the work setting and with their manager also affect their values and expectations. Therefore managers will have to live with the results of their behaviors toward individuals and with the results of the organizational script for those individuals.

Goal-Setting Theory

At the most basic level, goal-setting theory is concerned with the effect of goals on individual performance. Some view goal-setting theory as an extension of process theories of motivation. The emphasis is on the intended outcomes and the motivational process that the establishment of the intended outcomes has on the behavior of the individual. Goal-setting theory suggests that goals are associated with enhanced performance because they mobilize effort, direct attention, and encourage persistence and strategy development.[22]

Locke and Latham developed a sophisticated theory of individual goal setting and performance.[23] They claim that an assigned goal influences a person's beliefs about being able to perform that task (labeled *self-efficacy*) and encourages the acceptance of those goals as personal goals. Both factors in turn influence performance. Goals can be implicit or explicit, vague or clearly defined, and self-imposed or externally imposed.

Many studies have shown that relative to general do-your-best goals, job performance is enhanced by the setting of specific goals.[24] Some studies suggest that people will accept and work hard to attain difficult goals until they reach the limits of their capabilities. However, as goals become difficult, they may be rejected, and performance will suffer.[25] Activity 6–4 provides an opportunity to experience some powerful notions of goal-setting theory as a motivational mechanism.

Other Aspects of Motivation

Group Influence on Individual Motivation

Many people think of motivation as something built into the individual: It is part of a person's character—one either has it or one doesn't. However, an individual's self-image is deeply imbedded in groups he or she has been a part of in the past. Personal identity is a composite of the groups (family, friends, religious, work, and other) that the individual has been a member of, past and present. (This will be discussed in Module 11.) An individual's response to new situations is often based on what he or she thinks a specific group would or would not do under the conditions.

This dependency on others is part of the human condition. One reason is that there are few absolutes for judging new social situations; in social interaction, the available guidelines for how to behave usually come from past experience or how others are reacting. In more objective conditions, such as walking through a doorway or driving a car, immediate feedback as to whether one is doing all right is received in the form of cues coming to the sensory system from physical objects. Meaning comes from the interaction with the physical object and is almost always highly predictable, reliable, and stable. Alternative ways of responding to an inanimate object are limited. In social situations highly variable patterns can be used, since these situations are more ambiguous and provide less predictable feedback. Inadequate feedback makes for ambiguity and greater dependency on others. Dependence on others when confronted with ambiguity seems almost automatic. The group norms that result can greatly influence behavior and motivation.

In addition to overcoming ambiguity, conformity to group norms can become part of the individual's system of goals to be attained in the fulfillment of needs. Maslow's description of safety and love needs provides insight into this. Safety needs, according to Maslow, originate in a baby's fear of being dropped, loud noises, flashing lights, and so on. Avoidance of harm becomes a goal. There is a real need for predictability, as Stanley Schachter notes:

> From these and similar observations, we may generalize and say that the average child in our society generally prefers a safe, orderly, predictable, organized world which he can count on, and in which unexpected, unmanageable or other dangerous things do not happen, and in which, in any case, he has all-powerful parents who protect and shield him from harm.[26]

There is an underlying fear of change and a preference for familiar rather than unfamiliar things. The love needs include acceptance by others (belongingness needs). Fear of rejection is an important aspect of conformity to group norms.

An experiment by Schachter provides insight into the nature of both the safety and love needs. This experiment studied the relationship between anxiety and affiliation (belongingness or social needs). College students participating were subjected to one of two conditions designed to produce anxiety. For "high anxiety," the subjects were told they would receive a series of electric shocks (for medical research) and that these would be intense and painful. For the "low-anxiety" condition, subjects were told that they should not let the "shock" trouble them because they would enjoy the experiment. The two groups were, of course, kept separate, and they were unaware of the two conditions. While waiting to undergo the shock experiment, the individuals were given their choice of waiting alone in a room or waiting in a room where other subjects were present. The results were that in the group that had been told individuals were to receive the intense shock, 63 percent of the subjects indicated they would like to wait with other subjects rather than alone. In the group that had been told individuals were to receive the milder shock treatment, only 33 percent of the subjects chose to be together.

The significance for management theory of the interrelationship between group norms and needs is that work itself, as provided for in the script in the formal organization, does not automatically take care of all the needs of the individual. When the person first arrives on the job, the strangeness and unpredictability of the situation produce a threat to the safety needs. One response to threat, as the Schachter experiment showed, is to seek out other people; people clump and cluster together to satisfy belongingness and safety needs. Thus management, which will be perceived by the new employee as associated with any threat felt, is not turned to for assurance, but fellow employees are. The individual is almost automatically willing to give his or her allegiance to peers in return for the supportiveness they offer. Conformity to group norms brings acceptance; failure to do so brings rejection.

Relationship of Motivation to the Human Organization

In our discussion in an earlier module of the differences between the formal and the human organizations (Module 4), we did not analyze why actors play their roles somewhat differently than is called for in the script. Motivation is the primary reason. Because the formal organization often does not provide for all the needs of the individual, it can generate frustrations. To achieve need fulfillment, the individual will find ways of doing things that are different from the system's expectations but will still permit him or her to do an adequate job.

Consideration of motivation theory makes it possible to formulate the human organization concept as that system of interrelated shared expectations (social norms, values, roles, statuses) determining the behavior of the actors that (1) completes the requirements called for in the script (much of the behavior will be identical with that depicted in the formal organization), (2) is not adequately provided for in the script but is functionally necessary (for example, lack of information flow can lead to informal channels of communication), and (3) satisfies those human needs or overcomes those frustrations that were not taken into consideration when the formal organization was designed.

The more management is unaware of, and unresponsive to, factors 2 and 3 above, the more the energy of employees will be directed against productivity and management against the establishment. Informal cliques and groupings will develop, either covertly or overtly, with their own group norms, communications systems, and informal leaders. To avoid this, management's goal is the integration of individual needs and organizational needs. The problem is to produce the climate, policies, and practices whereby individuals can attain their personal goals by achieving organizational goals. In shaping the human organization, the manager must be able to work with all three of these areas of behavior in an atmosphere of openness, two-way communication, and employee involvement.

Frustrating Events and Their Effects

Our discussion of motivation so far has shown that it is just as necessary to be concerned about what turns people off as with what turns them on. The blue-collar blues result in high costs when turnover and absenteeism soar. The toll for individuals is also great, as measured by stress-related diseases associated with different occupations. One study of 23 occupations showed the highest job satisfaction and lowest rate of stress-related diseases existed for family physicians, a profession in which individuals work an average of 55 hours per week.[27] In contrast, assembly-line workers—who do not have excessively long hours, unwanted overtime, large work loads, or particularly great demands for concentration—reported the most boredom and the greatest dissatisfaction with their work load as well as the highest levels of anxiety, depression, irritation, and somatic disorders. This strong evidence of strain, the researchers found, is attributable to job insecurity, to a lack of social support from immediate superiors and other workers, and to a lack of opportunity to use individual skills and abilities or to participate in decision making.[28]

The conclusion was that dissatisfaction increases with the degree of discrepancy between the demands of the job and the desires of the worker. Another source of **frustration,** in addition to the nature of the work, is management practices. Many managers believe keeping people under pressure is an effective motivator; this is the concept of "management by pressure." Some even believe it best to keep people guessing about where they stand with the boss or on the career promotion ladder so they will continually try to prove their worth. There are major problems with this, such as the question of how much pressure is meaningful in terms of influencing people in a positive way. People also respond differently to frustration—an event that may not even be observed by one person might cause another person extreme discomfort.

Some Managerial Implications and Programs

Generalized Approaches

Job enrichment, to be discussed in Module 13 on work and organization design, is well known as one approach that centers on the assumption that there are generalized needs throughout the work force that are responsive to management programs; that is, all employees should respond well to enriched jobs. Behavior modification programs (discussed later in this module) have in the past 20 years gained widespread attention as a generalized approach. This method has been used in companies such as General Electric, Standard Oil of Ohio, and Michigan Bell. Recently employee profit-sharing plans and bonus systems have gained considerable prominence.

Profit-Sharing Plans

Employee participation in work planning programs is frequently reported as a method to link employee compensation with organization profits. It is an old idea that has attracted new interest as a means of increasing productivity and quality. The Scanlon Plan, which goes back to the 1930s, is a program in which employees are involved in making and integrating suggestions into the company's operating processes. A formula is used to distribute a percentage of the resulting cost savings and profits to employees. The plan has been used for many years by the Lincoln Electric Company of Cleveland and has benefited both the company and the employees. A unique and relatively recent development of profit-sharing plans is the employee stock ownership plan.

Employee Stock Ownership Plans (ESOPs)

ESOP activities have been spreading at an increasing rate over the past decade. It is estimated that 10 million workers, comprising 10 percent of the private sector work force, are participating in **employee stock ownership plans** (ESOPs) with assets of about $20 billion in 7,500 companies, about 1,500 of which are majority or fully employee-owned.[29] There are three main types of ESOPs:

1. *The nonleveraged ESOP.* The company contributes stock or cash to buy stock in a trust that buys workers shares, which workers receive upon retirement or leaving the company.
2. *The leveraged ESOP.* Workers' ownership is established with money the company borrows to invest in company stock for the workers. The company guarantees that it will make periodic payments to the worker-ownership trust to amortize the loan.
3. *The tax-credit ESOP.* The company gets dollar-for-dollar tax credit for stock purchased for workers.

Research indicates that ESOP companies showed an average annual productivity increase,[30] improved employee motivation,[31] and increased growth rate of two to four times that of companies where employees did not own stock.[32]

Pygmalion and Motivation

As we saw in Module 2 on expectations and learning, the self-fulfilling prophecy (SFP) or **Pygmalion effect** is a major social phenomenon with far-reaching implications. In a recent study, a unique and practical model that pulls together leadership, expectation, motivation, and performance at work was proposed.[33] (See Figure 6–7.)

Figure 6–7
A Model of Self-Fulfilling Prophecy at Work

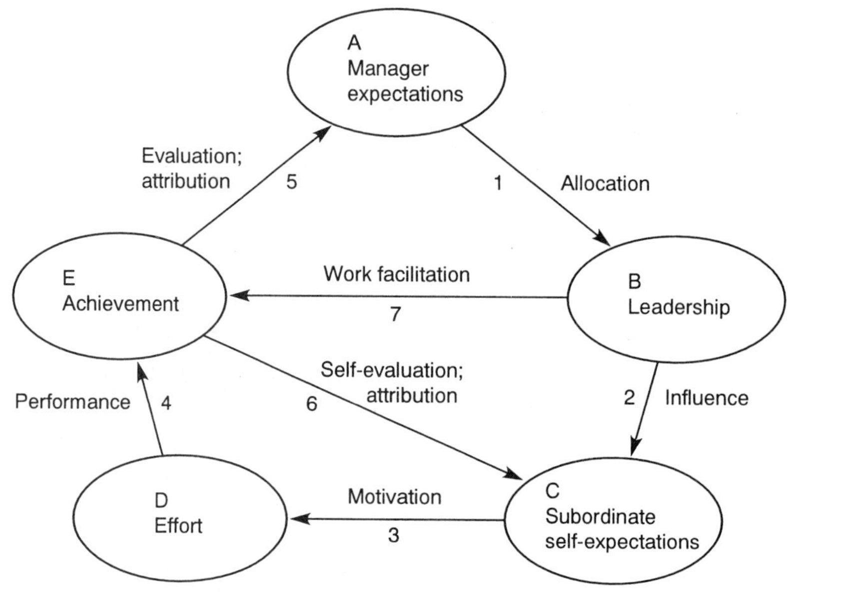

Source: Reprinted by permission of the publisher, from *Pygmalion in Management* by Dov Eden (Lexington, Mass.: Lexington Books, D. C. Heath and Company, copyright 1990 Lexington Books).

The model encompasses five interrelated variables: manager expectations, leadership, subordinate self-expectations, effort, and achievement. The manager's performance expectations for a subordinate influence the leadership dynamics between the manager and the subordinate. As a result, the subordinate raises his or her expectations, which increases the motivation to exert a greater deal of effort on the job, the outcome of which is improved performance and better achievement. Dov Eden's research demonstrated that the combination of raising self-expectations and setting specific, hard goals increases performance. Furthermore, this line of research and its findings provided additional support for the combined effect of Pygmalion and goal setting on motivation. This combined effect appears especially promising in increasing motivation and performance.[34]

Individualized Organizational Policies and Practices

The idea of adapting company policies and practices to meet individual needs is somewhat like a legislature passing laws that do not apply to everyone. Obviously this could entail more management time, and laws that presumably apply to everyone equally but are intended to satisfy individual differences and could be perplexing to those for whom they are intended. One of the best-known attempts in this regard is the practice of flexible work schedules, in which workers have a choice of how their required weekly hours are to be distributed throughout the week.

An article by E. E. Lawler describing problems and promises of providing for individual differences in organizations concludes

> The research on reward systems, job design, leadership, selection, and training shows that significant individual differences exist in how individuals respond to organizational policies and practices. Because of this, an effective normative organization theory has to suggest an organization design that will treat individuals differently. Existing normative theories usually fail to emphasize this point. There are, however, a number of things that organizations can do now to deal with individual differences. These include cafeteria-style pay plans and selective job enrichment. Unfortunately, a fully developed practical organization theory based upon an individual

difference approach cannot be yet stated. Still, it is important to note that approaches to shaping organizations to individuals are developing. It seems logical, therefore, to identify these and other similar efforts as attempts to individualize organizations. It is hoped that the identification of these efforts and the establishment of the concept of individualization will lead to two very important developments: the generation of more practices that will individualize organizations and work on how these different practices can simultaneously be made operational in organizations. Only if these developments take place will individualized organizations ever be created.[35]

Managing Individuals According to Their Differences

An enduring controversy has existed between those who say, ''Treat people the same,'' and those who advocate, ''Manage each person differently since people have different experiences, abilities, and needs.'' This dilemma is faced by parents raising children, teachers guiding students, and coaches training athletes as well as by managers. To explore this issue, the boss–subordinate role-playing situation of Activity 6–4 is provided.

Behavior Modification

A very different kind of practical technique that has been attracting much managerial attention is **behavior modification.** Based especially on the work of B. F. Skinner, behavior modification insists that internal states of mind (such as ''needs'') are misleading, scientifically unmeasurable, and in any case hypothetical. Instead, what managers and behavioral scientists need to pay attention to is behavior—the observable outcomes of situations and choices, what people actually do. This approach to behavior rests on two underlying assumptions. First, human behavior is seen as determined by the environment. Second, human behavior is subject to observable laws (such as the laws of physics or chemistry) and thus can be predicted and changed. Behavior is changed by rewarding it, ignoring it, or punishing people for using it. The behavior modification view says that behavior is a response to a combination of specific stimuli and other environmental factors (such as time and previous experiences).

Continuous reinforcement rewards every occurrence of the desired behavior. (You give your dog a biscuit every time he sits up.) This is the quickest way to get a person to act in the desired way. *Extinction* rewards no behavior; you ignore the behavior (a two-year-old's tantrum or your dog's chasing his tail instead of sitting up). Behavior receiving no external reward will be less frequent than rewarded behavior. *Intermittent reinforcement* rewards some responses but not others according to a preset schedule (rewarding the dog only after five successful sits). Intermittent reinforcement establishes the desired behavior more slowly than continuous reinforcement, but has longer-term effects. Moreover, intermittently reinforced behavior is less easily extinguished than continuously reinforced behavior.

In behavior modification (or *operant conditioning,* to use its more formal name), consequences are arranged for some voluntary behavior that is desired. For instance, workers are praised for properly doing their jobs. The most effective reinforcements seem to be specific, detailed, and concrete praise about how and what the employee has done, closely and directly related to the desired behavior. Thus, rather than saying ''Good job, Jones,'' the supervisor says something like ''Jones, your use of the new package format has really increased—the record says you're making over 90 percent use on your shipments, and, as I watch, I can see you've got a good system.''

Behavior modification has had some notable successes. At Emery Air Freight, to use a classic case, managers thought workers were not using containers to combine small package shipments as often as they could. A study showed containers were used less than half of the times they could be. A behavior modification program resulted in significant improvements in container use that saved the company some $650,000 annually, and the improved behavior persisted over several years. Other companies are also using varied forms of behavior modification, among them General Electric, B. F. Goodrich, and Michigan Bell. Of course, lots of good managers and supervisors (and parents) have used it for years without the fancy name. There are some concerns about *why* it works, however.

While Skinner's reinforcement suggests that the consequences themselves govern behavior, a close look at Emery Air Freight suggests that feedback and goal setting played as much a part of the success story as reinforcement. A high, explicit goal was set, and workers were given training on how to attain it. Employees were provided with timely, accurate reports on their performance, which they themselves monitored. Hence they reinforced themselves by direct access to performance information. So at any time, they knew where they stood on reaching their performance goals.

Most behavior modification programs to date have been applied at operating levels—to clerical help, production workers, or mechanics, for instance. Behavior modification is most easily applied to relatively simple jobs, where critical behaviors can be easily identified and specific performance goals can be readily set. For managerial jobs, these key factors may be more difficult to apply. Further, it's not clear that supervisor praise, recognition, and feedback are enough. After some years, Emery had to introduce new reinforcers, such as special luncheons, because the old ones had become routine.

Criticisms of behavior modification include the charge that it's essentially bribery and that workers are already paid for performance. Because it disregards people's attitudes and beliefs, behavior modification has been called misleading and manipulative. Particularly where money is involved, one critic has noted that there is little difference between behavior modification and "some key elements of scientific management presented more than 60 years ago by Taylor."[36] Another criticism is that behavior modification does not take into consideration group norms, which can have an antiorganization character, such as group norms to restrict production. Indeed, behavior modification improperly used can generate much group resistance.

Why does it matter whether behavior modification works because of reinforcement or because of goals? Because you, as a manager, will need to know what the essentials are for getting the performance you want—whether those essentials are praise or self-administered feedback. Moreover, Emery was careful to avoid setting groups or individuals in competition with one another. Instead, people were encouraged to compete with their own previous records. This appears to be an important factor that you, as a manager, should know about.

Successful behavior modification requires the following:

1. A careful analysis of the job to identify specific key behaviors for targeting.
2. Careful, explicit communication to employees of what is wanted, including both behaviors and concrete, measurable goals.
3. "Reinforcers" to attach consequences to desired behaviors. Most often used are praise and recognition. (Union agreements may make other reinforcers—like money or promotions—unavailable.)
4. Concrete, continuous feedback or feedback soon after performance that workers can use to check on themselves.

The evidence suggests that behavior modification and goal setting, creatively applied, do seem to improve *some* performance at *some* levels. The thoughtful manager will be wary of any simple solutions, instead paying close attention to the weaknesses and problems of many approaches, and combining approaches for their strengths.

International Viewpoint on Motivation

Studying theories of motivation can lead us to assume that we are dealing with "human nature"— the way people really are. We must be aware that most research for these theories has been done by Americans with Americans, although some of

Herzberg's work included cross-cultural comparisons. We must realize that American motivation patterns and social character arise out of unique history; they are not universal—to a degree they differ from those of other cultures. As we have seen earlier, cultural diversity plays an important role in shaping individuals' behavior.

This becomes very relevant when we hear that some managers and companies attempt to apply management practices that were developed in other cultures, assuming that because they worked well in another culture they will work well in their own. Furthermore, industries need to expand the awareness they already have of the cultural differences in motivation that exist between different regions of the United States. This is shown in the relocation from the industrial Northeast, where union practices and attitudes affect productivity, to the Sunbelt states, where past economic conditions have left the population more compliant to rigorous work standards.

The United States is an achievement-oriented society that has historically encouraged and honored individual accomplishment and the attainment of material prosperity.[37] The American dream tells us that with hard work and perseverance, we can attain anything. Individualism, independence, self-confidence, and speaking out against injustice and threat are important elements of American culture. Materialism and the concomitant rewards of living well are basic goal systems in our motivation patterns.

In contrast to American motivation characteristics, Howard, Shudo, and Umeshima found the Japanese motivation and values to be quite different, with obvious implications for management practices.[38] Their research showed that Americans put greater value on individuality, while Japanese place greater value on socially oriented qualities. The social orientation of the Japanese may be traced to Confucianism, which stresses a rigid hierarchy in a collective society, where members are expected to maintain absolute loyalty and obedience to authority. The stress on dependency and security are part of the Japanese upbringing, whereas autonomy and early independence are typically American. In their corporate life, Japanese show great dependency and are highly conforming and obedient in return. Japanese management recognizes the inhibiting effects this character has on creativity and innovation; at present they are emphasizing the need to integrate programs into their schools that will free up and develop the creativity and ingenuity they envy in America.

As of late, work motivation in mainland China seems to be an issue of concern. The problem of low work motivation that was identified by foreign researchers and practitioners was a forbidden topic of investigation for Chinese researchers until the end of the Cultural Revolution.[39] Factors that have been postulated as responsible for low motivation and productivity include lack of an effective reward–punishment system, "unscientific" work quotas, the problematic promotion–wage system, lifetime employment, and an ineffective "political work-system."[40]

We discussed McClelland's work on achievement in this module. Adler reviewed the cross-cultural research on achievement and found it relatively robust across cultures.[41] For example, managers in New Zealand appear to follow the pattern developed in the United States. However, the literature would show that the word *achievement* itself is hardly translatable into any language other than English. However, countries characterized by a high need for achievement also have a high need to produce and a strong willingness to accept risk. Anglo-American countries such as the United States, Canada, and Great Britain follow the high-achievement motivation pattern, while countries such as Chile and Portugal follow the low-achievement motivation pattern. (Admittedly, these broad generalizations are based on very limited research data.)

Implications for managerial style, practices, and motivation planning for U.S. firm operating branches in foreign countries are apparent. The social character, the values, and the cultural practices of each country must be taken into consideration when planning and operating the human organization. Corporations operating abroad have long known this but have often not taken it sufficiently into account. The U.S. Foreign Service pays close attention to developing an awareness of these differences for its people operating abroad. It provides considerable schooling for its diplomats preparing for life in a new country, and many American corporations do likewise.

Summary

Some understanding of motivation can be gained by examining your own work experience and that of fellow participants, and then sorting out factors accounting for ''best'' and ''less than best'' performance. Activity 6–1 for this purpose yields results similar to Herzberg's dissatisfiers (those factors that make workers unhappy when they are not present) and motivators (those factors that provide opportunities for self-direction and challenge). Motivation is commonly thought of as being inherent in the individual in the sense that one either has it or does not have it. When defined as psychological energy directed toward goals, all behavior is motivated; goals are the direction for achievement of wants or avoidance of threats. All ''nonproductive'' behavior can be viewed as attempts to avoid or counteract threats.

Theories of motivation can be classified as either content or process. The four content theories of motivation—Maslow's need hierarchy, Herzberg's motivation-hygiene theory, Alderfer's ERG theory, and McClelland's achievement—focus on the specific factors that motivate people. The four process theories—expectancy, equity, goal setting, and reinforcement—focus on the elements that foster individual choices of behavioral patterns and the forces that will increase the likelihood that specific behaviors will be repeated over time.

We explored critical aspects of motivations, such as the group influence on individual motivation, the relationship between the human organization and motivation, and frustrations and their effect on motivation. This module focused on understanding motivation dynamics at work; therefore, the last section explored specific managerial implications and programs: profit-sharing plans, employee stock ownership plans, employee involvement programs, Pygmalion and motivation, and behavior modification. Finally, motivation in the global context of work was discussed.

Study Questions

1. When this book's authors created the classroom workshop model, which of the following viewpoints did they use: horticultural, engineering, or human resources? Give reasons and illustrations to support your answer.
2. Your manager tells you Herzberg's theory applies to himself and other managers he knows so his advice is to forget about other fancy theories of motivation. If he is the type of manager you can talk to, how would you respond?
3. What is meant by *intrinsic* and *extrinsic* factors in motivation? To what theories do these apply? Why are these important distinctions for a manager to remember in planning for employee motivation?
4. How do Herzberg's dissatisfiers fit into Maslow's hierarchy of needs? How do his motivators fit into the hierarchy?
5. The discussion on leadership asked whether leaders are born or made. How do McClelland's and Eden's works affect the answer to this question?
6. Compare and contrast any one content theory of motivation and any one process theory of motivation.
7. What is the basic management issue when you manage people according to their individual needs, abilities, and experiences? What actions can supervisors take to manage according to individual differences while trying to avoid the problems inherent in such an approach?
8. If you were the human resources manager of a large corporation and the executive office told you to prepare a report on installing an employee profit-sharing program, what major topics would your report include?
9. Explain the phrase, ''Motivation is culture-bound.''

10. Thorndike's law of effects states that behavior that appears to lead to positive consequences tends to be repeated, while behavior that appears to lead to neutral or negative consequences tends not be repeated. Which of the theories does this law describe? Give reasons for your answer.

Endnotes

1. D. M. McGregor, "The Human Side of Enterprise," *Management Review* 46, no. 11 (1957).

2. F. J. Landy and W. S. Becker, "Motivation Theory Reconsidered," in *Research in Organizational Behavior,* vol. 9, L. L. Cummings and B. M. Staw, eds. (Greenwich, Conn.: JAI Press, 1987), pp. 1–38.

3. R. A. Katzell and D. E. Thompson, "Work Motivation: Theory and Practice," *American Psychologist* 45, no. 2 (1990), pp. 144–53.

4. For the best discussion of this theory, see Frederick Herzberg, "One More Time: How Do You Motivate Employees?" *Harvard Business Review* 46 (January-February 1968), pp. 53–62.

5. For a critique of Herzberg's work, see E. E. Lawler III, *Motivation in Work Organizations* (Monterey, Calif.: Brooks/Cole, 1973), pp. 69–72.

6. The ERG theory discusses frustration of the growth needs. See C. P. Alderfer, *Existence, Relatedness, and Growth* (New York: Free Press, 1972); and C. P. Schneider and C. P. Alderfer, "Three Studies of Measures of Need Satisfaction in Organizations," *Administrative Science Quarterly,* December 1973, pp. 489–505.

7. A. H. Maslow, "A Theory of Human Motivation," *Psychological Review* 50 (1943), pp. 370–96.

8. C. P. Alderfer, *Existence, Relatedness, and Growth* (New York: Free Press, 1972).

9. C. P. Alderfer, "An Empirical Test of a New Theory of Human Needs," *Organizational Behavior and Human Performance* 4 (1969), pp. 142–75.

10. D. C. McClelland, "Power Motivation and Organizational Leadership," *Power: The Inner Experience* (New York: Livington Publishers, 1975), pp. 252–71.

11. D. G. Winter, *The Power Motive* (New York: Free Press, 1973), pp. 108–9.

12. L. L. Cummings and C. J. Berger, "Organization Structure: How Does It Influence Attitudes and Performance?" *Organizational Dynamics* 5 (Autumn 1976), pp. 34–49.

13. D. C. McClelland, "Power Motivation and Organizational Leadership," p. 269. Also see D. C. McClelland and R. S. Steele, *Motivation Workshops* (New York: General Learning Press, 1972) for the type of training program used.

14. U. Pareek, "Motivational Analysis of Organizational-Behavior (MAO-B)," *The 1986 Annual, Developing Human Resources* (1986), pp. 121–28.

15. J. S. Adams, "Toward An Understanding of Inequity," *Journal of Abnormal and Social Psychology* 67 (1963), pp. 422–36; J. Brockner, J. Greenberg, A. Brockner, J. Bortz, J. Davy, and C. Carter, "Equity Theory and Work Performance: Further Evidence of the Impact of Survivor Guilt," *Academy of Management Journal* 29 (1986), pp. 373–84; R. C. Huseman, J. D. Hatfield, and E. W. Miles, "A New Perspective on Equity Theory: The Equity Sensitivity Construct," *Academy of Management Review* 12 (1987), pp. 222–34; and J. Greenberg, "Cognitive Reevaluation of Outcomes in Response to Underpayment Inequity," *Academy of Management Journal* 32, no. 1 (1989), pp. 174–84.

16. See, for example, M. E. Tubbs, D. M. Boehne, and J. G. Gahl, "Expectancy, Valence, and Motivational Force Functions in Goal Setting Research: An Empirical Test," *Journal of Applied Psychology* 78, no. 3 (1993), pp. 361–73.

17. V. H. Vroom, *Work and Motivation* (New York: John Wiley & Sons, 1964).

18. M. J. Stahl and D. W. Grisby, "A Comparison of Unit, Subjectivity and Regression Measures of Second Level Valences in Expectancy Theory," *Decision Sciences* 18 (1987), pp. 62–72; and H. J. Klein, "An Integrated Control Theory Model of Work Behavior," *Academy of Management Review* 14, no. 2 (1989), pp. 150–72.

19. R. J. House, H. J. Shapiro, and M. A. Wahba, "Expectancy as a Predictor of Work Behavior and Attitudes: A Reevaluation of Empirical Evidence," *Decision Sciences* 5 (1974), pp.

481–506; and S. T. Connolly, ''Some Conceptual and Methodological Issues in Expectancy Theory Models of Work Performance,'' *Academy of Management Review* 1 (1976), pp. 37–47.

20. L. W. Porter and E. E. Lawler III, *Managerial Attitudes and Performance* (Burr Ridge, Ill.: Richard D. Irwin, 1968).

21. For an extensive discussion of the impact of groups on individuals in organizations, see J. Richard Hackman, ''Group Influences on Individuals,'' *Handbook of Industrial and Organizational Psychology,* Marvin D. Dunnette, ed. (Skokie, Ill.: Rand McNally, 1976), pp. 1455–1525. Hackman pays special attention to the effect of group norms and influences on member performance effectiveness.

22. A. M. O'leary-Kelly, J. J. Martocchio, and D. D. Frink, ''A Review of the Influence of Group Goals on Group Performance,'' *Academy of Management Journal* 37, no. 5 (1994), pp. 1285–301.

23. E. A. Locke, and G. P. Latham, *A Theory of Goal Setting and Task Performance* (Englewood Cliffs, N.J.: Prentice-Hall, 1990).

24. See, for example, G. P. Latham, and T. W. Lee, ''Goal Setting,'' in E. A. Locke, ed., *Generalized from Laboratory to Field Settings* (Lexington, Mass.: Lexington Books, 1986), pp. 100–17.

25. See, for example, D. E. Terpstra and E. J. Rozell, ''The Relationship of Goal Setting to Organizational Profitability,'' *Group & Organization Management* 19, no. 3 (1994), pp. 285–94.

26. S. Schachter, *The Psychology of Affiliation: Experimental Studies of the Sources of Gregariousness* (Stanford, Calif.: Stanford University Press, 1959), pp. 12–19.

27. ''Boring Jobs Are Hardest on Health, A Study of 23 Occupations Reveals,'' *ISR Newsletter,* Institute for Social Research, University of Michigan, Ann Arbor, Spring 1975, pp. 5–6.

28. Ibid., p. 6.

29. Two thoughtful and comprehensive books on the subject have been written by J. R. Blasi, *Employee Ownership: Revolution or Ripoff* (Cambridge, Mass.: Ballinger, 1988); *The New Owners* (New York: Harper Business, 1993).

30. T. R. Marsh and D. E. McAllister, ''ESOP Table: A Survey of Companies with Employee Ownership Plans,'' *Journal of Corporation Law* 6, no. 3 (1981), pp. 552–623.

31. *ESOP Survey: 1990* (Washington, D.C.: ESOP Association of America, 1990).

32. M. Trachman, *Employee Ownership and Corporate Growth in High Technology Companies* (Oakland, Calif.: National Center for Employee Ownership Publications, 1985).

33. D. Eden, *Pygmalion in Management: Productivity as Self-Fulfilling Prophecy* (Lexington, Mass.: Lexington Books, 1990), p. 70.

34. D. Eden, ''Pygmalion, Goal Setting, and Expectancy: Compatible Ways to Boost Productivity,'' *Academy of Management Review* 13, no. 4 (1988), pp. 639–52; D. Eden, ''Self-Fulfilling Prophecy as a Management Tool: Harnessing Pygmalion,'' *Academy of Management Review* 6 (1984), pp. 64–73; and D. Eden and A. B. Shani, ''Pygmalion Goes to Boot Camp: Expectancy, Leadership, and Trainee Performance,'' *Journal of Applied Psychology* 67 (1982), pp. 194–99.

35. E. E. Lawler III, ''The Individualized Organization: Problems and Promise.'' © 1974 by the Regents of the University of California. Reprinted from *California Management Review* 17, no. 2 (1974), p. 90 (conclusion) by permission of the Regents.

36. E. A. Locke, *The Myth of Behavior Mod in Organizations,'' Academy of Management Review,* October 1977.

37. J. T. Spence, ''Achievement American Style, The Rewards and Costs of Individualism,'' *American Psychologist,* December 1985, pp. 1285–94.

38. A. Howard, Keitaro Shudo, and Miyo Umeshima, ''Motivation and Values among Japanese and American Managers,'' *Personnel Psychology* 36 (1983), pp. 883–98.

39. See, for example, O. Shenkar and S. Ronen, ''Structure and Importance of Work Goals among Managers in the People's Republic of China,'' *Academy of Management Journal* 30 (1987), pp. 564–76; and M. M. Yang, ''Between State and Society: The Construction of Cooporateness in a Chinese Socialist Factory,'' *The Australian Journal of Chinese Affairs* 22 (1989), pp. 36–60.

40. See, for example, P. Jin, ''Work Motivation and Productivity in Voluntarily Formed Work Teams: A Field Study in China,'' *Organizational Behavior & Human Decision Processes* 54 (1993), pp. 133–55.

41. N. J. Adler, *International Dimensions of Organizational Behavior* (Boston: Kent, 1986), pp. 129–30.

Activity 6–4: Motivation through Goal Setting

Objectives:

a. To explore problems of managing individuals according to their differences.

b. To provide a model for coaching by goal setting.

Task 1:

Individuals are to form dyads with someone outside of their own team. (*Note:* Participants usually enjoy a change at this point in the course.)

Tear out Appendix G, the general information sheet for "Motivation through Goal Setting." The instructor will read this aloud while the class follows.

Dyads will decide who is to play Chris Birch, the supervisor, and who is to be Pat King, the professional employee.

Turn to your role assignment sheet in Appendix G and tear it out, taking care not to look at the role to be played by your partner. Study your role for about 10 minutes, thinking how you would play it.
(Time for introduction and study: 20 minutes)

Task 2:

The instructor will start the role playing by announcing that Pat has just entered the chief's office for the appointment that Pat requested. Play your role naturally, based upon how you would feel if you were in the situation described. When facts or events arise that are not covered by the roles, make up things that are consistent with the way it might be in a real-life situation.
(Time for role playing: 10 minutes)

Task 3:

When the role playing is stopped, form triads among those who played Birch or those who played Pat. Triads are to discuss the following questions:

(1) How did you feel about being in this situation?

(2) What could Birch or King have done to lessen this problem in the first place?

(3) What things did the other dyad member do that made it easier for you or more difficult for you?

(4) What kinds of solutions did you agree upon?

(Time: 10 minutes)

Discussion led by instructor:

Questions are to be taken one at a time and are to be responded to first by King triads and then by Birch triads to get at the differences in perception arising from the roles. (See *Instructor's Manual* for summary.)
(Time: 20 minutes. For 50-minute class sessions, class discussion can take place immediately after the role playing without the triad part of the exercise.)

Activity 6–5: Motivational Analysis of Organization-Behavior (MAO-B)

Objectives:

a. To examine a behavioral model of motivation.

b. To provide students with the opportunity to diagnose and analyze their own motivation.

c. To compute individuals' operating effectiveness.

Task 1:

Individuals working alone should complete and score the survey.

Task 2:

Individuals in a small group are to share their scores and interpret the results. Each group is to complete the following tasks:

a. Identify common themes.
b. Discuss the implications of individuals' motivation to team performance.
c. Develop an action plan to overcome the motivational issues.

Motivational Analysis of Organizations-Behavior (MAO-B) Inventory

Instructions: This inventory can help you to understand how different motivations can affect your behavior and your performance at work. There are no "right" or "wrong" responses; the inventory will reflect your own perceptions of how you act at work so you will gain the most value from it if you answer honestly. Do not spend too much time on any one item; generally, your first reaction is the most accurate.

Read each statement below and decide which of the numbered columns to the right best describes how often you engage in the behavior or have the feeling described. Circle the appropriate number next to each statement to indicate your response.

	Rarely/ Never	Sometimes/ Occasionally	Often/ Frequently	Usually/ Always
1. I enjoy working on moderately difficult (challenging) tasks and goals.	1	2	3	4
2. I am overly emotional.	1	2	3	4
3. I am forceful in my arguments.	1	2	3	4
4. I refer matters to my superiors.	1	2	3	4
5. I keep close track of things (monitor action).	1	2	3	4
6. I make contributions to charity and help those in need.	1	2	3	4
7. I set easy goals and achieve them.	1	2	3	4
8. I relate very well to people.	1	2	3	4
9. I am preoccupied with my own ideas and am a poor listener.	1	2	3	4
10. I follow my ideals.	1	2	3	4
11. I demand conformity from the people who work for or with me.	1	2	3	4
12. I take steps to develop the people who work for me.	1	2	3	4
13. I strive to exceed performance/targets.	1	2	3	4
14. I ascribe more importance to personal relationships than to organizational matters.	1	2	3	4
15. I build on the ideas of my subordinates or others.	1	2	3	4
16. I seek the approval of my superiors.	1	2	3	4
17. I ensure that things are done according to plan.	1	2	3	4
18. I consider the difficulties of others even at the expense of the task.	1	2	3	4
19. I am afraid of making mistakes.	1	2	3	4
20. I share my feelings with others.	1	2	3	4
21. I enjoy arguing and winning arguments.	1	2	3	4
22. I have genuine respect for experienced persons.	1	2	3	4
23. I admonish people for not completing tasks.	1	2	3	4
24. I go out of my way to help the people who work for me.	1	2	3	4
25. I search for new ways to overcome difficulties.	1	2	3	4
26. I have difficulty in expressing negative feelings to others.	1	2	3	4
27. I set myself as an example and model for others.	1	2	3	4
28. I hesitate to make hard decisions.	1	2	3	4
29. I define roles and procedures for the people who work for me.	1	2	3	4
30. I undergo personal inconvenience for the sake of others.	1	2	3	4
31. I am more conscious of my limitations or weaknesses than of my strengths.	1	2	3	4
32. I take interest in matters of personal concern to the people who work for me.	1	2	3	4
33. I am *laissez-faire* in my leadership style (do not care how things happen).	1	2	3	4
34. I learn from those who are senior to me.	1	2	3	4
35. I centralize most tasks to ensure that things are done properly.	1	2	3	4
36. I have empathy and understanding for the people who work for me.	1	2	3	4
37. I want to know how well I have been doing, and I use feedback to improve myself.	1	2	3	4
38. I avoid conflict in the interest of group feelings.	1	2	3	4
39. I provide new suggestions and ideas.	1	2	3	4
40. I try to please others.	1	2	3	4

41. I explain systems and procedures clearly to the people who work for me.	1	2	3	4
42. I tend to take responsibility for others' work in order to help them.	1	2	3	4
43. I show low self-confidence.	1	2	3	4
44. I recognize and respond to the feelings of others.	1	2	3	4
45. I receive credit for work done in a team.	1	2	3	4
46. I seek help from those who know the subject.	1	2	3	4
47. In case of difficulties, I rush to correct things.	1	2	3	4
48. I develop teamwork among the people who work for me.	1	2	3	4
49. I work effectively under pressure of deadlines.	1	2	3	4
50. I am uneasy and less productive when working alone.	1	2	3	4
51. I give credit and recognition to others.	1	2	3	4
52. I look for support for my actions and proposals.	1	2	3	4
53. I enjoy positions of authority.	1	2	3	4
54. I hesitate to take strong actions because of human considerations.	1	2	3	4
55. I complain about difficulties and problems.	1	2	3	4
56. I take the initiative in making friends with my colleagues.	1	2	3	4
57. I am quite conscious of status symbols such as furniture and size of office.	1	2	3	4
58. I like to solicit ideas from others.	1	2	3	4
59. I tend to form small groups to influence decisions.	1	2	3	4
60. I like to accept responsibility in the group's work.	1	2	3	4

Instructions: Transfer your responses from the MAO-B inventory to the appropriate spaces on this sheet. If you circled the number 2 to the right of item #1, enter a 2 in the space after the number 1 below; if you circled a 4 as your response to item #13, enter a 4 in the space to the right of the number 13 below, and so on until you have entered all your responses in the space below.

A	B	C	D	E	F
1. _____	3. _____	5. _____	10. _____	12. _____	8. _____
13. _____	15. _____	17. _____	22. _____	24. _____	20. _____
25. _____	27. _____	29. _____	34. _____	36. _____	32. _____
37. _____	39. _____	41. _____	46. _____	48. _____	44. _____
49. _____	51. _____	53. _____	58. _____	60. _____	56. _____
A total _____	B total _____	C total _____	D total _____	E total _____	F total _____
a	**b**	**c**	**d**	**e**	**f**
7. _____	9. _____	11. _____	4. _____	6. _____	2. _____
19. _____	21. _____	23. _____	16. _____	18. _____	14. _____
31. _____	33. _____	35. _____	28. _____	30. _____	26. _____
43. _____	45. _____	47. _____	40. _____	42. _____	38. _____
55. _____	57. _____	59. _____	52. _____	54. _____	50. _____
a total _____	b total _____	c total _____	d total _____	e total _____	f total _____

Now sum the numbers that you have entered in each vertical column and enter the totals in the spaces provided. These totals are your scores for the approach-avoidance dimensions of each of the six primary motivators of people's behavior on the job. Transfer those totals to the appropriate spaces in the two middle columns below.

Achievement	A (approach) _____	a (avoidance) _____	OEQ _____
Influence	B (approach) _____	b (avoidance) _____	OEQ _____
Control	C (approach) _____	c (avoidance) _____	OEQ _____
Dependence	D (approach) _____	d (avoidance) _____	OEQ _____
Extension	E (approach) _____	e (avoidance) _____	OEQ _____
Affiliation	F (approach) _____	f (avoidance) _____	OEQ _____

To compute your operating effectiveness quotient (OEQ) for each motivator, find the value for your approach (capital letter) score for the motivator along the top row of the table that follows, and then find your avoidance (lower-case letter) score for that motivator in the left column. The number in the cell that intersects the column and row is your OEQ score for the motivator. Transfer that score to the tally marked "OEQ" at the bottom of the previous page. Do this for each motivator.

Avoidance Scores	Approach Scores															
	5	**6**	**7**	**8**	**9**	**10**	**11**	**12**	**13**	**14**	**15**	**16**	**17**	**18**	**19**	**20**
5	0	100	100	100	100	100	100	100	100	100	100	100	100	100	100	100
6	0	50	67	75	80	83	85	87	89	90	91	92	92	93	93	97
7	0	33	50	60	67	71	75	78	80	82	83	85	86	87	87	88
8	0	25	40	50	57	62	67	70	73	75	77	78	80	81	82	83
9	0	20	33	43	50	55	60	64	67	69	71	73	75	76	78	79
10	0	17	28	37	44	50	54	58	61	64	67	69	70	72	74	75
11	0	14	25	33	40	45	50	54	59	60	62	65	67	68	70	71
12	0	12	22	30	36	42	46	50	53	56	59	61	63	65	67	68
13	0	11	20	27	33	38	43	47	50	53	55	58	60	62	64	65
14	0	10	18	25	31	36	40	44	47	50	53	55	57	59	61	62
15	0	9	17	23	28	33	37	41	44	47	50	52	54	56	58	60
16	0	8	15	21	27	31	35	39	42	45	48	50	52	54	56	58
17	0	8	14	20	25	29	33	37	40	43	45	48	50	52	54	56
18	0	7	13	19	23	28	32	35	38	41	43	46	48	50	52	54
19	0	7	12	18	22	26	30	33	36	39	42	44	46	48	50	52
20	0	6	12	17	21	25	29	32	35	37	40	42	44	46	48	50

Operating Effectiveness Quotients

When you have completed this process for all of your scores, you will have a numerical picture of what typically motivates your behavior at work, whether you respond positively (approach) or negatively (avoidance) to each of the six typical motivators, and how your responses to each motivator influence your operating effectiveness.

Source: This questionnaire was designed by Dr. Udai Pareek. The survey is reprinted here with permission of University Associates, San Diego, Calif. 92121. All rights are reserved.

Activity 6–6: The Centurion Finance Case

Centurion Finance Company, a company specializing in making personal loans, was one of the largest Canadian finance companies. The company had over 300 branches in Canada as well as a small operation in England, which had seven branch offices. This case deals with the operation of the division in the United Kingdom.

The personal loan business involved three activities: (1) *loan making,* which began with a customer's request for a loan, and continued with the investigation of the applicant's job, general background, and credit history; (2) *collections,* the contacting of customers (by phone, letter, or personal calls) who were delinquent in their loan payments; and (3) *business development,* visiting retail outlets and initiating finance plans with them. The greatest part of a branch's outstanding loans came from personal loans rather than finance plans.

People usually sought assistance from personal loan companies because they found themselves in financial difficulty and unable to borrow from a bank. The interest rates charged by personal loan companies were significantly higher than those charged by banks or savings and loan companies, a reflection of the differences in the risks involved in the loans the institutions made.

The essential challenge in the personal loan business was guessing right on marginal loan prospects. Prospective clients fell into three groups:

1. Good credit risks—those who had credit experience, job stability, and family responsibilities. This was by far the smallest group of customers because most of these people could obtain bank loans.
2. Medium credit risks—individuals who were deficient in one or more of the above areas.
3. Poor credit risks—those who lacked job stability, had poor credit experience, were overloaded with debt, were single, and had no fixed residence.

Segregating groups 1 and 3 was relatively simple. However, in order to be profitable, the loan company needed to determine which of the medium-risk types would repay a loan. Usually this involved significantly more than just a cursory examination of the applicant. It could involve checking with employers, neighbors, all of the credit bureaus, plus any other possible sources of information about the borrower. In the major urban areas in Canada, this investigation process had become almost routine due to the presence of fast, reliable credit-checking services. In England, however, the credit bureaus were both slow and less reliable. As a result, a great deal of digging and ingenuity was necessary in the investigation process there.

The U.K. Operation

The seven branches of Centurion Finance in the United Kingdom were located in Manchester, Nottingham, Croydon, Romford, Watford, Tottenham, and central London. Croyden, Romford, Watford, and Tottenham were in the greater London area.

Centurion started operations in England 10 years ago. An office on Bond Street, which was later moved around the corner to Oxford Street, was the beginning. Two Canadians from the head office were sent to England to begin operation of this branch. After eight months of operation, delinquency rates were extremely high and the branch was unprofitable. The analysis of the reliability of British credit-reporting agencies had been inadequate. Subsequently, more care was taken with investigations and, eventually, the branch became profitable. In the interim, four employees had been hired locally and a new branch was opened in the suburb of Croydon. Over the next eight years, five more branches were opened.

Fred O'Reilly, one of the original Englishmen hired at the first office in Bond Street, was the division manager. After working for the company for two years in

England, O'Reilly had gone to Canada and worked in company branches and at the head office for three years. He then returned to England as division manager. Reporting to him were the seven branch managers. In three of the branches, the manager was supported by two assistant managers. The other branches were supported by one assistant manager. Each assistant manager had two or three staff representatives reporting to him or her. Each branch had three to five staff representatives.

The branch manager's role had several dimensions. First, the branch manager was ultimately responsible for making a loan. Usually either the assistant manager or a staff representative interviewed the potential customer, completed the subsequent investigation, and made a recommendation to the manager. The branch manager was also responsible for coordinating business development and reducing delinquent customers. Business development was handled by the manager or the assistant manager, while delinquency reduction and collections were handled by the assistant manager and the staff representatives.

In England, the law placed restrictions on advertising by loan companies. Interest rates could not be stated, and literature pertaining to the borrowing of money could not be sent without authorization. Essentially, all that could be advertised was the company name, address, phone number, and the words *personal loans.* These restrictions, which did not exist in Canada, made increasing the total volume of personal loans somewhat difficult. The initiation of finance plans with retailers was totally dependent on personal calls.

In the larger branches, one of the staff representatives was usually assigned outside calls, which meant that he or she spent 65 to 70 percent of his or her time on calls to delinquent customers.

After individuals were hired by the company, they spent the first four or five months learning the business by studying the company manual and by assisting one of the staff representatives. They were gradually eased into the day-to-day branch routine under the supervision of the branch manager or the assistant manager.

The Transfer Policy

Employees in England were discouraged from emigrating to Canada to work for the parent company. One executive at the head office said that the reason for this unwritten policy was that "Canadians don't like to do business with someone with a British accent." He also mentioned the differences in operating conditions between England and Canada and the difficulty in adapting from one culture to another.

The manager of the Tottenham branch had the following comments:

> I have been with Centurion for six years now; I don't see any opportunities here for a while. There are three other managers with more seniority than I have and they are all relatively young. I asked Fred O'Reilly if I could be transferred to Canada where, I am quite sure, the opportunities for promotion would be substantially better because there are more branches, more divisions, and more jobs. Anyway, Fred told me that the company wouldn't guarantee me anything if I went to Canada—not even an assistant manager's position. That was discouraging to say the least.

Fred O'Reilly had this to say about the policy:

> It's bad, but then that's the way it is. We just can't have them all going to Canada. The head office doesn't like the prospects of being overrun. Besides, from what I've experienced, Canadians don't like being beaten out of a promotion by a Brit. I've spoken to headquarters about the situation, but I guess nothing can be done.
>
> I know that it's getting harder and harder to keep people on the job. They enter the company; go like a shot through the training, and after about seven or eight months realize that it will be a long haul before they reach manager or even assistant manager. At this point, they either let their work slide, doing just enough to get by, or they leave the company entirely. This means we've lost a lot of money in terms of the time spent training them. In fact, either way we get hurt. Right now, I know there are seven managers who are eyeing my job; but I'm still young and happen to like it here. I have lots of free time and it will be a while before I move on.

> Last year we had a manager's position open in Watford. I had to fire the manager there. The bastard was screwing the company. He had a fiddle going with a couple of used car dealers in the area. As a result of that mess, delinquency in that office was almost 25 percent. (The overall British delinquency rate was 7 percent, and the Canadian rate was 4 percent.)
>
> It just so happened that at this time there were three individuals working as assistant managers. They had all been hired at the same time. Each of them spotted the opening and worked for it. Outstandings in those three offices jumped, and their delinquencies fell. However, it came time to make the decision, and two people had to lose. What could I do? I explained to them that we would be opening more branches in the future, and I gave them a salary increase. There was nothing else that could be done; I just hope they would understand. The three men were all top notch; it was a hard decision to make.
>
> When it comes time to appoint a manager for the new branch, I know we're going to lose a good man. We've got a real problem here! How do you keep them motivated when the outlook for promotion is this bad. I've tried shuffling managers and assistants around; I've created extra assistant manager positions, but it just seems that anything I try doesn't quite have the effect of a real promotion. I wish to hell something could be done!

Nigel Martin, the assistant manager who received the promotion, said that he felt he had lost two good friends when he got the job. He said that in the time since the choice had been made, relations between them had gotten slowly better, but he felt that things would never be quite the same. Martin also made a comment that had been made by other managers: "When I finally realized I had gotten it, the manager's job, that is, there was a hell of a letdown. I remember saying to myself, Where do I go from here?"

Allan Sinfield, one of the two assistant managers who did not get the promotion, commented that when he realized a position was opening up he had "worked his head off." He expressed disappointment at being passed over. When asked about the future, he said, "I don't know what will happen if I don't get the promotion the next time."

Employee turnover figures reflected the difficulties O'Reilly faced. Three of the 10 assistant managers had left the company last year, a 30 percent turnover rate. The Canadian turnover rate for the same position was half as high. Of the 25 staff representatives, 12 had resigned last year, a 45 percent turnover. The Canadian turnover rate for the same position was 10 percent. In terms of purchasing power, company salaries in the United Kingdom were equivalent to those in Canada. While the starting salary for staff representatives was not high, it was about 20 percent above average wage rates in the community. The top branch manager's salary was three times the starting staff representative's salary.

Company growth in England was impossible to project accurately, but all the branches were increasing their outstanding loans significantly. The head office had more branches planned, but as yet no specific details were available. Fred O'Reilly thought it would be at least eight months until the next one opened, and after that, probably a year before the next branch opened.

As branch outstandings increased, more staff representatives were needed. Centurion had been hiring about three individuals every two months in order to cover the increase in workload and the high turnover.

There were a great number of personal loan companies in England; however, most were very small, with only one or two offices. Very few were as large as Centurion. One other North American finance company had operations in England. The American company, Futura Finance, had been operating in England for six years. It had opened 12 branches. Although no reports were available on Futura's profitability, it was rumored that the American company was going to open two more branches within the next six months.

Discussion Questions

1. What are the potential causes of the company's turnover?
2. Is promotion the only motivation involved in situations like these? What other motives might exist? How can the company tap them?

3. If you were Fred O'Reilly and headquarters refused to consider changing the company's transfer policy, what alternatives would you have for dealing with this situation?
4. What would your plan of action be? What would you do? When would you do it; that is, what specific steps would you take? What benchmarks for success would you use, and how long would you expect it would take to get results?
5. Why do you favor this plan over the alternatives?

7 Perception and Attribution

Learning Objectives

After completing this module you should be able to

1. Describe the perceptual process.
2. State the internal and external determinants of individual perception.
3. Appreciate the impact that perceptual problems have on organizational life.
4. Understand your own perceptual process and barriers to accurate perception.
5. Describe how the attribution process influences perception and individual behavior.
6. Gain insights into the role that Pygmalion and self-fulfilling prophecy can play in the perceptual process at work.
7. Understand the perceptual challenges in management.
8. Identify the basic managerial actions that can help overcome the barriers for accurate perception.

List of Key Concepts

Attribution process
Cognitive dissonance
Denial
Distortion
Expectancy effects
Left-brain mode of functioning
Perception
Perceptual process
Premature closure
Projection
Rationalization
Right-brain mode of functioning
Stereotypes

Module Outline

Premodule Preparation

The instructor may assign either one or a combination of the following as a presession activity: Task 1 of Activity 7–1 (''Exploring Perceptual Issues via Dan Dunwoodie's Problem''); the questions at the end of Activity 7–3 (''The Elaine Martin Case''); and Task 1 of Activity 7–5 (''Male–Female Interface on Women in Management'').

Activity 7–1: Exploring Perceptual Issues via Dan Dunwoodie's Problem

Objective:

To have small groups identify and define the problem in a case study so that the process can be studied through the analysis of contrasting results presented by the groups.

Task 1:

Participants are to read the case study "Dan Dunwoodie's Problem" which follows. Each team is to answer the following three questions on the case study:

(1) What is the problem?

(2) What is the principal cause?

(3) What action should Dan Dunwoodie take?

(Time: 15 minutes)

Task 2:

Each team first presents its results on problem definition, which the instructor lists on the board. Then the same procedure is followed for causes. After these have been listed, the action recommendations are given and listed. During the process of listing the contrasting results from the various teams, team members are not to challenge or discuss the solutions. Questions may be asked for clarification. When the data are all out, there should be open challenges and discussion of differing points of view and of the feasibility of the suggested actions.

The class should develop at least one criterion for deciding upon the problem; a decision should be reached as to what would be the best solution from the standpoint of the criteria developed. (Time: 30 minutes)

Case Study: Dan Dunwoodie's Problem

Up to this point I have been doing very well. At 27 years of age I am chief of an economic analysis branch in the United Automobile Manufacturing Company. I was hired personally by John Roman, my division chief, who interviewed me at the university where I was completing my MBA. John had expressed interest in several of my qualifications: BA in economics from an outstanding university, four years of work experience as an analyst in industry, and a specialty in information systems while working on my MBA.

When I entered on duty three months ago, John gave me guidance as follows:

> Economic analysis functions and processing at United need updating. Analysts are substantive experts and do not comprehend the importance of management, nor the possible application of information systems to managerial decision making. They keep insisting that judgmental processes cannot be automated; they resist suggestions that they can augment their activities by using computers. After you have had three to six months to learn your job, you are to come up with recommendations for organizational and procedural changes in your branch. You are to keep in close touch with your peers, the other branch chiefs in the division, all of whom have been with the company for five or more years.

(Their responsibilities were almost identical to mine, except each branch had different economic specialties.)

I assumed my responsibilities with great energy and soon saw many possibilities for developing the effectiveness of my branch. I worked evenings and weekends on a new plan. As I developed ideas, I would try them out on each of the other branch chiefs. They were helpful and responsive. One objection did arise from Carl Carlson, chief of

Exhibit 1

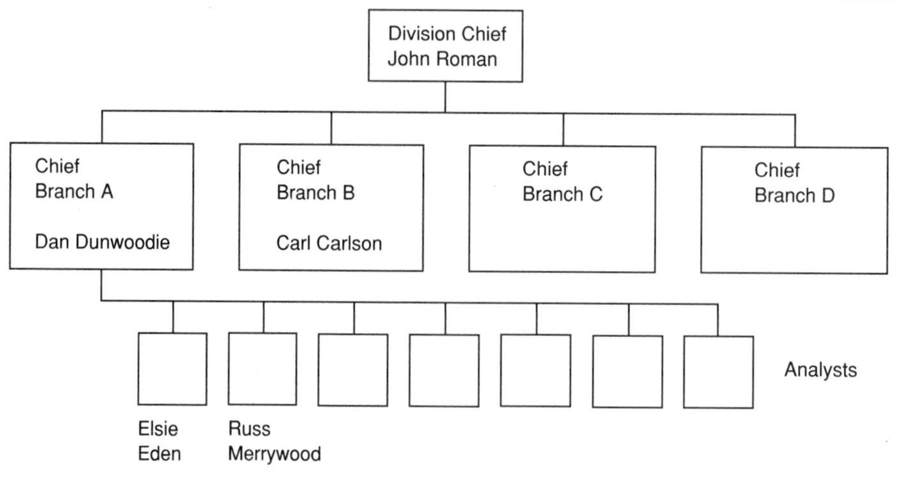

Branch B, who criticized some of the information systems suggestions. (Carl was regarded in the division as the next man in line for John's job. See Exhibit 1.)

At the end of three months with United, I presented my plan to my entire branch in a briefing session, complete with a statement of objectives, charts, and expected results. In response to my request for their reactions, two people spoke up. One was Elsie Eden, who was a contemporary of John and the branch chiefs. (I had heard she would have had my job if she had been willing to take an extensive computer training program.) The other was Russ Merrywood, also an old-timer, who had been passed over for advancement. (I had also heard that Russ had money and was not too committed to his job, although I find that his work is excellent.) My plan was well thought out, and further clarification of various details appeared to satisfy all questions raised.

On a Wednesday afternoon, I gave the same oral briefing to John (division chief), who showed enthusiasm and pleasure. He promised me an early decision and asked for a copy of my written report for further study. On Thursday afternoon, I received the report back with the notation, "Sounds great. Proceed soonest with entire plan with the exception of paragraph 6, which I wish to study further." (Paragraph 6 contained an information system suggestion concerning which Carl had expressed disapproval to Dan.)

I spent Friday in meetings with my branch making initial plans for implementing the new program. Over the weekend I continued on my own to make final plans.

Early Monday morning I was asked to come to the division chief's office. I then learned that John had reversed his decision, and no changes were to be put into effect at this time. John appeared rather brusk and said he did not have time to discuss the decision. Later that day, I learned that John had attended a dinner party at Russ's house over the weekend.

Activity 7–2: Mirroring Gender: Perceptual Exploration

Objectives:

a. To heighten students' awareness of their perception of themselves, their perceptions of members of the opposite sex, and the perceptions of themselves by the opposite sex.

b. To elicit data for improved working relationships between the sexes.

Task 1:

Students are to be divided into same-sex groups of not more than seven students in a group. (Ideal size is five students to a group.) Each group is to respond to two questions:

a. How do you see yourselves as women (or men)? Generate a list on a flip chart paper using words or short phrases that describe your characteristics or traits individually as a woman (or man) or as a group of women (or men). For example, I see women as being intuitive, good listeners.

b. Make a second list that describes how you think members of the opposite sex see you as a group, or as a member of your sex. For example, I think men see us—as women—as nurturing, chatty, always wanting to shop, . . .

In the development of these lists, students should use a brainstorming process that eliminates the need for agreement or consensus, that includes each individual's contributions, and that does not involve any judgment or evaluation on anyone's part. (Time: 15 minutes)

Task 2 (Class Sharing):

The lists should be taped to the walls of the room for all to see. Each group reads its list aloud to the entire class. The only discussion at this stage should be questions of clarification or explication.
(Time: 10 minutes)

Task 3:

a. The students should look at their lists and silently reflect on what is there. The students are to try to identify and write down some notes about the tone (negative and positive), intensity, patterns, and themes.

b. Individuals are to share their reflections in the groups.

c. The groups are to address the following question: What would be the ideal working relationship with the opposite sex?

(Time: 10 minutes)

Task 4:

a. Spokespersons will report to the class.

b. The instructor will facilitate further discussion related to the work, content, and process of some of the issues that were raised.

(Time: 10 minutes or longer if time is available)

Source: This activity was contributed by Dr. Judith White, Loyola Marymount University, Management Department, Los Angeles, Calif. 90045-2899. We are grateful to Dr. White.

Introduction

Perception and attribution, the third major core concepts for understanding behavior in organizations (the first two being diversity-personality and motivation), provide a framework and a useful tool for understanding effectiveness at the individual, group, intergroup, and organizational levels. The subject has been dealt with indirectly up to this point. Underlying the dialogue process of Module 2 was the question of what differences existed in the way the participants and the professor were perceiving important contextual aspects of the subject to be studied. The study of leadership styles in Module 3 included the question of how managers perceive themselves and how they are perceived by others. Small group membership within the human and formal organizations was seen to provide the basis for self-identity and emergent role system. Understanding motivation involved focus on a person's self-image.

Perception and Perceptual Differences in Daily Life

Perception is a fascinating subject that is being studied in many areas of daily life. The politicians are concerned about how they are perceived by the public and how their images can be improved and maintained; the U.S. diplomat wants to know how representatives of other nations with whom he or she will negotiate perceive this country; the advertiser must determine how ads and products will be seen by consumers. Law students, in many schools, are required to take courses in psychology and psychiatry to improve their self-awareness. As one law school dean said, "When you go into the courtroom, you are part of the problem; the better you know what part of it you are, the better you can control and influence the situation." In mental health, the therapist attempts to help the patient build a favorable self-concept and change his or her self-image so that it is more consistent with the way the person is perceived by others, thus reducing misunderstandings in interpersonal relations. Intelligence officers must know how their agents perceive themselves in relation to the operation in which they are engaged and how they see the intelligence officer and his or her country, in order to understand, predict, and control the agent's activities.

Everyone is aware that we all see things somewhat differently, but this is a complicated and difficult area—few people are aware of the differences to the degree that they actually exist. Blind spots develop to obscure specific happenings. Police surrounded a hotel and conducted a shootout with snipers firing from the hotel roof; some police officers were killed. Only one body was found on the roof after the firing stopped; the other suspects presumably escaped during the battle. It was not until some weeks later that the official investigation revealed that only one assailant was ever on that roof. The police and the television reporters, under the pressure of excitement, "saw" several assailants firing. Were police officers actually killed by the ricocheting bullets of other police in this setting, which maximized perceptual distortion?

Blind spots can distort a person's perception consistently over time, as one of this book's authors has become painfully aware of from time to time. He and his wife attended a husband–wife workshop for helping couples become more aware of one another. The first exercise required two couples to get together; each person in the foursome was to take a turn saying what he or she appreciated most about his or her spouse. The author spoke for several minutes of the love, trust, and support he had received over years of married life. After all four had completed their turns, his wife reproached him, saying, "I never thought you would say what you did about me." When asked why she felt this way, she replied, "I have done some good things with real estate. I have designed and built a home. I know how to run a home more economically than almost anyone I know." She also enumerated other accomplishments.

What she was saying was that her self-esteem and self-appreciation were based on a lot more than she heard her spouse say he appreciated in her. She had abilities and skills that made her an effective person and that she had developed well over the years. She was also saying that the author was not fully aware of her abilities and that appreciation for love and affection were only part of her needs. The exchange in the supportive atmosphere of the workshop, where he was prepared to hear it, made him realize that even after years of married life, he did not appreciate her as a complete person, and he was perceiving her differently than she was perceiving herself. Learning of this enduring blind spot proved to be a most valuable discovery and provided the basis for dialoguing on the marriage relationship for some time thereafter. The women's liberation and equal opportunity movements have made men very conscious that women, like men, want recognition for their abilities, talents, and competence, and that women deplore sexist stereotypes of women.

Another example of perceptual differences is the differing recollections that are brought out dramatically in legal hearings in which two or more witnesses are interrogated on the same event. The degree of differences in the testimony varies, but some difference almost always exists.

There are many applications of the concept of perceptual differences to management theory and to the various levels of effectiveness. Some of these will be discussed following the section on determinants of perception.

Determinants of Perception

Perception can be broadly defined as a process by which an individual screens, selects, organizes, and interprets stimuli. As such, an individual's perception is what an individual is experiencing at a given moment, based on a number of factors. These include data being received from the five senses (sight, smell, taste, touch, and hearing), data in the memory system, emotions, feelings, needs, wants, and goals. It is important to realize that what individuals experience at any given moment is based primarily upon what goes on inside them (the internal factors affecting perception) rather than what is happening outside them in the external world (physical objects and social interactions).

The degree of influence on the individual of internal and external factors is illustrated in Figure 7–1. It can be assumed that the more pressure the individual is under from physical or mental stress or from external sources (noises, violence, and so on), the greater will be the influence of the internal factors. Figure 7–1 is not intended to be exhaustive; it presents only broad areas for consideration relevant to the determinants of perception. The following sections discuss the internal factors listed in the figure.

Figure 7–1 Relationship between Factors Determining Perception That Are Internal to the Individual and Those That Are in the External World

Internal factors	External factors
Physiological	Physical objects
Past experience	People
Psychological	Social interactions
Motivation	
Defense mechanisms	
High percentage of influence	Low percentage of influence

Physiological Factors

It is impossible to separate physiological and psychological factors, they are so closely blended. No real purpose could be served by trying to make precise distinctions. We are all aware that our outlook, abilities, and emotions are affected by the state of our health. The effects of drugs (particularly LSD and other hallucinatory agents) on perception have been widely publicized.

An example of a physiological cause of peceptual differences is color blindness. One student reported his experience of undergoing an Army physical examination during induction. Standing in line at a medical station, he could hear those ahead of him calling out "49" as they looked at a printed chart of different-colored circles of various sizes. When his turn came, he looked at the patterns formed among the color spots and called out the number he saw, which was 36. He was pulled out of the line for further testing and learned that he was partially color blind and was not perceiving shades of green and red, although he could identify the vivid basic colors. Thinking back on past experiences, he recalled that he had at times not seen certain aspects of distant scenes reported by others, but he had not thought too much of it. Once the test proved his disability, he became aware that he often was not experiencing what others were experiencing in this regard. Many subtle differences between people exist and influence how they see things, but there may be no awareness of the physiological factors that account for the differences.

Past Experience

It is widely hypothesized that everything experienced by the human being from birth on (some say from in the womb on) is stored in the memory system and is available for recall under certain conditions. Often discussed in this regard is the research of Wilder Penfield, M.D., at McGill University's Department of Neurology and Neurosurgery and the Montreal Neurological Institute in Montreal.[1] Penfield's patients were fully conscious when he conducted exploratory research of the cerebral cortex during surgery in which local anesthesia was used. Using an electrode to stimulate different regions of the brain, Penfield found the patients could vividly recall, or it might be appropriate to say "relive," remote past experiences. Penfield describes his findings as follows:

> Recollections which are clearly derived from a patient's past memory can sometimes be forced upon him by the stimulating electrode. The psychical experience, thus produced, stops when the electrode is withdrawn and may repeat itself when the electrode is reapplied. Such psychical results have been obtained from stimulation of certain areas of the temporal cortex, but from no other areas of the brain.
>
> A series of brief examples may be given.
>
> First is the case of S. B. Stimulation at point 19 in the first convolution of the right temporal lobe caused him to say, "There was a piano there and someone playing. I could hear the song, you know."
>
> When the point was stimulated again without warning, he said, "Someone speaking to another, and he mentioned a name, but I could not understand it. . . . It was like a dream." The point was stimulated a third time, also without warning. He then observed spontaneously, "Yes, 'Oh Marie, Oh Marie!' . . . Someone is singing it." When the point was stimulated a fourth time, he heard the same song and explained that it was the theme song of a certain radio program.
>
> When point 16 was stimulated, he said, while the electrode was being held in place, "Something brings back a memory. I can see Seven-Up Bottling Company . . . Harrison Bakery." He was then warned that he was being stimulated, but the electrode was not applied. He replied, "Nothing."
>
> When in another case, that of D. F., a point on the superior surface of the right temporal lobe was stimulated within the fissure of Sylvius, the patient heard a specific popular song being played as though by an orchestra. Repeated stimulations reproduced the same music. While the electrode was kept in place, she hummed the tune, chorus and verse, thus accompanying the music she heard.
>
> The patient, L.G., was caused to experience "something," he said, that had "happened" to him before. Stimulation at another temporal point caused him to see a man and a dog walking along a road near his home in the country.
>
> Another woman heard a voice which she did not quite understand when the first temporal convolution was stimulated initially. When the electrode was reapplied to approximately the same point, she heard a voice distinctly calling, "Jimmie, Jimmie, Jimmie." Jimmie was the nickname of the young husband to whom she had been married recently.
>
> In these examples it seems to make little difference whether the original experience was fact, dream or fancy; it was a single recollection that the electrode evoked, not a mixture of memories or a generalization. The electrical current was often of not greater voltage than the minimum, or threshold, value required to secure responses from the Rolandic sensorimotor cortex.[2]

Penfield goes on to discuss the vivid nature of the recollections of his patients:

> Under the compelling influence of the stimulating electrode, a familiar experience appears in a patient's consciousness whether he desires to focus his attention upon it or not. A song goes through his mind, probably as he heard it on a certain occasion; he finds himself a part of a specific situation, which progresses and evolves just as in the original situation. It is, to him, the act of a familiar play, and he is himself both an actor and the audience.
>
> The subject feels again the emotion which the situation originally produced in him, and he is aware of the same interpretations, true or false, which he himself gave to the experience in the first place. Thus, evoked recollection is not the exact photographic or phonographic reproduction of past scenes and events. It is reproduction of what the patient saw, heard, felt and understood.
>
> In many cases, it has been evident that the evoked memory is more detailed than anything the patient could possibly summon for his own consideration. It is not fused with other, similar experiences. In this respect, evoked recollection differs from the normal recollection of the past, where single experiences may be indistinguishable from other, similar experiences.[3]

Our knowledge in the area of memory and recall is most limited, and we do not know the extent to which, or whether, all experience is recorded in the brain. But it is safe to assume from this and much other research that the memory traces are vastly greater than any individual is conscious of, and these traces do affect perceptions and actions even though the individual may not be aware of them.

One mechanistic analogy would be to liken the mind to a computer system in which there is a large memory storage bank. In order to use these data, a program must be written giving the directions. Instead of programs, the mind has coding systems that organize the memory data into units; these are usable in the perceptual processes when the brain gives the directions for their use.

Codes of Past Experience

''Society'' is a meaningfully organized element in the mental context; a complex system of expectations exists in each person's brain of how people should, ought, and must behave under both general and specific circumstances. It does not exist out there in the real world, but only in the expectation system of all members as to how they are to interact with one another. This includes expectations organized around social roles, norms, customs, symbols, and so on. Life around us is automatically meaningful because of this major aspect of the memory system.

Among other important blocks of codes are knowledge, facts, theories, beliefs, attitudes, and language. These are codes that are widely shared by people in the same society or in subgroupings of that society. There are also many codes of past experience that are unique to the individual and shared with only a few or with no one. The overlap between the coding systems of people with similar experiences is a fundamental requirement of communication. (This is explored in Module 8 on communication.)

Psychological Factors

Of the many psychological factors that could be discussed, we will focus on only two: motivation and defense mechanisms. Abilities, skills, intelligence, and the cognitive processes are among others that could be included here.

Motivation

Feelings and Emotions: All experience is accompanied by emotions and feelings, which are integral components of the learning process. The individual is not aware of this most of the time. As you read this text, feelings you have had in the past toward education, classrooms, teachers, or your parents' attitudes toward learning are all present and influence what you are reading. Codes of past experience also have a feeling component. A good classroom demonstration to alert students to this can be done with a dollar bill borrowed from one of the class members. The instructor holds the bill up before the group and asks if any one has any feelings about it. The response is low. He then proceeds to tear the dollar through the center. There are gasps: ''You simply don't do that. It's against the law.'' All of the emotion learned in past experiences with money is brought forth, even though a moment earlier no one felt he or she had any feelings about the dollar.

The attachment of feelings to words becomes evident in learning a foreign language. In English, the phrase *I am hot* is socially acceptable to express the feeling that the atmospheric temperature is too high. In German, the identical phrase, *''Ich bin heiss,''* has only the meaning that the person is sexually aroused. An American making the translation to express the former condition would find the Germans reacting in ways other than expected. (In German, the way to comment on high atmospheric temperature would be *''Es ist mir warm,''* or ''It is warm to me.'')

As tourists in a foreign country, people frequently find they can spend the local currency like play money; they have not developed the feelings about it that they have about their own currency. American children going to live abroad will learn easily all the dirty words of the new country and shout them about in public, an activity they would not do with opprobrious language in English. When cautioned on this, their reaction could be that it is a fun language; they have not learned the ''no-no'' feelings they had with such words in their own language.

The point to stress here is that feelings and emotions affect your perceptions all the time, even though you might not be aware of it.

Goals, Needs, and Wants: What your goals and needs are at a specific time are major determinants in perception. The principle that *perception is selective* means that the individual is not experiencing all of the external world to which he or she is exposed at a given moment; the person only experiences those aspects of it (cues) that are being selected out by the internal determinants. Needs demonstrate this nicely. Three people standing on the same street corner perceive the identical street scene selectively. The sailor on shore leave sees only the woman in the miniskirt walking away from him. The businessman, late for an appointment, sees only the clock on a sign above the woman. The third man sees only the restaurant sign above the clock; it's noon and he is hungry.[4]

Defense Mechanisms

Objects, events, or social interactions that arouse fears or concerns in an individual are often dealt with psychologically in a manner of which the person is unaware. These are defense mechanisms the brain develops to cope with the person's fear or concern.

Denial: One of the most frequent defensive responses is **denial.** Here things that individuals would like to do but that are socially unacceptable are dealt with by the brain processes so that people eventually believe they do not want to do those things. The individual is also opposed to anyone else doing them. This is evident in all the "no-no" areas, such as sex, aggression toward others, envy, and desire for power. A woman may hate a man she loves because she unconsciously realizes she cannot have him, but she really is convinced of the hate. An individual with strong status needs may claim he does not really want any recognition for his deeds. Not being able to make much money may lead to expressions of delight with simple living. The *psychology of opposites* is an apt phrase for denial, which can indeed affect how an individual perceives certain behaviors of self and others.

Projection: We will illustrate projection in terms of a well-known story. A young man visited a psychiatrist, who asked him why he had come for treatment. The man indicated that he did not know, that his parents had sent him because they thought he was acting strangely, but he did not think there was anything wrong. The doctor said maybe he could determine if there was a problem by asking a few questions. He then took out a piece of chalk and went to a small blackboard in the office and drew a straight vertical line about 10 inches long. He asked, "Tell me, what do you see here that I have drawn?" The young man replied, "It's a naked woman." The doctor said, "Very good. Now what is this?" He then drew an identical vertical line about six inches to the right of the first. The man replied, "It's a naked man." "And now what do you see?" asked the psychiatrist, as he drew a horizontal line between the two lines, forming an H shape. "It is a naked man and a naked woman and they are in bed together making love." The psychiatrist then gave his diagnosis. "I can see you are very sick. You really have some serious sex problems." The young man was upset and said, "Doc, what do you mean, me having all the sex problems? You're the one drawing all those dirty pictures!"

This story illustrates denial, but the main point is that the patient was projecting his own needs onto some external object. **Projection** means interpreting the world and the actions of others in terms of your own wants, needs, goals, desires, impulses, fears, and so on. If you are feeling aggressive and hostile, you may feel that it is those people out there who are hostile and causing all the trouble. If you are in love, you may believe most young couples you see walking on the street are in love. If you are a fearful person, you may perceive everything that happens in negative terms. If you think everyone is unfriendly, chances are you are really unfriendly and are attributing it to others. Of course, you may be unaware of this and immediately deny it if it's brought to your attention. Projecting one's own tendencies onto others, and not being aware of it, is a natural brain process that operates most strongly when the individual is feeling defensive. Thus it distorts the perceptual processes in terms of the internal determinants interfering with the reception of what is really out there—the external factors.

A number of other defense mechanisms are useful to know about. You may wish to pursue this in your outside reading.

Left-Brain and Right-Brain Processes in Perception

The Presumptions of Logic and Rationality in Organizational Life

Organizations are created to achieve a purpose. Reasoning and logical thinking are processes essential to goal analysis. Planning, organizing, directing, and controlling are basic activities for goal achievement. Therefore, what people do at work must make sense. This viewpoint is so pervasive that it is difficult for many to comprehend that some people do not behave as if it were correct. Henry Mintzberg, in a fascinating article, distinguishes between planners, who operate predominantly with this viewpoint, and managers, who often are working on the basis of their intuitions and insights. He relates this to the study of the left- and right-brain hemispheres and he hypothesizes planners to be left-brain–dominant, while more effective managers are right-brain–dominant.[5]

A summary of relevant functions of the two hemispheres suggests right-brain– and left-brain–dominant individuals perceive problems and generate solutions somewhat differently.[6] The **left-brain mode of functioning** is logical, rational, and based upon analytical reasoning and causal relationships. Thought is linear, sequential, and factual; it involves language and mathematical analysis. In contrast, the **right-brain mode of functioning** is intuitive and insightful. It is holistic, simultaneously processing and synthesizing total impressions, experience, and feelings. Spatial relationships and comprehension of visual images are right-brain functions, as are certain nonverbal processes such as pattern discrimination. Mintzberg sees lawyers, accountants, and planners as left-brain–dominant, while artists, sculptors, politicians, and managers are right-brain–dominant.[7] Analyzing versus synthesizing, and thinking versus intuiting are essential differences.

J. S. Livingston, commenting on the arrested career growth of Harvard MBAs 15 years after graduation, sees their training as leading to ''analysis paralysis'' rather than to the needed abilities of problem and opportunity finding.[8] This would appear to have some consistency with the Mintzberg thesis, and it suggests that perceptual functioning relevant to problem solving is somewhat different for more or less successful managers, whether or not it can be accounted for by left- or right-brain dominance.

E. S. Ferguson makes a similar analysis of the differences between systems engineers using scientific modes of thought and technicians using nonscientific modes.[9] Reviewing the intellectual history of technological development, he concludes,

> Much of the creative thought of the designers of our technological world is nonverbal, not easily reducible to words; its language is an object or a picture or a visual image in the mind. It is out of this kind of thinking that the clock, printing press, and the snowmobile have arisen. Technologists, converting their nonverbal knowledge into objects directly (as when an artisan fashioned an American ax) or into drawings that have enabled others to build what was in their minds, have chosen the shape and many of the qualities of our manmade surroundings.[10]

As science progressed, universities trained engineers in systems engineering, and the value of the nonverbal knowledge of the technician became less well recognized. Ferguson sees a danger that engineers will lose flexibility in solving problems and making decisions unless this is integrated into their training.

The Effect of Unconscious Motivation on Perception: When defining organizational behavior, we made the point that there would be no study of behavior if it were all completely rational. (See Figure 1–1.) Gaining some understanding of irrationality in behavior can improve the probability of managing effectively. Groupthink is an outstanding example of a team being dominated by irrational forces, while participants remain unaware of the impact of emotion on their behavior. Yet people always seem to find a ''logical'' reason for what they do. This is known as **rationalization,** which means finding a good reason rather than the real reason for what one does. The research of Gazzaniga and his colleagues gives us some understanding of unconscious behavior and our ability to rationalize.[11]

Working with split-brain patients—epileptics who had undergone surgical separation of the nerve system that connects the two brain halves and enables them to communicate with each other—they designed some fascinating experiments to illustrate the differentiated processes of the left and right portions of the brain. They would flash a stimulus picture to the left visual field. (The left side of the body is controlled by the right side of the brain.) But the patient could not name the stimulus because the right side of the brain receiving the image has no ability to produce language. (Only the left brain recognizes and uses language.) However, in one case a number of objects were laid out beneath the table top where they were not in view but the patient's left hand could feel them. The patient proceeded to pick out the object with the left hand even though he could not name it. The right hemisphere knew the meaning of the noun even though it did not have the language. Gazzaniga described a further experiment:

> The experiment requires each hemisphere to solve a simple conceptual problem. A distinct picture is shown to only one hemisphere; in this case the left sees a chicken claw. At the same time the right hemisphere sees a picture of a snow scene. Placed in front of the patient is a series of cards that serve as possible answers to the implicit questions of what goes with what. The correct answer for the left is a chicken; for the right a shovel.

A typical response is that of P. S., who pointed to the chicken with his right hand and the shovel with the left. After his response I asked him why he did that; he looked up and without a moment's hesitation said from his left hemisphere, ''Oh, that's easy. The chicken claw goes with the chicken, and you need a shovel to clean out the shed.'' Here was the left brain explaining why the left hand was pointing to a shovel when the only picture the brain recalled seeing was a claw. The left brain is not privy to what the right brain saw because of the brain disconnection. Yet the patient's very own body was doing something. Why was it doing that? Why was the left hand pointing to the shovel? The left brain's cognitive system needed a theory and instantly supplied one that made sense, given the information available.[12]

Cognitive Dissonance

Other research providing insight into rationalization, or self-justification, is that of Festinger on **cognitive dissonance.**[13] The theory is simply that one's behavior needs to be consistent with one's beliefs or the individual will experience feelings of dissonance. If one's behavior is in conflict with one's beliefs, the individual will tend to change the behavior or else change the belief to relieve the conflict feelings. In Festinger's experiments, students employed to do monotonous tasks were given small monetary rewards to lie to recruits and tell them the work was interesting; after engaging in this behavior, they developed more favorable attitudes toward their tasks. The relationship between reward and attitude change is more complicated than this, but the body of research supports the idea that beliefs are often changed to justify one's behavior. In the work world, a primary example is that of the salesperson. When first introduced to a product, salespeople might become aware and concerned about its shortcomings. After selling it for a while and receiving the compensation, they may become sincerely convinced the product is first-rate. They may hear warnings, but the denial process comes easily. Stockbrokers and financial advisors have sometimes been so convinced of the worth of a questionable item they recommended that they overpurchased the item for themselves and often pushed it on family and loved ones; we assume these actions provide reinforcement to the self-justification process.

Business consultants often take advantage of cognitive dissonance by charging high fees, the assumption being that if clients have more money invested in the activity, they will be predisposed to think highly of the service and heed the advice better. Presumably clients will unconsciously think that if they paid so much for the service, it must be good and they had better follow the guidance or they would have been wrong in the first place and wasted their money. The behavior, following the advice and favorable thoughts about the advice, reduces or prevents any feelings of dissonance.

Stereotypes

The term **stereotypes** implies modular (constructed as units) perceptions in which visual, factual, emotional, and feeling elements are all integrated into a fixed pattern of viewing persons, problems, activities, or objects. Within a social cognition framework, stereotypes function to reduce information-processing demands, to define group membership, and to predict behavior based on group membership.[14] The term has a negative connotation in that it implies a closed system in which no new information is taken into the modular unit; it is perceived as a source or excuse for social injustice; it is based on little information; it rarely accurately applies to specific individuals.[15] Also, the strongest stereotypes (such as racial stereotypes) are aggressively biased against a group. Even a positive stereotype (for university graduates), such as a company policy that only university graduates are promotable, shuts out information and reduces objectivity. However, stereotyping is not a negative process; rather, it is a neutral, subconscious cognitive process that increases the efficiency of interpreting environmental information that can lead to inaccuracies and/or negative consequences.[16] Recently a cognitive model of stereotyping in the workplace has been proposed by Loren Falkenberg.[17] (See Figure 7–2.)

The classification of individuals and their status assignments provide the background for delineating the processes underlying the maintenance and revision of stereotypes. Inaccurate stereotypes are maintained through interpreting behaviors of minority-status individuals in the workplace that most often lead to actions and behavior expectations that result in enhanced stereotypes. Three processes stimulate the development of more accurate stereotypes: (1) storing distinct or unexpected information in memory, (2) storing personal information on an individual with increased personal interactions, and (3) increasing recognition of individuals working in various occupational roles. Stereotypes can have a self-fulfilling prophecy, such as everyone believing an employee has great potential, and the beliefs come true. Recently the Pygmalion effect has been popular in management as a concept to help managers shape the destiny of employees or to help individuals shape their own personal growth.

The Pygmalion Effect

The influence of perception and expectation on the potential of people to grow, or not to grow, depending upon the labels accorded them, has been dramatically demonstrated by the Pygmalion effect.[18] Rosenthal and associates conducted experiments in an elementary school in which all students were given a nonverbal IQ test.[19] The teachers, who were not informed of the experimenter's true purpose, were told the IQ tests identified a number of children who were "intellectual bloomers." Each teacher was given the names of 20 percent of the students in each of their classes who fell into this classification for high intellectual growth. In reality, the 20 percent named were randomly selected and were in the average IQ range for their classes. The general results were that the intellectual bloomer groups did show a significant gain in IQ over the rest of the class. The difference in the students existed only in the minds of the teachers, who assumed they were working with brighter students.

The experimenters explained the Pygmalion effect, based upon their observations, to be due to four factors: The teachers (a) created a warm, supportive learning climate for their special students, (b) gave them more feedback on their performances, (c) gave them more material and more difficult work, and (d) gave them more opportunity to ask questions and respond. This experiment showed that student growth was stimulated by raising the expectations of the teacher that the child could achieve—the expectations were beyond what would have been expected if the teacher had seen these students as average. The point raised earlier that social attitudes and stereotypes generate

Figure 7–2
Information-Processing Strategies Leading to Maintenance and Revision of Stereotypes

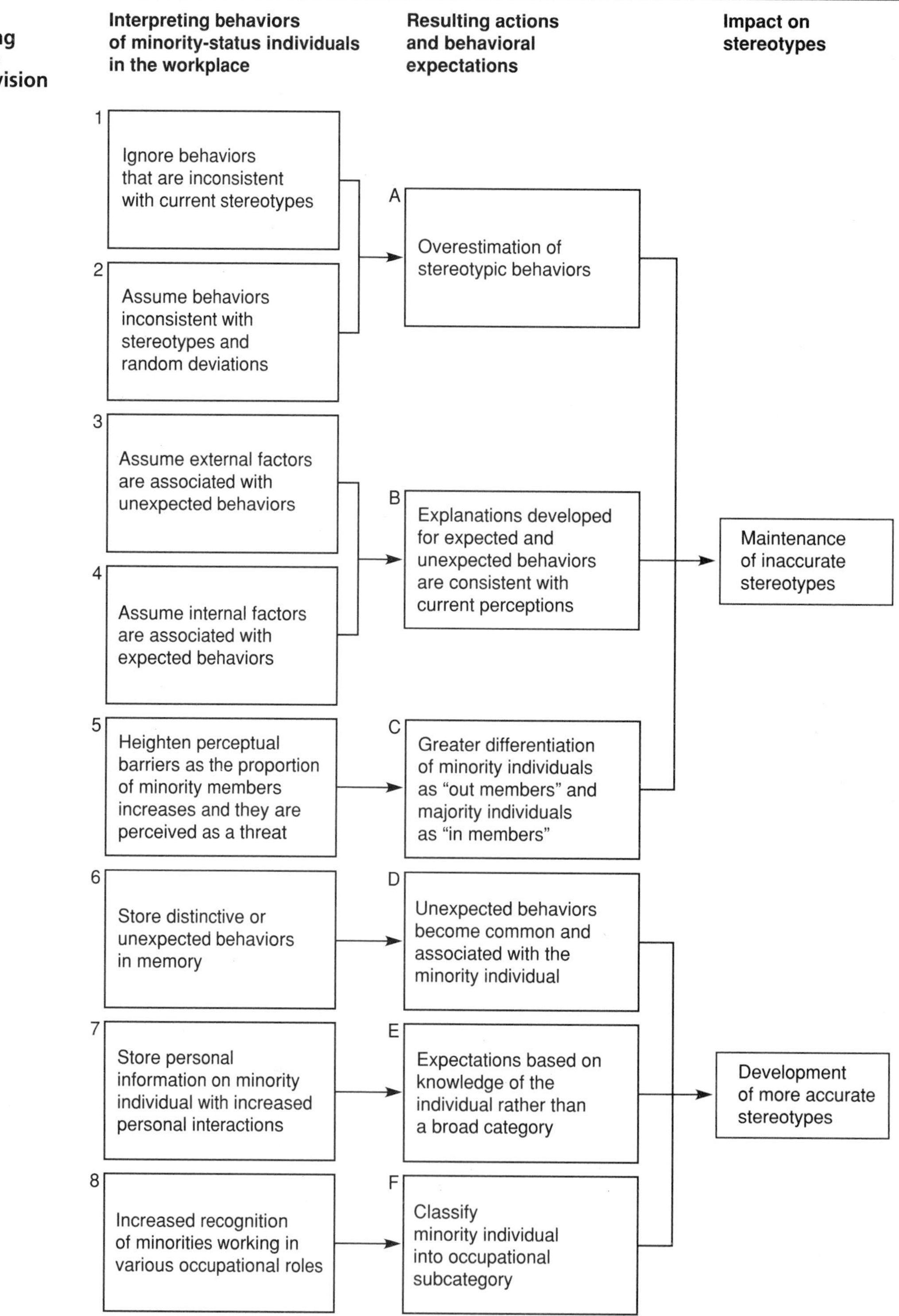

Source: Adopted from Loren Falkenberg, "Improving the Accuracy of Stereotypes within the Workplace" *Journal of Management* 16, no. 1 (1990), pp. 107–18.

expectations that are a deterrent to change was also demonstrated by another aspect of the Rosenthal experiments in which there was some tendency for low-income children with high IQs to be viewed negatively by their teachers. When these children passed the expectations of their teachers, they were somewhat resented.

Although Rosenthal's experiments have been evaluated as controversial by reviewers (one reason being that the results have not always been easy to replicate), they will strike a note of truth for many managers who have seen employees sponsored and labeled in order to influence them to move into management positions. To have a high executive label a young professional as a real "comer" can start a career. In Washington, D.C., an Ivy League degree can move one up the ladder of some agencies.

Since the early 1980s, an increasing number of studies attempted to replicate the Pygmalion paradigm with adults. Professor Dov Eden has led the research frontier on the Pygmalion phenomenon with adults.[20] Some of the best studies on the Pygmalion effect among adults have been conducted in military organizations. In one of the studies, military trainees were randomly assigned to three groups and were described to their instructors as possessing high, regular, or unknown "command potential." Data indicated that trainees who had been labeled as having high potential significantly outperformed trainees in each of the other groups on objective measures.[21] In a different study, the same effects were obtained by raising supervisors' expectations toward their subordinates as a group.[22]

At a personnel review board meeting in one company, the executive conducting the meeting described one young professional employee as having outstanding potential and dismissed the individual's mistakes the record showed with the comment, "He needs an opportunity to grow by falling on his face a few times." At a later point, he commented on the mistakes of another subject as "goofing more than you would expect." The record of the second individual actually was stronger in terms of background preparation and achievement in the company, but the comment of the chairperson went unchallenged.

Managers generally pride themselves on their ability and objectivity when judging people. But consider the implications of employee appraisal systems, particularly in large organizations. Some type of a scale is typically used to rate people in their performance and it is highly probable over a period of time that a manager's employees become typed as "outstanding," "average," "below average," and so on. If we apply what we learned of the Pygmalion effect—as articulated and summarized by Dov Eden and his book *Pygmalion in Management: Productivity as a Self-Fulfilling Prophecy*[23] and in his review article "Leadership and Expectations"[24]—the chances are rather low that the employee labeled as "average" or "below average" will ever be perceived as outstanding, even if performance improves.

The Pygmalion effect has been dramatically described in another form in Maxwell Maltz's book *Psycho-Cybernetics,* which has widespread popularity in management growth workshops.[25] Maltz, a plastic surgeon, noted that some of his patients who underwent a surgical transformation from an ugly face to a beautiful face showed a marked change in their lives; they developed more self-esteem and confidence. However, others continued to experience feelings of inadequacy and inferiority just as if they were still "ugly." From his studies, he concluded that those who had grown through the facial change had also undergone an inner change; they had developed a new self-image to correspond to the new beautiful face. Their expectations of change resulted in new behaviors that "worked" and brought them an increase in satisfaction.

Attribution Theory

One way to understand the relationship between perception and individual behavior is **attribution theory.** Attribution theory focuses on the process by which individuals interpret events around them as being caused by a relatively stable portion of their environment.[26] The underlying assumption is that individuals are motivated to understand the causes of particular events in their environment. According to attribution theory, it is the perceived causes of events, not the actual events, that influence individuals' behavior.

The attribution process includes four phases: (1) A particular behavioral event triggers a cognitive analysis that (2) focuses on what causes the event, (3) followed by a modification or reinforcement of previous assumptions of causality that (4) leads to behavioral choices regarding future behavioral events. For example, an individual who received a bonus will attempt to attribute the bonus to some underlying cause. If the employee perceives the explanation for the bonus to be the fact that he is a hard worker and consequently concludes that working hard leads to rewards in this organization, he will decide to continue to work hard in the future. Another employee may attribute his bonus to the fact that she is a ''team player'' and decide that it make sense to continue to be a team player for that reason. In both cases, individuals have made decisions affecting their future behavior based on their attributions.

The attribution process provides insights into the understanding of the behavior of other people. A central question in the attribution process concerns *how* perceivers determine whether the behavior of another person stems from internal causes (such as personality traits, motives, and emotions) or external causes (such as the situation or other people). In making attributions, people focus on three factors:

Consensus—the extent to which others, faced with the same situation, behave in a manner similar to the person perceived.

Consistency—the extent to which the person perceived behaves in the same manner on other occasions when faced with the same situation.

Distinctiveness—the extent to which the person perceived acts in the same manner in different situations.[27]

In the context of managing work and managing others, managers cannot assume that their attributions will be the same as their employees' attributions. The managerial challenge is to understand both the attributions that employees make and the ones that the manager makes of a specific event. This will enhance the manager's ability to work effectively with others.

Perceptual Challenges in Management

Management research has found large perceptual differences among individuals at different levels of the managerial hierarchy. In a study by N. R. F. Maier and associates, 58 manager and subordinate pairs were asked questions concerning the job duties of the subordinate.[28] Only 46 percent of the pairs agreed on more than half of the topics. More striking was the difference for the obstacles standing in the way of the subordinates' performance; in this category only 8 percent of the pairs were in agreement on more than half of the topics discussed. It would appear that either the subordinates were not fully aware of what their superiors expected of them, or the superiors did not know what work the subordinates were required to perform. In either case, the question can be raised as to how much communication occurred between the levels to provide understanding of the job requirements.

Part of the difficulty arises from authority and status differences, which inhibit individuals from communicating freely with their superiors about important job matters. Thus the different perceptions of subordinates and superiors are likely to remain differences. This problem of communications is illustrated in Table 7–1 based on a study by Floyd C. Mann in a large public utility, which was reported by Rensis Likert.[29] This table presents the results obtained when the top staff and the foremen were asked to give their ideas of how free the foremen felt to discuss important things about their jobs with the top staff. A similar question was asked of foremen and workers concerning how free the workers felt to discuss their work with the foremen. The first row indicates that between 85 and 90 percent of the top staff and the foremen think their

Table 7–1

Extent to Which Subordinates Feel Free to Discuss Important Things about Job with Superiors (as Seen by Superiors and Subordinates)

	Top Staff Says about Foremen	Foremen Say about Themselves	Foremen Say about the Men	Men Say about Themselves
Feel very free to discuss important things about the job with my superior	90%	67%	85%	51%
Feel fairly free	10	23	15	29
Not very free	—	10	—	14
Not at all free	—	—	—	6

Source: Data from unpublished studies by Floyd C. Mann of power plants in a public utility. From *New Patterns of Management,* p. 53, by Rensis Likert. Copyright © 1961 by McGraw-Hill Book Company. Used with permission of McGraw-Hill Book Company.

subordinates feel "very free" to discuss important job matters with them. However, only about half the men and two-thirds of the foremen say that they feel very free to discuss important matters with their superiors. Superiors are more likely than subordinates to think that communications between them are good.

The data in Tables 7–1 and 7–2 again show the striking differences in perception between superiors and subordinates concerning how well the communication processes are being carried out. These tables concern perceptions about superiors' use of subordinates' ideas and opinions in problem solving on the job.

Table 7–2

Extent to Which Superiors and Subordinates Agree as to Whether Superiors Use Subordinates' Ideas and Opinions in the Solution of Job Problems

	Top Staff Says as to Own Behavior	Foremen Say about Top Staff's Behavior	Foremen Say as to Own Behavior	Men Say about Foremen's Behavior
Always or almost always get subordinates' ideas	70%	52%	73%	16%
Often get subordinates' ideas	25	17	23	23
Sometimes or seldom get subordinates' ideas	5	31	4	61

Source: Data from unpublished studies by Floyd C. Mann of power plants in a public utility. From *New Patterns of Management,* p. 53, by Rensis Likert. Copyright © 1961 by McGraw-Hill Book Company. Used with permission of McGraw-Hill Book Company.

Some insight into the reasons for the inconsistent responses seen in these tables is provided by the following:

> One reason for the lack of a consistent pattern between supervisory behavior as reported by the supervisor and the response of subordinates is the discrepancy that exists at times between what a supervisor says he does and his actual behavior. Often a supervisor may not be aware of this discrepancy and may actually believe he is doing what he reports. There is evidence that some supervisory training programs increase this discrepancy. They seem to change the verbal response of a supervisor more than they change his actual supervisory behavior.[30]

That this discrepancy can be substantial is shown by the data in Figure 7–3, which were also collected by Mann in his study of a utility. As Likert notes, "These data show the discrepancies between what supervisors report they do and the way their subordinates see them behaving."[31] Many recent studies verify this difference in perception among all levels of the hierarchy. It appears to be an almost universally persistent problem of organizational life. Most organization development or effectiveness programs (to be discussed in later modules) include communications designs to overcome this problem.[32]

Self-Boss Perceptions of Managers

There is some tendency at all levels of the hierarchy for supervisors and managers to see themselves as better communicators than their superiors. We have demonstrated this in many management workshops, using the following exercise. Participants

Figure 7–3
Comparison of Supervisors' Description of Their Behavior with Employees' Description of Their Experience

	Asked of supervisors: "How do you give recognition for good work done by employees in your work group?" Frequency with which supervisors say "very often":	Asked of employees: "How does your supervisor give recognition for good work done by employees in your work group?" Frequency with which employees say "very often":
"Gives privileges"	52%	14%
"Gives more responsibility"	48%	10%
"Gives a pat on the back"	82%	13%
"Gives sincere and thorough praise"	80%	14%
"Trains for better jobs"	64%	9%
"Gives more interesting work"	51%	5%

Source: *New Patterns of Management* by Rensis Likert. Copyright © 1961 by the McGraw-Hill Book Company, Inc. Used with permission of McGraw-Hill Book Company.

complete a questionnaire indicating on a 10-point scale (from poor to outstanding) a number of their abilities as a manager, such as administrator, problem solver, and communicator. These rating sheets are picked up; the next day participants are given an identical sheet and asked to rate their bosses on the same abilities. Both questionnaires are completed anonymously to increase the validity of the ratings and protect the individual respondent. Sheets are identified for matching purposes by a code number the individual selects.

The results from one such study of middle managers in the federal government are shown in Table 7–3. The upper part of the table shows that in topics dealing with task completion (problem solver and administrator) the respondents tended to see their bosses as either as good as or better than themselves. In areas of communication (ability to communicate with subordinates, willingness to stand up for subordinates, and candidness), this is true to a lesser degree—as many as 46 percent of respondents indicated that they believe they are better than the boss in these attributes.

The degree of intensity of feelings on these factors is shown in the lower part of Table 7–3, which gives the total number of scale points, for the total sample, by which

Table 7–3

Midcareerists' Self-Boss Perceptions of Managerial Abilities ($N = 48$)

	Solve Problems	Administer	Communicate with Subordinates	Stand up for Subordinates	Candidness
Percentage saying					
My boss is better	40%	29%	35%	29%	31%
No difference	29	38	19	31	23
I am better	31	33	46	40	46
	100%	100%	100%	100%	100%
Total number of scale points by which respondent said					
Boss is better	34	26	27	16	38
I am better	37	44	57	62	50

respondents felt they exceeded the boss or were exceeded by the boss. The results were quite pronounced. When individuals think their bosses are better than they on a certain ability, they do not see their bosses as much better. But when they see themselves as better, they tend to see themselves as considerably better. This is most apparent on the item ''stand up for subordinates,'' where the 29 percent of the respondents who considered their bosses better gave the bosses a total of 16 points, whereas the 40 percent who considered themselves better allotted themselves 62 points. It is least true in the more task-oriented area of problem solver. The communicate and administer factors all involve more interpersonal relations, which may account for the degree to which individuals felt more intensely why they were better.

Significance of Perceptual Differences

The principal point to be made about perceptual differences is that no one perceives with complete objectivity. The determinants of perception are in operation all the time. A positive aspect of this process is that the world can be made immediately meaningful for the individual by his or her codes of past experience. Coding is a normal function of the brain processes, as are the defense mechanisms that protect the individual against being overwhelmed with fears and anxieties.

The disadvantages of perceptual differences are related to the fact that most people rely on the meanings coming from their codes without realizing that the perceptions are primarily from internal determinants rather than from the external world. Stereotyping people, for instance, can shut out new data required to understand others; stereotypes lead to **premature closure,** that is, drawing conclusions too quickly. Identifying someone as a hippie, jock, nerd, frat boy, or minority member provides the already packaged data of what such people are like without bothering to understand the person further.

Stereotypes related to management, employees, unions, and other categories of people serve a similar function in the work world. Stereotypes fulfill the needs of people (particularly when they're frustrated for ready answers) and are major communication problems in organizational life.

Reducing Perceptual Differences and Distortion

The major thrust of this presentation on perceptual differences has been to emphasize the need for people to be more aware of the ever-present distortion and differences in everyone's perceptions. This is the first step in reducing these differences and the most difficult to learn. Alertness to the differences is required for improvement of effectiveness. It could be said that the theory, concepts, and social technology of this text are generally directed toward helping participants with problems related to this area. For example, a recent study—see Table 7–4—that focused on reducing sex stereotyping identified students' perceptions of how men and women can promote equal ways of relating at work.[33]

As we have seen in this module, overcoming barriers to accurate perception is a major undertaking. Yet, if we are to fully utilize human potential, it is a must. Since workplace diversity is becoming the increasing reality for most organizations, managers are charged with finding ways to reduce distortions such that the potential of the human asset can be realized. Communications theory and techniques are most relevant in this process; these will be explored in the communication module.

Summary

Perceptual differences between people and groups are a major problem area for many fields of study, including foreign affairs, politics, advertising, mental health, and interpersonal relations. In management, perceptual problems are pervasive. Recognition of

Table 7–4
Student Perceptions of How Men and Women Can Promote Equal Ways of Relating at Work

What women do/can do to promote equal relationships between the sexes:

- Be assertive and confident; take selves seriously.
- Be knowledgeable and well organized.
- Support each other more.
- Network with men; mentor men.
- Push for day care, pay equity, parental leaves (flexibility in workplace).
- Do not ignore or promote sexist behavior at work; don't let it go by.
- Don't negate or undermine selves. (For example, don't play dumb.)
- Aspire to higher positions.
- Break traditional home roles (equality in personal relationship).
- Don't perpetuate stereotypes (male or female)—break the mold.
- Be patient and understanding with men (but challenge them to change).

What men do/can do to promote equal relationships between the sexes:

- Ask women their opinions; take them seriously.
- Don't just look at women as "girls," but see them as partners and team members.
- Involve women in decision making; don't patronize them.
- Delegate responsibility to women; trust them.
- Acknowledge and respect women's talent and ability.
- Compliment women on their work and performance.
- Approach women for advice and input.
- Compete with women like they are "one of the gang."
- Listen better; don't interrupt women.
- Share power more readily; mentor women.
- Don't stereotype women.
- Share in child rearing and housework.
- Give more support to women (networks, mentoring); be an ally.
- Accept interdependence in marriage.
- Acknowledge to the organization that family issues are men's issues too.
- Support other men in working through personal change; be patient.
- Don't ignore sexist behavior by male colleagues—"challenge to change."
- Don't "obsess" on work/career success—be willing to let go a little.
- Let go of masculine stereotypes.

Source: M. Maier, "The Gender Prism," *Journal of Managerial Education* 17, No. 3, 1993, p. 306. Used with permission.

their existence is of major importance in understanding organizational behavior. The problems are inherent in the nature of the perceptual process.

The determinants of perception are primarily internal to the individual, rather than arising from observed external objects or social interaction. Internal factors can be divided into physiological, past experience, and psychological categories. Codes of past experience and the motivational and defensive processes can filter and greatly distort what the individual is perceiving. The influence on perception of the differentiated processes of the left and right halves of the brain was discussed, with emphasis on the role of the right brain on unconscious behavior such as groupthink.

Perceptual differences are normal functions of the brain processes that help make life immediately meaningful. However, they do shut out data that are needed for more objective meaning. Awareness of these processes and particularly of one's own blind spots is seen as a primary need for understanding organizational life and improving all four levels of managerial effectiveness. Approaches to overcoming problems of perceptions and perceptual differences are explored throughout the book via a variety of experiential activities.

Study Questions

1. Identify and describe the key elements in the perceptual process.
2. "Organizational dialoguing" (see Activity 2–1) is also a model for individual dialoguing between a company representative and a client. Assume you are employed

by a major accounting firm and are assigned your first client. Using the individual dialoguing model, what questions are you going to explore that could facilitate your relationship with the client?

3. Why do we emphasize the need to have some understanding of unconscious motivation in the field of OB?
4. Explain the phrase "expectations determine perception." If you are a manager of a number of employees, half of whom have a college education and the other half only a high school background, how can this concept provide you some guidance for supervision?
5. Why are defense mechanisms studied in the field of perception?
6. N. R. F. Maier's findings on differences in perception between bosses and subordinates have been found to be so pervasive in organizational surveys that all managers need to understand them. What can be done about these differences?
7. An expert in product quality made the following statement recently: "I've met people who said, 'I've stopped buying Japanese electronics components because the quality seems to have suffered." Analyze this statement while illustrating your knowledge of perception.
8. What perceptual errors by managers foster special problems in the assessment of worker performance?
9. Some argue that perception plays a critical role in the problems that women and minorities in management experience at the workplace. State your position and provide your reasons while incorporating what you have learned about perception.

Endnotes

1. W. Penfield, "Memory Mechanisms," *A.M.A. Archives of Neurology and Psychiatry* 67 (1952), pp. 178–98, with discussion by L. S. Kubie et al.

2. Reprinted from W. Penfield, "Memory Mechanisms," *A.M.A. Archives of Neurology and Psychiatry* 67 (1952), pp. 178–80. Copyright © 1952 A.M.A. Permission granted by A.M.A. and Dr. W. Penfield.

3. Ibid., p. 183.

4. D. Fabun, *Communication* (Beverly Hills, Calif.: Glencoe Press, 1968); J. C. Cutting, "Perception and Information," *Annual Review of Psychology* 38 (1987), pp. 61–90; B. M. DePaulo, D. A. Kenny, C. W. Hoover, W. Webb, and P. V. Oliver, "Accuracy of Person Perception: Do People Know What Kinds of Impressions They Convey?" *Journal of Personality and Social Psychology* 52 (1987), pp. 303–15.

5. H. Mintzberg, "Planning on the Left Side and Managing on the Right," *Harvard Business Review,* July-August 1976, pp. 49–58.

6. Primarily based on R. E. Ornstein, *The Psychology of Consciousness* (San Francisco: W. H. Freeman, 1972).

7. Mintzberg, "Planning on the Left Side and Managing on the Right."

8. J. S. Livingston, "Myth of the Well-Educated Manager," *Harvard Business Review,* January-February 1971, pp. 79–89.

9. E. S. Ferguson, "The Mind's Eye: Nonverbal Thought in Technology," *Science* 197, no. 4306, pp. 827–36.

10. Ibid., p. 835.

11. M. S. Gazzaniga, "The Social Brain," *Psychology Today,* November 1985, pp. 29–38; J. Levy, "Right Brain, Left Brain: Fact and Fiction."

12. Ibid., p. 30.

13. L. Festinger, *A Theory of Cognitive Dissonance* (Stanford, Calif.: Stanford University Press, 1957).

14. R. D. Ashmore and F. K. Del Boca, ''Sex Stereotypes and Implicit Personality Theory: Toward a Cognitive-Social Psychological Conceptualization,'' *Sex Roles* 5 (1979), pp. 219–48; and D. Christensen and R. Rosenthal, ''Gender and Nonverbal Skill as Determinants of Interpersonal Expectancy Effects,'' *Journal of Personality and Social Psychology* 42 (1982), pp. 75–87; K. Deaux and M. E. Kite, ''Gender Stereotypes: Some Thoughts on the Cognitive Organization of Gender-Related Information,'' *American Psychology Bulletin* 7 (1985), pp. 123–44; A. H. Eagly and V. J. Steffen, ''Gender Stereotypes Stem from the Distribution of Women and Men into Social Roles,'' *Journal of Personality and Social Psychology* 46 (1984), pp. 735–54; M. E. Heilman, M. C. Simon, and D. P. Repper, ''Intentionally Favored, Unintentionally Harmed? Impact of Sex-Based Preferential Selection on Self-Perceptions and Self-Evaluations,'' *Journal of Applied Psychology* 72 (2987), pp. 62–68.

15. B. E. McCauley, C. L. Still, and M. Segal, ''Stereotyping: From Prejudice to Prediction,'' *Psychological Bulletin* 87 (1980), pp. 195–208; G. V. Bodenhausen and R. S. Wyer, ''Effects of Stereotypes on Decision Making and Information-Processing Strategies,'' *Journal of Personality and Social Psychology* 48 (1985), pp. 267–82; J. P. Fernandez, *The Diversity Advantage* (New York: Lexington Books, 1993); L. Gardenswartz and A. Rowe, *Managing Diversity* (Burr Ridge, Ill.: Richard D. Irwin, 1993); U. Hentschel, G. Smith, and J. G. Draguns, eds., *The Roots of Perception* (Amsterdam: North-Holland, 1986); E. T. Higgins and J. A. Bargh, ''A Social Cognition and Social Perception,'' *Annual Review of Psychology* 38 (1987), pp. 369–425; E. S. Jackson, *Diversity in the Workplace* (New York: Guilford Press, 1994); G. N. Powell, *Gender and Diversity in the Workplace* (Thousand Oaks, Calif.: Sage, 1994).

16. L. Falkenberg, ''Improving the Accuracy of Stereotypes within the Workplace,'' *Journal of Management* 16, no. 1 (1990), pp. 107–18.

17. Ibid., p. 110.

18. According to Greek legend, Pygmalion, a king of Cyprus, created an ivory statue of a maiden known as Galatia. He fell in love with the statue, and at his prayer Aphrodite gave it life. In George Bernard Shaw's *Pygmalion,* a professor polishes the language and manners of a cockney flower girl until he is able to pass her off as a princess, only to fall in love with her. *My Fair Lady* is the musical version of Shaw's play.

19. R. Rosenthal, ''The Pygmalion Effect,'' *Psychology Today,* September 1973, pp. 56–63.

20. A. S. King, ''Self-Fulfilling Prophecies in Training the Hard-Core: Supervisors' Expectations and the Underprivileged Workers' Performance,'' *Social Science Quarterly* 52 (1971), pp. 369–78.

21. D. Eden and A. B. Shani, ''Pygmalion Goes to Boot Camp: Expectancy, Leadership, and Trainee Performance,'' *Journal of Applied Psychology* 67 (1982), pp. 194–99.

22. D. Eden, ''Pygmalion without Interpersonal Contrast Effects: Whole Groups Gain from Raising Manager Expectations,'' *Journal of Applied Psychology* 75 (1990), pp. 394–98.

23. D. Eden, *Pygmalion in Management: Productivity as a Self-Fulfilling Prophecy* (Lexington, Mass.: Lexington Books, 1990).

24. D. Eden, ''Leadership and Expectations: Pygmalion Effects and Other Self-Fulfilling Prophecies in Organizations,'' *Leadership Quarterly* 3 (1992), pp. 271–305.

25. Maxwell Maltz, *Psycho-Cybernetics* (New York: Pocket Books, 1966).

26. H. H. Kelley, ''The Process of Causal Attributions,'' *American Psychologist* 28 (1973), pp. 107–28; and F. Fosterling, ''Attributional Retraining: A Review,'' *Psychological Bulletin,* November 1985, pp. 495–512.

27. Kelly, ''The Process of Causal Attribution.''

28. N. R. F. Maier, L. R. Hoffman, J. J. Hooven, and W. H. Read, *Supervisor–Subordinate Communications in Management* (New York: American Management Association, 1961).

29. Rensis Likert, *New Patterns of Management* (New York: McGraw-Hill, 1961), p. 47.

30. Ibid., p. 91.

31. Ibid.

32. For example see R. R. Blake and J. S. Mouton, *The Managerial Grid* (Houston: Gulf, 1964); and G. S. Odiorne, *Management by Objectives* (New York: Pitman, 1965).

33. M. Maier, ''The Gender Prism: Pedagogical Foundation for Reducing Sex Stereotyping and Promoting Egalitarian Male–Female Relationships in Management,'' *Journal of Management Education* 17, no. 3 (1993), pp. 285–314; A. McKee and S. Schor, ''Confronting Prejudice and Stereotypes: A Teaching Model,'' *Journal of Management Education* 18, no. 4 (1994), pp. 447–67; E. L. Perry, A. Davis-Black, and C. T. Kulik: "Explaining Gender-Based Selection Decisions: Synthesis of Contextual and Cognitive Approaches," *The Academy of Management Journal* 19, no. 4 (1994), pp. 786–820.

Activity 7–3: The Elaine Martin Case

Elaine Martin, a summer student intern in the Topanga Valley branch of BancWest, was angry and worried. It was July 6, and she had just experienced another unpleasant incident involving assistant branch manager Joe Andrews in which she felt herself to be unfairly discriminated against. Elaine's working relationship with her supervisor was deteriorating rapidly, and she was becoming increasingly anxious about the probability of receiving a bad performance appraisal at the end of the summer. Elaine wondered what she could do to improve the situation.

The Summer Intern Program

With headquarters in Los Angeles, BancWest was one of California's largest banks. Through a bank holding company it operated banks in several other western states. The hiring and training of all bank personnel was the responsibility of BancWest's corporate human resource department.

The position of assistant branch manager was a key position in the bank's retail operations. In a typical branch, the assistant manager was responsible for customer service, operations, personnel administration, security, and expense control. Training for this position was accomplished by either (1) 12 months of continuous work/study (available to university or college graduates or BancWest employees without college degrees) or (2) three summer intern segments (available to outstanding students currently enrolled in college). Student trainees learned primarily through on-the-job training, which was supplemented by self-instructional materials, workshops held at BancWest's regional training centers, and supervisory field visits from corporate training officers.

Three years ago, Elaine Martin was hired by the bank's human resource department as a summer intern for the position of assistant branch manager. She had just completed her first year at Golden State University, and the idea of a career in banking appealed to her. Elaine was told she would work in the Topanga Valley branch, a convenient 15-minute drive from her family's home.

Before starting in June, Elaine met with the corporate training officer to whom she had been assigned. The trainer gave Elaine a training manual and explained its use in conjunction with resource materials located in the branch office. He told Elaine:

"A lot of your evaluation will be based on how effectively you can use the manual and resource books. You don't have to memorize the contents, but you *must* be able to find any information you're asked for quickly. Like all trainees, you'll get a half day each week to study, and the questions I ask at review time will test your knowledge thoroughly.

"But more than simply knowing how to locate information, you must be able to deal with people. Some branch staff resent having to train 'college types' who will become their superiors, so this might cause you some problems. And don't be taken in by any staff who might try to take advantage of you. If they help you for an hour, you owe them an hour in return—no more!

"Ultimately, you're responsible for developing yourself, but I am available by telephone at any time, and I'll be out to see you in early July and late August for your performance reviews. I'll be in touch with the assistant branch manager to explain my objectives for you, and I'll send him our manual about how to develop interns—and, of course, the assistant branch manager will also review your performance at the end of the summer."

Elaine worked as a teller at Topanga Valley branch throughout the summer two years ago. This job, although interesting at first, soon became routine and boring for her. Last year, during the second summer, Elaine worked in the checking and savings areas, about which she said, "The assistant manager told me I'd be doing checking for a month, and savings for the next, but she actually put me on checking for a week, savings for a week, then back again on checking. She didn't know what she was doing! But I didn't do anything about it because I hadn't been given any overall goal to achieve.'' This summer (at the end of her junior year as a business administration major) Elaine returned to the Topanga Valley branch for her third and final summer in the internship program, this time as a trainee in the loan department.

The Topanga Valley Branch

The Topanga Valley Branch was located in a suburban residential area in Southern California, adjacent to a regional shopping mall. The area was experiencing significant growth, and the branch's increasing business reflected that growth. Several new positions (a branch administration officer and three part-time tellers) had been added to the branch staff early in the year, bringing the total number of employees to 17.

The position of branch administration officer was held by 24-year-old Bob Grimes. He was responsible for certificates of deposit, foreign exchange, securities, credit ratings, and lines of credit. The loan supervisor, Terri Bradshaw, a woman in her late 30s, was responsible for the computerized daily reports and many other records concerning personal and corporate loans that had been approved by the branch's loan officer, who reported directly to the branch manager. Checking supervisor Mary Simpson at 58 was the senior branch employee. She was responsible for all checking matters—opening new accounts, NSF checks, special checking account service, overdrafts, and so forth. The 29-year-old savings supervisor, Pam Ortiz, was responsible for all savings accounts and for the daily balancing of machine output from the tellers. Beth Tolliver, the 40-year-old teller supervisor, was in charge of the work of the tellers. All of these individuals reported to the assistant branch manager.

Joe Andrews, the new assistant branch manager, had been appointed at the beginning of the year. A former truck driver in his late 20s, Andrews had completed the 12-month training program at the bank's largest branch in the region. Andrews was a junior college graduate.

The branch building was small and compact. Two glass-enclosed offices (one for the manager, the other for the loan officer) were located immediately inside the door. An L-shaped counter provided work space for customer service by tellers and supervisors. The desks of the loan, checking, and savings supervisors were located side by side behind the section of the counter where customers came for transactions other than the routine deposits, withdrawals, check cashing, and so forth handled by the tellers. The assistant branch manager's desk was located in a corner where he had an unobstructed view of the entire customer service area. The branch administration officer's desk was located alongside.

Elaine's Summer Experience

When Elaine reported for work in June, she was asked to meet with the branch manager and the assistant branch manager. The manager told Elaine about her summer responsibilities—training and working in loans, assisting at the counter, and doing other duties as assigned. The manager firmly stated his expectations:

''I know there are things you're supposed to learn for head office, but you're working in our branch, and we want you to work under our rules. This year will be different from the past two summers. This year, your performance will be measured on your demonstrated management ability—on doing your work well, but especially on gaining the respect of other employees. You'll get no differential treatment as an intern and business student. You'll be treated as a full-time employee, which includes doing counter work like everyone else—and as you know, counter work constitutes about 50 percent of the job. We can't allow you any time off to read or study for head office tests because it wouldn't look right to the other employees. It wouldn't be fair to them. And keep in mind that your future in the bank depends on your receiving a good staff report, which Joe will write at the end of the summer.''

Talking to a friend late in June, Elaine described her work situation:

''I was supposed to receive two weeks' training on loans from Terri, who would then be available to handle special assignments for the loan officer or the assistant manager, or go on vacation, while I took over the position for her. But her husband got sick and she's been away a lot, so I only received two days' training. But Terri's fun! She's not the brightest person, but she works hard, and I really like her. She gets along well with customers and helps staff members who get behind in their work.

"I liked Joe Andrews at first. He's a hard worker and can be quite nice, but he has a terrible temper and yells at everybody when things are going badly. He's young—has only been with the bank for four years and has been an assistant manager for one. Joe took over at the Topanga Valley branch in January and inherited an awful mess! Things were really bad, and there was a lot of pressure on him—records and reports to fix up, personnel problems, the works. I wouldn't want to be in his shoes. I don't have the patience to deal with so many problems. And in spite of having so much responsibility, he has no real decision-making authority.

"A lot of things still need to be fixed up, but he can't get the people to work harder. For one thing, the checking supervisor won't even go to the counter! Mary is an older woman and would probably be fired except that her husband has a position high up in the bank. Of course, counter work is 'extra,' and she has a lot of work to do every day, but people keep coming to the counter in front of our desks to open new accounts, buy certificates of deposit, open or use safety deposit boxes, and so on. They all need help, and a lot of the counter procedures are long and involved. If you get behind in your regular work, you have to stay and work overtime.

"People think I'm OK handling loans on my own because they know I grasp things quickly. It's really hard, though, and the assistant manager doesn't help. He's always hassling me about going to the counter, and he tells me what to do in front of people. How can I gain their respect? I can't reach my management goals for this summer if he keeps on. I'm in a double bind. To get a good rating, I have to meet the corporate trainer's expectations that I'll learn the job and technical aspects, as well as Joe's demands that I perform ordinary branch services and conduct myself as a manager, gaining the staff's respect.

"I'm feeling frustrated, angry, and on edge almost all the time. Many times when Pam, Mary, and I (and Terri too if she's in) are working and somebody comes up to the counter, Joe tells *me* to go to the counter. He tells me in front of everyone, which makes it look as if I'm not doing anything. I don't mind going to the counter and doing my share, but he always sees me when I'm sitting down. You see, he hated doing counter work when he was a trainee, so he pushes it at me—'Do counter, counter, counter!'

"Sometimes when I ask the person at the counter, 'Can I help you?' the person will say, 'No, I'm waiting for Pam,' or someone else. So I sit down, and Joe comes around the corner, taking in the scene of people waiting and me sitting down. Right away I feel really uptight as he looks at the counter and looks at me. Sometimes he asks the customer, 'Are you being looked after?' and other times it's just the eye contact. Right away I know he's thinking I'm terrible, even though I know I went to the counter. Other times, I may be sitting there with nothing to do, because I work pretty fast. The others try to make themselves look busy, making personal phone calls and so on, but I won't. I'll go to the counter though, but I don't stay there gabbing to the customers about their four kids or their vacation or whatever, like Pam and Terri do.

"I know it's not my imagination that Joe's got the idea that all women are second-class citizens, and that he is not interested in advancing their careers. He actually told me that when the present branch administration officer moves on, he wants a young, ambitious *man* to replace him, not a woman. He said a man will work hard at the job because he wants to go far in the bank, while a woman will just do as much work as she *has* to. He said this in his usual coarse way, with a couple of sexist jokes thrown in, which he probably picked up from his truck driver friends—he still drives a truck on weekends.

"Today was the last straw. I was in the loan office, talking to the loan officer about discounts. I wanted to learn more so that I could explain loans to customers. When customers ask the rest of the staff, they say they don't know and send them to the loan officer. I know she has a lot to do, and I figured it would be good if I could help her out a bit. Well, Joe phoned the loan officer while I was in there, and said, 'Tell Elaine to go to the counter—it's busy.'

"I really got upset. I was so mad I almost cried—or screamed! I had to walk right across the bank, and Mary, Terri, and Pam were just sitting there. Sure they had work to do, but I was working, too, and that made me feel terrible.

"When I saw the doctor recently about my headaches and stomach problems, he said there was no physical cause he could find. He thought it was pressure from the job. I'm feeling so frustrated! I want to do a good job and meet my goals, but nobody can possibly have any respect for me when I'm treated so badly. I'm sure to get a poor staff report at performance review time, and I just don't know how to change things."

Discussion Questions

1. Describe Elaine's perceptions of the other employees in the bank.
2. How do you suppose they might see her?
3. What are Elaine's options in dealing with this situation?
4. If you were Elaine, what would you do? Why?

Activity 7–4: Prejudices and Stereotyping

Objectives:

1. To heighten learners' awareness of their own prejudices and stereotypes.
2. To develop awareness of the effects of one's own prejudices and stereotypes on one's behavior.

Task 1:

The instructor will facilitate 10 minutes of class brainstorming to generate names of groups and persons the students know to have been targets of some form of prejudice, discrimination, or stereotyping.

Task 2:

The instructor will facilitate 5 to 10 minutes of brainstorming that focuses on the specific characteristics or traits they know to be associated with these groups that contribute to the stereotyping or prejudiced attitude and behavior.

Task 3:

a. Students are to find a group on the board that they can associate themselves with and gather in small similar groups. The students might cluster themselves into a group of African-Americans, Latinos, white males, physically disabled, and so on.
b. Each group selects a reporter who may take notes and who will summarize the discussion and report it to the class. Each group should
   1. Identify (following a few minutes of reflection) a specific time when you experienced some form of discrimination or prejudice because of your identity as a member of this particular stereotyped group.
   2. Describe what occured, who was there, what you did, and what you felt at the time.
   3. Talk about what you feel now and what you think had happened. What has influenced your feelings and thinking since that particular incident?

Task 4:

In the larger class, individuals are asked to share some of their experiences. The instructor will facilitate class discussion around common themes and issues, emphasizing the common and painful experience of suffering from discrimination, prejudice, and stereotyping.

Task 5:

Go back to the same small groups. Each individual will

a. Think of a time when you consciously or unconsciously discriminated against someone, perpetuated a stereotype, or supported some prejudiced attitudes or behaviors.
b. Describe what occurred, who was there, what you did, what you felt and thought at the time, and your current thoughts and feelings.

Task 6:

a. In the larger class, individuals are asked to share some of their experiences. The instructor will facilitate class discussion around common themes and issues, emphasizing the importance of awareness as the first step toward understanding and perhaps changing behaviors, and the need to be patient and forgiving as change occurs.
b. The instructor will facilitate a discussion about the application to the workplace.

Source: The basic ideas in this activity are adopted from the work by Drs. Anne MeKee of the Wharton School, The University of Pennsylvania, and Susan Schor of Pace University. The activity in its present form was developed by Dr. Judith White, Loyola Marymount University, Management Department, Los Angeles, Calif. 90045-2899. We are grateful to Drs. McKee, Schor, and White.

Activity 7–5: Male–Female Interface on Women in Management

Objectives:

a. To explore perceptions of male and female participants on the abilities of women to perform in management positions.
b. To elicit views on the most favorable relationships for men and women working together.

Task 1 (Homework):

Study the following "The Silicon Technologies Corporation" case. Answer the first question at the end of the case study by preparing notes on the worksheet accompanying the case.

Task 2 (Classroom):

a. Women participants are to form groups of five to seven persons. Men are to meet in similar groups. The groups should be intermingled to avoid having men clustered on one side of the room and women on the other. Each group will elect a spokesperson.
b. The arguments (listed on worksheet) given by male members of the human resources board are to be discussed to decide on the degree of validity for each item. The spokespersons should make a list of the points raised.

(Time: 15 minutes)

Task 3:

a. Male groups are to report their conclusions to the class. When they have completed their reports, female groups will report. (*Note:* While the reports are being made, no dialogues among groups are to take place. This is not a confrontation. It is an attempt to learn what the true perceptions of men and women are concerning the arguments in the case study.)
   (Time: 15 to 20 minutes)

b. Open dialogue between the groups to take place for the purpose of clarification.
(Time: 10 minutes)

c. A brief lecture will be given by the instructor on the validity of the arguments.
(Time: 10 minutes)

Case Study: The Silicon Technologies Corporation

Silicon Tech has a Human Resources Review Board, which meets periodically to consider promotions, placements, and other personnel actions. The board includes representatives from different departments, at this time consisting of

Duke, executive officer

Chong, Human Resources Management

Marcos, Research and Development

Sam, Finance

Sonya, Marketing

Rod, Production

Today they are meeting without Sonya, who is out of town on a marketing survey. As the meeting gets underway, Duke, the chairperson, is talking.

DUKE: Chong, what do you have for us today?

CHONG: Our first case for promotion is Barbara Sidaris, who wants to give up her accounting job to accept an assistant manager position in Production. You all have copies of her file.

There was silence as all gave attention to the promotion papers on Barbara. The first to speak was Rod, the Production representative.

ROD: I think we ought to defer action on Barbara's case until Sonya comes back. It's really the only fair thing to do.

CHONG: I find that an interesting statement. What are we supposed to assume from that? That you have some doubts? Are you saying that those present cannot make a fair judgment on a woman moving into a management position?

ROD: No, not at all. It's only because Sonya generally acts as advocate for women candidates here.

DUKE: Rod, your statement seems to imply there is something wrong with this promotion recomendation.

ROD (*appearing flushed*): I didn't mean it that way.

DUKE: Maybe this is a good time to open up and speak frankly. I have the feeling that when Sonya is here, you guys are really not leveling on some of the cases involving promotion of women into management positions. Rod, why don't you start? You obviously do have some concern in this case or you wouldn't have made that statement about fair treatment.

ROD: This is a good time to speak out because I think it is for the good of the company to have hardball personnel reviews instead of glossing over potential problem areas just because we might be regarded as biased against women.

DUKE: And in this case that means what?

ROD: Alright, look at Barbara's absentee record. Each year she has used up all her sick leave. If she were a manager and had that record, it would be deplorable.

SAM (FINANCE): Barbara is one of my department's people, and in all fairness to her, she is an outstanding professional. They don't come any better. As an accountant over the past five years, she has been one of our most productive people, always putting in extra time when required. It is because she is so successful that she wants to go on to new experiences and challenges, and we support her 100 percent.

MARCOS (R&D): While I'm impressed with Barbara and her record, I'm glad Rod raised the issue of women in management because it is something we have to face with the males all the time. There are some resentments. Many men feel women are too emotional at times to make good management decisions. Using all of one's sick leave is right to the point. Are there times of the month when women's judgments are not the best? Women speak so openly today about their periods that it's nothing for a woman worker to say she is not working well, or ask to go home, because it is "that time of the month."

CHONG: Is this an important productivity issue? We haven't heard about it from managers.

MARCOS: What I hear from my people is a lot of support for women as professionals in specialist positions, but not in management. My engineers feel women are more content in the specialized roles; they are just being pushed by the press and the women's movement into leadership types of responsibilities whether they want them or not. The absentee record raises the question as to how seriously the individual wants to be a model for other employees. We have to be careful not to create an atmosphere of pressure that makes women feel it is wrong not to push for managerial jobs.

CHONG: It seems a lot is being made over one little blemish on a woman's record. If this were a man, we would probably be saying he needs the opportunity to grow and develop more managerial viewpoints.

DUKE (*laughing and responding to Marcos's comments*): The *Sunday Times* editorial section had a highly provocative item by a right-wing columnist in which he maintained that history clearly shows 99 percent of the great leaders were men, and therefore it is genetically determined that men assume leadership and that followers accept men as leaders. He describes Ronald Reagan's appeal as that of the tribal chief and father moving naturally and instinctively ahead as millions fall in behind him.

CHONG: One implication of that view is that women are not aggressive enough. In this case I would like to point out that Barbara is aggressive, or the word being used is *assertive,* and still is not offensive to most men. At least I've never heard any complaints in this regard.

SAM: You are so right. She's generally regarded as a most attractive and personable woman.

ROD: You guys can be so positive in your comments, because she will not be joining your management staff. We are the ones taking her in. One of my concerns is that she is too feminine; not only is she a sexy lady, she also dresses the role to an extent, smells lovely, and wears a little eye shadow, which is really out of place. For men who work with women like that, it is distracting.

SAM (*laughing*): Like for you, Rod?

ROD (*guffawing*): Yep, I find her distracting. But seriously, it takes a lot more effort to integrate a woman into a management job than it does a man. Even other women will tell you they prefer to work for a male boss. And males know how to be part of the team; women often don't know how to be a team member.

MARCOS: Yeah, women generally don't know how to play the power game and men don't know how to respond to women when they do.

CHONG: You can give her a key to the executive john, Rod, so she will find out what the team is thinking.

DUKE: With all the objections you have raised, Rod, it sounds to me like the Production Department has decided not to support Barbara for the opening you have as assistant manager? Am I right?

ROD: Oh, hell no! We're very strong on Barbara. The feeling among our people was unanimous to accept her over all the male candidates we interviewed.

DUKE: Well, then, why are we going through all these motions? You've raised so many doubts.

ROD: Someone suggested we let down our hair a bit while Sonya was not here and that started us off. I felt others in this room might have some doubts.

DUKE: How do the rest of you feel about Barbara's promotion?

MARCOS: I certainly support it, but as a help to Rod, I recommend that Chong have lunch with her and tell her of the board's concern; her full use of sick time looks like she is just using it for vacation, which is not appropriate for a manager. Also, that she might be more conscious of the unwritten dress code among professional women and tone it down a bit.

ROD (*grinning*): Don't tell her to tone it down too much.

SAM: When you guys get tired of an antiseptic atmosphere, come over to Finance, where loveliness is cultivated. Our accountants have the figures.

DUKE: I'm going to assume the vote is unanimous. Also, to put what has been said into perspective, I want to point out that the performance of the women we have in management positions has been first-rate. Further, I personally dislike the idea of reducing femininity as an important element of organizational climate. What's next, Chong?

Questions for Discussion

1. Discuss each of the reasons advanced by the men of the Human Resources Review Board as to why women are not as qualified as men for management positions. There is validity in all the arguments. What is the nature and degree of validity in each of them? Use the accompanying worksheet to record your responses.
2. What is going on in this case?

Worksheet for Activity 7–5

Reasons women are not as qualified as men for manager positions as stated or implied by the Silicon Tech Human Resources Review Board.	Your position on the nature and degree of validity for each of the reasons.
1. The women's libertion movement does not really represent what American women want.	
2. History shows few women leaders, which is evidence of . . .	
3. Women in business prefer specialist professional roles but are pushing for management positions because of pressure from the women's movement.	
4. By temperament women are not as aggressive or competitive as men, implying they are too gentle to be in management.	
5. Women's biological makeup produces emotional factors that could at times adversely influence decision making or interpersonal relations.	
6. Many women do not like to work for women bosses.	
7. Women are not as good as men in team activities.	

8 Communication

Learning Objectives

After completing this module you should be able to:

1. Identify and describe the basic elements in the communication process.
2. Appreciate the relationship between diversity, personality, perception, motivation, and communication.
3. Understand the different levels of communication.
4. State the internal and external determinants of interpersonal communication.
5. Identify the potential barriers in the communication episode.
6. Describe the methods to overcome potential communication barriers.
7. Understand your own barriers in the communication process and some of the actions that you can take to overcome them.
8. Identify some of the basic components of intragroup communication.
9. Identify some managerial actions that can help overcome the barriers for communication in organizational settings.

List of Key Concepts

Communication
Communication media
Communication networks
Computer networks
Decoding
Encoding
Interpersonal communication
Intragroup communication
Intragroup conflict
Kinesic behavior
Message
Nonverbal communication
Paralanguage
Proxemics
Semantics
Superordinate goals

Module Outline

Premodule Preparation

The instructor may assign either one or any combination of the following activities as a presession task: Task 1 of Activity 8–1 (''Communication, Coaching, and Goal Setting'') or Task 1 of Activity 8–2 (''Exploring Communication Barriers'').

Activity 8–1: Communication, Coaching, and Goal Setting

Objectives:

a. To develop your awareness of the human resources that you bring to the work situation.

b. To provide an opportunity to practice discussing your own resources with two other persons.

c. To practice listening and paraphrasing.

Task 1:

As homework, complete the ''Questionnaire on Coaching and Goal Setting'' that follows before coming to class so that you will have notes for participating in this exercise. The questionnaire is intended as a guide, and you may use any other approach or questions you feel would be more helpful to you for performing your role in the triads discussed in the following paragraphs. The questionnaire is for your own use; you will not be asked to hand in any written work on this.

Task 2:

In the classroom, the permanent teams are to form into triads.

The roles. During the exercise each participant will have an opportunity to fulfill all three roles. For instance, during the first 15-minute session, participant A will be the teller, participant B will be the listener, and participant C will be the observer. Participants will rotate through the three roles as they complete the sessions as follows:

The role of teller. Individuals will talk about their resources and goals in the way that is most meaningful, using notes from the questionnaire if needed. It is better, however, to speak spontaneously.

The role of listener. Individuals will paraphrase back to the teller what they hear the teller saying. Listeners have to determine how long they should let the teller talk before interrupting to paraphrase. Waiting until the end of the session is too long; interrupting at the end of each sentence is too short. Listeners are not to take notes and are to give the teller their full attention. The paraphrasing must be acceptable to the teller. Questions may be asked for clarification, but remember this is not an interrogation or an interview, so probing is not appropriate. The intent is for people to talk about themselves in a way that is meaningful to them. Questions for any purpose other than clarification can lead the teller into talking about topics that are not really of central concern.

The role of observer. How well do the listeners carry out the role? Do they paraphrase well? How do you feel about the way the teller talked? Make notes if you wish, and be prepared to give any feedback you want to when the instructor indicates you are to come into the interaction. The observer is not to enter into the discussion until the designated time—this will be difficult for some.

Task 3:

The instructor is to indicate when the exercise is to start. If the time allowed for each session is 10 minutes, the instructor should stop the teller and listener after 7 minutes and allow 3 minutes for the observer to give feedback and for the triad to discuss the activity. If the time allowed is 15 minutes, the teller and listener are to be stopped at 10 minutes, thus leaving 5 minutes for the observer to interact. (Time for each session: 7 or 10 minutes, depending upon the length of the interval the instructor has chosen. Although 15 minutes is desirable, the time available during the class will be a determining factor.)

The observer gives feedback to the teller and listener in accordance with the role description in Task 1. Other possible questions to discuss: How did the talkers feel about their roles? What problems were there with them? How did the listeners feel about their roles? What problems were there with them?
(Time: 3 or 5 minutes, depending upon the length of the interval)

Continue these activities until all three participants have performed all roles. (*Note:* It is important for the instructor to control the timing of the intervals for the teller and listener and for the observer feedback sessions; otherwise each individual will not get a fair share of the air time.)

Task 4:

Class discussion of the exercise provides a good opportunity for participants to share opinions on these questions:

- How did you feel about
  (1) Talking about yourself?
  (2) Listening to someone talk about himself or herself?
  (3) Paraphrasing what you heard?
  (4) Having someone paraphrase back to you?
  (5) Being a listener?
  (6) Being an observer?
- What is the value of being able to talk about one's resources?
- What other skills are involved in coaching besides (1) understanding how individuals perceive their resources and goals and (2) listening?

Questionnaire on Coaching and Goal Setting

Introduction

The motivation to work may be thought of as the interaction between three areas: (1) the individual as a human resource, (2) the requirements of a particular job, and (3) the character of the work climate. The degree to which individuals are effective and derive satisfaction in their professional assignments depends upon the extent to which these three fit together harmoniously.

Factors in each of these areas that might be relevant to your motivation to work include

1. *The individual as a human resource.* This would include your abilities, skills, experience, education, interests, interpersonal skills, attitudes, temperament, goals, and the broad area of psychological needs such as for achievement, status, recognition, power, acceptance by others, influence, and control. These and many other factors can give you the potential of high performance on certain types of job requirements.
2. *The nature of the job and its specific requirements.* It is assumed there is a range of different types of jobs for which you are suited, depending on your resources. Most of us have some awareness of the nature of work for which we think we are most suited and that encourages us to perform with the highest degree of motivation and involvement.
3. *The work climate.* This can be thought of as, first, relationships between people—between you and your boss, you and your peers, or you and your subordinates. The climate has certain values and norms that characterize the atmosphere and either promote or hinder your effectiveness as an individual.

The Manager as a Coach

A role of the supervisor-manager that is emphasized is that of a coach to employees. This is of value because it helps develop the full potential of people and makes the organization fully aware of its human assets. From this knowledge, decisions can be made for selection, placement, assignments, rotation, career planning, promotion, and so on.

This questionnaire is intended to permit you to practice being both employee and coach as the roles relate to motivation and goal setting. A similar exercise has been used in industrial supervisory training in which trainees complete a questionnaire focused upon the three areas discussed.

Read through the questionnaire and then reread the description of the activity so you will know how you are to use the notes you will make on the questions. (*Note:* This questionnaire is for your own use and is not to be handed in or shown to others unless you desire. Write your answers on extra sheets of paper if enough room has not been provided on the form.)

Name ______________________________ Date ______________________

Questionnaire on Coaching and Goal Setting

PART I: YOU AS A RESOURCE (What I bring to the job)

In answering this question, think in terms of your human resources as described in the introductory section. Use extra sheets of paper where necessary, since little room is provided here.

1. What do you regard as some of your major strengths: abilities, work habits, needs, goals, temperament, etc. (Note: Do not try to ''sell'' yourself. Just state honestly how you see yourself.)

PART II: APPLICATION OF YOUR RESOURCES

The first question gives you an opportunity to think of your resources, which might include many assets you do not use frequently. Now think specifically in terms of how you perform in different areas. (You do not have to confine your answers to a work situation—school, recreation, work, church, etc., are fine.)

1. What are some things you do well and would like to do more of? Why?

2. What are things you do not do so well, but would like to do better? Why?

3. What are things you have done and would prefer not to do more of? Why?

4. What are some things you have not done, but would like to do?

5. Can you recall something you have done in the past couple of years that you felt was innovative?

6. What new skill would you like to acquire in the year ahead?

7. List three brief statements of your characteristics that you would like to improve or reinforce.

8. List three brief statements of your characteristics that you would like to minimize or reduce.

9. What I want most out of my job is:

10. What I would like to achieve in the next five to ten years is:

PART III: THE WORK CLIMATE

1. The type of relationship I want with my boss that can provide me the support I need to achieve my needs and goals is:

2. The type of work climate in which I will be most effective is:

3. Three things I do that are especially helpful for other people are:

4. Three things I would like to do better in order to be more helpful to others are:

(Use extra sheets of paper where necessary.)

Notes:

1. This exercise is designed to give you the opportunity to sample an aspect of the broad area of goal setting, coaching. Obviously the times provided for this exercise are unrealistic, and the individual will probably prefer to select some aspect of the questionnaire and concentrate on it. Complete coverage is not the intent here.

2. *If you prefer to discuss questions on the topic of resources and goals not presented here, please feel free to do so.*

Activity 8–2: Exploring Communication Barriers

Objectives:

a. To identify communication barriers.

b. To explore emotional blocks in the communication process.

c. To appreciate the complexity of the communication process.

Task 1 (Individual Work):

Read the episode that follows the instructions and respond to the following questions:

1. What are the barriers to accurate communication in the episode?
2. How did each of the barriers affect the communication process?
3. What suggested course of action will you give Professor Shrink and Bob Aware?

Task 2:

The class is divided into groups of three. Each group will role play the continuation of the discussion between Bob Aware and Professor Shrink. (Two individuals will play the roles of Bob Aware and Professor Shrink. The third person will be the observer and provide feedback on the role playing.)

"Bob Aware Meets Professor Shrink"

Scene 1: Professor Shrink is on the faculty of a graduate school of business at a large university where executive programs are conducted. He is a middle-aged man with hair just above his collar and a large horseshoe mustache. He wears the latest style of glasses but is conservatively dressed. Shrink is sitting in his office one day when an executive from one of the education programs comes in and addresses him.

VISITOR: Professor Shrink?

SHRINK: (*standing up and offering his hand*): Yes. Can I be of help?

VISITOR: Yes. I am in one of the programs here and need some guidance. I'm Bob Aware and . . .

SHRINK (*interrupting and smiling*): Oh, "be aware," that's interesting!

AWARE: I've heard you run some great communication workshops and I think I would be interested. You see, I am realizing more and more that the communications gap is very real. I really don't understand many of the young people who are coming into my company, and I also feel concerned that I don't know where my own son is coming from. The world is changing so fast, I am experiencing future shock right now.

SHRINK: I like your attitude very much. You could probably get a good deal out of some of the sessions we are running. Would you like to hear a little more about them?

AWARE: I certainly would.

SHRINK: Let me run through briefly the communication sequence, the learning model we use in all our workshops. If you will permit me to take about five minutes to explain the theoretical framework, we can go back and discuss it. (*Aware nods his consent as Shrink walks over to a small blackboard on the wall and writes "Dialogue Sequence.*[1]*"* Now when two people or two groups of people do not understand each other and find themselves in conflict, there are certain dialoguing steps through which they can work their way out of it so they can work or live together better. The first of these is listening (*he writes "1. Listening Skills" on the board as he speaks*), which is . . .

AWARE (*jumping to his feet, interrupting, and speaking rapidly*): Listening? Boy, if there is one thing I am good at it's listening. I've had 15 years of hearing everything my employees say. I'm known for my good ear. At home I hear everyone of my family members out and understand all they say. I can even "read" my little dog. We can skip the listening phase and go right into communicating. I want to learn more about communicating.

SHRINK (*who had been standing with his hand poised at the blackboard, waiting for the word flow to stop*): Mr. Aware, I hear what you are saying. You feel you really are good at listening and do not need that type of learning experience. I think if you will permit me to run through this four-step sequence so you will see the entire process in operation, you will be able to judge whether or not this is something that will be useful to you. So let me continue. After people have learned to listen to each other and can paraphrase back what they have heard with the degree of understanding that permits the other person to say, "You are reading me right," they can proceed to the second phase, which is confrontation. (*Shrink writes "2. Confrontation Skills" on the board.*)

AWARE (*again jumping to his feet and interrupting*): Confrontation skills! That is exactly what I need. I really have to be able to confront people in a more meaningful way. How to get my feelings out in a way that does not turn everyone off is a big problem. I am really enthused about this, Professor. When do we start?

SHRINK: That is a good point you made and we will try to help you on that, but let me run through the entire dialogue sequence so you can make a decision once you have the total picture. Confrontation refers to facing up to both your true differences and your areas of agreement after you have gained the understanding from the listening phase. The third skill area is in looking for alternatives (*writes "3. Searching Skills" on the board*) that are open to the two parties and may help them to work better together. The fourth area is that of implementing (*writes "4. Coping Skills" on the board*) the decision we make after examining the alternatives. The four steps are a cycle that the two parties can go into whenever they encounter a barrier to communication.

AWARE: Professor, I am most enthused. I don't need the listening training, but the other sounds excellent. When do I start?

SHRINK: We have four workshops starting in the morning. One is a black–white, in which we have 10 blacks who have come here for a confrontation experience; 10 executives will meet with them for two hours a day for three days. There is also a woman's lib group of 10 women from business who wish to meet with 10 of you. In addition there will be a boss–subordinate group and a generation-gap group; the latter will have 10 students who live in a commune not too far away.

AWARE: That's what I want, the generation-gap workshop. Please sign me up.

SHRINK: Fine. Let me give you some guidance. When you meet with the group tomorrow, your task is to find out where they are. Pretend you are a radio receiver and that the only thing you can do is to pick up all the signals that are coming in. What is it that the young people are broadcasting? Can you really learn what it is they are saying, in terms of both content and what they are feeling?

AWARE: Sure, that should be easy for me. No trouble. But why can't we go right into confrontation?

SHRINK: You really can't confront until you learn what you are to confront. Now, tomorrow, be here at 8 AM for your first session. It will run two hours. After it is over, come by here for a chat and let me know what you have learned about them. (*Aware departs, promising to do that.*)

Scene 2: Next morning, Shrink's office. Aware enters.

SHRINK: Well, how did it go?

AWARE: These kids make absolutely no sense. The only think they can think about is to tear down the establishment. Everything is wrong. The system is wrong, the older people are wrong. And worst of all, they don't have any plans of their own. They just make no sense whatsoever. (*He continues with the same theme.*)

SHRINK: So what I hear you saying is that they are not rational or logical and are destructive without new ideas. And you are also not feeling very happy about them or your experience. Am I right? (*Aware nods.*)

SHRINK: Let me see if I can be helpful so it will be a better experience when you have your second session tomorrow. Let us go back to our radio receiver model. You are just trying to pick up all the signals that are coming in. Everything they are sending. Now don't think in terms of just what is *rational* and *logical.* You also have to pick up all the *emotions* and *feelings* that are being sent. What you need to determine is, How are they experiencing life at this time? How are they perceiving the world, their life at the university and in the commune, and people like you? So don't get thrown off by logic and rationality. Can you try that? (*Aware, looking somewhat discouraged, indicates he will and departs, with Shrink patting him on the back.*)

Scene 3: Next morning, after the workshop.

SHRINK: Good morning, Bob! Sit down and tell me what you have learned about where those young people are at.

AWARE: Professor Shrink, those kids are lying. They distort everything our generation has done. They are misrepresenting us all. Can you imagine them living in communes and wanting the rest of us to do so? Why they smell to high heaven! All that unwashed hair and those dirty, smelly feet. And all that foul language. I can take four-letter words from men, but to hear them from the lips of young ladies is terrible.

SHRINK: So, you feel they are basically dishonest and are not attempting anything meaningful; they're just trying to be offensive? (*Aware nods and Shrink continues.*) I'm sorry this has not been a good experience. Why don't you give it a try again tomorrow. Use the radio receiver model again, but this time try to think of the radio as a completely neutral source. Don't judge or evaluate the information as it comes in. Don't think of it as good or bad; it is just data as to how they see life and why. Give it one more try.

Scene 4: The third morning.

AWARE (*entering, obviously irritated and upset*): Professor, I have been coming here for three days and those kids have not heard one damned thing I have been telling them. They are completely hopeless.

SHRINK: Mr. Aware, I am going to have to be very confronting with you. When you came in here on the first day, I judged you to be open to new learning and as really wanting to gain new communication skills. Instead, you have learned nothing, have only stood in judgment of the young people, and have persisted in broadcasting without receiving.

AWARE (*completely shocked and becoming angry*): Now I am beginning to understand what this is all about. You believe what they believe. You are one of them. That's why you wear that long hair and those glasses. I see it all now. This is a plot! This is a plot! You are trying to change me. You are trying to change me.

Introduction

Communication is one of the primary areas for understanding human behavior. In organizational surveys, communication has always been ranked high as a problem by managers. A survey of managers in three countries found that communication was ranked as a key barrier to organizational effectiveness by 74 percent of the responding companies in the United States, 63 percent in Great Britain, and 85 percent in Japan.[2] A recent study of leading companies concluded that effective managers strategically use communication to manage tough organizational changes.[3] Communicating effectively seems to be an area of increasing concern for most managers.[4]

Communication is the primary area of focus for understanding human interactions and learning methods of changing one's own behavior and influencing that of others. This is an area in which individuals can make great strides in improving their own effectiveness. It is also the point of major conflicts and misunderstandings between two people, between members of a team, between groups, and within the total organization as a system. This is one reason communication workshops are probably more widespread than any other type. Sensitivity training deals with helping people communicate better, and family counseling sessions and group therapy are communication-oriented. Management workshops deal with it much as we do in this course.

In this module we will continue to build on previously presented theories of personality, motivation, and perception. We begin with a review of the relationship between personality, motivation, perception, and communication. An examination of the basic components of the communication process is followed by a review of the different levels of communication. Finally, interpersonal communication, the group's effects on the communication process, and the cross-cultural context of communication are explored.

The Relationship among Personality, Motivation, Perception, and Communication

The nature of the personalities involved, the perceptual process, and motivation deeply affect communication. What two people communicate about is determined by who they are and by how they perceive themselves and the other person in the situation. How they perceive will depend on their motivation (goals, needs, defenses) at the given moment. This relationship is illustrated in Figure 8–1.

The communicated idea is so closely related to the personality, perceptions, and motivations of both the sender and the receiver that misunderstandings are built into the nature of the process. In addition, the method of communication—face-to-face, telephone, electronically via computer network or via voice mail technology, meetings, formal reports, and memorandums—is likely to influence the nature of the communication episode. Overcoming the natural barriers to communication is a major objective in communicating meaning. Before we begin to examine some of the barriers to accurate communication, let's review briefly the communication process.

Figure 8–1 Relationship among Core Concepts of Motivation, Perception, and Communication

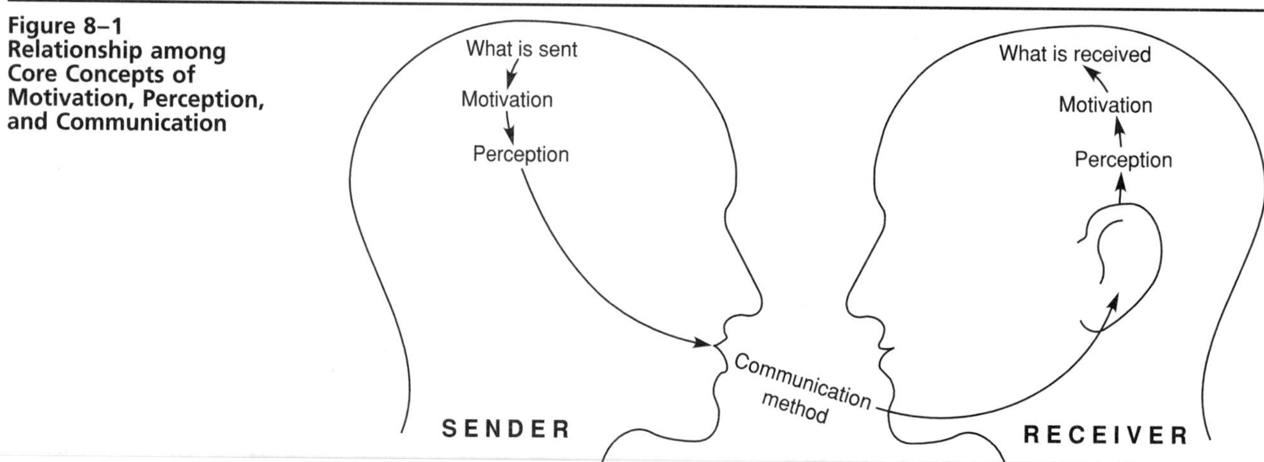

In communication, all transfer of meaning filters through the motivational and perceptual determinants of the sender and receiver.

The Communication Process

At the most basic level, **communication** is the transfer of information from one person to another. As such, the communication episode entails the transfer of information from one person (the sender) to another (the receiver) by some method (the channel). Yet communication is complex and problematic, as we shall see. The process involves five elements: the sender, the message, the medium, the receiver, and feedback. The sender–receiver link (the channel) can be a telephone wire or computer signal, sound waves (the voice), or a written message, to name a few. One key difficulty is noise or interference in the channel, which distorts the message. Noise can be literally that, as when you try to hold a conversation in the same room with a band or a loud engine. Any other signal in the channel of communication besides the desired message can be thought of as noise. A beautiful symphony that prevents me from hearing a customer's request, static that disturbs a computer signal, or the poor quality of a photocopy that prevents me from reading a memo—all these are noise. However, there are other sorts of noise whose sources are in the sender and receiver themselves. Communications are heavily interactive with perceptions, attitudes, and interpretations, being both dependent on them and an important factor affecting them. Figure 8–1 outlines some of these connections.

Still another factor affecting communications is the process of encoding and decoding. Any message to be sent must first be encoded. We formulate our meanings in words, for instance, to hold a conversation; in special circumstances, we use special codes. (The signals of the quarterback on the football field; the special language of surgeons during an operation; the slang with which we communicate with our buddies; the specially ordered, cryptic conversation of air traffic controllers and pilots, or the dispatcher and police units all offer examples.) If the sender and receiver aren't using the same code, accurate communication will not take place even if there is no noise in the channel.

Language is one obvious sort of code, and words and their meaning are a significant source of potential miscommunication where sender and receiver understand different meanings for the same word.

Levels of Communication

A variety of classifications of communication levels can be found in the literature. Some make the distinction between verbal and nonverbal communication; some make the distinction between verbal and electronic communication; some make the distinction between different electronic communication media; and some make the distinction among various other types of communication: intraindividual (e.g., a message is sent from sensory organ to the brain), interpersonal (e.g., a message is sent between two individuals or more within the same group), intraorganizational (e.g., a message is sent between two groups or subsystems within the same organization), and interorganizational (e.g., a message is sent between two organizations). In this module, we examine communications at the interpersonal levels.

Interpersonal Communication

As we have seen, at the most basic level, communication is a process that occurs when an individual sends and receives messages through a chosen method of communication in an effort to create meaning in his or her mind or in the mind of others. Figure 8–1 illustrates the multiple elements that participate in the interpersonal communication episode. Each of the elements not only plays a critical role in the communication process, but also serves as a source of potential barriers for accurate communications.

Barriers to Accurate Communication

There are many barriers to accurate communication: conflicting assumptions, inadequate information, semantics, emotional blocks, nonverbal communication barriers, cultural barriers, inadequate communication networks, and limited communication methods and technology. Four of the barriers that will be presented here have a basis in the factors included in the discussion of perception in the previous module. The barriers become apparent by asking what two people need to have in common to communicate. By way of helping answer this question, we might ask, If you were an explorer in a jungle area and encountered a native who had never had any contact with the world outside of his own isolated tribe, what could you communicate with him about? The answer is that you could exchange meaning—through sign language—only about those things with which both of you had had past experience: food, shelter, temperature, elimination, birth, death, facts about the environment such as where the sun rises and sets, and so on. The codes of past experience have to be shared by both parties before meaning can be exchanged.

Conflicting Assumptions

When one individual sends a communication to another, he or she is assuming that the receiver will use the same codes of past experience in interpreting the message that were used in sending it. The receiver, in turn, will assume that the codes he or she uses to give meaning to the message are the same as those used by the sender. This is probably best illustrated by humorous stories that set a person up with one set of assumptions and codes and then switch to an entirely different set in the punch line.

Unfortunately, daily communication between people is frequently distorted because each uses slightly different assumptions and codes, but they make the assumption that each is using the same system; there is no punch line to help them out. This *assumed overlap of codes* is incorrect a large percentage of the time, but it is not realized by the participants and the misunderstanding goes undetected.

Organizational life, with its hierarchy of superiors and subordinates, is an ideal culture for nurturing the problems of conflicting assumptions. Employees and bosses perceive many aspects of the subordinate's job duties and the obstacles to performance of them differently as we discussed in the module on perception. The boss may well not be the communicator he or she believes, as indicated in Tables 7–1 and 7–2. The organizational climate usually generates an atmosphere in which subordinates fear they might appear to be stupid if they ask too many questions; often they assume they understand what is being passed down but they really do not. Thus conflicting assumptions are apt to abound between levels of the hierarchy, between sections, and between people in the organization.

Figure 8–2 illustrates the problem of conflicting assumptions, or assumed overlap, in the codes of past experience that are active in communication. Each individual's codes of past experience are unique, but to an extent they overlap with those of other individuals in general (as between the explorer and the native) and with those of country, town, social class, family, and so on. The major problem in communications, then, is that each individual is inclined to assume that people with whom he or she interacts are using the same coding systems. That this is not the case often goes undetected.

Inadequate Information

Frequently a manager does not provide enough information for those receiving assignments to do the jobs adequately.

Semantics

Semantics (word usage) is a major source of communication failure. Most words in the dictionary have multiple meanings. An illustration is the word *charge:*

You *charge* someone a fee for doing a service.

You *charge* something you purchase when you want to pay later.

You *charge* a battery when you want it to provide electricity.

You *charge* an official with duties to perform.

You *charge* a horse into battle against an enemy.

You get a *charge* out of something funny.

Figure 8–2
Assumed Overlap of Codes of Past Experience in Communication

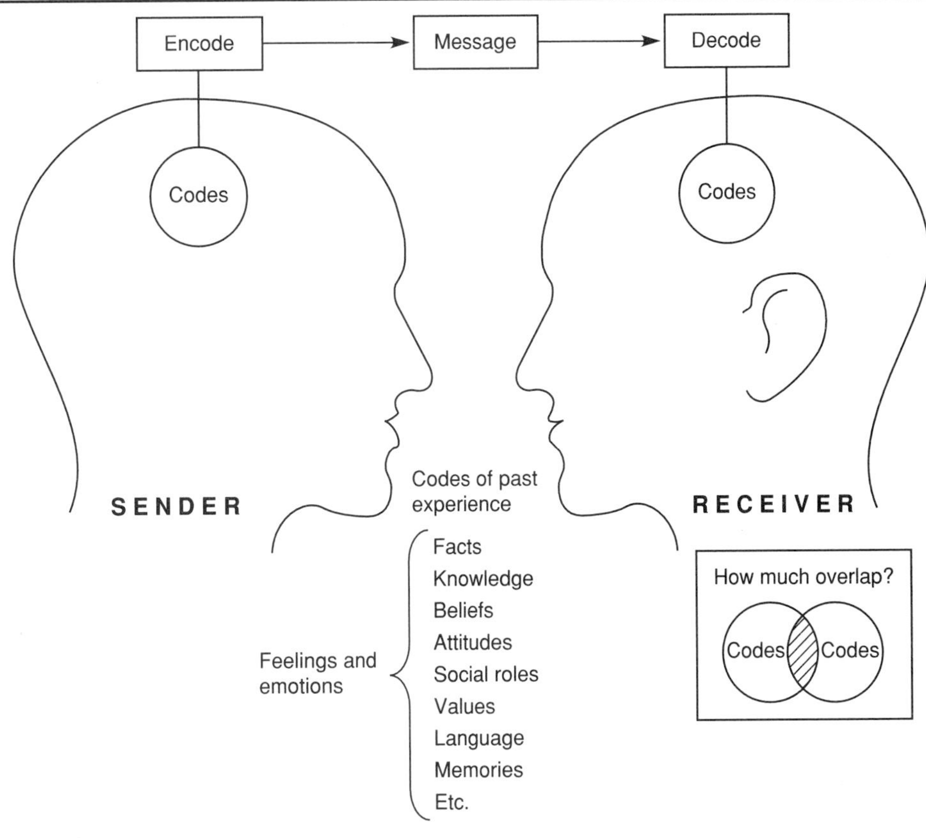

Communication between two persons involves transfer of meaning, which assumes that both individuals use the same coding system. Since each individual's codes are unique, there is never the degree of agreement (overlap) between the two coding systems that either party assumes. Thus conflicting assumptions are primary barriers to communications.

You place a *charge* of powder into a cannon.

You *charge* a criminal for crimes committed.

You *charge* a rifle when you level it at the enemy.

A favorite word for discussion in management courses is *fast,* which can have meanings that are directly opposite: A color is fast when it won't run, while a horse is fast when it runs well.

When two individuals are using different meanings of the same word and do not realize it, a barrier to meaning exists that may go undetected. The phrase ''meanings are in people, not words'' is commonly used in management workshops. You cannot assume the meaning you give a word will be the one the receiver uses in decoding the message.

Emotional Blocks

All experiences and all learning have an emotional and feeling component. The Penfield brain research reported earlier revealed that recall of past experiences includes not only the event and content but the feelings that accompanied them at the time they occurred. Figure 8–2 also represents this in the codes of past experience, all of which are learned with a feeling component. The significance of this for communications is that any time the codes of past experience are used, the feelings and emotions are present to influence both sender and receiver at the time the message is exchanged. Most of the time neither is aware of this, although the feelings are intense and are a part of the content. Sometimes, however, the content does not indicate the feelings, but the individual is transmitting nonverbal signals of which he or she is not aware though they are being received by others.[5]

Love and affection can distort communications, but the term *emotional blocks* seems to be used most often in the sense that defense mechanisms are operating; denial and projection are examples. (See Module 7 on perception.) This area was explored in Module 5 on personality and diversity, when the Parent, Adult, and Child concepts used in Thomas A. Harris's book *I'm OK—You're OK* are discussed.[6] Most of us have definite ideas of the ways certain things should be done and the way people ought to behave under given circumstances. When the message we receive is contrary to these ideas of what is right and proper, the feelings we have will distort or even block out the incoming messages.

Nonverbal Communication Barriers

Activity 8–3 focuses on the critical role that **nonverbal communication** plays in the communication episode that many times serves as a confusing or reinforcement element. Learning to be aware of nonverbal communication can help in understanding the communication episode as well as in setting the stage and deriving a holistic meaning of the communication message. Here are a few basic types of nonverbal communication:

Body motion or **kinesic behavior**—gestures, facial expressions, eye behavior, touching, and any other movement of the limbs and body.

Physical characteristics—body shape, physique, posture, height, weight, hair, and skin color.

Paralanguage—voice quality, volume, speech rate, pitch, nonfluencies (e.g., *yaa, um,* and *ah*), laughing.

Proxemics—ways people use and perceive space (for example, seating arrangements and conversational distance).

Environment—building and room design, furniture and interior decorating, light, noise, and cleanliness.

Time—being late or early, keeping others waiting, and other relationships between time and status.

Cultural Barriers

Communication Networks

The nature of the communication network that the individual is a part of might create an additional barrier. Communication can be examined by focusing on how and what individuals communicate as well as by focusing on the communication relationships among individuals. **Communication networks** involve oral, written, and nonverbal signals between two or more individuals. For example, the pattern of signals will flow between a manager of a produce department in a large food store and the other managers while, at the same time, another pattern of signals will flow between the manager and his or her immediate subordinates and all the other individuals with whom the manager interacts. A manager's network extends laterally (with other managers at the same level) and vertically (with a direct superior or direct subordinates). From this point of view, communication networks can be quite complex, and they have the potential to create barriers to understanding.

Communication Methods and Technology

The method or the tool chosen to transfer the message from the sender to the receiver plays a key role in the communication episode. With the advancement of technology, we are capable of assembling and electronically storing, transmitting, processing, and retrieving words, numbers, and sounds around the globe. Computer networks enhance our communication accuracy not only within the small unit or between two individuals, but also between large units located in different geographical areas. Yet, limiting the communication episode to the computer's screen—which allows for the use of two of the senses only—can be a major barrier in the communication episode.

Communication, as an exchange of meaning, is bounded by culture. As we have seen in Figure 8–2, **encoding** describes the producing of a symbol into a message and **decoding** describes the receiving of a message from a symbol. Furthermore, the message sender must encode her or his meaning into a form that the receiver will recognize. Translating meaning into words and behaviors (i.e., into symbols) and translating the words and behaviors back again into meaning is based on a person's cultural background, which is not the same for every person.[7] Since cross-cultural communication occurs between two individuals from different cultures, it can lead to much miscommunication. Recent research indicates that the greater the differences between the sender's and the receiver's cultures, the greater the chance for miscommunication.[8] Miscommunication in this context is the result of misperception, misinterpretation, and misevaluation. The following example was provided by Nancy Adler:

> Since in Cantonese the word for "eight" sounds like "faat," which means prosperity, a Hong Kong textile manufacturer Mr. Lau Ting-pong paid $5 million in 1988 for car registration number 8. A year later, a European millionnaire paid $4.8 million at Hong Kong's Lunar New Year auction for vehicle registration number 7, a decision that mystified the Chinese, since the number 7 has little significance in the Chinese calculation of fortune."[9]

Cross-cultural communication occurs when a person from one culture communicates with a person from another culture. Miscommunication in the cross-cultural context occurs when the receiving person (from the "other" culture) does not receive the sender's intended message. Coupling individual diversity with cross-cultural differences dictates that one must assume significant differences between the sender and receiver. Furthermore, cross-cultural perceptions seem to play a role in the cross-cultural communication episode. People from diverse cultures tend to view the world differently, while at the same time they stereotype individuals from other cultures. As we have seen in the previous module, perceptual patterns are neither innate nor absolute. They are selective, learned, culturally determined, consistent, and inaccurate.[10] Managing the cross-cultural communication episodes presents a set of challenges for organizations and managers of the multinational corporation. Yet some of the skills that are explored in the next section provide the necessary foundation.

Managers' Role in Managing Communication: Overcoming the Barriers

Managers' role in fostering the communication process is critical. Beyond a self-assessment about their own communication style, methods, and competencies, managers can ensure a work environment in which employees feel that they can communicate openly at all times. A recent study found that two-way communication is a critical element in fostering continuous improvement and organizational learning.[11]

Practicing Communication Skills

Each manager must practice communication skills until they become second nature. *Paraphrasing,* for example, is one of the more useful skills practiced in numerous professions. Diplomats spend considerable (sometimes endless) time making sure they understand views of the representatives of other countries. Television journalists frequently pause in their interviews to feed back what they think they have heard. Supervisors giving instructions to employees find it useful to say, "Now, tell me what you are going to do so we will be sure we are in agreement." One top executive we observed had called six other executives together for a preliminary discussion of a problem area. He asked each person to use five minutes to present his initial views on the matter. As each individual finished, he would summarize what he had heard, ask if he understood correctly, and then ask questions if he had any. After all six had spoken, the executive summarized and integrated their views and then led a discussion concerning what steps should be taken to study the problem.

A middle-level manager informed us that paraphrasing was one of the most meaningful ways to handle a complaint at the initial stage.

> Give the person the time needed to fully express the problem. When the person is through, summarize what you have heard and see if there is agreement on the complaint. Then say you will look into the matter and discuss it further at a later date. This has the advantage of not feeling pressured to make an uninformed decision on the spot, of letting the individual know he or she has been heard, and of giving the individual time to cool off.

Paraphrasing is a useful tool when a disagreement arises. One exercise frequently used in communication workshops is to have a group of people sit in a circle and carry on a discussion on a controversial topic such as the Arab–Israeli conflict in the Middle East or arms limitations. After one person has expressed her view, the next person to respond must paraphrase to the last speaker's satisfaction what has just been said before he expresses his own views. This is continued for the entire discussion. Individuals usually find they are so preoccupied with what they are about to say that they forget to listen to what is being said. (Your class might want to try this as an additional exercise if there is time.)

Awareness and Understanding

Learning that communications problems do exist and studying some of the theory and concepts that might account for them is an initial step. This means learning not only at the content level but also at the dynamic level of what goes on between you and other people when you communicate. It is difficult for some people just to understand that others are not perceiving the world as they do.

Social Technology

Knowledge of the techniques and methods available to help administrators in overcoming communications problems is a major objective of this text. Managers must learn what technology is available and how to use it for all four levels of effectiveness. Practice is necessary in dialoguing, listening, paraphrasing, perceptual checking, and so on.

Creating a Supportive Organizational Climate

The organizational atmosphere is all-important. If it is threatening and suppresses expression of individuals' feelings, there will be serious breakdowns in communications at all levels of the hierarchy. Modern management theory recognizes that a manager's skills must include the handling of feelings and emotions of employees as much as how to work with logic and rationality; the consequences of not developing these skills are that employees' emotional blocks will divert energy into nonproductive or antiorganizational channels. Supportiveness and two-way communication, as basic values of the organizational culture, can reduce employees' feelings of defensiveness.

Self-Awareness

It is assumed that the more managers are aware of their own needs, goals, feelings, and defenses, the better they will be able to cope with their own growth and behavior. This means being able to communicate with yourself. It means knowing what your strengths are in interaction situations and what part of the problem you represent. The section on "I'm OK—You're OK" in Module 5 was directed toward this area of development.

Giving and Receiving Feedback

The impact one person has on another can be a major barrier to communication. Managers need to have some idea of the impact they are having if they are to influence others effectively. Producing an organizational atmosphere in which there is two-way feedback between superior and subordinates is one area of development. Some organizations are having employees fill out anonymous evaluation forms concerning their supervisors and managers. The data become the subject of general discussion between the superior and subordinates as to how the superior's behavior is affecting the progress of the work. Training workshops dealing with communications, leadership, and self-awareness can be helpful in attaining insight into the impact one is having on others; learning how to give others feedback without offending them and learning how to receive feedback without being offended are currently stressed.

Working with the Motivation of Others

In Frederick Herzberg's theory, helping individuals use their own internal dynamos—the motivators—can increase both productivity and satisfaction. A manager can work at the level of trying to produce the conditions in the work situation that augment this result, but he or she also needs to make efforts to understand what motivates each individual. This can be explored in goal setting, in daily conversations when this appears appropriate, and in watching the behavior of the individual. Activity 8–1 focuses on this subject.

Coaching and Goal Setting

Goal setting as an organizationwide practice can help overcome communications barriers. When a boss and a subordinate sit down periodically to define the subordinate's goals, which are part of the organization's goals, many of their perceptual distortions will be greatly reduced. At the same time, the individual's personal goals, what he or she would like to attain careerwise from the present situation and in the coming years, can be an integral part of the process. Discussion of progress and feedback from the supervisor as to how well the individual is doing should be accomplished as the need arises, based on events as they occur. Saving up these discussions for yearly review produces barriers to communications; not only does the subordinate lack the information and guidance needed, but unexpressed feelings can build up and interfere with performance. Milestone points for specific review and revision of the goals should be part of the procedure to ensure that nothing is overlooked.

Coaching is a very broad topic, and only two limited aspects of it will be considered here. The first concerns developing the manager's attitudes about the employee as a human resource who brings assets to the work situation that need to be nurtured if the employee is to grow and be productive. The manager as a coach needs to know how employees think of themselves in terms of their strengths and what goals they perceive as being meaningful in order to develop and use these strengths. When a manager finds that an employee's opinion in these regards is different than his own, important data for coaching the employee in his or her performance and career become available.

A second aspect of coaching is developing listening skills, which can help the manager determine accurately what the employee is saying about himself or herself. Paraphrasing, as a listening skill, is one way to try to get objective data from others without imposing one's own preconceptions onto what is being said. Asking nonleading questions for clarification is another; "I'm not sure what you are telling me. Could you give me that again more slowly?" does not lead the individual from his or her own trend of thoughts. As an example of a leading question, consider the response to a mother who expressed concern about her teenage son, who had always been a good student, good to his parents, and helpful around the house, but who, during the past six months, had shown all the opposite behaviors. The person who was supposed to have been the listener asked, "Do you suppose he might be on drugs?" Even if the mother did not have a problem when she came, she did when she left.

Activity 8–1 ("Communication, Coaching, and Goal Setting") provides an opportunity to further develop your awareness of the critical role that communication plays in facilitating individual goal setting. In this activity, it is assumed that the best way to learn to work with human resources is to go through the process of thinking about one's own resources and goals. Most of you will not have formulated your thinking in this regard, and you may feel you are groping. It is better to start thinking about this now than to wait until you are confronted with the problem in an actual work situation.

Students in this course sometimes say they do not like to talk about themselves because they may appear to others either to be bragging or to have too few resources to talk about. The fact they have come this far in their education indicates they do have resources to talk about and they had better think about goals if they are to continue to grow. Recruiters often want the individual being interviewed to talk spontaneously in terms of interests and what he or she does well in an authentic manner that indicates some degree of self-esteem, not just a selling job. Throughout a career, an individual can expect bosses to periodically ask, "Tell me, how do you see yourself in terms of your job? Where do you want to go? What do you want to do? What do you want from your job? Are there abilities you have that are not being used or that you want to develop?" Some inhibitions in answering such questions can be overcome by practice in a situation such as we saw in Activity 8–1 earlier in this module.

Current Challenges

The communication episode is a complex process that involves many different dimensions. New forms of communications have emerged over the past decade. Although face-to-face communication is vital to individual, group, and organizational effectiveness, the major technological leap has introduced alternative advanced communication technology that helps overcome some limitations of interpersonal interaction. The transformation of communication-driven technology has been accelerated as a result of increased global competition and the emerging of the global markets. E-mail, communication networks (such as local area networks and wide area networks), electronic bulletin boards, real time video conferencing, and further development of software (such as groupware software) that allows individuals and teams to work together on a problem while located in different places are likely to become more of the norms in communication.

While globalization and technological development are driving the emerging new forms of communication, the challenge of understanding the impacts of the new communication technologies and attempting to manage them increases. For example, think of yourself as a part of a team where each member is in a different geographical location. You are linked via a local area network and a groupwide software program. The team is trying to solve a problem but is not able to see each other or talk to each other orally. But you are able to send messages back and forth, and every person on the team is able to take part in the exchange via the computer screen.

Based on what we have covered in this module, what are some of the barriers for accurate communication that your team is likely to experience? What will be the effect of this barrier on your team? The scientific community is only beginning to investigate the new advanced communication technology and its impact on the behavior and effectiveness of individuals and teams. In Module 16 on the management of technology and information, we explore further some of these issues.

Communication is also faced with the increased challenge of diversity at the workplace and globalization. As we have seen, diversity and cultural differences can play a major role in creating barriers to accurate communication. Ethnocentrism—the tendency to consider the values, norms, and customs of one's own country to be superior to those of other countries—has been shown to hinder the communication process.[12] Figure 8–3 presents Nancy Adler's suggestions for overcoming cross-cultural barriers to communication.

Summary

Communication has often been ranked as a key problem of organizational life. Communication is closely interrelated with the other core concepts of personality, diversity, perception, and motivation previously reviewed. Messages to be communicated are formulated from the sender's motivation (intent) and perception of the relevant context.

Figure 8–3
What Do I Do If They Do Not Speak My Language?

Verbal behavior

- *Clear, slow speech.* Enunciate each word. Do not use colloquial expressions.
- *Repetition.* Repeat each important idea using different words to explain the same concept.
- *Simple sentences.* Avoid compound, long sentences.
- *Active verbs.* Avoid passive verbs.

Nonverbal behavior

- *Visual restatements.* Use as many visual restatements as possible, such as pictures, graphs, tables, and slides.
- *Gestures.* Use more facial and hand gestures to emphasize the meaning of words.
- *Demonstration.* Act out as many themes as possible.
- *Pauses.* Pause more frequently.
- *Summaries.* Hand out written summaries of your verbal presentation.

Attribution

- *Silence.* When there is a silence, wait. Do not jump in to fill the silence. The other person is probably just thinking more slowly in the nonnative language or translating.
- *Intelligence.* Do not equate poor grammar and mispronunciation with lack of intelligence; it is usually a sign of second-language use.
- *Differences.* If unsure, assume difference, not similarity.

Comprehension

- *Understanding.* Do not just assume that they understand; assume that they do not understand.
- *Checking comprehension.* Have colleagues repeat their understanding of the material back to you. Do not simply ask if they understand or not. Let them explain what they understand to you.

Design

- *Breaks.* Take more frequent breaks. Second-language comprehension is exhausting.
- *Small modules.* Divide the material into smaller modules.
- *Longer time frame.* Allocate more time for each module than usual in a monolingual program.

Motivation

- *Encouragement.* Verbally and nonverbally encourage and reinforce speaking by nonnative language participants.
- *Drawing out.* Explicitly draw out marginal and passive participants.
- *Reinforcement.* Do not embarass novice speakers.

Source: Adopted from N. J. Adler, *International Dimensions of Organizational Behavior* (Boston, Mass.: PWS-Kent, 1991), p. 69. Used with permission.

The meaning of the message to the receiver is filtered through the receiver's perceptual frame of reference and own needs and defenses.

Eight barriers to communication are conflicting assumptions between sender and receiver, cultural differences, nonverbal communication barriers, limited communication methods and technology, inadequate information, semantics, inadequate communication networks, and emotional blocks. The latter area is complicated by the tendency of the receiver to evaluate and judge the message rather than understand the meaning. Listening for logic and rationality, while ignoring the emotional and feeling content, also interferes with the transmission of meaning. Ways to overcome these barriers and improve communications include developing awareness and understanding, social technology applications, a supportive organizational climate, and self-awareness.

A variety of activities were developed to enhance improved communication skills. Activities 8–1 and 8–2 provide the experiential base for understanding the communication process and the development of basic skills of coaching and goal setting. Activity 8–3 provides the opportunity to explore the dynamics of nonverbal communication.

Communication is a complex phenomenon and a multilevel concept that can have an impact on behavior at the individual, group, and organizational levels. In this module, communication was examined and studied at the interpersonal and intragroup levels. As we will see in Part 4, communication influences key organizational processes such as creativity, innovation, work design, and the management of quality. Improving the communication process is an ongoing managerial challenge that requires continuous effort.

Study Questions

1. "In the communication process, meaning is in the mind of the sender and the receiver." Explain this statement.
2. Of the barriers to communication given, which is the most basic? Why?
3. What is the "dialogue sequence" described in the Professor Shrink scene? How could it be relevant to business organizations? To interpersonal relationships?
4. Several methods are given for overcoming barriers to communication. Give examples from your own experience of how these methods worked. Give examples of other methods that have worked for you or others you know.
5. Discuss the relationship between communication and perception.
6. Discuss the relationship between communication, diversity, and expectations.
7. We discussed a few ways for overcoming barriers to communication. Provide an example from your group's experience that illustrates how you overcame communication barriers.
8. What are some of the similarities and differences between interpersonal and intergroup communications?
9. What does goal setting have to do with communication at both the interpersonal and intergroup levels?

Endnotes

1. Variation of this dialogue sequence can be found in C. Rogers, *On Becoming a Person* (Boston: Houghton Mifflin, 1961), chap. 17; Floyd Mann, "Handling Misunderstanding and Conflict," in *Current Perspectives for Managing Organizations,* B. M. Bass and S. D. Deep, eds. (Englewood Cliffs, N.J.: Prentice-Hall, 1970), pp. 476–80; and Gordon Lippitt, *Quest for Dialogue* (Lebanon, Pa.: Sowers, 1966).

2. R. R. Blake and J. S. Mouton, *Grid Organizational Development* (Houston: Gulf Publishing, 1968), p. 4. Many recent studies reaffirmed Blake and Mouton's results.

3. M. Yong and J. E. Post, "Managing to Communicate, Communicating to Manage: How Leading Companies Communicate with Employees," *Organizational Dynamics* 22 no. 1 (1993), pp. 31–43; Berlo, D. K. *The Process of Communication: An Introduction to Theory and Practice.* New York: Holt, Rinehart & Winston, 1960; Burger, P., and B. M. Bass. *Assessment of Managers: An International Comparison.* New York: Free Press, 1979; Cheney, G. "The Rhetoric of Identification and the Study of Organizational Communication," *Quarterly Journal of Speech* 69 (1983), pp. 143–58; Fabun, D. *Communications.* Beverly Hills, Calif.: Glencoe Press, 1968; Gibson, L.; J. M. Ivancevich; and J. H. Donnelly, Jr. "The Communication Process," in *Organizations: Behavior, Structure, Processes,* rev. ed. Dallas, Tex.: Business Publications, 1976, pp. 161–85; Goldhaber, G.; M. Yales; D. Porter; and R. Lesniak. "Organizational Communication," *Human Communication Research* 6 (1978), pp. 76–96; Haney, W. V. *Communication and Organizational Behavior.* Homewood, Ill.: Richard D. Irwin, 1973.

4. See, for example, W. A. Gudykunst, *Bridging Differences* (Thousand Oaks, Calif.: Sage, 1994); Chu, Leonard L. "Mass Communication Theory: The Chinese Perspective," *Media Asia* 131 (1986), pp. 14–19.

5. See Carl Rogers's concept of congruence in communication. C. Rogers, *On Becoming a Person* (Boston: Houghton Mifflin, 1961), pp. 338–46.

6. T. A. Harris, *I'm OK—You're OK* (New York: Harper & Row, 1969).

7. N. J. Adler, *International Dimensions of Organizational Behavior* (Boston, Mass.: PWS–Kent, 1991); Kohls, L. Robert. *Survival Kit for Overseas Living* (Yarmouth, Maine: Intercultural Press, 1979), pp. 30–31.

8. B. J. Reilly and J. A. DiAngelo, "Communication: A Cultural System of Meaning and Values," *Human Relations* 43, no. 2 (1990), pp. 129–40; Prekel, T. "Multi-Cultural Communication: A Challenge to Managers." Paper delivered at the International Convention of the American Business Communication Association, New York, 1983.

9. N. J., Adler, Ibid., Page 65.

10. N. J. Adler, Ibid., p. 68.

11. Young and Post, "Managing to Communicate."; Putti, J. M.; S. Aryee; and J. Phua. "Communication Relationship Satisfaction and Organizational Commitment," *Group and Organization Studies* 15, no. 1 (1990), pp. 44–52.

12. See, for example, N. J. Adler, *International Dimensions of Organizational Behavior* (Boston, Mass.: PWS-Kent, 1991).

Activity 8–3: Nonverbal Communication

Objectives:

1. To complete small group tasks without any verbal communication.
2. To explore individual and group reactions when verbal communication is cut off and only nonverbal communication can be used. To test your tolerance for ambiguity.
3. To demonstrate that shared expectations (group norms and roles) are spontaneously generated.
4. To provide behavioral data for a theoretical discussion of communications in this module.

Task 1 (A Structured Task):

Participants are to put their books aside and are not to refer to them again until this exercise and the discussion following it have been completed.

All chairs and tables are moved to the sides of the room. Members of a team or group (five to seven people) stand in a close circle facing one another.

The instructor will ask participants to become completely silent before giving instructions and will ask them not to speak until this exercise in nonverbal communication is completed.

The instructor will present a poster for all to see upon which the "Shoe Store" problem (included in the *Instructor's Manual*) is written. Teams are to reach a consensus on the correct answer. Only nonverbal (no written or spoken) communication is to be used.
(Time: 5 minutes)

When the instructor indicates the time is up, each team is to report its solution to the class. Three minutes are then allowed for discussion of the results among team members, after which the instructor will provide the correct solution.

Task 2 (An Unstructured Task):

Participants are to remain completely silent until this exercise is completed.

Each group is to carry on, as a team, any activities or conversational topic of its own choosing for seven minutes. No spoken or written communication, only nonverbal communication, is to be used. You might want to start by expressing to each other your feelings about this class and then move on to other activities as a team. Use the space in this room in any way you wish.
(Time: 7 minutes)

Task 3:

The instructor will stop all the activity, asking everyone to remain silent until the next instruction has been given.

Take one minute to try to get in touch with your feelings. How are you feeling now, and how were you feeling during the exercise, about the interaction in which you just took part? When the instructor indicates the time is up, you are to speak. Each participant should be given an opportunity to share feelings with the group. (Time: 1 minute of silence and 3 to 5 minutes for sharing)

Individuals are called on to share how they felt about the experience. (Time: 10 to 15 minutes)

Task 4:

Each group is to discuss the following:

(1) What shared expectations developed in the group as to what was to be done and how members should or could behave? These may be thought of as group norms.

(2) What roles developed among the members?

(3) Did any subgrouping take place?

(Time: 5 minutes)

Each group is to report its findings. The instructor will add observations of what norms and roles he or she saw evolving in each group.

PART 3 MANAGING TEAMS

Review

Part 2 interrelated the four conceptual areas of personality and diversity, motivation, perception, and communication. Part 1 helped to establish the boundaries and process of the course. Part 2 continued to explore the relationships between the core conceptual areas that are at the root of human behavior in organizational settings. Figure A provides a conceptual road map that summarizes the relationship between the four core concepts and effectiveness. We have found this road map to be a good analytical tool to begin the study of human behavior in organizational settings. Before we progress to study the effects of key organizational processes on individual, group, and organizational behavior, we need to investigate the nature of group behavior.

Figure A
Relationships among Four Core Concepts for Understanding Organizational Behavior at Individual, Group, Intergroup, and Organizational Levels

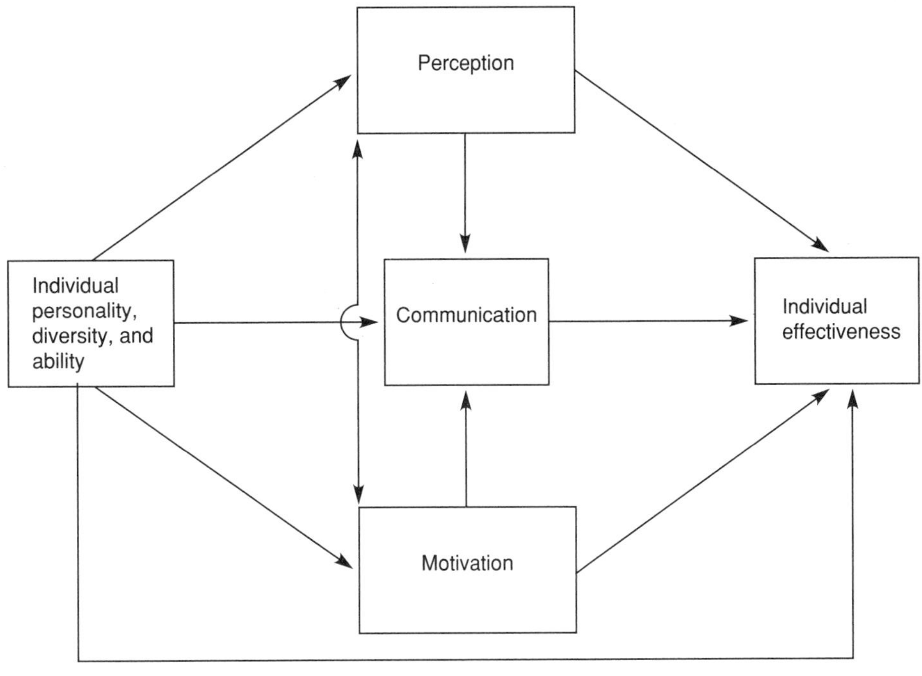

Preview of Part 3

Small group dynamics will be a major focus of study throughout this course because work groups and teams are the basic unit of organizational life. As the course progresses, new aspects of group effectiveness will be introduced so they can be applied to your classroom group. Modules 9, 10, and 11 concentrate directly on the small group and provide material on team skills, small group theory, and team building or team development. Module 12 focuses on the dynamics between teams. We approach the study of work groups and teams with the process learning model, which first provides an experience from which you can develop theory and concepts.

Thus, at the beginning of Module 9, group problem solving is explored in Activity 9–1 (''Mountain Survival Exercise''), Activity 9–2 (''Important Days Task''), and Activity 9–3 (''Task 21''). These are similar exercises, and your instructor will most likely assign only one of them to you. These activities should help you to understand (1) the difference between a group and a team and (2) why teams are so often used in organizations.

These activities are a good introduction to the subject of team effectiveness and the individual behaviors that help to improve team effectiveness. We then discuss individual versus group decision making as well as the circumstances where group problem solving or participative management is most appropriate. The module examines the role of the manager in facilitating group decision making and problem solving, explores ways in which creativity in problem solving can be enhanced, and shows some specific ways in which teams are used in organizations.

Module 9 ends with three additional activities that you may be assigned. The Group Skills Development activity is followed by ''Who Gets the Overtime?'' which is an exercise in decision making where there is no single right answer. The third, ''Decision Making— Japanese Style,'' shows the impact of culture on group processes.

Module 10 focuses on group dynamics. It begins with two activities: ''An Initial Inventory of Group Dynamics'' and ''A Card Game Called *Norms,*'' both of which are designed to help you focus on some of the dynamics at work in your classroom group. The module explores in detail the factors that affect group development and performance, including leadership, group structure, and member composition. The phenomena of social loafing and cohesion are also discussed. The module ends with two activities to help you further explore the dynamics of your classroom group: ''Individual Role Assessment'' and ''Status on the Campus.'' Finally, two case studies provide an opportunity for you to apply the concepts discussed in the module.

Module 11 describes ways to improve team effectiveness, both before a team starts operating and after it has begun its work. The activities and cases in Modules 9 and 10 should have demonstrated the possibility that dysfunctional behavior can exist in teams and work groups, and this module briefly examines ways to prevent and cure this behavior in systematic interventions to enhance team performance. The module contains two activities. The first provides an opportunity for you to revisit your team development goals; the second activity—''Team Building in a Hospital Setting''—illustrates the team-building process via a case study that presents a situation where team building is needed and gives you the chance to outline an intervention program.

Finally, Module 12 focuses on the dynamics between teams in organizational settings. As such, the module presents a framework that can guide the examination of the dynamics between two or more work teams. Intergroup communication processes and the dynamics of conflict are focal points for the module. A significant portion of the module is devoted to conflict handling. Three activities—''Ambiguity, Conflict, and Interteam Dynamics,'' ''The Prisoners' Dilemma,'' and ''The SLO Corporation''—provide opportunities to have concrete experiences of the complex interteam dynamics and their effect on human behavior and performance.

9 Group Problem Solving and Decision Making

Learning Objectives

After completing this module you should be able to

1. Understand the differences between teams and groups.
2. Understand the basic skills that contribute to effective team membership.
3. Explain the role that synergy plays in group problem solving.
4. Understand the rational group problem-solving process.
5. Understand the consensus process in team activity.
6. Gain insights into the dynamics of creativity in group problem solving.
7. State the conditions under which group decision making or participative management is most effective.
8. Understand how problem-solving teams are used in organizations and how groups may be more creative.

List of Key Concepts

Brainstorming
Consensus process
Creativity
Group
Group problem-solving process
Groupware
Interpersonal skills
New product development teams (NPDT)
Nominal group technique
Participative management
Quality control circles (QCC)
Rational problem solving
Self-managing team
Synergy
Team

Our colleague Professor David Peach, Management Area, Cal Poly State University, took the lead on the revision of this module. We are grateful to Dave.

Module Outline

Premodule Preparation

Activity 9–1: Mountain Survival Exercise*

and/or

Activity 9–2: Important Days Task

and/or

Activity 9–3: Task 21

Objectives:

a. To demonstrate problem solving as a small group skill.

b. To show that group solutions can be superior to those of individuals under certain conditions.

c. To identify the types of behavior on the part of team members that facilitate problem-solving effectiveness.

Task 1:

a. Individuals, working alone, will complete the "Mountain Survival Task" in Appendix I, the "Important Days Task" in Appendix J, or "Task 21" in Appendix K. (Time: 10–15 minutes)

Task 2:

a. Individuals are to sit with their regular teams; it will not be necessary to appoint a spokesperson for this exercise.

b. Teams are to solve the problem as a team and arrive at a team solution for the problem. In doing so, the team should try to reach consensus and not use majority vote, trading, or averaging in reaching decisions.

Consensus is a decision process for making full use of available resources for resolving conflicts creatively. Consensus is difficult to reach, so not every ranking will meet with everyone's complete approval. Complete unanimity is not the goal—it is rarely achieved. However, each individual should be able to accept the group rankings on the basis of logic and feasibility. When all group members feel this way, you have reached consensus and the judgment may be entered as a group decision. This means, in effect, that a single person can block the group if he or she thinks it necessary; at the same time, individuals should use this option in the best sense of reciprocity. Here are some guidelines to use in achieving consensus:

1. Avoid arguing for your own rankings. Present your position as clearly and logically as possible, but listen to the other members' reactions and consider them carefully before you press your point.
2. Do not assume that someone must win and someone must lose when discussion reaches a stalemate. Instead, look for the next most acceptable alternative for all parties.
3. Do not change your mind simply to avoid conflict. When agreement seems to come too quickly and easily, be suspicious. Explore the reasons and be sure everyone accepts the solution for similar or complementary reasons. Agree only to positions that have objective or logically sound foundations.
4. Avoid conflict-reducing techniques such as majority vote, splitting the difference, or coin tosses. When a dissenting member finally agrees, don't feel that that person must be rewarded by having her or his own way on a later point.
5. Differences of opinion are natural and expected. Seek them out and try to involve everyone in the decision process. Disagreements can help the group's decision because with a wide range of information and opinions, there is a greater chance that the group will hit upon more adequate solutions.†
6. As the teams work on a solution to the problems, no references, books, or other aids are to be used. The group results are to be recorded in the column titled "Team Rankings" (or "Group Score" for the "Task 21" activity). The individual

* Source: Special permission for reproduction of the Mountain Survival activity is granted by the authors, Professors Fremont E. Kast and James E. Rosenzweig, Graduate School of Business Administration, University of Washington. All rights are reserved, and no reproduction should be made without express approval of Professors Kast and Rosenzweig. We are grateful to them.

† Special permission for reproduction of this is granted by the author, Jay Hall, Ph.D., and publisher, Telemetrics International. All rights reserved.

rankings completed prior to the exercise should not be changed; they will be scored later.
(Time: 30–45 minutes)

Task 3:

a. The correct answer to the exercise will be provided by the instructor.
b. Individuals will calculate a total error score for their own solutions as follows:

If Your Answer Is	If Key Is	Difference between the Two Is
15	4	11
5	7	2
11	2	9
etc., for all items	etc.	etc.
	Total Error Score*	

* Add up without regard to pluses and minuses.

c. Calculate the team score in the same manner.
d. Calculate the average score for the individuals in your group by adding all scores and dividing by the number of members.
e. The instructor will record and display the results for all teams. Tables 9–1 (for "Mountain Survival Exercise" and "Important Days Task") and 9–2 (for "Task 21") are provided for you to record them.
f. Discussion question: Why were the group solutions in this activity superior to those of the average of the individual team members or, for some teams, superior to the "best" individual member?

Table 9–1

Error Scores for Individuals and Groups on "Mountain Survival Exercise" or "Important Days Task" for Your Class

	Before Discussion		After Group Discussion			
Group	Average Error Score of Group Members	Error Score of Most Accurate Group Member	Group Error Score	Gain or Loss over Average Error Score	Individuals in Group Superior to Group Score	Gain or Loss over Most Accurate Individual
1						
2						
3						
4						
5						
6						
7						
8						
Overall Average						

Table 9–2

Correct Answer Scores for Individuals and Groups on "Task 21" for Your Class

	Before Discussion		After Group Discussion			
Group	Average Score of Group Members	Score of Most Accurate Member	Group Score	Gain or Loss over Average Score	Individuals Superior to Group Score	Gain or Loss over Most Accurate Member
1						
2						
3						
4						
5						
6						
7						
8						

Introduction

Your participation in classroom groups provides an opportunity to gain an understanding of three aspects of small group effectiveness: (1) team skills that facilitate the achievement of group goals, (2) characteristics of a group that influence its ability to solve problems and make decisions effectively, and (3) the dynamics of small groups. Even more important for you, participation in a classroom group provides you with a setting where you can assess and develop your *own* skills in influencing the activities of groups in which you participate. Group problem solving and decision making are the subject of this chapter, with an emphasis on the potentially creative forces (**synergy**), in group processes.

We start with a definition of teams. A discussion of team skills is based on the three premodule activities, which allow you to explore team problem solving and synergy. Coverage of group versus individual problem solving is followed by a discussion of group decision making, and an exploration of managerial actions that should foster creativity and improve group problem solving and decision making. Finally, the utilization of group problem solving and decision making in organizations is reviewed. A questionnaire is included to aid you in assessing your personal skills in operating as a team member so you can develop these skills in your team activities as the course continues.

Teams

Work groups and teams have been referred to as "the building blocks of excellent companies."[1] Committees, task forces, quality circles, product development teams, and self-managed teams are all features of today's organizations.

At the most basic level, a **group** can be defined as "a set of three or more individuals that can identify itself and be identified by others in the organization as a group." Groups in organizations can be either *formal* (i.e., a formal part of the organization, created by management) or *informal* (created by the members themselves, largely out of day-to-day interaction between individuals). Alderfer advocated the organizational behavior view of groups, which encompasses both the sociological (external relations) and psychological (internal relations) aspects of group operations in this definition:

A group is a collection of individuals (1) who have significantly interdependent relations with each other, (2) who perceive themselves as a group, reliably distinguishing members from non-members, (3) whose group identity is recognized by nonmembers, (4) who, as group members acting alone or in concert, have significantly interdependent relations with other groups, and (5) whose roles in the group are therefore a function of expectations from themselves, from other group members, and from nongroup members.[2]

Katzenbach and Smith define a **team** as "a small number of people with complementary skills who are committed to a common purpose, set of performance goals, and approach for which they hold themselves mutually accountable."[3] They distinguish between work groups such as committees and teams on the basis that the former's performance is a function of what its members do as individuals, while team performance includes both individual performance and what they call "collective work products" that reflect the joint, real contribution of team members and that are greater than the sum of their individual contributions.[4]

This difference between real teamwork and simple group membership and the skills that lead to performance differences in teams are demonstrated by the premodule activities.

Discussion of Premodule Preparation's Results

Table 9–3 summarizes the results of the Mountain Survival Exercise for 12 groups of college students. Table 9–4 does the same for Task 21. You should find that these results are similar to the ones you obtained in your groups, although because the exercises are not conducted under controlled conditions, results may vary due to such artifacts as the time allotted for both individual and group decision making. However, if we use the group average score as an approximation of the individual group members' capability in the situation faced by the group in the exercises, in general, the groups did better than the average individual. In many cases, the groups performed better than their best individual member. This clearly demonstrates Katzenbach and Smith's notion that a team is more than the sum of its parts and produces performance levels greater than the sum of all the individual bests of team members.[5]

Table 9–3
Summary of Group Performance on the Mountain Survival Exercise

Number of Groups	Average Individual Score	Average Group Score	Average Gain	Average Low Score	Number of Group Scores Lower than Best Individual Score
12	56.2	40.8	6.6	43.3	4

Table 9–4
Summary of Group Performance on Task 21

Number of Groups	Average Individual Score	Average Group Score	Average Gain	Average Low Score	Number of Group Scores Lower than Best Individual Score
18	5.9	16.9	11.1	9.3	0

Why were group scores superior to those of individuals? We must look at several aspects of the exercise in seeking an explanation.

1. Three conditions appear relevant: (1) There was a definite answer to all problems, (2) the problem could be solved by logic or reason in the case of Activities 9–1 and 9–2, and (3) for all problems, each person had some relevant information or point of view but no member had it all. More information resources were available to the group—if the group made use of them.

2. A **problem-solving process** was used. If you followed the experiential learning cycle, your team has been developing some sequence or steps to its problem-solving process. If you followed the **rational problem-solving process** model, steps you might have followed include (1) agreement on goals, (2) shared understanding of what the problem is, (3) shared understanding of ground rules for the way the group will work, (4) shared understanding of the basic assumptions and priority issues in solving the problem, (5) consideration of alternative solutions, (6) development of criteria to evaluate alternatives, (7) choosing the best alternative, and (8) checking the alternative chosen against the problem statement. Some researchers argue that this process has a left-hemisphere focus. If the process that you followed is less orderly, systematic, or linear, you probably followed a more *intuitive problem-solving process* (which some researchers call a *right-hemisphere focus*). Some differences in the scores received by different teams may be attributable to differences in the effectiveness of their problem-solving process.

3. The **consensus process** was used. If you followed the instructions, your team was developing (or improving) communication skills that could augment the problem-solving process. It is often important to (1) get input from all, (2) listen to all views, (3) be willing to change your views if someone else's makes more sense, and (4) assume conflict can be creative in generating ideas.

Thus, effective team problem solving involves both effective problem-solving skills and effective **interpersonal skills.** Those interpersonal skills include careful listening plus supporting and encouraging the contributions of all members. For example, a team can adopt a practice whereby, when communication problems arise, members feel comfortable paraphrasing what they hear one another say to make sure all understand what is being said (e.g., "Do I hear you saying . . . ?"). This technique involves learning to listen until it is clear what a person is saying and then paraphrasing what is said to the satisfaction of the speaker. Where there is no awareness on the part of the team members that a communication problem has arisen, periodic summaries of what has been discussed can ensure that all are on the same wavelength. Similarly, some individuals have learned that saying something like "Here's the problem *I'm* having with what you said," is a more effective response than "That's a stupid idea." The former response is less likely to generate defensive behavior and is more likely to encourage complete communication and contribution to the group's effort.

Just like problem-solving skills, interpersonal skills can be learned and practiced. Individuals who learn the skills of listening and communicating can apply them in any situation; they become part of the interpersonal skills that improve the person's effectiveness in any group. Differences in group performances on this module's activities may also be a function of how well the group's interpersonal processes operate. Effective teams work on improving their interpersonal processes.

Individual versus Group Problem Solving

In your class's operation of the problem-solving activities, you may have observed instances where the group score was higher than the best individual score. Such was the case with 4 of the 12 groups whose performance is outlined in Table 9–3. There, in four of the groups, the group outcome was worse than that of the best members. Thus, while in general groups performed better than the average of their members, and most of the time better than their best member, this was not always the case. Some groups would have been better to use the solution of their best member, *assuming, of course, they knew who that was!*

Thus, no generalization can be made that group problem solving is superior to individual effort. Variables such as the type of problem; the talent, ability, education, and experience of the individuals; the time available; organization and national culture; leadership; and group process are all relevant as are many other factors.

There is evidence that the capacity of groups to perform better than their best individual member increases with the time that individuals have worked with each other in teams.[6] Other research has suggested that the superiority of teams is a function of their capacity to develop valid information about the members' relative expertise.[7] Hackman and Morris observe that, in sum, there is substantial agreement among researchers and observers of small task groups that something important happens in group interactions that can affect performance outcomes. There is little agreement about just what that "something" is, whether it is more likely to enhance or depress effectiveness, and how it can be monitored, analyzed, and altered.[8]

One problem in applying research findings to managerial situations concerns the methods used in experimental studies. By necessity they are done in the laboratory, with the necessary controls to examine specific variables. This has little comparability to the conditions under which real work teams operate. Real teams can learn to critique and redirect their actions, a flexibility not possible in experimental studies, nor perhaps as likely to occur, given that the stakes, risks, rewards, and punishments for real work teams are significantly different than those for laboratory teams.

In truth, group process can both enhance and detract from team performance. In reality, organizations—for a variety of reasons, some of them discussed below—cannot avoid using groups and teams for problem solving and decision making. Thus, the real questions for managers do not involve individual versus group decision making. The real questions are (1) Where is group decision making most appropriate? and (2) How can teams be made more effective?

One primary factor affecting group performance is the degree of proficiency in team action that a group can develop. This proficiency is aided by effectiveness training for individual members, such as leadership, problem-solving, and communications workshops. It also requires on-the-job training in the use of these skills by the work team after the individuals have had the advantage of separate training. If group effectiveness is to be enhanced, time must be allotted for these activities.

Group Decision Making and Participative Management

The problems involved in Activities 9–1, 9–2, and 9–3 had a ''right'' or preferred answer. While such problems are indeed faced by organizations, these are not the only type of problems that exist. Very often, organizations face situations with a number of viable alternative solutions. Activity 9–5 (''Who Gets the Overtime'') at the end of the module presents such a situation.

In that activity, the leader is instructed to behave in a particular manner. Is that the only way to handle the problem? Is it the best way? What are the alternatives?

Victor Vroom, Phillip Yetton, and Arthur Jago have developed a model that can provide the answers to these questions. They first suggest that there are five ways in which decisions can be made:

1. The manager solves the problem by himself or herself, using the information available at the time (AI style).
2. The manager obtains the necessary information from employees and then makes the decision himself or herself (AII style).
3. The manager consults with subordinates individually, getting their ideas and suggestions, and then makes a decision (CI style).
4. The manager consults with subordinates as a group, again getting their ideas and suggestions, and then makes a decision (CII style).
5. The manager explains the problem to the employees as a group, and the group makes the decision (GII style).[9]

The model suggests that there are five key attributes to problem situations: time, information, quality, employee commitment, and employee development. It lists eight problem attributes that allow these factors to be taken into account in decision making:

1. *Quality requirement (QR).* How important is the technical quality of the decision?
2. *Commitment requirement (CR).* How important is employee commitment to the decision?
3. *Leader's information (LI).* Does the leader have sufficient information to make a high-quality decision?
4. *Problem structure (ST).* Is the problem well structured?
5. *Commitment probability (CP).* If the leader makes the decision alone, will subordinates be committed to the decision?

6. *Goal congruence (GC).* Do employees share the organizational goals to be attained in solving this problem?
7. *Subordinate conflict (CO).* Is conflict among employees over preferred solutions likely?
8. *Subordinate information (SI).* Do employees have enough information to make a high-quality decision?[10]

To decide on a decision-making style, the manager follows a decision tree incorporating the eight problem attributes, asking the question in each attribute of the problem at hand, as shown in Figure 9–1.

Figure 9–1 **The Vroom–Yetton–Jago Decision Model**

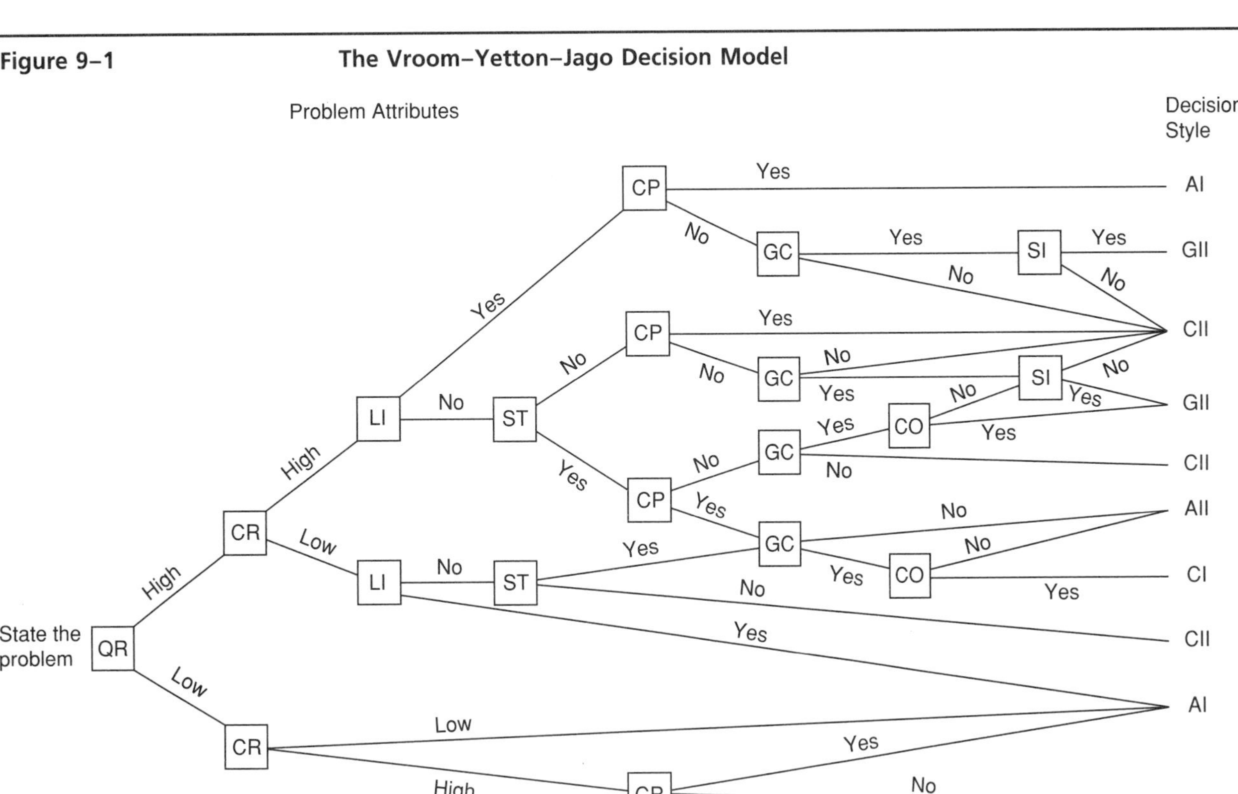

Source: Victor H. Vroom and Arthur G. Jago, *The New Leadership* (Englewood Cliffs, N.J.: Prentice-Hall, 1988), p. 184. Printed with permission.

Note that only one of the styles in the model is what is conventionally called **participative management.** Others are consultative and autocratic. The model is a contingency model, which seeks to identify the situations under which particular forms of employee influence are most appropriate. In brief, it suggests that full participation is not *always* an appropriate style for the leader to use, although at times it is *very* appropriate. In light of this model, it may be argued that the participative style has been overused, a view supported by recent research results that find low relationships (so low so as to be insignificant) between participation, productivity, and employee satisfaction.[11]

Review the "Who Gets the Overtime?" activity using the Vroom–Yetton–Jago model. What decision-making style would be appropriate?

Other Factors

Although the Vroom–Yetton–Jago model incorporates a number of important variables, still other variables may affect the choice of decision-making style:

1. *Personality of the manager.* Managers who feel most comfortable making all the decisions and who have difficulty allowing others to be involved should not attempt to use participation. If they do not believe in it, they should assume that employees

will detect this and feel they are being manipulated if they are asked to become involved.

2. *Skill and ability of the manager.* The manager's abilities in managing group problem-solving activity and in conflict resolution have been shown to affect the results of participative management attempts.[12]
3. *Organizational climate.* If the organization's climate and culture are strictly authoritarian, it is difficult for any single manager to follow a participative style.
4. *Employee personality.* Some employees do not work well in participative situations, but rather prefer to work in highly structured situations where they are told what to do.[13]

The Role of the Manager as Facilitator in Group Decision Making

Although group decision making is not necessary in every problem situation, where it is used, its efficacy rests with the manager who is responsible for facilitating the process. In deciding to proceed with a group decision, the manager has to address several key issues before the group or team can begin to function:[14]

1. *Assignment boundary.* Tasks given to teams are often complex. This requires that the manager clearly define the group's task, its responsibility and authority, and the requirements and performance criteria that the team is expected to meet.
2. *Assessment of assignment resources.* Once the assignment boundaries are defined, the manager may need to divide the assignment into manageable tasks and examine the resources available for the assignment. Time, knowledge, skills, and competing system demands are some of the resources that are likely to have an impact on the decision-making process. An attempt to address and resolve the resource issues prior to the formation of the group will aid the team's performance.
3. *Team formation.* Decision-making groups are often formed to deal with complex tasks that are beyond the ability of any one individual. Identifying the individuals that have the needed knowledge and skills as well as the individuals that are likely to be affected by the decision will provide the group with the appropriate resources to deal with the task. Appointing a leader at the start of the group or ensuring that the groups selects a leader as a first task is often a good idea.

The role of the manager in group decision making can be that of a chairperson who guides the consensus process while trying not to influence others to adopt his or her solution. In playing the role of the supervisor in "Who Gets the Overtime?" individuals sometimes adopt a completely passive manner. The supervisor in this situation (or similar ones) could choose to be highly active and still permit the employees to make the decision. Here are some ways the manager-as-chairperson can facilitate this process:

1. Set the stage and clarify expectations.
   a. Help the group members get acquainted (if this is the first meeting of a new group).
   b. Review the agenda for the meeting or, if this is a continuation of prior meetings, review the progress made to date.
   c. Introduce the problem by asking what would be a fair way of deciding who should get the overtime.
   d. Have the group decide what criteria should be used. Explore alternative options.
   e. Let the group decide what method, procedure, or decision-making process will be used to arrive at a decision. Review the alternative methods. Some of the

methods discussed below (such as brainstorming and nominal group technique) may be useful.

2. Do not takes sides or give your own views.
3. Make sure all employees have time to express their views.
4. Control conflict by having each person ''own'' his or her feelings without attacking another person—say where you are without ''laying it on'' the other person. (It is much more acceptable to say, ''I think seniority is a better way to decide this than one's personal needs,'' than ''Chris's ripping us off by contributing to the overpopulation problem.'') Also, remember that conflict can be creative when it is focused on issues rather than personalities.
5. Protect those who are verbally attacked. Create a supportive atmosphere.
6. Focus on the agreement about the reasoning and its logic rather than on the agreement about the choice itself.
7. Do not manipulate the process so it will come out the way you would like to have the problem decided. Others usually become aware of your *hidden agenda* and may resent it.
8. At the end of the meeting, review the task, the agenda, the decision method, and the decision. If the group has a follow-up meeting, spell out the task ahead, its schedule, and the responsibilities of the members to be completed before the next meeting.[15]

When exposed to this type of leadership, employees can learn the team skills implicit in this behavior and, by example, learn to make a decision without the supervisor, if called on to do so.

Organizational Skills

A systems approach to organizational effectiveness must provide for the development of the group skills of both individual managers and the teams they direct. Figure 9–2 provides a model of four goal areas for the attainment of these organizational skills. To move in the direction of the goal areas, development is needed in two types of group skills for both individuals and groups: *emotional* and *task skills.*

For the individual, skills related to influencing social and emotional relationships include abilities both to be supportive of others and to confront others when necessary. Communication skills such as listening, paraphrasing, and appropriate expression of feelings and support are examples. For the team, acquiring these skills means developing the climate of relationships in which interactions can be facilitated and the use of all other skills can be optimized.

Task skills are more directly related to getting the group's tasks accomplished. An individual can learn certain roles in a group, such as clarifying what is going on or keeping the discussion on target. (A more complete discussion of group roles can be found in the next module.) In addition to group skills, such as those you experienced in the problem-solving exercises earlier in this module, teams can learn planning and implementation techniques such as Management by Objectives. The critiquing of the progress achieved at a given moment or after a completed activity has much to offer for future improvement of the group's operation if it is done objectively in a nonthreatening climate.

There are definite techniques for attaining improvement in the four goal areas shown in Figure 9–2. Some of these have been discussed or will be in future modules. Module 11 will discuss team building, but before focusing on techniques and skills, we will attempt to develop a more general understanding of group dynamics in Module 10.

Figure 9–2
Goals and Organizational Skills

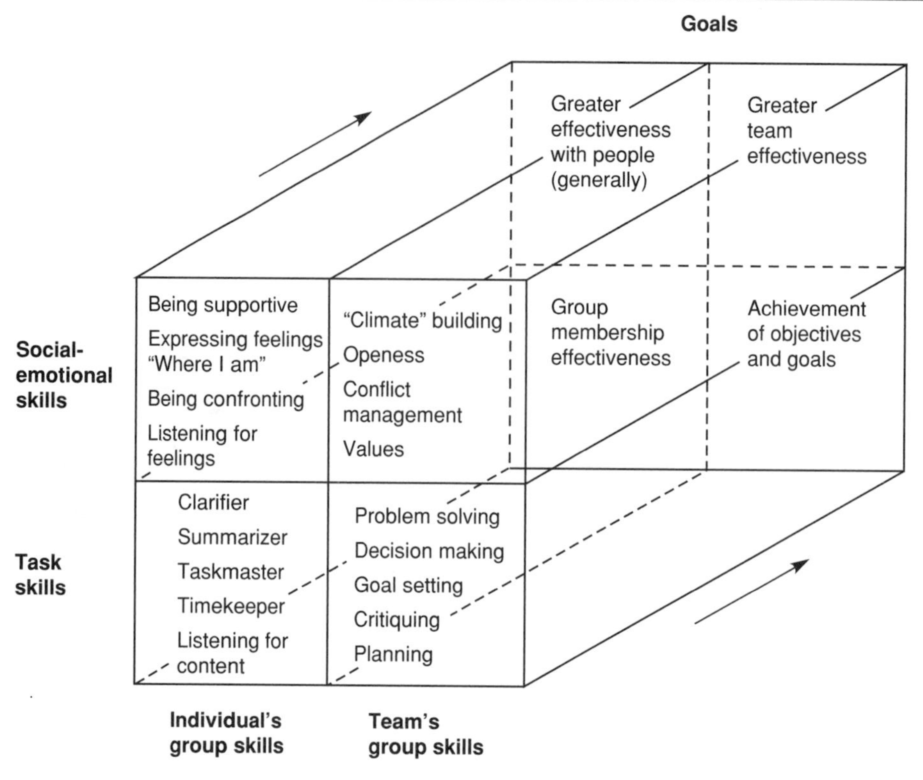

Creativity and Group Problem Solving

An integral element of the synergy process in group problem solving involves creativity. As individuals interact around ideas, an issue, or a problem, a novel solution may emerge that no individual has identified earlier. **Creativity** is defined as an individual's ability to take bits and pieces of seemingly unrelated information and synthesize the pieces into new understanding or a novel, useful idea. Creativity is discussed in Module 15, which focuses on the phenomena of creativity and innovation in the organizational setting. For the purpose of this section, we will explore two techniques that are likely to foster creativity in group problem solving and decision making: brainstorming and the nominal group technique.

Brainstorming

One well-known method for developing creative ideas and decision alternatives through group participation is **brainstorming.** Ground rules generally followed are

1. Everyone spontaneously expresses all ideas, no matter how extreme they may appear.
2. Ideas belong to the group, and all members are encouraged to rework or elaborate upon them.
3. Evaluation of ideas does not occur until the generation process has been completed.

Nominal Group Technique

The **nominal group technique** is a highly structured group problem-solving process[16] in which the focus is on the rational process of problem solving. Ground rules normally followed are

1. During a period of silence, individuals independently write down their ideas.
2. Each individual in turn shares one of his or her ideas at a time, following a round-

robin reporting process. Ideas are written on a chart for all to see. No discussion is allowed during this phase.

3. After all ideas have been recorded, members discuss the ideas only for the purpose of clarification. No criticism is permitted.
4. A preliminary vote takes place to reduce the number of alternatives.
5. An in-depth discussion of the remaining ideas then occurs.
6. An independent silent vote takes place, and the group's solution is determined by the votes.

The nominal group technique is an orderly, efficient, rational process that encourages full participation and meaningful discussion. Research findings suggest that this method seems to have a clear advantage under conditions of high stress and conflict. Other research suggests that while most individuals feel relatively satisfied with their level of involvement, some show resistance to the forced method of decision making.

Application of Problem-Solving and Decision-Making Teams

Organizations use a variety of teams—both problem-solving and decision-making. Let's discuss three recent applications of teams in organizations: self-managing teams, new product development teams, and quality control circles.

Self-Managing Teams

Self-managing teams are groups of employees who work on relatively whole tasks (such as assembling a car or a major auto component) and who manage their own performance. Many self-managing teams work without direct supervision. One recent survey found that almost half of all Fortune 1000 companies were using self-managed work teams, with even more planning their use.[17]

The important characteristics of self-managed teams are (1) employees with a variety of skills who perform interrelated tasks and who are responsible for making a product or delivering a service and who (2) work together closely (face-to-face interaction) with (3) discretion over decisions such as work assignments, work scheduling, and work methods and sometimes even team member selection and training.[18]

One recent study found that self-managing teams were rated higher than conventionally managed work groups in quality of work life (QWL) areas such as job satisfaction, personal growth satisfaction, social satisfaction, and organizational commitment. Self-managed work groups were also found to perform better than conventionally managed work groups in terms of both quantity and quality of work.[19]

New Product Development Teams

New product development teams (NPDT) have emerged as a viable tool within highly competitive technology-based industries for enhancing the product development process. NPDTs are small groups of employees who collectively have the knowledge and skills needed to solve the problem of developing a new product, from conception through manufacturing and distribution—"from design to delivery." These teams are often composed of individuals from a variety of functional areas, such as marketing, finance, design engineering, process engineering, and manufacturing.

Research has shown that NPDTs are highly effective in facilitating the development process,[20] shortening product development time, and increasing cooperation between functional groups within the organization.[21] These teams typically succeed if they effectively obtain information and resources from others (both inside and outside the organization), use the information and resources to create a viable product, and gain support for the product from others (both inside and outside the organization).[22] In a fashion similar to the use of NPDT, organizations can create multidisciplinary teams to service or support a single large customer.

Quality Control Circles

Quality control circles (QCC) are small groups of workers from the same work area who are given training in problem solving, statistical quality control, and group processes. (We discuss quality in depth in Module 14.) They meet regularly to discuss ways to improve the quality of their work and to solve job-related problems. The concepts of QCC originated in Japan, and are considered by many to be the most famous Japanese organizational innovation to date.[23] While results of the use of quality circles have been mixed in both the United States and Japan,[24] the most important potential of QCCs is the continuing organizational dialoguing they promote between managers and the work force.

Electronic Enhancement of Group Decision Making

One of the most rapidly developing fields is the use of computer technology to enhance group problem solving and decision making. (We explore the relationships between technology, information technology, and human behavior in Module 16.) Computer-based forms of brainstorming (electronic brainstorming) have been developed.[25] Computer programs that allow for sharing information via computer networks are called **groupware.** Though it's still relatively new, use of this technology has produced impressive productivity gains.[26] Research studies on groupware are just beginning to appear, but one study indicated that its use improved group conflict resolution processes,[27] while another found that groups using electronic communication have more difficulty in reaching consensus than do groups meeting face to face and also appear to be more willing to take risks.[28]

Group Decision Making and the Cultural Context

Culture influences the ways decisions get made in organizations. When we think of decision making in the global context, the following questions come to mind: Do groups from different cultures perceive problems in the same way? Do they use the same decision-making processes? Do they gather similar types and amounts of information while investigating the problem? Do they follow the same thinking patterns? Do they construct similar types of solutions? Do they use similar strategies for choosing between alternatives? Do they implement their decisions in the same ways? The answer to each question is no.[29]

The cultural context within which groups exist plays a critical role in preference for and the performance of individual versus group problem solving. While in some cultures (e.g., the United States and Great Britain) there is a strong belief in the importance and centrality of the individual, in other cultures (e.g., China and Taiwan) there is a strong belief in the importance of collectivism.[30] Thus we find that people's choice of either individual or group problem solving and their actual behavior and performance are likely to be affected by their cultural heritage. We also find that culture can affect performance in a particular context. One study showed that managers from collectivist cultures performed worse when working alone, as opposed to working in a group with which they identified.[31]

As an example of the impact of culture on decision-making processes, within the Japanese culture, a unique consensual decision-making process exists. There are two components to this process—*ringi* and *nemawashi*—through which Japanese managers involve subordinates in considering the future direction of their companies. Individuals and groups who have ideas for improvement or change will discuss them widely with a large number of peers and managers. During this extensive informal communication process, some kinds of agreements (*nemawashi*) are hammered out. At this point, a formal document is put forward and circulated for signatures or a personalized stamp (the seal) of every manager who is considered relevant to the decision (called a *ringi*).[32] Only after all the relevant managers put their seals on the proposal is the idea or suggestion implemented. Activity 9–6 at the end of the module illustrates this unique group decision-making process.

Summary

Aspects of both team problem solving and decision making have been explored in this module, and differences between the two activities have been discussed. Behaviors that enhance group problem solving have been outlined as well as conditions under which both individual and group decision making (participative management) may be effective. The manager's role in facilitating group decision making was covered as well as techniques for enhancing group creativity. Several ways in which organizations use problem-solving teams were outlined.

Study Questions

1. What is rational group decision making? Why is it useful?
2. What is the consensus process? How is it of value to your teams in this course? What is its relationship to synergy?
3. Athletic coaches train teams in techniques to win the game or to achieve peak performance. In what kinds of skills can managers train work teams? Give specific examples.
4. Students often remember Activity 9–5 ("Who Gets the Overtime?") as an attempt to illustrate the effectiveness of group decision making. Was it effective? Why do you think so?
5. What are some considerations in deciding whether to allow a group to participate in decision making?
6. Assume that you are a manager and have decided to use group decision making for a problem affecting the productivity of your team. What issues should you consider before the first group meeting? How would you go about managing the meeting? What would be some pitfalls to avoid?
7. Identify the different phases in the group problem-solving cycle. At which phases did your group encounter problems in the activities in this module? Why? What steps will you take to avoid these problems in the future?
8. Identify one method to improve your classroom group's problem-solving effectiveness. What specific steps would you take to facilitate the process?
9. In what ways are quality control circles and new product development teams different? How are they alike?
10. How does culture affect group problem-solving effectiveness? How might U.S. culture affect a team's performance?

Endnotes

1. T. J. Peters, *Thriving on Chaos* (New York: Alfred A. Knopf, 1988).

2. C. P. Alderfer, "An Intergroup Perspective on Group Dynamics," in *Handbook of Organizational Behavior,* J. W. Lorch, ed. (Englewood Cliffs, N.J.: Prentice-Hall, 1986).

3. J. R. Katzenbach and Douglas K. Smith. *The Wisdom of Teams: Creating the High Performance Organization.* Boston: Harvard Business School Press, 1993.

4. *Ibid.*

5. *Ibid,* p. 112.

6. W. Watson, L. K. Michalson, and W. Sharp, ''Member Competence, Group Interaction, and Group Decision Making: A Longitudinal Study,'' *Journal of Applied Psychology* 76 (1991), pp. 803–9.

7. P. W. Yetton and P. C. Bottger, ''Individual versus Group Problem Solving: An Empirical Test of a Best-Member Strategy,'' *Organizational Behavior and Human Performance* 29 (1982), pp. 307–21.

8. J. R. Hackman and C. G. Morris, ''T-Group Tasks, Group Interaction Process, and Group Performance Effectiveness: A Review and Proposed Integration,'' in *Advances in Experimental Social Psychology,* Leonard Berkowitz, ed., vol. 8 (New York: Academic Press, 1974), p. 49.

9. V. H. Vroom and P. W. Yetton, *Leadership and Decision Making* (Pittsburgh, University of Pittsburgh Press, 1972), p. 13.

10. V. H. Vroom and A. C. Jago, *The New Leadership* (Englewood Cliffs, N.J.: Prentice-Hall, 1988), p. 184.

11. J. A. Wagner III, ''Participation's Effects on Performance and Satisfaction: A Reconsideration of Research Evidence,'' *Academy of Management Review* 19, no. 2 (1994), pp. 312–30.

12. J. Hall, ''Decisions, Decisions, Decisions,'' *Psychology Today,* November 1971; and A. Crouch and P. Yetton, ''Manager Behavior, Leadership Style, and Subordinate Performance: An Empirical Examination of the Vroom–Yetton Conflict Rule,'' *Organizational Behavior and Human Decision Process* 39 (1987), pp. 384–96.

13. D. Collins, R. A. Ross, and T. L. Ross, ''Who Wants Participative Management?'' *Group and Organizational Studies* 14 (1989), pp. 422–45.

14. G. P. Hubler, *Managerial Decision Making* (Glenview, Ill.: Scott, Foresman, 1980), Chapter 9.

15. W. Alan Randolph and Barry Z. Poner. *Getting the Job Done! Managing Project Teams and Task Forces for Success,* rev. ed. Englewood Cliffs, N.J.: Prentice-Hall, 1992.

16. A. L. Delbecq, A. H. Van de Ven, and D. H. Gustafson, *Group Techniques for Program Planning: A Guide to Nominal and Delphi Processes* (Glenview, Ill.: Scott, Foresman, 1975); J. M. Bartunek and J. K. Murningham, ''The Nominal Group Technique: Expanding the Basic Procedure and Underlying Assumptions,'' *Group and Organization Studies* 9 (1984), pp. 417–32; and G. E. Burton, ''The 'Clustering Effect': An Idea-Generation Phenomenon during Nominal Grouping,'' *Small Group Behavior* 18 (1987), pp. 224–38.

17. E. E. Lawler, S. A. Mohrman, and G. E. Ledford, Jr., *Employee Involvement and Total Quality Management: Practices and Results in Fortune 1000 Companies* (San Francisco: Jossey-Bass, 1992).

18. P. S. Goodman, S. Devadas, and T. L. Hutchinson, ''Groups and Productivity: Analyzing the Effectiveness of Self-Managing Teams,'' in *Productivity in Organizations,* J. P. Campbell, R. J. Campbell, and Associates, eds. (San Francisco: Jossey-Bass, 1988), pp. 295–325.

19. S. G. Cohen and G. E. Ledford, Jr., ''The Effectiveness of Self-Managing Teams: A Quasi-Experiment,'' *Human Relations* 47 (1994), pp. 13–43.

20. W. E. Souder, *Managing New Product Innovation* (Lexington, Mass.: Lexington Books, 1987).

21. J. R. Hackman and R. E. Walton, ''Leading Groups in Organizations,'' in *Designing Effective Work Groups,* P. Goodman, ed. (San Francisco: Jossey-Bass, 1986).

22. R. Burgelman, ''A Process Model of Internal Corporate Venturing in the Diversified Major Firm,'' *Administrative Science Quarterly 31* (1982), pp. 223–44.

23. P. Lillrank and N. Kano, *Continuous Improvement: Quality Control Circles in Japanese Industry* (Ann Arbor: University of Michigan Press, 1989).

24. R. E. Cole, ''Japan Can But We Can't,'' IAQC Conference Presentation, Louisville, March 1981.

25. R. B. Gauupe, L. M. Bastianutti, and W. H. Cooper, ''Unblocking Brainstorming,'' *Journal of Applied Psychology* 76, no. 1 (1991), pp. 137–42.

26. David Kirkpatrick, ''Why Microsoft Can't Stop Lotus Notes,'' *Fortune,* December 22, 1994, p. 142. This article reported returns on investment from use of groupware ranging from 179 to 351 percent.

27. M. S. Poole, M. Holmes, and G. DeSanctis, ''Conflict Management in a Computer-Supported Meeting Environment,'' *Management Science* 37 (1991), pp. 926–53.

28. Sara Kiesler and Lee Sproull, ''Group Decision Making and Communication Technology,'' *Organizational Behavior and Human Decision Processes* 52 (1992), pp. 96–123.

29. N. J. Adler, *International Dimensions of Organizational Behavior,* 2nd ed. (Boston: PWS–Kent, 1991), p. 162.

30. G. Hofstede, *Culture's Consequences* (Newbury Park, Calif.: Sage, 1984).

31. P. C. Earley, ''East Meets West Meets Mideast: Further Explorations of Collectivistic and Individualistic Work Groups,'' *Academy of Management Journal* 36 (1993), pp. 319–48.

32. P. Sethi, N. Namiki, and C. Swanson, *The False Promise of the Japanese Miracle* (Marshfield, Mass.: Pittman, 1984).

Activity 9–4: Group Skills Development

Objective:

To help individuals identify specific group skills that they would like to develop.

Task 1:

Individuals are to complete the attached "Questionnaire on Group Skills Development."

Task 2:

a. Individuals are to share with their group the list of skills to which they assigned top priority.

b. The group should brainstorm about how it can help each individual accomplish his or her goals.

c. Each individual in collaboration with the group is to develop an action plan (for each individual) that will help him or her accomplish these learning goals or team skills.

Questionnaire on Group Skills Development

Below are skill areas in which participants in past courses have indicated an interest in developing greater proficiency. Please indicate the degree to which you have an interest in developing greater skills effectiveness by checking the appropriate position on the scale to the right of each item.

Skills Areas	*Not Interested*	*Somewhat Interested*			*Very Interested*			*Highly Interested*		
1. Expressing my viewpoints clearly and logically	1	2	3	4	5	6	7	8	9	10
2. Convincing or persuading others of my ideas or views	1	2	3	4	5	6	7	8	9	10
3. Gaining or holding the attention of others	1	2	3	4	5	6	7	8	9	10
4. Listening attentively so I can understand others' ideas and perceptions	1	2	3	4	5	6	7	8	9	10
5. Paraphrasing back what someone says so I can determine if I am "hearing"	1	2	3	4	5	6	7	8	9	10
6. Paraphrasing back what someone says so the other person feels reassured that I'm listening	1	2	3	4	5	6	7	8	9	10
7. Asserting myself more	1	2	3	4	5	6	7	8	9	10
8. Asserting myself without stepping on others' toes	1	2	3	4	5	6	7	8	9	10
9. Getting my share of "air time"	1	2	3	4	5	6	7	8	9	10
10. Being less dominating, opinionated, or dogmatic	1	2	3	4	5	6	7	8	9	10
11. Being more open-minded about the views of others	1	2	3	4	5	6	7	8	9	10
12. Feeling less intimidated by the way others express their views	1	2	3	4	5	6	7	8	9	10
13. Feeling less defensive when others don't agree with me	1	2	3	4	5	6	7	8	9	10
14. Being less nervous and more confident in speaking	1	2	3	4	5	6	7	8	9	10
15. Taking criticism better	1	2	3	4	5	6	7	8	9	10
16. Coping with people who are different than I am (e.g., differences in age, sex, race, religion, fraternity, sorority)	1	2	3	4	5	6	7	8	9	10
17. Confronting conflict when it arises between myself and another person	1	2	3	4	5	6	7	8	9	10
18. Having a harmonizing influence on the group (e.g., helping shy people open up; getting others to listen to each other; getting group members more involved and enthusiastic; helping group members to be more comfortable in their relations)	1	2	3	4	5	6	7	8	9	10
19. Leading the group discussion	1	2	3	4	5	6	7	8	9	10
20. Taking control when the discussion gets out of hand; keeping discussion on target	1	2	3	4	5	6	7	8	9	10
21. Facilitating the group discussion to get maximum output	1	2	3	4	5	6	7	8	9	10
22. Dealing with conflict between group members	1	2	3	4	5	6	7	8	9	10
23. Manipulating the group's interactions so they will come out the way I feel is best	1	2	3	4	5	6	7	8	9	10

Note: When you have finished, go back over the above items and circle the numbers of those to which you would give top priority.

Activity 9–5: Who Gets the Overtime?

Objectives:

a. To examine group decision making as a process.
b. To identify some issues concerning participation of employees in decision making.
c. To explore the role of the leader in group decision making.
d. To use role playing as a learning method.

(*Note:* This activity's objective is neither to advocate the use of group decision making nor to demonstrate how it should be done. Rather, we are exploring the issue of group decision making based on your experience in the exercise.)

Task 1:

a. The instructor will briefly discuss role playing. There are a number of ways to role play, and it is used for a variety of purposes. In this case, each member of your team will be given a role in a group decision-making problem. You will be comfortable doing this if you follow this guidance: Remember that this is not a theatrical production. You are not being asked to take the lead in the school play. All you are asked to do is play yourself as you would feel if you were in the situation described in the role you will be given. For instance, pretend you are taking a final examination and the professor comes up to your desk, picks up your exam paper, tears it up, and says, "You fail the course. You have notes and books on the floor beside you and under your desk and I've seen you looking down there. Also, you were glancing at the examination paper of the student next to you." You decide to appeal your failure grade to the dean. What are all the possible arguments you could use to defend yourself? (Take two minutes now and discuss this with two of your fellow students.) This situation could be role played by you, with someone else playing the role of the dean, whose viewpoint would probably be different from yours. The roles of our exercise are similar in that you will have some idea of how you would behave if you were in the situation described. One more point about role playing: Remember that you are role playing not only for what you can learn from it, but also to give the other role player the opportunity to see what it is like to interact with, and learn from, you in this situation. That is, in this course you are responsible for the learning of others.

b. Tear out the instruction sheet "Who Gets the Overtime?" in Appendix L, but be careful not to look at any of the individual role sheets while doing so. The instructor will read this instruction sheet aloud while the class follows it. This sheet can be referred to by the participants at any time during the role playing if they need to do so.

c. Each team is to arrange itself in a circle and elect the supervisor (Kim) for this specific exercise. (*Note:* If the class is not working in permanent teams, participants are to form groups of six and elect a supervisor for this exercise.) Starting clockwise from the supervisor, the role assignments are as follows:

A woman in the group should assume the role of Sara. (If there is no woman in the group, of course, she has to be played by a man.) If only five members are present, eliminate the role of Fran. If only four are present in the team, a member of a six-person team should be borrowed temporarily for this exercise.

Turn to your own role assignment sheet in Appendix L and tear it from the book. After you have read the role description and understand it, turn it face down and use it as a name card so your team members can identify your role name during the exercise. Do not tell others what your role instructions are. When the exercise begins, play your role naturally, without referring back to your sheet. Remember, when facts or events arise that are not covered by the roles, make up things that are consistent with the way it might be in a real-life situation.

When Kim has studied and understands the supervisor's role, she will stand. When the supervisors for all groups are standing, the instructor will give the signal to begin the exercise. When Kim sits down, assume Kim has just entered the office and greet Kim with a hearty "Good morning!" Kim will tell you what to do from this point on. (*Note for Kim:* If you have only five on the team, including yourself, announce to your group that Fran called in sick and read them Fran's role. Fran is to be taken into consideration in arriving at the solution.)

Observers, if there are any, are to be assigned one to a group for the purpose of observing and, possibly, reporting to the class at the end of the session how the decision was made. Observers are not to enter into the process.

(Time: for introduction, 10 minutes; for role playing, 20 to 25 minutes; for discussion, 20 minutes or longer. This exercise generates a range of rich data, and it is well to reserve discussion time to extend into the second hour.)

(*Note:* Teams completing role playing before the time has run out should proceed with Task 2. Skip Task 2 and go directly to Task 3 if teams all finish at about the same time.)

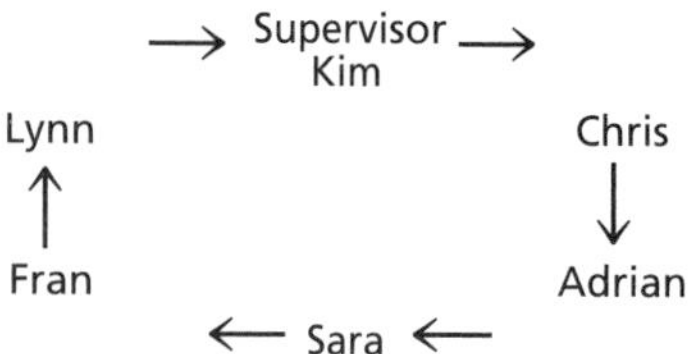

Task 2 (Only for Teams Finishing Task 1 Early):

After deciding who gets the overtime, the team should assume it is reconvening as a committee of supervisors to deliberate and decide the same case. To whom would this committee give the overtime? Why?

Task 3:

a. When the role playing is completed, the instructor will ask each supervisor to give the name of the person in the role play who got the overtime. The names are to be listed on the blackboard for all groups (using the chart form below), but no discussion is to take place at this time. The listing provides the class with information as to which groups agree and disagree with their choice.

Group	Who Got the Overtime?	How Was Decision Made?
#1		
#2		
#3		

b. The instructor will now interview each group on the following:

   a. How was the decision made? (List the elements of these decision processes on the board for each team.) What are the similarities and differences among the decision processes? What criteria were used? (List on the board.) What procedures could be used to bring more objectivity into the process if the group were to start over again—assuming the leader left the problem entirely up to employees to solve?

   b. Was this a good way to make the decision for this particular problem? Why?

   c. What issues (points of controversy) were raised by the group decision making?

   d. How did the supervisor feel about the role she or he was given? How did the employees feel about the role played by the supervisor? How could the supervisor have actively guided and facilitated the process and still let the employees make the decision?

   e. If the supervisor had decided not to let the employees make the decision, what other methods could he or she have used to arrive at the decision?

Which of the alternatives, including group decision, would you have preferred?

f. How did each Sara feel about her role?
(*Note:* This has to be done from the standpoint of sharing feelings with others. The atmosphere of listening for understanding without confrontation or argument is important. The differing reactions and the way the Saras perceive their roles can provide insight into the area of male–female interface in a work group.)

g. For teams that finished both Tasks 1 and 2, were there any differences in the decisions for the two circumstances?

Source: This activity follows the design developed by Norman R. F. Maier's exercise "The New Truck Dilemma" in N. R. F. Maier, A. R. Solem, and Ayesha A. Maier, *Supervisory and Executive Development* (New York: John Wiley & Sons, 1957). This exercise is printed here with the special permission of Dr. Maier.

Activity 9–6: Decision Making—Japanese Style

Objectives:

a. To provide you with the opportunity to experience a decision-making process within the Japanese context.
b. To heighten student awareness of the Japanese style of consensual decision making (*ringi/nemawashi*).

Task 1:

Within the Japanese culture, a consensual decision-making process emerged—one with two components: *ringi* and *nemawashi*—through which Japanese managers involve subordinates in considering the future direction of their companies. According to this process, ideas for improvement or change that are general in nature are widely circulated to a large number of peers and managers. An extensive informal communication process, in which agreements (called *nemawashi*) are hammered out, is usually followed by a formal document stamped with the seal of every manager who is considered relevant to the decision (called *ringi*). Your instructor will explain briefly the Japanese decision-making process and then assign you a task. Each individual is to spend five minutes on his or her set of ideas; these will be written on a piece of paper.

Task 2:

Teams are to meet, with the oldest group member nominated as the group leader (called *kacho*). Teams deliberate over the assignment.
(Time: 15–20 minutes)

The *kachos* are to meet in a "fish bowl situation" to hammer out some sort of initial agreement.
(Time: 15–20 minutes)

The class has to decide how to proceed with the process and the discussion. The goal is to produce *ringi* document(s) to be signed by all the managers considered relevant to the decision.

Task 3:

The instructor will facilitate a class discussion on the decision-making processes, a comparison of the Japanese consensual decision-making process to other decision-making models, and the cultural context of decision making.

Some Alternative Tasks:

a. Design a reward structure and processes that would facilitate learning in this course.
b. Design a final examination process that is both a good learning experience and a valid means of evaluating performance.
c. Develop a proposal for a new student club in the business school.

d. Design a structure and processes for admitting new students into the program.

e. Design a structure and processes for graduate placements in the work environment.

Source: This activity was contributed by Professor William Van Buskirk, La Salle University, Philadelphia, Pennsylvania 19141.

10 Small Group Dynamics

Learning Objectives

After completing this module you should be able to

1. Explain the basic elements and processes of small group dynamics.
2. Identify the factors affecting the evolution and performance of groups.
3. Discuss the differences between the emergent role system and the required role system.
4. Describe the role that the manager can play in facilitating the development and performance of a group.
5. Appreciate the effect of group cohesion on group performance.
6. Identify the developmental stages of groups.
7. Gain insight into the complexity of group dynamics.

List of Key Concepts

Cultural values
Deviant
Group cohesiveness
Group development
Group dynamics
Group maturity
Group structure
Groupthink
Maintenance role
Norms
Role differentiation
Small group leadership
Social loafing
Task role

Our colleague David Peach, Professor of Organization Behavior and Human Resources Management, took the lead on the revision of this module. We are grateful to him.

Module Outline

Premodule Preparation

Activity 10–1: An Initial Inventory of Group Dynamics

Objectives:

a. To give you the opportunity to reflect on your group experience thus far in the course.
b. To help you develop an appreciation for the many elements that play a role in the evolution of a group.
c. To help you diagnose the current stage of development of your group, such that you would be able to improve its effectiveness.

Task 1:

a. Working alone, jot down as many norms as you can think of that emerged in your group. Briefly describe each norm (not more than a one-line sentence per norm).
b. Reflecting on your experience with your group, identify the different roles that individuals have taken on.
c. List additional elements that you believe influenced the evolution and progress of your team.

Task 2:

a. Each team is to elect a spokesperson.
b. Each team is to compile a list of the norms that emerged that are agreed upon by the team and provide an example of the norm wherever appropriate.
c. Each team is to compile a list of the roles that evolved that are agreed upon by the team.
d. Each team is to compile a list of elements that are agreed upon that influenced the evolution of the team and its effectiveness.
e. The instructor will call upon spokespersons, one at a time, to name the elements, norms, and roles. These will be written on the board. Examples will be requested for clarification.
f. The instructor will give a short lecture on this subject.

Task 3:

a. The teams are to discuss the different norms and roles that emerged in the groups and examine their effects on the groups' effectiveness.
b. Teams are to identify norms and roles that they would like to see change and devise an action plan to execute and monitor the changes.

Activity 10–2: A Card Game Called *Norms*

Objective:

To help classroom teams establish norms.

Task 1:

Cut out the 12 cards for this exercise found in Appendix M. Shuffle the cards. Cut out the blank cards that will be used for group responses. Keep the blank cards separate. Cut out the Agreement Form, Appendix M, and save it for use at the end of the exercise.

Task 2:

Take turns drawing cards (which represent situations that may occur in your team) and reading them aloud. The person drawing the card should serve as facilitator until the next person draws a card.

a. Discuss times that things similar to the experience listed on the card have happened to you when you've been assigned to work in groups.
b. As a group, decide what your team would do if such a situation happened. Each person is then to write out the group's answer on a blank card. At the end of this exercise, each team member will have a complete deck of cards.
c. As a group, decide how your team will prevent such occurrences and what norms and sanctions your team will institute to guard against such occurrences. These should also be written on cards.
d. Develop additional scenarios of situations you think might occur and repeat steps a, b, and c.
e. Have all group members agree to abide by your norms and sanctions and sign their names on the Agreement Form.

Source: This activity was contributed by Professor Alice Walton, College of Business Administration, University of Detroit Mercy, Detroit, Mich. 48219-0900. We are grateful to her.

Introduction

In Module 9 we introduced some characteristics of small group activities, emphasizing the development of group skills for greater team effectiveness. We also discussed several uses of small groups and teams in the work setting. We will now take a closer look at small group processes and characteristics to provide you with knowledge of small group dynamics and an understanding of the social group that develops within the work group. Understanding the dynamics of small group operation should help you improve the operation of your class team and other groups of which you are a member.

As a primary frame of reference in studying group dynamics, remember that *whenever a group of strangers or whenever two or more people come together to perform a task, the web of group dynamics spontaneously begins to spin.* (Sounds magical, and maybe it is!)

Group Dynamics Defined

The small work group is a primary focus of the study of organizational behavior because it is here the social system (what we will call the *emergent role system*), which is a primary determinant of behavior, is spontaneously generated. One good definition of **group dynamics** is from Knowles:

> [Group dynamics] refers to the complex forces that are acting upon every group throughout its existence which cause it to behave the way it does. We can think of every group having certain relatively static aspects—its name, constitutional structure, ultimate purpose, and other fixed characteristics. But it also has dynamics aspects—it is always moving, doing something, changing, becoming, interacting, and reacting, and the nature and direction of its movement is determined by forces being exerted upon it from within itself and from outside. The interaction of these forces and the resultant effects on a given group constitute its dynamics.[1]

A knowledge of small group dynamics is essential for your understanding of the social system of the group, what we will call the *emergent social system.* You will also find it helpful in analyzing the interactions in your classroom team for, whenever a group of individuals comes together to perform a task, predictable patterns of behavior will develop. Thus, we may also define *group dynamics* as the pattern of interactions among group members as a group develops and achieves goals.[2] The influence of the individual on the group and the group on the individual, and the interrelationships between groups and the interaction of groups with the larger institutions of which they are a part are the primary focus in the study of group dynamics.

To start our investigation into the topic of group dynamics, we have used Activity 10–1 ("An Initial Inventory of Group Dynamics") and/or Activity 10–2 ("A Card Game Called *Norms*"). Next we will discuss small group dynamics in terms of their purpose, structure, process, and developmental stages. Our learning can be integrated through the use of either the Claremont Instrument Company case or the Performance Appraisal Task Force case.

Factors Affecting Group Development and Performance

As Activity 10–1 has demonstrated, many factors affect the development and performance of teams. These elements can be clustered into six broad categories: context, purpose, member composition, structure, processes, and leadership. Figure 10–1 shows key components of the six elements.

Figure 10–1
Factors Affecting Group Development and Performance

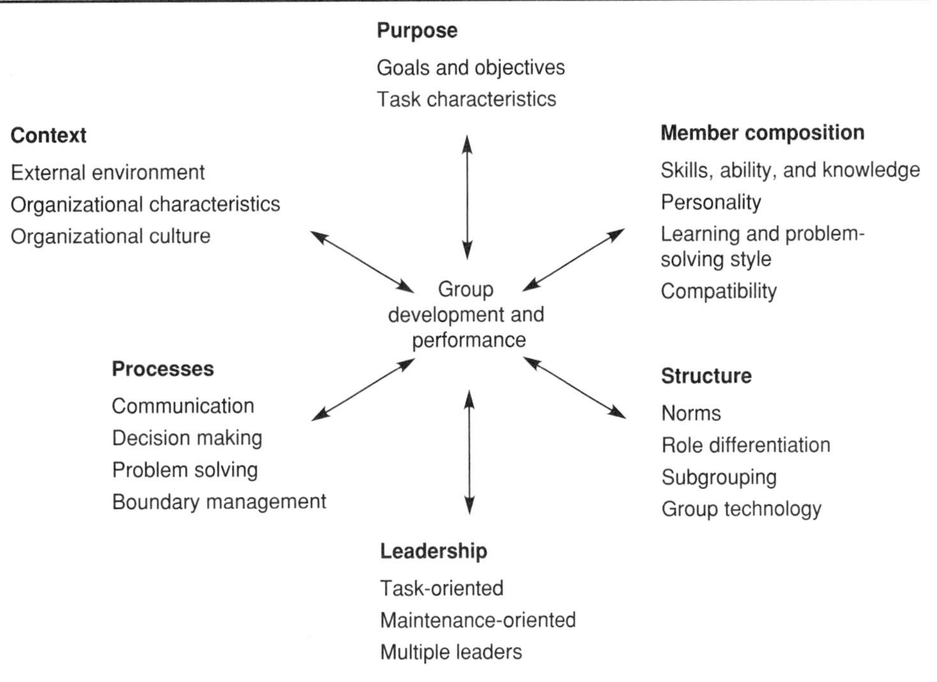

Context

Context refers to the environment in which groups operate. It refers to both the organizational environment and the environment external to the organization. Contextual factors influence both the evolution of a group and its performance as well as all the other (internal) factors.[3] A group's contextual factors might include (1) *organizational characteristics* such as business strategy, production technology, organization structure, management philosophy and practice, information technology, decision-making processes, reward and punishment systems, control systems, and working conditions, (2) *organizational culture* (e.g., norms, values, attitudes toward strategy and goals, actual operating procedures, and power structure), and (3) the characteristics of the organization's *external environment,* which could include factors such as industry characteristics; competitive pressures; technological change; economic, social, political, and legal expectations and requirements; customers; and suppliers.

Purpose

All small groups have *goals and objectives* to attain. They are the reason the members have come together and the primary determinants of the interaction of people out of which patterns of behavior will emerge. The purpose of a group can be clearly defined—as would be the case with work teams—or loosely defined (or collectively recognized)—as would occur with a meeting of a group of friends held to satisfy the social needs of the members. Goals are powerful inducements for action. Clearly defined goals are critical for effective group performance.[4] The specific content of the goal and the kind of goal (competitive versus cooperative, for example) will influence the evolution and performance of the group.[5] Furthermore, the group's specific *task characteristics and requirements* will be determinants of its performance. These include required activities and interactions, the required level of interdependence among group members to accomplish the task,[6] and the task's time frame and deadlines.[7] Coupled with group member composition, they set the stage for group performance.

Processes

The process elements of decision making and problem solving were discussed in Module 9. *Boundary management* refers to the management of the relationship between a team and other teams or other organizational entities, a process related in part to context and purpose elements, which have already been discussed. The other major element, communication, is discussed in Module 8, but we will consider here the impact on the location of individuals within the channels of communication.

The effects of location on performance and satisfaction have been summarized by Swap[8] in his review of the experimental work done on communications networks by Cartwright and Zander.[9] Swap saw an important determinant of a group's decision-making effectiveness to be the communication structure of the group—who is allowed to communicate with whom. An extract of that review follows.

We might want to know the answers to a number of questions relating to a network: How *satisfied* will each of the group members be? How *efficiently* will they be able to accomplish a task or make a decision? Will any one member come to be viewed as a *leader*? To answer these questions, let us return to the social psychologist's laboratory.

You are one of five subjects in an experiment. Each of you is given a card with five symbols taken from a group of six (circle, triangle, and so on). Only one of the symbols appears on each subject's card. The task of the group is to determine the identity of that common symbol as quickly as possible. The five subjects all sit around a table divided by partitions. In each partition is a slot through which subjects can exchange written messages. Which slots are open or closed determines the nature of the communication network. You may be in a position where you communicate with only one other subject, or two, or perhaps all four corresponding to the patterns shown in Figure 10–2. These are just four of the many possible networks. A double arrow indicates that a communication link is two-way; that is, a slot permits both sending and receiving messages. (While some networks include one-way channels—such as putting a message in a suggestion box—they are relatively rare, and will not be considered here.)

Perhaps the most important characteristics of communication networks are their centrality and the degree of centrality of a given member within the network. Centrality may be viewed as the degree of *connectedness* among the people in the network. In Figure 10–2, the wheel is highly centralized, with C maintaining communications with all other group members. The circle is less centralized as each member maintains but two communication links.

Let's summarize the major findings that have emerged from research on communication networks. First, a given member's centrality is strongly related to his or her satisfaction with the group experience. This relationship is particularly strong among people with relatively dominant personalities. Second, people who are placed in central positions in the network come to be viewed as *leaders* by the other group members. Virtually all group members agree that C is the leader in the wheel, but there is no

Figure 10–2
Four Different Communications Networks

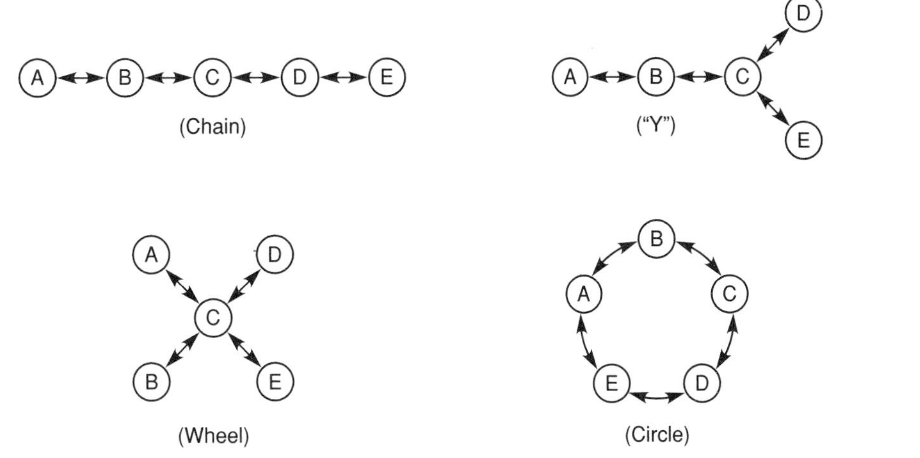

Source: Walter C. Swap and Associates, *Decision Making* (Beverly Hills, Calif.: Sage Publications, 1984), pp. 55. Reprinted by permission of Sage Publications, Inc.

consensus about leadership in the circle. Third, the performance of the group (measured by such factors as speed, accuracy, and rate of learning) is strongly affected by its structure. For simple tasks, such as information gathering described in the preceding experiment, the more centralized networks perform better. For more complex activities such as those requiring somebody (i.e., the central person) to operate on the information after it is collected, centralized groups perform more poorly. We might speculate that the result will be particularly pronounced when the central person is basically incompetent. But a further explanation comes from the fourth general finding: Decentralized groups as a whole are more satisfied with their group experience than are centralized groups. While the wheel may have one satisfied person (the "leader"), there are four peripheral, unhappy members. Participants in a circle network, on the other hand, are all equally central or peripheral and share equally in the group responsibilities. This higher degree of group satisfaction might contribute to the finding that such decentralized (democratic) groups outperform others on more challenging tasks.

The effectiveness of group decision making should clearly vary with the complexity and nature of the group task and with the type of communication structure. A highly centralized structure should be most effective with simple decisions and when a competent leader holds the central position. For more complex, discretionary tasks, a more decentralized communication structure should produce both better decisions and greater member satisfaction.

Member Composition

Some key elements in this category relate to the characteristics of the individuals and the group-formation process. Personality characteristics and the level of knowledge, ability, and skills plus the similarities and differences among members, the level of compatibility among individuals, learning styles, problem-solving styles, and preferred roles are all integral parts of group evolution and performance.

As we saw in Module 5, beyond the unique similarities and differences that exist between individuals' personalities and learning styles, research has indicated that all four dominant learning modes are critical for group effectiveness. Thus, the extent to which group members are compatible will influence the group's performance. Similar conclusions can be drawn regarding individual problem-solving styles. The particular combination of member styles will affect the group's evolution and its outcomes.[10] For example, a group composed of four strong "accommodators" and one "diverger" is likely to fall short in its ability to objectively analyze the situation, may have difficulty identifying the main issue or problem, will lack insight in the identification and exploration of alternative solutions, and may fall short in the choice of the best solution.

Studies have also shown that a heterogenous group in terms of abilities and experiences can have a positive effect on group performance, particularly when that group's tasks are diverse, because a wide range of competencies are needed. On the other hand, groups with a more homogenous makeup may have less conflict, better communication, member satisfaction, and lower turnover.[11]

Other individual characteristics that can influence group performance are individual flexibility in terms of task assignments[12] and preference for a group work. Individuals who prefer to work in groups tend to be more satisfied and effective in those settings.[13]

Structure

Group structure refers to certain psychologically shared properties of the group that result from both formal and informal interactions of its members. Structural elements that influence group performance can be divided into two categories: the formal and the informal. Formal structural elements are those that are imposed by the organization, most importantly the design of the group's tasks. Informal elements are those that develop out of the group's operation.

Formal Elements—Work Design

Work design is discussed in Module 13. Work design influences the activities and interactions of group members. One recent study showed that the design of group tasks that provided for skill variety, task identity, task significance, autonomy, and feedback had a positive influence on group productivity, satisfaction, and effectiveness.[14] Since the subject of work design is extensively covered in a later chapter, we will not discuss additional details here, but merely note that work design is indeed an important element to be considered in understanding group performance and developing enhanced group performance.

Informal Elements

As a group develops, *recurrent patterns* of relationships occur. Furthermore, group technology is developed. There are three dimensions of group technology: (1) task predictability, (2) problem analyzability, and (3) interdependence. There are also three properties of group structure: (1) *connectiveness* (the extent to which group members identify with the goals of other members in their group), (2) *vertical differentiation* (the number of different levels of the organizational hierarchy represented in a group), and (3) *horizontal differentiation* (the number of different job areas represented in a group). Beyond the unique recurrent patterns of relationships, group technology and group structure affect overall group performance.[15]

The recurrent patterns are shared psychologically by group members in that all come to know and are influenced by the patterns, whether they are consciously aware of them or not. This psychological sharing may be thought of as being in the general area of emergent attitudes. However, since we need more specific concepts to aid us in analyzing group behavior, we will work with terms such as *norms* and other structural components, including *status* and *role differentiation.*

In order to understand shared expectations that emerge in the group, we must know the process by which two or more persons spontaneously, often unconsciously, come to share expectations and assumptions of what is appropriate or meaningful behavior. These can be thought of as unwritten, informal guidelines that group members develop and accept without realizing it.

Development of Norms: **Norms** *are expectations shared by group members of how they ought to behave under a given set of circumstances.* The idea of a norm carries with it a range of behaviors that are acceptable, so there is some variability for individuals. Work attitudes are an example. A work team made up of individuals who believe in giving an honest day's work to their employer could readily develop a high-productivity norm, whereas one composed of individuals who believe business rips off workers could develop a low-productivity norm. One work team having half of each type might have only a shared expectation that "we will never agree on productivity."

Group members are often unaware of their norms and that these norms influence member behavior. Freudians have always assumed that there are subconscious and unconscious mental processes that influence our behavior, and norms often exist at the level of group subconsciousness. When participants in our courses write a term paper on their teams' interactions, it is surprising how few norms they have observed. (Are you making entries in your journal on the norms you assume to be developing in your group? One way to identify norms is to observe behavior of the group, particularly in relation to the behavior of an individual member. Is the group upset by the behavior, for example, of being late or not being prepared? If so, does that identify behavior that the group feels is appropriate or inappropriate? The same can be said for behavior that the group rewards with praise.) We offer this hint because it is important first to become aware of the consequences of certain norms and then to become knowledgeable of how teams can develop and shape their own norms for the purpose of improved effectiveness. Earlier in this text, in Activity 8–3 on nonverbal communications, you became more aware of how unaware people are of the spontaneity of the development of norms. There are also several case studies in which you can analyze the existing norm structure of work groups.

Work groups often spontaneously develop an emergent role system with norms that are contrary to management goals, but that satisfy their own needs and reduce their frustrations. If you have analyzed The Slade Company case, you have seen an example of this kind of situation. Integrating the required and the emergent systems so they are compatible is an ever-present management challenge.

Values play a special role in the formation of norms. **Cultural values** provide an example of this. Values tell us what is moral, worthwhile, good, or beautiful. For individuals, values have been developed and reinforced through a lifetime of experiences. When team members in this course meet for the first time, often they espouse values related to democracy, fair treatment, and honesty. They frequently develop such group norms as "Let everyone have a fair share of the air time," "Let's not play manipulative games," and "Let's be open and level with one another."

So how do values and norms differ? Values may be thought of as "criteria or conceptions used in evaluating things (including ideas, acts, feelings, and events) as to their relative desirability, merit, or correctness."[16] Values can be held by a single individual; norms cannot because they emerge from the interactions in the group. Norms are rules of behavior, but values are critical for evaluating behavior and other things. Further, norms carry sanctions, but values never do. This distinction is important because management teams in particular need to be in agreement on the basic operating values from which their system of norms is derived. We frequently find that management teams are in conflict over values, such as short-run profits versus longer-range organizational viability or rate of return on investment versus market share. Consultants find values clarification is usually a priority need in high-level team-building sessions. You may recall from your own experience with Activity 4–3 ("Values in Business") how emotionally loaded the area can be.

If you were assigned Activity 10–2 ("A Card Game Called *Norms*"), you will have had the opportunity to identify and establish norms in your classroom group.

Role Differentiation

Whenever two or more people come together to work on a common purpose, **role differentiation** occurs; that is, patterns of behavior for each individual develop that tend to become repeated as activities progress. Roles can be classified into those that are focused on achieving the tasks of the group, ones that build and maintain favorable relationships among group members, and those that serve individual needs, sometimes at the expense of the group.[17]

Task Roles

Individuals who assume **task roles** are interested in getting the job done. They often emerge as the informal leaders of work groups. Roles that fall in this category include

- *Initiator*—Offers new ideas both on ways to solve problems and on ways for the group to approach its task or organize to do its work.

- *Coordinator*—Coordinates group activities, connects different ideas and suggestions, and clarifies relationships.
- *Information seeker*—Seeks out facts and information and clarifies ideas. *Opinion Seekers* are variants of this role.
- *Information giver*—Offers facts and information that are relevant to the group's task. *Opinion givers* are variants of this role.
- *Recorder*—Keeps track of the group's activities and progress to date. May write down ideas. *Summarizers* are a variant of this role and act to provide a verbal summary of activity to date or decisions made by the group.
- *Evaluator-critic*—Offers assessments of the group's operation as well as evaluations of ideas and suggestions made by group members.
- *Timekeeper*—Works to keep the group on schedule and to help ensure that the group makes productive use of the time available to it.

In any group these roles may be played by one or many individuals.

Group-Building and Relationship Maintenance Roles

Individuals who assume relationship roles are often the most popular members of groups because they work to facilitate social and emotional relationships among group members. They are often the social leader of the group. Examples of the types of roles in this category are

- *Encourager*—Supports the activity of other group members, praises contributions, and agrees with suggestions.
- *Gatekeeper/expediter*—Keeps individuals from monopolizing the discussion, encourages participation by everyone, and keeps the discussion moving.
- *Standard setter*—States both output and process standards and goals for the group to achieve; assesses group performance in terms of these standards and goals.
- *Observer/commentator*—Acts as a detached observer, commenting on both group process and outcomes.
- *Followers*—Passive but friendly group members.

Individual Roles

These roles are expressions of individual personalities and individual needs. Sometimes individuals act in a manner that is detrimental to group performance. Individual roles include

- *Aggressor*—Verbally attacks other team members and their contributions.
- *Blocker*—Refuses to concede a point even when confronted with group unanimity; stubborn and unreasonable at times.
- *Dominator*—Attempts to control the group and the discussion.
- *Recognition seeker*—Needs to be the center of attention.
- *Avoider*—Seeks to avoid becoming involved with the group; passive, avoids commitment.

Other types of individual roles include self-confessor, playboy, help seeker, and special-interest pleader. You may be able to think of other classifications based on your group experience. One student saw Wonderwoman, Superman, cynic, cheerleader, white knight, and Florence Nightingale among her team members.

The significance of role differentiation is that these patterned relationships develop in a group and become part of the members' shared expectations of what ought to be done and what is appropriate or acceptable behavior. Knowledge and awareness of different roles provide the manager or team leader with a basis not only for understanding what is taking place but also for developing useful roles and discouraging dysfunctional roles in the group. Activity 10–3 at the end of this module lets you observe and discuss the individual roles performed in your classroom group.

Status

Status was defined in Module 7 as the degree of esteem, respect, or prestige an individual commands from others. Status operates in group settings, and group members acquire common perceptions for respecting other members on numerous dimensions. If problem-solving and analytical abilities are important in the group, members will, over time, rank one another from the highest to the lowest ability in this regard. Other dimensions of status include ability to judge the motivation and the capabilities of others, professional knowledge, experience, interpersonal skills, personal appearance, "personality," and any other area valued by the group, including items like a car to transport the group or an apartment where the group can meet comfortably. An overall status that is dependent on a combination of these factors is accorded to group members. One of the most important is the degree to which a person conforms to the norms of the group. High conformers have high status; low conformers have lower status. However, group pressures toward uniformity vary. Some norms are absolutes, while others permit a range of behaviors—what is called *wiggle room.* Group leaders usually have more freedom than the other group members to try new behavior.

Awareness of Status: Participants often write in their papers that there were no differences in status among members of their group. This failure of observation may be because they think it is unfair to label people or to ridicule some. However, status always exists in groups and affects behavior and performance. You need to think of it, first, as the characteristics one brings to the group (such as family background or what course of study the individual is pursuing) and, second, as the degree to which a person conforms to the norms of the group. Another way of thinking about status is that of credibility (What's my credibility in this group?). Acceptability is another dimension (How can I improve my acceptability in this group?). Listening more attentively to others is a possible answer to this question. Good journal entries can enhance your awareness of status factors and have implications for growth in your understanding of how your status can influence others. Activity 10–4 at the end of the module can help you identify status elements that operate in your everyday life and subsequently identify status elements that may be influencing the operation of your classroom group.

Rejection of the Deviant

A **deviant** is an individual whose behavior differs from what is regarded as standard. In a group sense, a deviant is one who does not subscribe to the group's norms. Stanley Schachter conducted laboratory experiments with college students and found some interesting reactions of small groups toward individuals who take an unchanging position in opposition to the majority.[18] In each group he had three "stooges" who played three different roles: One would agree with whatever majority position arose; the second—called the *slider*—would take the opposite position but would change toward the majority gradually; and the third, who was the deviant, took the opposite position and did not change. In those groups where there was high cohesiveness among the members (see the discussion of cohesiveness below) and where the subject under discussion was of high relevance, communications were directed toward the slider and the deviant in attempts to convince and persuade them. Communication toward the deviant fell off toward the end of the meeting; the slider was accepted and the deviant rejected.

The dynamics of deviant behavior in groups is a complex phenomenon that has a significant effect on the development of a group. (Have you ever been in a group in which one member constantly violated accepted norms of behavior? Can you imagine the effect of such behavior on a group?) A *scapegoat* or *covert role player* is an individual in a group who is unconsciously assigned the role of absorbing emotions on behalf of the group. For example, the scapegoat can be blamed for the failures of the group; he or she also allows the group to avoid an unpleasant true examination of its behavior and performance.[19]

Subgroupings of Members

Subgroupings are recurrent patterns of relationships among individuals within the group that become established. Some of these relationships are temporary and some are enduring. These subgroups may be dyads (pairs) or triads (trios). A positive dyad is two persons supporting each other's views; a negative dyad is composed of opposing persons; a third possibility is one person who finds someone attractive but meets with rejection. Such subgroupings are not always readily apparent to members. Triads are supposedly the most unstable of all groups because they almost always break down into a pair and one.[20]

Observers, more often than group members, can identify subgrouping patterns. Greater awareness and sensitivity to this can help team members become more objective. For instance, subgrouping tends to become associated with seating arrangements. A fixed pattern by which each member always sits in the same place or members from one unit always sit next to one another can reinforce any feelings associated with subgrouping.

Participants often write that there were no subgroupings and comment that everyone was equally independent; however, subgroupings always exist to some degree. Sociometric techniques can readily bring out the underlying basis for subgrouping (attraction to or identification with other people or rejection). Ask the question, ''What team member would you most like to go to a movie with?'' Rank all members from ''most like to'' to ''least like to.'' The teams' responses could be listed on a diagram showing the interrelationships among members. The same ranking could be done with a number of questions relating to different aspects of relationships—for example, ''Who would you most like to have on your debate team?'' These underlying feelings can be the basis of subgroupings though they might not be apparent on the surface or influence the team greatly. See if you can make journal entries that show an enhanced ability to observe subgroupings and their influences on the team.

Leadership

Leaders in small groups play a critical role in fostering the evolution of the group and its performance. Studies in group dynamics have emphasized the importance of the emergent leader in the accomplishment of group tasks. The group leader or leaders are seen as roles that emerge within the group just like the other differentiated roles discussed earlier in this chapter. Module 3 provided an overview of leadership orientations and some of the current knowledge about the role of leaders in organizational settings.

In the context of **small group leadership**, we would like to add the following points based on recent research. First, two types of leadership functions in small groups have been found to influence group performance: *monitoring* (obtaining and interpreting data about performance conditions and events that might affect them) and *taking action* (creating or maintaining favorable performance conditions).[21] Second, the performance of both task-oriented and maintenance-oriented leadership roles influence group process and group effectiveness.[22] Third, two categories of leaders' behavior—*performance monitoring* (collecting performance data), and *performance consequences* (establishing rewards and punishments for performance)—have been found to be a requirement of leaders' optimal performance in small groups.[23] Finally, effective leaders of effective teams manage the teams' boundaries—defining goals and direction and placing constraints on team behavior.[24] It is also important to note that all the factors that influence group development and performance (summarized in Figure 10–1) are greatly influenced by group leaders.

Other Aspects of Small Group Dynamics

Group dynamics is a field that has been intensively studied. Only a few of the concepts associated with it have been touched on so far in this book. In this section, we examine several other concepts that have relevance for the manager: social loafing and free riding, cohesiveness, homogeneity, and group development.

Social Loafing and Free Riding

Social loafing is an effect first noted by a German psychologist named Ringleman, who measured individual and group effort on a rope-pulling task. He found that the effort extended by a group was less than the sum of individual efforts. Subsequent psychological experiments have found this effect to exist in other group settings.[25] The term *free rider* refers to a person who obtains benefits from being a member of a group but who does not bear a proportional share of the costs of providing those benefits.[26] These effects have been noted to increase as group size increases.[27]

The reasons why these effects have been found can be attributed to individual perceptions about other group members' efforts, to individual laziness, and to the fact that individual effort is hidden or less noticeable in a group setting. Other factors that have been identified are an indifferent group climate, unimportant or meaningless group tasks, low expectancy of being able to master the task, the presence of a highly qualified group member, and pressures to conform.[28]

Clearly social loafing and free riding can be detrimental to group performance. This tendency can be dealt with by attempting to make individual contributions or tasks identifiable or perceived as unique.[29] It can be reduced by controlling the size of groups (with five to seven members generally seen as ideal). Social loafing and free riding can also be controlled by rewarding cooperative behavior and by encouraging the development of norms that encourage full contribution to the group effort by all members.

Cohesiveness

The term **group cohesiveness** refers to the attractiveness of the group to its members—the degree to which members desire to stay in the group. Unlike structure and process characteristics, which can be shaped by the team, cohesiveness is an outcome of how group members interact.

Research tends to support the assumption that members of highly cohesive groups, as contrasted to those of low cohesiveness, communicate better, are more cooperative, and are more responsive to group influence; they also tend to achieve accepted goals more efficiently and to have higher satisfaction.[30] Does this mean that cohesive work groups have better performance than less cohesive groups? Although many studies over the past 30 years have demonstrated mixed results in attempting to answer this question,[31] one recent summary study found a consistent, small relationship between cohesion and productivity. The study found that the effect was much stronger in "real" (as opposed to laboratory or experimental) groups.[32]

Cohesiveness leads to trust, confidence, and acceptance among members. The pressures toward conformity give the group more influence over the individual,[33] and the individual shows greater commitment and loyalty.[34] Members of highly cohesive groups tend to have higher self-esteem and are less anxious than those of less cohesive groups.

Highly cohesive groups are by definition fulfilling important needs of group members. This has several implications:

1. If the group can become more aware of the needs being fulfilled by the group for each member, it can improve its support of those needs.
2. If your team members in this class were more aware of the team skills you desire to develop, they might be more helpful in this regard.
3. One of the goals of team building (discussed in the next chapter) is to become aware of the skills, abilities, and strengths of each member so that they can be integrated into the work activities of the group wherever feasible. This has the potential of increasing cohesiveness and individual satisfaction.

Groupthink

Groupthink is a mode of thinking that individuals engage in when pressures toward conformity become so dominant in a group that they override appraisal of alternative courses of action. High cohesiveness, insulation of the group from outsiders, lack of methodological procedures for search and appraisal of alternatives, directive leadership, a complex and changing environment, and high stress with a low degree of hope for finding a better solution than the one favored by the leader or other influential members were found to be conditions that can trigger groupthink behavior.[35] The following are the characteristics and symptoms of groupthink as articulated by Irving Janis:

1. An illusion of invulnerability is shared by all or most members of the group, which creates excessive optimism and encourages high risk taking.
2. Collective rationalization discounts warnings that might lead members to consider their assumptions before they commit themselves to a major policy decision.
3. An unquestionable belief in the group's morality inclines members to ignore ethical or moral consequences of their decisions.
4. There are stereotyped views of the enemy leaders as too evil to warrant genuine attempts to negotiate, or as too weak and stupid to counter whatever risky attempts are made to defeat their purpose.
5. Direct pressure on any member who expresses strong arguments against any of the group's stereotypes, illusions, or commitments makes clear that this type of dissent is contrary to what is expected of all loyal members.
6. Self-censorship of deviations from the apparent group consensus reflects each member's inclination to minimize the importance of self-doubts and counterarguments.
7. There is a shared illusion of unanimity concerning judgments conforming to the majority view (partly resulting from the self-censorship of deviants, augmented by the false assumption that silence means consent).
8. Self-appointed mindguards (members who protect the group from adverse information that might shatter its shared complacency about the effectiveness and the morality of its decision) emerge.[36]

Janis developed groupthink theory in analyzing the failed Bay of Pigs invasion of Cuba. Groupthink has also been implicated in the Nixon White House staff's handling of the Watergate affair and the Air Traffic Controllers Union's approach to the strike in 1981, which resulted in the discharge of most of its members.

One dramatic example of groupthink is NASA's managerial actions associated with the January 1986 accident that destroyed the space shuttle *Challenger.* The mindguarding function has been well documented. Before the launch, the engineers voted unanimously to recommend a delay in the launch because the O-rings might not work in low temperatures. In the past, Thiokol engineers had been asked to present considerable evidence to support a launch. This time they were asked to prove that no launch should occur. The engineers' recommendation was never relayed by management up to the top level in NASA, where the final decision to launch was made.[37] The presidential commission investigating the accident concluded that space agency officials were at certain critical points ill informed and "mesmerized" (a good synonym for *groupthink*) by past successes. When the Marshall Space Flight Center was criticized, the *Los Angeles Times* reported

> "Everybody in a position of responsibility has to ape the boss in order to maintain their position," he said. "They have to have the same noxious attitude. Dissent is a bad word." To some employees at Marshall, the criticism was welcome news. Engineer William C. Bush, a long-time critic of the center's management, said the commission's description of the Alabama facility's isolationism from the rest of NASA was well deserved. "Marshall management has an 'us vs. them' mentality and equates dissent with disloyalty," Bush said.[38]

These highly publicized examples of groupthink may give you the false impression that the phenomenon only happens "out there" and can't or doesn't happen to you. Student team projects frequently get into a groupthink mode that negatively affects their results. One team, in considering its (poor) performance on the Mountain Survival activity ruefully concluded that the group quickly latched onto the idea of walking out and never considered the problems with that alternative and never considered the alternative of staying at the crash site. A former student recently told us that what she remembers most about her organizational behavior class is the groupthink she experienced with her classroom team. She reported that she sees it often in her work relationships and regards guarding against it as a major responsibility in team management.

Groupthink can be prevented by the following steps:

- Appointing a team member to serve as a *devil's advocate* to question the group's assumptions and actions.
- Bringing in outside experts to evaluate the group's processes.
- Testing the group's ideas on outsiders.
- Having the leader avoid stating his or her position before the group reaches a decision.
- Once a decision is made, carefully reexamining the alternatives.[39]
- Having the leader alleviate time pressures on the group or, if this is not possible, focusing on issues and encouraging dissension and confrontation, or scheduling special meeting sessions.[40]

Homogeneity–Heterogeneity of Group Membership

How are group productivity and satisfaction influenced by similarities and differences in the type of people making up the group? A group composed of individuals of similar personalities, intellectual levels, abilities, experiences, and viewpoints lacks the variety of assets available for activities such as group problem solving that we find in a group whose individuals differ in these regards. However, if the differences among members in these characteristics are too extreme, it could be difficult for group members to work together.[41] Increased demographic similarity in groups is associated with greater social integration; higher social integration is in turn associated with lower turnover.[42]

Thus, in selecting group members, both cohesiveness and homogeneity–heterogeneity need to be considered. As C. R. Shephard observes,

> Similarity is an aid to developing cohesion; cohesion in turn is related to the success of a group. Homogeneity, however, can be detrimental if it results in the absence of stimulation. If all members are alike, they may have little to talk about, they may compete with each other, or they may all commit the same mistake. Variety is the spice of life in a group, so long as there is a basic core of similarity.[43]

However, cohesiveness has an elusive quality. It is difficult to provide direct guidance on how to make a group more cohesive since cohesion (just like high productivity) seems to be the result of other forces. Shephard sees both cohesion and productivity as being associated with successful groups. In addition to high cohesion and high productivity, he sees successful groups as groups in which ''objectives, role differentiation, values and norms, and membership criteria are clear and agreed upon, and in which communication is open and full.''[44]

Group Development and Group Maturity

Group cohesiveness and the operation of norms occur over time. Like individuals, groups develop over time and reach developmental maturity. **Group maturity** has been described as existing when

1. Members are aware of their own and each other's assets and liabilities vis-à-vis the group's task.
2. These individual differences are accepted without being labeled as good or bad.
3. The group has developed authority and interpersonal relationships that are recognized and accepted by its members.
4. Group decisions are made through rational discussion. Minority opinions and/or dissent is recognized and encouraged. Attempts are not made to force decisions or false unanimity.

5. Conflict is over substantive group issues such as group goals and the effectiveness and efficiency of various means for achieving those goals. Conflict over emotional issues regarding group structure, process, or interpersonal relationships is at a minimum.
6. Members are aware of the group's processes and their roles in them.[45]

Group Development

Development is a process by which a system adapts to internal and environmental forces. Throughout this book we have noted that individual development is driven by the interaction of biological, psychological, and social elements. Groups that function in a relatively homogeneous environment tend to progress through similar patterns of development. A number of group development models have been advanced in the literature. These models can be classified into three categories: performance models, emotional climate models, and revolt models.[46] Table 10–1 provides a comparative summary of a representative model from each of the categories.

Table 10–1

Group Development Models: A Comparison

	Forming	Storming	Norming	Performing	Adjourning
Tuckman and Jensen (1977) (Performance Model)	Activity to determine nature and parameters of task	Engender emotional responses, resistance, ineffectiveness	Open exchange of relevant interpretations	Constructive task activity	
	Inclusion	**Control**	**Affection**		
Schutz (1958) (Emotional Climate Model)	In or out	Top or bottom	Near or far		
	Uncertainty	**Group**	**Competition**	**Termination**	
Hartman and Gibbard (1974) (Revolt Model)	Revolt	Fusion-utopia	Intimacy		

The *performance models* are based on the assumption that groups resolve issues as preparation to completing task performance. The group develops or moves through a clear hierarchy of stages toward more efficient and effective group work. Not all groups move through all stages, but may become stuck at a particular level of development. The *emotional climate* models do not contain stages of task performance but rather describe a progression of emotional concerns in the group. The stages build hierarchically toward closer relationships between members. The *revolt models* are based on the notion that groups proceed predictably toward a rebellion against the leader or leaders. The group develops by working through complex dynamic relationships between the members and the leader(s).

For illustration purposes, we describe an emotional climate development model developed by H. J. Reitz.[47]

1. *Orientation.* People wonder how authority and power will be distributed. What is our purpose? How will we carry out the activities? What are the rules? What will my role be? How will I appear to others? How can I influence what is going on? This is a period of getting organized. The function of many of the behaviors is to ward off anxiety. The individuals' needs for status, attention, and acceptance are involved. Some individuals respond by withdrawal, not talking, doodling, or yawning. Others respond by being assertive, overtalkative, or aggressive; others respond by attempting to please. People seek to avoid anxiety by depending on the structure of leadership, rules, goals, and activities.
2. *Conflict.* Even though there is an initial settling in and the group seems somewhat stabilized, individual needs are not satisfied. Eventually this results in the challenging or testing of the leadership or role structure or the rules and goals that are devel-

oping. Subgroupings are apt to form around these issues, some supporting what has been established so far, others opposing or offering alternative approaches.

3. *Cohesion.* During the conflict phase, emotions are more easily expressed and some tension release takes place. A redistribution of leadership power may occur and members' roles become more clearly defined. Some issues raised during the conflict stage are resolved, so the authority structure and members' role clarification result in feelings of belongingness, feelings that "we have been through this together."
4. *Delusion.* The good feelings of having resolved many of the issues of authority may not last long. Group members still face issues concerning emotional aspects of interpersonal relationships. How intimate are they to become? How much are they willing to reveal about their feelings? Can they accept individual differences? The delusion arrives because the increased group acceptance that members feel around the authority and power issues can lead them to believe—erroneously—that there are no interpersonal problems. Conflict is apt to be smoothed over until the group members realize obstacles do exist, and they move into the next phase.
5. *Disillusion.* The euphoria of the delusion stage wears off as uncertainties around interpersonal issues remain. Subgroupings may form around the degree of socializing versus task orientation.
6. *Acceptance.* If the group has work to do and if there is the pressure of goals and deadlines ahead, these forces will greatly influence resolution of residual authority and intimacy problems. Such pressures bring rationality into the forefront and provide the base for individuals to play roles furthering problem resolution and acceptance of the group. Achievement of goals can greatly augment the movement toward maturity as described above.

Summary

Some concepts of small group dynamics have been described to demonstrate their applicability to the emergent role system of work groups and to your classroom teams. Group development and group performance are affected by six general factors: the group's purpose, the group's composition, the context within which the group operates, the group's structure, the group's processes, and the group's leadership.

Within groups, recurrent patterns of relationships occur that are based on shared expectations. Of particular importance are the group's norms. Individuals follow norms to perform their roles and to ensure status and acceptance in the group. Subgrouping among members occurs from role interactions and from attraction and rejection. Some group members may not put forth full effort, and social loafing may occur.

High group cohesiveness is associated with several factors. Too much of either homogeneity or heterogeneity in group membership is dysfunctional to group performance. High cohesiveness is also related to group maturity. Groups go through developmental stages as members struggle with both tasks and interpersonal relationships. Effectiveness requires avoiding hang-ups en route to group maturity. A major hazard faces groups that become highly cohesive. They can develop groupthink, which can lead to inappropriate or incorrect action.

Study Questions

1. What is group dynamics? Why is an understanding of group dynamics essential for any team manager or group member?
2. In what way can group norms be considered a part of group structure?
3. Leadership is listed as a factor that influences performance. The other factors discussed are also influenced by team leaders. Develop an example of such influence for each of the other factors.

4. The disadvantages of groupthink are outlined in this module. Can you think of any advantages arising from groupthink?
5. What generalizations can be made concerning the relationship between homogeneity/heterogeneity and team effectiveness?
6. Think of any team you now are or have been a member of. How would you rate it on the six points given on group maturity?
7. Reflect on your group experience in this course thus far. Identify the different factors that affected the development of the group. What course of action would you take to improve the group's performance? Why?

Endnotes

1. M. Knowles and Hulda Knowles, *The Introduction to Group Dynamics* (Chicago: Follet, 1972), p. 14.

2. For a more complete definition of this complex subject, see Dorwin Cartwright and Alvin Zander, eds., *Group Dynamics: Research and Theory,* 3d ed. (New York: Harper & Row, 1968).

3. D. L. Gladstein, ''Groups in Context: A Model of Group Effectiveness,'' *Administrative Science Quarterly* 29, no. 4 (1984), pp. 499–517.

4. R. A. Guzzo and R. J. Campbell, ''Group Performance and Intergroup Relations in Organizations,'' in *Handbook of Industrial and Organizational Psychology,* vol. 3, M. D. Dunnette and L. M. Hough, eds. (Palo Alto, Calif.: Consulting Psychologists Press, 1992), pp. 269–313.

5. R. W. Napier and M. K. Gershenfield, *Groups: Theory and Experience,* 4th ed. (Boston, Mass.: Houghton Mifflin, 1989).

6. G. P. Shea and R. A. Guzzo, ''Group Effectiveness: What Really Matters?'' *Sloan Management Review,* Spring 1987, pp. 499–517.

7. C. J. G. Gersick, ''Time and Transition in Work Teams: Toward a New Model of Group Development,'' *Academy of Management Journal* 31, no. 1 (1988), pp. 9–41.

8. W. C. Swap and Associates, *Group Decision Making* (Beverly Hills, Calif.: Sage, 1984), pp. 55–58. The extract given here is reprinted by permission of Sage Publications, Inc.

9. Cartwright and Zander, *Group Dynamics.*

10. J. E. Diskill, R. Hogan, and E. Salas, ''Personality and Group Performance,'' in *Group Processes and Intergroup Relations,* C. Hendrick, ed. (Newbury Park, Calif.: Sage, 1987), pp. 91–122; and D. A. Kolb, I. M. Rubin, and J. M. McIntyre, *Organizational Psychology: An Experiential Approach to Organization Behavior* (Englewood Cliffs, N.J.: Prentice-Hall, 1984.)

11. J. A. Pearce and E. C. Ravlin, ''The Design and Activation of Self-Regulating Work Groups,'' *Human Relations* 40 (1987), pp. 751–82; and S. E. Jackson, J. F. Brett, V. I. Sessa, D. M. Cooper, J. A. Julin, and K. Peyronin, ''Some Differences Make a Difference: Individual Dissimilarity and Group Heterogeneity as Correlates of Recruitment, Promotions, and Turnover,'' *Journal of Applied Psychology* 76 (1991), pp. 675–89.

12. E. Sundstrom, K. P. DeMuse, and D. Futrell, ''Work Teams: Applications and Effectiveness,'' *American Psychologist* 45 (1990), pp. 120–33.

13. T. G. Cummings, ''Designing Effective Work Groups,'' in *Handbook of Organizational Design,* vol. 2, P. C. Nystrom and W. H. Starbuck, eds. (New York: Oxford University Press, 1981), pp. 250–71.

14. M. A. Campion, G. J. Medsker, and A. C. Higgs, ''Relations between Work Group Characteristics and Effectiveness: Implications for Designing Effective Work Groups,'' *Personnel Psychology* 46 (1993), pp. 823–47.

15. F. R. David, J. A. Pearce, and W. A. Randolph, ''Linking Technology and Structure to Enhance Group Performance,'' *Journal of Applied Psychology* 74 (1989).

16. J. W. VanderZander, *Sociology* (New York: Ronald Press, 1965), pp. 64–65.

17. K. D. Benne and P. Sheats, ''Functional Roles of Group Members,'' *Journal of Social Issues,* Spring 1948, pp. 41–49; and L. R. Hoffman, ''Applying Experimental Research on

Problem Solving in Organizations,'' *Journal of Applied Behavioral Science* 15 (1979), pp. 375–91.

18. S. Schachter, ''Deviation, Rejection, and Communications,'' *Journal of Abnormal and Social Psychology* 46 (1951), pp. 190–207.

19. J. Eagle and N. Newton, ''Scapegoating in Small Groups: An Organizational Perspective,'' *Human Relations* 34 (1981), pp. 283–301; and G. Gemmill and G. Kraus, ''Dynamics of Covert Role Analysis,'' *Small Group Behavior* 19, no. 3 (1988), pp. 299–311.

20. T. Caplow, *Two against One* (Englewood Cliffs, N.J.: Prentice-Hall, 1968).

21. R. J. Hackman and R. E. Walton, ''Leading Groups in Organizations,'' in *Designing Effective Work Groups,* P. S. Goodman, ed. (San Francisco: Jossey-Bass, 1986), pp. 72–119.

22. D. L. Gladstein, ''Groups in Context: A Model of Task Group Effectiveness,'' *Administrative Science Quarterly* 29, no. 4 (1984), pp. 499–517.

23. J. L. Komaki, M. L. Desselles, and E. D. Bowman, ''Definitely Not a Breeze: Extending an Operant Model of Effective Supervision to Teams,'' *Journal of Applied Psychology* 74, no. 3 (1989), pp. 522–29.

24. J. R. Hackman, ed., *Groups That Work (and Those That Don't)* (San Francisco: Jossey-Bass, 1990), p. 496–97.

25. B. Latané, K. Williams, and S. Harkins, ''Many Hands Make Light the Work: The Causes and Consequences of Social Loafing,'' *Journal of Personality and Social Psychology* 37 (1979), pp. 822–32.

26. R. Albanese and D. D. Van Fleet, ''Rational Behavior in Groups: The Free-Riding Tendency,'' *Academy of Management Review* 10, no. 2 (1985), pp. 244–55.

27. J. M. Beyer and H. M. Trice, ''A Reexamination of the Relations between Size and Various Components of Organizational Complexity,'' *Administrative Science Quarterly* 24 (1979), pp. 48–64.

28. J. F. Verga, ''The Frequency of Self-Limiting Behavior in Groups: A Measure and an Explanation,'' *Human Relations* 44, no. 8 (1991), pp. 877–94.

29. G. R. Jones, ''Task Visibility, Free Riding, and Shirking: Explaining the Effect of Structure and Technology on Employee Behavior,'' *Academy of Management Review* 9, no. 4 (1984), pp. 684–95; and K. H. Price, ''Decision Responsibility, Task Responsibility, Identifiability, and Social Loafing,'' *Organizational Behavior and Human Decision Processes* 40 (1987), pp. 330–45.

30. M. E. Shaw, *Group Dynamics: The Psychology of Small Group Behavior* (New York: McGraw-Hill, 1976), pp. 232–33.

31. P. E. Mudrack, ''Group Cohesiveness and Productivity: A Closer Look,'' *Human Relations* 9 (1989), pp. 771–85.

32. B. Mullen and C. Copper, ''The Relation between Group Cohesiveness and Performance: An Integration,'' *Psychological Bulletin* 115, no. 2 (1994), pp. 210–27.

33. Cartwright and Zander, *Group Dynamics,* p. 104.

34. P. R. Nail, ''Toward an Integration of Some Models and Theories of Social Response,'' *Psychological Bulletin* 100 (1986), pp. 190–206; and G. E. Overvold, ''The Imperative of Organizational Harmony: A Critique of Contemporary Human Relations Theory,'' *Journal of Business Ethics* 6 (1987), pp. 559–65.

35. I. L. Janis and L. Mann, *Decision Making: A Psychological Analysis of Conflict* (New York: Free Press, 1977); and C. Posner-Weber, ''Update on Groupthink,'' *Small Group Behavior* 18 (1987), pp. 118–25.

36. I. L. Janis, *Victims of Groupthink,* 2d ed. (Boston: Houghton Mifflin, 1982).

37. R. Jeffrey Smith, ''Shuttle Inquiry Focuses on Weather, Rubber Seals, and Unheeded Advice,'' *Science,* February 28, 1986, p. 909.

38. M. Dolan, ''Fletcher Pledges NASA to Make Technical, Management Reform,'' *Los Angeles Times,* June 10, 1986, part I, p. 10.

39. I. L. Janis, *Groupthink: Psychological Studies of Policy Decisions and Fiascoes,* 2d ed. (Boston: Houghton Mifflin, 1982).

40. G. Moorhead, R. Ference, and C. P. Neck, ''Group Decision Fiascoes Continued: Space Shuttle Challenger and a Revised Groupthink Framework,'' *Human Relations* 44 (1991), pp. 539–50.

41. M. E. Shaw, *Group Dynamics: The Psychology of Small Group Behavior* (New York: McGraw-Hill, 1976), pp. 232–33.

42. C. A. O'Reilly III, D. F. Caldwell, and W. P. Barnette, "Work Group Demography, Social Integration, and Turnover," *Administrative Science Quarterly* 35 (1989), pp. 21–37.

43. C. R. Shephard, *Small Groups* (San Francisco: Chandler, 1964), p. 118.

44. Ibid., p. 124.

45. L. N. Jewell and H. J. Reitz, *Group Effectiveness in Organizations* (Glenview, Ill.: Scott, Foresman, 1981), pp. 14–15. (Based on W. Bennis and H. Shepard *A Theory of Group Development* (San Francisco: Jossey Bass, 1974).

46. M. McCollom, "Reevaluating Group Development: A Critique of the Familiar Models," in *Groups in Context,* J. Gilette and M. McCollom, eds. (Reading, Mass.: Addison-Wesley, 1990), pp. 134–54.

47. H. J. Reitz, *Group Behavior in Organizations* (Homewood, Ill.: Richard D. Irwin, 1981).

Activity 10–3: Individual Role Assessment

Objectives:

a. To identify individual roles being played by members of a group.

b. To relate those roles to group performance.

c. To provide team members with feedback on their group performance.

Task 1 (Homework):

For each member of your classroom group (other than yourself), write down words that describe their behavior in the group. Next, review the section of the text describing individual roles. Do any of the roles described fit any members of your group? Which ones? Finally, which members can best be described as task leaders? As social (group maintenance) leaders? Your journal may be of use here.

Task 2 (Group Meeting):

1. Write each member's name on the board. Under each name write the words written down by other team members, including any specific roles identified. Indicate any individuals identified as task or social leaders.
2. Discuss the functionality of the roles observed in the group. To what extent do they help or hinder group performance?
3. Identify any roles that are not being performed (e.g., critic/evaluator). Does the lack of this role inhibit the group in any way or reduce its performance?

Task 3 (Classroom—Optional):

Without naming individuals, report back to the class the types of roles found in your groups. Given the larger sample size of the class, how many different roles are found? Are there any roles not found? Why might this be so?

Activity 10–4: Status on the Campus

Objectives:

a. To identify status as it operates on a college campus.

b. To examine the role of status on classroom and group operation.

Task 1 (Homework):

Make a list of characteristics that define high status or low status on your campus. In doing so, think of individuals that you view as "cool" or "awesome" and identify what makes them so. You can do the same thing with individuals who lack these characteristics. As another approach, you could try to define what is meant by cool, awesome, or outrageous behavior, and then try to identify individuals who possess those characteristics.

Task 2 (Classroom):

Based on individual contributions, develop a class list of factors and behaviors that lead to high status on campus. Identify items for which there is a high degree of consensus.

Task 3 (Group Meeting—Optional):

Using the list of status factors developed in the class, identify the extent to which group members possess these elements. Any group member who has a high number of status elements would be identified as having a high degree of external status. Do you have individuals like this in the group? Does high external status affect the role that the individual(s) plays in the group? Why or why not?

Activity 10–5: The Claremont Instrument Company

Objective:

To examine the human dynamics in the context of the firm.

Task 1 (Homework):

Individuals are to read the case and answer the questions at the end of the case.

Task 2:

The instructor will facilitate class analysis of the case.

Background:

The following case is a widely used Harvard classic that provides an excellent opportunity for the use of the models covered thus far to analyze employee behavior. After studying the case, prepare written answers to the questions in the assignment at the end.

The horseplay of the work group and the resulting accident raise questions for the managerial action that can be explored through the role playing that is suggested in the next activity, "Ed (Edna) Masters' Problem."

Case Study: The Claremont Instrument Company

One of the problems facing the supervisory staff of the Claremont Instrument Company was that of horseplay among employees in the glass department. For some time this question had troubled the management of the company. Efforts had been made to discourage employees from throwing water-soaked waste at each other and from engaging in water fights with buckets or fire hoses.

Efforts to tighten up shop discipline had also resulted in orders to cut down on "visiting" with other employees. These efforts were made on the grounds that whatever took an employee away from his regular job would interfere with production or might cause injury to the employees or the plant machinery. Production was a matter of some concern to the officials of the company, particularly since the war. In spite of a large backlog of unfilled orders, there were indications that domestic and foreign competition in the relatively near future might begin to cut into the company's business. Anything

Source: Copyright © by the President and Fellows of Harvard College. Harvard Business School case 9-406-032. This case was prepared by H. Craig under the direction of Paul R. Lawrence and Ralph M. Hower as the basis for class discussion rather than to illustrate either effective or ineffective handling of an administrative situation. Reprinted by permission of the Harvard Business School.

which could help to increase the salable output of the company was welcomed by the officers; at the same time, anything which might cut down overhead operating expenses, or improve the quality of the product, or cut down on manufacturing wastage was equally encouraged.

The Claremont Instrument Company had been located for many years in a community in western Massachusetts with a population of approximately 18,000. The company employed approximately 500 people. None of these people were organized in a union for collective bargaining purposes. The company produced a varied line of laboratory equipment and supplies. Many of its products were fabricated principally from glass, and over the years the company had built up a reputation for producing products of the highest quality. To a considerable extent this reputation for quality rested upon the company's ability to produce very delicate glass components to exacting quality standards. These glass components were produced from molten glass in the glass department. Exhibit 1 presents a partial organization chart of the company. The entire glass department was located in one wing of the company's main factory. In this department the glass components such as tubes, bottles, decanters, and glass-measuring devices were made from molten glass. Some of these glass parts were produced by hand-blowing operations, but most of them were produced on bottlemaking machinery which in effect blew the molten glass into a mold. This operation of blowing the glass by hand or by machine was the most critical operation in the department and required a high degree of skill. Immediately following the blowing operation some of the parts were "punched." The "puncher" was a mechanical apparatus into which the glass components were placed; as the machine revolved, a small gas flame melted the glass in a small area and blew a hole in the glass component. Next the parts were placed on a mechanical conveyor where they were annealed by an air-cooling process. Then the parts were picked off the conveyor by women known as packers, whose duty was to inspect them for defects of many kinds and to give them temporary packaging in cardboard cartons for transit to other parts of the factory. The final operation in the department was performed by sealers, whose job it was to seal these cardboard cartons and place them in stacks for temporary storage. Exhibit 2 is a floor plan of the glass department.

The glass department was operated on a continuous, 24-hour, seven-day-a-week basis, because of the necessity of keeping the tanks of molten glass hot and operating all the time. Four complete shifts worked in the department. The different shifts rotated as to the hours of the day they worked. Roughly, each shift spent two weeks at a time on the day shift, on the evening shift, and on the night shift. Each shift worked on the average five days a week, but their days off came at varying times throughout the week. The glass department was located in a separate wing of the plant, and the employees of the department used a special entrance and a special time clock.

Each of the four shifts employed about 23 people. Each shift had its own foreman and assistant foreman and hourly workers as indicated in Exhibit 1. All these workers were men, with the exception of the packers. The foreman was a full-time supervisor, but the assistant foreman usually operated a glass machine and only substituted for the foreman in his absence. The furnace men prepared the molten glass for the glass blowers while the floormen cleaned up broken glass and other waste and filled in on odd jobs.

An inspector from the quality-control department and a maintenance man from the maintenance department were assigned on a full-time basis to each of the four shifts.

The inspector worked with the packers and was responsible for the quality of all glass components. The maintenance man was responsible for the maintenance and satisfactory operation of all machinery in the department.

Several physical conditions made work in the glass department unique in the plant. The fact that the glass furnaces were located in this department meant that the department was always unusually hot. The glassblowing machines were run principally by compressed air, and each movement of a machine part was accompanied by the hiss of escaping air. This noise combined with the occasional sound of breaking glass made it impossible for the members of the department to converse in a normal tone. An oil

Exhibit 1
Partial Organization Chart

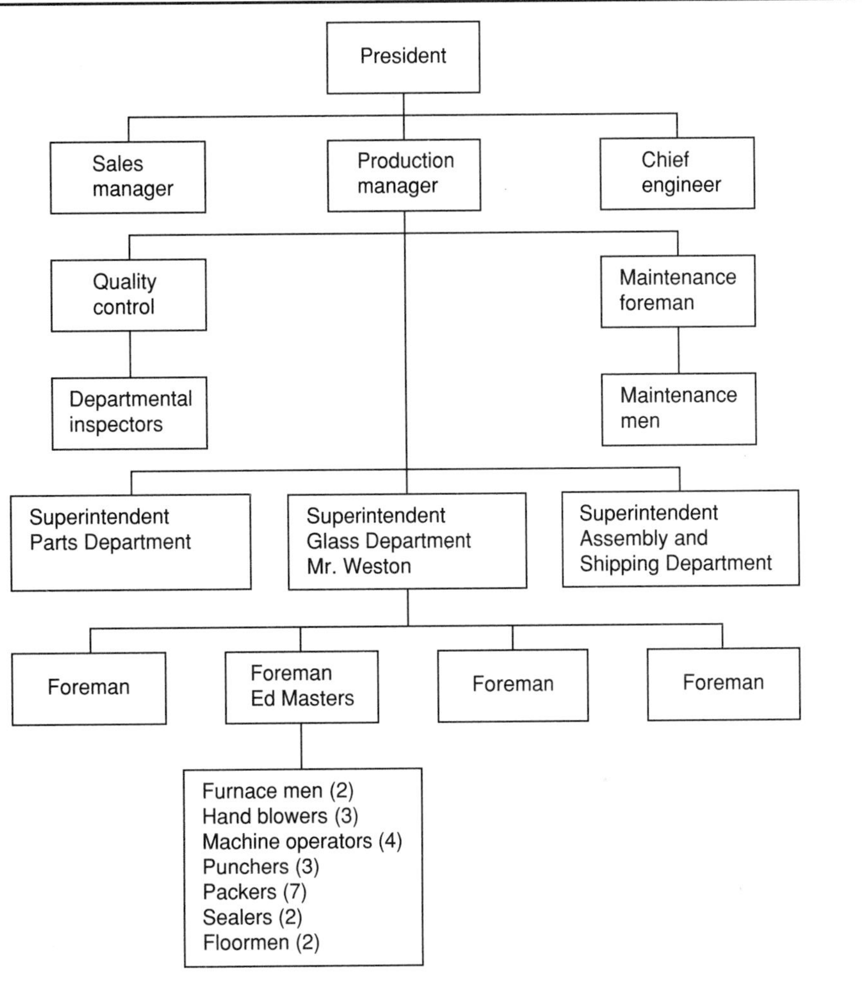

Exhibit 2
Floor Plan of Glass Department

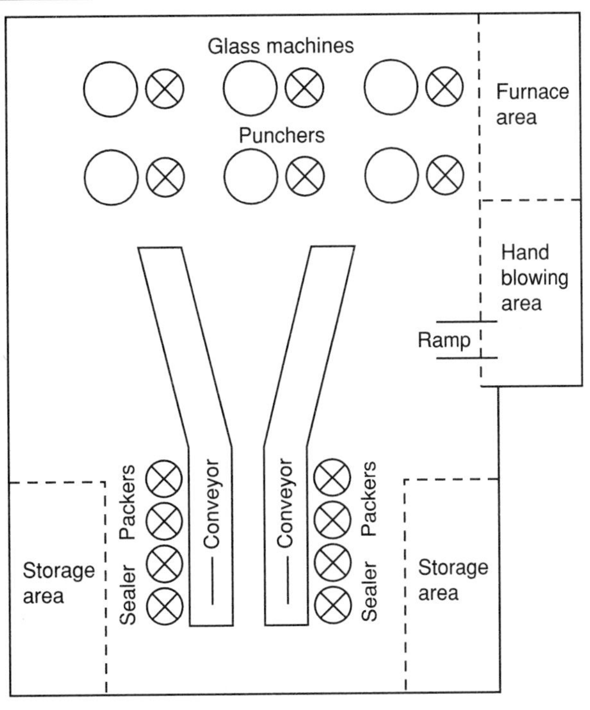

vapor was used to coat the inside of the molds on the glass machine, and when the hot glass poured into the mold, a smoke was given off that circulated throughout the department.

Ralph Boynton, a student at the Harvard Business School, took a summer job as one of the floormen on one of the shifts working in the glass department. While on this job, he made the above observations about the Claremont Instrument Company in general and the glass department in particular. In the course of the summer, Ralph became particularly interested in the practice of engaging in horseplay, and the description that follows is based on his observations.

The foreman of Boynton's shift, Ed Masters, had worked a number of years in the glass department and had been promoted to foreman from the position of operator of one of the glass machines. In Ralph's opinion the foreman was generally liked by the shift employees. One of them commented to Ralph, "If everything is going okay, you don't see Ed around. If anything goes wrong, he's right there to try and fix it up." Another one of them commented, "He pitches right in—gives us a hand—but he never says much." Frequently when a glass machine was producing glass components of unacceptable quality, Ralph noticed the foreman and the maintenance man working with a machine operator to get the machine in proper adjustment. On one occasion Ralph was assigned the job of substituting for one of the sealers. Shortly after Ralph had started work, Ed Masters came around and asked how he was doing. Ralph replied that he was doing fine and that it was quite a trick to toss the cartons into the proper positions on the stack. Ed replied, "You keep at it, and it won't be long before you get the hang of it. You'll be tired for a while, but you'll get used to it. I found I could do it and I am a '97-pound weakling.' "

Ralph also picked up a variety of comments from the employees about one another. The shift maintenance man, Bert, referred to the men on the shift as "a good bunch of guys." One of the packers referred with pride to one of the machine operators, "That guy can get out more good bottles than anybody else." On one occasion, when the glass components were coming off the end of the conveyor at a very slow rate, one of the packers went around to the glass machines to find out what the trouble was. When she came back she reported to the rest of the packers, "Ollie is having trouble with his machine. It's out of adjustment but he will get it fixed in a few minutes." Ralph noticed that a record was kept of the total daily output of each shift of packers. These women seemed anxious to reach a certain minimum output on each shift. When the components were coming through slowly, he heard such comments as "This is a bad night." If the work had been coming slowly, the packers regularly started "robbing the conveyor" toward the end of the shift. This was the practice of reaching up along the conveyor and picking off components for packaging before they reached the packer's usual work position.

A short time after Ralph started to work, the company employed another new floorman for the shift. This new man quickly picked up the nickname of "Windy." The following were some of Windy's typical comments: "My objective is the paycheck and quitting time." "I love work so much I could lay down and go to sleep right beside it." "These guys are all dopes. If we had a union in here, we would get more money." "I hate this night work. I am quitting as soon as I get another job." Most of the other employees paid little attention to Windy. One of the sealers commented about him, "If bull were snow, Windy would be a blizzard." One night Windy commented to three of the men, "This is a lousy place. They wouldn't get away with this stuff if we had a union. Why don't the four of us start one right here?" None of the group replied to this comment.

Ralph had a number of opportunities to witness the horseplay that concerned the management. At least one horseplay episode seemed to occur on every eight-hour shift. For example, one night while Ralph stood watching Ollie, one of the machine operators, at his work, Ollie called Ralph's attention to the fact that Sam, the operator of the adjacent machine, was about to get soaked.

"Watch him now," Ollie said with a grin, "last night he got Bert and now Bert is laying for him. You watch now." Ralph caught sight of Bert warily circling behind the machines with an oil can in his hand. Sam had been sitting and quietly watching the bottles come off his machine. Suddenly Bert sprang out and fired six or seven shots of water at Sam. When the water hit him, Sam immediately jumped up and fired a ball of wet waste which he had concealed for this occasion. He threw it at Bert and hit him in the chest with it. It left a large wet patch on his shirt. Bert stood his ground squirting his can until Sam started to chase him. Then he ran off. Sam wiped his face and sat down again. Then he got up and came over to Ollie and Ralph. Sam shouted, ''By Jesus, I am going to give him a good soaking.'' Ollie and Ralph nodded in agreement. Later Ollie commented to Ralph, ''It may take as long as three hours for Sam to work up a good plan to get even, but Bert is going to get it good.''

Sam was ready to get back at Bert as soon as he could be lured close enough to the machine. Sam pretended to watch his machine but kept his eye out for Bert. In a little while Bert walked jauntily by Sam's machine. They grinned at each other and shouted insults and challenges. Bert went over to a bench to fix something and Sam slipped around behind his machine, pulled down the fire hose, and let Bert have a full blast chasing him up along the conveyor as Bert retreated. Sam then turned off the hose, reeled it back up, and went back to his machine.

All the other employees on the scene had stopped to watch this episode and seemed to enjoy it. They commented that it was a good soaking. Bert came back to the machines after a while, grinning, and hurling insults while he stood by Sam's machine to dry off from the heat of the machine. The other operators kidded him some, and then everyone went back to work seriously.

A little later the foreman came through the department and noticed the large puddle of water on the floor. He instructed Bert to put some sawdust on the puddle to soak up the water. Ralph was told later that Ed Masters had told Bert, ''I want more work and less of this horsing around.'' A few minutes later Ed Masters and Bert were discussing a small repair job that had to be done that evening.

On another occasion Ralph asked Ollie what he thought of the horseplay. Ollie commented, ''It's something each guy has to make up his own mind about. Personally, I don't go in for it. I have got all the raises and merit increases that have come along, and I know Bert hasn't had a raise in over a year. Whenever something starts, I always look back at my machine so that I can be sure that nothing goes wrong while I am looking away. Personally, I just don't care—you have to have some fun, but personally, I don't go in for it.''

Just at this point Al, one of the punchers, came down from the men's lavatory ready to take his turn on one of the punch machines. He was a moment or two early and stood talking to Sam. Ollie got up from where he had been talking to Ralph and started to holler, ''Hey, Al—hey, Al.'' The other operators took up the chant, and all of them picked up pieces of wood or pipe and started drumming on the waste barrels near their machines. Al took up a long piece of pipe and joined in. After a minute or two, one of the operators stopped, and the drumming ended quickly. Al lit a cigarette and stepped up to take the machine for his turn.

Ralph later had an opportunity to ask Bert what he thought of the horseplay. Bert said, ''You have to have some horseplay or you get rusty. You have to keep your hand in.'' Ralph noted that Bert's work kept him busy less than anyone else, since his duties were primarily to act as an emergency repairman and maintenance man. Ralph asked, ''Why doesn't Ollie get into the horseplay?'' Bert replied, ''Ollie can't take it. He likes to get other people, but he can't take it when he gets it. You have got to be fair about this. If you get some guy, you are surer than hell you will get it back yourself. Now you take Sam and me. We've been playing like that for a long time. He don't lose his temper, and I don't lose mine. I knew I was going to get that hose the other night; that was why I was baiting him with a squirt gun.''

Ralph asked, ''Does Ed Masters mind it very much?'' Bert answered, ''Hell, he's just like the rest of us. He knows you've got to have some of that stuff, only he gets bawled out by the superintendent if they see anything going on like that. That's why we don't play around much on the day shift. But the night shift, that's when we have fun. The only reason we don't squirt the foreman is because he's the foreman. As far as we're concerned, he is no different from us. Besides he ain't my boss anyway. I'm maintenance. I don't care what he says.''

About the middle of the summer, the superintendent of the glass department returned from his vacation and immediately thereafter an effort was made by him through the foremen to tighten up on shop discipline. The men on the machines and the punchers were forbidden to walk up to the other end of the conveyor to talk to the packers and sealers and vice versa. The foreman started making occasional comments like ''keep moving'' when he saw a small group together in conversation. On one occasion a small group stood watching some activity outside the plant. Ed came by and quite curtly said, ''Break it up.'' Everyone seemed quite shocked at how abrupt he was.

About this same time, the word was passed around among the employees that a big push was on to step up the output of a certain product in order to make a tight delivery schedule. Everyone seemed to be putting a little extra effort into getting his job done. Ralph thought he noticed that the foreman was getting more and more jumpy at this time. On one occasion Ed commented to some of the employees, ''I am bitter today.'' One of the machine operators asked him what the trouble was, and Ed made some comment about a foreman's meeting where the superintendent was telling them that the playing around and visiting would have to stop.

One night a short time later, Ralph saw that preparations were being made for an unusually elaborate trap for soaking Jim, one of the sealers who had recently begun to take part in the water fights. A full bucket of water was tied to the ceiling with a trip rope at the bottom in such a way that the entire contents would be emptied on Jim when he least suspected it. Many of the employees made a point of being on hand when the trap was sprung. It worked perfectly, and Jim was given a complete soaking. Ralph thought Jim took it in good spirit since he turned quickly to counterattack the people who had soaked him. Shortly after all the crew had gone back to work, Ruth, one of the packers, was coming down the ramp from the area where the hand-blowing operations were performed. She was carrying some of the glass components. Ruth slipped on some of the water that had been spilled during the recent fight and fell down. She was slightly burned by some of the hot glass she was carrying. Those who saw this happen rushed to help her. The burn, while not serious, required first-aid attention and the assistant foreman went with Ruth to the company dispensary for treatment. Ralph thought that the employees all felt rather sheepish about the accident. Ruth was one of the more popular girls in the department. The word went around among the employees that a report on the nature and cause of the accident would have to be made out and sent to higher management. Everyone was wondering what would happen.

Case Assignment

Prepare written notes on the following questions. When answering questions 1, 2, and 3, guide your analysis by referring to Figure 4–1 (''Operational Blueprint''). Remember to analyze the background and script factors as if the actors were not yet on the scene. For question 5, refer to Figure 4–2 (''Actors Playing Their Roles'') and to the small group dynamics concepts in this module.

1. What important external background factors are going to influence managerial practices and/or behavior of employees? (Use only those mentioned in the case and not all those listed in Figure 4–1.)
2. What internal background factors are going to influence employee behavior?
3. *Script:* What is the required role system for the work group in the Glass Department in terms of activities, interactions, and attitudes?
4. Considering only the operational blueprint factors you have analyzed in the preceding questions, make a list of (a) satisfactions, and (b) frustrations employees in the Glass Department would experience when fulfilling their required roles.

5. *Actors Playing Their Roles:* Now look at the daily drama in the Glass Department with the actors present. Describe how the emergent role system differs from the required one by focusing on the norms that control behavior.
6. Make a complete list of norms (shared expectations of acceptable behavior) of the emergent role system in the Glass Department.
7. What needs are satisfied, or frustrations lessened, by the emergent role system (norms and status system) that were not satisfied by the required role system? Make a list of these.

Activity 10–6: Ed (Edna) Masters' Problem

Objectives:

a. To examine managerial-action alternatives in the Claremont Instrument Company.
b. To illustrate the basic role conflict of the first-line supervisor.

Introduction:

At the end of the case study, Ruth slipped in the water that had been thrown on the floor during horseplay. She was only slightly burned, but a report to higher management on the nature and cause of the accident was required. Let's assume Ed Masters later told the employees—somewhat peevishly probably—that his boss, Mr. Weston, had just asked Ed to come to his office to discuss the matter.

Task 1:

Class participants are to form groups of six. Half the groups will be assigned the role of Ed Masters (or Edna Masters for women in the group). The other half will be assigned the role of the employees in the Glass Department.

Ed Masters groups will (a) try to anticipate what Mr. Weston's position will be when he discusses the subject and (b) decide what viewpoints Masters should express to Weston.

Employee groups will also try to anticipate Weston but will decide what position Ed Masters should take from their viewpoint.
(Time: 10 minutes)

Task 2:

Each Ed Masters group will select one of its members to role play its position before the class. The instructor will select one from among these.

As the role playing opens, Ed Masters has just entered Mr. Weston's office for the meeting. The instructor, playing the role of Mr. Weston, will follow the role-playing instructions in the *Instructor's Manual* while the class acts as observers.
(Time: 10 minutes)

At the conclusion of the meeting, Ed Masters will meet with one or more of the groups of employees for an exchange of views on his meeting with Weston.
(Time: 5 minutes)

Task 3 (Class Discussion):

a. What are the issues brought out by the role playing?
b. What alternative actions could management take in this case using the consequences of productivity, worker satisfaction, and organizational health as criteria?

What is the basic role conflict built into first-line supervision? How might first-line supervisors view this conflict in a way that will improve their effectiveness?

Activity 10–7: Performance Appraisal Task Force

Objectives:

a. To learn the distinction between process and content in analyzing group dynamics.
b. To apply theories of group development in analyzing one group's interactions.
c. To observe the processes of leadership influence and coalition formation in group interaction.

Task 1 (Homework):

(*Note to instructor:* Assign one of the two questions below to half the class or to half the teams in the class, and the other question to the other half, so that a range of data will be generated for analysis of this case.)

Read the following case study, "The Performance Appraisal Task Force," and prepare a written answer to the following question:

1. Analyze the case by paying attention to dynamics relevant to group development, like self-oriented versus group-oriented behavior, task avoidance, dependency, counterdependency, overt and covert conflict, and subgroup formation. Diagnose what stage or phase the group is in. Particular emphasis should be placed on providing specific examples from the case to justify your diagnosis.
2. Analyze the case from the perspective of leadership, authority, and influence. Describe how these dynamics are played out over the course of the meeting.

Task 2 (Classroom):

a. Teams are to decide on appropriate answers to the question assigned in Task 1. (Time: 20–25 minutes)
b. Team spokespersons are to report their answers to the class. Open class discussion follows.
(Time: 25–30 minutes)

Case Study: The Performance Appraisal Task Force

A task force has been created by the general manager of Division X of a medium-sized plastic fabrication firm. The task force's mission is to recommend a system of performance appraisal (PA) for the entire division. The task force has met twice in the past. At the first meeting it was decided that they needed greater clarification of the task and decided that Eric should go ask the general manager exactly what they should be doing. At the second meeting Eric reported back that the general manager wasn't much clearer and seemed to simply want the group's best thinking. Following this there was a rambling discussion and the meeting ended with a decision to meet for one hour the day after next.

(Meeting comes to order as Paul initiates.)

PAUL: I came across a really interesting article on performance appraisal in *Organization Dynamics* and I made copies for all of you. (*He passes them out.*) It's about how they set it up at Rohm & Hauss and I thought it made a lot of sense.

ERIC: I'm sure this will be very helpful, Paul, but before we look at any specific system I think we should begin by defining our objectives more clearly. For example, I was thinking, is this PA system going to be mainly used for promotion decisions, like

Source: This case study was contributed by Gervase R. Bushe. Special permission for the reproduction of this exercise and case study is granted by the author, Professor Gervase R. Bushe. We are grateful to Professor Bushe.

Exhibit 3

Third Meeting

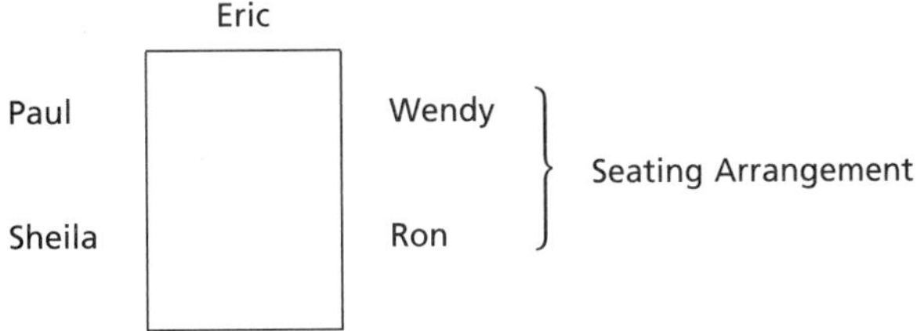

making sure that good people move up in the organization? Or is it supposed to be used mainly for salary and merit decisions?

SHEILA: Or how about, Is it supposed to help develop management?

WENDY: It's pretty clear that there are a lot of ways to skin this cat. I've been wondering if we might not be taking on too big a task, especially with our limited knowledge in this area. I guess what I'm saying is that I really think we need to get some outside expertise in here on this.

PAUL: Boy, our senior managers are really not on the ball; know what I mean? Just look at this committee. The least they could do is be specific about what they want us to do. Lately they seem to keep blowing it.

ERIC: Oh I think they do a pretty good job.

WENDY: Personally I find it encouraging that they're thinking of putting in a PA system. I mean its about time this company started to manage human resources in a systematic way.

PAUL: Well, what about that screw-up on the Bently account. Instead of just holding back, working out the bugs and delaying shipment for a week, they ordered Rodgers to ship a box full of scrap again and the account went down the drain. One thing you have to say about Rohm & Hauss, whatever they ship is 100 percent!

SHEILA: Did you hear about what happened with that task force on consolidation? They made a report to the brass last Monday after working their tails off for two months and Dan swears two of them were asleep for most of the presentation. I mean literally asleep.

ERIC: Well look; we've got a job to do and I think we should just get down to doing it.

WENDY: There's obviously a lot of ways to look at PA and probably a lot we won't think of, so, let's face it, we need some expertise. As it turns out, I have the name of a consulting firm that comes well recommended.

SHEILA: But will they give us the money to hire a consultant?

WENDY: Good question. Eric should go ask.

PAUL: Hold on a second. Who are these consultants?

WENDY: They're personnel specialists with, apparently, a wide range of expertise. I know they've done work for Celanese and Duo-Plastic and they . . .

PAUL: Celanese!?! They're losing money hand over fist. And they're doing that dumb "quality is free" hype. I don't think I want one of their consultants.

WENDY: Well, we could look into other personnel specialists.

PAUL: Frankly, I don't like asking the company to spend money that way. Obviously they've asked us to be a task force because they think we have what it takes and I'd sure like a shot at it first. I've been reading up on PA and it seems pretty clear that to make something like this work, it has to be every manager's responsibility.

RON: Maybe we should start by listing all the things we think a PA system could do.

ERIC: Good idea, Ron, but first I just want to get clear if the group wants me to go see the general manager about a consultant.

PAUL: I thought we decided to try without one for awhile.

SHEILA: I don't know that anybody decided anything, but I do think it's a good idea to get some additional information and just educate ourselves. But there are lots of ways we could do that.

PAUL: I could distribute other stuff I've read.

ERIC: Great, I'd like to see that.

SHEILA: Me too.

PAUL: Good, I'll have my girl get the stuff out to you.

WENDY: Oh Paul, I can't believe you still say "my girl." (*general laughter*)

SHEILA: You know, what really bugs me is that the secretaries call themselves *girls.*

PAUL: Well, what does it really matter? Words are just words. You can call me a *boy.* I don't care.

ERIC: You might not say that if you were black. (*general laughter*)

ERIC: Well, this is all good fun, but I think we need to be pushing forward. It seems to me we have to define our objectives here more clearly before we can move ahead.

WENDY: I think it's pretty obvious that the key here is to develop a system that allows us to monitor and rationalize our human resources within the framework of the organization's strategic plan.

SHEILA: But shouldn't it also provide information about the state of human resources that can be fed into strategic planning?

WENDY: Exactly what I mean.

PAUL: Well, I'm not sure what you mean.

SHEILA: All she's saying, Paul, is that the PA system should help management make decisions taking into consideration the manpower implications of them.

WENDY: Well, that's not exactly what I meant.

PAUL: Personally, I want a PA system that's going to give me a clear idea of just what I'm being evaluated on and I think that's what most people want. They want to know what their boss thinks they should be doing and how well he thinks they're doing.

SHEILA: So you want to see it used mainly as a feedback mechanism.

PAUL: Well, what's wrong with that?

SHEILA: I wasn't saying there's anything wrong with that.

RON: Maybe we should keep a list of all these ideas.

SHEILA: OK. We've got two so far.

ERIC: I think the main point of a good PA system is to make sure that everyone gets treated as fairly as possible, especially when it comes to promotions.

WENDY: Oh yes, I think that's critical.

PAUL: Don't forget the motivational aspects too.

WENDY: Which motivational aspects are you referring to?

PAUL: Well, the idea that if people know what's expected from their boss and get feedback on it, it'll motivate them. Like this article I'm going to send you talks about tying a PA system into an overall MBO program that really helped increase employee motivation at Terex.

ERIC: What's MBO?

WENDY: MBO—Management by Objectives—and I've heard that that MBO stuff just doesn't work.

PAUL: Why do you say that?

WENDY: Well, they tried at National Semi and I have a friend who works there and it created such a mess they just disbanded it after 10 months.

PAUL: But the article said it worked wonders at Terex. Other places too?

WENDY: You know, Paul, you can't believe everything you read. I'll bet it was written by some consultant trying to generate business. Like do you see all those stories on quality circles these days? But I heard that they're really all falling apart because we're not like Japan.

SHEILA: Yeah, it really bugs me all the stuff we keep hearing about Japan—Japan this, Japan that. If we had their labor rates and government support, we'd be doing just as well if not better.

WENDY: I think that it's true to some extent, but it's also true that they just have a different culture so different things will work there than here.

ERIC: I'll say it's different. We spent part of our last vacation in Tokyo and I couldn't believe how so many people can live in so little space. It'd drive me crazy in short order.

PAUL: Well, I don't know what all this has to do with performance appraisal.

ERIC: Quite right, Paul. We should get back on track. Now . . . what were we doing?

SHEILA: Ron was keeping a list of our ideas.

RON: No, I only suggested we should keep a list.

ERIC: Maybe you ought to be keeping that list for us, Ron.

RON: Frankly, there's so much digression going on here that it's hard for me to stay tuned in.

PAUL: You're not kidding. This meeting seems more like a sewing bee than a business meeting.

WENDY: Well, I wouldn't know since I've never been to a sewing bee. Have you, Paul?

SHEILA (*laughing*): You know, even when I was a kid, I knew I didn't want to sew and stuff.

PAUL: Look, we're really getting nowhere. Eric, will you please take charge of this meeting and get us moving in some direction.

ERIC: I thought we *were* making some progress on defining objectives.

PAUL: You know, it really pisses me off that the objectives haven't already been defined by senior management. If they treated quarterly profit targets the same way, nothing would get done around here. I wonder what would happen if we just told them it's impossible to do this without them taking a clear stand.

SHEILA: A stand on what?

PAUL: Well, for example, is the PA system going to be a personnel program or a line management function?

RON: You think it should be a line function, don't you?

PAUL: Damn right. Don't you agree, Eric?

WENDY: Management has to be involved, but I think it's clear that we would also need personnel specialists to administer and run it and make sure it's working properly. Like, we'd probably need to train managers in how to give constructive feedback, use the system, and all those kinds of things.

PAUL: Oh, just what we need, more training.

SHEILA: But, Paul, whatever system is used, we'll need to teach people how to use it, won't we?

PAUL: I don't want to do any teaching.

SHEILA: I didn't mean that we—this task force—would actually do the teaching. I meant the company will have to teach people.

PAUL: Well, I don't see what's so difficult. You just tell managers to write down their subordinates' objectives and then rate them and then tell them their ratings. What's so tough about that?

WENDY: But can you trust that managers really will give people honest feedback?

PAUL: That's the problem these days, no respect for authority. When guys like Eric and me joined this company, back then people respected their boss.

WENDY: You haven't said a word yet, Ron. What do you think?

RON: I guess people are a lot less willing to respect someone just because of their position than they used to be.

WENDY: No, I mean what do you think the objectives of a PA system should be?

RON: Well, I agree with a lot that's been said. You know, I don't really know.

WENDY: Maybe it'd help us reach some consensus if we talked about what we'd personally want the outcomes of a PA system to be.

SHEILA: OK. I think I'd like to know how I stand compared to other managers in my department.

ERIC: You mean people would know each other's ratings?

SHEILA: Sure, why not?

PAUL (*muttering*): I don't believe it.

ERIC: Hold on a second; I don't know if that's such a good idea. I mean, well, it could be very bad for morale, you know, it . . .

WENDY: Are you advocating management by secrecy?

ERIC: No, of course not. It's just that it could create some very sensitive situations and, anyway, wouldn't it make it more likely that managers wouldn't give honest feedback? I mean, that's what you're concerned about, isn't it?

WENDY: Maybe it would force them to be more careful and precise in their appraisals.

PAUL: As far as I'm concerned, my rating should be between my boss and me.

SHEILA: But don't you want to know how you're doing in relation to everyone else?

PAUL: I do know. I just have to look at the quarterly reports.

SHEILA: OK, but not everybody's work is directly reflected in profit reports.

RON: I don't think any one person's work is reflected in profit reports.

WENDY: I agree. In fact, if you extend that idea, maybe we should be appraising a team's performance instead of individuals.

ERIC: Well, that's a novel idea. And speaking of novel ideas, I could sure use a break to get rid of some of this coffee I've been drinking.

SHEILA: Great—I could use a smoke.

(*Meeting breaks up for 10 minutes.*)

11 Work Team Effectiveness: Team Building

Learning Objectives

After completing this module you should be able to

1. Explain the relationship between team building and team effectiveness.
2. Describe the potential problems that work teams face.
3. Diagnose the potential problems that your classroom team faces.
4. Describe the phases in team-building intervention.
5. Explain the roles that perception, communication, and motivation play in team effectiveness.
6. State the variations of team-building activities.
7. Appreciate the roles that team members and team leaders play in improving team effectiveness.

List of Key Concepts

Action orientation
Family groups
Hidden agenda
Special groups
Team building
Team effectiveness
Team style

Module Outline

Premodule Preparation

Activity 11–1: Revisiting the Team—Team Development

Objectives:

To review the progress and effectiveness of your team.

Task 1:

Individuals working alone are to complete the attached questionnaire on team development scales. The instrument is similar to the one that you completed at the end of Module 4.

Task 2:

Teams are to meet.

a. Discuss each item on the scale. Identify and discuss the similarities and differences in the ratings. Work toward developing a consensus rating.
b. Look back at the individual and team scores generated by the end of Module 4. Discuss the similarities and differences of the ratings. What conclusions can you draw from the comparison? Did you meet the goals that you established?
c. Study the goals and identify team goals that you would like to attain by the end of the course.

Name ________________________________ Date ________________

Questionnaire on Team Development Scales

Climate Scales

1. The degree to which my team shows enthusiasm and spirit:

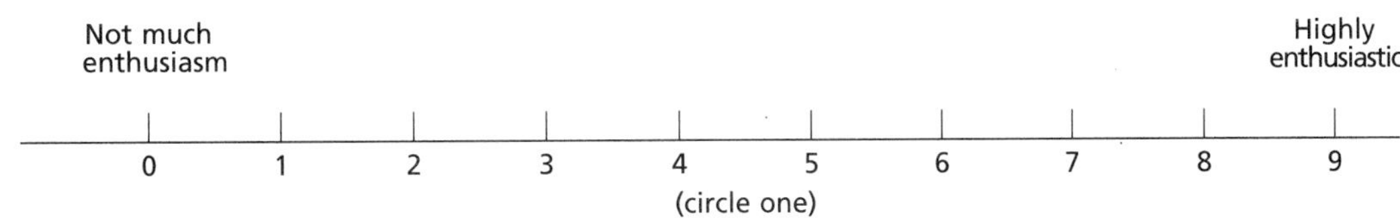

2. On humor I would rate the team

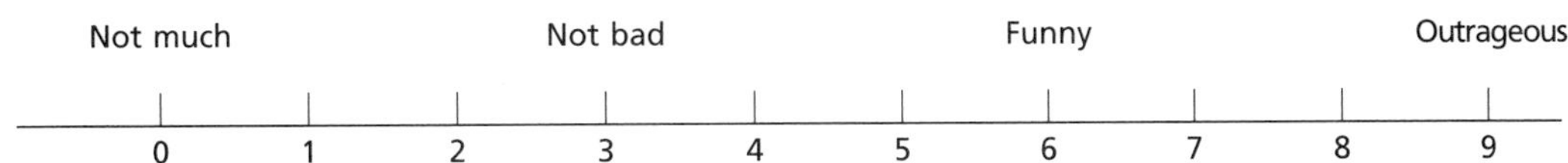

3. My team is

_____ mostly task-oriented

_____ more task-oriented than social

_____ equally task and social in orientation

_____ more social than task-oriented

_____ mostly social

People Scales (How We Regard One Another as Human Beings)

4. The degree to which we are interested in one another as people is

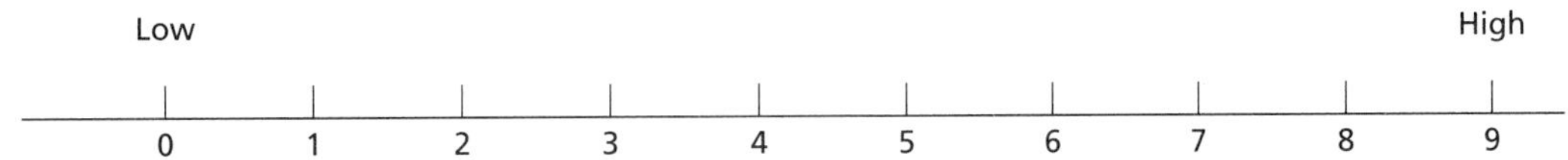

5. Our regard for each individual as a resource (knowledge, skills, abilities, viewpoints) for group goal achievement is

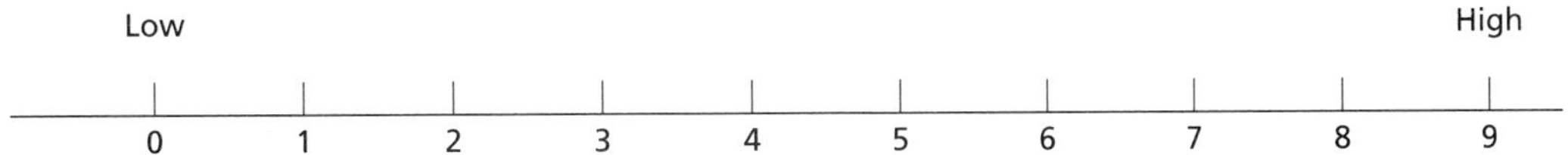

Productivity Scales (Goals, Work Accomplishment, Commitment)

6. Team's task achievement goals:

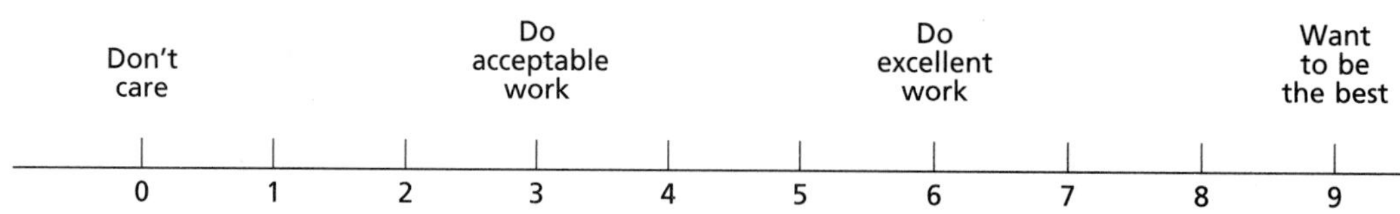

7. Actual quantity of work produced:

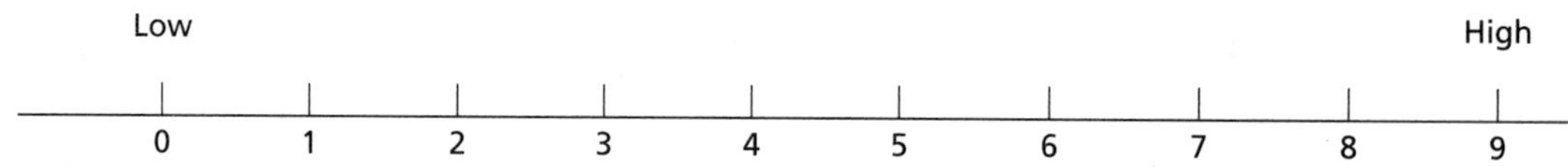

8. Quality of work produced:

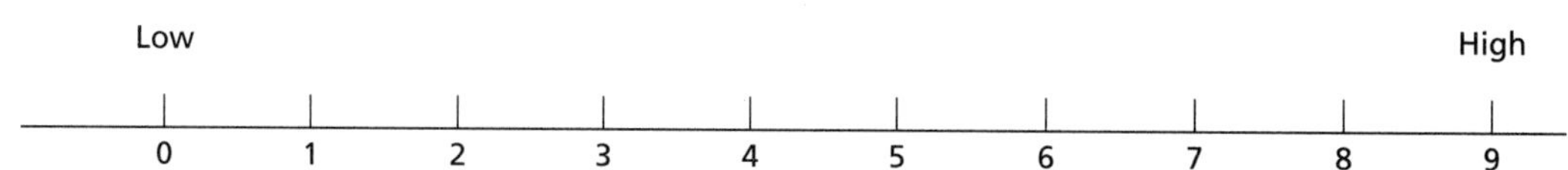

9. Interest in learning:

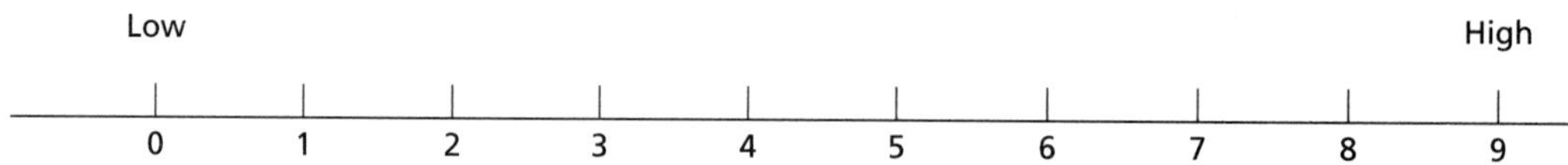

Process Scales (Participation and Communications)

10. Participation (check one):

_____ 1 to 2 members contribute the most

_____ 2 to 3 members contribute regularly

_____ 3 to 4 members contribute regularly

_____ 4 to 5 members contribute regularly

_____ all members contribute regularly

11. An input from all members is sought before decisions are made:

_____ never _____ sometimes _____ often _____ always

12. Where the team falls on the ''handling-conflict'' scale:

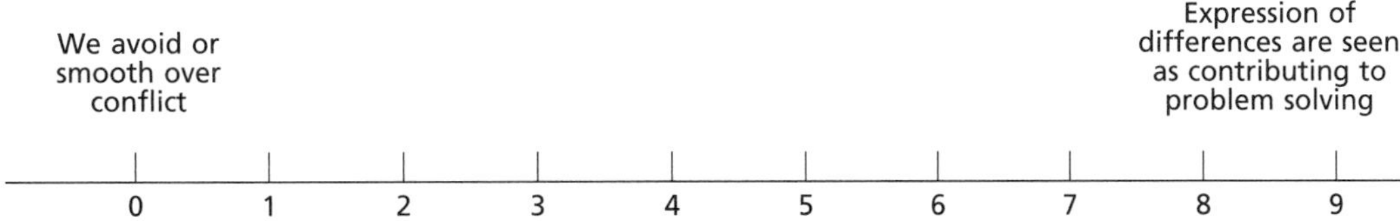

13. Openness in communications:

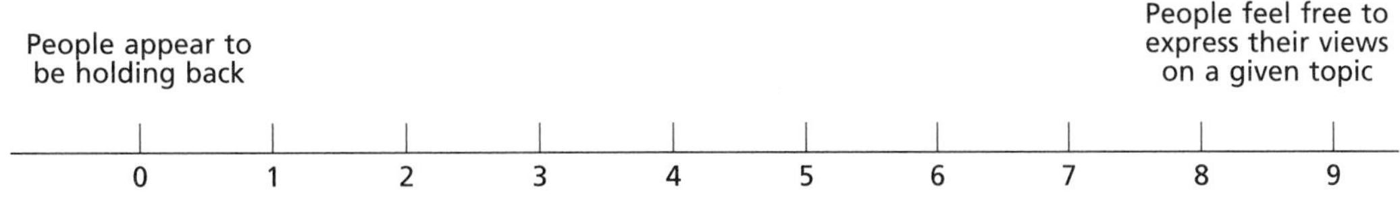

14. Expression of personal feelings:

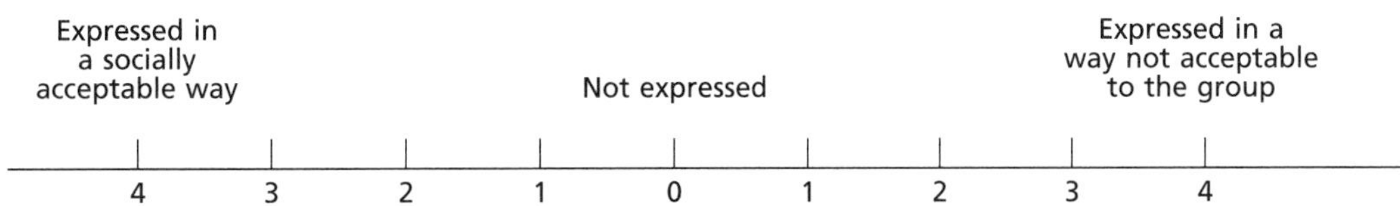

15. Degree to which we listen and actually hear each other's views:

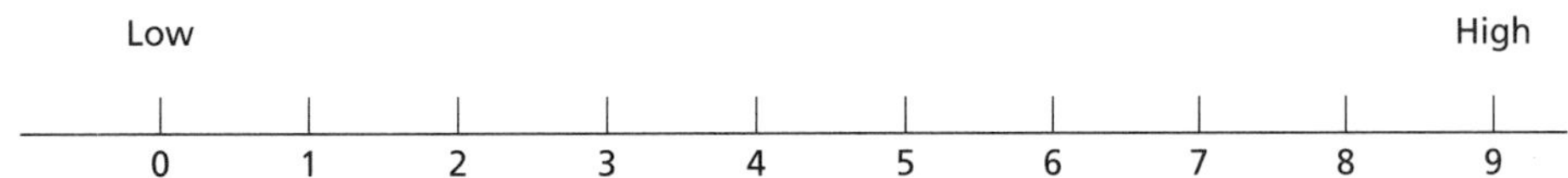

Comments: Make notes of anything you would like to feed back to the team about how members work together, or how effectiveness could be improved, that is not already suggested by the scales.

Team Goals

The scales of this questionnaire pertain to attitudes, processes, and skills that can make a team more or less effective under the conditions in which we work in this course. They thereby suggest goals for improvement of team effectiveness. (*Note: It should not be assumed that these attributes apply to the effectiveness of all teams under all conditions. Whether the specific goals suggested are appropriate depends upon the specific conditions of the situation.*)

Scale attributes should be regarded as interacting with and reinforcing one another. The following examples illustrate this and suggest some of the consequences.

Productivity

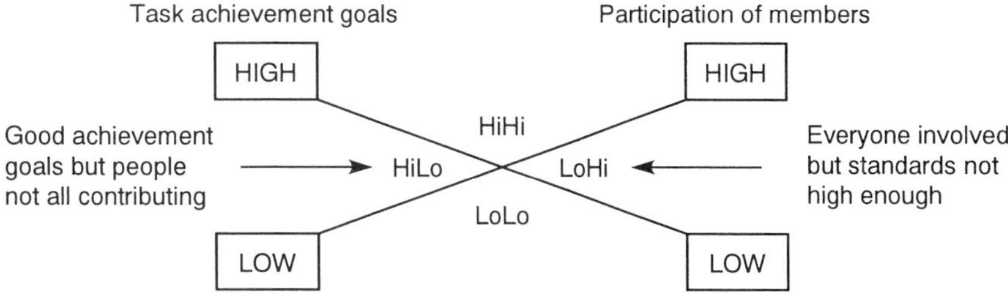

Quality of involvement

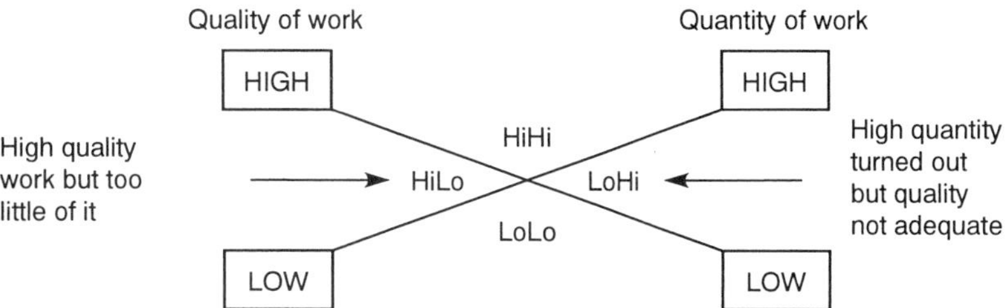

Regard for people

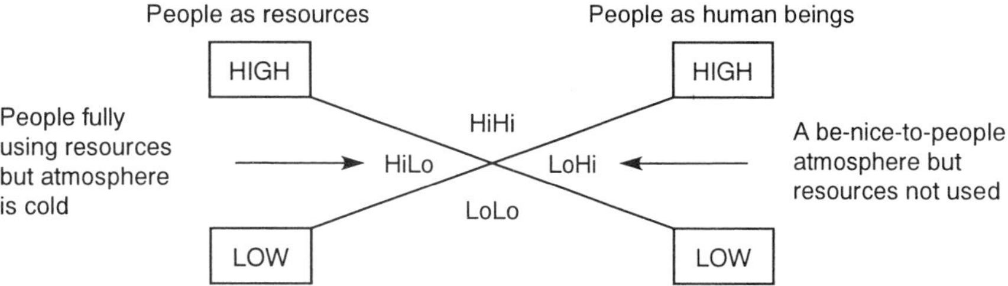

Introduction

Teams form a critical link between the individual and the organization. They function to accomplish tasks that cannot be performed by one individual or to fulfill individual needs not met by the formal organization. As teams such as top management teams, product development teams, quality circles, task forces, project teams, become more and more a part of the way organizations operate, it becomes increasingly important to understand their effectiveness and impact. Modules 9 and 10 focused on small group behavior and dynamics. This module examines **team effectiveness** from an integrative growth perspective. As we have seen, personal growth focuses on the development of interpersonal skills that help an individual be more effective in any situation.

It also stresses the need for personal goal setting to help the individual achieve greater fulfillment. This module focuses on the development of work teams and the ongoing challenge of improving their effectiveness. We start with a look at the evolution of teams via Activity 11–1. The comparison with Activity 4–4 illustrates the need for team-building activities. An examination of the problems of work teams that call for team-building effort is followed by a review of team-building goals and phases. Finally, we examine the effectiveness of team building within the international context.

Why Team Building?

If you were assigned one of the activities that began Module 9, you should have seen that some teams are more effective than others in solving problems or making decisions. Effective problem solving and effective team operation do not necessarily occur naturally. They have to be worked at. Module 9 suggested a number of ways in which both team members and team leaders can improve team effectiveness. In Module 10 we examined group dynamics and saw that the dynamics of a team are very complex and that at times dysfunctional behavior can occur. The ultimate goal of these modules and the team activities that accompany them is to improve your capacity to work effectively as a team member—initially in your classroom team, but ultimately in the organizations in which you will spend your career.

The discussion in those modules focused on improving team performance. Indeed, a continuous improvement focus to team activity should be part of every team's (and team leader's) effort.[1] However, insofar as effective team operation is not necessarily natural, and insofar as problems with team operation can indeed develop, **team building,** which can be defined as a process for helping a team to diagnose its problems and become a more effective working unit[2], is an activity that managers and managers-to-be need to be aware of and understand. This module is designed to further identify problems that work teams can experience and to describe techniques for helping groups solve those problems. The emphasis of team building is the team, and team building is a *collaborative* process.

The use of team building in organizations is not as new as the use of teams. Many of the team-building methods and techniques have been developed in the aerospace industry. That industry was an early user of product development teams, which are teams set up for the life of a project, which is of limited duration. Users of these teams found that assembling groups of individuals from different functional areas and with different disciplines did not automatically create effectively functioning teams. Thus time spent during the group's formation on goal setting and team membership skills was useful in facilitating the team's operation. When teams developed operating problems, time spent on identifying those problems and developing solutions for them improved team performance.

Team Building at Team Start-up

While team-building efforts aimed at solving teamwork problems are probably more common than efforts aimed at preparing a team to work effectively within itself, such efforts are becoming more frequent, as organizations come to realize that it is often easier to prevent problems from occurring than it is to fix the problems after they have occurred. Thus time is often set aside as a team is formed to help the team understand and effectively work through the early stages of group development.

In this type of effort, the likes of Activity 9–1 (''Mountain Survival Activity'') are often used. Such exercises give teams the opportunity to experience and test their problem-solving ability and to understand what types of behavior are necessary to have an effective team. Another type of activity is that done by the Outward Bound Leadership School (and others) in which the team experiences a number of different outdoor activities in which they must work together and learn to trust each other to pass physical tests or accomplish objectives such as crossing a river or climbing a steep mountain. Such activities are analogous to a football team, which engages in play study, practice, and drills, and plays intrasquad or preseason games before the regular season starts.

To continue the analogy, such teams continue to practice and work on problems that develop during the season. The same is true in organizations, where even with good preparation, problems may develop with team operation, and team building efforts can be made to solve those problems. Those efforts can be similar to those discussed above. To understand the types in initial team-building efforts that might be useful and the activities that might be used after a team has begun operating, we will examine some problems that work teams can develop.

Problems of Work Teams

There are certain recurring problems that teams typically encounter if the interaction patterns of the members have not been specifically shaped to avoid them. The problems have been widely described in the management literature, and we have observed that they frequently characterized the behavior of participants of this course, particularly those who undertake the outside team project of Appendix A. Let's discuss some major problems.

Action Orientation

The need to get things underway in organizations and to keep the momentum going frequently results in insufficient time for planning. In executive team-building sessions, this lack becomes evident when the team starts to discuss its goals and objectives. Prior to the meeting, they might have believed they were in accord, but when each person is asked to make a separate list of goals and rank them in order of priority, considerable discrepancies appear. Here it's evident that insufficient time has been allotted to the development of shared goals, and lack of coordination of efforts and problems of overlapping role responsibilities are brought to the surface. In other situations, members of a team are aware of differing views of their goals but have not faced the conflict.

Some teams who have used the Mountain Survival activity at the beginning of Module 9 have experienced some of the problems attached to an **action orientation.** In that exercise, some teams immediately start figuring out how to get out of the place they are in, without considering that attempting to leave is an alternative—in fact a better one than attempting to walk out. Similarly, participants who make the outside survey in the self-directed team task exercise of Appendix A will often soon recognize that they have not carefully defined the problem of their survey and have devoted insufficient time to planning. As a result, the survey data they collect will be difficult to interpret. The pressures to go right to constructing the questionnaire are so great that they plan superficially. These faults are true to a lesser degree of executives in workshops; they often do not spend enough time defining the problem of a case study they are assigned and must go back and start over after they are well underway.

An interesting study that illustrates the dominance of task orientation over other considerations is summarized below:

The parable of the Good Samaritan was put to the test recently by two Princeton University psychologists studying bystander behavior in emergencies.

In the experiment . . . 40 unwitting theological students on their way across campus encountered a groaning, coughing "victim" slumped in a doorway.

Sixty percent of the subjects kept right on walking.

Prior to encountering the "victim," subjects in the experiment were asked to prepare a three-to-five–minute impromptu talk on a specific topic—some on vocations and others on the parable of the Good Samaritan.

Equipped with a map and instructions to go to another laboratory to tape the speech, subjects were told they were either already late for the session (high-hurry condition), that they were expected momentarily (immediate-hurry condition), or that they could take their time (low-hurry condition).

The hurry condition of the subject proved significant as to whether he would stop to help the victim. Of the 16 students (40 percent) who did stop,

53 percent were low-hurry subjects.

40 percent were intermediate-hurry subjects.

7 percent were high-hurry subjects.

A person in a hurry is likely to keep going. Ironically, he is likely to keep going even if he is hurrying to speak on the parable of the Good Samaritan.[3]

Action orientation frequently leads to inadequate definition of the objectives and problems of the team, poor planning, and lack of consideration for human factors.

Use of Time

Closely associated with action orientation is how the team uses time. Many work groups are concerned about wasting time in meetings. Since planning often involves ambiguity and abstract thinking, there is pressure to get it over with and to get on to something more concrete. Planning requires blocks of time to permit the generation of ideas and allow synergy to take place. Teams must develop the expectation that a four-hour period, a day, or a weekend might be needed.

The effects of poor distribution of time are perhaps most evident in university life, where the practice is to schedule faculty or committee meetings for one hour once a week because teaching schedules and room availability makes it most difficult to arrange longer blocks of time. Meetings in the evening and on weekends are against faculty norms. So each committee meeting, scheduled for an hour, makes little progress because of the long start-up time, which requires recapitulation of what was covered the week before, trying to pick up the continuity of the planning, and carrying it further.

Team Style

Work groups develop a style of operation. (The models presented in Module 10 apply here.) **Team styles** embrace the expectations team members have about meetings. Autocratic-style meetings tend to be avoided except when they are needed to get information out and get reports back; corporate-style meetings are likely to be highly procedural and committeelike and are held for more purposes than are really necessary; permissive-style meetings are apt to be frequent and held just for the conversation; retired-on-the job meetings may never take place; and professional–manager meetings would be of the team action type discussed in this module. The patterns of member expectations that accompany each of these styles become so frozen in the minds of team members that they cannot be changed without considerable effort, frequently only with the assistance of outside expertise.

Work Habits and Skills

Many organizations are unaware that work groups can develop skills almost like individuals can. Making the improvement of group work habits and skills a goal and providing the time for this purpose is rarely considered.

Only in sports and the military services is training for effective interaction patterns accepted as a necessity. The ideal that time should be devoted to this purpose has come late to business and government organizations.

One-to-One Relationships with the Boss

The rivalries among team members that arise from one-to-one relationships in the managerial hierarchy are extremely difficult to avoid. An effective manager must meet with the team members one at a time for some purposes and with the entire team for others. (This was illustrated in the Vroom–Yetton–Jago decision-making model discussed in Module 9.) Determining how to do this so maximum trust will prevail and rivalries will be kept low is a continuing challenge. Edgar H. Schein notes,

> The successful manager must be a good diagnostician and must value a spirit of inquiry. If the abilities and motives of the people under him are so variable, he must have the sensitivity and diagnostic ability to be able to sense and appreciate the differences. Second, rather than regard the existence of differences as a painful truth to be wished away, he must also learn to value differences and to value the diagnostic process which reveals differences. Finally, he must have the personal flexibility and the range of skills necessary to vary his own behavior. If the needs and motives of his subordinates are different, they must be treated differently.[4]

While this view may sound reasonable, it is extremely difficult to practice. The fact that people are complex and need to be treated differently can run contrary to the ideal of fair treatment as perceived by employees. For example, in a team-building session involving an executive and the middle-level managers reporting to him, one manager said he would like to discuss how money available for management development and training was to be allotted in the coming year. He stated that he had not felt right during the past year when he received $600 to attend a one-week workshop but learned that $1,500 had been spent for another team member. The boss then asked, ''But John, didn't you get just what you asked for?'' John replied, ''Yes, I did, and I was very satisfied with what I gained from the workshop.'' The boss went on to say that the other employee had also gotten what he had asked for, and that his main concerns had been both satisfying the team members' requests and making sure that the training of each also met organizational needs; following this flexible policy meant that assigning a fixed sum to each individual would not be meaningful.

When the team discussed this, it was obvious that all were concerned about receiving their fair share of the training funds, but they concluded that they would like to have the present policy continued. John said that he felt better about it now that it had been discussed. The boss stated that it had not occurred to him that his flexible policy would be questioned as long as it met the needs of the team members; he then asked if there were other things he was doing that were being experienced as perhaps not completely fair; other practices were discussed. If this dialogue had not taken place, the executive might not have become aware that his flexible practices of treating people according to their needs had to take into consideration how team members perceived his actions from the point of fairness. Given that this occurred during a team-building session, we can begin to see how such sessions allow feelings and issues to be addressed—feelings and issues that, if not dealt with effectively, might affect the relationships between team members, with a corresponding impact on the team's operation.

Hidden Agendas

Rivalries, distrust, ambitions, concern about looking bad, foolish, or unknowledgeable, and other factors can cause individuals to avoid saying openly how they feel or what they want. The interactions and communications of individuals in meetings are apt to be complicated by these **hidden agendas.**

Variations of Team-Building Efforts

Organizations, managers, and teams face many issues, and these change continuously. As such, team-building efforts have different emphases or purposes have emerged over the past several decades. Team-building efforts can be classified into four general types:[5]

1. *Interpersonal processes.* This effort assumes that teams operate best with mutual trust, open communication, and an attempt to build team cohesion. The intervention involves candid discussion of conflicts and relationships between team members. The purposes are to resolve interpersonal conflict and to create open communication between individuals who work on the same team.[6]
2. *Role definition.* This effort assumes that some major sources of problems within a team are role conflict and role ambiguity. The intervention focuses on clarifying individual role expectations and group norms and the developing shared understanding of the roles and responsibilities that each individual carries in the effort.[7]
3. *Goal setting.* This approach assumes that individual performance in a team setting is influenced to a large extent by the specificity and shared understanding of goals and objectives. The intervention involves clarifying the team's general objectives and goals, defining specific tasks and subgoals to be accomplished within a specific timetable, measuring performance, and using feedback loops.[8]
4. *Problem solving.* This is the most often used intervention. Such an activity is generated when someone identifies a problem within the team. What follows is a complete team problem-solving cycle of gathering data, analyzing data, finding causes, understanding solutions, choosing a solution, planning an action, and implementing and evaluating the action.[9]

Team building can be directed at two different types of groups: **family groups** (which are intact, ongoing work teams) and **special groups** (groups that may have a limited life span, such as start-up teams, special project teams, and task forces).

Goals of Team Building

The four types of team-building efforts just listed are likely to be found in any team-building effort. However, "unless one purpose is defined as the primary purpose, there tends to be considerable misuse of energy."[10] If interpersonal problems are great, that may be the central focus. If planning, objectives, and role definition are a major area of confusion, more time will be spent on these. But the major overall purpose of team building is the application of behavioral science knowledge and technology to improve the team's effectiveness. Here are some specific and generic team-building activities:

1. Achieving consensus on objectives and goals of the team. This may include adding, dropping, or redefining goals.
2. Identifying problems preventing the achievement of these goals.
3. Developing team-planning, goal-setting, problem-solving, and decision-making skills and improving the work habits of the team, such as the use of time.
4. Diagnosing the present team style and determining what would be its preferred style of operating. This means looking at the system of norms and values that determine the team's manner of interacting and changing it. Moving toward the professional manager style requires learning and practicing the communication skills of leveling, saying where one is at, listening and paraphrasing, perceptual checking, and so on.
5. Utilizing fully the individual resources of team members. Some members have strengths, expertise, and ideas they do not think are integrated into the group's activities. They may have concerns about this that should be worked through.
6. Developing action agendas, assigning responsibilities, and setting specific dates for follow-up of the activities identified as important during the session.

Obviously, these activities are too extensive to be covered in a work retreat covering a two-or-three–day period; they can only be regarded as new behavior patterns that are launched in the session and must be practiced and worked into the behavioral system of the team and its members. The permissive-style pitfall of "groupiness" for its own sake must be avoided, and the professional manager emphasis on goals, results, and high standards through integrated team action has to be understood.

Changing the System versus Changing the People

Changing the norms and interaction patterns within a team, between teams, or within an organization is a primary goal in applying behavioral science methods to organizational life. If a team has norms such as distrust or hidden agendas, it is easy to assume that it's made up of people who cannot work together—that it is the individuals who are at fault. Changing such a team to one that has norms of openness, leveling, and so on may be difficult—the situation has to be right for change, but it can be done. The behavioral scientist has to recognize that there are no bad people, just inappropriate system of norms, values, and interaction patterns. This is a great oversimplification, but it indicates working assumptions that set the direction of efforts in team building or in organization development programs. This does *not* mean that individuals on teams are *never* replaced. It simply is a statement of the assumptions that are in place as team-building efforts are begun.

How a Team-Building Workshop Is Planned and Conducted

There are many variations of the generalized model for a team-building workshop presented here. The specific form will depend on the team members involved and their problems as well as on the consultant's professional orientation. Generally, the format includes four steps: interview with the manager, dialogue with the team, interview with team members, and presentation of the problem data at the workshop.

Interview with the Manager

First, the consultant meets with the manager to discuss the situations that have led the manager to decide to have a team-building workshop. The consultant informs the manager of the general goals of such a workshop and determines how the manager feels about the team examining its own behavior, particularly the manager's willingness to get feedback from the team members on how they feel about his or her style of management and practices. If the manager is not receptive to these ideas, the team-building experience may not have much potential.

Dialogue with the Team

The consultant and the manager meet with all those who are to attend the session, and the consultant describes the goals, agenda, and procedures of the workshop and the agreement with the team manager. An atmosphere of openness and trust must be created at this time, and a commitment of involvement should be obtained from the group.

Interview with Team Members

The consultant interviews each team member privately, assuring each of confidentiality but indicating that problems identified by more than one member will be listed openly for discussion at the workshop. The questions addressed in the interview are designed to diagnose the problems of the team.

Presentation of the Problem Data at the Workshop

The workshop should be held at a site away from the workplace and probably should last two or more days, depending on the problems and the number of people involved. Early in the session the consultant provides a feedback summary of problems that have been presented. This is generally put on large flip-chart sheets that are hung on the walls so that all can see and discuss them. From this point on, the progression of the workshop is designed by the consultant to best suit the needs of the team. For instance, in one workshop of 16 people made up of a division chief, three branch chiefs, and 12 section chiefs, the section chiefs requested that the division and branch chiefs sit in a center circle and openly discuss among themselves how they felt about all the problems they saw on the charts. The section chiefs would listen. After that the section chiefs would discuss the problems among themselves, with the other chiefs listening. A dialogue would follow. They did this, and the design for the workshop was developed out of this spontaneous beginning.

At some time during the workshop, all six goals of team building may be worked on to some degree, but the design has to be flexible and spontaneous, and the topics are best addressed when the appropriate time arises. The consultant has a variety of techniques to move the team in the direction of the goals. These include using models of leadership styles, case studies, training films, and involvement exercises such as those used in this book. It is helpful if the consultant has had T-group training and experience so as to help the team cope with their feelings and conflicts. The consultant's interviews will have provided considerable data on how the participants feel about each other. Although the consultant is not able to reveal these feelings to the group directly, because of the pledge of confidentiality, if the workshop is successful, the feelings will be brought out by the participants themselves as they become more open. The consultant must be able to be supportive of the members if they need support at that time. Although this set of steps can be found in most team-building programs, practitioners emphasize on different phases; Dyer presents a 33-item checklist for identifying whether a team-development program is needed and whether the organization is ready to begin such a program.[11] Burke argues that it is important to use Beckhard's four-purpose list of goal clarification, roles and responsibilities, procedures and processes, and interpersonal processes in the order that they are listed.[12] Others focus on the interrelationship between process and content of team-building interventions.[13]

How Effective Are Team-Building Activities?

The results of team-building activities can be classified into three main areas: (1) results specific to individuals, (2) results specific to the team's dynamics and operations, and (3) results that have an impact on the team's relationships with other teams, departments, and so forth. Although most reported results are descriptive in nature, a few empirically based studies shed some light on the effectiveness of team-building efforts. In a study conducted with hourly employees in an underground metal mine, team building was found to have a positive effect on the quality of the teams' performance.[14] In a field experiment with command teams of seven combat companies that underwent team-building workshops, researcher D. Eden was able to show that the experimental companies (in comparison to the control companies) significantly improved in teamwork, conflict handling, and communications.[15] Another study with 18 logistics units that went through a team-building workshop demonstrated that team building failed to improve organizational functioning, although subjective reports of the personnel who participated in the workshops were very positive.[16]

An empirical investigation that attempted to compare the effects of team building and goal setting on productivity of hard-rock miners in an underground metal mine resulted in inconclusive results.[17] This study joins an overall inconclusive body of empirical research on the effectiveness of team building. Although positive results were found in 29 of the 36 studies reviewed in one study[18] as well as in 19 of the 30 studies reviewed in another study,[19] both authors concluded they could make no firm statements regarding the effectiveness of team building with respect to individual and team performance. The challenge as identified by the researchers is in the development of an appropriate research methodology and measures.

An experiment conducted with MBA students who were randomly assigned to four-member teams (half of which received team-building training) and were engaged in complex and interactive decision-making tasks revealed the following results: Teams that received team-building training were initially more cohesive and obtained superior economic performance during the early stage of the simulation. As time progressed, teams that did not receive the training became more cohesive and improved their economic performance but not up to the same level as the teams that received the training.[20] A unique investigation into performance of 32 teams' teamwork revealed that with the exception of one team, all had improved attitudes, effectiveness, and performance.[21] Finally, a study that focused on team members' exchange quality in a unionized plant revealed that employees managed under a team-oriented system (following team-building activities) reported higher team member exchange quality than did those managed under a more traditional system.[22]

Summary

The team-building movement has been growing as managements attempt to cope with the explosive changes in technology and the business environment. Types of problems lessening team effectiveness include too much action orientation at the expense of planning; poor use of and failure to provide adequate time; norms of the autocratic, corporate, and permissive styles; inadequate work habits and team skills; a pattern of one-to-one relationships between the boss and team members; and hidden-agenda game playing. The goals of team building include defining objectives and problems as well as improving group skills and interpersonal relations. A general design for a team-building workshop was described.

Study Questions

1. Describe the relationship between group dynamics and team building.
2. What are some challenges faced by team leaders as they try to facilitate team effectiveness?
3. Discuss the variations of team building.
4. To what extent did the activities your classroom team engaged in help get the team off to a good start? Were the activities adequate for that purpose? What else might have been done?
5. ''Every team can use team building.'' Do you agree or disagree? Why?
6. Identify the reasons that would lead a manager to utilize a team-building intervention.
7. Discuss the phases and activities during a team-building effort.
8. How would you use PAC/TA in a team-building effort?
9. What areas should be considered for evaluating the effectiveness of team building?
10. Discuss the effect of team building on creativity, innovation, and quality improvement.

Suggested Reading

William G. Dyer. *Team Building: Current Issues and New Alternatives.* 3d ed. Reading, Mass.: Addison-Wesley, 1995.

Larry Hirshhorn. *Managing in the New Team Environment: Skills, Tools, and Methods.* Reading, Mass.: Addison-Wesley, 1991.

Dennis C. Kinlaw. *Developing Superior Work Teams.* Lexington, Mass.: Lexington Books, 1991.

Jack D. Orsburn, Lina Moran, Ed Musselwhite, and John Zenger. *Self-Directed Work Teams.* Homewood, Ill.: Richard D. Irwin, 1990.

Endnotes

1. For a discussion of the difference between team development and team building, and specific programs for team development, see Dennis C. Kinlaw, *Developing Superior Work Teams* (Lexington, Mass.: Lexington Books, 1991).

2. W. G. Dyer, *Team Building, Issues and Alternatives,* 2d ed. (Reading, Mass.: Addison-Wesley, 1987), p. 6.

3. *APA Monitor,* November 1973.

4. E. H. Schein, *Organizational Psychology,* 2d ed. (Englwood Cliffs, N.J.: Prentice-Hall, 1970), pp. 71–72.

5. E. Sundstrom, K. P. DeMeuse, and D. Futrell, "Work Teams: Applications and Effectiveness," *American Psychologist* 45, no. 2 (1990), pp. 120–33; and M. Beer, *Organization Change and Development: A System View* (Santa Monica, Calif.: Goodyear, 1980).

6. R. E. Kaplan, "The Conspicuous Absence of Evidence That Process Consultants Enhance Task Performance," *Journal of Applied Behavioral Science* 15 (1979), pp. 346–60.

7. W. Bennis, *Changing Organizations* (New York: McGraw-Hill, 1966).

8. E. A. Locke, K. N. Shaw, L. M. Saari, and G. P. Latham, "Goal Setting and Task Performance," *Psychological Bulletin* 90 (1982), pp. 125–52; and E. A. Locke, G. P. Latham, and M. Erez, "The Determinants of Goal Commitment," *Academy of Management Review* 13 (1988), pp. 23–39.

9. P. F. Butler and C. H. Bell, Jr., "Effects of Team Building and Goal Setting on Productivity: A Field Experiment," *Academy of Management Journal* 29, no. 2 (1986), pp. 305–28.

10. R. Beckhard, "Optimizing Team-Building Efforts," *Journal of Contemporary Business* 1, no. 3 (1972), pp. 23–32.

11. W. G. Dyer, *Team Building: Issues and Alternatives* (Reading, Mass.: Addison-Wesley, 1987).

12. W. W. Burke, *Organizational Development* (Boston: Little, Brown, 1982).

13. P. G. Hanson and B. Lubin, "Team Building as Group Development," *Organization Development Journal* 4, no. 1 (1986), pp. 27–35.

14. P. F. Buller, "The Team Building–Task Performance Relation: Some Conceptual and Methodological Refinements," *Group and Organization Studies* 11, no. 3 (1986), pp. 147–68.

15. D. Eden, "Team Development: Quasi-Experimental Confirmation among Combat Companies," *Group and Organization Studies* 11, no. 3 (1986), pp. 133–46.

16. D. Eden, "Team Development: A True Field Experiment Employing Three Levels of Rigor," *Journal of Applied Psychology* 70 (1985), pp. 94–100.

17. P. F. Buller and C. H. Bell, "Effects of Team Building and Goal Setting on Productivity: A Field Experiment," *Academy of Management Journal* 29, no. 2 (1986), pp. 305–28.

18. K. P. DeMeuse and S. J. Liebowitz, "An Empirical Analysis of Team Building Research," *Group and Organizational Studies* 6 (1981), pp. 357–58.

19. R. W. Woodman and J. J. Sherwood, "The Role of Team Development in Organizational Effectiveness: A Critical Review," *Psychological Bulletin 88* (1980), pp. 166–86.

20. J. Wolfe and D. D. Bowen, "Team Building Effects on Company Performance," *Simulation and Games* 20, no. 4 (1989), pp. 388–408.

21. C. E. Larson and F. M. J. LaFasto, *TeamWork* (Newbury Park, Calif.: Sage, 1989).

22. A. Seers, "Team-Member Exchange Quality: A New Construct for Decision-Making Research," *Organizational Behavior and Human Decision Processes* 43 (1989), pp. 118–35.

Activity 11–2: Team Building in a Hospital Setting

Objective:

To demonstrate the application of team-building activities to improve effectiveness in an organizational setting.

Task 1:

a. Read the following case study, "Time for a Change."

b. Based on the limited information presented, make a list of factors and actors that influence the group's work. (You might want to use the "blueprint and the actors" described in Module 4 as a guide.)

c. Through what set of activities did the consultants lead and guide the group?

Task 2 (Classroom):

Participants are to share their responses to the questions in Task 1 and develop a shared understanding of them. Teams are to discuss the following questions:

a. What are the chances of the group succeeding in resolving the problems at SHM? Why?

b. Is this group the one to which these issues should be addressed? Why or why not?

c. What steps can be taken to resolve the nursing issue? What specific changes will each group have to make? What forces make it likely or unlikely that these changes will occur?

d. What kind of specific team-building activities would you recommend for each group? How would you overcome some of the potential roadblocks?

Team ideas will be shared with the whole learning community and serve as the basis for class discussion.

Case Study: Time for a Change at Suburban Health Maintenance

For centuries the relationship between physicians and nurses has generally been that physicians give orders and nurses carry them out. Only recently, with the increasing professionalization of nursing and nurses' desires to be treated as equals, has the traditional physician–nurse relationship been called into question. These days, it seems, physicians and nurses don't work very well together except when they are in the process of providing care to patients. Nurses often feel overlooked and unappreciated by their professional superiors; physicians, on the other hand, feel that nurses should simply comply with their requests. Often, neither party finds the relationship very satisfactory.

One unusual group of physicians and nurses at Suburban Health Maintenance (SHM) decided to change all that. They were in a unique position to do so; as part of a health maintenance organization (HMO), the same physicians work with the same nurses every day, week in and week out. In most hospitals, nurses stay put while physicians dart in and out, leaving a concise but unreadable set of orders for the nurse to follow as they go to their next patient.

Physicians and nurses at SHM faced a different situation—they had to learn to live with one another. This was not only because they worked together all the time; like most HMOs, SHM was committed to holding down membership costs for their patients. This meant utilizing nurses as much as possible in the delivery of care to help minimize the use of expensive physicians' time. This meant that the group had to work

Source: This case was contributed by William A. Pasmore. We are grateful to Professor Pasmore.

together smoothly and try to avoid the problems besetting traditional nurse–physician relationships.

Over time, members of each group came to know their counterparts on a first-name basis; this was something they hadn't experienced in other places they had worked except in a few rare instances. Nevertheless, problems still remained, the worst of which was the inability of SHM to attract and retain good nurses.

SHM had several health centers throughout the city that were coordinated by a central administrative group. The south-side center wasn't located in the best of neighborhoods, but the organization was dedicated to continuing its service to the racially mixed population surrounding the facility. Unfortunately, the location of the south-side center made it difficult to attract qualified nurses since jobs were plentiful in safer parts of the city.

The chronic understaffing of the south-side facility and the low level of skills possessed by those nurses who could be hired caused physicians to complain to the administration about the quality of nursing care. As time went on and the problem was not resolved, some complaints were made directly to an already frustrated nursing management group. It was rumored that some physicians had reprimanded nurses in front of their peers and patients, deploring the poor quality of care being provided by nursing. Of course, such outbursts caused more nurses to leave the already troubled facility and seek employment elsewhere; a vicious circle was beginning to take form.

In most health care organizations, that would have been it—cold war would have begun. Administration would be called on to solve the problem—but as a third party, it would be almost powerless to act. The administration at SHM did what it could; it raised the pay of nurses, but the problem remained. What made SHM different from other health care organizations, however, was the feeling of "being in it together." Nurses and physicians were not exactly aligned in their views of the situation, but they did agree to sit down and talk about it. Representatives of the nursing management group and a number of key administrative physicians representing the medical group met to hammer out an understanding. Administrators responded to an invitation to attend.

The first few meetings of the group were routine. Consultants had been used to design the meetings, and the roles that were specified for the participants managed to keep the cap on the volcano of misunderstanding long enough for the groups to realize that they were actually in agreement about the problems that faced SHM's south-side facility.

By the third meeting, it was discovered that the physicians really didn't have a very clear idea of what activities nursing management engaged in besides responding to complaints from doctors. It was felt that if physicians had a clearer idea of what nurses did, they would not be so quick to complain about nursing's lack of responsiveness to their needs.

Nursing management agreed to take responsibility for preparing a description of their roles, which they would present at the next meeting. What was uncovered during that meeting left the consultants and administrator of the south-side HMO wondering what action needed to be taken to meet the demands of both groups. Some of the issues discussed at that meeting appear in the following list.

1. *Waste of nursing management time on clerical tasks.* The members of nursing management spend an incredible amount of time doing clerical work. This work consists of such things as making out schedules, providing staff coverage where needed, scheduling vacations, and maintaining records on employee absenteeism and tardiness. Repeated requests have been made to computerize the system so that attention could be paid to more important matters, but the downtown office has decided that the computerization of these things is low in priority compared to other things that need to be done.

At one time, the nursing supervisor made a request for a clerical support person to do the work; the request for the position went downtown and came back classified as a union position. This meant that a union employee would be involved in scheduling nursing management time and have access to confidential management information. This situation was clearly unacceptable to the nursing supervisor, and she canceled her request for the position.

Attempts at delegating these functions led to dangerous lack of coordination among the nursing departments. Because each department head was unaware of the schedules of other departments, situations developed that left the health center seriously understaffed.

2. *Discipline problems.* Nursing management itself is overworked and short-staffed. They can't be everywhere at once. Employees have taken advantage of the situation by coming to work late, leaving early, and taking long breaks in between. Nursing management would like to install time clocks to help control the situation. The facility, which was in use before SHM purchased it, once had time clocks, and they are currently being stored in the building. However, the downtown office will not allow them to be installed because then employee policy would not be the same throughout the area.

3. *Budgeting.* The budgeting process is a nightmare. The process begins in May for the next year and usually doesn't conclude until July of the subsequent year. Until the budget is approved, no capital purchases can be made, so even if capital expenditures are eventually approved, the equipment may not be purchased until over a year after it's needed. The process is long and drawn out because the central office must do a careful evaluation of the requests from all of the health centers and the physicians to determine the priority of needs, taking into account the revenue available. The top administrator has expressed a strong conviction that funds should not be given to the health centers unless the need for them can be justified since financial resources are tight.

4. *Supply.* Even the procurement of normal usage items can be problematic. Orders are placed through the central warehouse, which purchases large quantities of supplies at discounted prices for the entire organization. If the items requested are out of stock, the ordering party is usually informed within a week's time. If the item is desperately needed, arrangements can then be made to place a special order or borrow supplies from another hospital. This whole process is cumbersome.

5. *Influence.* Nurses in the organization do not receive attention when they raise complaints. For example, when the health center ran out of plaster for making casts, a nurse was told to contact supply immediately. When she called, she was put on hold several times. The chief of surgery then called personally, and the response was instantaneous. The same situation is repeated when dealing with maintenance, dietary, and other hospital support.

At the end of the meeting, the nurses and physicians agreed that something needed to be done about the situation. Both groups looked to the administrator and the consultants for suggestions.

12 Dynamics between Teams

Learning Objectives

After completing this module you should be able to

1. Describe the basic elements in the dynamics between teams.
2. State how the interactions between teams or groups affect their performance.
3. Identify some basic components of intergroup communication.
4. Recognize barriers to intergroup cooperation and the actions that can be taken to overcome such impediments.
5. Understand the relationships between group problem solving, decision making, group dynamics, and intergroup behavior and performance.
6. Describe several approaches that can be used to foster effective outcomes between teams and groups.

List of Key Concepts

Accommodating orientation
Assertiveness
Avoidance orientation
Collaborating orientation
Common enemy
Competitive orientation
Compromising orientation
Conflict
Conflict prevention through change programs
Conflict-handling mode
Cooperativeness
Intergroup communication
Interteam/intergroup conflict
Social intervention approaches
Strategic intention
Superordinate goals
Team management

Module Outline

Premodule Preparation

Activity 12–1: Ambiguity, Conflict, and Interteam Dynamics

Introduction:

Most of this course's group activities to date involved problem solving and decision making. For each, you were given specific situations and techniques with which to work. Exploring what happens to a group when it is confronted with an ambiguous, less-structured task is the purpose of this exercise. Your team is to meet outside class for a period of two hours to complete Task 1.

This exercise deals with two subjects: management of diversity and managers promoting competition among employees. These have been controversial issues in business and government organizations for many years. Everyone has opinions on these subjects, which become apparent when they search their minds carefully. This exercise will tap your reservoir of opinion.

In this exercise, please use no books, articles, or other reference material. This task is to be completed entirely from the interaction of minds, through sharing of knowledge and opinions, and via the synergistic development of ideas.

Task 1:

Teams are to meet outside class to examine their knowledge and attitudes on the topic and answer these questions:

a. What are the advantages and disadvantages of diversity at the workplace? To aid you in developing as complete a list as possible, groups might first compare and contrast homogenous and heterogenous units in as many subjects as possible. (*Note:* There are a number of diversity aspects that we have not discussed in this course.)
b. What are the advantages and disadvantages of promoting competition among employees and among teams?
c. Under what conditions should a manager promote competition among his or her employees and teams? When should competition not be used as a management technique?

Prepare your answers on one to three (not more) typewritten pages, using outline (not essay) form, but be complete enough so the reader will understand the point you are making. (*Note:* Your team's completed answers should be delivered to the instructor at a designated time prior to the next class meeting so copies can be made. These copies will be used in Task 2.)

Task 2:

Your team and another team will be assigned in class the task of comparing the lists developed in Task 1. Each member of your group will be assigned to a dyad with a member of the other group. Dyad partners are to supply each other with copies of their team reports from Task 1. Each is to study the other's and contrast it with his or her own. The papers are to be discussed in detail so that complete understanding of the intent of the lists is communicated.

At the conclusion of the discussion, an agreement is to be reached by the dyad as to which team paper represents the better solution for the assigned task. For this purpose, each dyad has 20 points to divide up and assign to the papers. Thus one paper could have a 20 and the other a 0 (or any other division of the points), but the judgment cannot be 10 to 10 since a final discrimination must be made. If there are an odd number of teams in the class, representatives from each of the last three teams will meet as triads; they will have 30 points to distribute but there can be no 10-10-10 final judgments.
(Time: 30 minutes)

(*Note:* The *Instructor's Manual* has important guidance on how to conduct this case.)

Task 3:

After all dyads and triads have reached their conclusions, participants are to return to their teams. They will have two minutes to discuss their experience. The instructor will list the results on team charts on the board. This will be followed by a discussion and interpretation of the results.

Task 4:

A short lecture on the process involved will be given by the instructor.

Introduction

One way to think about an organization is to conceptualize it as a collection of interrelated groups operating at various levels of the organizational hierarchy. As such, in any firm, a high degree of intergroup interaction is vital to the organization's success. The ability to diagnose and manage interteam interactions is essential to the firm because (1) in most organizations, teams need to work with other teams to accomplish their goal, (2) the interdependency between the teams often creates dependency relationships that might foster conflict, and (3) conflicting team goals and the emerging dynamics between teams might influence the effectiveness of the firm.[1] Even in small companies, the production group must interact with the marketing/sales group and both must interface with the accounting, human resources, and finance groups.

In the context of this module, we go beyond the definition of a *group* presented in Modules 9, 10, and 11, which focused on person-to-person relations. In this module, a *team* or *group* refers to (1) any one of the types of groups and teams previously mentioned, (2) a department or a business unit, or (3) any formal or informal classification of employees based on geographical location, hourly versus permanent workers, race, gender, ethnic background, religion, occupation, educational background, and so on.[2]

Determinants of Intergroup Performance

Intergroup behavior occurs when two groups interact. As we have seen in Modules 4, 9, and 10, each group is likely to have its own characteristics and uniqueness, but all groups operate within a larger organizational context composed of both the formal and the human organization dimensions. These entail policies, rules and procedures, goals and reward systems, culture, work flow, decision-making processes, and so forth. To fully understand the behavior and performance of the marketing and manufacturing departments in a specific organization, we need to know about their interaction with one another, with the different departments in the organization, as well as the interaction between the organization and its environment.

As a broad skeleton, beyond the nature of the formal and human organizations, intergroup behavior and outcomes are influenced by the following key elements: the nature and characteristics of the task (which will be examined in Module 13), the degree of required group interdependence (the frequency and quality of interactions among groups), the group's time and goal orientations, and the bases for the interaction (such as information flow requirements and integration requirements). Figure 12–1 presents a partial schema of intergroup behavior and performance.[3]

The quality of the intergroup outcomes is influenced by the ability of all the parties to the interaction to meet all the requirements. As we have seen in Modules 9 and 10, managing team dynamics is a complex managerial task. Managing intergroup dynamics is more than just managing two teams; it requires the ability to also manage the dynamics between two teams that together form a larger entity with its own complex dynamics.

Intergroup Communication and Conflict

Special problems of leadership (Module 3), diversity and personalities (Modules 1 and 5), communication (Module 8), self–other perception (Module 7), and win–lose motivation (Module 6) exist in the area of intergroup relationships. Intergroup activities are greatly influenced by the fact that **conflict** is built into both the individual and the society. While this conflict can be destructive, it can also lead to problem solving and creativity when it is understood and coped with appropriately. To this end, conflict has been studied at a number of levels: within the individual, between individuals, within

Figure 12–1
Intergroup Behavior: A Partial Schema

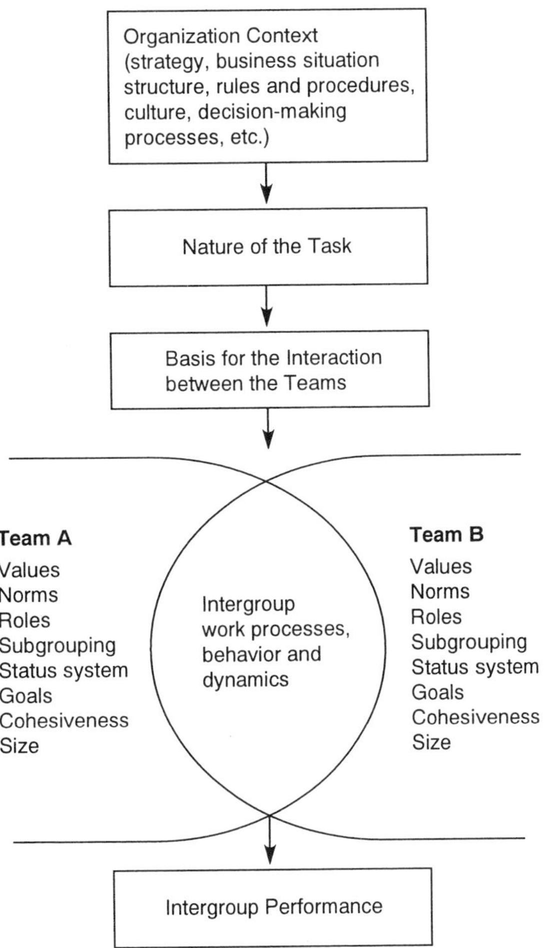

small groups, between groups and categories of people, between institutions, and between nations. We will focus first on theories about individuals and their relationship to small groups. Then we will apply these ideas to intergroup relations.

Conflict within the Individual

The socialization process, by definition, shapes the individual's drives and creates certain needs to make him or her a well-functioning member of society. This means he or she will conform to the group behaviors, values, customs, and standards and will not gratify individual wants and desires totally at the expense of others. This process is not without its toll to the comfort of the individual because it creates lifelong tensions and psychological conflicts.

The psychoanalytic approach to studying this phenomenon has emphasized the internal conflict people experience as they cope with their drives, needs, wants, and fears on the one hand, and their internalized "parent" (the society that has been programmed into their mental processes) on the other. They feel compelled to obey society's dictates or suffer self-disapproval and guilt. In the extreme, this dynamic conflict results in psychosis, a state in which the individual has been overwhelmed by these opposing forces. Even when adequately coped with, the individual's psychological defense mechanisms can readily be aroused when confronted with certain types of frustration. Once aroused, fear and anger can be available for displacement on available (presumably offending) targets. One indication of mental health is the maintenance of a self-image that facilitates the achievement of needs in a manner acceptable to society as the person has experienced it.

Conflict and Group Identity

By the time an individual is an adult, identity includes an integration of all the groups (family, school, social, work) he or she has been a part of, or has become aware of, that satisfy needs. The values, beliefs, behaviors, and life-styles of the groups with which the individual has had experience or has admired make up an important aspect of self-image, while the values, beliefs, behaviors, and life-styles of groups he or she has rejected or not admired are perceived as ''not me.'' Muzafer Sherif uses the concept of *reference groups,* which he defines as ''those groups to which the individual relates himself as a member or aspires to relate himself psychologically.''[4] Reference groups with which the individual identifies may be thought of as *positive,* whereas those the individual rejects may function as *negative reference points.* As discussed in Module 7, perception of an ongoing experience is meaningful primarily because the brain has programmed past experiences into categories; included in these categories would be such reference groups.

Another aspect of this is that the better I know ''who I am,'' the better ''who I am not'' can be differentiated. Deciding what is ''me'' and what is ''not me'' is a continuing mental process. Anything that (1) suggests that what is ''not me'' might be better than what is ''me'' or (2) could attack or deprive the individual spontaneously arouses defensiveness. The popularity of the great put-down in contemporary humor reflects the need of individuals to feel superior and put those who are ''not like I am'' in their places. Reliance upon status, material objects, symbols, and social organization membership is one way of assuring the individual of who he or she is and, moreover, is not. Club bylaws often define not only what ''we stand for'' but have restrictions against admitting those who are ''not us.''

One significance of the reference group concept is that it sometimes makes meaningful the actions of an individual that seem completely incongruent with what is known of that person. In one case, it was difficult to understand how a high school boy who was from a ''good'' middle-class family, had excellent school grades, was a church member, and was highly thought of by many teachers could be guilty of vandalizing certain teachers' offices. Then it was learned that he was a part of a group of boys who believed they had to punish certain male teachers they thought behaved in a sadistic way toward students. The norms of the group included bringing to justice those who had been untouchable in the past in that no suffering student had ever won a grievance against them. A member's status and acceptance in this group could only be maintained by helping vandalize the offices of the offending teachers.

Most frequently, we try to deal with individuals as individuals and are unaware of the forces acting upon them from the groups with which they identify. The informal cliques in which employees participate are excellent examples of this. Rate busters in factories are either deviants from an employee group (a negative reference group for them) or are ignorant of how the group feels about their behavior.

Intergroup Conflict

This attachment to groups and the accompanying concern, apprehension, or distrust for other groups can be almost instantaneous. Warren G. Bennis reports the following, which would appear to support this.

> Jaap Rabbie, conducting experiments on intergroup conflict at the University of Utrecht, has been amazed by the ease with which conflict and stereotype develop. He brings into an experimental room two groups and distributes green name tags and pens to one group, red pens and tags to the other. The two groups do not compete; they do not even interact. They are only in sight of each other while they silently complete a questionnaire. Only 10 minutes are needed to activate defensiveness and fear, reflected in the hostile and irrational perceptions of both ''reds'' and ''greens.''[5]

Recall also that one of the elements of Janis's groupthink (Module 10) is stereotyped thinking toward other groups.

The most famous field experiment on in-group/out-group dynamics and the reduction of **intergroup conflict** was conducted by Sherif and associates in 1954. At a summer camp they succeeded in creating two groups of boys, each of which developed norms of its own that included hostility to the other group. Then through further experimental arrangements, they succeeded in overcoming both groups' hostility.

Robert R. Blake found many of the same findings to be valid when business executives were the subjects.[7] He and his associates brought 20 to 30 executives together in two-week workshops. They were formed into groups that developed the norms, group structure, and cohesiveness that characterized Sherif's subjects in the first phase. Two executive groups were then given an identical problem for which they were to find the ''best'' solution; these solutions were later evaluated. Under these conditions, win–lose power struggles spontaneously occurred. Each group enhanced its own position and downgraded its adversary's. Negative stereotypes arose toward the adversary. Intellectual distortion occurred; points upon which the two teams were in agreement were minimized or not recognized, and differences were highlighted. When representatives of the groups met to negotiate, the loyalty of the representatives to their groups became more important than logic. A representative who conceded was seen as a traitor by the group; a winner was a hero.

We have run numerous intergroup exercises in management workshops to provide an experiential base for examining the dynamics of in-group/out-group relationships. The competitive reactions are so spontaneous, demonstrating what past research has documented, that subjects often become too involved to draw back and look at the learning opportunity offered by the situation. Some keep insisting that the other group is wrong without ever understanding the process being illustrated. What better evidence of the process? University students performing the same activity as the executives are much calmer and low key in their reactions. However, the win–lose dynamics are very evident. Most students say they definitely wanted to win for their team, but they did not wish to make the person with whom they were ''problem solving'' look too bad so they held out for just enough points to win. For the most part they do show more problem-solving orientation than the more combat-experienced executives. Activities 12–2 and 12–3 illustrate this point.

In the Sherif and Blake research discussed, the conflict is reciprocal between specific adversary groups, which might be thought of as between teams. A similar relationship exists to some degree in the interface of categories, such as male–female, black–white, minority–nonminority, and boss–subordinate. The data in Tables 7–1, 7–2, and 7–3 on perception support the proposition that the interface between levels of the hierarchy is characterized by differences in the way the members of the levels perceive their own and others' behaviors. Whenever people of one category perceive themselves or their roles differently than do those with whom they interface, the potential for conflict exists.

Dealing with Intergroup Conflict

Some of the primary determinants of intergroup conflict arise from the greatly augmented rates of change in the general culture. Changing markets, changing technology, and changing availability of resources mean that organizations must be designed to cope continuously with changing circumstances. Changes in emphasis on human values and standards of living are accompanied by rising expectations of the public, which are never more than partially satisfied, leaving a reservoir of tensions and frustrations available for displacement.

Competition for scarce resources is generally agreed to be a major factor in initiating and perpetuating conflict in organizations. The scarce resources may be in innumerable forms, such as materials available, opportunities for promotion, power, recognition and status, attention from the boss, or competent secretaries. Since the scarce-resource condition always exists, how can intergroup conflict in organizations be lessened? How can behaviors facilitating coordination among functionally integrated units be enhanced? A number of theories, strategies, and techniques are relevant to achieving this goal. The following sections discuss several of these.

Awareness of Intergroup Dynamics

It is essential to help people develop both the intellectual and experiential learning necessary to understand the probability that everyone will become spontaneously enmeshed in the win–lose trap. Knowledge alone will not overcome reactions that experience has built into our reflexes, but it may provide the base for preventative measures or for guidance out of the trap once it has been entered. Workshops and education programs are important techniques, but awareness of both causal and remedial measures must become a part of the organizational culture. Future modules will discuss organizational change and development methods as a systematic approach to developing organizational value systems and interaction patterns. Values related to avoiding the win–lose trap or groupthink hopefully can be accepted throughout the organization. The ideas discussed in this section also could come to characterize the working climate.

Recognition of the "Common Enemy"

Competition is a part of every American's education. Rivalry for grades or victory in sports—and all the accompanying values and behaviors—are carried from the school right into the organization. Managers often use the word *team* in the same win–lose sense they would use it on the ball field. While the coordination that helps an athletic team win is also needed to help an organization achieve its goals, promoting competition between functionally integrated units of an organization can be highly dysfunctional. Nevertheless, a common view among managers is that competition between employees is healthy because they see competition as one of the more effective motivating forces. The main point is that competition is not "good" or "bad" in itself, and the manager has to determine under what conditions it is functional or dysfunctional.

Some research evidence indicates that intergroup hostility between teams can be reduced when a **common enemy** is introduced.[8] Since all industrial organizations are in competition for their markets, emphasis on the common enemy of the closest competitor provides an opportunity for pitting the organizational team against an outsider as the team to beat.

Some readers will object to this procedure on various grounds, such as ethics or concern over whether the behavior developed against "the enemy" might not be turned back onto the organization. Rensis Likert advocates a more constructive approach, based on research of the management style and performance of the various offices of the sales force of a large company that operates nationally.[9] One finding was that the high-producing offices typically adopted group methods of management; the manager and the salespeople used group problem solving, group coaching, and group goal setting. Likert contrasts this approach with providing contest awards for highest sales by individuals. When the salespeople are pitted against one another this way, they do not share information about markets, leads, techniques, or problems. He concludes, "The best performance, lowest costs, and the highest levels of earnings and of employee satisfaction occur when the drive for a sense of personal worth is used to create strong motivational forces to *cooperate* rather than *compete* with one's peers and colleagues."[10] As an alternative, an individual can compete with a past record or strive to achieve goals set individually or group goals set by his work group.

Development of Superordinate Goals

Sherif's experiment illustrated the potential of reducing intergroup conflict through the achievement of goals that are important to both groups. Organizations cannot function without the attainment of **superordinate goals**—primary goals of an organization or competing groups that exceed those of individuals or subgroups—yet intergroup conflict and failure to coordinate are major deterrents to organizational effectiveness. While many reasons for these reactions are irrational in the sense that people are resisting working together, at least a part of the problem can be attributed to a lack of shared understanding as to what the goals are. Consultants who conduct team-building workshops often focus on this. Generally, members of a top-management team assume they all know the objectives and goals toward which they are working, but when they are asked to list the goals and rank their priorities, considerable variance is often found. Subordinates of the team indicate that these confusions are pushed down into the hierarchy and become a factor in interdivisional conflict.

The current surge for the development of shared organizational vision in industrial, government, and educational institutions can be seen as an attempt to identify the superordinate objectives and the objectives of each unit that function to achieve them. When everyone works toward a set of individual, unit, and organizational objectives, the information level of all employees in carrying on their coordinated efforts is systematically raised, and perceptual distortion and communication problems are reduced. Fighting can arise spontaneously if two units assume they are working on the same objectives when this is not the case. The personality–communication–perception–motivation relationship we have been suggesting is directly applicable here.

Conflict-Handling Modes

The notion that intergroup conflict can never be totally resolved or eliminated dictates the need to explore different ways in which groups can deal with such conflict. Kenneth Thomas proposed that two main dimensions underline the intentions of the group to be involved in a conflict situation: (1) **cooperativeness**—the degree to which the group wants to satisfy the concerns of the other group—and (2) **assertiveness**—the degree to which the group wants to satisfy is own concerns.[11] The two dimensions plotted in Figure 12–2 are reflected in five **conflict-handling modes.**

Figure 12–2 Two-Dimensional Model of Ways to Handle Conflict

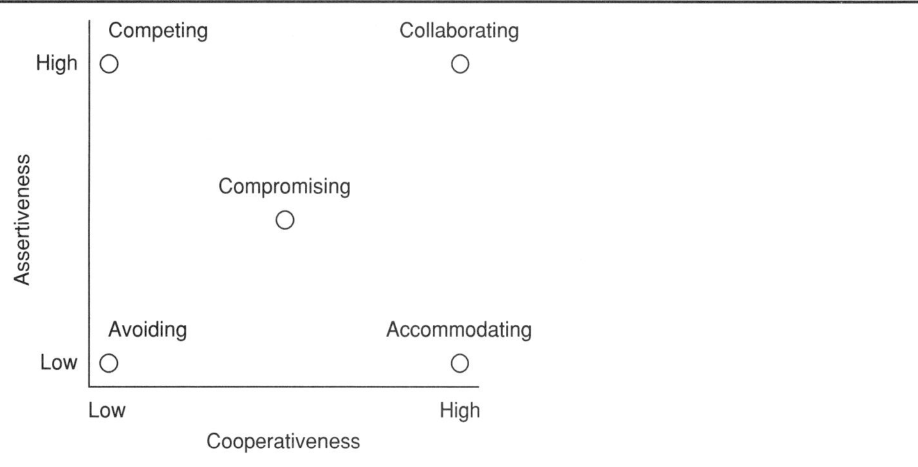

Source: Adapted from T. Ruble and K. Thomas, "Support for a Two-DImensional Model of Conflict Behavior," *Organizational Behavior and Human Performance* 16 (1976), p. 145.

The **avoidance orientation** implies an unassertive, uncooperative approach in which both groups neglect the concerns involved by sidestepping the issue or postponing the conflict by choosing not to deal with it. The **competitive orientation** implies winning at the other's expense. This is an assertive, uncooperative mode in which the groups attempt to achieve their own goals at the expense of the other through argument, authority, threat, or even physical force. The **accommodating orientation** reflects an unassertive, cooperative position where one group attempts to satisfy the concerns of the other by neglecting its own concerns or goals. The **compromising orientation** reflects the midpoint between the styles. It involves give-and-take by both groups. Both groups gain and give up something they want. The **collaborating orientation** is an assertive, cooperative mode that attempts to satisfy the concerns of both groups. It is different from the compromising orientation in that it represents a desire to satisfy fully the concerns of both groups.

The appropriate mode depends on the nature of the situation, the task, and the people involved. Each of these five modes is used at one time or another. This taxonomy of conflict-handling modes has been interpreted in a number of ways, including behaviors, styles, and strategies. Recent development of this framework suggests that these modes actually represent the **strategic intentions** of the groups involved in terms of what they attempt to accomplish in satisfying their own and other's goals.[12] Figure 12–3 captures the appropriate situation for each of the five modes, as identified by chief executives.

Figure 12–3
Appropriate Situations for Five Strategic Intentions

Conflict-Handling Modes	Appropriate Situations
Competing	1. When quick, decisive action is vital (e.g., emergencies). 2. On important issues where unpopular actions need implementing (e.g., cost cutting, enforcing unpopular rules, discipline). 3. On issues vital to company welfare when you know you're right. 4. Against people who take advantage of noncompetitive behavior.
Collaborating	1. To find an integrative solution when both sets of concerns are too important to be compromised. 2. When your objective is to learn. 3. To merge insights from people with different perspectives. 4. To gain commitment by incorporating concerns into a consensus. 5. To work through feelings which have interfered with a relationship.
Compromising	1. When goals are important, but not worth the effort or potential disruption of more assertive modes. 2. When opponents with equal power are committed to mutually exclusive goals. 3. To achieve temporary settlements to complex issues. 4. To arrive at expedient solutions under time pressure. 5. As a backup when collaboration or competition is unsuccessful.
Avoiding	1. When an issue is trivial, or more important issues are pressing. 2. When you perceive no chance of satisfying your concerns. 3. When potential disruption outweighs the benefits of resolution. 4. To let people cool down and regain perspective. 5. When gathering information supersedes immediate decision. 6. When others can resolve the conflict more effectively. 7. When issues seem tangential or symptomatic of other issues.
Accommodating	1. When you find you are wrong—to allow a better position to be heard, to learn, and to show your reasonableness. 2. When issues are more important to others than yourself—to satisfy others and maintain cooperation. 3. To build social credits for later issues. 4. To minimize loss when you are outmatched and losing. 5. When harmony and stability are especially important. 6. To allow subordinates to develop by learning from mistakes.

Source: Kenneth W. Thomas, "Toward Multi-Dimensional Values in Teaching: The Example of Conflict Behaviors," *Academy of Management Review,* 1977, 2, Table 1, p. 487.

Social Intervention Approaches

Workshop methods are used to reduce conflict and promote collaboration, such as changing a win–lose condition to a win–win problem-solving situation. One general design can be accomplished in a one- or two-day workshop.[13] Representatives of the two groups (such as management–labor, production–sales, or, in government, personnel–security or administrative services–line functions) agree that they have serious problems and are committed to exploring thoroughly avenues of better cooperation. First, they work in separate team rooms to develop a statement of how each group sees itself as behaving toward the other group. The items from this statement are listed on a large pad. Each group then makes a list of items that outline how it perceives the other group as behaving toward it. The two groups meet and share their lists. This provides an opportunity for them to explore, in an objective setting and under the guidance of a consultant, what problems of perception, communication, and interaction they are having. This process is somewhat similar in function to the organizational dialoguing—"Where are you? Where am I?"—used in Module 2.

A second phase might be for each team to work separately on a list of factors it considers essential for an ideal working relationship. These are also shared and explored; an agreed-upon model might be analyzed. A third phase would be preparing a list of tasks the two units would have to accomplish in the future or a list of problems that must be solved. An action agenda is agreed upon; times are set for completion of the items on the agenda, and further meeting arrangements are made to discuss progress. In recognition that interaction skills must be practiced, follow-up meetings are set to maintain the newly improved relationships.

This design can be extended to more than two units, but this can become very time consuming. In a meeting of sales, research and development, and production departments, for example, the three could end with a general contract of how they are to work together, and each could have a separate contract with each of the other two pertaining to matters not involving the third unit.

Richard Beckhard describes a design to work with intraorganizational problems that he refers to as a *confrontation meeting.*[14] In this case the top manager meets with the entire management group and the discussion goes through five phases: climate setting, information collecting, information sharing, priority setting and group action planning, and organization action planning. The top-management team meets immediately after the confrontation to plan actions and then makes its decisions known to the management group. A follow-up meeting with the entire management group should take place four to six weeks later for feedback and further planning. The success of this model will depend on the degree to which an atmosphere of openness and trust exists in the organization so that actual problems can be fully explored and dealt with.

Team Management

The one-to-one style of management has been characterized as creating conflict, rivalry, and suspicion among those reporting directly to a manager. The atmosphere of distrust provides no incentive for the team members to discuss their relationships when they do meet as a group with the boss; considerable game playing is apt to take place at these meetings. The rivalries among members, who are all managers, generally get pushed down into the hierarchy so that the employees reporting to them also become involved in interdepartment rivalries. Team development methods to overcome this aspect of conflict were covered in Module 11.

Likert advocates the *linking pin* concept as one method of avoiding problems associated with the rigidly traditional, hierarchical, one-to-one arrangement between boss and subordinates in the management structure.[15] Likert's position is that each person in the nonsupervisory structure must be a member of an effective work group and must be skilled in both leadership and membership functions and roles. Each work team needs to develop the type of group skills and means of communicating that will enable members to influence one another and their superior. Each member is a linking pin between the work group of those reporting directly to him or her and the work group consisting of that person's boss and those reporting to the boss. The organization is thus made up of a series of overlapping work groups in which each manager performs a linking function between groups of two levels of the hierarchy.

Likert provides for increased coordination between different functional areas by developing a multiple overlapping group structure through lateral as well as vertical linkage. Vertical linkage may take the form of committees or temporary work projects that provide for the lateral communication between groups.

Conflict Prevention through Change Programs

Too often managers are concerned about conflict only when a firefighting operation becomes necessary. An aggressive concern for effectiveness methods that have preventive and coping activities as an integral part of the overall program is more purposeful. Discussion of the macro approaches to organizational effectiveness, such as Likert's System 4, will be saved for Module 17; however, brief reference should be made to Likert's views on management of conflict to illustrate this point.[16] His System 4 is a behavioral description of managerial practices that, when applied throughout an organization, has the potential of increasing effectiveness considerably. Certain aspects of the total approach contribute to the prevention and resolution of conflict. These include

- Linking pins and the linking process.
- The nature of System 4 leadership.
- Contributions arising from supportive behavior, integrative goals, deemphasizing status, and use of consensus for productive problem solving (win–win).
- Principles of System 4 organizational structure.[17]

Intergroup Communications

Perceptual stereotyping, communication barriers, and win–lose motivation are all increased during intergroup relations. Intergroup conflict can be better understood by first considering conflict within the individual. In the socialization process, individuals learn the conforming behaviors of society at the expense of freely fulfilling their own drives and desires; this process can generate internal conflicts that could easily be directed against other people. A second aspect of socialization is that the individual develops a self-identity, which can be thought of as an integration of all the groups he or she has been a member of or has admired; these are termed positive reference groups. Groups that individuals have rejected provide negative reference points in perceiving others. Knowing an individual's reference groups makes his or her behavior more understandable. The tendency of people to cluster together when threatened or frustrated tends to make such a group a positive reference group, while outsiders become negative reference points.

Recent research indicates that groups of strangers can develop in-group/out-group attitudes within a very few minutes. Sherif's experiments indicate how easily cohesive groups of boys can fall into the win–lose trap; Blake has shown executives are also highly susceptible. Ways to avoid the win–lose trap include awareness of the dynamics of intergroup conflict, recognition of a common enemy, development of superordinate goals, and certain social intervention strategies, such as workshops set up to solve the conflict. Team management concepts such as Likert's linking pin also are directed at overcoming problems of conflict and increasing coordination.

Summary

Intergroup dynamics is a complex phenomenon and a multilevel concept that can have an impact on behavior at the individual, group, and organizational levels. In this module, intergroup dynamics was examined and studied at the interpersonal and intergroup levels within the organizational context. A short review of the determinants of intergroup performance was followed by an exploration of intergroup communication and conflict.

Next, we discussed a variety of ways for handling intergroup conflict. Finally, five strategic intentions were presented for handling conflict in a variety of situations. This module's activities—12–1 (''Ambiguity, Conflict, and Interteam Dynamics''), 12–2 (''The Prisoners' Dilemma''), and 12–3 (''The SLO Corporation'')—provide an opportunity to develop the ability to diagnose and handle intergroup conflict. As we will soon see in Part 4, intergroup dynamics influence key organizational processes such as the management of work and organization design, of quality, of creativity and innovation, and of technology and information technology. Improving intergroup dynamics is an ongoing managerial challenge that requires continuous effort.

Study Questions

1. Identify and describe some determinants of intergroup performance.
2. Define the term *intergroup conflict.* What makes intergroup conflict a complex phenomenon?
3. Discuss the relationship between intergroup communication and intergroup conflict.

4. What is the relationship between intergroup conflict and groupthink?
5. Identify a group of which you are a member and another group that can affect your group's performance. Describe the two groups. Discuss the interdependences between the groups. How does each group affect the performance of the other group?
6. We discussed a few ways to reduce intergroup conflict. From your own experience, give other methods of coping with conflict that you have used or seen others use meaningfully.
7. Compare and contrast any two of the modes for handling intergroup conflict.

Endnotes

1. See, for example, R. A. Guzzo and G. P. Shea, "Group Performance and Intergroup Relations in Organizations," in M. D. Dunnette and L. M. Hough, eds., *Handbook of Industrial and Organizational Psychology,* vol. 3, 2d ed. (Palo Alto, Calif.: Consulting Psychological Press, 1992), pp. 269–313.
2. H. C. Triandis, L. L. Kurowski, and M. J. Gelfand, "Workplace Diversity," in H. C. Triandis, M. D. Dunnette, and L. M. Hough, eds., *Handbook of Industrial and Organizational Psychology,* vol. 4, 2d ed. (Palo Alto, Calif.: Consulting Psychological Press, 1994), pp. 769–827.
3. For a more comprehensive model, see R. M. Steers and J. S. Black, *Organizational Behavior* (New York: Harper Collins, 1994), pp. 264–68.
4. M. Sherif and C. Sherif, *Social Psychology* (New York: Harper & Row, 1969), p. 418.
5. Verbal communication from Rabbie to Bennis in W. G. Bennis and P. E. Slater, *The Temporary Society* (New York: Harper & Row, 1968), p. 66.
6. M. Sherif, O. J. Harvey, B. J. White, W. R. Hod, and C. Sherif, *Intergroup Conflict and Cooperation* (Norman: University of Oklahoma Book Exchange, 1961). Also see Sherif and Sherif, *Social Psychology,* Chapter 11.
7. R. R. Blake, H. A. Shephard, and J. S. Mouton, *Managing Intergroup Conflict in Industry* (Houston: Gulf Publishing, 1964), Chapter 2.
8. Sherif and Sherif, *Social Psychology,* p. 255.
9. Rensis Likert, *The Human Organization* (New York: McGraw-Hill, 1967), pp. 52–59.
10. Ibid., pp. 73–75.
11. K. W. Thomas, "Conflict and Negotiation Processes in Organizations," in M. D. Dunnette and L. M. Hough, eds., *Handbook of Industrial and Organizational Psychology,* vol. 3, 2d ed. (Palo Alto, Calif.: Consulting Psychologists Press, 1991), pp. 653; and K. W. Thomas, "Conflict and Conflict Management: Reflection and Update," *Journal of Organizational Behavior* 13 (1992), pp. 265–74.
12. Ibid.
13. See H. A. Hornstein, B. B. Bunker, W. W. Burke, M. Gindes, and R. J. Lewicki, *Social Intervention* (New York: Free Press, 1971), pp. 355–56; Richard Beckhard, *Organization Development: Strategies and Models* (Reading, Mass.: Addison-Wesley, 1969), pp. 33–35; and Blake, Shephard, and Mouton, *Managing Intergroup Conflict in Industry,* App. 1.
14. See Hornstein et al., *Social Intervention,* p. 213.
15. Likert, *Human Organization,* Chapters 4 and 10.
16. Rensis Likert, *New Ways of Managing Conflict* (New York: McGraw-Hill, 1976).
17. Ibid., p. 7.

Activity 12–2: The Prisoners' Dilemma: An Intergroup Competition

Objective:

To explore the dynamics of intergroup competition and its effect on performance.

Task 1:

Using your permanent teams, break teams into pairs, designating one team Red and the other Blue. If there are an odd number of teams, members of the extra one should be divided among the other teams, but no Red or Blue should have more than eight members for this activity. The instructor will indicate whether there are to be observers. Be sure that each set of Red and Blue teams is sufficiently isolated from the other sets so they can carry on their interactions without disturbing the others. Do not communicate with the other team until the instructor indicates the exercise is to start.

Tear out the Prisoners' Dilemma Tally Sheet from Appendix N, and study the directions. Your instructor will answer any questions you have about scoring. (Time: 10 minutes)

Task 2:

Your instructor will tell you when to begin. You will have three minutes to make a team decision. When the instructor tells you to do so, enter your team's decision on the tally sheet.

Choices of the teams for Round 1 will be announced and the scores entered.

Task 3:

After all rounds have been completed, take a moment to note your reactions to the competition.

a. What impact did the ban on communication with the other group have?
b. Did you or others in your team become aggressive? Want to compromise? Feel frustrated? Withdraw?
c. How might a situation like this develop in a working organization?

Task 4:

Your instructor will lead a discussion of the exercise, drawing on the insights of observers and participants' notes. A lecture on intergroup competition will conclude this exercise.

Source: Reprinted from J. William Pfeiffer and John E. Jones, eds., *A Handbook of Structured Experiences for Human Relations Training,* vol. 3 (San Diego, Calif.: University Associates, 1974). Used with permission.

Activity 12–3: Interdivisional Competition at the SLO Corporation

Objective:

To explore the dynamics of interdivisional competitions and their effect on performance.

Task 1 (Individual):

Individuals are to read the following case.

Case Study: The SLO Corporation

The SLO Corporation, founded 25 years ago by Mr. Bright, is a success story. Mr. Bright, who is the president and the majority stockholder, rules with a heavy hand and is involved in all company decisions. The two major divisions, manufacturing and marketing/sales, have been in constant conflict. Over the years, Mr. Bright assumed the role of the linking pin and arbitrator between the two divisions. Furthermore, at this

Source: This activity is similar to many that have been developed previously. The original exercise was developed by Sherif, *Intergroup Relations and Leadership,* and further developed by many others, notably Robert Black. This activity is a further modification of one found in D. A. Kold, J. S. Osland, and I. M. Rubin, *Organizational Behavior: An Experiential Approach,* 6th ed. (Englewood Cliffs, N.J.: Prentice-Hall, 1995), pp. 291–93.

point on any issue of importance, the two divisions communicate through him. As a successful company, SLO has grown at an average annual rate of 9.5 percent in sales, which makes the company an above-average performer in the industry. The managers of the two divisions are composed of individuals with somewhat different educational background: 65 percent of the manufacturing division managers are engineers, 15 percent with business degrees, 5 percent with some other university degrees, and 15 percent with no college education; 65 percent of the managers of marketing/sales have business-related degrees, 15 percent have engineering degrees; 5 percent have some other university degrees, and 15 percent have no degrees.

Mr. Bright's surprise sale of his stock to Steel Co. Inc. has made SLO Corporation a wholly owned subsidiary that must now operate without Mr. Bright. Known for its participative orientation, Steel Co. Inc. sends its executive vice president, Mr. Aquire, to meet with SLO people and get a clearer picture on the status of affairs, how to proceed in the process of selecting and appointing a new president (i.e., should it be a person from within SLO or an outsider), and what kind of person the president should be.

Following a few meetings, Mr. Aquire sends the following short memo to members of the manufacturing and marketing/sales divisions:

> I have asked your division heads to call a divisional meeting for the purpose of establishing criteria for choosing the new president. Each one of you should come to the meeting with five criteria on a piece of paper. The outcome of the meeting should be a report listing the criteria with a short description. You are also being asked to rank order the criteria.

Task 2:

The instructor will split the class into an even number of teams, each with the same number of team members. Half of the teams will represent manufacturing and the other half will represent marketing/sales. Each individual and team is to assume the role of a member from the assigned division. Each team is to meet separately and work on its task. Each member is to make a clear copy of the criteria developed by the team; this copy is to be shared with a member of the other division.
(Time: 20 minutes)

Task 3:

To review the reports and evaluate them, individuals will be paired with a person from the other division. Each person is to share the report and discuss it with the partner. Your task is to decide which set of criteria is better, and assign points accordingly. As a team of two, you are given 100 points to be assigned. There must be a preference indicated (e.g., 54–46, 52–48, 80–20). Your task is to focus on the content of the criteria that you are evaluating.
(Time: 20 minutes)

Task 4:

a. Go back to your original team and total the number of points that each member brought back.

b. Each individual is to share the process that they have gone through. What occurred between you and the representative from the other division?

c. Brainstorm with the team about an alternative strategy that might work better.

(Time: 20 minutes)

Task 5:

Meet again with your partner from the other group to review and give each other feedback focusing on both content and process.

a. *Content* would include a discussion on your ability to focus on interests or positions, invention of options for mutual gains, and insistence on the use of objective criteria.

b. *Process* would include a reflection on the process that you have used, the way the conflict was handled, the conflict styles that were used, and what kind of negotiations were used.

c. Develop an agreement around a potential repeat of this activity. That is, knowing what you know now, how would you improve the negotiation session?

(Time: 15 minutes)

Task 6:

Meet with your original teams and discuss the following:

a. How did the team operate during the preparation for the first meeting with the representatives from the other division?

b. How did the team handle the outcomes from the first negotiations? What was the climate in the team? What effect did losing or winning have on the team?

c. How willing were you to receive feedback and help from a member of another team? How easy is it for you to work with a member from the other group to develop a winning criteria list?

d. What is the climate in the team now after the activity?

Task 7:

The instructor summarizes the activity, facilitates a class discussion, and provides a minilecture.

PART 4 MANAGING KEY ORGANIZATIONAL PROCESSES

Part 3 interrelated the four conceptual areas of personality, motivation, perception, and communication to the management of teams. The last two modules in Part 3—managing work team effectiveness and managing the dynamics between teams—set the stage for the exploration of key organizational processes. This part explores the relationships between the main conceptual areas and key organizational processes. The organizational processes—work and organization design, quality, creativity and innovation, and technology and information technology—are examined as key processes that are pivotal to individual, team, and organizational effectiveness.

Work and organization design are considered in Module 13. The focus is on the design principles of organizations and work as well as on the design process. Under increasing competitive conditions, companies are searching for more flexible ways of organizing human and other resources via redesigning total organizations, departments, work units, and jobs. This module reviews several comprehensive approaches to organization design: information processing, sociotechnical systems, and self-design. Following a snapshot review of alternative forms of structure, we explore work design orientations that emphasize both individuals and groups. The roles that leadership, group and intergroup dynamics, perception, communication, and motivation play in the process of the different work design orientations are addressed.

Quality and the management of quality are the focus of Module 14. Quality is a major theme in recent best-selling books, seminars, and journals. In this text, quality is perceived as a key organizational process that influences individual, team, and organizational effectiveness. A discussion of the importance of quality, its history, and its salient principles is followed by the identification of management mechanisms, structural support configurations, tools, and techniques that can foster the continuous improvement process.

Creativity and innovation are two processes that lately have been termed critical for organizations' effectiveness and survival. Module 15 examines the creative process, explores the organizational characteristics and managerial actions that can foster creativity, identifies stages of the innovation process, describes key organizational elements that influence the innovation process, and considers the interplay between creativity, innovation, and human behavior.

The last module in this part—Module 16—focuses on the management of technology and information technology. In this text, technology and information technology are perceived as key organizational processes that must be managed. Both have direct effects on human behavior, organizational behavior, and organizational effectiveness. The growth of information technology systems is changing the nature of work and human interaction. As such, we review some advances of information technology and examine the challenge that they present to managers and organizations alike. The roles that perception, communication, leadership, group and intergroup dynamics, work design, and creativity and innovation play in shaping managing technology and information technology are addressed.

The experiential approach continues to be the underlying foundation of the learning process of this part. Each of the four modules includes one to three experiential activities and two cases. The instructor will make the appropriate choices of mix of activities and sequence based on time availability.

13 Work and Organization Design

Learning Objectives

After completing this module you should be able to

1. Appreciate the importance of integrating goals, structure, and people through comprehensive organization design.
2. Describe the basic dimensions involved in comprehensive organization design.
3. Identify the different ways of grouping people into departments and integrating their efforts.
4. Describe three types of work teams fostered in private industry.
5. Explain the job characteristics approach to job enrichment.
6. Identify design-related problems in different organizational settings.
7. Appreciate that there are many successful ways to approach work design at individual, group, and organizational levels.

List of Key Concepts

Continuous quality improvement (CQI) team
Design dimensions
Differentiation
Flexible work schedule
Forms of structure
Fractal organization
Horizontal organization
Information processing design approach
Information technology
Integration
Job characteristics approach
Job engineering
Job enlargement
Job rotation
Job sharing
Lean production system
Macro organization design model
Motivational potential score (MPS)
Network organization
Off-line team
Organization design
Part-time, temporary, and leased employees
Quality circle
Scientific management
Self-design approach
Sociotechnical systems design approach
Sociotechnical systems (STS) team
Strategic organization design
Total quality management (TQM) team

This module was revised by our colleague Michael Stebbins, Professor of Organization Design, College of Business, California Polytechnic State University, San Luis Obispo, California 93407. We are grateful to Professor Stebbins.

Module Outline

Premodule Preparation

The instructor may assign either one of the following two activities. If time permits both might be used.

Activity 13–1: Designing a Student-Run Organization That Provides Consulting Services

Objectives:

a. To appreciate the importance of the total organization on group and individual behavior.

b. To provide a beginning organization design experience that will be familiar to students.

Background:

The Industry Advisory Council for your school has decided to sponsor a student-run organization that will provide business consulting services to nonprofit groups in your community. The council has donated $20,000 toward start-up costs and has agreed to provide office space, computer equipment, and other materials as needed. The council hopes that the organization will establish its own source of funding after the first year of operation.

Task 1:

The dean of the school wants you to develop alternative designs for the new organization. Your task is to identify the main design dimensions or factors to be dealt with in establishing such an organization, and to describe the issues that must be resolved for each factor. For example, you might provide an organization chart to help describe structural issues involved. You may also have to think about (1) groups in the community that could use your help and (2) problems they face before jumping ahead with your design. Remember, though, your task is to create the organization that will provide services, not to provide an in-depth look at the types of services provided.

You and your team are to brainstorm design dimensions to be dealt with and to develop a one- or two-page outline that can be shared with the entire class. You have one hour to develop the outline and select two people to present your design. Assume that you will all be involved in the new organization, filling specific positions.

Task 2:

After the brainstorming period, the spokespersons will present the group designs and answer questions from the audience.

Task 3:

The instructor will comment on the designs and discuss additional factors that might be important for the success of this organization.

Activity 13–2: The Woody Manufacturing Company: Start-up Design

Objective:

To apply the concepts learned in the module about work design at the individual, group, and organizational levels in designing the Woody Manufacturing Company.

Task 1 (Individual Assignment):

a. Read the following case study of the Woody Manufacturing Company.

b. Review carefully the module and choose the design orientation that you feel can best guide you in developing the design for Mr. Woody.

c. Write down your thoughts on alternative management structures, pay systems, and allocation of work to individuals and groups.

Task 2 (Team Work):

a. Get together in your team and develop a proposal for Mr. Woody that, if followed, would help him fulfill his vision.

b. Prepare a five-minute presentation. Your typewritten team proposal is due prior to your team presentation in Mr. Woody's conference room.

Case Study: The Woody Manufacturing Company

Mr. Woody, the owner/operator of a small furniture company specializing in the manufacture of high-quality bar stools, has experienced a tremendous growth in demand for his products. He has standing orders for $750,000. Consequently, Mr. Woody has decided to expand his organization and attack the market aggressively. His stated mission is ''to manufacture world-class products that are competitive in the world market in quality, reliability, performance, and profitability.'' He would like to create a culture where ''pride, ownership, employment security, and trust'' are a way of life. He just finished a set of interviews, and he has hired 32 new workers with the following skills:

Four skilled craftspeople.

Ten people with some woodworking experience.

Twelve people with no previous woodworking experience or other skills.

One nurse.

One schoolteacher.

One bookkeeper.

Three people with some managerial experience in nonmanufacturing settings.

Mr. Woody (with your help) must now decide how to design his new organization. This design will include the management structure, pay system, and the allocation of work to individuals and groups. The bar-stool–making process has 15 steps:

1. Wood is selected.
2. Wood is cut to size.
3. Defects are removed.
4. Wood is planed to exact specifications.
5. Joints are cut.
6. Tops are glued and assembled.
7. Legs/bases are prepared.
8. Legs/bases are attached to tops.
9. Bar stools are sanded.
10. Stain is applied.
11. Varnish is applied.
12. Bar stools are sanded.
13. Varnish is reapplied.
14. Bar stools are packaged.
15. Bar stools are delivered to the customer.

Mr. Woody currently manufactures three kinds of bar stools (pedestal, four-legged corner, and four-legged recessed). There is no difference in the difficulty of making the three types of bar stools. Major cost variations have been associated with defective wood, imprecise cuts, and late deliveries to customers. Mr. Woody must decide how to organize his company to maintain high quality and profits.

He has thought about several options. He could have some individuals perform the first step for all types of bar stools; he could have an individual perform several steps for one type of bar stool; or he could have a team perform some combination of steps for one or more bar stools. He wonders whether how he organized would affect quality or costs. He's also aware that while the demand for all types of bar stools has been roughly equal over the long run, there were short periods where one type of bar stool was in greater demand than the others. Because Mr. Woody wants to use his people effectively, he has committed an expert in work design to help him set up an optimal organization.

Introduction

''The limiting factor in achieving society's goals is quite often the manner in which resources are organized.''

Jay Galbraith, 1977

Organization and work design can be a key element influencing how well organizations and people perform. The design of work and jobs is an ongoing challenge and is evolving as a specialized field of study in academia and as a tool for change. Organizations have unique histories, purposes, cultures, and environments; they usually evolve through trial and error rather than being developed all at once through deliberate organizational planning and design. While we might say that companies in an industry are in the same business, they often do not view their tasks the same way or pursue the same strategies and ways of organizing. For example, Alpha Health Care Corporation is a relatively new managed care company in the health care industry. Alpha competes with long-established health maintenance organizations (HMOs) such as Kaiser Permanente, but does not build and own hospitals, operate its own medical groups and clinics, or directly provide medical services in the traditional Kaiser Permanente mode. Alpha has a different mission and follows a market-driven strategy that results in faster growth and greater flexibility. Compared with Kaiser, it does not have a complex hospital hierarchy nor does it need to be concerned with matters such as hospital accreditation or help from hospital volunteers. It leaves these decisions up to community hospitals and other providers that choose to participate in the Alpha network. The point is that organizations take on different tasks and are configured in different ways. The differences in configuration can be explored at the total-organization, department, work group, and job levels to find out how design affects organizational success.

Comprehensive Approaches to Organization Design

Work design at the organizational level has developed over the past 40 years both as a field of academic study and as a process for improving organizations. A recent comparison of organization design perspectives identified 10 design schools of thought or orientations that can be used to guide redesign programs.[1] Three of the orientations are comprehensive; that is, they provide guiding models, they spell out design principles, they provide a redesign process, and they have an empirical track record of applications in different settings.[2] All three approaches have been applied to diverse organizations during the corporate downsizing era. The orientations are *information processing theory, sociotechnical systems theory,* and *self-design.*

The Information Processing Design Approach

Jay Galbraith is credited with establishing the information processing orientation to design. According to information processing theory, **organization design** is most usefully defined as a decision-making process.[3] The decision-making process includes choices about goals, tasks to be accomplished, technology to be adopted, ways to organize, and ways to integrate individuals into the organization.[4] The key is finding a balance or fit among these decisions, and doing it in a way that is in step with the changing environment. Attention to customers, changing market needs, and desired outcomes makes the overall process **strategic organization design.** A comprehensive redesign program might involve strategic planning activities, reengineering of core work processes through (for example) computer and telecommunications enhancements, creation of a new formal structure, development of management systems to provide better coordination, and, finally, efforts to develop a new organizational culture, work group norms, and values. Increasingly, information technology plays a role in each of these activities.

The growth of information technology (IT) and its pervasive use in all sectors of the economy is a familiar trend in the 1990s. **Information technology**—including voice messaging, on-line transaction processing, electronic mail, teleconferencing, and other computer and telecommunications advances—are fundamentally changing the nature of the workplace. (See Module 16 for more on this topic.) The potential for IT innovations is exemplified by a recent Andersen Consulting company project at UCAR Carbon of Clarksville, Tennessee. With expert advice from Andersen's consultants, the company eliminated its big assembly line production setup and formed new worker teams in manufacturing, order processing, and other mainstream work areas. Now one employee with a workstation connected to a computer network can respond to a customer's request for price quotes within minutes, in place of an old system that relied on time-consuming information gathering and contacts among affected departments. Workers in the assembly teams gain access to vital order information on the same network, and the new system sets the wheels in motion to replenish customer inventories on demand.[5]

Information technology advances have resulted in a new **macro organization design model.** The model (see Figure 13–1) is an outgrowth of the information processing theory proposed by Jay Galbraith and further enhanced by David Nadler and Michael Tushman. Briefly, design begins with analysis of the company's business situation. Managerial assessments of the environment and business situation help determine the organization's goals and strategies. Goals and strategies in turn influence decisions about tasks and work processes. Based on these strategic decisions, managers decide the best ways to group employees into departments, coordinate department activities, and provide additional integration by adopting various support systems. All design choices are influenced or driven by information technology and cultural variables. Emergent behavior and business results are directly tied to the quality of managerial choices made throughout the design chain.

Figure 13–1
Macro Organization Design

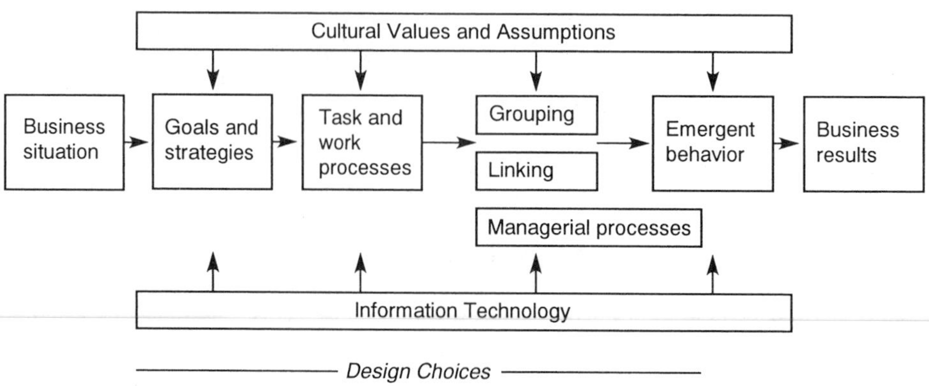

Now that an overall macro organization design model has been offered, we will demonstrate **design dimensions** and relationships by offering an example. Consider the simple case of a dentist starting a new practice in a small town. He is not the only dentist in town, and he must gradually build a practice in competition with others in a 40-mile district. Initially the dentist does everything himself. That is, he takes appointments, greets patients, provides his own workstation setup, cleans teeth and performs other dental services, cleans the office, orders supplies, and sends out the bills. Soon he is working a 12-hour day and his wife has taken over the billing. Considerable time passes with other adjustments made. Five years later he is the leading dentist in the district and has a markedly different operation. Now he has a much larger office facility, an office manager, three dental hygienists to clean teeth, three dental assistants, an information specialist who deals with outside insurance companies and runs an automated billing system, and a part-time dentist who asists with patient overloads. Office cleaning has been contracted out, as have various supply, financial, tax, and legal services. The dentist has a sophisticated electronic data interchange (EDI) with vendors that automatically triggers purchase orders for supplies and speeds billing to major insurance carriers. His entire staff is trained in data entry and inquiry activities. What happened during the five-year period?

Initially the dentist was content with the idea of doing everything himself. Coordination was easy since the dentist handled all transactions personally and a single brain did the integration. With increasing patient demand, variety of services needed, and related business activities, the dentist was in an overload situation. At first, he made piecemeal decisions, such as hiring a receptionist and contracting a cleaning service. After a time, he contacted a business consultant to rethink his entire practice. Over a one-year period, the dentist, the consultant, and an architect investigated new work design possibilities, did some strategic planning, developed an ideal practice model, created a set of plans for a new office facility, and developed business systems to complement the patient care changes. His wife and employees were included in the planning activities to contribute ideas and help with practical applications. The processing of information in the expanded practice was also a key consideration. At a predicted high volume of patient demands, the proposed future office required new information processing capacity. The consultant helped the dentist create new capacity, primarily through new computer systems. The planning work culminated in a move to a new office facility, installation of state-of-the-art equipment, expanded staffing, and employee training activities; these activities occurred over a three-month period. Computers and information technology innovations were used at each step of the way, and the dentist is now poised to adopt new technologies as his practice moves into the 21st century.

This case illustrates that total organization design requires an assessment of information processing requirements to perform a task that is to be matched by new information processing capacity. That capacity can include a new structure or hierarchy, new roles and other mechanisms to help integrate the work, and new management systems. In the case of the small dental office, the choices were limited yet profound. While the office retains a pleasant and caring small-office work climate, the volume of work and productivity have leaped ahead. Both people and technical considerations were covered in the organization redesign.

The Sociotechnical Systems Design Approach

Whether the organization is big or small, it must consider people concerns as well as technology during a redesign project. This concept was recognized by founders of the sociotechnical systems (STS) school of design as early as 1948. Eric Trist of the Tavistock Institute in London coined the term *sociotechnical* to describe the interrelatedness of social and technical subsystems within organizations. The principle of joint optimization of these subsystems is the backbone of STS theory. An organization will function best if the social and technical systems are designed to fit the demands of each other and the environment.[6]

STS is a diverse and flexible approach to design. It demands a careful analysis of each situation (contingency perspective) and encourages managers to develop options rather than insisting on the idea that there is one best way to organize. It has strong ties to quality of work life (QWL) experiments and is also associated with autonomous work groups, self-inspection of work quality, job enrichment, team orientations, and other design principles covered in this module. STS programs have been implemented in many countries, notably in British coal mines, in textile mills in India, in diverse Norwegian, Dutch, and Swedish companies, and in American manufacturing firms. Recent attention has been directed to design programs in high-technology businesses and to knowledge workers.[7] We explore STS theory and planned change process in Module 17.

The Self-Design Approach

Self-design is an outgrowth of STS theory. Thomas Cummings, a leading self-design author, contributed to the STS school of thought in earlier decades. The **self-design approach** encourages managers to plan and to implement their own strategy/structure change programs. The design process is neither simple nor quick. Managers and employees are trained in project planning, diagnostic, process, and design skills needed to run the program. Self-design emphasizes the need for practice in design implementation, assessment, and continual modification of the organization. The process is dynamic and cyclical and encourages organizational learning from design experimentation.

Figure 13–2 shows the self-design process model. Briefly, the foundation for self-design is employee and manager training. People must prepare themselves for activities that differ substantially from daily routines. New conceptual and empirical knowledge is needed to conduct a redesign project; otherwise redesign will be superficial. Also, the values and outcomes the organization is trying to promote must be specified, and the people involved must undertake diagnostic work to determine how well the organization is currently performing. These activities lead to an initial definition of organizational issues and agreement on design criteria. Design criteria are standards that guide design activities by specifying the purposes the new design must satisfy. They will help designers choose among design alternatives and influence the best design. From this point the process is hard to delineate since the extent of change needed is unknown. The existing design might need fine-tuning, a competitor's design might be imitated, or drastic redesign might be in order. Additionally, there may be a need to have different groups of employees generate designs, test them against design criteria and realities of the workplace, and decide on the best overall design. Even when there is agreement by designers, the job is not over, as different constituents must provide input to the final design. Constituents might force the work back to zero by questioning the original diagnostic work and design criteria. Although it's still new, self-design promises to be a fruitful approach for the coming century. Self-design programs have recently been conducted within companies in the telecommunications, aerospace, electronics, software, and pharmaceutical industries.[8]

Activity 13–4 provides additional material on self-design theory plus an opportunity to redesign a small bakery operation using self-design concepts. Organization structure is a major focus in all redesign projects. We turn now to consider forms of structure and related concepts.

Forms of Structure

The term *structure* has many meanings. Research studies on organizations have identified *structural variables* such as the number of levels in the hierarchy, formalization (the amount of written documentation, as in policies and procedures manuals, job descriptions, and the like), standardization (the extent to which activities must be performed in a uniform manner), and degree of centralization. Form of structure refers to

Figure 13–2 **Self-Design Process Model**

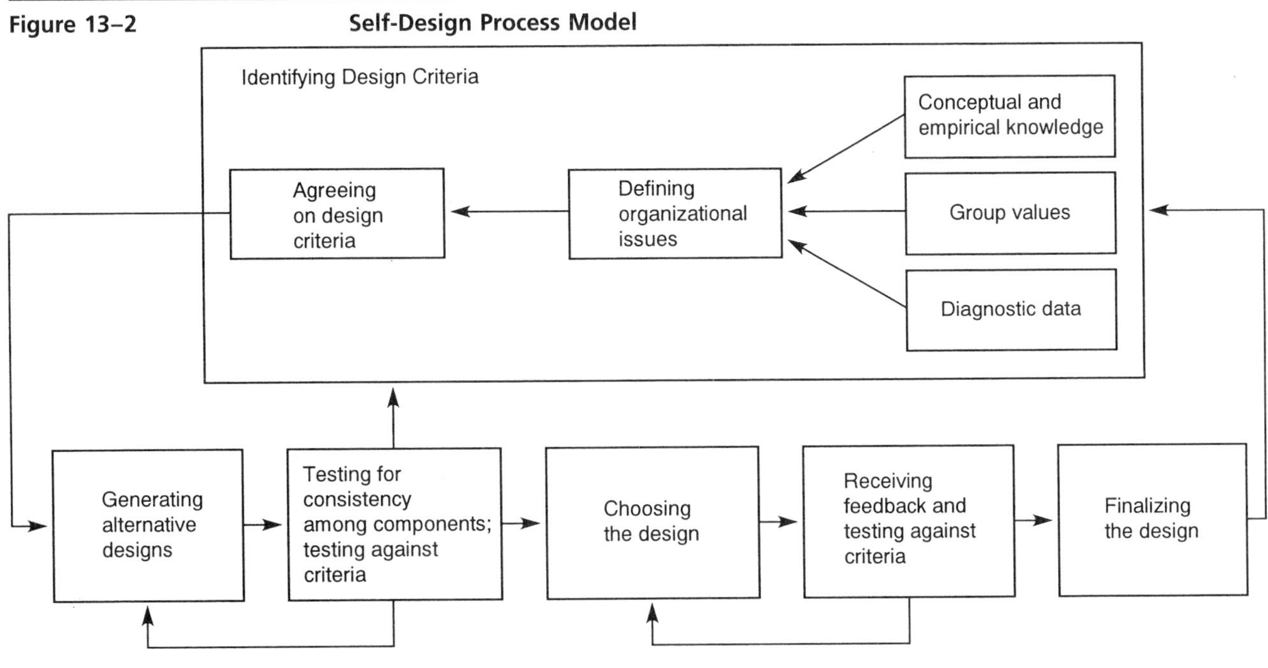

Source: Adapted from S. A. Mohrman and I. G. Cummings, *Self-Designing Organizations* (Reading, Mass.: Addison-Wesley, 1989).

the method of grouping employees together into work units, departments, and the total organization. Finally, structure includes *organizational processes* such as reward systems that foster cooperation and integration of diverse work activities. Since a comprehensive look at structure is beyond the scope of this book, we provide a brief abstract of common forms of structure and organizational processes.[9]

Simple Form

In our previous dental practice case, a simple form of structure exists. The dentist is owner/operator of a small business and clearly has a hand in all aspects of the enterprise. While he has a modest division of labor through delegation of certain activities to support personnel, he can personally perform every function if needed. The dentist has established the foundation for a functional organization, but the organization will not be the functional form until managers of specialty units are appointed and given some discretion to make decisions. Many small businesses do not grow in size beyond the capabilities of the owners as direct supervisors.

Functional Form

Organizations that group personnel on the basis of function performed, work process, and specialized knowledge, training, or academic discipline have chosen the functional form. Typically, as the organization grows, **differentiation** of specialty units occurs, with managers appointed for each unit. Again, using our dentist example, if activities are delegated, **integration** or coordination must still be achieved. For example, the dentist knows that he must reserve time in his own schedule to check the work of his dental hygienists. Likewise, he must work closely with the support staff on instructions provided to patients so that both patients and providers are aware of what is to take place following the visit. The left hand must know what the right hand is doing if the patient is to receive integrated dental health care. Figure 13–3 shows a functional form of structure.

Moving away from the services industry to a manufacturing example, a small production plant will typically have departments with names such as Production, Sales, Finance, Engineering, Purchasing, Information Technology, and Personnel. As the company grows, additional hierarchy and differentiation is created. For example, as a plant

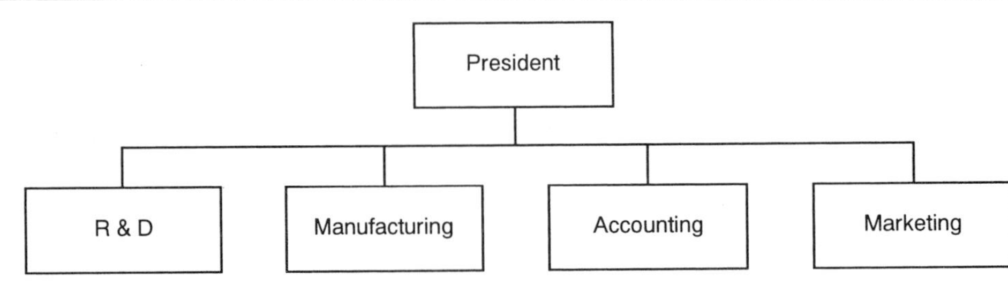

Figure 13–3
Functional Form of Structure

expands from 500 to 2,000 employees, the three-person personnel office may be enlarged to include separate units such as plant security, labor relations, salary and benefits, training, and workers' compensation, each headed by a supervisor. As the personnel department grows, the department manager must ensure that her own supervisors and employees are communicating and must be concerned about how personnel services are being received by managers and employees throughout the plant. The plant manager, as a generalist, will be preoccupied with coordination to a great extent, as departments must cooperate in getting quality products to the customer on time. A similar scenario exists for larger services companies, government offices, and nonprofit organizations.

Certain advantages and disadvantages are associated with the functional form of structure. Functional organizations tend to be efficient and work well when the business situation and outside environment are generally stable. Employees are hired into junior positions and develop skills under the direction of senior workers and managers. On the negative side, people in functional organizations often develop parochial viewpoints, and interdepartmental cooperation can be poor. Resolutions of interdepartmental conflicts and other decisions are often pushed up the hierarchy, slowing things down and blocking needed changes. As the company's products and customers expand, other forms of structure appear more attractive to top management.

Product or Self-Contained Form

With increasing company size, product divisions or other self-contained units are often created to replace the single-function organization. In our manufacturing example, a new product created at the company's plant may enjoy immediate success, diverting attention from mainstream products. If demand for the new product increases, there will be pressure to retool the factory or construct an entirely new facility. With greater diversification of products and greater diversification in customers and markets served, the company may choose to reorganize according to its major products. When this occurs, each product group gains discretion to design, produce, and distribute its products in ways that are consistent with the competitive environment. When personnel are grouped according to product line, service performed, or project, then a product or self-contained form of organization has been created, as Figure 13–4 shows.

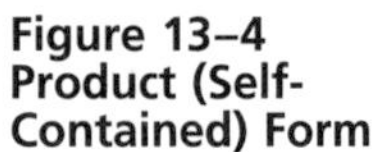
Figure 13–4
Product (Self-Contained) Form

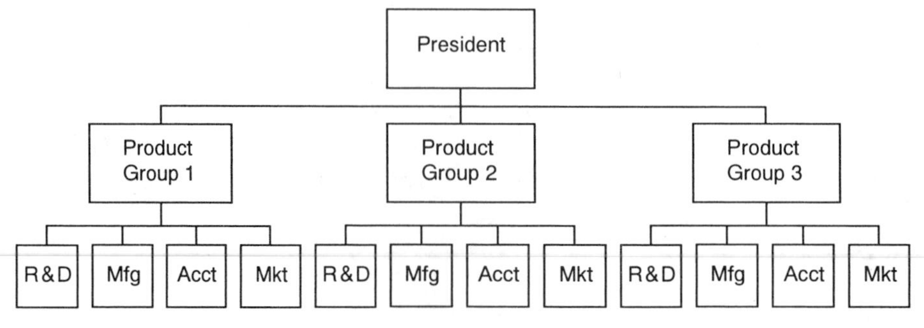

At the corporate level, companies with the product form often have certain functions such as public relations, legal, compensation, and finance units as staff executive offices. These corporate units work with the president and product division personnel to establish certain common policies, practices, services, and controls for the entire company. Cases of staff/line cooperation and conflict are widely experienced in organizations having larger size. Recently there have been efforts to decentralize certain corporate and division staff units to operating groups so that the operating groups are better able to manage support services.

Advantages associated with the product form include greater responsiveness to a changing environment, improved cooperation and coordination among functional groups with each product division, decision making closer to the customer, and improved customer satisfaction. Disadvantages include duplication of resources, difficulties coordinating company activities that cross product lines, and a reduction of knowledge and technical specialization compared to the functional form. Companies such as IBM that are moving to greater product division independence find it more difficult to integrate activities and standardize across product lines.

Mixed or Hybrid Form

As a practical matter, many organizations have mixed or hybrid forms rather than following the pure forms of structure listed above. One of the mixed forms is *matrix* structure (Figure 13–5), which allows a focus on two dimensions at the same time. For example, a pure matrix structure in an aerospace firm has functional engineering departments and project offices. Most employees work in functional departments under the day-to-day supervision of functional bosses, but are also assigned to one or more project teams. Project managers work with functional managers and employees to ensure that projects are accomplished on time with high quality and attention to costs. Changing competitive environments in many industries have pushed companies toward matrix and other experimental forms. For global competition, some companies have organized by country and types of products. Other emerging forms of structure will be discussed at the end of this module.

Figure 13–5
Matrix Form

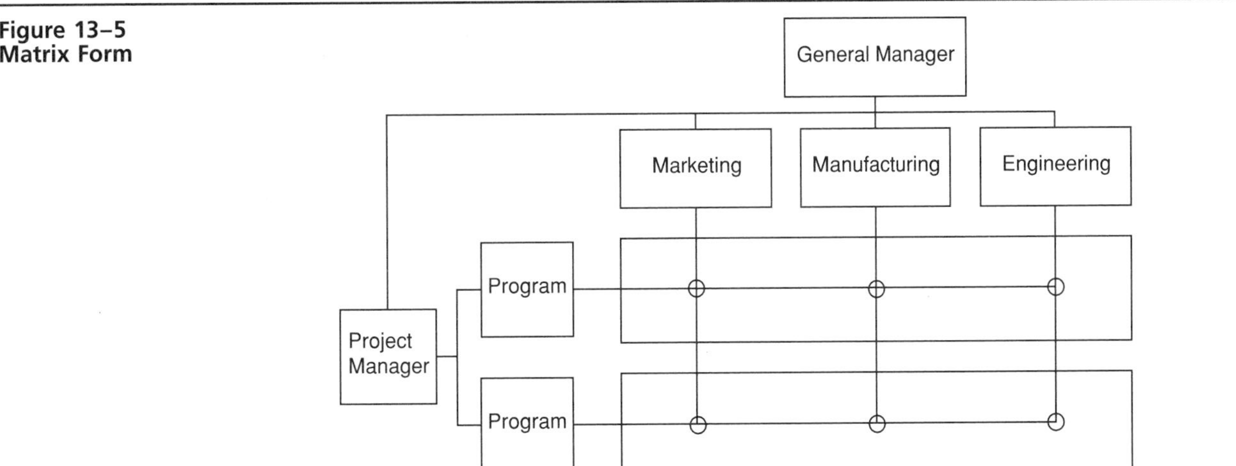

Horizontal and Flexible Organizations

A recent theme in the writings of organization design experts has been the need for greater horizontal or cross-unit coordination and integration within organizations of all types. Jay Galbraith's book *Competing with Flexible Lateral Organizations* shows us how to build *lateral organization capabilities* to match company goals and strategies.[10]

Simply put, lateral organization capability means that people get things done by working across organizational units rather than relying on the managerial hierarchy. The organization is decentralized with free flow of information. Galbraith observes that lateral coordination begins with informal, voluntary cooperation. Our dentist office example offers open and continuous sharing of information by the dentist and his employees, usually on a face-to-face basis. Galbraith provides a more complex example of an investment bank where people in different departments implement fast-moving deals for their clients. Where coordination requirements are great, the bank might establish formal groups such as new product teams to ensure that diverse experts and groups take responsibility for new product success. If there is any need for new product oversight, the bank might also appoint a coordinator or integrator person to further strengthen coordination. The concept of flexibility is closely tied to horizontal coordination. Companies want flexibility in responding quickly to rapidly changing situations. By adopting various types of lateral organization, they are better able to adjust to the changing environment.

Beyond lateral organization capability, the concept of the **horizontal organization** includes organizing around processes and adoption of information technology. Organizations are beginning to integrate closely related functions into *core processes.* An example of a core process for a manufacturing company is a mingling of sales, shipping, installation, service, and billing. Reengineering of activities in these functions eliminates much duplication and interdepartmental strife. All functions use the same information systems and the customer can call a single number to find out the status of an order. Similar core process reengineering opportunities exist for new product development and manufacturing. The combined use of lateral organization capability, organizing around processes, and information technology produces competitive advantage for the company. Time-based competitiveness, quality assurance, and productivity move upward with adoption of the horizontal organization.[11]

William Pasmore's book *Creating Strategic Change: Designing the Flexible, High Performing Organization* shows managers and employees how to manage in turbulent times.[12] A key concept is changing design dimensions at the same time (or in a systematic fashion) as if the organization is redesigned from scratch. Pasmore believes that (1) people should become active participants in their own redesign change programs and (2) managers should train people to be flexible, adopt flexible technology, and create flexible work. People doing the work can decide whether to adopt formal mechanisms to coordinate the work, or whether informal and voluntary ways of bringing things together on behalf of customers will work best.

Work Design—Emphasis on Groups

New organization designs rely on teams of all types. Modules 9, 10, 11, and 12 explore the nature and dynamics of teams. Recent research suggests that more than half of all major U.S. corporations are exploring some form of team-based work system.[13] Much of the current interest in teams is driven by Japanese work practices, and the team systems in use are grouped into the following categories: *sociotechnical systems (STS) teams, lean production teams,* and *off-line teams* such as quality circles and continuous quality improvement groups.[14]

Competitive Advantage through Teams as a Core Structure Concept

Early efforts to design work around groups can be traced to the experiments conducted by the Tavistock Institute in London in the late 1940s and early 1950s. The research projects led by Trist, Emery, and their colleagues in the coal mining, textile, and electronics industries found that clustering jobs into work teams yielded better results than more functional divisions of labor. For example, in coal mining, STS consultants found that newly invented systems and equipment requiring workers to specialize and to work on big platforms failed. Inventors and engineers expected miners to make the switch from traditional, family-member teams to factorylike working conditions that optimized technology. Downsizing the platforms and returning to other concepts that worked successfully with the traditional small teams eventually generated the expected gains in production.[15]

Sociotechnical Systems Teams

Today **sociotechnical systems teams** are found in diverse industries and nations. Perhaps the most widespread application has been in Scandinavia, stemming in part from Volvo's Kalmar plant success in Sweden and strong government support for STS experimentation in Norway and Sweden. Other widely cited examples of STS design include General Foods in Topeka, Leyland's plant in West London, Procter & Gamble, and Shell Canada.[16] Sociotechnical systems teams, often called *autonomous work groups,* integrate the requirements of social and technical systems. Sociotechnical systems teams feature high worker autonomy in decision making, no first-line supervisors, frequent job rotation, cross-training with an emphasis on learning, and a sound physical work environment. Teams decide specific work assignments, work schedules, work process, quality control procedures, rewards, and other activities that might be performed by management. Gulowsen developed the following detailed criteria of work team autonomy:[17]

1. The group has influence on qualitative goals.
2. The group has influence on quantitative goals.
3. The group decides questions of internal and external leadership.
4. The group decides what additional tasks to take on.
5. The group decides when it will work.
6. The group decides on questions of production method.
7. The group determines the internal distribution of tasks.
8. The group decides on questions of recruitment.
9. The group decides on questions of internal leadership.
10. The group members determine their individual production methods.

Theoretically STS is a general framework that should allow for many types of integration among social and technical systems. Technical systems are not viewed as dominant, but rather as equipment and operations to be shaped through worker input. In practice, nearly all STS design-based organizations have adopted autonomous work groups as a central feature of design, with varying success at modifying technology to meet worker needs.

Lean Production Teams

Japanese influence on the movement toward teams in industry is unmistakable. The label **lean production systems** is synonymous with Japanese manufacturing facilities. Lean production systems feature customer-driven priorities, just-in-time delivery between customers and suppliers, low internal inventory, reduced steps in work operations, high worker participation via work teams, and broad team responsibilities for monitoring quality and planning work activities. The commitment to continuous improvement in all aspects of operations is also strong. In the United States, Nippondenso Manufacturing of Battle Creek, Michigan, provides a clear example:

> We saw machinery tightly packed together, with automated movement of parts from machine to machine such that raw materials flowed quickly through to the loading dock where trucks were dispatched every 12 minutes as part of a just-in-time delivery system. Workers were hustling from station to station; fork lift trucks were moving quickly to deliver raw materials and unload finished product. Despite the hustle, we observed that people also found time to make eye contact, smile, and even briefly converse with us as visitors. There was little inventory visible anywhere in the plant. In each work area, there were highly visible clusters of red, yellow, and green lights (the andon system) to indicate when the line was running (green light) and when

workers wanted to consult about a possible quality or inventory problem (yellow light), and when a worker needed to shut down the line (red light). Further, near each part of the production line, a "hot corner" meeting space was provided for each team, featuring a table, chairs, and a filing cabinet. Charts were displayed tracing key "measurables" on quality, safety, productivity, progress in building skills among team members, as well as rewards and communications information.[18]

At Nippondenso Manufacturing, people give their own work areas a personal touch with house plants, pictures, cartoons, and other personal effects—in both production and administrative office environments. The entire Battle Creek plant environment is designed to encourage communications and emphasize common purpose. Early evidence suggests that lean production systems such as the one at Battle Creek are highly dependent on team concepts, although the degree of actual team control over work operations and decision making and employee reaction to the system deserve further research.

Off-Line Teams Such as Quality Circles and TQM Groups

A third development in work design has been the proliferation of **off-line teams** such as quality circles (QC), **continuous quality improvement (CQI) teams,** and **total quality management (TQM) teams.** These groups do not operate on a daily basis, but instead take "time out" periodically to address workplace issues. The **quality circle** movement was strongest in the 1970s and 1980s, but has withered as lean production systems and comprehensive TQM systems have come to the fore. From a work design perspective, quality circles are part of a parallel organization created to address work-related issues that the formal organization has not resolved. Quality circles are supplemental organizations that coexist alongside the formal organization; they draw on organizational resources, skills, and knowledge to make improvements. Quality and Total Quality Management are reviewed in depth in Module 14.

Off-line teams are typically established to solve problems that extend beyond natural work groups; their major benefit is probably quick reaction to quality and operations problems. In the case of CQI and TQM teams, success may be dependent on the group's contacts with the formal hierarchy and its ability to be involved in implementation of recommendations. At the outset, team members are trained in quality improvement philosophy and principles, group processes, and statistical analysis methods. Given trained and capable team members, quality improvement groups have unique potential to address internal and cross-department problems.

Work Design— Emphasis on Individuals

As discussed above, modern work design orientations have moved away from individual-focused approaches to group- and organization-focused theories. Historically, however, work design had a strong job engineering foundation, and emphasis on narrowly defined tasks that could be easily performed and monitored. Therefore, it is worthwhile to study both the traditional and newer approaches to job design. We will begin with scientific management.

Job Engineering/ Scientific Management

The **scientific management** approach to job design, often referred to as the **job engineering** approach, was coined by Frederick W. Taylor and further developed by his associates Frank and Lillian Gilbreth.[19] As a supervisor in a shop, Taylor noticed that workers were operating their machines at differing speeds, that workers were devising their own methods to perform their duties, that there was no incentive to increase production, and that many workers did not have the desire, skills, or training to perform their duties appropriately. Trained in mechanical engineering, Taylor set out to develop a way in which management and workers could develop the most efficient work procedures. Through experimentation he was able to determine how tasks were to be performed, the proper tools necessary for maximum efficiency, and the amount of work that an employee could be expected to perform.

Four major ideas about work design are embodied in Taylor's comprehensive strategy. First, work is a cooperative effort by management and workers to ascertain the one best way of performing a job. Second, tasks should be specialized, and work should be designed, wherever possible, so that the individual performs a minimal number of tasks that are easy to master. Third, work should be studied using scientific methods to quantitatively determine how each segment of the work or task should be performed regardless of who actually performs the task. There should be standardization of tasks, methods, and time frames as key work design criteria. And finally, managers should train, develop, and supervise employees so that the work is performed according to scientific methods, and managers should motivate employees by giving monetary bonuses accordingly.

The work design process (that is, the actual set of activities based on the scientific management orientation) was developed by R. C. Davis. It includes five steps.[20] First, a process analysis is conducted to determine the stages of production. Second, a motion study—the analysis of the movements of a person doing a task—is conducted. Third, a time study—the analysis of the time it takes to complete different job tasks—is recorded. Fourth, based on the results of the first three phases, standards are determined, experimented with, and modified. Fifth, the standards are applied and used for planning and control and the appropriate reward is allocated for task accomplishment.

Scientific management was an innovative concept in the early 1900s that led quite naturally to the ways that work was analyzed. The emphasis was to develop efficiency through specialized and standardized work tasks. Furthermore, Taylor's work led to a set of *time and motion* studies that sought to eliminate wasted movements and simplify work patterns. The methods developed by Taylor and the Gilbreths are the bases of the time and motion studies conducted today in many industries.

Job Enlargement, Job Rotation, and Job Enrichment

Maximizing efficiency only through time and motion studies and worker–machine interfaces (the scientific management view) creates fractionalized and boring jobs. As characteristics of the work force changed and employees and the unions demanded a better quality of work life, new work design strategies emerged. Job enlargement, job rotation, job sharing, and flexible work schedule strategies emerged to respond to job boredom. By adding more tasks (**job enlargement**), by moving employees among different tasks over time (**job rotation**), and by dividing a job between two or more employees (**job sharing**), individuals had greater job and task variety, skill variety, and freedom and challenge.

An example of job enlargement might entail a worker on the auto assembly line whose initial job was to install a car's front seats. As a result of the redesign program, the same worker may install the front seats, the door panels, and the steering wheel. The thinking behind the job enlargement program is that by increasing the variety of tasks and skills, the employee's interest in the work being performed will be increased.

Organizations that have a series of routine jobs that cannot be enlarged or enriched might choose to rotate employees from one job to another. Job rotation also is a good work design strategy when the employee does not find the activity challenging. At that point the employee would be rotated to another job at the same level that requires a similar set of skills. The assembly-line worker whose initial job was to install front seats year-round now would rotate every work shift to another task: installing back seats the next shift, door panels the shift after, then electrical panels, and so on.

As the impact of job enlargement was being explored, a new movement started to emerge. Frederick Herzberg, the advocate of *job enrichment,* put forward some work design principles for scientific job enrichment and reported positive results with them. As we saw in Module 6, according to Herzberg, "job enrichment seeks to improve both task efficiency and human satisfaction by means of building into people's jobs, quite specifically, greater scope for personal achievement and its recognition, more challenging and responsible work, and more opportunity for individual advancement and growth.''

The theoretical basis for the early formulation of job enrichment, the design principles, the implications, and some of the issues associated with this view can be found in Herzberg's *two-factor theory* of motivation discussed in Module 8.

The Job Characteristic Approach

To meet some of the limitations of job enrichment, researchers and practitioners began to concentrate on the characteristics of jobs and their relationship with work satisfaction and motivation. The **job characteristics approach** (a middle-ground theory that draws on both management practice and psychological theory and at the same time builds on the work of Herzberg and others) was developed by Hackman and Oldham.[22]

The theory is composed of five core job dimensions (skill variety, task identity, task significance, autonomy, and feedback), which influence three critical psychological states (experienced meaningfulness, experienced responsibility, and knowledge of results), which in turn affect a number of personal and work-related outcomes (high internal work motivation, high-quality work performance, high satisfaction with work, and low absenteeism and turnover). The relationships among the core job dimensions, critical psychological states, and outcomes are moderated by an individual's need for growth.

According to the job characteristics model (Fig. 13–6), any job can be described in terms of its ''core job dimensions,'' which are said to contribute to the formation of the employee's ''critical psychological state.'' The dimensions are defined as follows:[23]

Figure 13–6
The Job Characteristics Model

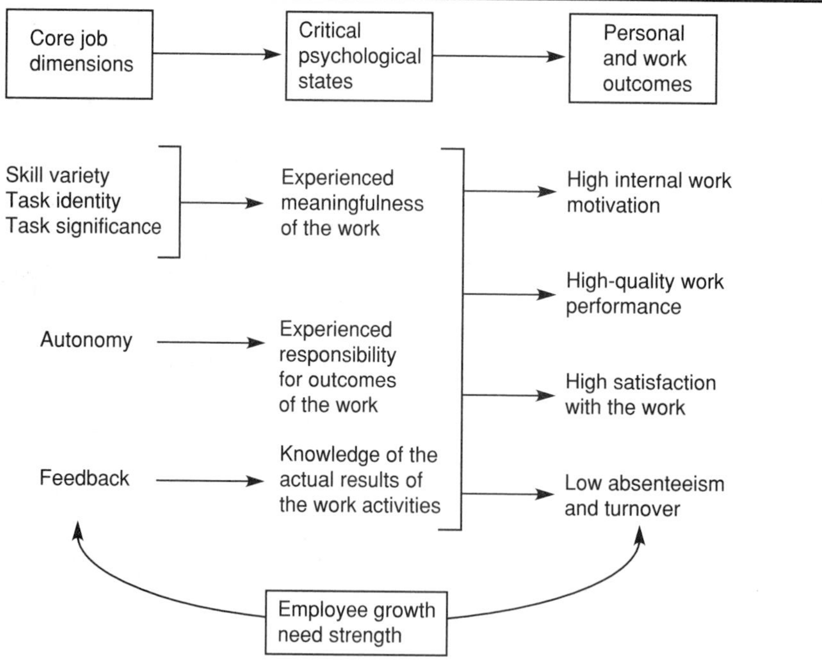

Source: J. R. Hackman and G. R. Oldham, *Work Design* (Reading, Mass.: Addison-Wesley Publishing, 1980), p. 90, Fig. 4.6. Reprinted with permission.

Skill variety—the degree to which a job requires a variety of different activities that involve the use of a number of different skills and talents.

Task identity—the degree to which the job requires completion of a whole and identifiable piece of work, that is, doing a job from beginning to end.

Task significance—the degree to which the job has a substantial impact on the lives or work of other people, whether in the immediate organization or in the external environment.

Autonomy—the degree to which the job provides substantial freedom, independence, and discretion to the individual in scheduling the work and in determining the procedures to be used in carrying it out.

Skill variety, task identity, and task significance contribute to the psychological state of experienced meaningfulness of work. Autonomy contributes to experienced responsibility for work outcomes. Feedback contributes to the knowledge of work results. The model further advocates that three psychological states affect employees' satisfaction and motivation. The three psychological states are

Experienced meaningfulness: The person must experience the work as generally important, valuable, and worthwhile.

Experienced responsibility: The individual must feel personally responsible and accountable for the results of the work he or she performs.

Knowledge of results: The individual must have an understanding, on a fairly regular basis, of how effectively he or she is performing the job.

The growth need strength—which refers to an individual's need to learn, need for accomplishment, and need for challenging work—moderates how people will react to work at two important points in the model. The first point is the link between the five core job dimensions and the three psychological states. The second point is between the psychological states and the outcome variable. High growth need individuals are more likely to experience the psychological states than are low growth need individuals at the first moderating point when jobs are enriched by the five core job dimensions. High growth need individuals are more likely to respond favorably to the psychological states than are low growth need individuals.

An important aspect of the job characteristic model is the **motivational potential score (MPS).**[24] The MPS is a way to measure the degree that the five core dimensions are perceived in the work itself. These dimensions are measured using the Job Diagnostic Survey (JDS), a questionnaire developed by Hackman and Oldham. The significance of this aspect is that it establishes a value for evaluating work prior to and following work redesign. The MPS is calculated as follows:

$$\begin{array}{c}\text{Motivating}\\ \text{potential}\\ \text{score}\end{array} = \frac{\begin{array}{c}\text{Skill}\\ \text{variety}\end{array} + \begin{array}{c}\text{Task}\\ \text{variety}\end{array} + \begin{array}{c}\text{Task}\\ \text{significance}\end{array}}{3} \times \text{Autonomy} \times \text{Feedback}$$

As with many models and theories of human behavior, some believe that there is a need for more methodological and theoretical improvements in regards to (1) the proposed theoretical relationships,[25] (2) the model's ability to predict performance, (3) the measurement of job characteristics,[26] (4) its failure to account for the influence of organizational contexts on employee responses to task, and (5) the psychometric properties of the instrument itself.[27] Although the model proposed by Hackman and Oldham is not the final answer, it provides a useful framework for understanding and guiding work design explorations.

Job Sharing, Flexible Work Schedules, Part-Time Workers, and Contracting Out

With increasing work force diversity and greater attention to payroll costs, many companies have adopted flexible employment practices. Some of the practices have origins in social movements of the 1960s and 1970s, while others became common in the recent era of downsizing and restructuring. **Flexible work schedules** give employees the latitude and freedom (often within established parameters) to determine their own work schedule. Four types of work scheduling have been semi-institutionalized: *compressed work week* (for example, a reduction in days per week from five days at eight hours per day to four days at 10 hours per day), *permanent part-time employment* (as in sharing a job with another person), *rotated shift work* (such as morning, afternoon, or evening on a rotated basis), and *flextime* (allowing employees to determine when they start and finish work within a given time frame). Employees are usually required to be present during certain daily core hours under flextime.

Some flexible employment practices represent the dark side of human resources management in the 1990s, as viewed by employees. The threat of unemployment resurfaced in the 1980s and continues into the 1990s under tight product market competition. Because of the aging baby boom generation, unemployment affects more older workers with higher income loss and greater difficulties obtaining reemployment. Major cuts within middle management and staff ranks have extended insecurity of employment to white collar workers. In the 1990s restructuring is a strategic decision to redeploy the organization's resources.[28] Downsizing continues in the face of prosperity. Part of restructuring involves holding a portion of jobs for **part-time, temporary, and leased employees;** this allows managers to staff the workplace according to peaks and valleys in work demands, while driving down wage and benefit costs. Part-time and temporary employees commonly receive lower wages and fewer benefits. Increasingly, employers are also reviewing noncore work activities and administrative services to determine whether contracting out is feasible. Contracting out or what some call out-sourcing is the use of other firms with specific expertise to perform tasks that the organization chooses not to carry out in-house. Contracting out functions such as information systems support and training reduces overhead and the number of staff support employees. These trends are expected to continue into the next decade.

Designs for the 21st Century

The age we live in demands learning and flexibility. Planning and traditional management functions are still valuable, but must be loosened to recognize changing business conditions. In designing organizations to meet the new challenges, we can learn from authors such as William Ouchi (*Theory Z*), Tom Peters (*Thriving on Chaos* and *Liberation Management*), David Nadler (*Organizational Architecture*), and Jay Galbraith (*Competing with Flexible Lateral Organizations* and *Organizing for the Future*).[29] New forms of structure are emerging to meet challenges associated with global competition, and they promise to create both societal benefits and problems. Let's explore two of the new organizational forms: the network structure and the fractal organization.

Network Organizations

The idea of adopting forms of structure that can flexibly adjust to the environment has great appeal to executives in leading organizations. One of the new forms, the network structure, blends traditional management concepts such as the value of management planning and controls with market concepts such as exchange agreements. Network forms of structure rely heavily on contracting out and outsourcing in lieu of owning and operating functions internally. Network arrangements have a long history. In the construction industry, an example is a general contractor who relies on subcontractors to perform the bulk of construction work on (say) an expensive home. Subcontractors bid on plumbing and other aspects of a job, giving the general contractor some discretion and cost control without the headaches of total management of the resources involved. The subcontractors are aware of the interdependencies with other parts of the network and are willing to share information, cooperate with each other, and customize their contribution to fit the overall design. In contrast with this construction industry example, the network structure applied to industrial organizations is a relatively new concept. Movement toward the network form became apparent in the 1980s when international competition and rapid technological change forced restructuring of U.S. industries and companies. Companies downsized to their core areas of competence and established alliances with independent suppliers and distributors. The new industrial firm network structure brought suppliers, producers, and distributors together in unique arrangements that could be stable and long-lasting, or be dynamic and exist for a single project. Moreover, large companies now use networks *within* existing structures to achieve market benefits by having divisions of the company buy and sell outside the firm as well as within. The network form has been observed in semiconductor, computer, automobile, farm equipment, motorcycle, athletic shoe and apparel, and health care organizations among others.[30] Figure 13–7 shows an example.

Figure 13–7
Dynamic Network Form

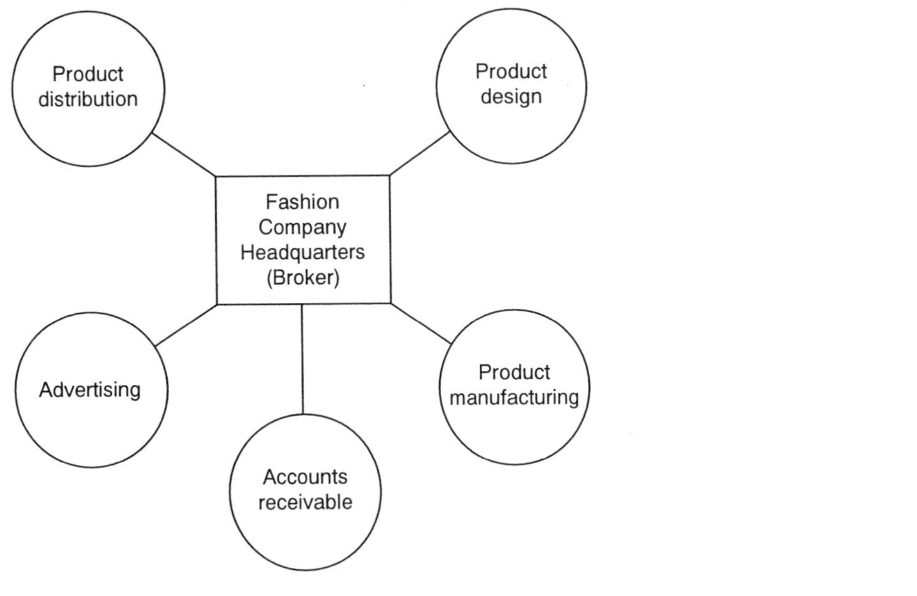

Fractal Organizations

William Pasmore notes that one of the most exciting developments to emerge in the physical sciences is the discovery of the fractal, which is a basic building block of complex and chaotic-appearing systems.[31] In brief, fractals are repetitive images that appear when computers run programs based on nonlinear equations; order in chaos. Pasmore's example of this phenomenon in everyday life is an antique quilt in which each geometric shape (for example, a diamond) is repeated, first on a tiny scale and then on larger and larger scales. The resulting quilt is not a picture of chaos, but of order. Each midsize pattern is a holographic piece of the entire structure; in it is the code that enables the rest of the quilt to be assembled. There is room in the quilt for local variation, as long as shared rules are followed. Figure 13–8 shows a quiltlike fractal organization design.

The analogy is that individuals are the small diamonds in the quilt within organizations. Individuals vary in qualities and characteristics, but do fit into the larger structure of the organization. Individuals share certain basic values, pursue common goals, and act as part of the whole. Periodically, people with the same backgrounds and perspectives come together to explore issues in depth and to advance the state of their knowledge. At other times large assemblies with the entire range of diversity in the system come together to consider problems faced by the whole organization, gain the perspective of the quilt maker, and make certain that the overall pattern is emerging as planned. Knowledge has much to do with success. While most accountants in the finance department know relatively little about steel making in a basic steel company, it helps if a few accountants understand steel making just as it helps if a few steel makers know about accounting.

As Japanese organizations have learned, it is valuable to have employee mobility across organizational functions. In our *organizational quilt* it is possible to acquire diversity through the temporary inclusion of individuals with different characteristics. Each unit has access to resources possessed by the larger organization. The more flexible individuals are, the more flexible the overall organization can be. The organization functions with a mix of specialists with master skills and enough generalists for flexibility. Moving away from the limits of our quilt analogy, organizational units can vary in size and other characteristics to meet local conditions without destroying the symmetry of the larger organization. That is, different-sized production plants can be created

Figure 13–8
Fractal Organization Design

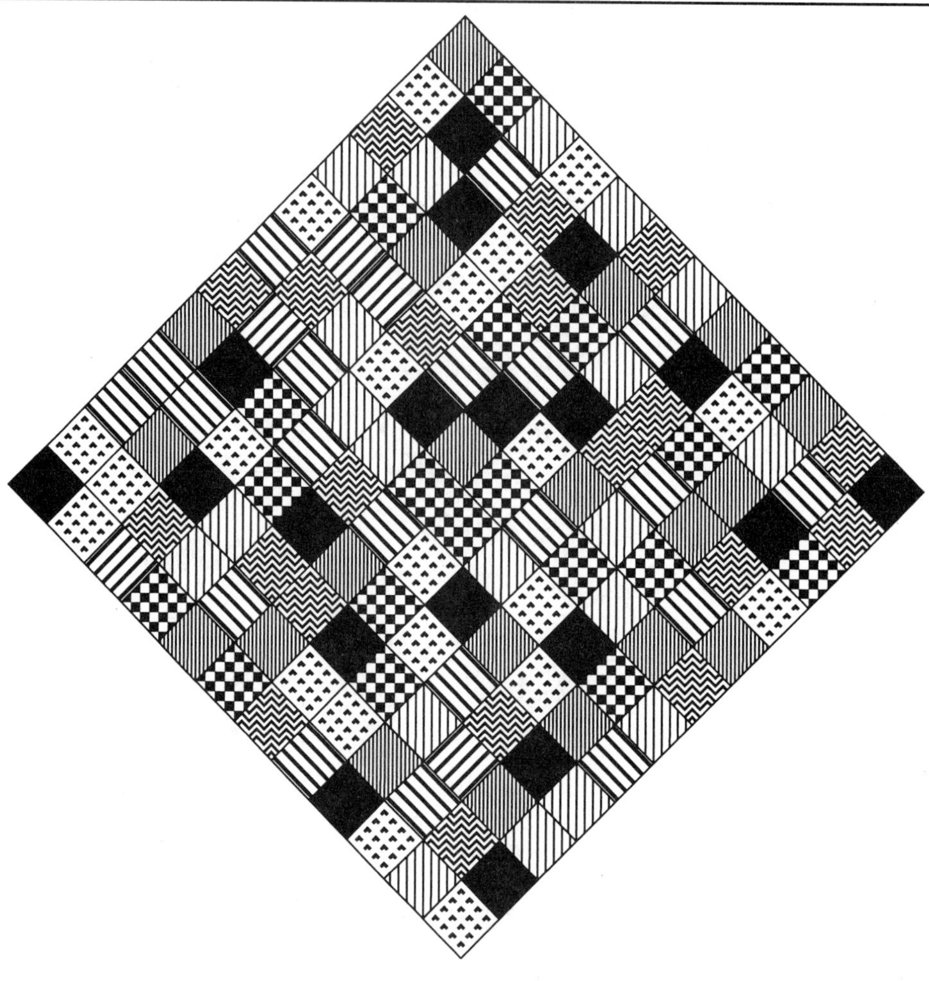

Source: Adopted from W. A. Pasmore, *Creating Strategic Change: Designing the Flexible, High Performing Organization* (New York: John Wiley & Sons, 1994).

to meet specific business needs, new units can be quickly formed to capitalize on a research breakthrough, and scientists at diverse locations can contribute to problem solving at one division of the company through telecomputing and other information technology.

Pasmore believes that the fractal organization, in contrast with other high-performing systems, has similar patterns at the top and bottom of the organization. That is, multiskilled, self-managing teams are good at the shop floor level as well as at corporate headquarters. Corporate units are patterned after the rest of the quilt, and can be staffed by people who come from other parts of the organization on a temporary basis. The fractal organization does not have a specific new organization chart. Fractal design offers flexibility for managers and organization designers, both in the total design and in local work units.

Summary

Under increasing competitive conditions, companies will explore more flexible ways of organizing human and other resources. Design of the total organization, departments, work units, and jobs is a complex undertaking. We have discussed several design orientations to facilitate work redesign. The information processing and sociotechnical systems models are the leading total design approaches. Both models recognize the importance of information technology, the need for lateral coordination, and the value of team concepts. Recent experiments with team concepts such as sociotechnical system teams and off-line quality improvement teams have produced major benefits and are expected to continue into the 21st century. At the individual job level, job enrichment, job rotation, and flexible employment practices will increasingly be tried in the workplace.

The way work is designed influences the performance, effectiveness, productivity, and satisfaction of individuals in organizational settings. Work redesign is a key organizational process that promises to have profound impact in many industries. Decisions that managers make regarding work design, while they contain many contingencies, determine organization success. Accordingly, the knowledge of different organization design approaches, their strengths and weaknesses, and the extent to which they fit specific organization cultures will be increasingly valuable to managers in the 21st century.

Study Questions

1. Why is design an important consideration at this point in history?
2. Explain the importance of "fit" in organization design.
3. Compare and contrast the information processing and STS approaches to organization redesign.
4. List the main forms of structure and describe their advantages and disadvantages.
5. How do STS teams differ from off-line teams?
6. What are some major differences between the early approaches to work design (job engineering, scientific management) and more recent approaches (job enrichment, job characteristics approach)?
7. Will job enrichment work in every work situation? What factors can make it difficult to implement job enrichment?
8. Discuss the relationship between work design, expectations, motivation, and leadership.

Endnotes

1. A. B. (Rami) Shani and M. W. Stebbins, "Organization Design: Emerging Trends," *Consultation: An International Journal* 6, no. 3 (1989), pp. 187–194.

2. M. W. Stebbins and A. B. (Rami) Shani, "Organization Design: Beyond the 'Mafia' Model," *Organizational Dynamics,* Winter 1989, pp. 18–30.

3. D. Nadler and M. Tushman, *Strategic Organization Design* (Glenview, Ill.: Scott Foresman, 1988), p. 10.

4. J. R. Galbraith, *Organization Design* (Reading, Mass.: Addison-Wesley, 1977), p. 5.

5. M. W. Stebbins, J. A. Sena, and A. B. (Rami) Shani, "Information Technology and Organization Design," *Journal of Information Technology* 9, no. 3 (1995). In press.

6. For additional material on the evolution of STS theory, see W. A. Pasmore, *Designing Effective Organizations: The Sociotechnical Systems Perspective* (New York: John Wiley, 1988); J. C. Taylor and D. F. Felten, *Performance by Design: Sociotechnical Systems in North America* (Englewood Cliffs, N.J.: Prentice Hall, 1993); and A. B. (Rami) Shani and O. Elliott, "Sociotechnical Systems in Transition," in *The Emerging Practice of Organization Development,* eds. W. Sikes, A. Drexler, and J. Grant (La Jolla Calif.: University Associates, 1988), pp. 187–98.

7. See, for example, W. A. Pasmore and K. Gurley, "Enhancing R&D across Functional Areas," in *Making Organizations Competitive,* ed. R. H. Kilmann (San Francisco: Jossey-Bass, 1991); and M. W. Stebbins, and A. B. (Rami) Shani, "Organization Design and the Knowledge Worker," *Leadership and Organization Development Journal* 16, no. 1 (1995), pp. 23–30.

8. There is a growing literature on self-design. See, for example, B. Hedberg, P. Nystrom, and W. Starbuck, "Camping on Seesaws: Prescriptions for a Self-Designing Organization," *Administrative Science Quarterly* 21 (1976), pp. 41–65; S. A. Mohrman and T. G. Cummings, *Self-Designing Organizations: Learning How to Create High Performance* (Reading, Mass.: Addison-Wesley, 1989); K. E. Weick, "Organization Design: Organizations as Self-Designing Systems," *Organizational Dynamics,* Autumn 1977, pp. 31–46; and K. E. Weick, "Organizational Redesign as Improvisation," in *Organizational Change and Redesign,* eds. G. P. Huber and W. H. Glick, pp. 346–76. (New York: The Free Press, 1993).

9. See R. L. Daft, *Organization Theory and Design* (St. Paul, Minn.: West Publishing, 1995), for foundation material on structure and design.

10. J. R. Galbraith, *Competing with Flexible Lateral Organizations,* 2d ed. (Reading, Mass.: Addison-Wesley, 1994).

11. T. Stewart, "Are You Flat, Lean, and Ready for a Bold New Look? Try High Performance Teams, Redesigned Work, and Unbridled Information," *Fortune,* May 18, 1992, pp. 93–98.

12. W. A. Pasmore, *Creating Strategic Change: Designing the Flexible, High Performing Organization* (New York: John Wiley, 1994).

13. P. Osterman, "How Common Is Workplace Transformation and Who Adopts It?" *Industrial and Labor Relations Review* 47, no. 2 (January 1994).

14. J. Cutcher-Gershenfeld and 14 other authors, "Japanese Team-Based Work System in North America: Explaining the Diversity," *California Management Review* 37, no. 1 (Fall 1994).

15. See E. Trist and K. Bamforth, "Some Social and Psychological Consequences of the Longwall Method of Coal Getting," *Human Relations* 1 (1951), pp. 3–38.

16. F. E. Emery and M. Emery, "Participative Design: Work and Community Life, Parts 1–3," in *Participative Design for Participative Democracy,* ed. M. Emery (Canberra: Australian National University, Center for Continuing Education, 1989); and Taylor and Felton, *Performance by Design.*

17. Gulowsen's work is based on P. G. Herbst, *Alternative to Hierarchies* (Leiden, The Netherlands: Nijhoff, 1976); E. Thorsrud, "Democracy at work: Norwegian Experiences with Non-bureaucratic Forms of Organization," *Journal of Applied Behavioral Science* 13, no. 3 (1977), pp. 410–21; and M. Elden, "Sociotechnical Systems Ideas as Public Policy in "Norway: Empowering Participation through Worker-Managed Change," *Journal of Applied Behavior Science* 22, no. 3 (1986), pp. 239–55.

18. Cutcher-Gershenfeld et al., "Japanese Team-Based Work System," p. 47.

19. F. W. Taylor, *The Principles of Scientific Management* (New York: Harper & Row, 1911); and Frank Gilbreth and Lillian Gilbreth, *Cheaper by the Dozen* (New York: Harper & Row, 1947).

20. R. C. Davis, *The Fundamentals of Top Management* (New York: Harper & Row, 1951).

21. F. Herzberg, "One More Time: How Do You Motivate Employees?" *Harvard Business Review* 46 (1968), pp. 53–62.

22. J. R. Hackman and G. R. Oldham, "Motivation through the Design of Work: Test and a Theory," *Organization Behavior and Human Performance* 19 (1976), pp. 250–79.

23. J. R. Hackman, "Work Design," in *Improving Life at Work,* eds. J. R. Hackman and J. L. Suttle (Santa Monica, Calif.: Goodyear, 1977).

24. J. R. Hackman and G. R. Oldham, *Work Design* (Reading, Mass.: Addison-Wesley, 1980).

25. R. M. Steers and R. T. Modway, "The Motivational Properties of Tasks," *Academy of Management Review* 2 (1977), pp. 645–58.

26. T. D. Wall, C. W. Clegg, and P. R. Jackson, "An Evaluation of the Job Characteristics Model," *Journal of Occupational Psychology* 51 (1978), pp. 183–96.

27. K. H. Roberts and W. Glick, "The Job Characteristics Approach to Task Design: A Critical Review," *Journal of Applied Psychology* 66 (1981), pp. 193–217.

28. S. Freeman and K. Cameron, "Organizational Downsizing: A Convergence and Reorientation Framework," *Organizational Science* 4, no. 1 (1993), pp. 10–29.

29. See W. G. Ouchi, "Markets, Bureaucracies, and Clans," *Administrative Science Quarterly* 25 (1980), pp. 129–41; Tom Peters, *Thriving on Chaos* (New York: Knopf, 1987); D. A. Nadler, M. S. Gerstein, and R. B. Shaw, *Organizational Architecture: Designs for Changing Organizations* (San Francisco: Jossey-Bass, 1992); Galbraith, *Competing with Flexible Lateral*

Organizations and J. R. Galbraith and E. E. Lawler, *Organizing for the Future: The New Logic for Managing Complex Organizations* (San Francisco: Jossey-Bass, 1993).

30. For a closer look at network organizations, see R. Miles and C. Snow, ''Organizations: New Concepts for New Forms,'' *California Management Review* 28, no. 3 (1986); and C. C. Snow, R. E. Miles, and J. Coleman, ''Managing 21st Century Network Organizations,'' *Organizational Dynamics,* Winter 1989, pp. 18–30.

31. Pasmore, *Creating Strategic Change,* p. 219.

Activity 13–3: Colonial Automobile Association: Job Design Inventory

Objectives:

a. To analyze jobs on different job dimensions.

b. To involve students in a job enrichment opportunity.

Task 1:

Read the Colonial Automobile Association case, with a special focus on Susan Quayle's job as claims adjustor. Then work alone to complete the following worksheet. (*Alternative:* The instructor may ask you to focus on one of your past jobs instead, and follow the same steps listed below.)

a. With the instructor's direction, list knowledge and skills Susan must have to perform her job. Group the knowledge and skills under the various job dimension categories. For example, under Skill Variety, the job requires communication and computer skills among others.

b. After listing required knowledge and skills on the five dimensions, rate Susan's job using the worksheet's seven-point scale. Assign a score for each dimension and enter it to the left.

c. Predict Susan's degree of general job satisfaction using the same scale.

Task 2:

a. Individuals share with other members of the group their lists of knowledge and skills required, and ratings on all job dimensions.

b. The instructor will provide Susan's own ratings for comparative purposes. Strengths and weaknesses will be discussed.

c. The instructor will give a brief lecture on job characteristics and job enrichment theories, preparing students to rebuild Susan's job.

Task 3:

Group members use job enrichment theory and their own ideas to rebuild Susan's job.

a. Individuals work alone to list job enrichment ideas and other design options.

b. Groups discuss their ideas and prepare a consolidated list of the most promising ideas.

c. A spokesperson from each group reports out to the entire class.

d. The instructor comments on the proposed changes and discusses additional ideas raised by students in past OB classes.

This activity was contributed by Professor Michael Stebbins, College of Business, California Polytechnic State University, San Luis Obispo, California 93407. We are grateful to Professor Stebbins.

Scale: 1 = Extremely low
2 = Very low
3 = Somewhat low
4 = Neither high nor low
5 = Somewhat high
6 = Very high
7 = Extremely high

__________ *Skill variety.* The degree to which the job requires a variety of activities that challenge her or his skills and talents.

__________ *Task identity.* The degree to which a job requires completion of a whole and identifiable piece of work (doing a job from start to finish).

__________ *Task significance.* The degree to which the job has a substantial impact on the lives or work of other people.

__________ *Autonomy.* The degree to which the job gives freedom, independence, and discretion to the individual in scheduling the work and carrying it out.

__________ *Feedback from the job.* The degree to which the worker, in carrying out the work activities, gets direct and clear information about the effectiveness of her or his performance.

__________ *Overall job satisfaction.* A global rating of satisfaction with all aspects of the job.

Case Study: Colonial Automobile Association

In 1989, Susie Quayle interviewed for a position with Colonial Automobile Association (CAA), in hopes of landing a job as a claims adjustor with the firm. Two days following her interview, she received a phone call from Mr. Taylor, manager of the claims department at CAA, offering her a position as an adjustor—level I. All college graduates started at adjustor–level I throughout CAA.

Prior to arriving at CAA, Susie Quayle, like all of the other entry-level adjustors, was required to spend approximately two and one-half weeks training, learning how to operate the company computer, filling out computerized claim forms, and filling out all of the paperwork required as part of the task of being an adjustor. In training, management stressed the importance of maintaining "a high level of customer service." Management believed that high customer service translated into higher overall productivity; thus management was measured on productivity (i.e., the number of claims processed and completed monthly).

The theme of productivity carried over into motivation and job enrichment at CAA, which consisted of monthly contests between adjustors based largely on volume of processed claims. Subrogation contests, an effort to retrieve money from outstanding claims in favor of CAA, was another area in which management tried to stimulate employee motivation by offering bonuses to employees who collected the firm's outstanding claims.

Following her preparation training at the corporate office, Ms. Quayle assumed her position as a claims adjustor at the Colonial offices in Palo Alto, California.

Colonial AA–Palo Alto

CAA–Palo Alto employed 15 entry-level claims adjustors at a modest salary of $1,800 per month. Each adjustor was responsible for processing 10 to 15 new claims daily. The nature of these claims varied from auto accidents to vandalism to injuries. In addition to new claims filed daily, each adjustor was responsible for all pending claims in her file. (The statute of a claim in the state of California is three years.)

Processing claims included roughly 45 minutes of interaction with the customer or claimant. Additional time to prepare and file paperwork as well as to follow up with the respective parties involved was necessary. For example, one auto claim could conceivably involve (1) the CAA client, (2) the claimant, (3) the claimant's insurance company, (4) a rental agency, (5) an injured party, (6) medical expertise, (7) auto body quotes, (8) police reports, and (9) a decision as to who is liable (at fault).

When Susie Quayle arrived at CAA, she found over 200 pending claim files at her cubicle. These files belonged to the individual whom she replaced. Overwhelmed at the sight of over 200 claim files, she had no idea what to do. So she decided to ask the adjustor working adjacent to her cubicle. He told her not to worry about it because he had about 250 pending files of his own.

Following this brief conversation, Susie's telephone range. She politely answered the phone and engaged in a conversation with a rather abrupt and agitated customer. Unable to help the customer, she jotted down his problem and a phone number, promising to return the call as soon as she could find a solution.

Susie's day continued with more phone calls from disgruntled customers demanding resolution from the insurance company. Her daily mail included new insurance claims.

Energetic and determined to get the job done, Susie maintained a positive attitude toward her work for several weeks. However, her outlook changed as more claims rolled in on a daily basis, mail began to pile up, phones rang off the hook, customers continued to complain, management's pressure to control monthly targets mounted, and outside parties to claims demanded instant resolution. To say the least, Susie Quayle was overwhelmed.

Distraught by pressures at work, Susie engaged in an after-work discussion with several of her peers. She asked each adjustor whether they were going through similar challenges and pressures. One adjustor pointed out that Susie should not take the problems too seriously. ''Everyone is overworked and underpaid. Just take a day or two off once in a while,'' he said. Susie brought up management's goal of meeting its monthly claim targets and was told by another adjustor that ''management doesn't really care as long as we come close. The worst thing that can happen is that your name is posted at the end of the month with the number of completed claims next to it.'' She added, ''I would rather have my name and claims posted than have my goofy picture on the 'adjustor of the month' plaque at the reception desk.'' As for the subrogation contest, Susie was told not to bother with it because it was not worth the bonus for the amount of time spent on each file. As one adjustor noted, ''Besides, Bill Baron wins every month because he has been here the longest (18 months) and knows how to cut corners.''

Activity 13–4: Kate and Jake's Flaky Cakes—A Self-Design Simulation

Objectives:

a. To demonstrate the use of self-design theory within a familiar setting.
b. To provide students an experience in organizational problem solving.
c. To demonstrate the iterative nature of self-design and the principle of continuous learning.

Task 1:

This activity is based on a short case supplemented by role descriptions for people in the Kate and Jake's organization. You are to read the case plus an assigned role description along with other material provided by the instructor before attending class.

Task 2:

The instructor will introduce the activity and present materials on the self-design approach including steps in the design process. Groups will be formed with 9 to 11 members each. Participants should review the case and then each person should discuss her or his own responsibilities as covered in the role description, as well as problems experienced in performing the work. The case and the roles can be found in Appendix Q.

Task 3:

Each group should agree on the main issues and write them down. The next step is to formulate design criteria. A list of criteria must be recorded before the group moves to Task 4.

Task 4:

Each group will generate one alternative design to address the current situation. The design should be summarized on a flip chart, white board, or chalk board so that the rest of the class can view it. The group should elect two people to act as spokespeople.

Task 5:

Spokespeople for each group will present their respective designs. If the room allows it, the rest of the class can move to the group's workstation for the presentation.

Task 6:

The instructor will lead a discussion on (1) the designs proposed and (2) learning about self-design as a process.

Source: This activity was contributed by Saraf Anjali and Chris Roth. We are grateful to them for their contribution.

14 Managing Total Quality

Learning Objectives

After completing this module you should be able to

1. Describe the evolution of the total quality concept.
2. Explain the reasons why managing total quality is a key organizational process.
3. Appreciate the variety of total quality philosophies, frameworks, and approaches.
4. Describe the key features of Total Quality Management.
5. Compare and contrast Total Quality Management and the economic theory of the firm.
6. Gain an insight into the relationship between total quality and individual, team, and organizational behavior.

List of Key Concepts

Continuous improvement
Parallel learning structure
Quality
Quality control
Quality improvement
Quality planning
Service quality
Statistical process control (SPC)
Structural support configuration
Total quality control
Total Quality Management (TQM)
Zero defects

Module Outline

Premodule Preparation

The instructor may give either of the following activities as a premodule assignment.

Activity 14–1: Quality, Human Behavior, and Performance: An Exploratory Investigation

Objectives:

a. To explore the meaning of quality.
b. To investigate the effect of quality on human behavior and performance.

Task 1 (Individual—Homework):

Individuals are to interview a manager about his or her perceptions of quality and its meaning in their organization. The interview should be scheduled for about 45 minutes. Here are some questions that might help you begin the joint exploration:

a. Tell me a little about what you do here.
b. What does quality mean to you?
c. What does quality and/or Total Quality Management mean in your firm?
d. Please describe any continuous improvement effort initiated in your company. Who were/are the key actors in the program? How was the program implemented? Identify the specific phases and/or activities. What effect did the program have on individual and team behavior? What effect did the program have on performance and productivity?
e. What were the effects of the program on the way everyday business was conducted?
f. Discuss the strengths and weaknesses of the quality effort.

Task 2 (Team—Homework):

a. Individuals are to meet in their teams and share their findings and learning.
b. After reviewing the findings, the team is to identify similarities and differences between the managers' perceptions.
c. Prepare a two-page synopsis of your team findings and a five-minute presentation to the class.

Task 3 (Classroom):

a. The instructor will have each team share its learning with the class.
b. Based on the teams' findings and the current body of knowledge, the instructor will facilitate a class discussion about the meaning of quality and human behavior.
c. The instructor will give a short lecture on the interface between the process of managing quality and human behavior.

Activity 14–2: The Travel Agency: A Case of Quality Management

Objectives:

a. To explore the mean features of quality in a small business environment.
b. To investigate the effect of quality on human behavior and performance.

Task 1 (Homework):

Participants are to read the case on The Travel Agency and answer the questions at its end.

Task 2 (Class):

The instructor will facilitate class discussion based on the individuals' answers.

Case Study: The Travel Agency

Patricia Wood sat back and reviewed her past quarter's performance figures again. Even though the local economy had been somewhat sluggish recently, she had the feeling that The Travel Agency was nearly 15 percent behind the previous year's second-quarter revenue numbers. As she pondered the implications of the balance sheet in front of her, Pat remembered a recent seminar on Total Quality Management (TQM) and how speakers noted the importance of quality in a service operation as a competitive strategy. As she put away the budget files and locked the office, Pat made a mental note to find her meeting records and review the quality concepts that had been presented.

History

Pat had started The Travel Agency in 1978 and had experienced steady growth to nearly $1.7 million in booking revenues in the past year. The office, located within easy walking distance from downtown Santa Bahia, now had five full-time employees plus two part-time people. The city had only 50,000 residents but a high proportion of professionals and upper-middle–class demographics. Currently, Pat estimated the agency's market position at number three in the city with just over 17 percent of the total travel agency business. Recently, Pat had created a new division that catered exclusively to the "carriage trade" by offering upscale ocean cruise vacations. Though the business as a whole was doing well, Pat believed that changes in the travel industry were eroding her profits. The air travel business yielded a steady 8 to 10 percent margin. Cruise margins were somewhat larger at 12 to 17 percent. But customers were demanding more service, and the travel providers (airlines, cruise lines, hotels, etc.) were asking the agencies to provide additional freebies. Pat was proud that all of her agents were certified travel consultant (CTC) professionals. This certification required that the agents take special courses that were highly recognized by industry standards. Pat had a standing policy of encouraging visibility, and she was a frequent participant at business seminars and travel expositions. She had a high profile in the local community in social and professional areas, and she was one of the first women invited to join the Rotary Club. She attempted to stay current on industry trends, and recently she asked a business school student team from the local university to review The Travel Agency and to make recommendations for the coming decade. The comprehensive report included many good suggestions, but the bottom line was that in a fixed-percentage business, profit was dependent on increased volume.

The Industry

The travel agency industry serves both leisure and business travelers in nearly equal proportions. Transportation deregulation (specifically airline deregulation in 1978) has changed the framework of the industry during the past decade. Agency booking has grown from $20 to $80 billion over the past 10 years. During the same time, the number of agencies has grown from 14,800 to more than 30,000. Two-thirds of these have average booking revenue of less than $2 million. Cruise sales were 15 percent of agency sales (1989), followed by hotels (11 percent), car rentals (8 percent), rail (4 percent), and other (4 percent). Air transportation continues to dominate agency business at 58 percent of revenues. The industry expects cruise business to continue to rise during the 1990s. Domestic travel accounts for 70 percent of agency sales today. Average agency revenue was $2.6 million in 1989, and the typical agency employed 6.3 people. Nearly 68 percent of agencies are single-location, 19 percent are branches, and 13 percent are home-office locations. Most (86 percent) are not affiliated with any association for corporate travel and fewer (61 percent) are nonaffiliated for vacation travel.

Source: This case was contributed by Professor Ray M. Haynes. College of Business, California Polytechnic State University, San Luis Obispo, California 93407. We are grateful to Professor Haynes.

Technology has played a vital role in the expansion of the travel agency industry. The most significant factor is the wide-scale proliferation of computerized reservation systems (CRS). There are several systems on the market, each identified with a major trunk airline. The SABRE system, offered by American Airlines, commands more than 50 percent of the market with 15,500 agency customers. Others include APOLLO (United), SYSTEM ONE (Texas Air/EDS), and WORLDSPAN (Delta, TWA, and Northwest). Worldwide several smaller systems are emerging. A travel agency with a CRS terminal can find the lowest fare and best schedule, can book and confirm all air and ground services, and even can issue a boarding pass along with the ticket within a matter of minutes. The larger CRS providers offer accounting packages, frequent flier tracking, and a host of attendant software to help manage agency operations.

The second area of technology implementation is electronic funds transfer. The industry clearinghouse, Airline Remittance Corporation (ARC), clears all accounts for both carriers and agencies on a weekly basis. Should funds not be available, penalties and reserve bonds can be invoked that deplete the already small margin for the agencies. The avalanche of special fares, restricted tickets, and changing fare structures have made daily agency operations an administrative nightmare for many.

The travel agent functions as a knowledge broker by providing both individuals and groups with high-speed access to the wide range of travel information. The agent facilitates customer selection of travel arrangements and provides the necessary documentation, including tickets, visas, currency exchanges, transfers, and special-handling needs. The agent must possess a high level of technical skill to operate the gateway systems (CRS) while maintaining an expertise in dealing with people. In both areas, the agent must constantly train and develop both cybernetic and social techniques. The electronic interfaces are constantly developing new and improved features that require continued education of the travel agent. The traveler is becoming more sophisticated and often requires special attention regarding both real and imagined needs. The travel agent has emerged from being a schedule reader and ticket writer into a full-fledged professional consultant. Combining the complex travel environment with the necessary technical and social skills means that the successful agent must be flexible, intelligent, and open to change to remain efficient and effective in a dynamic regulation- and rule-based operations arena.

Pat's Dilemma

Pat knew from the consultants' report that her performance numbers were generally better than the industry ratios, but she also knew that The Travel Agency needed higher productivity to continue to grow. Her notes from the seminar on quality and productivity indicated several relationships that she thought would be useful for her planning.

First, there was the basic definition of *productivity* that considered the ratio of input to output. She knew that outputs were aggregate booking revenues and that inputs were the resource costs of securing the output level. Productivity could be raised by either increasing outputs or reducing inputs. Pat reasoned that if the market was sluggish, she might have to focus on the input side—and, like any service, this meant people. More specifically, the people were the employees of The Travel Agency.

Second, she came across a definition of *service quality* in a service operation. The speaker had emphasized how the customer is directly involved in a service and the quality of the service is based on the level of satisfaction achieved. The diagram was something like this:

CUSTOMER's → EXPECTATION → EXPERIENCE → SATISFACTION

If the experience is better than the expectation, satisfaction—and quality— are high. If the experience is less than the expectation, satisfaction—and quality—are low. If the experience equals the expectation, satisfaction—and quality—are average. Furthermore, marketing and advertising create the expectation, the actual service operation delivers the experience, and human behavior establishes the relationship between the two.

Third, the concept of Total Quality Management (TQM) requires that all of the people involved in the operation are aware of the quality emphasis and the underlying rationale. Pat reasoned that for a service operation like The Travel Agency, she had three sets of people groups involved. Pat and the employees of the agency formed one group, the customers using their service were another, and the actual service providers (airline, hotel, etc.) formed a third group. Each group certainly had expectations of quality, uniquely defined within its own expectation–experience scenario. However, each group had some degree of appreciation of the group interrelationships because of the high people contact nature of the service delivery involving all three groups.

Now that Pat had reviewed some of the basic quality concepts, she felt ready to start conducting a more detailed analysis of her business within a framework of TQM.

Total Quality Management

Pat realized that TQM was not really a technique that could just be turned on and assure her that quality would improve. It seemed that TQM was more of a basic philosophy that required active participation on the part of management to really understand all major business factors that could have an impact on quality. TQM was highlighted as being an ongoing process that could be approached from the standpoint of continuous improvement in incremental stages. She read that the Japanese even had a word for this process, *kaisan.*

Pat began her analysis with the least controllable group, the service provider. She reviewed several quality issues associated with three key provider segments. In general, all were subject to getting the best possible value for Pat's customer, but recently other aspects offered factors that must be considered from a quality perspective. The airlines were fighting the issue of on-time performance and overall business stability. In the past decade, several major airlines, including Braniff, People Express, and MUSE, had succumbed to competitive pressures and gone out of business. Others, such as Eastern and Continental, teetered on the brink of bankruptcy and disrupted service. Based on these observations, Pat identified business stability, on-time performance, and the actual route (direct, via a hub, nonstop) as being vital quality factors for her customers. Therefore she maintained a careful watch on the providers and continually discussed options with her agents for them to consider when booking any customer in the future. If a customer insisted on a specific carrier, route, or fare, the agent was encouraged to discuss the ramifications of this selection in a tactful manner. The same issues were explored with respect to rental cars (airport location, free mileage, age of cars) and hotels (location, limousine service, room amenities, extras). In effect, Pat created a quality checkoff list for evaluating the provider selection. This aspect of choosing the actual provider was complicated by the dynamic fare environment and ticket restrictions. However, The Travel Agency endeavored to keep its customers informed on any special considerations that should be evaluated.

Attention to the user's/customer's expectations became the next area that Pat analyzed with respect to quality performance. She realized that her company offered virtually the same services but could remain an effective competitor by focusing more on the actual "services" delivered by the agent to the customer. She knew that each service "encounter" or customer transaction was highly individual and that her business had been built on the concept of truly personalized service. She recommended that her agents really take time to listen to the customer and make an effort to understand his or her particular needs. Even though the extra time spent on each customer could reduce the total volume of business that an individual agent could handle during a day, they all concurred that the special handling would pay off in being able to better match the customers' expectations to the actual travel arrangements. By creating a symbolic "brand loyalty" to The Travel Agency, Pat believed that the amount of repeat business would outweigh a pure volume orientation. A customer feedback survey was conducted to assist in establishing exactly what the customers' standards of excellence were with respect to traveling and using a travel agent.

Finally, Pat turned her quality audit analysis to her own employees. All five of them were seasoned professionals, and their average tenure with The Travel Agency was more than five years. Since Santa Bahia was a small town, salaries and perks were not as critical as in a large metropolitan area. However, Pat had always treated her employees as family and recognized work anniversaries, birthdays, and special accomplishments with regularity. She decided that one area that could be of interest was a stronger identification with The Travel Agency. She wanted them to think of their daily activity as being more than just going to work at a "job." After some discussion, she decided to initiate some team-building activities that included short seminars on quality and productivity facilitated by a local university professor. The second part of the employee plan was to make them actual "owners" in the travel company so she asked her attorney to look into distribution of small quantities of common stock. As a private corporation, the stock issue would be essentially symbolic, but she thought it might encourage the employees to think of The Travel Agency as their "own" company to a small degree and, as such, work just a little bit harder to do their jobs well. Pat's sense of whimsy took over for the final segment. She decided to have several high-quality cotton polo shirts made up with the company's logo design. These were distributed to the employees in a variety of colors to be worn during nonworking hours to show identification with The Travel Agency—their own company! Pat knew that these were tried and true human resource techniques that had been effectively used by many large and small companies, including America West Airlines, TRW, and General Motors. Paying attention to employees was a significant part of improving productivity in the famous Hawthorne studies. By combining attention, education, a sense of ownership, and humor, Pat believed that she could build an unbeatable esprit de corps that matched her employees' quality perceptions.

Finally, Pat gave some thought to the impact of technology in her business. She had been an early user of the SABRE CRS but decided to splurge and upgrade to American's new CRS, using PCs instead of dedicated terminals. The concept was to provide users with increased productivity through higher transaction rates and extended features. Next, she decided to add an answering service that would give her customers a prerecorded message identifying the agency's hours plus any weekly "specials" that were available. In order to give special attention to her cruise customers, a dedicated telephone line and number were added to the office rotary for direct access. Pat also planned to look into some of the newer electronic billing and payment mechanisms available through ARC and local financial institutions.

Endgame

Pat sat down and reviewed her notes and analyses with respect to the informal quality audit of The Travel Agency and proposed areas of concentration. Experience and discussion seemed to point to a potential for increasing the perceived and actual quality levels in her business. She knew it would not all happen tomorrow but felt confident that a gradual implementation would be rewarding to all participants in the business.

What do you think about her conclusions and quality implementation plan? The following questions may help direct your analysis of The Travel Agency, considering the topics presented in the chapter.

Questions

1. Given the information in the case, describe the nature and characteristics of The Travel Agency while using some of the organizational concepts described in Module 4.
2. What are some unique characteristics of the technical system or technology utilization in the travel industry?
3. How does the CRS technology seem to affect (1) human behavior, (2) design of work, and (3) individual and agency performance?
4. Consider each part of the quality assessment and plan described for The Travel

Agency. Discuss any major problems or opportunities that you would suggest Pat add to her evaluation.

5. Consider the general approach to conducting a quality audit. Would this activity be significantly different for a manufacturing organization compared to a service operation?

Introduction

The need to manage quality products and services continues to be a dominating force in the middle 1990s. The ability to manage the quality of products and services is dependent on the quality of the working relationship between human beings at the workplace. W. Edwards Deming and Joseph Juran started sending this basic message around 1950. Companies in every industrial sector would agree that to be competitive in the changing global market, firms need to better manage the quality of products and services.[1] The American Society for Quality Control and the Association for Quality through Participation estimate that there were over 250 books in the last 10 years with the word *quality* in their title. Most companies are beginning to compete based on quality.[2] The relationships among people and quality often take on special characteristics. The quality of our technology, the quality of our products or services, and the quality of our relationships with relevant others (whether they are peers, subordinates, leaders, customers, or suppliers) add emotional intensity to the workplace. This module examines major features of quality—as fundamental elements of organizational behavior—and their interdependent relationship with human behavior.

The Concept of Quality

Quality as a concept has been contemplated throughout history.[3] Yet, during the past decade, the concept of quality and its dynamics have captured the imagination of managers, organizational members, customers, scientists, and organizational consultants. Quality has become a buzz word across disciplines as business people, researchers, consultants, and organizational development experts strive to compete successfully in a rapidly changing global business environment. Quality is an area that is attracting a lot of action, research, and dialogue in a variety of business disciplines. Many definitions and perspectives of quality can be found. Furthermore, quality is often examined, studied, and implemented by organizations under a variety of labels such as *quality control, quality control circles, self-design teams, self-managed teams, quality assurance, quality service, customer focus, total quality control, quality function deployment, continuous improvement, reengineering,* and *Total Quality Management.*

Review of some of the written material reveals that for some people, quality is a way of thinking; for some, it is an approach to conducting and managing work; for some, it is a management philosophy; for some, it is a work method; for some, it is just another management ploy; for some, it is a religion or a cult; for some, it is a way to relate to the customer; for some, it is a movement toward an improved work environment and working conditions; for some, it is a way to optimize organizational resources; for some, it is an outcome such as a ratio in the reduction of number of product defects (many times being measured by defective parts per million); yet for some, it is the dynamics of behavioral processes rather than a finished product.

A recent study that focused on employees' perception of quality found two clusters of quality constructs: a quality orientation that individuals seem to have internalized and a quality orientation that is more company-specific. Here is a partial list of definitions of *quality* as articulated by organizational members: integrity of numbers, job security, defect-free incoming materials, up-front relationship with vendors, no functional defects, testing verification, error-free software, doing the best job you can, communication between group members, doing things the right way, working well as a team, good workmanship, and meeting customer requirements. Yet at the same company, individuals' perceptions of what quality means to the company generated the following partial list: 100 percent on-time delivery, perform as per specifications, design of the future, quality of end product, customer satisfaction, long-term cost reduction, management of resources, and self-inspection. The content and generated meaning of the construct seems to vary within and between work units as well as between levels, regardless of similarities in the work, organization goals, structures, and work processes.[4] The study concluded that quality seems to be a dynamic phenomenon formulated as a result of interactions between people in multiple work settings. The work group dynamics that the individual is an integral part of, the socialization process that individuals go through, and the process of socially constructed reality[5] might help explain the differences. Thus development of a shared meaning of quality is a process that must be managed.

In a generic sense, **quality** can be viewed as a set of processes, supporting structural configurations, and production methods in either a manufacturing or service environment that economically produce quality goods or services that meet and/or exceed the customers' requirements and/or expectations. To add to this complexity, customers or users might view quality in many different ways—for example, in terms of performance, features, reliability, conformance, durability, responsiveness, competence, courtesy, serviceability, aesthetics, access, and perceived quality. We cannot understand quality and the management of quality without a review of its unique evolution.

Quality: A Historical Note and Competing Frameworks

Quality as a business process has been with us for millennia. In its original form, quality was reactive and inspection-oriented; today, while the discipline is still evolving, quality-related processes and activities are becoming more of a formal part of every organizational member.[6] The roots of quality and its evolution in the United States can be traced back to the 1930s and the pioneering work of Deming, Juran, Feigenbaum, and Crosby.

The Deming Approach

W. Edwards Deming, a physicist and statistician, formed many of his theories on quality during World War II, when he worked at the U.S. Bureau of the Census. During that time, Deming taught members of various industries how to use statistical control to improve the quality of war materials. After the war ended, there was huge consumer demand for goods in the United States and relatively limited pressure for efficiency or quality. Because Japan was struggling to rebuild its economy, the Japanese were more open to Deming and his ideas. His message was simple: Study carefully what your customer wants, and then study and improve your product design and production techniques until the quality of the product is unsurpassed. In the 1960s and 1970s as foreign competition increased and as market boundaries broadened from domestic to worldwide, issues of quality and efficiency came to the forefront of managerial challenges in the United States. Furthermore, as foreign competition increased, a search for a competitive advantage occurred, which was defined in terms of customer satisfaction, cost-effectiveness, and effective product developments. During the late 1970s and early 1980s, total quality control concepts emerged as a vehicle for change that would allow an organization to compete and survive in the new worldwide markets.

Dr. Deming's lifelong mission was to seek sources of improvement. Deming's chain reaction (Figure 14–1) illustrates the implication of a focus on quality and improvement. Basically, the figure shows that when quality is improved by improving processes (''not by increased inspection''), the result is improved productivity. Improved productivity is achieved through many changes such as less rework, inventory inspections, need for capacity, and need to keep track of rework locations. Improved productivity in turn leads to lower costs and the potential for lower prices. For an organization, better quality and lower prices mean increased market share as well as the ability to stay in business and to provide more jobs. All this together gives the shareholder a solid return on his or her investment.

Figure 14–1
The Deming Chain Reaction

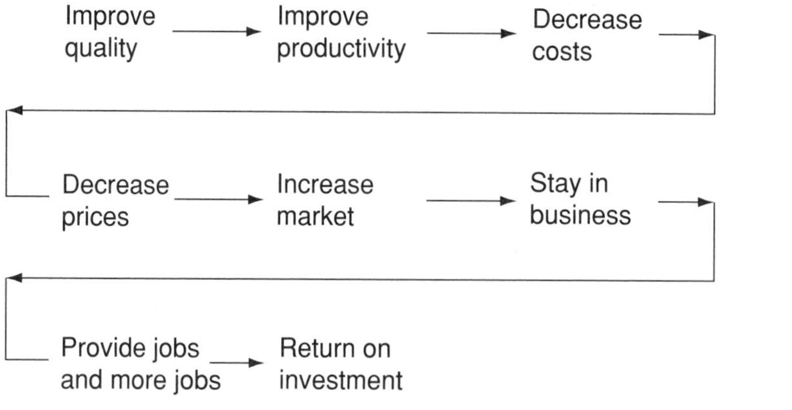

The development of the quality improvement movement was influenced by the work of many other practitioners and researchers. Among the most widely credited founding fathers we find Deming, Joseph Juran, Kaorn Ishikawa, Philip Crosby, Noriaki Kano, A. V. Feigenbaum, Masaaki Imai, and others who have been instrumental in setting the foundations for our knowledge about quality. Each of the founding fathers seems to have an underlying theory of management that emphasizes a different element of quality and accordingly provides a different framework.

For example, Deming's framework emphasizing the systematic nature of organizations, the importance of leadership, and the need to reduce variation in organizational processes[7] is anchored in his theory of management based on 14 principles: (1) Create consistency of purpose and plan, (2) adopt a new philosophy of quality, (3) cease dependence on mass inspection, (4) end the practice of choosing suppliers based solely on price, (5) improve constantly and forever the system, (6) institute training on the job, (7) institute leadership, (8) drive out fear, (9) break down barriers between departments and units, (10) stop requesting improved productivity without providing the tools and methods to achieve them, (11) eliminate work standards that prescribe numerical quotas, (12) remove barriers to pride of workmanship, (13) institute vigorous education and self-improvement, and (14) put everybody in the company to work to accomplish the transition.

Juran's Framework

Joseph Juran, an electrical engineer, started to work for Bell Systems in 1924 in its Hawthorne facility's Inspection Branch, which included 5,000 employees out of 40,000 in the facility. In 1926 Bell Systems encouraged its managers to implement statistical tools for product quality control. As a result of basic training courses in statistical methods, a new Statistical Control Department was formed. Juran (one of the founders of the department) began to formalize many of his theories on quality during and after World War II, in the four years that he was on loan to the federal government's War Production Board (WPB) that was created to harness the civilian economy to the war effort. One department at WPB had the job of helping industry meet the quality requirements of military goods. The focus of that effort was to offer free training courses in the use of statistical tools, notably control charts and sampling tables based on probability theory. Many of these tools evolved at Bell Systems during the 1920s.[8]

Following the war, Juran started to work as independent management and quality consultant. His first major book, *Quality Control Handbook,* was published in 1951.

Juran, like Deming, was invited to Japan in 1954 by the Union of Japanese Scientists and Engineers. Juran emphasizes that managing quality can be carried out through a trilogy of interrelated managerial processes: **quality planning, quality control,** and

quality improvements. Managing quality begins with quality planning. The purpose of the quality planning is to provide the operating forces with the means of producing products that can meet customers' needs, such as invoices and sales contracts. Once planning is complete, the plan is turned over to the operating forces. Their job is to produce the product as planned. If quality planning is conducted, there is a better chance that production will be efficient. Juran believes that the quality crisis of the 1980s was due to the lack of proper planning. He believes that many of the deficiencies in products and processes can be traced to deficient planning for quality.[9] Juran, unlike Deming, focuses on top-down management and technical methods rather than worker's pride and satisfaction.

In summary, Juran's 10 quality improvement management principles include (1) build awareness of opportunities to improve, (2) set goals for improvement, (3) organize to reach goals, (4) provide training, (5) carry out projects to solve problems, (6) report progress, (7) give recognition, (8) communicate results, (9) keep score, and (10) maintain momentum by making annual improvement part of the regular systems and processes of the company.

Feigenbaum and Ishikawa's Views

The term **total quality control** was first introduced by Feigenbaum in 1956 in his attempt to find a "way out of the dilemma imposed on businessmen by increasingly demanding customers and by ever-spiraling costs of quality, . . . a new kind of quality control, which might be called total quality control."[10] Ishikawa, quoting Feingenbaum, defined total quality control as "an effective system for integrating the quality development, quality maintenance, and quality improvement efforts of various groups in an organization so as to enable production and service at the most economic levels which allow for full customer satisfaction."[11]

Like Deming and Juran, Feigenbaum achieved visibility through his work with the Japanese. According to Feigenbaum, the underlying principle of total quality is that "to provide genuine effectiveness, control must start with the design of the product and end only when the product is in the hands of a customer who remains satisfied."[12] Some of Feigenbaum's early concepts and writing have had a profound effect on the quality movement. First, he sees the production process (and, later, service delivery), as an integrated process that originates with the customer—in terms of what the customer wants—and ends with the customer (customer satisfaction). Second, responsibility for managing this integrated process rests in the hands of management. Third is the need to define the role of the inspection function (defect prevention and line workers' responsibility for quality in order to reduce the need for inspection), the consequent reduction in costs of quality by building quality into the product (quality by design), and the usefulness of statistical quality tools (later to be known as *statistical process control*).

Kaoru Ishikawa's emphasis is on the need for total involvement and total organizational commitment to quality. Ishikawa's message to Japanese executives is that "through total quality control with the participation of all employees, including the president, any company can create better products (or services) at a lower cost, increase sales, improve profit, and make the company into a better organization."[13]

Crosby's Approach

Crosby provides a narrower view of quality. He defines quality in absolutes: (1) Quality is defined as conformance to requirements, not "goodness." (2) The system for achieving quality is prevention, not appraisal. (3) The performance standard is zero defects, not "that's close enough." (4) The measurement of quality is the price of nonconformance, not indexes.[14] Crosby stresses motivation and planning and does not dwell on statistical process control and the problem-solving techniques proposed by Deming and Juran. He argues that quality is free because the small costs of prevention will always be lower than the costs of detection correction, and failure. Here he emphasizes a program of **zero defects.**

All of these "founders" of quality believe that management and the system, rather than the workers, are the cause of poor quality. The experts seem to differ in their emphases. While Deming provides manufacturers with methods to measure the variations in a production process in order to determine the causes of poor quality, Juran emphasizes setting specific annual goals and establishing teams to work on them. Feigenbaum teaches total quality control aimed at managing by applying statistical and engineering methods throughout the company, while Crosby stresses a program of zero defects. Regardless of the differences in the orientations and emphases, most of the quality experts treat total quality as a critical organizational process that must be managed.

Quality in the 1990s and Beyond

In the increasingly competitive world of the late 1980s and early 1990s, quality is no longer optional; it is an essential part of business strategy. Data on customer preferences indicate that 8 out of 10 buyers now regard quality as equal to or more important than price. This emphasis on quality has forced many Western companies to reexamine their approaches to managing quality. A company's ability to compete in the industrial market of the 1990s is likely to include **Total Quality Management (TQM)** as a key element of business. TQM requires the transformation of a company's culture, the commitment of top management, and the involvement of all the relevant business constituencies such as the suppliers and customers. It is as its name says—total quality management.

One of the major challenges of quality concerns the need for the transformation of the organizational culture. (See Module 17.) For some, investigating their basic business assumptions and experimenting with alternative ways to manage, new work arrangements, and innovative work designs (see Module 13) can potentially improve quality, productivity, job security, and return on investment. Some authors argue that quality leadership (see Module 3) should be an integral component of management philosophy. A recently developed approach that can foster quality leadership, quality improvements, and the full utilization of organizational resources and that transforms organizational culture is total quality management.

Total Quality Management (TQM)

The growing number of organizations implementing unique TQM programs and the increasing number of studies published about TQM make the identification of its key features a challenge. Here we review some of its fundamental principles and briefly describe the TQM structural support configurations.

Basic Principles

Recently, seven total quality management basic assumptions or principles were identified for the 1990s:[15] (1) Quality is neither a technical nor departmental function but a systematic process that extends throughout the company. (2) The company's quality process should be structured to support both the quality work of individuals and the quality teamwork among departments. (3) The emphasis on quality improvement must take place in marketing, in development and engineering, in manufacturing, and, particularly, in services—not merely in production for factory workers only. (4) In this process quality must be perceived as what the buyer wants and needs; it must satisfy customer requirements. It should not be perceived as what the company needs to satisfy its requirements for marketing and production efficiency. (5) Quality improvements require the application of new technology, ranging from quality design techniques to computer-aided quality management measurement and control. (6) Widespread quality improvements are achieved only through the help and participation of the entire work force, not from the help of just a few specialists. (7) Finally, all of the preceding come about when the company has established a clear, customer-oriented quality management system throughout the organization, one that people understand, believe in, and want to be a part of.

A few organizational behavior themes can be derived from the preceding list of principles. (1) Open communications (see Module 8) and shared perceptions (see Module 7) within and between all levels of the organization are perceived as crucial for the success of quality programs. (2) Through a participative team effort (see Module 11) among management, engineer specialists, and workers, changes can be explored and implemented that will result in improved quality. (3) Because TQM is a strategic choice made by top management and consistently translated into guidelines for the functioning of the whole organization, the transformation process of a product from invoice to completed product must be carefully planned and skillfully managed. (See Module 13.) (4) Because each system with a certain degree of complexity has a probability of deviation, it can be understood through a variety of scientific methods and techniques. Concepts like Taguchi methods, value analysis, quality costing, control charts, and Pareto analysis should sound familiar to those of you who have previously taken production courses. Statistical process control (SPC), for example, is the most popular method used in controlling repetitive processes and activities. (5) An emphasis on product design (see Module 13) and on designing products with built-in quality is likely to help achieve high quality despite potential fluctuations on the production line. (6) Because the workers closest to the process are the ones who can inspect their output to assess the extent to which the product meets specifications, the development of self-regulating work systems (see Modules 9, 10, and 13) and the appropriate organizational culture (see Module 17) are critical. (7) **Continuous improvement,** a purposeful and explicit set of principles, mechanisms, and activities that are designed to achieve a continuous change in operating procedures and systems, is an integral part of quality.

Structural Support Configurations

As we have seen, Total Quality Management requires a system perspective. Furthermore, it involves the creation of some form of a multilayered team-based structure that functions parallel to the formal organization. Teams are the central facet of TQM. In order to describe this unique **structural support configuration,** new terms were recently coined, including *parallel hybrid organization, parallel participative organization,* and *parallel learning structure.*[16] Here we will focus on the parallel learning structure, which is perceived as a more generic term than the others. In a **parallel learning structure,** a specific division and coordination of labor is created that operates ''parallel'' (in tandem or side by side) with the formal hierarchy and structure and has the purpose of increasing the organization's ''learning'' (the creation and implementation of new quality-related solutions by organizational members).

The parallel learning structure is composed of multiple teams whose tasks are to inquire into quality issues, to recommend suggestions for improvements, and at times to implement the recommendations. The number of teams and their size, composition, and complexity depend on the nature of the organization and the scope of the TQM program. TQM uses many different types of teams—sometimes it is difficult to tell one from the other. Essentially, three types of teams are used most often: steering committee, problem-solving teams, and self-managed teams.[17] (See modules 9 and 10.) In most organizations, the teams are linked via some kind of structural arrangements. The parallel learning structure evolved as a mechanism and a place to house, guide, and nurture the quality improvement effort. Further discussion of parallel learning structures and their processes can be found in Module 17.

Delivering Quality Service

An integral part of total quality management for service-based organizations (e.g., banks, hotels, and airlines) is the delivery of quality service. In a service organization, quality often occurs during the delivery of the service, usually in an interaction between the customer and the provider; in this case, it is not engineered at the manufacturing plant and delivered intact to the customer. At the most basic level, the key to ensuring quality service is by meeting or exceeding what the customer expects from the service. Quality of service as perceived by the customer can be defined as ''the extent of discrepancy between customers' expectations or desires and their perceptions."[18] Recently a conceptual framework has been proposed to assess quality of service. (See Figure 14–2.)

Figure 14–2
Customer Assessment of Service Quality

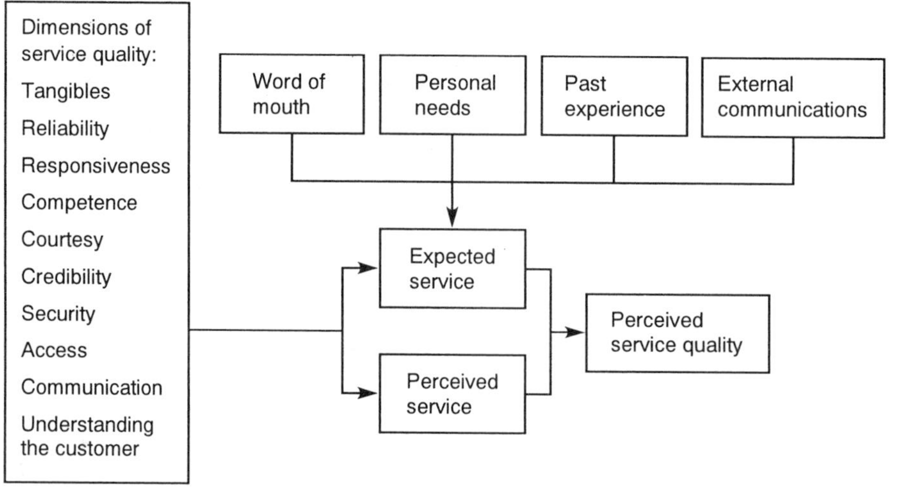

Source: Adapted with permission from V. A. Zeithaml, A. Parasuraman, and L. L. Berry, *Delivering Quality Service* (New York: Free Press, 1990), p. 23.

The framework suggests that there are 10 general dimensions that represent the valuative criteria customers use to assess **service quality;** that service quality is the discrepancy between customers' expectations and perceptions; and that key factors such as word-of-mouth communications, personal needs, past experience, and external communication influence customers' expectations. This framework ties together a few of the fundamental organizational behavioral themes that were explored in the first two parts of this book—namely, expectation dynamics at the workplace (Module 2), the role of perceptual differences (Module 7), and communication (Module 8)—to explain the phenomenon of service quality.

TQM, the Economic Model of the Firm, and Human Behavior

Recent studies argue that TQM is a challenge to conventional management processes and to the theories that underlie them.[19] Managing the total quality process requires major paradigm shift. To understand the broad implications, it's useful to consider how statistical process control, a technical tool of control, evolved into TQM, a philosophy that affects all functions and levels of the firm.

There is nothing revolutionary about **statistical process control.** It applies sampling theory to production processes in order to detect malfunctions faster than is possible with final inspection. But whereas SPC in its basic form simply determines when output is falling outside the boundaries of "acceptable quality," Deming, Juran, and Feigenbaum developed SPC into a tool for systematically analyzing variations and defects and, ultimately, for redesigning production processes to reduce variability. This has had important implications for the way work is done. First, it implies that the individual operator rather than a quality control engineer is best placed both to identify unacceptable variation and to take remedial action. This leads to changes in operations management that reversed trends of the past half-century such as deskilling, specialization, and increased supervision. SPC requires operator training and gives the operator more responsibility for performance, innovation, captial equipment, and the work environment. Second, SPC's emphasis on identifying and correcting the sources of variation directs attention to the linkage between production activities. Implementation of SPC treats the manufacturing process as a single integrated system, and operators and the line managers have to communicate and share knowledge in order to diagnose and correct problems. This emphasis leads naturally to the view of a production chain as a series of supplier–customer relationships.

Whereas SPC is a precise set of quality improvement techniques and processes, TQM extends quality improvement methods and processes to all functions and all management levels; TQM is a companywide philosophy of quality improvement. This philosophy contends that the firm's primary goal is to better meet customer requirements by improving the quality of products and processes. The far-reaching implications for management are fundamental. We illustrate the differences by comparing and contrasting the economic model of the firm with TQM. Table 14–1 summarizes the comparison.

Table 14–1
Emerging Management Paradigms: TQM and the Economic Model of the Firm

	TQM	Economic Model of the Firm
Organizational Goals	Serving customer needs by supplying goods and services of the highest possible quality.	Maximizing profit (i.e., of shareholder wealth).
Individual Goals	Individuals motivated by economic, social, and psychological goals relating to personal fulfillment and social acceptance.	Individuals motivated only by economic goals; maximization of income and minimization of effort.
Time Orientation	Dynamic; innovation and continual improvement.	Static optimization; maximizing the present value of net cash flow by maximizing revenue and minimizing cost.
Coordination and Control	Employees are trustworthy and are experts in their jobs; hence emphasis on self-management. Employees are capable of coordinating on a voluntary basis.	Managers have the expertise to coordinate and direct subordinates. Agency problems necessitate monitoring subordinates and applying incentives to align objectives.
Role of Information	Open and timely information flows are critical to self-management, horizontal coordination, and quest for continual improvement.	Information system matches hierarchical structure; key functions are to support managers' decision making and monitor subordinates.
Principles of Work Design	System-based optimization with emphasis on dynamic performance.	Productivity maximization by specializing on the basis of comparative advantage.
Firm Boundaries	Issues of supplier–customer relations, information flow, and dynamic coordination common to transactions within and between firms.	Clear distinction between markets and firms as governance mechanisms. Firm boundaries determined by transaction costs.

Source: Adapted from R. Grant, A. B. (Rami) Shani, and R. Krishuan, TQM's Challenge to Management Theory and Practice, *Sloan Management Review* 35, 2 (1994), p. 33.

For illustration purposes, we will focus our discussion on organizational goals only. A basic element of the conflict between TQM and the economic model is their fundamentally different goals. At the root of the economic model is profit maximization, which has been redefined more precisely to mean maximization of shareholder wealth. This principle is legally sanctioned in the requirement that boards of directors operate public corporations in the interests of shareholders. The shareholder value approach has yielded a set of management principles and decision rules. TQM emphasizes that the firm's primary objective is providing customer satisfaction. TQM does not reject the notion that a primary objective of the firm should be profit maximization, but views long-term profitability as an outcome of serving customers rather than as a driving force. The risk of using shareholder value maximization to guide decisions is that the firm loses touch with its serving the customer orientation. Deming is critical of short-term profitability as a guide to business performance and ''the futility of management by numbers.'' Thus, although shareholders take a backseat in quality management, their long-term interests are seen as convergent with quality goals.[20]

Quality Awards and Certifications

The pressure to establish quality processes within organizations is a global trend. An integral part of the efforts to improve quality has been institutionalized via awards and certifications. While some of the awards are national—such as the Malcolm

Baldrige Award, Deming Prize, Swedish Quality Prize, Australian Quality Prize, and Israeli Quality Award—others (such as the Shingo Award and the ISO certifications) are more global. The next few paragraphs review the Deming Prize, Malcolm Baldrige Award, and ISO Certification.

The Deming Award

The Deming Prize is a much cherished award sought by the management and employees of Japanese companies. Since its establishment about 35 years ago, the Deming Prize has been regarded as the highest honor for quality in Japanese industry. As Mr. Yotaro Kobayashi (president of Fuji Xerox Co., Ltd.) reported in competing for the 1980 Deming Prize, it was a process of finding out how to properly manage. The Deming Prize committee is headed by the chairperson of the Union of Japanese Scientists and Engineers, a distinguished scientific foundation. Every year, committee members are selected by the chairman from a pool of quality experts. Their assignment is to screen the candidates for the prize according to the previously defined criteria. Competition for the Deming Prize is severe; many companies spend years in preparation before they become eligible for consideration.[21]

The Deming Prize Survey Team concentrates on six criteria when evaluating a firm: (1) corporate policy, (2) the quality system and its management, (3) education and training, (4) execution, (5) demonstrated results, and (6) future plans. (See Figure 14–3.) Clearly, this systems viewpoint of quality forces candidates for the prize to evaluate their operations from top to bottom. The survey team visits all areas of the firm and listens to quality circle team presentations and discussions of quality improvement plans by top management and the managers of all major areas. Competition for the prize has become a unifying force within Japanese firms, moving the organizations toward better quality and improved processes, products, and services.

Figure 14–3 **Deming Prize Examination Criteria**

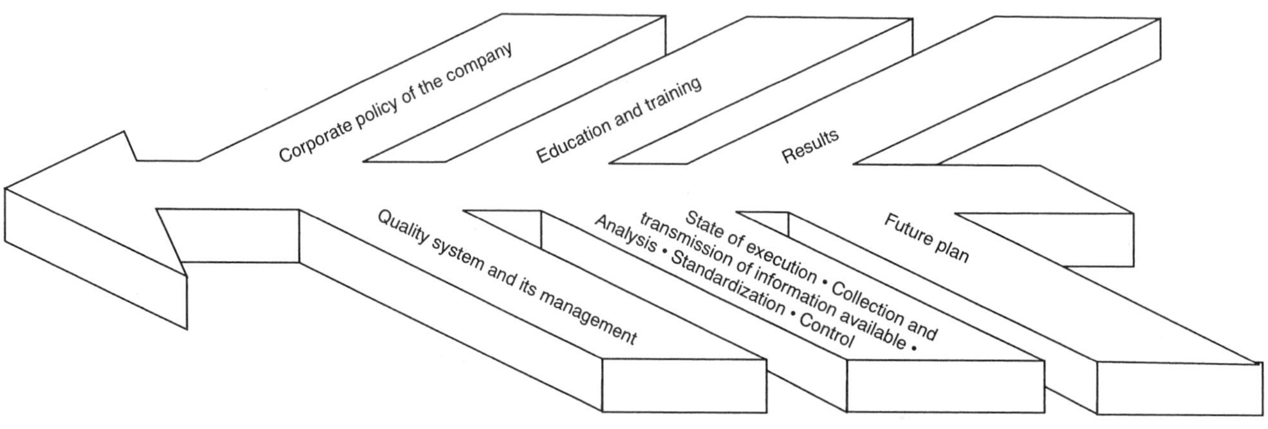

The Malcolm Baldrige National Quality Award

The U.S. Congress established the Baldrige Award to raise awareness about quality management and to recognize companies that have successful quality management systems. The award was named in honor of Malcolm Baldrige, who served as Secretary of Commerce from 1981 until his death in a rodeo accident in 1987. The award program—developed and managed by the National Institute of Standards and Technology (NIST) of the U.S. Dept. of Commerce with the cooperation and financial support of the private sector—recognizes quality achievements in three categories: manufacturing, service, and small business.[22]

The purpose of the Malcolm Baldrige National Quality Award is "to promote quality awareness, recognize quality achievements of U.S. companies, and to publicize successful strategies." The judging criteria for the award are clearly defined in the application guidelines. Figure 14–4 provides the criteria framework for the award.

Each criterion is allocated a maximum number of points: leadership, 100 points; information and analysis, 70 points; strategic quality planning, 60 points; human resources utilization, 150 points; quality assurance of products and services, 140 points; quality results, 180 points; and customer satisfaction, 300 points. Meeting the criteria is not an easy task. No company has received a perfect score of 1,000 points. Review of the distribution of the companies that have applied for the award through 1993 reveals that the top score was 875. The judging criteria take up 23 pages of application guidelines. U.S. corporations seem to use the application as a guide for managers and a checklist for internal quality standards and processes.

Figure 14–4
Baldrige Award Criteria Framework: Dynamic Relationships

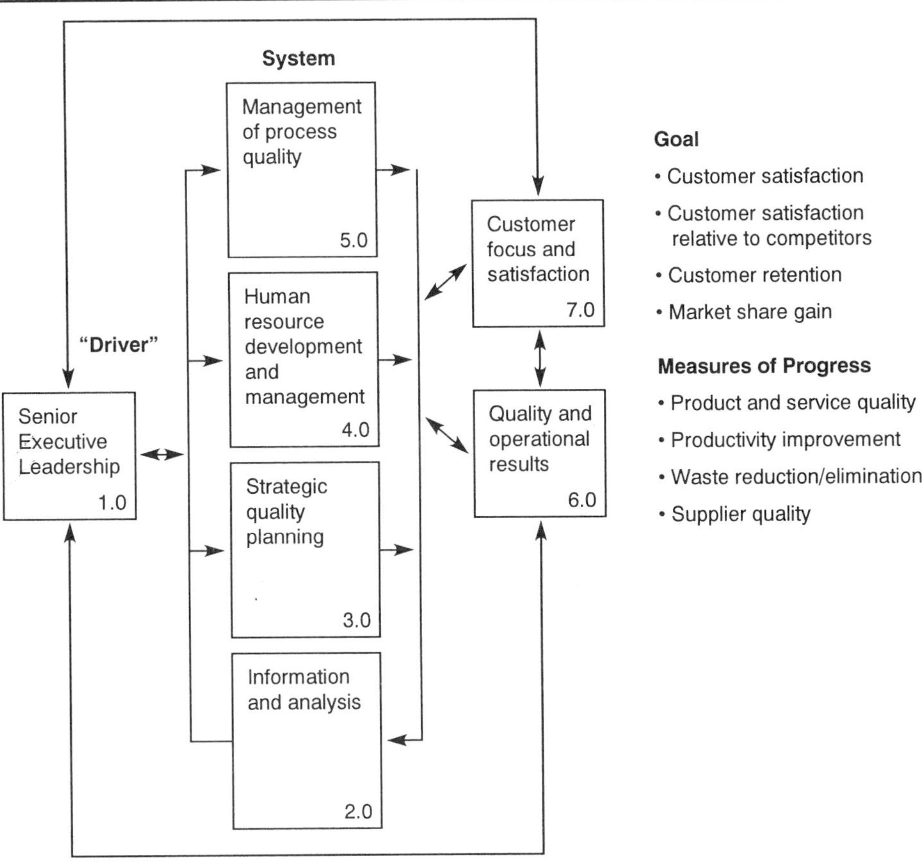

ISO 9000 Certification

Unlike the Deming and Baldrige prizes, the ISO 9000 series is not an awards program. It does not require a state-of-the-art system or any prescribed method of process quality control. ISO 9000 certification is generic and applies to all industries. As a set of requirements for quality systems, these series provide a common measuring stick for gauging quality systems. The ISO 9000 were finalized and published in 1987 by the International Organization for Standards. The agency is made up of 91 countries that are organized into many working commitees to harmonize increasingly international activities needed to produce products and services of high quality. The worldwide standards are divided into five subsets that establish the requirements for the management of quality. (See Table 14–2.)

The ISO standards are used by the 15-nation European Economic Community to provide a universal framework for quality assurance—primarily through a system of internal and external audits. The purpose is to ensure that a certified company has a quality system and processes in place to meet its published quality standards. In 1987 the United States adopted the ISO 9000 Series verbatim as the ANSI/ASQC Q-90 Series. As of 1992 more than 20,000 facilities in Britain had adopted the standards and

Table 14–2 Summary of ISO 9000 Standards

Standard	Content
ISO 9000	Provides definitions and concepts. Explains how to select other standards for a given business.
ISO 9001	Quality assurance in design, development, production, installation, and servicing.
ISO 9002	Quality assurance in production and installation.
ISO 9003	Quality assurance in test and inspection.
ISO 9004	Quality management and quality system elements.

become certified. Over 22,000 companies from the EC countries have registered. In the United States, 800 companies have adopted the standards. Japan has mounted a major national effort to get its companies registered. The impact of the standards is significant. Achieving the highest level, ISO 9001, requires a major tranformation and realignment of the firm and its behavior.

Summary

This module explored the management of quality as a key organizational process. We discussed the importance of Total Quality Management, reviewed its recent history, defined its salient principles, and identified the parallel learning structure as the structural support configuration that ''houses'' the continuous quality improvement efforts. Various quality awards and ISO 9000 certification seem to be major forces for firms' transformation. The management of quality is emerging as a driving force of organizational change. As such, it has a multiple-level impact on human behavior. Organizational choices made about the adoption of quality improvement philosophy coupled with the increasing demand for product quality and service quality has fostered the need to reexamine work dynamics (e.g., work design, communication networks, motivation, leadership, and teamwork) and the emergence of new organizational cultures.

Study Questions

1. ''Quality is one of the most critical organizational processes.'' State your position and provide your rationale.
2. A top executive claimed that management of quality is the responsibility of the workers. State your position and provide your rationale.
3. What are some key principles of Total Quality Management? How do they relate to human behavior?
4. Compare and contrast Deming's, Juran's, Feigenbaum's, and Crosby's views about quality.
5. Describe the effect that each of the quality awards is likely to have on organizational performance and organizational behavior.
6. How are expectations, perceptions, leadership, and quality of service related? Provide an example.

Endnotes

1. See, for example, R. Buzzell and B. Gale, *The PIMS Principles: Linking Strategy to Performance* (New York: Academic Press, 1987); and J. W. Dean and D. E. Bowen, ''Management Theory and Total Quality: Improving Research and Practice through Theory Development,'' *Academy of Management Review* 19, no. 3 (1994), pp. 392–418; R. E. Cole, P. Bacdayan, and

B. J. White, "Quality, Participation, and Competitiveness," *California Management Review* 35, no. 3 (1993), pp. 68–81.

2. See, for example, J. A. Belohlav, "Quality, Strategy, and Competitiveness," *California Management Review* 35, no. 3 (1993), pp. 55–67; and A. B. (Rami) Shani and M. Rogberg, "Quality, Strategy and Structural Configuration," *Journal of Organizational Change Management* 7, no. 2 (1994), pp. 15–30; E. E. Lawler, S. A. Mohrman, and G. E. Ledford, *Employee Involvement and Total Quality Management* (San Francisco: Jossey-Bass, 1992); G. E. Ledford, E. E. Lawler, and S. A. Mohrman, "The Quality Circle and Its Variations." In *Productivity in Organizations: New Perspectives from Industrial and Organizational Psychology,* eds. J. P. Campbell, and R. J. Campbell. (San Francisco: Jossey-Bass, 1988), pp. 255–94.

3. C. A. Reeves and D. A. Bendar, "Defining Quality: Alternatives and Implications," *Academy of Management Review* 19, no. 3 (1994), pp. 419–45; R. J. Schonberg, "The Quality Concept: Still Evolving," in *Total Quality Management,* ed. R. L. Chase (New York: IFS Publications, 1988), pp. 21–28.

4. A. B. (Rami) Shani, Y. Mitki, R. Krishnan, and R. Grant, "Roadblocks in Total Quality Management Implementations: A Cross-Cultural Investigation," *Total Quality Management* 5, no. 6 (1994), pp. 411–20.

5. Socially constructed reality is a process through which subjective experience gradually develops into a common stock of knowledge that is eventually perceived as everyday objective reality. This phenomenon is captured in P. L. Berger and T. Luckman, *The Social Construction of Reality* (New York: Anchor Books, 1967).

6. See, for example, H. I. Costin, *Total Quality Management* (New York: Dryden Press, 1994); M. Imai *Kaizan: The Key to Japan's Competitive Success* (New York: Random House, 1986); P. Lillrank, and N. Kano, *Continuous Improvement* (Ann Arbor, Mich.: University of Michigan Press, 1989); R. K. Reger, L. T. Gustafson, S. M. DeMarie, and J. V. Mullane, "Reframing the Organization: Why Implementing Total Quality Is Easier Said than Done." *The Academy of Management Review* 19, no. 3, pp. 565–84.

7. See, for example, J. C. Anderson, M. Rungtusanatham, and R. G. Schroeder, "A Theory of Quality Management Underlying the Deming Management Method," *Academy of Management Review* 19, no. 3 (1994), pp. 472–509; and W. E. Deming, *Out of the Crisis* (Cambridge, Mass.: MIT Press, 1982); Mary Walton, *The Deming Management Method* (New York: Dodd, Mead, 1986).

8. See, for example, J. M. Juran, "Made in USA—A Renaissance in Quality," *Harvard Business Review,* July–August 1993; and J. M. Juran, "The Upcoming Century of Quality," paper presented at the ASQC Annual Quality Congress, Las Vegas, May 24, 1994.

9. J. M. Juran, "The Quality Trilogy," *Quality Progress,* August 1986, pp. 19–24; J. M. Juran, *Juran on Planning for Quality.* (New York: Free Press, 1988).

10. Kaoru Ishikawa, *What Is Total Quality Control?* (Englewood Cliffs, N.J.: Prentice-Hall, 1985).

11. Ishikawa, Ibid page 90.

12. A. Feigenbaum, "Total Quality Control," *Harvard Business Review* 34, no. 6 (November-December 1956).

13. Ishikawa, Ibid, page 92.

14. P. Crosby, *Quality Is Free* (New York: Mentor Books, 1980).

15. A. V. Feigenbaum, "Total Quality Developments into the 1990s—An International Perspective" in R. L. Chase (Ed.) *Total Quality Management* (New York: IFS Publications, 1988) pp 3–10.

16. G. R. Bushe and A. B. (Rami) Shani, *Parallel Learning Structures: Increasing Innovation in Bureaucracies* (Reading, Mass.: Addison-Wesley, 1991); A. B. (Rami) Shani, and M. Rogberg, "Quality, Strategy, and Structural Configuration." *Journal of Organizational Change Management* 7, no. 2 (1994), pp. 15–30.

17. J. W. Dean and J. R. Evans, *Total Quality* (Minneapolis: West Publishing, 1994).

18. V. A. Zeithaml, A. Parasuraman, and L. L. Berry, *Delivering Quality Service* (New York: Free Press, 1990).

19. See, for example, R. M. Grant, A. B. (Rami) Shani, and R. Krishnan, "TQM's Challenge to Management Theory and Practice," *Sloan Management Review* 35, no. 2 (1994), pp. 25–35; B. Spector, and M. Beer, "Beyond TQM Programmes," *Journal of Organizational Change*

Management 7, no. 2 (1994), pp. 63–70; and D. A. Waldman, ''The Contribution of TQM to a Theory of Work Performance,'' *The Academy of Management Review* 19, no. 3 (1994), pp. 510–36.

20. For a detailed comparison of TQM against the economic model of the firm, see Grant, Shani, and Krishnan, ''TQM's Challenge to Management Theory and Practice.''

21. See, for example, S. B. Sitkin, K. M. Sutcliffe, and R. G. Schroeder, ''Distinguishing Control from Learning in Total Quality Management: A Contingency Perspective.'' *The Academy of Management Review* 19, no. 3 (1994), pp. 537–64; L. P. Sullivan, ''The Seven Stages in Companywide Quality Control,'' in *Total Quality Management,* pp. 11–20.

22. G. S. Easton, ''A Baldrige Examiner's View of U.S. Total Quality Management,'' *California Management Review* 35, no. 3 (1993), pp. 32–54.

23. See, for example, Shani & Bushe, Ibid.

24. F. Damanpour, ''Organizational Innovation,'' *Academy of Management Journal* 34, no. 3 (1994), pp. 555–90; R. Krishnan, A. B. (Rami) Shani, R. Grant, and R. Baer, ''The Search for Quality Improvements: Problems of Design and Implementation,'' *Academy of Management Executive* 7, no. 4 (1993), pp. 7–20.

25. J. D. Thompson, *Organization in Action* (New York: McGraw-Hill, 1967).

26. P. R. Lawrence and J. W. Lorsh, *Organization and Environment* (Boston, Mass.: Harvard Press, 1967).

Activity 14–3: Applying TQM in Making Paper Airplanes: A Simulation

Objectives:

a. To demonstrate the meaning of quality in production.
b. To explore the variety of elements that constitute quality.
c. To examine the different factors that can influence product quality.

Task 1:

Option A:

a. The instructor will demonstrate how to make the paper airplane.
b. Each class member practices a few times to ensure that he or she has the general idea of how to make one.
c. The instructor will assign each team into either assembly line A or B. One other team is to be the QA team; the size of this team should equal the number of production teams.
d. The instructor will give the teams about 10 minutes to read their roles (Appendix R) and design the assembly line, tasks, and processes.
e. The QA team will have to develop their specification that will guide the examination of the products produced.

Option B:

a. The instructor will assign each team into either assembly line A or B. One other team is to be the QA team; the size of this team should equal the number of production teams.
b. Each team will receive a prototype airplane from the instructor and study the prototype carefully.
c. Next the instructor will give the teams about 10 minutes to read their roles (Appendix R); the assembly line teams will have to figure out how to produce the airplanes and design the assembly line manufacturing flow.
d. The QA team will have to develop specifications that will guide the examination of the products produced.

QA Team

a. The instructor is to brief the QA team.
b. The QA team is to read its instructions (Appendix R) and prepare the specifications against which to examine the produced plans.
c. Each member of the QA team will observe one assembly line team.

d. The QA members are to supply each team with the raw material (i.e., paper) and record the number of pages allocated.
e. The QA individuals are to observe and record the actual manufacturing process and dynamics.
f. Following the completion of production, the QA team will test each of the plans against the specifications and produce a summary report that includes the following: (1) number of pages used, (2) number of planes produced, and (3) number of planes that passed quality assurance.

A and B Assembly Teams

a. The instructor will brief the assembly teams together.
b. Each team is to read the instructions for its assigned group (Appendix R).
c. The instructor will request that each team assign an assembly line supervisor.

Task 2 (Production):

a. Following a report from the supervisors that the teams are ready, the instructor will give the OK to start production.
(Time: about 10 minutes)
b. Each team must mark each one of its products via a name, logo, team number, or some such.

Task 3:

While the QA people are examining the products and producing the report, each team is to reflect on its production process, effectiveness, and output.
(Note: The next tasks are conditional upon time availability.)

Task 4:

The QA experts will join the team that they have observed. Each team will improve its task definitions, production process, roles, and work design.
(Time: 10 minutes)

Task 5:

Teams will be given 10 minutes to produce their products, while keeping tab on the use of raw materials.

a. At the end of the production process each team is to report on the approved products and use of raw materials.
b. Teams are to reflect on the production process, quality improvements, and team dynamics.

Task 6:

The instructor will facilitate class discussion about the quality improvements between the two production processes.

Activity 14–4: Continuous Improvement: The Paper Mills Case

Objectives:

a. To explore the main features of a successful continuous improvement process in a company.
b. To investigate the effect of quality improvement on human behavior and business performance.

Task 1 (Homework):

Participants are to read the case "The Paper Mills Corporation" and answer the questions at the end of the case.

Task 2 (Class):

The instructor will facilitate class discussion based on the individuals' answers.

The Paper Mills Corporation

The Corporation

The American–Israel Paper Mills Corporation Ltd. was founded in 1952 as a joint venture of Israeli and American investors. It was the first Israeli company whose shares were traded on the New York and Tel Aviv stock exchanges. Annual paper consumption in Israel increased from 10 kilograms to 110 kilograms per person on average between 1952 and 1994. The Paper Mills Corporation manufactures approximately 40 percent of the paper consumed in Israel. Most of its products are for the local market. In 1994 its sales amounted to $285 million. The number of employees in the corporation is 2,160. The plants are dispersed around 10 sites in Israel, but the main activity takes place in Hadera, a medium-sized city in the center of the country.

The corporation's policy is based on several targets and principles: attaining a profit for the firm's continuous existence and as a base for achieving its other targets; securing the existing market share and increasing the scope of sales to the local market; providing products and/or services that will meet customers' requirements and expectations; increasing productivity and improving product quality; decentralizing authority to the plants by delegating business, managerial, and operational responsibility; adopting advanced managerial approaches; fostering environmental quality and quality of work life; and contributing to immigrant absorption and to the community.

The central reason that motivated management to enter the field of quality improvement, as a systemwide program, was the need to reduce manufacturing costs and to improve the quality of the products. This was to increase profitability and also to keep up with rising overseas competition. For almost 40 years, the Israeli paper industry had enjoyed a monopoly of paper supply and price setting, and all of its products had a guaranteed market in Israel. The government's decision to remove protective customs barriers and open up the Israeli market to products from overseas served as a catalyst in exploring ways to reduce manufacturing costs and to improve the quality of the products and services. These circumstances also led to the decision to investigate potential markets overseas. Adopting innovative management systems and attaining ISO 9002 certification were established as the paths to growth and success.

The process chosen by the corporation entailed a gradual process with two sequential phases: first, develop a quality circle (QC) program within each of its four divisions; second, following the successful implementation of the QC programs to implement a Total Quality Management program. Furthermore, in the first phase, the Paper and Carton Product Manufacturing Division was the only division chosen to carry out the experiment.

The Paper and Carton Product Division

The Paper and Carton Product Manufacturing Division is located near the city of Hadera and includes three plants for manufacturing paper (white paper, brown paper, and domestic paper production plants) and four support and service units (engineering, projects authority, administrative, and production systems authority). (See Figure 14–5). The number of employees in the division is 800; it is the largest among the corporation's units.

Source: This case was written especially for this book by Professors Yoram Mitki, Ruppin Institute, Israel, A. B. (Rami) Shani, California Polytechnic State University, U.S.A., and Zvi Meiri Plant Manager, Israel.

Figure 14–5
The Paper Mill and Carton Division: Organizational Structure

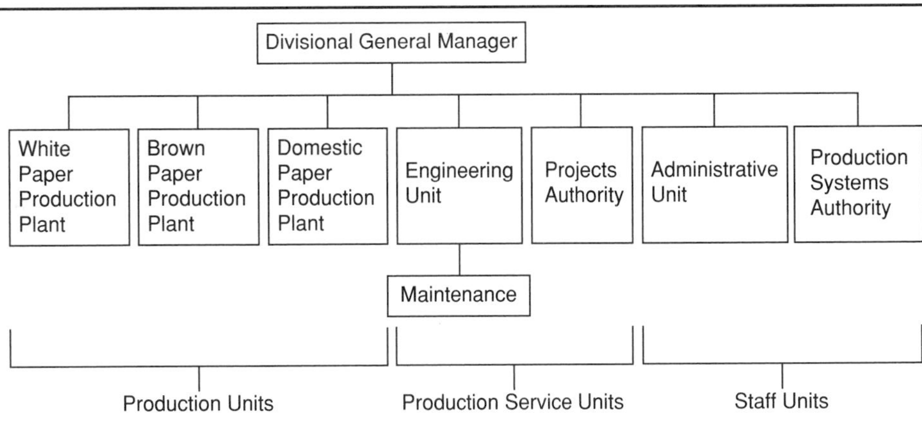

The Paper and Carton Manufacturing Division's business strategy is derived from the targets set by the corporation's management. It stresses several elements: the centrality of the customer in organizational perception; viewing product quality as the highest value; introducing an approach and habits for continuous improvement; developing advanced processes and innovative technologies; widespread implementation of team work; creating channels of communication at all levels and in all directions; and the management obligation to achieve these aims and to adopt and lead the required changes.

The initiative for entering the total quality program was led by the divisional general manager (GM). The first task was to create a divisional structure that is more conducive to learning and continuous improvements. Following a study of alternative design configurations, a design based on three semi-autonomous business units that is based on three different production processes was adopted and implemented. Among many advantages, this design was based on the production processes; provided clearer focus on processes, products, and services; and allowed for better integration between the support and staff departments and the production plants. (See Figure 14–6.)

Figure 14–6
The Paper Mill and Carton Division's New Structure

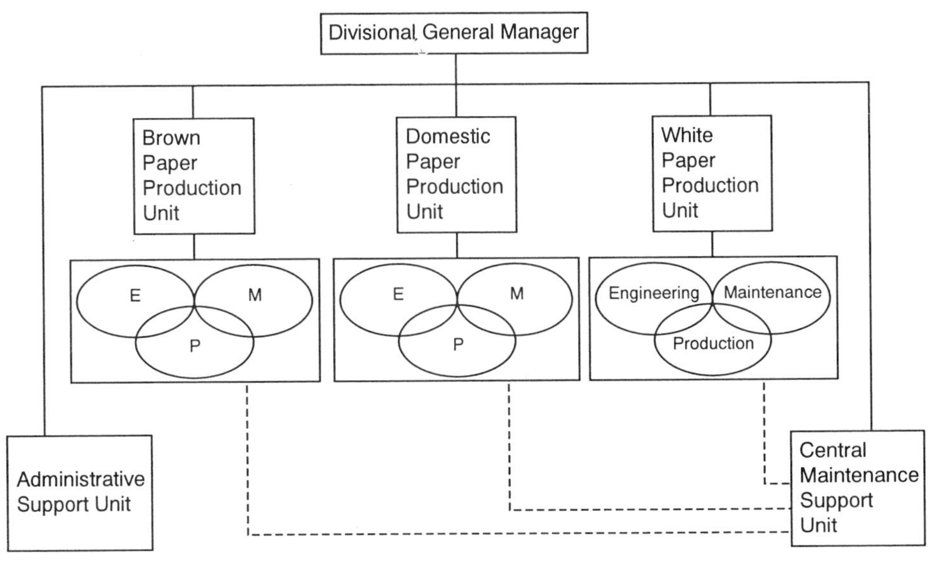

Following the restructuring of the division, the GM was interested in implementing a systemwide TQM program. Yet, at the start of 1987, the TQM approach was new in Israel, and data concerning results and implementation were scarce. Starting with a QC program was perceived as a safe first step that would likely yield the targets set by Corporate.

The risk of introducing QC is relatively low; the required investments for its implementation are also low. A quality circle structural configuration was established to house and guide the change effort. By the end of 1988, nine quality circles operated in the Paper and Carton Division. By the end of 1994, the program encompassed 45 quality circles, involving 630 workers (approximately 85 percent of all workers in the Paper Mills). The success of the QC program earned the division the first prize in 1991 as an organization excelling in the implementation of quality circles in Israel. The quality circles provided the infrastructure for the TQM effort that follows.

Based on the success of the QC program, a systemwide TQM program was launched during 1992. The program was set to accomplish the following objectives: It would supply products and services that would answer customer demands and expectations; every worker would take and receive full responsibility for his or her part in executing the work process; everyone would be responsible for quality; the company would choose suppliers who meet the quality policy and conform to the company's quality requirements; the management and the workers, as one, would lead the company to work quality improvement and to fulfill the aims and targets set in its policy framework; and the quality assurance procedure would be prepared according to the ISO 9002 principles and the corporation's quality policy.

The vision of the quality program is that of a long-term program that results in cumulative and continuous improvements. Accordingly, the program's implementation is gradual and its stages are constructed layer on layer. Successful existing activities and mechanisms that have already been implemented aid in widening and deepening the program. Table 14–3 summarizes the process of introducing the quality program thus far and indicates stages of its development.

The Learning Mechanism

The integration of quality in the division's business strategy, coupled with management commitment to a continuous quality program, resulted in the creation of a *Parallel Learning Mechanism.* This mechanism, operating parallel to the existing organizational structure, was charted with the responsibility of introducing and advancing the continuous improvement program. Its main functions are to translate the quality strategic targets into operative programs and to lead and guide its implementation. The Parallel Learning Mechanism is in charge of determining the tools, methods, systems, and rate of the program's implementation. This body is also responsible for the development of the essential learning processes, evaluation, and feedback. The Parallel Learning Structural Configuration includes a central Steering Committee headed by the divisional general manager; its participants are all the unit managers in the division and five members of the TQM Authority. The committee convenes once every two or three weeks in order to refine vision and general strategy, establish broad procedures, and review progress. The steering committee does not interfere in internal departmental topics chosen for handling by quality teams. It decides, at this stage, on interdepartmental or overall divisional processes needing improvement, appoints process improvement teams, and discusses and reviews recommendations presented by the teams.

The central quality steering committee is responsible for the ongoing daily operation of the quality program on both the logistic and the professional sides. This body is composed of the administrative unit head and four members, each of whom is in charge of one of the operative fields of the quality program; one person is responsible for QC, one for TQM, one for training, and one for finances. The central quality steering committee convenes at least once a week. The learning's structural configuration also includes seven clusters of different quality teams that report to the central quality steering committee: the quality circles (QCs), the process improvement teams (PITs), the internal customer–client improvement teams (ICCITs), communication improvement teams (CITs), lost time analysis teams (LTAs), statistical process control teams (SPCs), and cost-cutting teams (CCTs). The process improvement teams are composed of four to seven members from different units in the division; they function as an ad hoc team to address a specific topic. (See Figure 14–7.)

Table 14–3
An Overview of the Change Process

I. *Context*

A. Business situation—Dynamic business environment; increased competition; cancellation of protective customs on imports.

B. Business strategy—Maintain market share; achieve the European standard in quality and price (attain ISO 9002); identify market niches for export in the European market.

II. *The Nature of the Quality Program*

A. Vision — Improving effectiveness.
Developing a quality system while modifying the organizational culture to maintain competitiveness.

B. Orientation — Systemwide continuous improvement program; QC; SPC; BMT; team-based organization.

C. Key Events and Activities

1987 Managerial decision to enter the quality program; QC as first stage.
Workshops on quality circles for managers and setting up steering committees.
Building quality circle structural support configuration; implementing two experimental quality circles.

1988 First course in organization for quality circle leaders/facilitator.
Implementing nine quality circles.

1989 Increasing number of circles to 14.
Organizational survey for evaluating results of quality program.

1990 Publishing a manual for quality circle leaders/facilitator.
Crystallization of strategy, structural support configuration, and quality policy.

1991 Activating quality leaders/facilitator forum.
Number of quality circles increased to 30.
Fifth course for QC leaders/facilitator.
Plant management decides to implement Total Quality Management program.

1992 Establishing mechanism for implementing the TQM program.
Plant gains Quality Award of Israel Quality Association.
Two process improvement teams begin their activity.

1993 Seven process improvement teams active in plant.
Forty-two quality circles involving 600 participants (80 percent of all employees).
Eighth course for quality circle leaders.

1994 Five process improvement teams active in plant.
Forty-five quality circles involving 620 participants.
Completion of 10th course for QC leaders/facilitator.
Six pilot "internal customer–client improvement teams" formed.
Eight "lost time analysis teams" formed.
Twelve "cost-cutting teams" formed.
Attainment of ISO 9002 certification.

III. *The Parallel Learning Mechanism*

A. Goals
- To translate the strategic quality targets to an operative program.
- To provide the structural support and the linking pin between the different continuous improvement initiatives.
- To set the broad continuous improvement policies and to determine devices, systems, and rate for executing the program.
- To develop evaluation, feedback, and learning mechanisms.

B. The Structural Configuration

1. Key elements: The supplemental structure responsible for continuous improvement and organizational learning includes central steering committee, central quality steering committee, process improvement teams, quality circles, statistical process control teams, internal customer–client improvement teams, lost time analysis teams, communication improvement teams, and cost-cutting teams.

2. Key characteristics:

Formalization	High
Centralization	Moderate
Flexibility	Moderate
Integration	High

C. Involvement — High involvement of internal organizational customers and suppliers.
Low involvement of external organizational customers and suppliers.

D. Training — Multilevel learning programs.

E. Rewards — No direct monetary rewards for participation. Certificates of Merit, managerial appreciation, and social group events.

Figure 14–7 **The Paper Mill and Carton Division and Its Parallel Learning Structure**

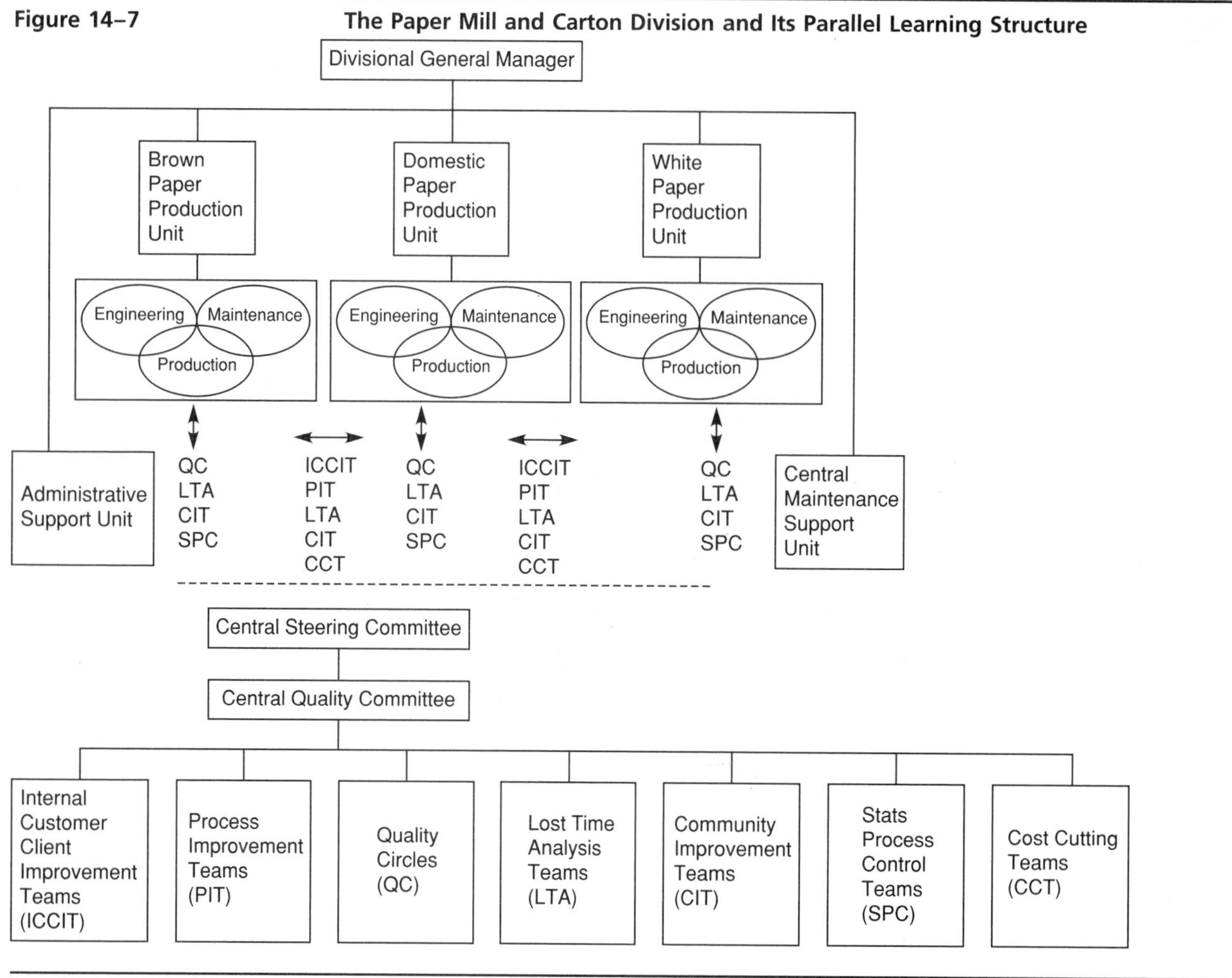

As the program evolves, the number of teams and the kind of teams change. For example, as this paper is written, there are 45 quality circle teams, seven process improvement teams, six pilot internal customer–client improvement teams, 50 communication improvement teams, eight pilot lost time analysis teams, and 12 cost-cutting teams. The quality circles, which include more than 85 percent of the entire plant staff, have operated continuously for the past five years. The QC teams improve work processes and production technologies in the organic departments and within the parameters of the processes that they are responsible for. Each of the 45 quality circles meets regularly every other week. A forum of quality circle leaders meets once every three months to clarify and solve organizational and logistical problems related to the QC and TQM activities. The leaders' collaboration assists in removing obstacles and in improving the implementation of the quality principles.

During 1994 internal customer–client improvement teams were added to the parallel learning structure. The purpose of the ICCITs was to establish another learning mechanism that will focus on the working relationships between the different units. Following a systematic process through which every unit had to identify its internal customers, the internal mapping of the customer chain was created. Six key chains were identified and proposed by the central quality steering committee and six pilot teams were created. The ICCITs received basic training and were given their charts. Following the outcomes and learning from the pilot ICCITs, the parallel learning structure will modify the process; divisionwide diffusion is planned to be executed by the end of 1995.

The parallel structural configuration and its dynamics with the formal organizational system influence its ability to achieve its aims in an effective manner. Knowing the structural characteristics of the quality program permits understanding of the internal dynamics of its operation and also permits making a comparison between it and other programs.[23] One characteristic is the degree of formalization of the program, which is expressed in the extent to which processes and procedures upon which the activity is performed in the organization are executed.[24] The level of formalization in the Paper Mills is high. (See Table 14–3.) The procedures and courses of action are clear and fixed, use of tools and methods is defined, the framework for convening is given in advance, and the communication and information-sharing mechanisms (including summaries of discussions and postperformance follow-up) are permanent and expected.

A second characteristic, the degree of centralization, refers to the measure of authority and autonomy for making decisions given the various units.[25] The level of centrality in the Paper Mills is moderate. Quality teams are given autonomy in everything related to process improvement and work efficiency proposals in the organic departments; 95 percent of the decisions taken in QC are also executed. But in interdepartmental or plantwide processes, the decisions are taken by the central steering committee. The process improvement teams' and the central quality steering committee's powers in these areas are relatively limited.

A third characteristic is the degree of flexibility that allows the program to adapt itself to new needs arising from internal and/or external changes. The flexibility level in the Paper Mills is moderate. The training set-up in the organization is based on perennial, annual, and monthly programs; almost all programs are planned from the standpoint of schedules and are budgeted for financially. The various units in the organization are planned in advance in order to release managers and/or workers for training. Organizational activity of this type reduces the scope of flexibility. At the same time, there is great flexibility for quality circles and steering committees to choose topics needing improvement. The selected processes can be adapted to varying states of reality.

The fourth characteristic is the program's degree of integration. This dimension measures the coordination and mutual nourishment performed between all the factors participating in it.[26] There is a high degree of integration in operating the program in the Paper Mills. The program is an integral part of the business strategy; it is clearly articulated; control and reporting mechanisms are in place; and the steering committee, which oversees this program, includes all the unit managers. Furthermore, the program is coordinated by the central quality steering committee (CQSC) and meets regularly to coordinate and review working processes. Members of the CQSC are also a part of the central steering committee. Another factor that contributes to integration is the permanent updating received by workers of all levels via periodic meetings with managers and via ongoing information sharing about every phase of the program.

Continuous Learning: Some Key Features

The Paper Mills' learning paradigm (as practiced and articulated during the past seven years) has a number of prominent characteristics. One characteristic concerns the learning aims. Learning is intended to achieve two purposes: (1) introducing values and new norms that are at the foundations of the quality culture that the organization is interested in embedding and (2) providing methods and tools (such as SPC and process analysis) that foster changes in work patterns and behavior.

A second characteristic concerns learning and understanding of the learning processes. In order to design suitable learning setups for its predetermined aims, the division implemented a system of cautious and gradual implementation. Experience was obtained first in one quality circle, in one process improvement team, or in one department; after evaluating the experimental program, specific ideas for improvement were articulated and systemwide diffusion took place.

A third characteristic relates to the organizational hierarchy involved in learning. Learning in the Paper Mills is performed at several organizational levels: individuals, groups, and an entire system (the plant). Learning is undertaken in organic teams (such as departmental teams or production shifts) as well as in mixed teams (for example, the steering committee and process improvement teams).

A fourth characteristic relates to the program's scope and time horizon. The training program in the Paper Mills is perennial and multirecurring. Long-term perspective enables the building of training routes that on the one hand are compatible with workers' and/or managers' needs and that on the other hand match the rate of the quality program's progress and the adaptations required to be made in it following changes in the business environment and/or the corporation's policy. The recurrence of organizing courses permits the establishing of a common base of knowledge for a large number of workers or teams, all of it according to their needs, the rate of their progress, and the function that they fill in the quality program. All of these characteristics make it possible to relate to the topic of learning as an ongoing process.

Results

Results of a quality program must be examined over a few years. A seven-year follow-up at the Paper Mills indicates that impressive results were achieved in performance measures, in developing processes, and in "hard" measures that express manpower behavior in the organization.

Performance Measures: Work hours required for producing a ton of paper were reduced over the past six years by 56 percent, from 16 work hours per ton in 1988 to 9 in 1994. The work hours reduction trend is illustrated in Figure 14–8. Furthermore, the average output of the four major paper production machines rose 10.7 percent between 1991 and 1994. (See Figure 14–9.)

Figure 14–8
Paper Production by Working Hours, 1988–94

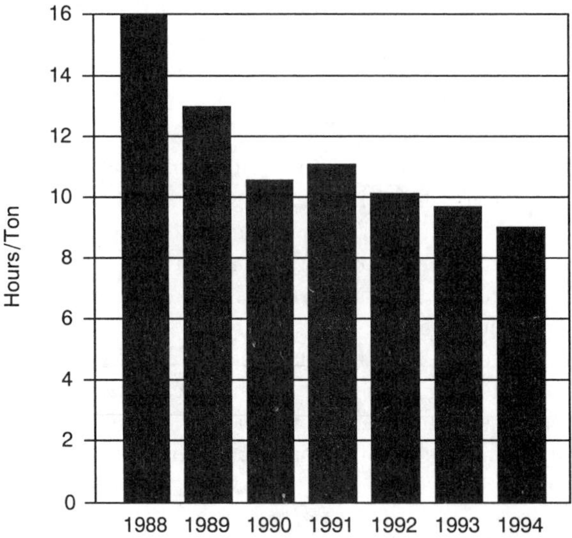

Water consumption for manufacturing a ton of paper went down by 55.4 percent without damaging the production process or the paper quality. In a growing country such as Israel, water conservation is a national target. Figure 14–10 illustrates the change in water consumption from 1989 to 1994.

Electricity in the manufacturing process is supplied from two sources; there is transmission line electricity and self-produced electricity. The self-produced electricity is cheaper by more than 2/3 than the linear form (linear electricity costing 1.5 kW/h). Between 1991 and 1994, a decrease occurred at a rate of 9.4 percent of linear electricity and there was an increase of 28 percent in self-produced electricity. This saved the corporation $515,000 per annum.

The raw material for paper manufacturing is based on fibers arriving from two sources: cellulose imported from overseas and waste collected in Israel. The corporation's objective is to reduce the use of cellulose as much as possible and to increase the use of waste. From 1991 to 1994, use of cellulose fibers for paper manufacture decreased by 7 percent, and recycled fiber consumption rose by almost 5 percent.

Figure 14–9
Paper Production Machines Output, 1991–94

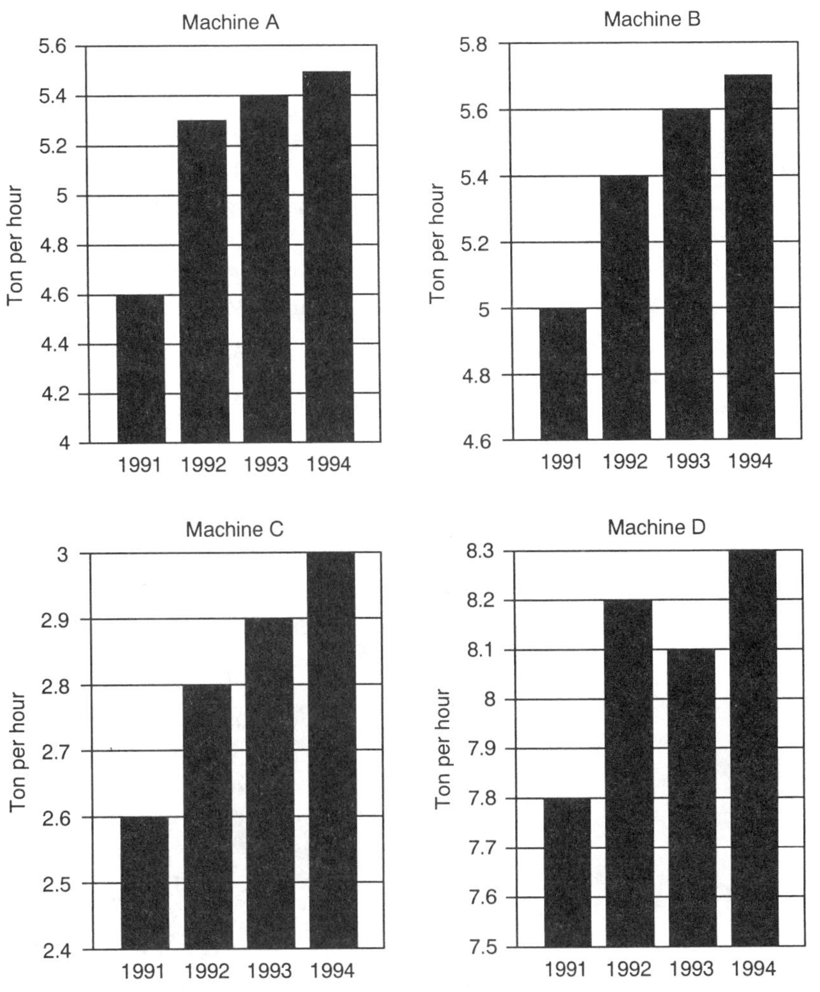

Figure 14–10
Water Consumption, 1989–94

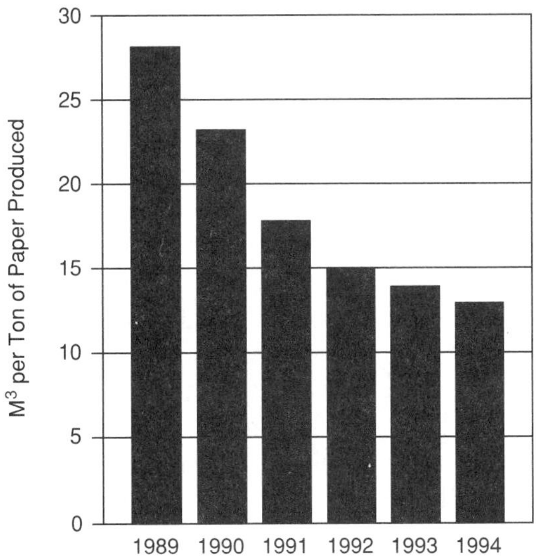

In the paper production industry, quality of products is measured by defect ratio per 10,000 sheets of paper. Defect ratios were reduced from 6.2 in 1991 to 5.5 in 1992 to 4.2 in 1993 to 3.84 in 1994. Customer satisfaction is measured in the industry by the number of complaints per month. The average number of complaints per month fell significantly from 8.8 in 1991 to 6.8 in 1992 to 4.5 in 1993 to 2.7 in 1994.

Improvement in Work Processes: Improvement in work processes is a key ingredient of a quality program. At Paper Mills, several processes were developed and improved on to make work more efficient, increase saving, and raise profits. One example is developing the de-inking (ink extraction) process. This process of treating paper waste and recycling it permits the exploitation of many elements of waste cleaning for paper manufacture. Waste can be used in this manner instead of cellulose, saving the division and the state the expense of foreign currency. Inherent in this is a contribution to environmental quality by preventing pollution from refuse that is not recycled.

A second example is developing an entire set-up of water recycling that includes instrumentation for cleaning water and fiber extraction (both of which are reused) and extracting dirt and various pollutants. The recycled water serves for the operation of some of the production machines, mainly those that manufacture cartons. Water recycling lowers the cost of water consumed, minimizes the division's dependence on fresh water supply, and reduces the amount of water flowing out into industrial waste.

Improvement in Work Behavior: One measure for testing the implications of the change program is the rate of worker absenteeism. Even though presence at work can be explained by many factors, quality program designers at the Paper Mills assumed that the investment in a worker, in training the worker, in enriching the job, and in improving the quality of life at work would influence workers' satisfaction and presence in the plant. An integral part of work at the Paper Mills Corporation is participation in professional training and development. During the past four years on an average, each employee received 36 hours of classroom training a year out of which 12 hours were devoted to TQM-related training and 24 hours were devoted to technical/professional training. Managers participate in 90 hours of training a year, most of which focused on TQM-related content over the past three years.

The average rate of absenteeism by workers was 18 percent in 1988, 16 percent in 1990, and 15 percent in 1992. By 1994 it had decreased to 10.5 percent. The cumulative rate of lost work days stemming from absenteeism, work accidents, and illnesses went down by 50 percent between 1988 and 1994. Finally, in 1988, there were 122 work-related accidents. Following a gradual drop, 46 accidents were reported in 1994.

Questions

1. Identify the key success factors in the quality management process at the Paper Mills Corporation.
2. How would Deming, Juran, Feigenbaum, and Crosby critique the quality improvement process implemented at the Paper Mills Corporation?
3. How did the process of managing total quality affect individual and team behavior?
4. Describe the effects of the total quality process on organizational performance.
5. You were asked by Mr. Meiri (general manager of the Paper and Carton Products Division) to generate some ideas on how to continue and improve the way quality is managed in his division. What would you propose?
6. The president of the Paper Mills Corporation asked you (as an expert who followed the successful implementation of total quality in his Paper and Carton Products Division) to help him get his other divisions to implement the total quality process. Propose an action plan.

15 Managing Creativity and Innovation

Learning Objectives

After completing this module you should be able to

1. Describe the creative process.
2. Identify the traits or characteristics that are related to individual creativity.
3. State managerial actions that can foster creativity in an organizational setting.
4. Explain the difference between creativity and innovation.
5. Describe the stages in the innovation process.
6. Explain the different types of innovation.
7. Gain insight into the key elements that influence the innovation process.
8. Understand the interplay among human behavior, group behavior, creativity, and innovation.
9. Gain insight into and appreciation for the complexity of managing creativity and innovation.

List of Key Concepts

Adaption-innovation model
Administrative innovation
Creative process
Creativity
Creativity-relevant skills
Domain-relevant skills
Dual ladders
Incremental innovation
Innovation
Innovation process
Person-oriented creativity
Innovation process
Process-oriented creativity
Product innovation
Product-oriented creativity
Radical innovation
System-maintaining innovation (SMI)
System-transforming innovation (STI)
Task motivation

This module was developed in collaboration with Dr. Carol Sexton, Department of Management, University of Otago, New Zealand. We are grateful to Dr. Sexton.

Module Outline

Premodule Preparation

Activity 15–1: Exploring Creativity in an Organizational Setting: 3M's Post-It Note Pads Case

Objectives:

a. To explore the organizational context for creativity and innovation.

b. To identify the variety of skills and competencies involved in creativity.

Task 1 (Homework):

Students are to read the case "3M's Post-It Note Pads" and respond to the questions at the end of the case.

Task 2:

Individuals are to share the answers in small groups. Each group is to develop a shared response, which will be presented and discussed with the class.

3M's Post-It Note Pads

In 1922, Minnesota Mining and Manufacturing inventor Francis G. Okie was dreaming of ways to increase sandpaper sales, the company's major product at the time, when a novel thought struck him. Why not sell sandpaper as a replacement for razor blades? The idea was that people could rub their cheeks smooth. The idea never caught on, but Okie went on at 3M and eventually developed a waterproof sandpaper that became a major staple in the auto industry. Okie's failure is as much legend at 3M as his successful idea.

The Company

3M was founded at the turn of the century by a doctor, a lawyer, two railroad executives, and a meat market manager on the shores of Lake Superior. Their purpose was to mine corundum, an abrasive used in sandpaper. Unfortunately the corundum mine yielded a mineral of no value to the sandpaper industry. Most of the original investors left, and those who remained turned to inventing. Their first success was an abrasive cloth used in metal polishing. Then Okie's wet or dry sandpaper came along. Since then, 3M has never stopped.

William L. McKnight is the legendary spiritual father of the company. McKnight worked himself up from bookkeeper through sales to chairman and chief executive. As a salesman, he pitched his products directly to furniture makers on the factory shop floors rather than to the purchasing agents. This became the 3M approach—get close to the customer. Scotch tape and masking tape were both developed to meet individual customers' needs. Part of McKnight's manifesto was "If management is intolerant and destructively critical when mistakes are made, I think it kills initiative." In addition to tolerating mistakes, the company rarely hires from outside (never at the senior level). The turnover rate among managers and other professionals is less than 4 percent. Divisions are kept small so that division managers are on a first-name basis with their staffs.

Source: Background on 3M was drawn from "Masters of Innovation," *Business Week,* April 10, 1989, pp. 58–63. This case is a shorter and modified version of "3M's Little Yellow Note Pads: Never Mind I'll Do It Myself," in *Breakthroughs!,* eds. P. R. Nayak and J. M. Kerrengham (New York: Rawson Associates, 1988), pp. 50–73. Used by permission.

New Product Development

A 3Mer comes up with an idea for a new product. He or she forms an action team by recruiting full-time members from technical areas, manufacturing, marketing, sales, and finance. The team designs the product and figures out how to produce and market it. Then the team develops new uses and line extensions. All members of the team are promoted and receive raises as the project develops. As sales grow, the product's originator can go on to become project manager, department manager, or division manager. There's a separate track for scientists who don't want to manage.

The result is that there are 42 divisions. Each division must follow the 25 percent rule: A quarter of a division's sales must come from products introduced within the past five years. In addition, there is a 15 percent rule. Virtually anyone at the company can spend up to 15 percent of the workweek on anything he or she wants to as long as it's product-related. Managers do not monitor very carefully their scientists' use of this 15 percent rule. If this policy were enforced rigidly, such action would undermine its intent and inhibit the creative energy of researchers. This practice (called *bootlegging* by members of the company) and the 25 percent rule are at the heart of one of 3M's most famous innovations, the yellow Post-It Note.

The Post-It Note

Unlike many of the incremental improvements and innovations made in product lines, the Post-It note pad was unique, a product entirely unrelated to anything that had ever been developed or sold by 3M. Post-It notes are ubiquitous in modern business because they do something no product ever did before. They convey messages in the exact spot where people want the messages, and they leave no telltale sign that the message was ever there at all.

This small but powerful idea was begun by a 3M chemist, Spencer Silver, refined by two scientists named Henry Courtney and Roger Merrill, and nurtured from embryo to offspring by Arthur L. Fry. Post-It revenues are estimated at as much as $300 million per year.

Post-It notes started out as another oddball idea—an adhesive that didn't form a permanent bond—with no perceptible application. In 1964, Silver was working in 3M's central research labs on a program called Polymers for Adhesives. 3M regularly sought ways to improve its major products. Tapes and adhesives were 3M's primary product lines, and adhesives that created stronger bonds were actively sought. Silver found out about a family of monomers that he thought might have potential as ingredients for polymer-based adhesives and he began exploring them.

In the course of this exploration, Silver tried an experiment, just to see what would happen, with one of the monomers and then to see what would happen if a lot more of the monomer was added to the reaction mixture, rather than the amount dictated by conventional wisdom. This in itself was irrational, as in polymerization catalysis, the amounts of interacting ingredients were controlled in tightly defined proportions according to theory and experience. Silver says, "The key to the Post-It adhesive was doing the experiment. If I had sat down and factored it out beforehand, and thought about it, I wouldn't have done the experiment. If I had really seriously cracked the books and gone through the literature, I would have stopped. The literature was full of examples that said you can't do this." To Silver, science is one part meticulous calculation and one part fooling around.

Silver describes what happened with the unusual concoction as a "Eureka moment"—the emergence of a unique, unexpected, previously unobserved and reliable scientific phenomenon. "It's one of those things you look at and you say, This has got to be useful! You're not forcing materials into a situation to make them work. It wanted to do this. It wanted to make Post-It adhesive."

The adhesive became Silver's baby. Silver started presenting this discovery to people who shared none of his perceptions about the beauty of his glue. Interested in practical applications, they had only a passing appreciation for the science embodied in Silver's adhesive. More significantly, they were "trapped by the metaphor" that insists that the ultimate adhesive is one that forms an unbreakable bond. In addition, Silver was immersed in an organization whose lifeblood was tape of all kinds. In this atmosphere, imagining a piece of paper that eliminated the need for tape is an almost unthinkable leap into the void.

Silver couldn't say exactly what it was good for. "But it has to be good for something," he would tell them. "Aren't there times," Silver would ask people, "when you want a glue to hold something for awhile but not forever? Let's think about those situations. Let's see if we can turn this adhesive into a product that will hold tight as long as people need it to hold but then let go when people want it to let go."

From 1968 to 1973, support for Silver's idea slipped away. The polymers for adhesives program ran out of funding and support, and the researchers were reassigned. Silver had to fight to get the money to get the polymer patented because there was no commercial application immediately present.

Silver was a quiet, well-behaved scientist with an amazing tolerance for rejection. Spencer Silver took his polymer from division to division at 3M, feeling that there was something to be said for such a product. He was zealous in his pursuit because he was "absolutely convinced that this had some potential." The organization never protested his search. At every in-house seminar no one ever said to Silver, "Don't try. Stop wasting our time." In fact, it would have violated some very deeply felt principles of the company to have killed Silver's pet project. As long as Silver never failed in his other duties, he could spend as much time as he wanted fooling around with his strange adhesive.

The best idea Silver could come up with on his own was a sticky bulletin board, not a very stimulating idea even to Silver. But 3M did manufacture them, and a few were sold, though it was a slow-moving item in a sleepy market niche. Silver knew there had to be a better idea. "At times I was angry because this stuff is so obviously unique," said Silver. "I said to myself, Why can't you think of a product? It's your job!"

Silver had become trapped by a metaphor. The bulletin board, the only product he could think of, was coated with adhesive—it was sticky everywhere. The metaphor said that something is either sticky or not sticky. Something *partly sticky* didn't occur to him.

Silver and Robert Oliveira, a biochemist whom Silver met in his new research assignment, continued to try selling the idea. Geoff Nicholson, who was leading a new venture team in the commercial tapes divison, agreed to see them. Nicholson knew nothing about adhesives and had just taken the position in commercial tapes. Silver and Oliveira were literally the first people to walk through his door. Nicholson says that he was "ripe for something new, different, and exciting. Most anybody who had walked in the door, I would have put my arms around them." Nicholson recruited a team to work on an application for the five-year-old discovery. One of these people, Arthur Fry (a chemist, choir director, and amateur mechanic), would make the difference. Fry had "one of those creative moments" while singing in the choir of his church. "To make it easier to find the songs we were going to sing at each Sunday's service, I used to mark the places with little slips of paper." Inevitably the little slips would flutter to the floor. The idea of using Silver's adhesive on these bookmarks took hold of him at one of these moments. Fry went to 3M, mixed up some adhesive and paper, and invented the "better bookmark." Fry realized that the primary application for the adhesive was not to put it on a fixed surface, such as the bulletin board, but on the paper itself. It was a moment of insight that contemplation did not seem to generate. Fry now has his own lab at 3M and often speaks to large groups of businesspeople about the climate for creativity at 3M. Silver is still in 3M's basement, working out of a cramped, windowless office in a large lab—a place where experimental ferment and scientific playfulness still reign.

The product was not perfected at the moment of Fry's discovery. It still took two more scientists on the Nicholson team—Henry Courtney and Roger Merrill—to invent a paper coating that would make the Post-It adhesive work. Silver said, "Those guys actually made one of the most important contributions to the whole project, and they haven't got a lot of credit for it. The Post-It adhesive was always interesting to people, but if you put it down on something and pulled it apart, it could stay with either side.

It had no memory of where it should be. It was difficult to figure out a way to prime the substrate, to get it to stick to the surface you originally put it on. Roger and Hank invented a way to stick the Post-It adhesive down. And they're the ones who really made the breakthrough discovery because once you've learned that, you can apply it to all sorts of different surfaces.''

To get the product to manufacturing, Fry brought together the production people, designers, mechanical engineers, product supervisors, and machine operators and let them describe the many reasons why something like that could not be done. He encouraged them to speculate on ways that they might accomplish the impossible. A lifelong gadgeteer, Fry found himself offering his own suggestions. ''Problems are wonderful things to have, especially early in the game, when you really should be looking for problems,'' said Fry.

In trying to solve the problem of one difficult phase of production, Fry assembled a small-scale basic machine in his own basement, which was successful in applying adhesive to paper in a continuous roll. The only problem was that it wouldn't fit through his basement door. Fry accepted the consequences and bashed a hole through the basement wall. Within two years, Fry and 3M's engineers had developed a set of unique, proprietary machines that are the key to Post-It notes' consistency and dependability.

Discussion Questions

1. Describe the creative process that resulted in the Post-It note pads as we know them today.
2. Identify the factors that fostered and hindered the creative process.
3. Describe the characteristics of Spencer Silver.

Introduction

Organization creativity and innovation are organizational processes that provoke continuing interest among managers and researchers alike.[1] At the surface level, organizational creativity and innovation are viewed as processes by which individuals working together in a complex social system create a valuable, useful new product, service, idea, procedure, or work process.[2] As such, they play a central role in the long-term survival of organizations and are key processes that must be managed.

In Module 4 we introduced the subject of environmental turbulence as the backdrop against which to understand the rapidly expanding use of behavioral science technology in the world of entrepreneurship and corporations. Alvin Toffler described this growing turbulence in *Future Shock* in 1970, which was followed by *Third Wave* in 1980. He has now completed his trilogy with *Powershift,* which claims that the accelerated dissemination of information has resulted in a shift of power and wealth.[3] From the old smokestack era with mass production of individual models requiring timely planning and changeovers, we have moved into the new computer-driven economies that make possible designer production and services tailored to specific client needs. The power vested in the stable financial institutions, which existed with the old industrial giants, has been diluted by the shift to designer financial systems and currencies, making a multitude of new enterprises powerful in a global production market. Threat of being outpaced by the continuous growth in the industrial and financial power of Japan and the Pacific Rim countries in the East and the European Community—particularly Germany—in the West creates intensive pressures for inventive ways for the United States to compete in the world arena. Adding to this mix are the economic and political turbulence (resulting, for example, from the manipulation of budget deficits as special interest groups assert power with the aid of modern media methods) and the social turbulence, arising from changing population demographics and a highly pluralistic society.

There seems to be little question that you and your peers will experience environmental change at an augmented rate never before experienced by humankind. Similarly, organizations in all phases of their life cycles will experience this whirlpool-type environment. In the past, organizational behavior practitioners have spoken of ''coping with change'' as a primary viewpoint for meeting this challenge, but more recently they have broadened this view to include a more proactive strategy of **innovation,** which emphasizes finding new products and new methods to enable organizations to maintain the lead in competitive endeavors. At present, the buzzwords *creativity* and *innovation* fill the work world vocabulary. Organizations like Asian Brown Bovery (ABB), General Electric, Ford, IBM, Intel, and Coca-Cola send their employees to training programs where they learn techniques for becoming more creative in their thinking. Numerous games and software are now available to teach people how to become more creative. But let us turn first to defining and exploring the relevant concepts. Next we will present a summary of some of the literature that describes strategies being used in organizations to attain a competitive edge regarding creativity and innovation. We begin by discussing creativity as an aspect of individual effectiveness and then move on to describing innovation in organizational effectiveness.

What Is Creativity?

Recently, an interactionist model of creative behavior was proposed.[4] The interactionist view suggests that **creativity** is the complex product of a person's behavior in a given situation. The situation is characterized in terms of the contextual and social influences that either facilitate or hinder creative accomplishments. The person brings with himself or herself to the situation cognitive abilities, personality traits, and noncognitive abilities. The interactionist view provides an integrative framework that combines important elements of personality (see Module 5), cognitive style and abilities, social psychology elements such as leadership dynamics (see Module 3), group dynamics (see Module 10), motivation (see Module 6), organizational elements such as work and organization design (see Module 13), and technology and information technology (to be examined in Module 16). Figure 15–1 captures the interactionist model of organizational creativity.

It is probably most useful to start with the view of cognitive psychology that the brain is a creative entity, continuously processing data for problem solving, understanding, and responding, mostly at the unconscious level. We are all creative because the brain is creative. Creative in this sense means processing data to come up with an answer, whether it be ''get out of the way of that oncoming truck'' (an unconscious response) or arithmetic reasoning (a primarily but not entirely conscious process). Webster's dictionary brings this into focus by defining *creativity* as ''the ability to bring something new into existence.'' Early experiments by Wolfgang Koehler add the element of ''insight'' to creativity.[5] Koehler placed a piece of fruit outside a chimpanzee's cage and beyond the reach of a stick in the chimp's hand. He placed a longer stick in the vicinity of the fruit. The chimp tried without success to reach the fruit with the short stick. After an extended pause, the chimp suddenly used the short stick to drag the longer one to him, and then used the longer stick to haul in the fruit. This sudden flash of insight into the right answer has been referred to as the *aha process* or *eureka process.*

Scientists long ago[6] developed a process to exploit the ''insight'' mechanism, and they show up on TV talk shows from time to time to tell about it. When confronted with a difficult problem, they systematically go through several stages:

1. Studying the problem area to realize its different aspects.
2. Saturating the brain with all available data.
3. Allowing incubation time during which the cognitive process at the unconscious level reform and reshape the data.
4. Awaiting enlightenment (insight).
5. Hypotheses testing.

Figure 15–1
Conceptual Links among Creative Persons, Processes, Situations, and Products

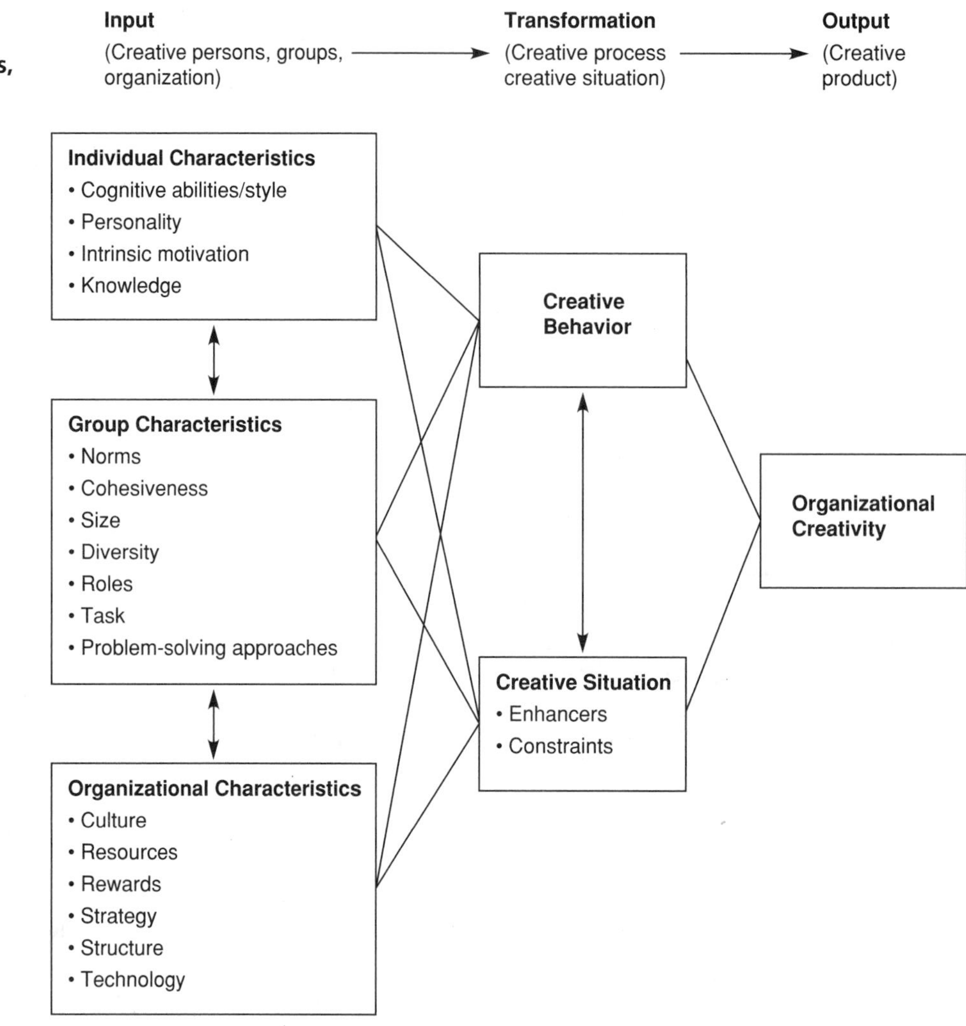

Source: R. W. Woodman, J. E. Sawyer, and R. W. Griffin, "Toward a Theory of Organizational Creativity," *Academy of Management Review* 18, no. 2 (1993), p. 309.

This process is used in many professions. Engineers are intensely aware of this inventive approach. Judges most often do not give decisions until time for incubation is allowed. Architects work and rework designs. All of us do this naturally, but awareness and practice can augment our effectiveness in both personal and work lives. (The next time you write a term paper, follow this procedure. After time for incubation, you will be surprised how much better than expected the material will fall into meaningful form so that you can write an excellent paper.)

Defining creativity as we have used it refers to brain functions of acquiring and processing data for purposes of problem solving, whether it be responses, answers, actions, or new ideas. This involves both unconscious and conscious processes.

As we have seen, the interactionist view would advocate the need to stress that in working organizations, everyone has potential for creativity—to solve problems and to give new ideas. Executives and managers with whom we have worked most always are looking for "creative people," assuming that "you've either got it (creativity) or you haven't," the implication being that there are very few who have it. Yet most consultant firms readily admit that their recommendations in managerial and organizational effectiveness surveys come primarily from internal sources: the employees they have interviewed. (Of course, these firms have performed the important function of judging the merits of each recommendation.)

There is further support for this idea. In Sternberg's studies, unskilled workers in a milk-processing plant always developed operating procedures that required the least physical efforts. The author reviewed other studies consistent with these findings and concluded,

> Beneath the surface of adaptation, however, lie continuing acts of creativity—the invention of new ways of handling old and new problems. Since creativity is a term ordinarily reserved for exceptional individuals and extraordinary accomplishments, recognizing it in the practical problem-solving activities of ordinary people introduced a new perspective from which to grasp the challenge of the ordinary.[7]

Carrying this idea one step further, there is additional evidence for widespread creativity in the multitude of unique ways in which disgruntled workers can come up with methods to resist or even sabotage management.

We know that there are some people who have more new ideas than others, but we also want to point out that the widespread (and self-fulfilling) expectation system of management overlooks the major contributions that the whole body of the employee system has to offer.

Distinguishing between Creativity and Innovation

Sociologists have long used concepts related to these subjects. Invention represents a completely new idea, often related to technology, that has an impact on societal institutions. Innovation is the reforming or reworking of old ideas to come up with something new. Both of these ideas would be included in our recent definition of creativity. We mention this here because the term *innovation* is currently being used in organizational settings in a trendy way to mean many things. In much of the literature discussing applications of creativity and innovation, the words are used loosely and often interchangeably. Current usage in organizational behavior defies definition of innovation as a concept. However, J. J. Kao's distinction between creativity and innovation is adequate for our purposes.[8] If creativity implies the vision of what is possible, then the term *innovation* suggests the implementation process by which inspiration leads to the practical results. Creativity involves problem solving that may lead to a useful idea. The term *innovation* is more suitably applied to decision-making processes: the decision to search for a new, useful idea; the decision to select the most useful idea; and the decision of how to implement the chosen idea.

Although creativity depends on many uncontrollable factors (such as the degree of knowledge available; the characteristics, skills, and motivation of the person or persons involved; and a good dose of chance or luck), innovation requires organizational choice and change that can be planned. Finally, an innovation when defined as implementation is not necessarily unique. Successful innovation may result from imitation or adoption of an innovation from another source.

Many people use the term *invention* when they are distinguishing creativity from innovation. However this distinction can be misleading about the nature of creativity. Most of us think of an invention as a tangible, usually technical, product or an idea that can be readily translated into a useful product. This is too limiting a view of creativity. Creativity involves characteristics of the individual exhibiting creative behavior and a process as well as a product.

Creativity can be defined from three perspectives: person-oriented, process-oriented, and product-oriented. The **person-oriented approach** to creativity studies patterns of personality traits and characteristics observed in individuals who exhibit creative behavior. Such creative behavior might include the activities of inventing, designing, contriving, composing, and planning.[9] The **process-oriented approach to creativity** examines the development of a new and valuable idea or product through the unique interaction of the individual with the available resources, settings, people, and situations. The **product-oriented approach to creativity** focuses on the production of novel and useful ideas by an individual or a small group of individuals working together. A full understanding of creativity requires an integration of these orientations. An agreement seems to exist that the creative behavior, the creative interaction, and the creative idea need not be successful, commercial, or applied.

Innovation, in contrast, generally refers to the successful application of a new idea to the firm. Success in this case refers to the actual translation of the idea into a useful product or process. An innovation may or may not be profitable or beneficial to the firm. Innovation is a process of developing and implementing a new idea, whether it is a new technology, product, or organizational process. Obviously, creativity can be a part of this implementation process.[10] It may involve recombining old ideas in a new way, a scheme that challenges the present order, or an approach perceived as new by those involved.[11] Note that the idea need not be a breakthrough idea such as superconductivity or a completely new organizational model; it need only be new, or perceived as new, to the organization. Given these distinctions between creativity and innovation, we next examine people's orientations toward creativity.

The Creative Person

The stereotyped image we have of the creative person originates from the mad scientist, the crazy artist, the computer nerd, or the absent-minded professor. We typically think of a collection of personality traits that immediately sets the individual off from others. Do such stereotypes hold? Outstanding creative people have been studied across fields to try to determine the common traits. Unfortunately the common traits do not come in a precise package that would help you to immediately identify a creative person.

The intelligence level has been of major interest. Exceptionally creative architects, mathematicians, scientists, and engineers usually score no higher on intelligence tests than their less creative peers. Testing suggests that a certain level of intelligence is related to creativity, but the correlation between the two factors disappears when the person's IQ is above 120. This lack of correlation is particularly important to know in a work setting because managers tend to believe that only the brightest people are apt to be creative. (Refer back to our previous discussion of creativity being widespread among workers.)

In general, the literature tends to show that expertise and intrinsic motivation are essential components of creativity—which is another way of saying that the individual has to know the field and want to do something about the problem. The following characteristics also have been related to creativity: high energy level, dedicated and effective work habits, a persistent and high level of curiosity, interest in reflective thinking, relatively little tie to reality, low level of sociability, unusual appreciation of humor, facility for producing humor, need for adventure, need for variety, self-confidence, tolerance of ambiguity, introversion, high need for autonomy, self-direction, and an impulsive personality.

Defining the creative person is not as easy as looking for people who display these characteristics. Not all creative people exhibit all of these characteristics. And many of these characteristics may be shared by people who are not perceived as especially creative.

The Organizational Context of Creativity

Creativity involves a special kind of problem solving. In organizational settings, attempts have been made to identify potentially creative people by observing their problem-solving behavior. Yet, as we have seen, individual creativity is a function of antecedent conditions (i.e., part reinforcement history), cognitive style and ability (i.e., divergent thinking), personality, relevant knowledge, motivation, social influences, and group, unit, and organizational factors.[12]

The Adaption-Innovation Model

The **adaption-innovation model**—and others—identify two types of people within organizations: adaptors and innovators.[13] *Adaptors* prefer structured situations, seek answers to the problem at hand, and are perceived by innovators as being rigid, conforming, "safe" people. *Innovators,* on the other hand, appreciate an unstructured work environment, seek to answer questions that have not yet been asked, and are perceived by adaptors as being impractical, abrasive risk takers. Although these types can both be found in all organizations and are both needed in the organization, research has found that both are capable of generating original creative solutions but from different problem-solving orientations. (See Figure 15–2.)[14]

Figure 15–2 **Characteristics of Adaptors and Innovators**

Implications	Adaptors	Innovators
For problem solving	Tend to take the problem as defined and generate novel, creative ideas aimed at "doing things better." Immediate high efficiency is the keynote of high adaptors	Tend to redefine generally agreed problems, breaking previously perceived restraints, generating solutions aimed at "doing things differently."
For solutions	Generally generate a few well-chosen and relevant solutions that they generally find sufficient but that sometimes fail to contain ideas needed to break the existing pattern completely.	Produce numerous ideas, many of which may not be either obvious or acceptable to others. Such a pool often contains ideas, if they can be identified, that may crack hitherto intractable problems.
For policies	Prefer well-established structured situations. Best at incorporating new data or events into existing structures of policies.	Prefer unstructured situations. Use new data as opportunities to set new structures or policies accepting the greater attendant risk.
For organizational "fit"	Essential to the ongoing functions, but in times of unexpected changes may have some difficulty moving out of their established role.	Essential in times of change or crisis, but may have some trouble applying themselves to ongoing organizational demands.
For potential creativity	Capable of generating original, creative solutions, but which reflect their overall approach to problem solving	Capable of generating original, creative solutions, but which reflect their overall approach to problem solving
For collaboration	High adaptors do not get along easily with innovators. Middle adaptors may act as bridges	High innovators do not get along easily with adaptors. Middle innovators may act as bridges.
For perceived behavior	Seen by innovators as sound, conforming, safe, predictable, relevant, inflexible, wedded to the system, and intolerant of ambiguity.	Seen by adaptors as unsound, impractical, risky, abrasive, often shocking their opposites and creating dissonance.

Source: Adapted with permission from M. J. Kirton, "Adaptors and Innovators: Problem Solvers in Organizations," in *Innovation: A Cross-Disciplinary Perspective,* K. Gronhaug and G. Kaufmann, eds. (Oslo: Norwegian University Press, 1988), p. 72.

Motivation and Creativity

We have argued that the personality traits associated with creativity are not enough to guarantee creative behavior. What motivates a person to be creative? The process is complex and involves both intrinsic and extrinsic motivation as well as skills and abilities. The components of individual creativity are shown in Figure 15–3.[15] The framework clusters three components of individual creativity: domain-relevant skills, creativity-relevant skills, and task motivation.

Domain-relevant skills are the general skills in the area (or domain) an individual must bring to the situation. If a person is working on a problem in microelectronics, then he or she must be knowledgeable, talented, and trained, for example, in electrical engineering.

Creativity-relevant skills are the "something extra" that makes the difference in creative performance. The individual's cognitive style is characterized by the ability to break out of old ways of thinking. The individual also depends on a *heuristic* (a general strategy that helps in approaching problems or tasks). A creative heuristic might be "when all else fails, try something counterintuitive" or "make the familiar strange." Finally, the individual's working style must be conducive to creativity. For example, persistence, a long attention span, and the ability to venture off in a new direction when the well-worn direction is not leading to a new idea are all characteristics of a creative work style. Creativity-relevant skills depend on training, experience, and also the personality characteristics mentioned earlier.

Regardless of the individual's skill level, it is **task motivation** that determines if these skills will be fully utilized. If a person is not motivated to do something, no amount of skills can compensate for the lack of motivation. The individual's attitude

Figure 15–3 Components of Individual Creativity

Domain-Relevant Skills	Creativity-Relevant Skills	Task Motivation
Includes	*Includes*	*Includes*
Knowledge about the domain Technical skills required Special domain-relevant "talent"	Appropriate cognitive style Implicit or explicit heuristics for generating novel ideas Conducive work style	Attitudes toward the task Perceptions of own motivation for undertaking the task
Depends on	*Depends on*	*Depends on*
Innate cognitive abilities Innate perceptual and motor skills Formal and informal education	Training Experience in idea generation Personality characteristics	Initial level of intrinsic motivation to the task Presence or absence of salient extrinsic constraints in the social environment Individual ability to cognitively minimize extrinsic constraints

Source: Adapted with permission from T. M. Amabile, "From Individual Creativity to Organizational Innovation," in *Innovation: A Cross-Disciplinary Perspective,* K. Gronhaug and G. Kaufmann, eds. (Oslo: Norwegian University Press, 1988), p. 149.

toward the task is simply the person's natural inclination either toward or away from the task—do I want to do this or not? The individual's perception of his or her motivation, however, depends on factors in the social and work environments. If an individual feels that there are extrinsic motivational factors in the environment intended to control his or her performance of the task (e.g., surveillance, evaluation, deadlines, competition, rewards, and restricted choices), his or her motivation to generate new ideas is likely to suffer. In contrast, if the person does not feel pressures to perform in a certain way or if the person is able to minimize or ignore such pressures, he or she is likely to have a higher level of motivation, even a "passion" for the project.

Creativity and Commitment

One additional element that may be related to the degree of intrinsic motivation is the individual's *commitment* to the organization (the degree to which an employee's personal goals are aligned with the organization's goals). Some authors have suggested that (1) there is a direct connection between level of commitment and motivation to engage in creative behaviors and (2) highly ideological organizations will produce more highly committed individuals.[16]

Creativity and Social Influence

What are the external influences that can operate on the individual, encouraging the display and development of creative potential in the organization? What can be done to increase creative behavior within the organization, that is, to turn a potentially creative person into an actively creative person? We have described some of the factors that can inhibit creativity, but several factors have been identified that have a positive effect on creative behavior. These factors can be organized into the general areas of freedom, support, and participation.[17]

Freedom: Freedom from external constraints can lead to creative behavior. The notion of freedom includes the following managerial actions:

1. Provide freedom to try new ways of performing tasks.
2. Permit activities or tasks to be different for different individuals.
3. Allow an appropriate amount of time for the accomplishment of tasks.
4. Allow time for non–task-related thinking and development of creative ideas.
5. Encourage self-initiated projects.
6. Respect an individual's need to work alone.
7. Encourage divergent activities by providing resources and room.

Support: Noncontrolling support can be given in the following ways:

1. Support and reinforce unusual ideas and responses of individuals.
2. Communicate confidence in the individuals.
3. Tolerate complexity and disorder.
4. Provide constructive feedback.
5. Reduce concern over failure.
6. Create a climate of mutual respect and acceptance among individuals.
7. Encourage interpersonal trust.
8. Listen to individuals.

Participation: Involving the individual in the decision-making process as well as the problem-solving process (participation) provides motivation that encourages creative behavior. Participation can be enhanced in the following ways:

1. Encourage individuals to have choices and be part of the goal-setting process.
2. Encourage involvement of those interested in the problem—don't limit involvement across jobs, departments, and divisions.
3. Challenge individuals to find new tasks and problems.
4. Encourage questioning.
5. Encourage a high quality of interpersonal relationships including a spirit of cooperation, open confrontation of conflicts, and the expression of ideas.

Freedom, support, and participation can be implemented in a variety of ways, depending on the situation. The application of these factors can reduce the extrinsic motivational factors that have a negative effect on creative performance.

Developing the Creative Process within the Organization

The ways of increasing creativity listed previously make up the organizational environment in which the creative process is to take place. The organization must introduce into this context a learning model for operational use. Individuals and teams must be made aware of the **creative process,** which we described in our discussion at the beginning of the chapter, and they must make a systematic effort to allow it to work. Thus, in stage 1, the problem is defined in all its dimensions, and decisions are made regarding who will be involved, who has the expertise, and what support is needed. Management needs to select people for participation who have the required domain-relevant skills and the task motivation ensuring high-level involvement. In stage 2, data are collected and all available sources are explored. Again, domain-relevant skills and creativity-relevant skills are essential. In stage 3, time lapse for the incubation of ideas and the injection of new data is allowed, with the recognition that there will be periods of no progress, that consultation and dialogues may be needed, and that dropping the effort temporarily may be useful. In stage 4, insight (hopefully) comes to the individual or the team in terms of useful ideas or solutions. Finally, in stage 5, some testing and verification is conducted to find out if the idea will be useful and if its implementation is possible.

Throughout the creative process, two types of thinking have been identified: divergent thinking and convergent thinking. Divergent thinking is creative thinking. By using divergent thinking, the individual creates new connections between ideas (as in making metaphors) and thinks of many possibilities and alternatives (as in brainstorming). In this type of thinking, a person's built-in censor is temporarily turned off. Convergent or critical thinking involves comparing and contrasting, improving and refining, screening, judging, selecting, and decision making. In the creative process, the individual moves back and forth between these types of thinking. In group settings, different individuals may be valued for their divergent or convergent skills.

Team Creativity

We have focused primarily on the role of the individual in creativity. Now we wish to refer you back to Module 9 where team problem solving and decision making were discussed. We noted that under certain conditions teams can achieve synergy—a group solution superior to that of the most accurate member's solution. One reason for this superior group solution was that the pool of knowledge in the group was usually greater than that of any individual. Another reason was creativity: Individuals built on others' ideas and produced new ideas. There were many factors at work. There seems to be little doubt that the interactive group process can be productive. However, managers must examine the conditions under which teams can be expected to be more creative or better solve problems than individuals. Certainly the conditions must be right. Expertise is often a major factor for including team members.

From Creativity to Innovation

Once a creative idea has been developed and verified, how does it become meaningful to the organization? The creative process described previously is commonly perceived as the first step in the process of innovation. It is a necessary first step to innovation, whether the innovation is a ground-breaking internal discovery or an idea brought to the organization from the outside. How the process unfolds is a function of the type of innovation, the innovation process itself, and key elements that influence innovation.

Innovation is rarely the work of one individual. As we saw, in the 3M case, many people, from scientists to managers, were involved in bringing that creative idea to commercial fruition.

Organizational Innovation

Types of Innovation

At the beginning of this module, we defined *innovation* as the successful application of a new idea to the firm. The idea may be a new technology, a new product, or a new organizational or administrative process. The innovation may be an imitation of a product, a person, or an idea used elsewhere, which becomes unique because it is placed within a new context.

We tend to think most often of innovations as **radical innovations** (discontinuous breakthroughs in technology).[18] Often, however, there is an **incremental innovation** (an improvement of a technology, product, or process). A series of incremental innovations can lead to radical innovation, as in the 3M case where Silver discovered the Post-It note adhesive while experimenting on improving traditional adhesives. Another distinction is between process and product innovations. A zero-defect quality control system is an example of a **process innovation. Product innovations** are usually the more visible of the two types, but not necessarily the more important. A product innovation can require process innovation.

Administrative innovations often affect the organization as much or more than technological innovations. New incentive systems and new communication network systems are just two examples of administrative innovations, as are new marketing and sales techniques.

Finally, it is important to make a distinction between **system-maintaining innovation (SMI)** and **system-transforming innovation (STI).** SMI refers to new ideas that enhance or improve some aspect of the business without changing the overall nature of how the organization operates. STI refers to a new idea that affects the fundamental aspects of organizing, requiring change in several of the subsystems or segments of the organization in order to fully implement the innovation.

Stages of the Innovation Process

Although there are many types of innovation, it is generally agreed that the **innovation process** for each is similar. Descriptions of the innovation process have been borrowed from many fields. Group development and problem-solving models,[19] decision process models,[20] and organizational change models[21] have all been applied to the innovation process.[19] These models as well as innovation process models have traditionally viewed the innovation process as occurring in a linear fashion in a series of discrete stages, generally from idea generation to adoption to implementation.[22] Although these activities occur in innovation, there is little empirical evidence for their occurrence in discrete stages. More recent research has found that the process is more ''fluid'' than stage theories would suggest.

The Minnesota Innovation Studies Program has been one of the most comprehensive research projects seeking to understand the process of innovation. Based on an in-depth review of longitudinal development of seven major innovations, the researchers of this study made six important observations about the process:

1. An initial shock to the organization precedes innovation. This shock may be new leadership, product failure, budget crisis, lack of market share, opportunity, or dissatisfaction of some kind.
2. Ideas proliferate.
3. While ideas are proliferating, setbacks and surprises are likely to occur.
4. These setbacks and surprises provide opportunities for trial-and-error learning and the blending of old and new ideas.
5. Restructuring of the organization at some or all levels occurs.
6. A hands-on approach of top management is evident all the way through the process.[23]

It is evident that this view of the innovation process is not a neat, step-by-step, easily planned activity. How the process unfolds is determined by the elements described next.

Key Elements That Influence the Innovation Process

Key Players and Roles

The previous description of the innovation process emphasizes the important role of top management in influencing innovation. Not only does top management provide resources for innovation, it also provides a vision of the organization and its members as innovative. In addition, several roles required in the innovation process have been described. As early as 1931, the phenomenon of innovation was being studied by J. Schumpeter, an economist.[24] His basic ''one-man theory'' described characteristics of the ''dynamic entrepreneur.'' This figure is still evident in small and new organizations. However, in larger organizations, it makes sense to view a variety of individuals who participate by playing different roles.

The *product champion* is the one who promotes the innovation and overcomes resistance to change. The product champion may or may not have formal power and influence within the organization, but this person has top-management support, which is necessary for success.[25]

The *technical innovator* is the inventor or the one who makes the most significant technical contribution to the innovation. In the 3M case this role may have been shared by Silver and Fry.[26]

The *technological gatekeeper* has been identified as the person who has both technical know-how and formal influence channels to other parts of the organization.[27]

Atmosphere or Climate

The organizational factors that were discussed as positively influencing creativity—freedom, support, and participation—also influence innovation, which is reasonable because creativity and innovation are viewed as parts of the same process. The climate or culture of the organization (the visions and goals, strategies, style of leadership, work setting, characteristics of the individuals, type of work, way people organize to get the work done, qualitative features of the context, and the values and norms of the people) may promote or inhibit innovation. How to measure the creative climate of the organization has been problematic. Using questionnaires and interviews, researchers have had some success discriminating between working climates that are more or less favorable to innovative outcomes.[28]

Organization Design

Managing work and the organization design process were discussed in Module 13. However, the relationship between organization design and innovation isn't definite. An early study of organizational innovation identified organic versus mechanistic organizations as likely to encourage innovation.[29] Bureaucracy, with its formal hierarchical levels, has often been identified as the mechanistic organization, whereas the organic organization has been described as flat. However, other researchers have argued that no one form of organization is superior to another in terms of being conducive to innovation; rather, it is the links for collaboration and problem solving throughout the organization that are important.[30] Reorganization during the process of innovation is likely to result in different designs as well as structures.

Incentives, Rewards, and Evaluation

We have seen that expected evaluation has been found to have a detrimental effect on creativity and that external incentives must stimulate intrinsic motivation. (See Module 6.) It is not so clear how reward systems contribute to creative and innovative effort. One view is that rewards based on seniority rather than performance tend to inhibit innovation and creativity, whereas merit-based systems, in which individual performance is rewarded, stimulate creativity. However, in Japan, where lifetime employment systems and seniority-based reward systems in large organizations are the norm, long-range thinking appears to be promoted, and there seems to be less necessity to resist new ideas (and freedom to fail) because a person's promotion and rewards are not based on short-term performance.[31] Innovative firms generally have innovative incentive and reward systems, which acknowledge both individual and group efforts in nonthreatening ways.

Job Design, Job Rotation, and Careers

Jobs that offer intrinsic motivation to perform well, that involve the employee, and that provide variety and autonomy tend to increase innovative levels of activity. (See Modules 6 and 13.) Recently, career planning involving **dual ladders** has gained a lot of attention. (Career planning is addressed in more depth in Module 18.) In a dual-ladder system, a high-performing individual may choose to climb the managerial or technical ladder, depending on his or her own personal preferences and goals. Companies such as 3M, Monsanto, Eastman Kodak, and General Mills have successfully implemented dual-ladder systems, which they've found lead to more open communications, are an aid in recruiting, and provide better advancement opportunities for people at all levels.[32] To be successful, the dual-ladder system requires the full commitment of management.

Management's Challenge

If creativity and innovation are both parts of a process that is becoming a greater and greater necessity in today's organizations, then managers must become aware of how this process can be managed. Innovation is not a simple, straightforward process. Innovation implies change, although not all change is innovation. Just as there is no one way to organize, there is no one way to encourage innovation. Innovation is risky, and the manager's role in this process can be likened to a balancing act. On the one hand, he or she must provide the stability, support, and security that free employees from the fear of failure. On the other hand, the manager must encourage risk taking, which is likely to result in new ideas that are beneficial to the organization as a whole.

Part of this challenge is to hire, train, and develop a set of individuals with not only a variety of specialized and technical skills and abilities, but also skills in problem solving, communication, conflict resolution, and team building. (See Modules 8, 9, and 11.) Another part of the challenge is to retain these employees not only through innovative reward and incentive systems, but also by providing the vision, resources, autonomy, and support they need.

This is far from an easy task. Innovative environments are turbulent, and the innovation process requires the management of change as an integral part of organizational and managerial routines. In addition to providing a free, supportive, and participative environment to encourage creative thinking, management must also deal with resistance to change, which is likely to occur in some parts of the organization when an innovation is developed. All of these elements demand that the manager be involved in an ongoing, creative problem-solving process. Creativity and innovation rely on creative and innovative management processes.

Cautions on Creativity

When expectations for creativity and innovation in the work world are high, there are bound to be counterproductive excesses. Young people may feel they will not be regarded as having high potential if they are not offering new ideas; and managers can feel they are not providing a supportive climate if they do not try new ideas. A "change for the sake of change" approach can be disruptive and must be guarded against. "If it's not broken, don't fix it," is often good advice.

Summary

In this module we have examined the organizational process that begins with creativity at the individual or team level and culminates in an innovation that contributes to the success of the organization as a whole. We have defined *creativity* as the brain functions of acquiring and processing data for the purposes of problem solving, whether it be responses, answers, actions, or new ideas. This involves both unconscious and conscious processes. A five-stage process for the individual to utilize in producing creative reactions was given. Innovation, in contrast, was used as the implementation process through which creative ideas are transformed into practical applications in the organization.

Study Questions

1. Creativity and innovation are different parts of the same process. Can an innovation occur without creativity? Discuss why or why not.
2. "The creative person is born, not made." Do you agree or disagree? Why?
3. Charlie likes to wrestle with a problem for several days or weeks, looking at it from all sides. Janet focuses on solving the problem efficiently and doesn't worry if she has considered all possible solutions. Which of the two is likely to be more creative? Why?
4. Sam loves his job because it is open-ended and he decides what to do each day. He works hard, often forgetting to quit at 5 PM. Discuss Sam's motivation.
5. List the five steps in the creative process. Identify the skills required at each step.

6. Think of an innovation that you would consider radical. How does it differ from an incremental innovation?
7. Mr. Jones has just returned from a short course on innovative management and has decided to reorganize his firm to increase innovation. He has isolated the scientists and design engineers in one building so they won't be disturbed by the production people and the marketing and sales forces. Is Mr. Jones's plan likely to increase innovative activity? Why?
8. Two employees of a high-tech firm began their careers with the firm as design engineers. Both are highly skilled, creative workers. Employee A now manages the production research department. Employee B has a private lab in the basement. Both are very satisfied. Discuss career choices and personal and organizational factors that led to this situation.
9. You are designing a new incentive and reward system for a research and development lab. All the employees have advanced engineering degrees, and the market for their skills is very competitive. How would you structure such a system?
10. Mrs. White has just been hired to run a large, nationwide temporary employment company. The former CEO suggests to her that she might be interested in attending a seminar on managing innovation. Mrs. White laughs and says, "Why would I want to do that? We're not concerned with innovation around here. That's something for managers of high-tech companies." Do you agree or disagree with Mrs. White? Explain your answer.

Endnotes

1. See, for example, S. G. Scott and R. A. Bruce, "Determinants of Innovative Behavior: A Path Model of Individual Innovation in the Workplace." *Academy of Management Journal* 37, no. 3 (1994), pp. 580–607.

2. See, for example, R. W. Woodman, J. E. Sawyer, and R. W. Griffin, "Towards a Theory of Organizational Creativity," *Academy of Management Review* 18, no. 1 (1993), pp. 293–321.

3. Alvin Toffler and Heide Toffler, *Powershift* (New York: Bantam Books, 1990); T. M. Amabile, "The Motivation to Be Creative," in *Frontiers of Creativity Research: Beyond the Basics,* ed. S. Isaksen (New York: Bearly Limited, 1987), pp. 223–54.

4. See R. W. Woodman and J. F. Schoenfeldt, "An Interactionist Model of Creative Behavior," *Journal of Creative Behavior* 24 (1990), pp. 279–90; and R. W. Woodman and J. E. Sawyer, *An Interactionist Model of Organizational Creativity,"* paper presented at the annual Academy of Management Meeting, Miami, 1991.

5. W. Koehler, *The Mentality of Apes* (London: Pelican, 1925/1957).

6. G. Wallas, "Stages of Control," *The Art of Thought* (New York: Harcourt Brace Jovanovich, 1926).

7. R. J. Sternberg, *The Nature of Creativity: Contemporary Psychological Perspectives* (New York: Cambridge University Press, 1988); R. J. Sternberg, and R. K. Wagner, *Practical Intelligence* (New York: Cambridge University Press, 1986).

8. J. J. Kao, *Managing Creativity* (Englewood Cliffs, N.J.: Prentice-Hall, 1991); D. Bohm, and F. D. Peat, *Science, Order, and Creativity* (New York: Bantam Books, 1987); J. R. Evans, *Creative Thinking* (Cincinnati: South Western, 1991).

9. J. P. Guilford, "Creativity," *American Psychologist* 14 (1950), pp. 469–79; J. P. Guilford, "Creativity Research: A Quarter Century of Progress," in *Perspectives in Creativity,* eds. I. A. Taylor and J. W. Getzels (New York: Aldine, 1975).

10. E. Rogers, *The Diffusion of Innovations,* 3rd ed. (New York: Free Press, 1983); and A. H. Van de Ven, "Central Problems in the Management of Innovation," *Management Science* (May, 1986), pp. 590–607.

11. G. Zaltman, R. Duncan, and J. Holbek, *Innovations and Organizations* (New York: Wiley-Interscience, 1973).

12. Woodman, Sawyer, and Griffin, ''Towards a Theory of Organizational Creativity,'' p. 296.

13. M. J. Kirton, ''Adaptors and Innovators: Cognitive Style and Personality,'' in *Frontiers of Creative Research,* ed. S. Isaksen (New York: Bearly Limited, 1987), pp. 282–304.

14. M. J. Kirton, ''Adaptors and Innovators: Problem Solvers in Organizations,'' in *Innovation: A Cross-Disciplinary Perspective,* eds. K. Gronhaug and G. Kaufmann (Norway: Norwegian University Press, 1988), p. 72.

15. T. M. Amabile, ''The Motivation to be Creative,'' in *Frontiers of Creativity Research,* ed. S. Isaksen (New York: Bearly Limited, 1987), p. 223–54.

16. R. L. Kuhn and G. T. Geis, ''A Cross-Organization Methodology for Assessing Creativity and Commitment,'' in *New Directions in Creative and Innovative Management,* eds. Yuji Ijiri and Robert Kuhn (Cambridge, Mass.: Ballinger Publishing Co., 1988), pp. 303–22.

17. S. G. Isaksen, ''Educational Implications of Creativity Research: An Updated Rationale for Creative Learning,'' in *Frontiers of Creativity Research,* ed. S. Isaksen (New York: Bearly Limited, 1987), p. 149.

18. M. Tushman and D. Nadler, ''Organizing for Innovation,'' *California Management Review* (Spring 1986), pp. 74–92; J. Galbraith, ''Designing the Innovating Organization.'' *Organizational Dynamics,* Winter 1982, pp. 5–25.

19. K. Lewin, ''Frontiers in Group Dynamics,'' *Human Relations* 1 (1947), pp. 5–41; and R. F. Bales and F. L. Strodtbeck, ''Phases in Group Problem-Solving,'' *Journal of Abnormal and Social Psychology* 46 (1951), pp. 485–95.

20. J. G. March and H. Simon, *Organizations* (New York: John Wiley & Sons, 1958); and M. D. Cohen, J. G. March, and J. P. Olsen, ''A Garbage Can Model of Organizational Choice,'' *Administrative Science Quarterly* 17 (1972), pp. 1–25.

21. G. W. Dalton, P. R. Lawrence, and L. E. Greiner, *Organizational Change and Development* (Homewood, Ill: Dorsey Press, 1970).

22. W. J. Abernathy and J. M. Utterback, ''Patterns of Industrial Innovation,'' in *Readings in the Management of Innovation,* eds. M. Tushman and W. Moore (Boston: Pitman 1975), pp. 97–150; M. Jelinek, and C. Bird-Schoonhoven, *Innovation Marathon: Lessons from High Technology Firms* (Oxford, England: Basil Blackwell, 1990); R. M. Kanter, ''Innovation—The Only Hope for Times Ahead?'' *Sloan Management Review,* Summer 1984, pp. 51–55.

23. R. Schroeder, A. H. Van de Ven, G. D. Scudder, and D. Polley, ''The Development of Innovative Ideas,'' in *Research on the Management of Innovation: The Minnesota Studies,* eds. A. H. Van de Ven, H. Angle, and M. Poole (New York: Harper & Row, 1990), pp. 107–34.

24. J. Schumpeter, *Theorie der wirtschaftlichen Entwicklung. Eine Untersuchung uber Unternehmergewinn, Kapital, Kredit, Zins und den Konjunkturzyklus,* 3rd ed. (Munich: Duncker & Humblot, 1931).

25. A. K. Chakrabarti, ''The Role of Champions in Product Innovation,'' *California Management Review* 17 (Winter 1974), pp. 58–62; Kjell Gronhaug, and Geir Kaufmann, *Innovation: A Cross-Disciplinary Perspective* (Oslo: Norwegian University Press, 1988).

26. T. J. Allen and S. I. Cohen, ''Information Flow in Research and Development Laboratories,'' *Administrative Science Quarterly* 14 (1969), pp. 12–19.

27. G. Ekvall and Y. T. Andersson, ''Working Climate and Creativity: A Study of an Innovative Newspaper Office,'' *Journal of Creative Behavior* 20 (1986), pp. 215–25; and R. M. Burnside, T. M. Amabile, and S. S. Gryskiewicz, ''Assessing Organizational Climates for Creativity and Innovation: Methodological Review of Large Company Audits,'' in *New Directions in Creative and Innovative Management,* eds. Yuji Ijiri and Robert Kuhn (Cambridge, Mass.: Ballinger Publishing Co., 1988), pp. 169–86.

28. T. Burns and G. M. Stalker, *The Management of Innovation* (London: Tavistock Publications, 1961).

29. J. L. Pierce and A. L. Delbecq, ''Organization Structure, Individual Attitudes, and Innovation,'' *Academy of Management Review* 2, (January 1977), pp. 27–37.

30. M. Jelinek and C. B. Schoonhoven, *Innovation Marathon* (Cambridge, Mass.: Basil Blackwell, 1990).

31. T. Kono, *Structure of Japanese Enterprises* (London: Macmillan, 1984).

32. M. F. Wolff, 'Revamping the Dual Ladder at General Mills,'' *Research Management,* November 1979, pp. 8–11.

Activity 15–2: Making a Metaphor

Objective:

To explore individual paradigms that affect individual creativity. A metaphor is a figure of speech in which we liken two objects or concepts that do not appear to be alike. Through metaphor we can make connections and discoveries that did not previously exist. We can make the familiar strange and thus challenge our way of thinking. In the 3M case, metaphors had to be changed so people could break through old mental sets.

Task 1:

Complete the following metaphors, choosing from one of the options given or making up your own.

Eating a fine dinner is like
a. Throwing a javelin a long distance.
b. Watching an hourglass drip sand.
c. Reading a popular novel at the beach.
d. Putting nail polish on your toes.

Raising a child is like
a. Driving from Seattle to New York.
b. Weeding your garden.
c. Building a fire and watching it burn.
d. Fishing for rainbow trout.

Playing a piano recital is like
a. Investing in the stock market.
b. Growing orchids.
c. Driving through rush hour traffic with your gas gauge on empty.
d. Fasting for three days.

Finding truth is like
a. Making banana nut bread.
b. Walking into a room and forgetting the reason why.
c. Navigating a sailboat through a violent thunderstorm.
d. Taking a test that has no wrong answers.

Task 2:

Share your metaphors with your group. Explain why you chose the metaphor you did. The instructor will facilitate a class discussion on the use of metaphors and creativity.

Source: This activity is adopted with permission from R. von Oeck, *A Kick in the Seat of the Pants* (New York: Warner Books, 1986), p. 72.

Activity 15–3: Fostering Creativity and Innovation in the Intercon Semiconductor Company

Objective:

To identify the organizational elements that affect innovation and creativity.

Task 1:

a. Students are to read the Intercon Semiconductor Company case.
b. Students are to analyze the case and provide answers to President Bergman's dilemma.

Task 2:

Class discussion will be facilitated by the instructor.

Case Study: The Intercon Semiconductor Company

Background and Company Evolution

Intercon was founded in 1961 as the first company worldwide to exclusively manufacture integrated circuits. The company's evolution resulted in six product line divisions and two specific market divisions. Each division designed, manufactured, and marketed its own products. The divisions were organized into the following groups: Metal-Oxide Semiconductor (MOS), Linear Large-Scale Integration (LSI) products group, Linear LSI, MOS Microprocessor, MOS Memory Bipolar Digital products groups, Logic, Bipolar LSI, Bipolar Memory, Military, and Automotive/Telecommunications. The Military and Automotive/Telecommunications divisions used products from each of the other six and packaged and tested them for their markets.

The company was headquartered on the East Coast with additional production facilities throughout the western United States and overseas.

In 1975, Intercon became a wholly owned subsidiary of U.S. Kunikon Corporation, a subsidiary of the European electrical and electronic multinational firm. Intercon operated independently of Kunikon, but relied on interchange of products and technology with Kunikon International.

The European firm bought and sold Intercon products under the Intercon name and supplied Intercon with innovative products. A Kunikon research laboratory located near Intercon headquarters housed scientists and technicians from both companies.

Intercon made most of its sales growth and reputation in bipolar technology, including programmable read-only memories (PROMs), integrated fuse logic (IFL), arrays, an 8-bit microcontroller family, emitter-coupled logic (ECL) and integrated shotkey logic (ISL) gate arrays, small-scale integration (SSI)/medium-scale integration (MSI) logic, and analog MSI/LSI circuits.

Though it was primarily seen as a generic transistor-transistor-logic (TTL) manufacturer, Intercon was developing as well into a producer of innovative very large scale integrated (VLSI) products and a supplier of metal-oxide semiconductor (MOS) products. Other developments included complementary MOS (CMOS) and n-channel MOS (NMOS) expertise and capacity. By 1983, production began of 256K NMOS read-only memories (ROMs), and the company achieved full production of MOS VLSI 8/16-bit microcomputers and peripherals. Intercon viewed its main strengths in production of MOS products including the 68000 16/32-bit microprocessor family, the NMOS and CMOS 8048/8051 8-bit midrange microcontroller family and static memory products such as ROMs, CMOS, EPROMs, CMOS static RAMs, and LSI CMOS and NMOS analog/digital signal processing circuits.

By 1983, Intercon had 18,000 employees and had grown since 1972 at a compounded annual growth rate of 26 percent (excluding the 1981–82 recession), outpacing industry growth by 7 percent. Revenues in 1983 were $600 million and were projected to triple by 1988.

Current Status of Company

Once the boom years were over, the company faced not only shrinking markets but competition from abroad in production effectiveness and pricing as well. Intercon underwent a major reorganization and a new reporting structure. In August 1985, Intercon announced a zero-defects warranty on all of its semiconductor products. It was the first IC company to offer the warranty. According to Quality and Reliability Director W. A. Stephens, zero defects is "really a selfish thing. It is the best way and the most cost-effective way to run a company." The zero-defects warranty was the result of several years of attempts to improve quality control. In late 1979, a 14-step quality improvement process had been initiated, based on Philip Crosby's "zero-defects" system. By 1985, the process of quality control had taken hold so that defects were eliminated at their source, through prevention, whereas previously a defect level of 1,000 parts per million had been acceptable.

Source: This case was developed by A. B. (Rami) Shani and C. Sexton.

Currently Intercon has over 15,000 employees, making it one of the largest companies in the semiconductor industry. Its relationship with the European-based Kunikon makes it the beneficiary of Kunikon's current overseas endeavors, including a joint venture with another multinational in the attempt to produce an unusually large memory chip. Kunikon is also researching gallium arsenide, which can process information 10 times faster than silicon; this is part of the corporate-directed effort to be first to the market with ultrahigh-speed superconductors, which will revolutionize the industry.

Intercon faces the same concerns that are faced by most large American-based semiconductor firms. In his April 1987 message, President Martin Bergman expressed the belief that Intercon had the fundamental strengths—the ability to respond quickly to the 1985 recession, the opportunities afforded by pooling strengths with Kunikon's worldwide organization, a zero-defects philosophy, and a nucleus of talented personnel—to respond to future shifts in the market.

Company Strategy

President Bergman believed that the restructuring of Intercon was designed to make it "more strategic, more competitive, and, ultimately, more profitable." According to VP of Sales and Marketing Mike Walker, there was one goal: "meeting the customer's every need. We have restructured this company with that single goal in mind."

A primary goal was to become a significant competitor in the worldwide market in MOS technology, while maintaining a leading edge in standard products in the linear division. LSI VP Martin Stanley remarked, "The challenge for us is to develop individual strategies within our product areas while maintaining a coordinated strategy between them—synergy in the marketplace that makes us as close to one-stop shopping as we can be."

Strategic Marketing Manager Linda Grant explained that "Learning the technology, our human resources, our processes, our customers, and our strengths and weaknesses in our markets is the beginning of developing strategic direction. Currently we are still a product-line–driven company. We have yet to develop the true market-driven–based strategy that is anchored in our strengths. Ideally we would try to match and deal with both a product and a market-based strategic plan. We don't have a clear direction where we are going to be or a clear sense of priority for the entire corporation. We don't have a cohesive overall priority-based strategy that is communicated by top management to the lower levels. Divisions do have their own strategies but we are not globally optimized without having the overall strategy and a clear set of priorities. We need to find the mechanism that will help us develop the shared vision for the entire corporation."

Business unit managers and functional managers within the units expressed concern over the market-driven orientation. "We need to be structured according to where the product is going. We lack product marketing engineers—people with engineering and technical backgrounds," stated Marketing Manager Martin. "We've still not made the full transition from our old philosophy. Products or devices fall between the cracks. Top management needs to decide whether we are market-driven or whether we can continue to drive the market. Doing both is confusing, both internally and in terms of our image."

The commitments to becoming a marketing-driven company and to having a zero-defects philosophy were considered key elements of strategy that would maintain and develop Intercon as the world leader in an industry where the large firms traditionally had difficulty in applying specifics because of the high degree of customer involvement. Application Specific Products (ASP) Marketing Manager Kelly Martin stated that the company "has the ability to bring something to the customer that he doesn't have—a highly reliable source of application-specific ICs."

Since the IC industry had become worldwide, a "global perspective and global presence" (in President Bergman's words) was required for success, and the relationship with Kunikon International afforded that presence and perspective. The relationship with North American Kunikon as well as the more recent relationship with Kunikon International were issues in the company strategy. According to R&D VP Paul

Bracken, "I believe that once you are in the multinational company you can, if you learn the system and learn the roles, do almost everything that you want. The economic struggle between us and Kunikon can either hinder us or explode into hyperactivity and very innovative work and products. The current struggle for autonomy between us and U.S. Kunikon does not permit us to take part in the innovation process as it is currently being conducted in other parts of the world. By limiting contact, you actually hinder the innovation process."

Harvey Sparling, vice president of Consumer/Standard Linear Products, noted an additional adjustment was necessary as part of Kunikon International. "We have a four-year strategic plan which we review quarterly. Kunikon requires us to have a five- to eight-year strategic plan."

Company Design

Figure 15–4 shows the company prior to the recent major restructuring. The company was designed along functional lines with the two major product groups—MOS and Bipolar—determined by technology.

Figure 15–4
Intercon Organizational Chart

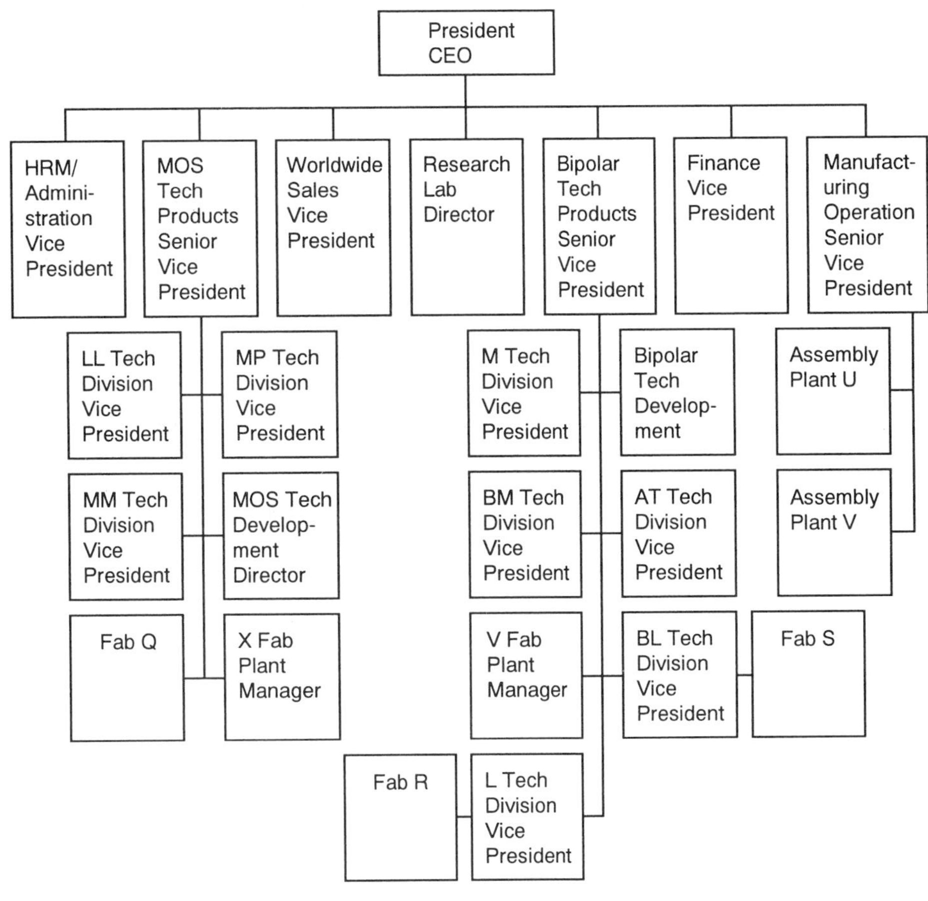

The new structure appearing in Figure 15–5 was designed to strip major product groups of their technological differences based on the major MOS and Bipolar technologies and restructure the company into groups differentiated by greater orientation to commodity versus leading-edge innovations products. The absolute number of divisions was reduced from eight to five to accommodate the pressure to find economies of scale. The technology development groups (which were previously separated within the two product groups) were combined into R&D. The new structure depended far more on integrated interfaces across functional groups within and across divisions and a more companywide team-oriented approach to making decisions about which new products to invest in.

Figure 15–5
Revised Intercon Organizational Chart

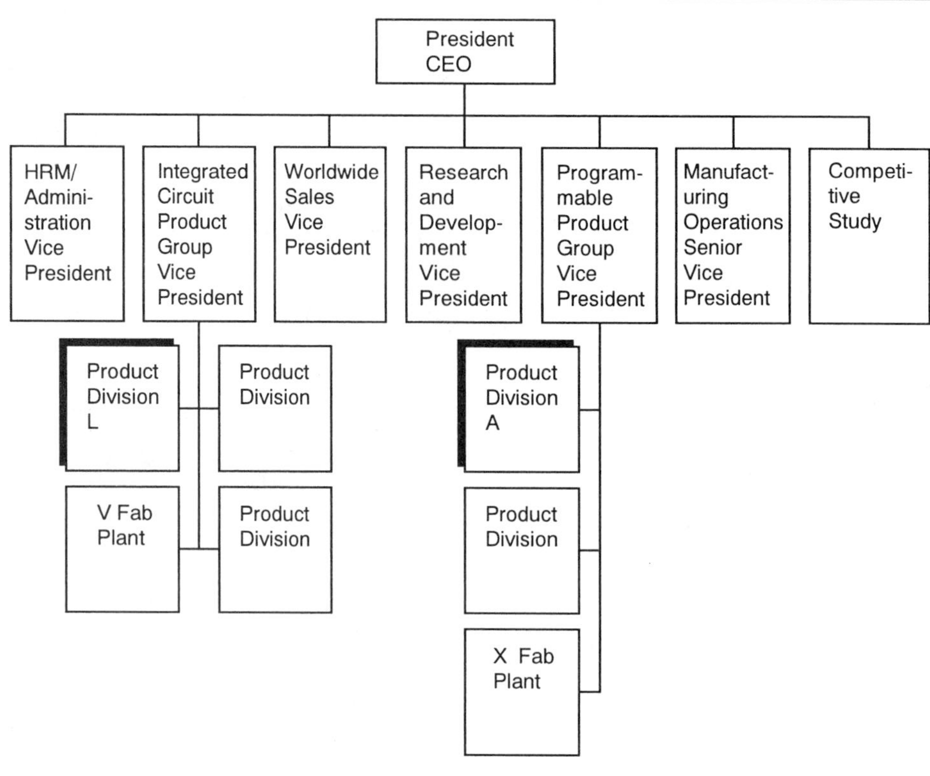

The current design was both strongly supported and questioned. Sales and Marketing VP Walker expressed the belief that how well the firm assesses the environment is the key to its success. The current business unit design supports the attempt to get closer and sense the environment by developing a network of relationships with the entire industry and utilize the process to collect all the variable information.

However, Linear Division VP Jonathan Lee remarked, "When I compare the business unit organization with the functional-based organization, I strongly believe that the functional organization has more advantages. The business unit structure fosters independence that results in limited sharing across the business unit boundaries."

Company Innovation

Although logic and bipolar memory were the mainstays of the company during its growth, Intercon sought to maintain its competitive edge by developing new products and areas of expertise. According to President Bergman, "The key to any company's success is product development, but we [need to] develop products that have clear and specific market segments to serve and that we are capable of manufacturing. The situation of the industry requires innovation, new product development, and a second-source house orientation. We need to make sure, however, that we keep developing new products in a timely fashion in order for us to continue our success and maintain our image. Designing the company so that it will accomplish innovation and will be a good second-source house is a challenge that we are still struggling with."

The company had committed major resources to innovation in the areas of application-specific and microprocessors. Moving from a technology-driven philosophy to a marketing-driven one had required, beyond product innovation, innovation in terms of methodology, processes, tools, strategy, and organizational structure.

According to R&D VP Bracken, "Innovation is more than the development of a concept into the product objectives specification that meets the business criteria and into product execution. It is actually the formulation of the concept itself. Management recognition and support of the new concept idea is innovation. It takes innovation on the part of management to recognize it."

VP of Programmable Products Kurt Nilssen stated that the company had identified four basic needs, including innovation. "We have technological needs—technology that we want to demonstrate—and customer needs—we develop good relationships with the customers and they identify for us their needs or problems requiring solutions. We have pure research needs, and finally we have innovative needs, namely, artificial expert systems. We are convinced that this is the direction to go."

Consumer Standard Business Unit Manager Jay Samuelson asserted that innovation is "what causes things to happen—25 percent of what we do should be geared toward this important asset."

Company Divisions

Figure 15–5 shows that currently there are two main product groups within the company and a total of five product divisions. The remainder of this case study will describe the dynamics of two major product divisions called Division L and Division A (one from each product group). Because the company is so complex, it was felt that an in-depth description of two divisions, identified by corporate as representative samples of company divisions, be made rather than provide a broad, but necessarily shallow overview of every division within the company. Division L and Division A exhibit two parallel company orientations with different strategic orientations for interfacing with the company and its competitive environment.

Division L

Design: Division L is made up of independent business units based on product orientation and an integrative marketing department for the entire division. Each business unit includes its own marketing department, design department, product engineering department, and test engineering department. The current divisional struggle is shown in Figure 15–6.

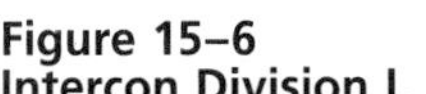

Figure 15–6
Intercon Division L

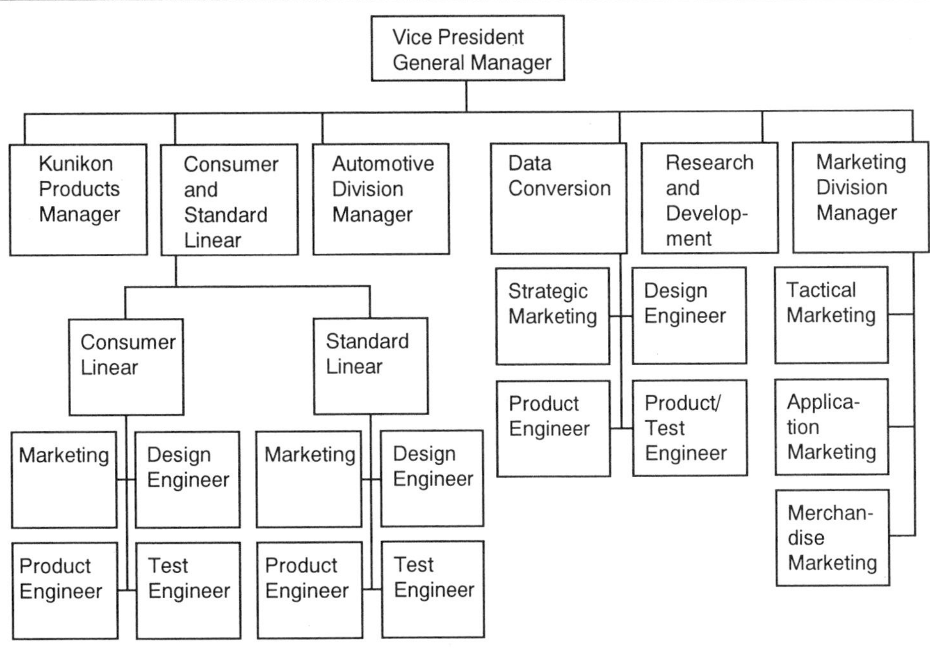

A key feature of the structure is the team concept. For example, the standard linear business unit is described as a *quality improvement team (QIT),* and the functional areas within the unit are designated as *make certain teams (MCTs).* Specific problem-solving activity is handled by *corrective action teams (CATs).* Though the team concept is stressed, the issues of individual differences and competition across functional boundaries have arisen. According to Standard Linear Product Engineer Manager

Duane Fulton, ''It is a constant war around here. We don't share the same goals. People do not confront each other. Many of the battles are fought under the table. There is conflict suppression on every issue.''

Standard Linear Marketing Manager Miles Wilson added, ''We are very fragmented within the division. The structure creates too strong boudaries, yet the definition of territory is not as clear.''

Strategy: Although Standard Linear Business Unit Manager Rex Fogelberg noted, ''We need to find the balance between technological and market innovation so that we can meet the needs of both our customers and our people,'' the tension involved in creating this strategic balance between technology push and market pull is pronounced.

Design Engineer Manager Eli Chou commented, ''The technological component should be represented higher up in the hierarchy. You cannot leave out the technology people. Marketing people tend to see what is out there now, what the customer wants. Technology tends to see what is in the future from a technology standpoint. Don't shut us middle management off by saying that we are marketing-driven.''

Division Manager Simon Adams summarized the division's concern over the market versus technology issue and the viability of the division and company's goals and strategies. ''The movement toward vertical marketing and product-specific markets is a series of concentrated efforts being made by the company. Yet it is often asked around here whether this is the right way to go and, if so, how should we proceed?''

Innovation: Innovation in this division is identified primarily as an engineering/design process, yet Consumer/Linear Test Engineer George Gasparian remarked, ''Product and test engineers should be involved in an earlier phase in a collaborative mode that might aid in stimulating design engineers to develop more innovative products.''

Product Engineer Manager Fulton agreed. ''The product engineer can be innovative by looking at the critical parameters within the time frame so that directions for their resolutions can emerge. The product engineer can be the igniter for innovation by the designers or test engineers.''

Design Engineer Manager Sharad Johal expressed the sentiment that management ''does not understand the problems that the design engineer faces. It is very hard to convince management to provide the funds to support the process. Management structure is not as responsive as it should be. Business managers dominate here. In other companies there is a technology director. Here we don't have that. The design manager feels alone. There is no forum for us, the middle management, to present our ideas or issues of technological challenges to the top. It is very difficult to get through to the hierarchy. It is like speaking two different languages.''

Throughout the division, engineers and managers expressed their views of what management might do to foster innovation:

''Managers should allow innovation to happen by keeping control over the work and by making sure that the designers or engineers have adequate tools.''

''Management needs to provide the freedom for development and at the same time create clearly defined boundaries so that things are not allowed to drift.''

''Management needs fewer time constraints. We need to rethink the time structured into one's week if we're really committed to new ideas.''

The Product Development Process (PDP): The PDP refers to the number and types of interactions and evaluations that occur between the initial formulation of an idea and its ultimate introduction into the market. It is an evolutionary process characterized by three major factors: research, development, and implementation. The PDP is variously described in the division. Some perceive it as beginning with the identification of new markets or a literature search for new ideas, while others see it as beginning with the new product release (NPR). Consumer/Standard Business Unit Manager Dave King identified 12 elements of the PDP (see Figure 15–7): the customer, marketing, design, characterization, data sheet specification, fabrication, die sort, assembly, final testing where cooperation takes place, quality assurance, production control, and sales—which lead directly back to the customer.

Figure 15–7
Product Development Process, Division L

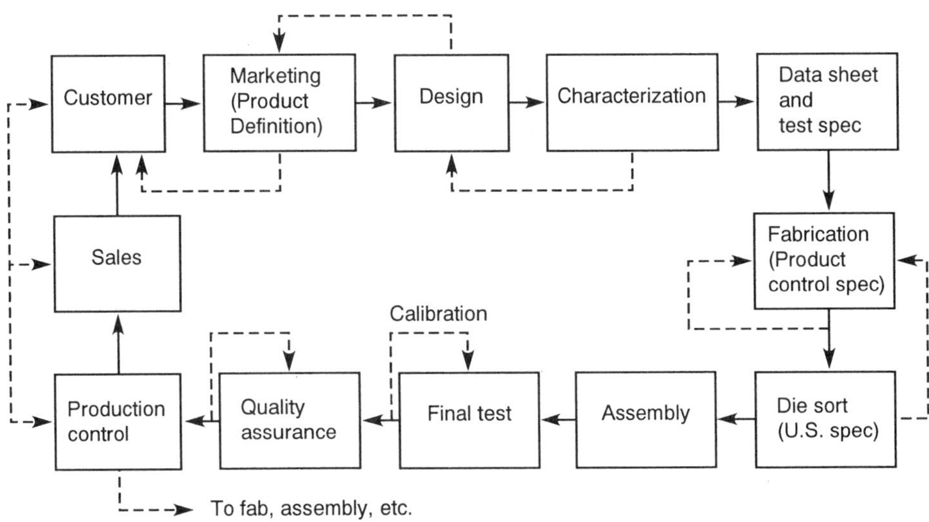

Although various stages of the PDP could be identified, a definite pattern was not always established. According to Marketing Division Manager Blake Lawler, "The PDP cannot always be sequential, especially in our case where the market moves too fast. As a result, there are times when the NPR is signed off after the product is already completely designed."

The importance of each phase and the order of the phases will vary throughout the division, depending on the function of the engineers. Test Engineer Gasparian felt that the "most critical and biggest problem is the phase where we determine how to test the product." Yet product engineer managers believed that product planning was the most critical.

The marketing-versus-technology question arises with regard to the PDP, ranging from marketing's "We are not fully incorporating the customer throughout the entire PDP," to Design Engineer Manager Johal's not seeing the need for "making the customer part of the PDP. The company probably has more to lose than to gain from it."

Business Unit Manager King remarked, "The design engineers are not close to the customers as they should be. We have a lot of holes in the specifications given by the marketing guys based on their understanding of the customers. It is at this stage that the discrepancy occurs around the interpretation of what the customer really needs."

Division Manager Adams main concern was "the relationship between the new product idea brought forward by the customer, the strategic marketing people, who believe they know the market (but who don't always know it), and design engineers, who are supposed to work together with the strategic marketing people and the customer. Being in the middle is problematic. Who has control over the product? Is it the customer, is it the engineer, or is it marketing?"

Division A

Design: The structure in Division A is a combination of functional-based and product-based design. The Programmable Linear Devices (PLD) group, which is the strongest and most stable group, is organized along functional lines. The semicustom group is formulated along product lines. The reorganized structure of Division A is shown in Figure 15–8.

Division members expressed various concerns about the effect of company structure and design on their division. PLD Design Engineer Paul Sakamoto commented, "The structure of the company gets in the way. The decision-making process is hindering, delaying the decision is causing us a lot of damage. Top-level management should delegate decision-making authority to lower levels and not centralize more and more decision making at headquarters."

Marketing Manager Andrea White was optimistic about further changes in the structure of Division A's marketing group. "Currently I am working on redesigning the

Figure 15–8
Intercon Division A

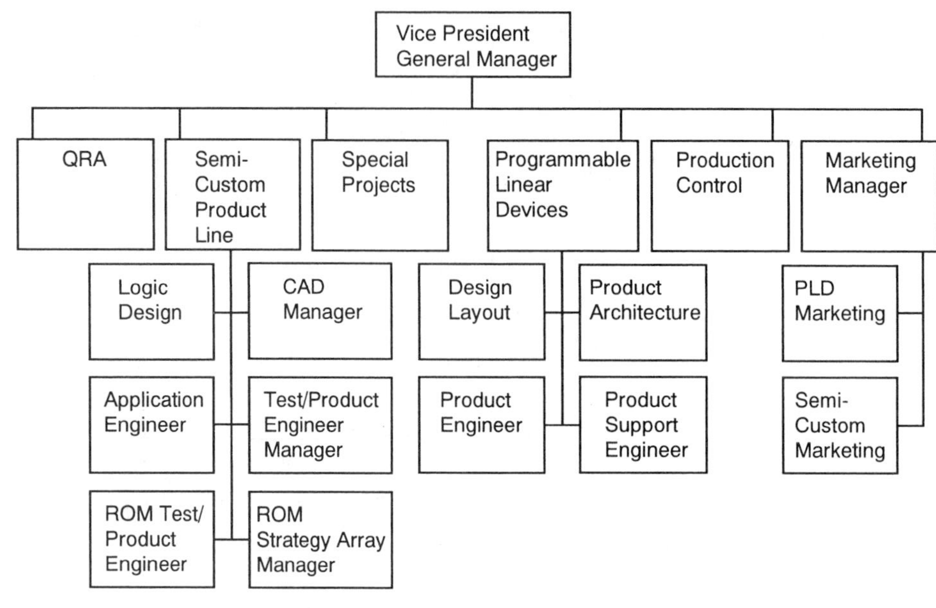

structure to include three subgroups: the strategic application group, the tactical marketing group, and the strategic business group. I believe this kind of design would help us accomplish our mission and position ourselves best in the marketplace and really enhance creativity and innovation. I believe that we can actually develop a long and lasting solid relationship with our customers.''

Semicustom Business Unit Manager Al Younger commented on the effect of organizational structure on the ability to innovate. ''We deliver sole-source products; therefore, we are limited in freedom to take risks. The bureaucratic procedures also hinder new product development. We need to try to minimize the bureaucratic process and to be sensitive to individual needs.''

Strategy: The market-driven aspect of company strategy is emphasized here. PLD Engineer Sakamoto remarked that ''We are a broad-line company, and as a result we are more market-driven. For the PLD group, we are driving the market. Lack of focus or clear direction is one of our struggles. The currently short-sighted view of top management is hindering the entire process.''

Various marketing personnel within the division made the following comments:

''There are things that we need to do to be viable in the market. The first priority is to satisfy customers, and the second priority is to develop new products and come up with new innovations.''

''The real challenge is to go out and segment the market.''

''We need to understand the marketplace first. Educating the customer is critical.''

PLD Marketing Manager Rod Ellsworth commented, ''Strategically, the technical reactive mode used to be our company's approach. Currently we are trying to break away from that mode. We have quarterly meetings with the field people and engineers to share ideas, and we make each party familiar with other current practices, thoughts, and ideas. In terms of decision making, a strategic roadmap is used as a criterion for making decisions.''

The role management played within the company appeared to many to be the key to the success of its strategy. Design Engineer Manager Elliot Shields remarked, ''Management today is entirely business bottom-line–oriented. They truly don't understand the complexity of what we do. Top management must understand that we need to differentiate ourselves from other companies, not just through bottom-line production of the same product. Management wants quick returns and therefore it's very tough, if not impossible, to be very innovative.''

Division Manager Mark Tenor noted, ''Senior management should provide vision. We have had serious problems with it. It is our fault that we did not provide it for our employees. I know where we are going as a division. I still have a lot to do in developing shared vision throughout the division. We are only one year old as a division.''

Innovation: In this division, the concept of innovation is frequently expressed in terms of product and technology development.

R&D VP Bracken described innovation as an ''interactive process. It is the ability to manage the three groups: design, layout, and computer-aided design (CAD).''

PLD Design Engineer Sakamoto said, ''Innovation is defining a new technology or process. Innovation is development of the right tool to integrate the products. Putting the tools in the design layout phase is where I will put my resources in order to foster innovation. We need to provide the design engineers with the state-of-the-art technological processes so that they can be innovative.''

Time, freedom, recognition, and stimulation are seen as requirements for innovation. Sakamoto believed it was important to give people the freedom to do the job, assign people the responsibility to a part, and let them know that its success is dependent on them without a continuous need for monitoring its progress. Upper-level management should know and be familiar with what their people do. They need to express appreciation and recognition and to provide equitable rewards. Top-level management should be concerned about the company.

Design engineers were generally in agreement about criteria for innovation:

''Stimulating the thinking process within the individual is critical for the manager in facilitating or fostering innovation. The challenge is to give people the time and the space that they need. Driving people to innovation is hindering innovation.''

''We need to find a way to recognize and acknowledge the innovative people and to provide people the time to think without special pressure. Short-term innovation is hindering the innovation process. Management needs to let people go and develop the product without too many other assignments. The tight schedule and the number of projects at any given time is hindering the ability to be really innovative.''

Division Manager Tenor commented, ''If innovation is a goal, we need to free the people that are innovative to do innovation. We need to free them from everyday operation functioning, and we truly need to stand behind them with the most updated state-of-the-art technology and processes.''

Product Development Process (PDP): Some descriptions of the PDP in this division are of highly technical, specialized stages; others describe more of a flow from the customer through the process and back to the customer. R&D Specialist Kenny Walsh defined the PDP as ''composed broadly of the following phases: idea, generation, new product review (NPR) document, NPR board review, design and layout, masks, fabrication, characterization phase, and code 1 (release for production).''

In contrast, Application Specific Marketing Manager White defined several phases in the PDP (see Figure 15–9): ''In the stimulation source phase there are three elements: technology, study, competitive study, and a study they I call seeing a 'better mouse trap.' Next we have the company phase, which leads to the idea generation element, which in turn leads to a feasibility assessment phase, followed by the initial market analysis phase. Market analysis is also exposure to the next phase, which is the customer.''

The PDP is perceived to have a variety of strengths and weaknesses in this division. Design Engineer Manager Shields noted, ''The time that it takes to pass the qualification process can take as much time as the entire design process. The more guidelines we have, the less flexible we are, and the less innovative we are going to be.''

Semicustom Business Manager Younger felt that ''Training the customer is the most critical thing. The customer will be as good as you train him. The company is not hiring the right people, the professional trainers.''

Figure 15–9
Product Development Process, Division A

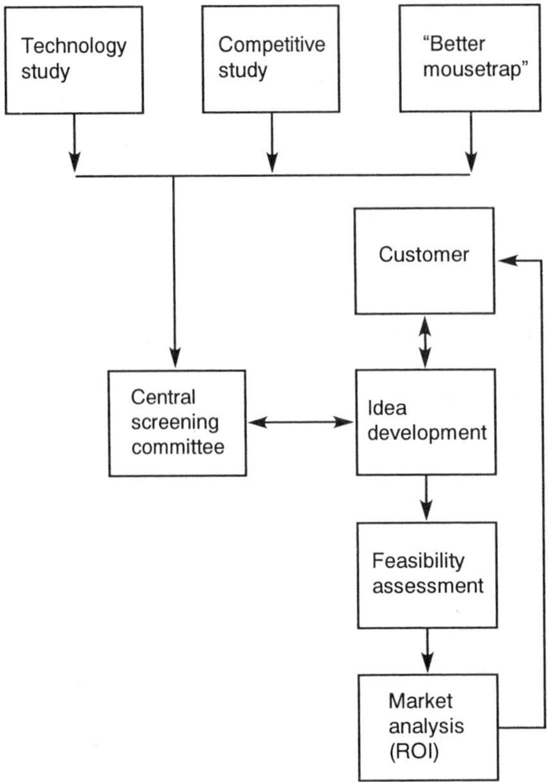

Division Manager Tenor commented on two weak points that he felt were hindering the innovation in the PDP. "First and most critical is our technology: manufacturing technology, process development technology, and design development technology. We are not using the most up-to-date technology on all three fronts. Second, we are weak at the concept definition. The Japanese have put a lot of resources to develop the next-generation technology. We have done very little with it. Furthermore, their designers are coming up with very good and creative design which is relatively new. Historically, they are very good at duplicating our designs, but now their designs are coming from unique, innovative ideas."

Sakamoto also remarked about the lack of resources. "We don't have enough resources to evaluate the up-to-date tools that we might need or can use. Integration of tools across groups is problematic in the integration and interface between the design and marketing. It should be worked on continuously."

Besides resources, time was also perceived as a critical factor. According to Marketing Manager White, "The amount of time that it takes to make a decision, the time to market, is critical. Once you start the PDP, you can do all you can to reduce the time, but if it takes a year from the first idea to the start of the design, you lose your market. We have a lot of ideas that were proposed that took too long, about a year on average."

Design Manager Shields added that "The rest of the PDP is pushed hard to cut time. This is wrong. You force the designers into using tricks to enhance the process to look better than it really is."

PLD Marketing Manager Ellsworth stated, "Technology is coming to bear faster than you can develop products for it. I believe that you need to stop at some point and not be driven completely by technology development."

President Bergman's Dilemma

As President Bergman prepared to meet with his top executives, he wondered what steps should be taken next by the company. Three things particularly troubled him.

First, how could he develop a better shared vision of the company's competitive strategy? Second, what could the company do to both foster and shorten the new product development process? Third, how could they achieve optimal alignment of the company's competitive strategy, organization design, and new product development process, while simultaneously maintaining zero-defect production and increasing bottom-line profit?

16 Managing Technology and Information Technology

Learning Objectives

After completing this module you should be able to

1. Describe the roles of technology and information technology as they affect behavior in organizations.
2. Describe the multiple effects of technology and information technology.
3. Understand the effect of technology on individual and group behavior.
4. Understand the effect of information technology on the organization.
5. Gain an insight into the information technology issues of the 21st century.

List of Key Concepts

Adaptors of IT
Adoptors of IT
Cell system
Client/server technology
Computer-integrated manufacturing (CIM)
Craft technology
Engineering technology
Fully integrated system
Information technology (IT)
Inventor of IT
Linked island system
Local area network (LAN)
Manufacturing technology
Nonroutine technology
Procedure-oriented IT
Routine technology
Service technology
Stand-alone system
Technical system
Technological complexity
Technology
Tool-oriented IT system

The module was contributed by James Sena, Professor of Management Information Systems, College of Business, California Polytechnic State University, San Luis Obispo, California 93407. We are grateful to Professor Sena.

Module Outline

Premodule Preparation

The instructor may assign either one of the following activities. If time permits, both activities might be used.

Activity 16–1: Management Challenge of the Software Development Firm

Objective:

To explore the managerial challenge of managing changes in technology and information technology.

Task 1 (Homework):

Students are to read the following case on The Software Development Firm and respond to the questions at the end of the case.

Task 2:

a. Individual students are to share their answers in small groups.
b. Each group is to then develop a joint response to be presented and discussed with the entire class.
c. The instructor will facilitate a class discussion of the main features of technology and information technology that have impacted the SDF firm and their potential impact and implications on organizational behavior.

Case Study: The Software Development Firm

A local area network (LAN) provides an ideal resource-sharing environment for organizational units that use data of importance to a number of departments or work groups. The SDF Company is a software development firm that recently underwent the transition from a stand-alone personal computer (PC) environment to a computerized system. Under the stand-alone environment, SDF personnel used PCs to support their work effort. These units were not connected; each worker operated independently of other personnel. The various units completed work using the PC for word processing, database management, spreadsheet analysis, and general record keeping. As the organization grew, the need either to connect these units or to adopt a centralized system, such as a minicomputer or mainframe system, became apparent. Data were being reentered and duplicated, and inconsistencies existed between both departments and individual workers in the use of computer software, the levels of expertise, and the compatibility and quality of data.

SDF produces utility software products for disk and file server management for personal computers and microcomputer networks. At SDF, it was implied and expected that all in-house computer work should operate using state-of-the-art equipment and software. The company's switch to a network system was in response to advances in computer technology and corporate processing needs.

SDF is organized into six departments: two software engineering groups, accounting, sales, marketing, and administration. The two engineering groups are divided along product development lines. Several work groups were formed to support the work of more than one department. Technical support works directly with engineering groups as well as the marketing department. International is a link-pin operation that combines both marketing and sales functions under a single work unit.

Every staff member has a personal computer on his or her desk. All of the machines are connected to a common network. The network complex consists of several file servers and multiple print servers. A file server is a microcomputer dedicated to supporting the communication among the various personal computers. The majority of

Source: This case was written by Professors J. Sena and A. B. Shani and is reported as part of a larger study in A. B. (Rami) Shani and J. Sena, "Information Technology and the Integration of Change: Sociotechnical System Approach," *Journal of Applied Behavioral Science* 30, no. 2 (1994), pp. 242–70.

data and software are stored on disk units on the file server. The PCs on the network all share and access these data concurrently. A print server is a PC to which a printer that can be shared is connected. Such units are not dedicated to printing—they can be used in the same way as any other PC on the network. Any user can send print work to these printer servers.

By using network software products, SDF was able to streamline all of its operations. Electronic mail reduced the overall time lag in phone/message tag. Voice mail was introduced to accommodate external communication; facsimile transmissions via and through the network eliminated delays in the traditional mail process. Paper flow became an automated process as opposed to a manual process. Mailings, label generation, correspondence tracking, and surveillance were accomplished at the touch of a button.

Software products that were being field tested could be monitored and tracked by the marketing staff from their offices. Coordination of effort in the development of the software products was enhanced through the sharing of software modules, which were available through the network file servers; this coordination ensured that each team member was using the same software and operating under the same standards. There were a number of occasions where engineering tested products internally using the network and the support staff as a test environment. At times, these internal tests created problems: work stoppages, inconsistent system performance, and system access malfunctions.

Within the support groups, the introduction of the network accounting package provided the mechanism to either reduce or streamline the paperwork regarding orders (for software products), requisitions for materials (e.g., sales brochures and promotions), and the delivery of merchandise to the wholesalers and dealers. Many standard manual tasks became automated.

For SDF, the introduction of a network system changed not only the technology but also the entire modus of working relationships. There were both subtle and profound changes. Correspondence among workers (especially via electronic mail, where privacy was ensured) allowed individuals to air out differences on issues and to share ideas. The frequency and duration of meetings, face-to-face discussions, written memos, and phone calls was reduced. A new plane of communication was introduced. At the present time, there is no control over this level of communication between workers. At SDF, the electronic desk facility for both the individual and the work group is being utilized on an increasing basis. Peer-to-peer communication (sending and receiving messages from/to other users without terminating the current task) on the workstation provided another communication facility. SDF also had developed a product that allowed a user to initiate and terminate work remotely. With this facility a user could control work on multiple PCs from a single system.

With the introduction of the network at SDF, intergroup and interpersonal dependencies increased. Virtually every department and each individual's work activity relied on common/shared databases. Standards were introduced for personal software applications on the network. Many of the standard software decisions were based on network capabilities and software licensing considerations. With the introduction of Windows 3.0, a shift toward windows-based software was advocated by senior engineering staff members. Excel and Word (both windows-based products) were designated as the company's only maintained network spreadsheet and word-processing packages, respectively. Needs for training, support, and incentives were not considered by senior management when they made the decision to standardize.

Rather than having each manager use spreadsheets on local drives, the controller established a template in the network version of Microsoft's Excel. Each department used the same template for its budgets and forecasts, and the data were entered dynamically, that is, fed through the accounting system and other related modules. The various budgets and forecasts were consolidated so that senior management could, on demand, examine the status of the company.

A technical log system used by technical support provided a barometer of this area's activity. The log included a record of all customer inquiries and complaints and the technical nature of these problems. This system was tied directly to the registered user database. The registered user database was compiled from completed and returned product registration cards. When a customer called and help was provided, the technician could verify that the caller was a registered user and could update the user database. The technician could also view a history of all previous communication activities with the customer. This data formed the nucleus for marketing, sales, and engineering support and enhancements. Figures on customer profiles, the nature of sales, noted problems, and any suggestions associated with products could be directed to and shared by various work groups.

With the introduction of the network, not only was there a redesign of work among the various organizational units at SDF, but also specific tasks were changed. Many manual or semiautomated tasks were computerized. Instead of being entered on a log sheet, the basic information from technical support calls was entered onto the technical log database.

Prior to the introduction of the network, each department constructed its own budgets and forecasts using whatever was appropriate (e.g., spreadsheets or handwritten notes). The move to the network and the use of standard software packages (e.g., Excel for spreadsheet analysis) facilitated uniform, consistent budgeting and forecasting. Accountability and budget tracking were available to the department managers, accounting, and senior management.

As a result of the implementation of the LAN, the clear lines of responsibility and use of information have become blurred. There have been conflicts regarding the content, entry, and recording of information. Before the network, all sales orders were handled by accounting, requisitions for materials were handled by production, and information requests were handled by marketing. Now any worker who has proper authority can initiate these entries.

Before the network was implemented, the accounting system consisted of accounts receivable, accounts payable, and general ledger software packages. Each package was fairly distinct—data were imported and exported in a common form. The software packages closely followed the work of the various accounting staff members. Sales orders were written manually, and entries were made by the accounts receivable clerk. Payroll was performed by an outside service.

After the LAN was implemented, the accounting system became totally integrated. An accounting package that provided inventory control, accounts receivable and payable, payroll, general ledger, project management, bank book management, general ledger, fixed assets, and spreadsheet interfacing was selected and placed on the network. This package became the foundation for the enterprise. Virtually all departments became involved in the entry, inquiry, reporting, and use of accounting information. Many issues relating to privacy, control, credit, accountability, and responsibility arose.

Because anyone could potentially initiate a sales order, some form of control over credit approval had to be established. Previously, accounting maintained tight control over the authorization of credit. Now, the credit process within accounting became one of handling exceptions. The access and use of sales and other accounting data were no longer the sole province of accounting. Regulation of materials such as computer or office equipment, software, and supplies affected the way the departments had done business. Previously a department had been able to acquire any needed equipment that it wanted as long as the cost was within its budget.

Even though the network system provided for the integration of inventory with the accounting system, the production department has been slow to participate in the integration. There was a separate physical facility for storage and production of inventory when the network was installed. Because of this physical separation, production continued to operate independent of the integrated accounting system, even though it had access to the network. Overall, there was similar resistance on the part of experienced users to adopt the standard software packages. Many users opted to use their favorite spreadsheet (e.g., Lotus) and word-processing (e.g., WordPerfect) systems.

Assignment

1. Describe the major characteristics of the technical system at the Software Development Firm.
2. How did the implementation of the LAN system seem to affect the other subsystems in the organization?
3. How did the implementation of the LAN system seem to affect human behavior?
4. What impact would the introduction of the LAN have on planning and control processes? On work design? On creativity and innovation?
5. How would the use of the LAN influence individual and organizational effectiveness?

Activity 16–2: Technology, Information Technology, and Human Behavior: An Exploratory Investigation

Objective:

To explore the role of technology and information technology in the management and behavior of existing organizations.

Task 1 (Homework):

a. Participants are to review current business publications (e.g. *Business Week, The Wall Street Journal, Fortune*) and identify a company that is reported to currently be addressing issues related to technology (distinct from information technology—e.g., use of sensors, intelligent agents, manufacturing processes).
b. Participants are to meet as teams. After reviewing the individual findings, they are to decide on the particular company for continued focus.
c. Participants are then to independently review and scan recent business publications (and perhaps perform a computer-based search) for references to the chosen company that would correspond to some of the following themes:
    1. How is the technological system described? What seem to be the characteristics of the technology? What terms or labels are used? How are they defined?
    2. Does the technical system appear to have an impact on the managerial system? On the design of work? On the human system? On human behavior? On individual, group, business unit, and/or organizational behavior?
    3. Is the technology distinct from or linked to information technology? How is the distinction or linking described?
    4. What seem to be the patterns or potential relationships among human behavior, technology, and information technology?
d. Participants are to meet in their teams to discuss the findings and responses to the four questions in part C and then are to develop a team response to each question.

Task 2 (Classroom):

a. The instructor will have each team present its findings for each of the questions with the entire class. Key points are to be recorded on the board.
b. Based on the various team findings, the instructor will facilitate a class discussion about current organizations, their technologies, and human behavior.
c. The instructor will then present a short lecture on the technical system and human behavior.

Introduction

"Thanks to technology, the world is going bonkers. And it's going to get more bonkers—bonker squared in a few years with bonker cubed on the way"

Tom Peters, 1994

The impact of technology and information technology on how organizations function and change has been nothing short of profound. To be competitive in the changing global market, firms need to improve their management of technology and information technology. Not only does information technology need to be managed, it also needs to be utilized and deployed to enhance the firm's competitive position. The relationships among people, technology, and information technology have special meaning and characteristics. Technologies themselves have no emotional capacity, though we still tend to imbue them with personalities to make our relationship with them more fulfilling. Information technologies, on the other hand, can become pervasive. People within the organization can become so focused on the gadgets and devices that they lose perspective of the goals and objectives of the firm. Pasmore argued that at a fundamental level, "It is our propensity to develop relationships with inanimate technological artifacts that explains why the interdependence between social and technical systems in organizations requires careful attention."[1] This module examines the major features of technology and information technology—as fundamental elements of organizational behavior—and their interdependent relationship with human behavior.

Technology

Technology at the most basic level is the tools, techniques, methods, devices, configurations, knowledge, procedures, and actions used by organizational members to acquire inputs, to transform inputs into outputs, and to provide outputs in terms of products or services to customers.[2] Organizational technology can include choices about raw materials, choices about how the technology is defined and presented, choices about work design or redesign, choices about control processes, choices about research and development, and in some sense choices about how to approach and utilize information technologies to support the infrastructure framed by the other technologies. The management of technology, then, transcends the concerns of production processes, machinery, and work procedures. The decisions made about the choices available and the processes used to arrive at those decisions are what differentiates one organization from another. In addition, any one of the technology-related choices is likely to influence choices made for many of the aspects of the organization on an ongoing basis. For example, a decision to modify production processes from batch production to continuous production implies a shift from efficiency to reliability.[3] Such areas as point-of-sale debit machines, automatic teller machines, toll-free phone numbers, and computerized reservation systems as well as traditional process-based operations like chemical processing are considered to be examples of continuous processing. A decision to apply one or more of these technologies will alter the relationship among the firm, its customers, and perhaps its suppliers. Furthermore, the relationship and work scope among and within the organizational units and the individuals in the organization are changed.

Technology as the Defining Feature of Organizations

A variety of classifications and categorizations of technology have been proposed by scientists and managers. The perception and definition of the **technical system** is strongly linked to any such proposed classification. One of the first typologies, proposed by Joan Woodward, organizes the firm according to its technological complexity and manufacturing processes.[4] The **technological complexity** dimension represents the extent of mechanization of the manufacturing process—a high technological complexity means that most of the work is done by machines. Based on these dimensions, three major categories of technology were identified: small batch and unit production (the manufacturing process is not highly mechanized and relies heavily on a human operator—for example, specialized optical equipment or custom-designed graphics), large batch and mass production (the manufacturing process is characterized by long production runs with standard parts—for example, most auto assembly lines), and continuous process production (the entire manufacturing process is mechanized and automated machines control the process—for example, nuclear power plants and chemical plants).

A research group at the University of Aston, England, classified technologies into three components: *operations technology* (the techniques used in the work flow activities), *material technology* (the nature of technologies used in the transformation process), and *knowledge technology* (the characteristics of the knowledge used in the organization).[5] A set of studies that focused on a wide range of technologies resulted in the classification of technology into three clusters: *long linked* (technology that involves series interdependence among subtasks, as in an assembly line), *mediating* (technology that links clients or customers with service providers in standard ways, and *intensive* (technology that involves the use of a variety of specialized techniques to bring about change in a specified object, such as the patient who is seen by various specialists in a hospital).[6] The key argument behind this set of studies is that each type of technology requires a different mode of coordinating the various interdependent performers who operate the technologies, which results in different patterns of planning, control, goal setting, work design, and human behavior.

In later research, it has been proposed that technology can be examined at both the organizational and departmental levels. At the organization level, technology can be divided into two types: **manufacturing technologies** (which include traditional manufacturing processes and advanced manufacturing systems) and **service technologies** (which include such services as law firms, consulting firms, schools, airlines, hospitals, hotels, and amusement parks). The department-level technologies focus on the distinct technologies and production processes operating within each department. The most influential work at the departmental level was conducted by Charles Perrow, who identified two dimensions of departmental activities: *variety* (which refers to the frequency of the unexpected events that occur in the conversion process) and *analyzability* (which refers to the degree to which work activities are analyzable).[7] These two dimensions form the basis for four major categories of technology: (1) **routine technologies,** which are characterized by little task variety that is highly analyzable (e.g., an auditors unit, a bank teller department, or a machine shop), (2) **craft technology,** which is characterized by limited task variety that is difficult to analyze (e.g., a fine glass manufacturing department, performing artists, or a physician in a hospital), (3) **engineering technologies,** which are characterized by a wide variety of tasks that are relatively easy to analyze (e.g., a law department, an engineering department, or a software technical support group), and (4) **nonroutine technologies,** which are characterized by high task variety with a conversion process that is difficult to analyze (e.g., an R&D department, software development group, or the staff assigned to strategic planning).

Of special note is mention of one of the technologies at the organizational level—that of advanced manufacturing systems. Building on early work in manufacturing-based computer support systems, such as material requirements planning (MRP), these systems have focused on more fully developed computer-based manufacturing. Studies have distinguished four levels of these systems: (1) **stand-alone systems** (e.g., robots and numeric control machine tools), (2) **cell systems,** which consist of equipment and materials for the production of parts (e.g., flexible manufacturing system, material requirements planning, bill of materials, and computer-aided engineering), (3) **linked island systems,** in which some cell systems are linked together to form production islands (e.g., picking lines, packaging and shipping operations, and pharmaceutical or cosmetic products that share selected process requirements), and (4) **fully integrated systems,** which link the entire manufacturing function and all of its interfaces through extensive information networks (commonly known as **computer-integrated manufacturing** or **CIM**).[8]

Mapping the Technological System at NT

As we saw in Module 13, the sociotechnical systems (STS) approach has become an increasingly popular organization design tool for examining and changing the workplace environment.[9] The sociotechnical perspective considers every organization to be made up of a *social subsystem* (the people) using tools, techniques, and knowledge (the *technical subsystem*) to produce a product or service valued by the *environmental subsystem* (of which customers form a part). A fundamental axiom of STS is that whatever decisions are made about or within any one of the organizational subsystems, those decisions should meet the demands of the other subsystems.

The scope of STS design extends beyond work design to encompass dimensions of organizational structure and strategy. The STS provides a useful framework for assessing the systemwide implications of new manufacturing technologies. Ensuring compatibility between the technical and environmental subsystem requires that new manufacturing technologies are effective in meeting the needs of customers and are capable of enhancing the competitive position of the firm.

Introducing new manufacturing technologies ultimately requires a redefinition of the relationship between the technical environmental subsystem through adjustments to the overall business strategy. To ensure compatibility between the technical and social subsystems, a balance needs to be struck between selecting new, compatible technologies and the nature of the existing social subsystems.

In order to understand the process by which firms manage the transition of the sociotechnical system as new manufacturing technologies are introduced, a study of the transformation process in Northern Telecom's manufacturing plant in Santa Clara, California, is presented herein. With the advances in telecommunications, Northern Telecom (NT) was well positioned to take advantage. It was the first to market digital switches in the late 1970s. And with the breakup of the Bell system in the United States, Northern Telecom had the opportunity to supply the operating companies. To sustain and increase its competitive edge, Northern Telecom needed to make strategic adjustments over time that encompassed realigning its technical subsystem with the environmental subsystem. To stay competitive, it needed to lower manufacturing costs, increase product quality, increase its responsiveness to customer requirements, and reduce the time to introduce new products.

With respect to Northern Telecom's environmental subsystem, operational objectives were established at the division level to reduce operating costs, reduce new product introduction intervals, improve incoming material quality, improve processing and outgoing process quality, reduce inventory, improve customer service, and increase market share. At the corporate level, it introduced an operational council to expedite the development of a companywide manufacturing strategy, to reduce inventory by 50 percent, to halve manufacturing overhead as a percentage of sales, and to increase customer satisfaction by 20 percent.

These environmental pressures for change focused initially on the technical system. In 1985, NT's manufacturing facility was best described as batch production organized on a job shop basis, with new manufacturing technology existing primarily as standalone systems. Its aim was to establish linked islands of automation that would form the basis for computer-integrated manufacturing extending to new product design, sales, marketing, field support, and divisional and corporate functions.

Such a step required an alignment of the technical subsystem with the social subsystem. In manufacturing operations, job specialization was high, most jobs were repetitive and skill requirements were low. The work force lacked the training and multiskilled flexibility required for integrated manufacturing. It also lacked the communication skills necessary for group-based working. Cultural, ethnic, and religious differences presented barriers to communication and cooperation. In addition, the departmental cultures were functionally differentiated and had a long-established hierarchical tradition.

Faced with the realities of the social subsystem, Northern Telecom extended the time horizon for the change process. Transitional steps were proposed including the reorganization of selected manufacturing processes to permit a continuous flow of product through consecutive stages of processing; just-in-time scheduling resulting in the near elimination of inventories; closer supplier coordination to reduce inventories of products and materials; warehouse automation to increase the efficiency of operations and reduce outside warehousing; and increased integration between manufacturing and design. Changes were made to enhance data sharing among design, manufacturing, testing, suppliers, and marketing. Figure 16–1 presents a map of the technological subsystem at NT.

Figure 16–1
Map of Technological Subsystem at NT

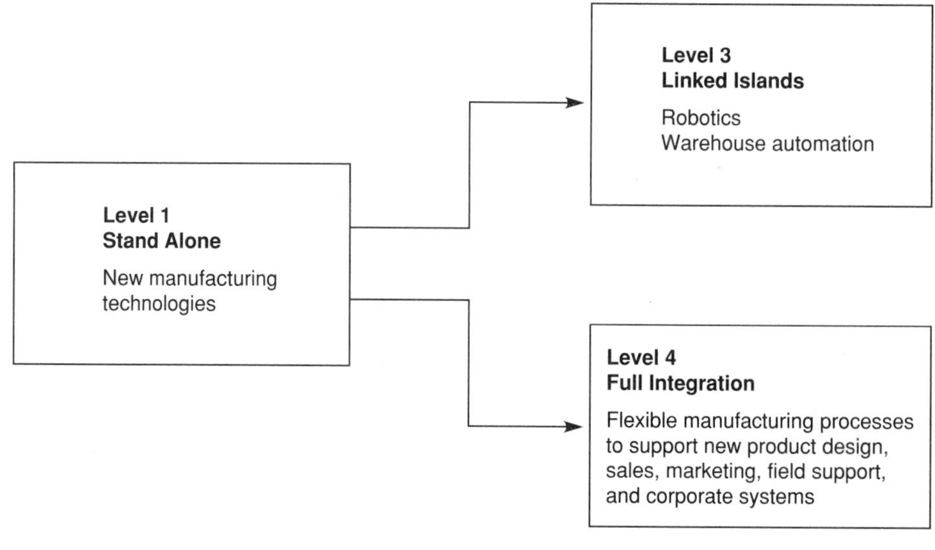

Simultaneous with the technology subsystem's transitional steps, changes in work design were also initiated. NT recognized the need for group-based rather than individual-based tasks. Training and educational efforts were initiated to build support for technological change. Group task design methods were introduced by making the group working with a team leader responsible for allocating individual job assignments, setting and meeting productivity and quality goals, and solving internal problems. There was a shift from bureaucratic control to self-regulation based on consensus in meeting common goals.

Differentiating between Technology and Information Technology

Technologies dealing with computers, communications, user interfaces, storage, software, artificial intelligence, robotics, and manufacturing all broadly fall under the umbrella of **information technology (IT).** The nature of the benefits originating from information technology depends on the information technologies themselves. (IT can be part of the production process of either the product or the service provided by the firm—e.g., automatic teller machines, robotics, cash recorders). IT can be used to exploit the production process through the use of specialized software. (For example, the installation of a **local area network [LAN]** would enable E-mail, group decision making, and so forth.) IT can also be an essential part of a new product or service (e.g., a car's on-board instrumentation).

An examination of the organizational technical system from a multiple perspective is likely to shed some light on the complexity of the technical system, its potential cause-and-effect relationships with other systems within the organization, and its potential effects on human behavior and performance. In the next section we review more closely the relationship between technology and behavior.

Information Technology

The growth of information technology systems and their pervasive use in industry is a familiar development in the 1990s. Information technology including executive information systems, groupware, voice messaging, on-line transaction processing systems, electronic mail, teleconferencing, object linking and embedding, and other computer and telecommunications advances are fundamentally changing the nature of the workplace.

Although controlled studies of IT impacts have been few, it is widely claimed that IT improvements require changes in organizational structure and managerial processes. Recent studies associate IT innovations and applications with corporate downsizing, elimination of organizational levels, improved cross-department coordination, and better interorganizational relationships. Some studies associate information technology advances with greater organizational flexibility, open flow of information, greater participation and voluntary input, and decentralization.[11, 12] Managers seem to also use IT for greater formalization, standardization, and centralization. Managerial philosophy and corporate culture have substantial bearing on the relationship between IT and structural characteristics.[13]

Advances in Information Technology

Information technology plays a vital role in supporting executive judgments about the external environment and internal organizational capability, experience, and competitive advantage. In today's rapidly changing environment, information about market conditions and product acceptance must get to senior managers quickly. Strategic information systems and executive support systems are two of the IT tools that allow rapid movement of information to executive decision makers. (See Figure 16–2.) Executives can also enter this information into expert systems to create profiles of the changing business situation and suggest new goals and strategies.

Figure 16–2
Selected Sample of Information Technology Innovations

Strategic

- Strategic Information Systems
- Executive Support Systems
  - Executive Information Systems
  - Expert Systems for Executives

Procedure-oriented

- On-line Transaction Processing Systems
- Networking Advances
  - Local-Area Networks (LANs)
  - Wide-Area Networks (WANs)
  - Client/Server Architectures

Tool-oriented

- Strategic Modeling and Decision Making
- Computer-Aided Software Engineering (CASE)
- Multiplatform Adoption
  - Standard Query Language (SQL)
  - Common Data Interfaces
- Electronic Communication
  - Electronic Mail (E-Mail)
  - Electronic Messaging
  - Teleconferencing
  - Groupware

Goals and strategies determine what critical tasks will be accomplished along with new work processes. **Procedure-oriented IT** innovations allow reconceptualization of basic tasks and work processes. These systems are used for repetitive tasks such as ordering and billing. They include transaction processing, management information and control, and formalized tactical and operational decision support. As applications are moved from the mainframe to local area networks, newer, more flexible software technologies are utilized. These systems facilitate changes and permit easier access to information stored in distributed data bases. In many cases, these systems are fundamental to the core technology or transformation process. Insurance, banking, investment, travel, and related organizations focus on selected transaction processing systems to conduct their external business operations. Within manufacturing firms, computer-aided design, computer-integrated manufacturing, and electronic document data interchange (EDI) with vendors and customers are being aggressively implemented. In these examples, procedure-oriented systems are mission-critical.

Tool-oriented IT systems are designed to help people communicate and make decisions at all levels and locations within the firm. Teleconferencing, electronic mail, voice mail, and groupware applications are usually categorized as tool-oriented systems. With the introduction of the PC and the later introduction of the local area network, the majority of managers and their staff used the computer as an extension of their work. The tool-oriented IT systems are comprised of end user software products ranging from spreadsheets (e.g., Excel and Lotus), word processing (e.g., Word and Wordperfect), data management (e.g., dBase and Access), and E-mail (e.g., ccMail) to groupware products (e.g., Lotus Notes) and software to assist in the data interchange with corporate systems (e.g., SQL servers). An example of the redesign potential enabled by tool-oriented systems is found at Mrs. Fields company. At Mrs. Fields (see Figure 16–3), cookie store managers at over 500 locations have access to the owner/founder and her corporate staff through E-mail and phone-mail systems that bypass the geographic district level managers. Store managers can expect answers to their operations inquiries within 48 hours, supporting the idea that Mrs. Fields is a flat organization with small-company procedures and culture.[14] In brief, procedure-oriented and tool-oriented systems produce dramatic changes in the way that tasks are carried out within organizations.

Figure 16–3
Mrs. Fields Store Managers Communicate via E-Mail and EDI Directly with the Corporate System

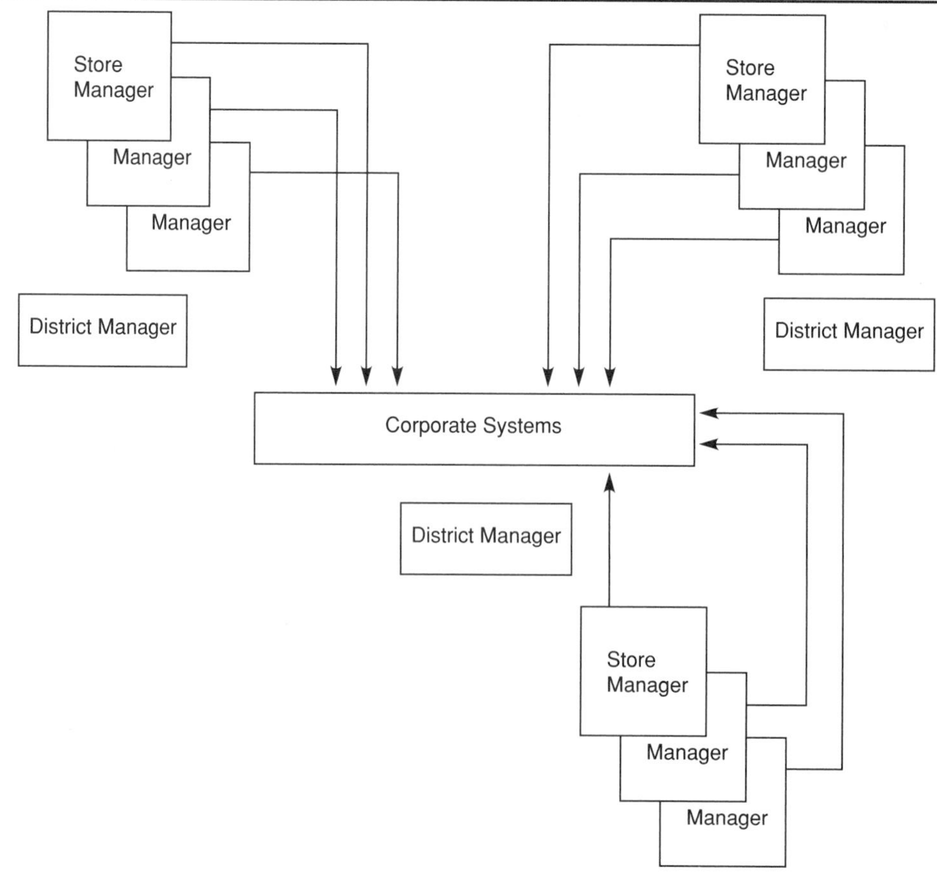

One specific tool that enables the transfer and access of information from computer systems located virtually anywhere—within the company, with its customers or suppliers, and even with the firm's competition—is that of **client/server technology.** To better coordinate manufacturing and retail operations, decision support software developer Manugistics, Inc., has teamed with market-data provider Nielsen North America to develop offerings that link point-of-sale systems with manufacturing applications. According to partners, the resulting supply-chain management system will help manufacturers and retailers enhance forecasting in an effort to reduce backlog and oversupply problems that currently plague every major industry.[15] Figure 16–4 shows the integrated system.

Figure 16–4 Manugistics System Ties Retail Data to Manufacturing

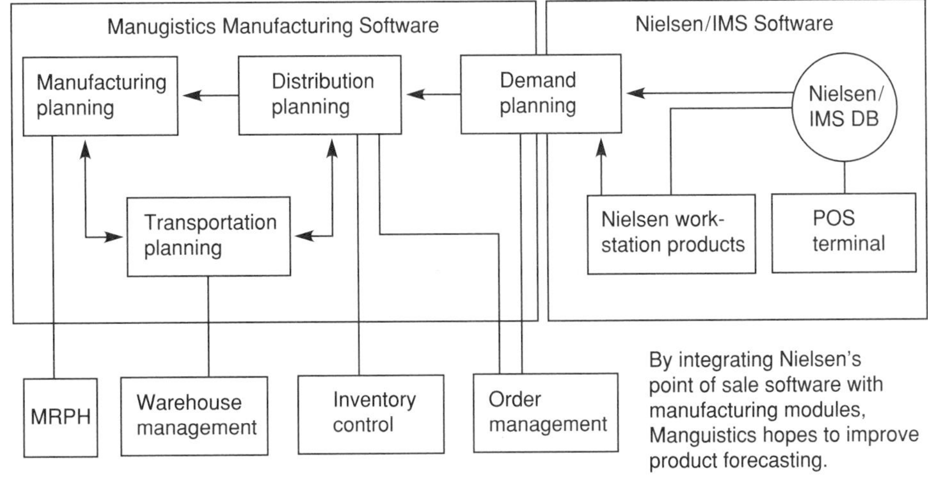

Information Technology and Organizational Behavior

The choices made by those who design and select both the technical system and the path to information technology utilization will affect the way people in organizations behave, how productive people will be, how teams will function, and how the organization performs. To understand the specific impacts of the technical system and the permeating influence of information technologies, we need to know the specific configuration of the technical system and the planned or anticipated deployment of information technologies. Given the dynamic aspects of information technology innovations, this may constitute a moving target. A recent study identified the following assumptions about the technical system: The same technology can be configured in a variety of ways to produce the same results; changes in any one component or in a set of components are likely to affect activities, interactions, and outcomes; technology is a heterogeneous rather than homogeneous concept in an organizational context; and technological changes evoke organizational changes.[16]

The impact of technology on organizational behavior is apparent at the individual, subunit or department, business unit, and organizational levels. Some of the effects are direct, immediate, and intended; others are indirect and unintended, and might surface at a later evolutionary stage. Any attempts to explore the effect of technology and behavior require an investigation of all levels and of the potential cause and effect among levels.

The most noticeable affect of the technical system on individual behavior has to do with productivity and performance. The nature of the technology is likely to impact how work is designed and the character of task activities. From a work design perspective (see Module 13), it can be argued that the introduction of technology or technological change is likely to affect the level of task variety, task autonomy, task significance, and feedback among core job dimensions. Beyond the direct impact on work design and productivity, technology indirectly affects the individual's psychological states such as self-perception and perception of self-worth; expectations about self and others and one's role; the psychological contract that the individual has established over time with the organization; work

Figure 16–5
The Effects of Technology on Organizational Behavior

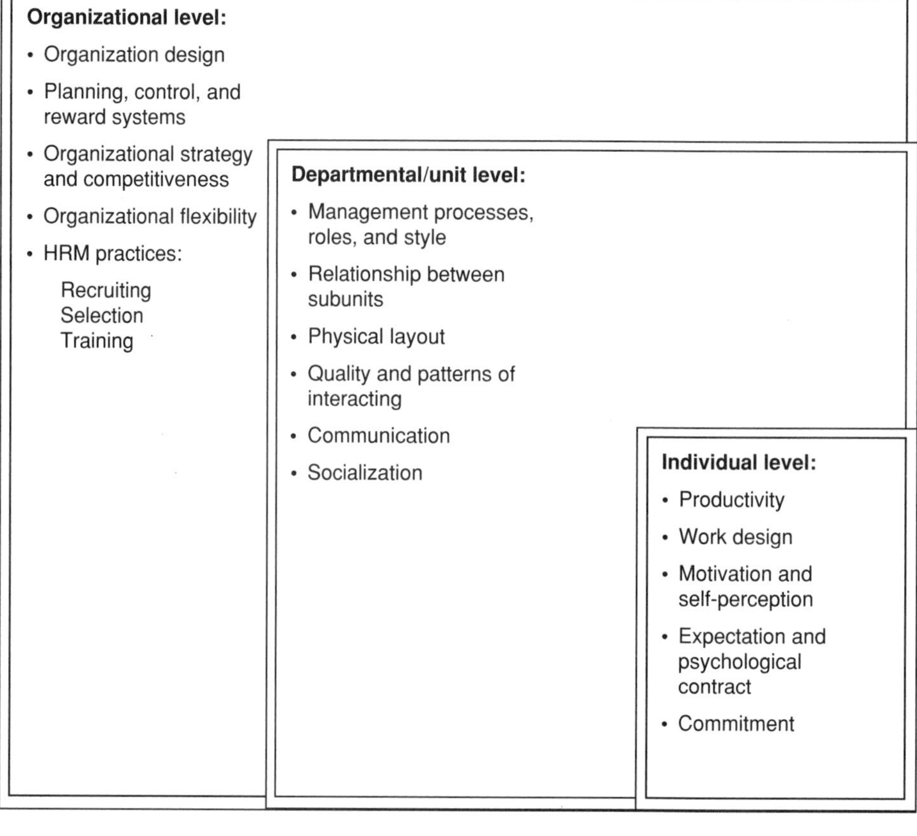

motivation; and, potentially, the level of individual commitment to the job and to the organization.

Organizational level:
• Organization design
• Planning, control, and reward systems
• Organizational strategy and competitiveness
• Organizational flexibility
• HRM practices:
Recruiting
Selection
Training
Departmental/unit level:
• Management processes, roles, and style
• Relationship between subunits
• Physical layout
• Quality and patterns of interacting
• Communication
• Socialization
Individual level:
• Productivity
• Work design
• Motivation and self-perception
• Expectation and psychological contract
• Commitment

An examination of the effects of the technical system at the subunit or department level reveals effects on basic management roles, processes, and styles; the quality of relationships between subunits and their communication patterns; and their physical layout. In a specific plant, the introduction of robotics on the manufacturing floor required a variety of changes such as revised physical layout of the assembly line; more integration between engineering, manufacturing, and maintenance; changes in the managerial roles from those that emphasized monitoring quality to those that stressed coaching and training; and changes in the reporting structure.

The technical system and the choices made about potential technological changes have an effect at the organizational level as well. Roles and relationships between functional areas and departments, the actual design and structure of the organization, planning and control processes, organizational flexibility and competitiveness, and human resource practices are all influenced by technology. As an example, Alaska's Fish and Game Department introduced front-end tools to help smooth application migration from mainfame computers to client/server technology. This move has allowed the department to streamline its computing enterprise, increase productivity, and cut computing costs.[17] This will enable the department to streamline the licensing process by having branch operations send data to Juneau electronically rather than sending hard copy to the main office for keying. This plan will link 1,500 vendors around the state.

A recent study identified four categories of information technology that are likely to impact organizations in the decade to come: (1) individual work support, (2) group work support, (3) advanced organizational automation, and (4) enhanced global communication.[18] As can be seen in Figure 16–6, the authors identified the specific types of information technologies that are likely to have influence on each one of the areas.

Figure 16–6
Information Technology of the Future

Individual Work Support	Group Work Support	Advanced Organizational Automation	Enhanced Global Communications
High-bandwidth portable computer	Groupware*	Electronic data interchange (EDI)*	Language speech translator
Knowbot	Cyberspace	Virtual reality sales	E-mail and voice mail*
Advanced forms of multimedia	Virtual reality for teams	Automated customer response systems*	Videophone and desktop videoconferencing
Virtual reality*			Videoconferencing*
Personal telephone and number			Telepresence
			International highway of business communications

* Already in use in certain corporations.

Source: L. Thach and R. W. Woodman, "Organizational Change and Information Technology," *Organizational Dynamics* 23, no. 1 (1994), p. 34. Reprinted by permission of the publisher.

Information Technology and the Organization

An obvious technology trend is that the cost of information technology is decreasing and its functionality is increasing at an exponential rate. "It has been observed that if automotive technology were to change at the same rate, a Rolls-Royce would cost less than ten dollars, give over one hundred thousand miles per gallon, and go at a speed of over one million miles per hour."[19] The benefits of IT can be summed up as savings of human work time. Work involves many transformations of information from one medium to another. There are many shadow activities consisting of unforeseen and foreseeable time-consuming activities (e.g., errors in typing, busy signals) that do not contribute to the end product. IT can improve the efficiency of such operations by automating all or some of the office automation processes; eliminating some of the transformation of medium; eliminating the shadow activities; and speeding up the information process itself.[20] Experience with many large multinational organizations has shown that corporations usually take one of three fundamental positions related to the competitive use of information technology. Corporations are either adoptors, adaptors, or inventors of information technology.[21] Some companies simply buy off-the-shelf products and do not undertake more than routine applications of their purchased systems. Their goal is usually either short-term survival or catching up with competitors. At this level, virtually any organization can increase its business advantage through the proper application of information technology products, but most **adoptors of information technology** must build (or rebuild) a basic technological foundation. IT adoptors can often be found in stagnant industries, in regions of depressed economies, or in companies with insufficient capital resources. However, a company may find itself in this position simply because of the failure of its senior management to recognize the competitive value of information technology.

Adaptors of information technology are developers and users who have already made information technology an essential element of their value-based planning. They have the awareness, capability, and funds to undertake internal development. They cultivate close working relationships with suppliers, which allow them to take advantage of developments in which timing is critical. These companies generally have developed applications that match those of their competitors. This includes maintenance and enhancement of existing applications as well as a focus on expanding and innovating new and existing applications.

Adaptors of information technology are found in expanding markets. They tend to be global in scope, operate with strong competition, and have rapidly changing products. They enter new markets by acquiring other businesses. Senior management members in adaptive corporations recognize the competitive value of IT and choose to involve IT as an integral part of the planning process.

Inventor companies are technology creators. **Inventors of IT** seek opportunity through scientific breakthroughs, and innovative use of state-of-art technology. Technology inventors are often found within the IT industry such as computer manufacturers and software vendors or suppliers. Some software development companies' overall objective is to tailor applications to companies' needs in a given area. As they do these developments, they simultaneously seek to develop resources needed for competitive technological advantage.

There may be a point where organizational effectiveness can be affected by a firm becoming too lean. There most likely is a certain minimum organizational size that must be maintained to be effective—particularly as a global marketer.[22] Networks are a form of information technology and new management technique that allows people to work together and achieve "scale power." Competitive pressures, increasing costs, "enlightened applications" of information technology, the threat of corporate control, and demands for executive accountability have induced firms to trim staff, reduce lines of business, and create autonomous subsidiary units. New technologies have reduced the optimum size of many businesses.

Information Technology, Work Design, and Organizational Flexibility

In the 1960s and 1970s, computers were used primarily for accounting and control systems. Most computing was centrally controlled and administered. In the 1980s, the personal computer was introduced, making local and departmental computer tasking possible. In the 1990s, the introduction of networks has brought together the critical computer facility with the departmental systems. Companies are now positioned to shape future tasks. Design decisions in computers' early decades emphasized IT for managerial control systems. Managerial decisions to group employees into departments and to link the departments through the hierarchy and linking roles were made first. (See Module 13.) Information systems and other IT choices were to support the basic managerial structure. The traditional view was that information systems choices followed virtually every other design choice to be made. Accordingly, an information systems plan was unnecessary if an overall strategic plan and an operational plan had not been formulated. New IT capabilities such as the widespread use and acceptance of local area networks have made it possible for management to reverse this sequence and identify situations in which other forms of IT drive consideration of task processes, grouping, linking, and managerial process alternatives. At the minimum, IT considerations play an important role in design choices concerning administrative grouping of employees, work location of employees, and coordination of employee activities across departments.

The IT connection to grouping decisions is illustrated by the dilemma of physical location of employees. In matrix organizations within the defense industry, executives must often decide whether to place technical employees such as systems engineers within multispecialty project teams (using a project matrix form of structure—see Module 13) or to place specialists within technical departments under the direction of functional supervisors (using a pure matrix form of structure). If this latter structure is chosen, project coordinators face the difficult problem of integrating diverse contributions from people working in diverse settings. The other extreme of grouping employees under project managers has the disadvantage of weakening professional expertise and training. Less experienced specialists are without mentors, and employees miss the ongoing support and problem solving from fellow experts in their fields. Recent advances with local-area networks and other IT systems allow reconsideration of grouping decisions. Many problems associated with matrix organizations can be alleviated through open communications among project coordinators, team members, and other specialists via local-area networks and groupware. For software development teams, the use of computer-aided software engineering tools can enhance productivity even if the team is dispersed throughout the organization.

Managerial Issues and Concerns for Technology into the 21st Century

The enabling information technologies today are faster, smaller, and cheaper. Each year advances in microchips, optoelectronics, and other building blocks make possible new products and services that bring more people into the Information Age. Equipped with speech recognition, a firm's computers will understand and serve as vanguards for human communication interfaces. Parallel processing divides work to get tasks done faster. Optoelectronics is speeding communication within and between computers. In data storage, better lasers are paving the way for denser storage and faster retrieval. Programmable software agents will do the grunt work for the firm—searching data bases or sorting E-mail. Object-oriented programming now offers very friendly user interfaces. Wireless connections keep workers in touch with each other. Asynchronous-transfer-mode (ATM) switches blend voice, video, and data calls without delay. Compression gets more traffic on the information superhighway without adding lanes.[23] The problem is knowing when to switch to new capabilities and knowing when new capabilities should not be employed even though they exist. The problems are management problems, not IT problems.[24] Automating the office is not a solution in itself or a goal—this could be a misuse of new information technologies. The office, instead, needs to be rethought in light of new capabilities and needs. Satisfactory substitutes for existing human interfaces have to be designed into any new system. Otherwise those working in our offices of the future could potentially sabotage the potentials of the new technologies.[25] IT offers the opportunity for organizations to react constructively to business turbulence and organizational change. Managing the impacts on knowledge workers is a crucial issue in developing and implementing information systems. The application of information technology to change work practices may provide personal opportunities and make jobs more interesting and challenging. It may also devalue job skills and make jobs tedious or even obsolete.

By far the most important issue facing businesses is to integrate information technology capabilities and perspective with their business operations and management.[26] The critical information technology people should be part of the business unit management team, helping to shape and implement strategy. They should truly be at the table of those teams to address opportunities. The point of decentralization and smaller units is to assign those people the targets and accountabilities that we expect from them and then give them the opportunity to pull together resources in a way that allows them to achieve those accountabilities. That includes access to information technology.

As firms become leaner, they most likely will change the structure of the workplace through the formation of work teams operating in business units. Business processes can form the link between high-performance work teams and the corporation at large. Organizing around processes, as opposed to functions, permits greater self-management and allows companies to dismantle unneeded supervisory structures.[27] Organizations need to be certain that they help people understand why change is needed in the first place. They have a right to know what is going on if they are to be partners in change.[28] Technology is capable of generating enormous amounts of information. The reengineering of organization structure is vital. Decentralizing old corporation hierarchies and empowering employees making and selling products are the first steps to improved productivity. Providing them with the right kinds of technology is the next critical step.[29] The organization's alignment with these new technologies is the third vital step.

Summary

Technology is the tools, techniques, methods, devices, configurations, knowledge, procedures, and actions used by organizational members to acquire inputs, to transform inputs into outputs, and to provide outputs in terms of products or services to customers. Information technology is a special subset of technology that deals with computers, communications, user interfaces, storage, artificial intelligence, robotics, and computerized manufacturing. The nature and benefit of any of these technologies depends on the organization, the organizational unit as a team, and the individuals as they interact and use the various technologies.

At the organizational level, technologies can be divided into two types: manufacturing and service. These technology types are a function of the service or production processes of the firm. IT can be part of the production process or service provided by the company. IT can also be used to exploit the production process through the use of specialized hardware and software. Innovations in IT have recently played a part in corporate downsizing, elimination of organizational levels, improved cross-department coordination, and better interorganizational relationships. IT also supports executives through improved communication with the external environment which may yield a competitive advantage.

We have presented a variety of classifications of technology. We clustered technologies according to (1) the interdependence of the tasks performed, (2) whether there was a requirement to link with customers and clients, and (3) which specialized technique the technology used. At the department level we identified two dimensions of departmental activity: variety and analyzability. These dimensions formed the basis for four major departmental uses of technology: routine uses of technology; craft; engineering; and nonroutine or high task variety. Within an organization focusing on manufacturing there may be a wide range of computer-based systems: stand-alone systems in machining, cell systems for flexible manufacturing, linked islands to form production systems, and full integration of the manufacturing processes. We concluded by noting that the choices made by those who design and select both the technology and the path to information technology utilization will affect the way people in organizations behave, how productive the people will be, and how teams will function. As such, technology and information technology must be treated as key organizational processes that requires vital managerial attention.

Study Questions

1. Although some argue that the technical subsystem is the defining feature of organizations, others argue that the technical system is only one of the many features that define organizations. State your position and provide your rationale.
2. Compare and contrast any two of the classifications of technology.
3. Describe a technical system in an organization that you are familiar with. How would you classify the system? How would Perrow, Woodward, or Thompson classify the same technical system?
4. Describe a technical system in an organization that you are currently working for or that you have worked for in the past. Describe the relationship between the technical system and human behavior. Examine how the technical system affects human behavior.
5. Discuss and contrast the relationship between technology and information technology.
6. Describe an information technical system in an organization that you are currently working for or that you have worked for in the past. Describe the relationship between the technical system and the use of information technology. Examine how the information technical system affects the business unit or group.
7. Review selected articles from *Business Week* or *Fortune* that deal with information technology. Describe the company and its use of these information technologies in terms of adoptors, adaptors, or inventors.
8. Using the various classifications of technology, develop a similar set of classifications for information technology wherein various forms of information technology are used to support the technology classification.

Endnotes

1. W. A. Pasmore, *Designing Effective Organizations* (New York: John Wiley & Sons, 1988), p. 51.

2. C. Perrow, ''A Framework for the Comparative Analysis of Organizations,'' *American Sociological Review* 32 (1967), pp. 194–208; D. A. Rosseau, ''Assessment of Technology in Organizations: Closed versus Open System Approaches,'' *Academy of Management Review* 4 (1979), pp. 531–42; F. E. Kast and J. E. Rosenzweig, *Organization and Management: A Systems and Contingency Approach* (New York: McGraw-Hill, 1985); and Pasmore, *Designing Effective Organizations,* pp. 55–57.

3. P. S. Goodman, T. L. Griffith, and D. B. Fenner, ''Understanding Technology and the Individual in an Organizational Context,'' in *Technology and Organizations,* eds. P. S. Goodman and L. S. Sproull (San Francisco: Jossey-Bass, 1990), pp. 45–86.

4. Joan Woodward, *Industrial Organization: Theory and Practice* (London: Oxford University Press, 1965).

5. D. J. Hickson, D. S. Pugh, and D. C. Phesey, ''Operations Technology and Organizational Structure: An Empirical Reappraisal,'' *Administrative Science Quarterly,* September 1969, pp. 365–78; J. D. Goldhar, and M. Jelinek, ''Computer Integrated Flexible Manufacturing: Organizational, Economic, and Strategic Implications,'' *Interfaces* 15, no. 3 (1985), pp. 94–105; P. S. Goodman, T. L. Griffith, and D. B. Fenner, ''Understanding Technology and the Individual in an Organizational Context,'' in *Technology and Organizations,* eds. P. S. Goodman and L. S. Sproull (San Francisco: Jossey-Bass, 1990), pp. 45–86.

6. J. Thompson, *Organizations in Action* (New York: McGraw-Hill, 1967).

7. C. Perrow, ''A Framework for the Comparative Analysis of Organizations,'' *American Sociological Review* 32 (1967), pp. 194–208; and R. Daft and N. Macintosh, A New Approach to Design and Use of Management Information,'' *California Management Review,* 21 (1978), pp. 81–92.

8. J. R. Meredith and M. M. Hill, ''Justifying New Manufacturing Systems: A Managerial Approach,'' *Sloan Management Review,* Summer 1987, pp. 49–61; and A. B. Shani, R. M. Grant, and R. Krishnan, ''Organizational Implications of New Manufacturing Technology: A Sociotechnical System View,'' *California Management Review* 34, no. 4, pp. 91–111.

9. A. B. (Rami) Shani and O. Elliott, ''Sociotechnical Systems Design in Transitions,'' in *The Emerging Practice of Organization Development,* eds. W. Sikes, A. Drexler, and J. Grant (La Jolla Calif.: University Associates, 1989), pp. 187–98; C. H. Pava, ''Redesigning Sociotechnical System Design: Concepts and Methods for the 1990s,'' *Journal of Applied Behavioral Science* 22, no. 3 (1986), pp. 201–21.

10. C. Francalanci, *Measuring the Impact of Investments in IT on Business Performances* HICSS Proceedings, 1994, p. 600.

11. G. B. Huber and W. H. Glick, ''Sources and Forms of Organization Change,'' in *Organizational Change and Redesign: Ideas and Insights for Improving Performance,* eds. G. B. Huber and W. H. Glick (Oxford, England: Oxford University Press, 1993), Chapter 1; D. J. Hickson, D. S. Pugh, and D. C. Phesey, ''Operations Technology and Organizational Structure: An Empirical Reappraisal,'' *Administrative Science Quarterly* 15 (1969), pp. 365–78; P. L. Nemetz, and L. W. Fry, ''Flexible Manufacturing Organizations: Implications for Strategy Formulations and Organization Design,'' *Academy of Management Review* 13, no. 4 (1988), pp. 627–38.

12. R. L. Daft, ''Implications of Top Managers' Communication Choices for Strategic Decisions,'' in *Organizational Change and Redesign,* Chapter 4.

13. A. B. (Rami) Shani and J. Sena, ''Information Technology and Structural Change,'' *Journal of Information Technology* 8 (1993), pp. 34–42; M. W. Stebbins, J. M. Sena and A. B. (Rami) Shani, ''Information Technology and Organization Design,'' *Journal of Information Technology,* 10, (1995), pp. 1–13.

14. T. Richman ''Mrs. Fields' Secret Ingredient,'' *Inc. Magazine,* October 1987, pp. 48–64.

15. Ted Bowen, ''Retail Gets Link to Factories,'' *PC Week,* December 5, 1994.

16. Scott Morton, *Corporations of the 1990's* (Oxford, England: Oxford University Press, 1991).

17. Aileen Crowley, ''Front End Tools Help Smooth Alaskan Application Migration,'' *PC Week,* December 19, 1994.

18. L. Thach and R. W. Woodman, ''Organizational Change and Information Technology,'' *Organizational Dynamics* 23, no. 1 (1994), pp. 30–46.

19. Crowley, "Front End Tools Help Smooth Alaskan Application Migration."

20. Reddy, Raj "A Technological Perspective on New Forms of Organizations," *New Forms of Organizations,* p. 235; G. R. Bushe, and A. B. Shani, *Parallel Learning Structures: Increasing Innovation in Bureaucracies* (Reading, Mass.: Addison-Wesley, 1991); M. L. Markus, and D. Robey, "Information Technology and Organizational Change: Causal Structure in Theory and Research," *Management Science* 34, no. 5 (1988), pp. 583–98.

21. C. Francalanci, P. Maggiolini, and P. Milano, "Measuring the Impact of Investments in Information Technology on Business Performance," *Proceedings of the Twenty-Seventh Annual Hawaii International Conference on Systems Science, 1994,* p. 612; and Louis Fried and Richard Johnson, "Planning for the Competitive Use of Information Technology," *Information Strategy: The Executive Journal,* Summer 1992, pp. 5–15.

22. Tom Peters, "Rethinking Scale," *California Management Review* 35, no. 1 (Fall 1992), pp. 7–29.

23. P. Coy, "The Enabling Technology Overview," *Business Week/The Information Revolution,* 1994, p. 54.

24. C. Thurow, "Preface to the Corporations of the 1990s", in *Corporations of the 1990's,* ed. Scott Morton (Oxford, England: Oxford University Press, 1991); D. Tapscott and A. Caston, *Paradigm Shift: The New Promise of Information Technology* (New York: McGraw-Hill, 1993); S. Zuboff, *In the Age of the Smart Machine: The Future of Work and Power* (New York: Basic Books, 1988).

25. P. Docherty, J. Sena, and A. B. (Rami) Shani, *Groupware, Team Performance and Organizational Productivity,* Working paper series (Stockholm: Stockholm School of Business, 1995).

26. "Double Duty CFO," *Financial Executive,* "Special Report: Information Management," July-August 1994, pp. 15–19.

27. Thomas Stewart, "Are You Flat, Lean, and Ready for a Bold New Look?" *Fortune,* May 18, 1992, pp. 93–96.

28. Stuart L. Stokes, *Controlling the Future: Managing Technology Driven Change* (Wellesley, Mass.: QED Information Systems, 1993).

29. Peter Sasson, "Basic Principles for Measuring IT Value," *IS Analyzer,* October 1992.

Activity 16–3: Department of Motor Vehicles (DMV): The Failed $44 Million Computer Project

Objectives:

a. To explore the major features of the technological system in the firm.
b. To investigate the effect of the information system on organizational performance.

Task 1 (Homework):

Participants are to read the case that follows, "The Department of Motor Vehicles," and answer the questions at the end of the case.

Task 2 (Class):

The instructor will facilitate class discussion based on individuals' answers.

Case Study: The Department of Motor Vehicles

Here is an excerpt from an article in the *San Jose Mercury News* on Sunday, August 14, 1984.

Source: This case was contributed by Professor James A. Sena. College of Business, California Polytechnic State University, San Luis Obispo, California 93407. We are grateful to him.

How the DMV Skirted Bidding Rules

In a deal that sidestepped state bidding laws, the Department of Motor Vehicles in 1990 and 1991 gave Tandem Computers, Inc., of Cupertino, California, three state contracts worth $1.7 million to perform major design and programming work on what turned out to be the DMV's failed effort to create one of the world's largest data bases.

The no-bid consulting contracts—which have come under scrutiny by state investigators looking into the disaster—are one of the most puzzling elements in the tangled tale of how the DMV wasted $44 million in taxpayer money trying to modernize the database that stores driving records of more than 30 million Californians.

The contracts assigned Tandem responsibility for "technical project leadership" and a "lead role in the application development methodology and the design and development of the DMV specific application software." But Tandem officials and the DMV say that the contracts were merely ways to funnel $1.7 million to consultants laboring on the project.

The project involved converting the DMV's massive IBM databases to a system that used Tandem computers and technology. The no-bid contracts in question involved consulting services for the Tandem system, including programming and database design. While those contracts allowed the DMV to hire the experts needed to keep the mired-down project from grinding to a halt, they also allowed the agency to evade competitive bidding laws for more than a year and kept the project's early troubles from coming to the immediate attention of state watchdogs and lawmakers. The failure of the DMV computer project was revealed by DMV officials at a legislative hearing in April 1994. After seven years, the DMV couldn't get the system to do what it had envisioned. At a May 1994 hearing of the Assembly Transportation Committee (one of several government bodies investigating the DMV project's failure), two Tandem representatives told the puzzled legislators that all the company did under the no-bid consulting contracts was pass the $1.7 million on to 18 independent consultants. Some of the consultants had been handling many of the major technical details of the complex project for the original project manager, the consulting firm of Arthur Young & Co., until the firm abandoned the project in June 1990. Figure 16–7 shows the events over seven years that led to the failure.

The Technology—What the DMV Was Trying to Accomplish

In 1987, the Department of Motor Vehicles was on the verge of completing a major technological feat: transferring its ancient, bulging databases from the old Sperry Univac computer systems it had built over the years to the brand-new IBM MVS environment that the state's Data Center had just installed.

As the project was winding down, the DMV got new marching orders from state lawmakers. They wanted the department to refuse to issue vehicle registration certificates to drivers who had no auto insurance. Unfortunately the DMV's database of driver's license information was separate from its database containing vehicle registration information. In simple terms, the two databases couldn't talk to each other so there was no way to match up uninsured drivers with their vehicles.

That's when the DMV's computer specialists hit upon what they saw as a solution to all of their problems. They would convert their flat-file database system, which could only provide information from one database at a time, to a relational database system, which could retrieve and massage information from a variety of databases simultaneously.

In late 1988, after a lengthy technological assessment, the DMV selected Tandem's Nonstop SQL relational database system, which can run only on Tandem computers. In December 1993, after five fitful years of trying to redesign and reengineer the DMV's assembler language application programs into a more sophisticated computer language the Tandems could understand, the DMV declared the project a failure. The agency is now seeking legislative permission to simply upgrade its current IBM system.

Some Case Observations

Many issues and information technology considerations are manifest in this almost unbelievable sequence of events. Let's first review the sequence of events as outlined in Figure 16–7. In July 1987, the DMV decided to convert its flat-file databases to a

Figure 16–7
DMV Summary of Events: Seven Years to Failure

July 1987	Department of Motor Vehicles officials decide to convert its old flat-file database system, which can provide information from only one database at a time, to a relational database system, which can retrieve and message information from a variety of databases simultaneously. They estimate it will take 64 months to complete and will cost $12 million.
Nov. 2, 1987	DMV now estimates costs at $28.5 million because of extended testing and pilot programs. Cost is deemed "modest . . . when compared to the total budget and the long-term benefits to be achieved."
April 1988	DMV sends out questionnaires to Tandem, IBM, Terradata, and Software AG so the companies can tell DMV what their relational database systems can do. Terradata and Software AG are eliminated from consideration. DMV plans a performance test between IBM and Tandem.
Sept. 6, 1988	DMV seeks bids for a project manager. Before the contract is awarded, the bid requirements will change seven times.
Dec. 23, 1988	A preliminary report of a performance test is published, announcing that Tandem's NonStop SQL system has been judged to be the best product, far outperforming the IBM DB2 system.
May 2, 1989	DMV first realizes that the Tandem system might be slower than what it is replacing and that the performance tests didn't measure what needed to be measured: average response time. Report notes, "Each user may have to run three or four times as many sessions to perform the same number of transactions they currently process in the same period of time."
May 16, 1989	Tandem is awarded its first contract, for $6.5 million, for a 12-CPU Tandem VLX system and a 4-CPU CLX system. DMV finances the purchase through Ford Motor Credit, which charges $84,248 for finance charges and $733,591 for interest. Taxpayers will make monthly payments of $180,478 for the next three years.
June 2, 1989	DMV opens bids for project manager. The Arthur Young consulting firm wins with a bid of $4.9 million.
March 1990	Ron Kuhnel, acting director of the Office of Information Technology, orders an independent evaluation of the DMV project by the Dept. of Finance budget office.
July 30, 1990	Monthly report from Computer Deductions Inc. (which is acting as DMV's consultant) says the "project is disoriented and not on the correct course."
Nov. 29, 1990	Dept. of General Services approves a $700,000 no-bid consulting contract for Tandem. The contract assigns Tandem responsibility for "technical project leadership" and "a lead role in the application development methodology and the design and development of the DMV specific application software." Tandem says the contracts are just a way to get money to the independent consultants.
Dec. 27, 1990	A purchase order is issued for six Tandem Cyclones and 140 gigabytes of storage for $11.9 million.
Jan. 9, 1991	DMV asks for another $700,000 for the Tandem no-bid consulting contract, boosting the contract total to $1.4 million.
March 12, 1991	A Finance Department audit report is released. The performance test did "not demonstrate the expected performance and benefits of the proposed new system," costs are being underreported and underestimated, and the project is far behind schedule, the report says.
May 15, 1991	DMV and Tandem sign an extension for $300,00 on the Tandem consulting contract through Sept. 30.
June 12, 1992	A confidential Tandem analysis of the DMV project concludes that the project won't be done until 1998 and will cost $155 million to complete.
Aug. 26, 1993	Tandem proposes to take over the DMV project with EDS, a Dallas computer company. Tandem wants a total of $41.7 million for consulting fees, additional hardware, and maintenance. EDS wants $30 million for consulting and $81 million for data processing services.
Dec. 22, 1993	DMV Director Frank Zolin informs Tandem that he has decided to abandon the Tandem system and go with another plan that uses IBM computers.
April 11, 1994	DVM informs the state Office of Information Technology that it is officially killing the project. The final report concludes, "It now appears that DMV management succumbed too readily to industry hype. The practicalities of what was being promoted by the technical industry were overly optimistic."
April 28, 1994	Assemblyman Jim Costa, D-Fresno, requests an audit of the DMV project to determine "how this massive misuse of taxpayer money could have occurred over so long a period of time."

relational system. This was a good strategy. It was not the first state or federal government agency to undertake this step. Industry had embraced relational database systems a good 10 years earlier. IBM had been encouraging its customers to make this move almost to the point where it would no longer support the simple flat-file database systems. The motor vehicle departments in both Texas and Washington had already converted their similar systems to relational databases.

The next major decision was the selection of hardware systems. The DMV made the decision to use Tandem's Nonstop SQL system instead of IBM's DB2 system. In 1988, Tandem's technology was not a proven commodity. IBM's DB2 was in use at most mainframe installations throughout the country. For some reason the DMV decided not to take the conservative approach. It chose an unproven computer technology. In retrospect many firms have employed Tandem's SQL system with a great deal of success. Such a system mainly focuses on online transaction processing systems where users are distributed throughout a region. The sheer size and volume of the databases could bring most computer systems to their knees. The newspaper article reported a variety of testing that indicated a mixed performance comparison between IBM's and Tandem's products.

It wasn't until after the DMV had decided to use and entered into a contract with Tandem that it opened bids for a project manager. The award was given to a management consulting firm, Arthur Young (AY). No mention is made of AY's experience with Tandem systems. It is doubtful that it had much experience because the technology was new and nontraditional. So, in effect, AY likely was intending to learn as it went along. Within a year (July 1990), it became apparent that AY did not have a master plan—"the project was disoriented and not on course." Tandem had to step in to ensure that its computer systems could be used properly; it was assigned technical project leadership. Somewhere along the line AY's services were terminated and specialists familiar with the Tandem system were employed under the guise of contractors paid on moneys funneled through Tandem. To salvage the system, Tandem proposed an alliance with EDS to take over the project (August 1993). Instead, the DMV decided to terminate the Tandem system and go with IBM computers (December 1993).

Assignment

1. What do you think were the two major contributory failures in the DMV project?
2. As a manger of technology, do you think the DMV made the right decision to employ the Tandem SQL computer solution in 1987?
3. Do you see any problems in the sequence of selecting the hardware vendor and then at a later time selecting the software implementors?
4. Do you think the choice to go with IBM as opposed to an alliance with Tandem and EDS was a good decision to make at the end of 1993? (Review what has happened with IBM mainframe computer system utilization and facility expansion since that time.)

Activity 16–4: Behavior, Technology, and Work Design: Speedy Delight and Shady Corner Cafe

Objectives:

a. To understand the concepts of work design, tasks, technology, and structure through personal observation and analysis of real organizations.
b. To identify the relationships among work design, technology, structure, and the human and formal organizations.
c. To compare and contrast two familiar organizations in terms of relevant characteristics or variables.

Task 1:

This activity requires that each of you—independently or in small groups—go out to observe two organizations. Spend 15 to 30 minutes observing (1) an independent, locally owned restaurant or cafe (we will call it the Shady Corners Cafe) and

(2) a fast-food service operation such as McDonald's, Burger King, Kentucky Fried Chicken, Taco Bell, or any similar owner-operated or franchised operation. (We will call this a Speedy Delight.)

You may make your observations individually or in small groups (two to three people). Perhaps the best way to begin is simply to go in as a patron, buy a cup of coffee, a hamburger, or a meal, and observe what happens. Ideally, you will be able to obtain additional information from the employees through informal discussion and interviews. This technique should not be too much of an imposition—after all, we are throwing business their way.

We do not want to structure your observations too much. You should be flexible in making up your own lists of similarities and differences for the two organizations. However, the individual observations form on the next pages provides you with some possible areas for consideration.

Task 2:

Teams are to meet and compare the observations. The attached "Group Composite Analysis" form lists areas for consideration.

Task 3:

A team spokesperson will be asked to provide a short presentation of the team's analysis. The written team comparative analysis is due at the beginning of the class session.

Task 4:

The entire class dicusses all the findings.

Source: This activity is a modified version of an exercise developed by Professors Fremont E. Kast and James E. Rosenzweig, University of Washington, Spokane, Washington. We are grateful to Professors Kast and Rosenzweig for their permission to include this activity here.

Individual Observations

	Shady Corners Cafe	Speedy Delight
Technical System Nature of equipment, degree of mechanization, and so on. (Include both cooking and service equipment.)		
How was the technical knowledge required to perform tasks developed in these two organizations?		
Products: Inputs and Outputs Standardization of product. How much variation is provided for customers?		
The degree of standardization or uniformity of raw material inputs.		
What are the outputs for customer satisfaction?		
What do customers seek in types of food and/ or service?		
Structure How are tasks divided? Degree of task specialization.		
How are tasks integrated?		
What are the authority patterns?		
Draw a simple chart of superior–subordinate relationships for each organization.		

	Shady Corners Cafe	Speedy Delight
Psychosocial System The age, background experience, and general characteristics of workers.		
Your impression of their motivation and satisfaction with their jobs. Why are they working there?		
Observations on the informal organization, group relationships, and so on.		
How do the technology and structure affect the human relationships?		
Customer and Environmental Relationships Who are the customers of these organizations?		
Have customers and employees established interpersonal relationships?		
How long (in minutes) are the customers in interaction with the organization?		
In the future, under what circumstances will *you* patronize the two establishments?		
Total Organization System Is there a pattern of relationships among the above factors?		
How easy would it be to duplicate each organization at another location?		
Are the factors that contribute to success or failure the same for both organizations?		
Other comparisons		

Group Composite Analysis

Share your observations and analysis with other members of your group. It is likely that each of you will have looked at a number of different organizations and therefore can extend your comparative analysis. Use the following framework for your group comparisons. Jot down key words or phrases for each area of analysis.

	Shady Corners Cafe	Speedy Delight
Technical systems		
Products: inputs and outputs		
Structure		

	Shady Corners Cafe	Speedy Delight
Psychosocial system		
Customer and environmental relationships		
Total organization system		
Other comparisons		

17 Managing Organizational Change and Development

Learning Objectives

After completing this module you should be able to

1. Appreciate the complex dynamics of managing change.
2. Explain the phenomenon of organizational culture and its underlying dimensions.
3. Describe the key factors that affect organizational culture.
4. Describe the relationship among organizational culture, change, development, and effectiveness.
5. Define the field of organizational change and development (OC&D).
6. Compare and contrast any two of the systemwide OC&D interventions.
7. Explain the roles that personality, perception, communication, and motivation play in OC&D efforts.
8. Discuss how OC&D can help foster creativity, innovation, and continuous improvements.
9. Explain some of the challenges that OC&D faces in the global arena.

List of Key Concepts

Action research
Continuous improvement (CI)
Eclectic planned change approach
GE's Work-Out Program
Grid organization development
Intervention
Organizational change and development (OC&D)
Organizational culture
Organizational development
Organizational diagnosis
Parallel learning structure
Planned change
Reengineering
Sociotechnical system (STS)
Systems 1 to 4
Total Quality Management (TQM)

Module Outline

Premodule Preparation

The instructor may assign one of the following two activities as a premodule assignment.

Activity 17–1: Andersson's Challenge at Berol Kemi

Objective:

To appreciate the process and role of organizational culture and the management of change.

Task 1 (Homework):

Participants are to read the attached case and respond to the questions at the end of the case.

Task 2 (Classroom):

a. Teams are to reach a shared perception of the major characteristics of Berol Kemi under Rolf Edebo's leadership.
b. Teams are to reach a shared perception of the major characteristics of Berol Kemi under Andersson's leadership.
c. Teams are to discuss the process of managing change. (For example, What was Edebo's approach? What was Andersson's approach? How was Edebo's approach different from Andersson's? What would have been the ideal process to change the organization?)

Task 3:

The instructor will have each team share with the entire class its perceptions of Berol Kemi's culture under the command of the two leaders.

Task 4:

The class will discuss the relationships between organizational culture, managing change, and its effects on organizational behavior and productivity.

Task 5:

The instructor will give a short lecture on organizational culture, managing change, and the role that the process plays in fostering or hindering effectiveness.

Case Study: Nobel Industries— The Case of Berol Kemi

This description of the Berol Kemi developments focuses on the period from the late 1970s to the early 1990s. This period starts and ends with changes in top management. We will however briefly touch on some of the challenges and later developments in what is now called Berol Nobel. Following a merger in 1988 the company is in the

Source: This case was written by T. Stjernberg and A. B. (Rami) Shani and was presented at the conference "Successful Business through People" at Cornell University in October 1992. The case was selected by a panel of key business leaders and experts in the Swedish Employers Confederation, the white-collar and blue-collar trade unions' confederations, and the Work Environment Fund as one of three illustrative cases for the conference.

midst of transformation. The company's top management feels a discussion of the current transformation process would be premature.

The question that faced the manager entering Berol Kemi in the late 1970s was, How do you create a new management philosophy and wide employee commitment to that philosophy, when entering a company in crisis and with downsizing likely in the near future?

The Berol Kemi developments in the late 1970s provide an example of how this may be done with very positive effects. A cooperative process resulted in the establishment of mutual commitment for business goals, high performance, and high quality of work life.

We will also briefly describe the work organization and wage system of one of the factories. That description focuses on the question, How may work be organized when complex, potentially dangerous chemical processes are to be monitored and controlled?

Berol Kemi: A State-Owned Company, 1973–88

From 1976 to 1978, Berol Kemi (owned by Statsföretag, the Swedish state-owned group) was bleeding heavily. With a turnover of SEK (Swedish Kroner) 500 millions, the loss was SEK 180 million in 1978. Statsföretag's marketing director, Ralph Edebo, had been opposed to buying Berol Kemi in 1973, but was placed as deputy representative on its shareholders' board. He was very critical of some of the Berol Kemi management investments in the mid-1970s and resigned from the board in 1976. When the top management of the Statsföretag Group in 1977 decided that new top management was needed in Berol Kemi, Edebo was asked to find a candidate. Six candidates were approached; all turned down the offer. Finally Edebo agreed to take the assignment as a project. One principal task was to study whether the company should be closed down. The alternative of closing down the company was going to cost the group SEK 300 million due to long-term contracts. Table 17–1 gives data on Berol Kemi in 1978.

Table 17–1
Berol Kemi in 1978

- 100 percent of the shares owned by Statsföretag, but operating with a shareholders' board with influential members in business and government (and with union representatives according to law).
- 1,200 employees, with head office and main production facilities for surface chemicals (raw materials for detergents etc.) at Stenungsund, about 30 miles outside Gothenburg, and additional production of cellulose derivatives at Örnsköldsvik in northern Sweden.
- Invoiced sales of SEK 500 million.
- Loss of SEK 180 millions.
- Estimated cost for shutting down SEK 300 million.
- 65 percent of production exported.
- One union with company representation for the factory workers (blue-collar) with almost all employees in this category as members. One union for salaried workers with about 95 percent membership. One union for graduate engineers with more than 95 percent membership. Together the two latter organizations form the PTK (the common negotiating organization for white-collar employees). In addition, the supervisors' union has members but no local organization.

Taking Command by Jointly Developing a New Management Philosophy and Structure

Two weeks after Edebo took over in February 1978, he called together 80 key persons, 25 of whom were union representatives. In advance a document was distributed, *Suggested Management Philosophy.* The three-day seminar started with a discussion of the suggested philosophy and issues such as prices, profits, profit center managers' authority, how to calculate results, and the management of information systems. The discussions led to an agreement about a management philosophy. During the evening 10 parallel groups worked to answer the question, Given this philosophy, how should Berol Kemi be organized? Similar suggestions were presented by 8 of the 10 groups in the morning of day 3. Edebo and the top-management committee discussed the suggestions until late that day and made an organizational chart that was presented and accepted by the board of directors the day after.

Thus within three weeks a new organization and management philosophy—widely accepted by middle management and union leadership as well as by the parent company—had been established.

A few weeks later a management control system was worked out, partly at a seminar with key persons and union representatives. By mid-March a process of rebudgeting started which led to the establishment of new cash flow targets and the identification of a possibility (and a necessity accepted by the unions) to reduce the staffing by 300 to 350 employees.

The Berol Kemi Model of the 1980s: Management and Unions in Close Cooperation

Berol Kemi became known for its employee participation in management and operations during the 1980s. Already before the changes in 1978, Berol Kemi had developed an elaborate system of advisory groups as the means for employees to become informed and to influence decision making. The general attitude to this system (according to Ralph Edebo) was that it created red tape but little influence and commitment. Edebo therefore asked the chairman of the factory workers' union to suggest a better system of employee participation.

The new system meant that 16 internal boards were formed, one for each division and one for each principal support unit. This included a board for strategic development. (Figure 17–1 shows the firm's structure in the 1980s.) Ralph Edebo exercised his decision-making power as chairman of the internal boards. All of these boards had union representatives. The management group board consisted of Edebo, the vice president of finance, the director of industrial relations, and two union representatives. They met every Monday for the entire morning. This group of people may be seen as the center of power in Berol Kemi. Meetings were characterized by a high degree of trust between top management and union representatives. All formal requirements for informing and negotiating with the employees, according to the codetermination act, were automatically taken care of through the activities of these boards. Only on five occasions during the 1980s were issues taken out from the boards for a more formal negotiation. Wage negotiations were done outside this model of influence according to general Swedish practice.

In the beginning of the 1980s, the employees gathered around the issue of saving the company. As managing director, Edebo felt that one of his main challenges during the 1980s was to energize the organization and to create continuous commitment and sharing of interests and goals. Sequential "Lifts" were launched. The first, "The Lift," was an internal marketing effort headed by the VP of personnel. One idea was to get every employee to suggest three ideas for improvement. This was followed by "The Computer Lift" when 80 percent of the employees participated in 40 hours of computer training during their free time. Participants also received a personal computer after the course. One effect, according to Edebo, was that the operators then managed to do most of the production planning and computer programming by themselves.

"The Total Quality Lift" during 1986 and 1987 was followed by "The Environmental Lift" in the late 1980s. "The Environmental Lift" meant 10 hours of instruction during employees' free time followed by a one-day excursion. According to Edebo, this Lift led to noticeable environmental improvements such as a 50-ton reduction in ethylene oxide released into the environment.

Berol Kemi became well known in Sweden for its participative work system as well as for its elaborate systems to encourage worker commitment. *LO-tidningen* (the paper published by the Swedish Confederation of Labor) called Berol Kemi "the best workplace in Sweden" in a feature article in 1989. Table 17–2 compares two indicators of the firm's quality of work life over a 13-year period (1978–91). Figures 17–2 and 17–3 show the firm's financial performance over that time. (The 1988 merger explains the leap in sales that year.)

Figure 17–1 **Berol Kemi in the 1980s**

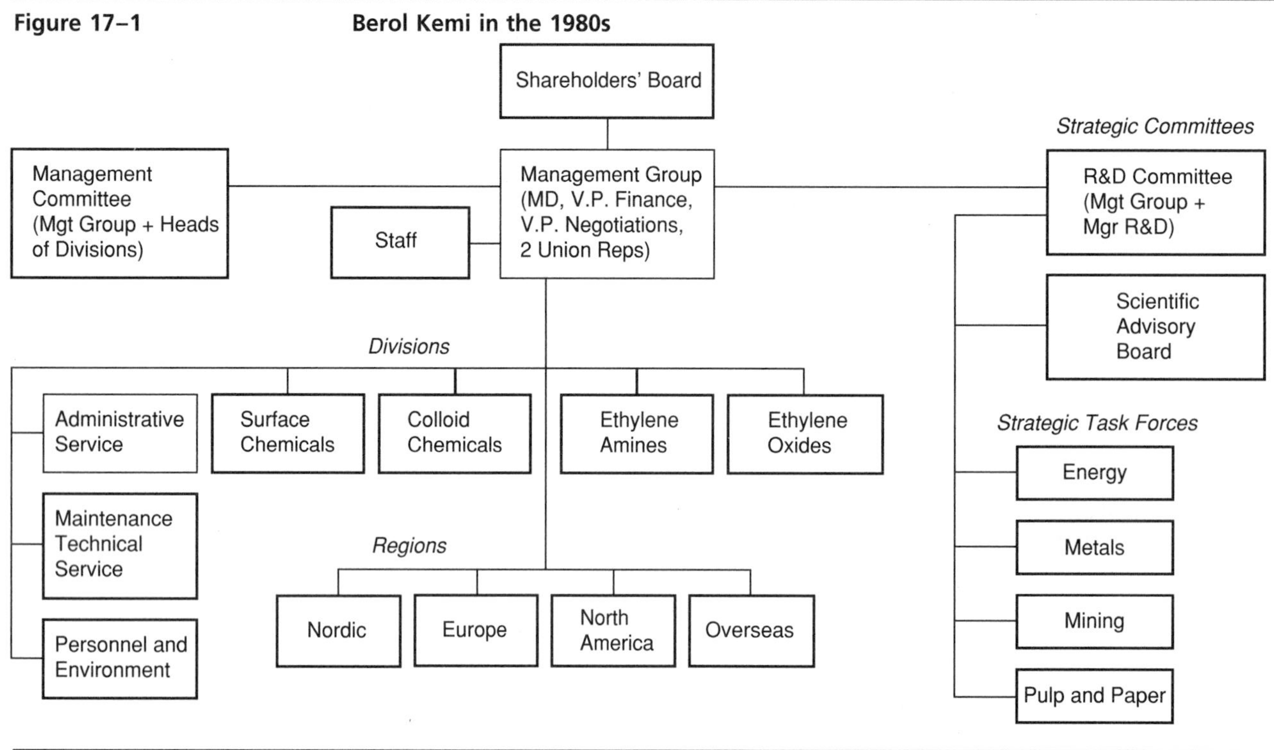

Table 17–2
Berol Kemi/Berol Nobel—Comparative Indicators of the Quality of Work Life

	Short Sick Leave		External Turnover		Number of Employees	
	Operators	Salaried	Operators	Salaried	Operators	Salaried
1978	5.6%	2.8%	6.3%	9.8%	336	448
1985	5.7	3.1	2.7	5.2	350	366
1991	2.9	4.8	3.3	3.0	447	459

Note: Short-term sick leave means sick leave less than one week. Most remarkable is the opposite trends in sick leave figures for the operators and salaried employees.

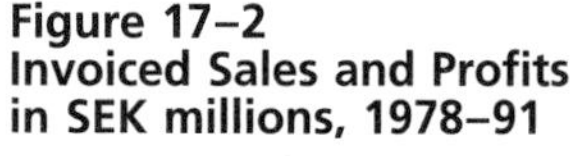
Figure 17–2
Invoiced Sales and Profits in SEK millions, 1978–91

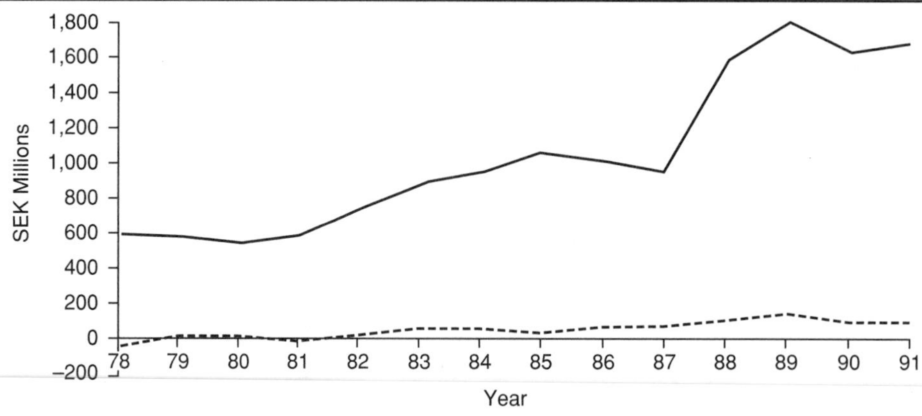

Figure 17–3
Profits (Exclusive of Financial Issues) as a Percentage of Invoiced Sales, 1978–91

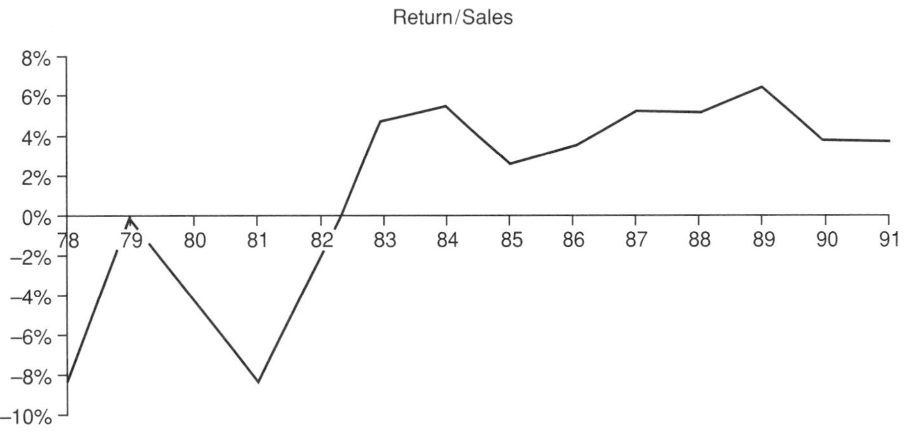

The Work Organization—Self-Managed Teams

Prior to 1978 the maintenance department initiated experiments with autonomous groups. When the new amines plant was started in 1977, the work organization was based on the principle that all members of each shift of six persons should be able to do all the tasks, including coordinating the team. A career ladder was established with plans for gradual buildup of competence, skills and pay. Tables 17–3, 17–4 and 17–5 present data on the amines plant.

Table 17–3
Production at the Amines Plant, 1980–90

	1980	1985	1990
Production (1,000 kg)	8,875	13,100	25,460
Workers (excluding loading)	35	36	38
Production (1,000 kg) per employee	253	364	670

Note: The increase in quantity means that the complexity of the production process has increased.

Table 17–4
The Amines Plant in 1992 (in Principle the Same Work Organization as in the 1980s)

- Part of the Ethylene Amines division that has 55 employees, including marketing, R&D, and production.
- Main products are ethylene amines produced according to a unique process.
- Forty-four employees in production; production manager, five engineers (working daytime and rotating the role of call on duty), logistics and loading (one manager and five workers on daytime), clerical support, five shifts of six workers rotating the roles of lab operator (the starting position), three outside operators, control room operator, and coordinator. During the nights and weekends, teams take full responsibility for the plant with a possibility to call the engineer on duty.
- Typical age of workers on the teams is 25, with a few workers in their 40s on each team. Twelve are coordinators, and three more will be appointed within a month.

Table 17–5
Wage System, 1978–92

1978: (1) Base pay plus (2) pay based on level of competence 1, 2, or 3 plus (3) pay based on experience after two years, plus (4) for employees in the amines plant and the maintenance unit, pay for being a coordinator during the period they actually worked as coordinator.

1985: Same as in 1978, but pay is based on experience in six intervals, after 2, 4, 5, 6, 8, and 10 years—adding SEK 200 per month for each step.

1992: Same as in 1985, but in addition to the pay as coordinator, when a person is actually working as coordinator, there is an extra fixed coordinator pay after one year, three years, and five years—adding SEK 250 in each step.

Pay levels: In 1992 pay for a factory worker with 10 years, experience who is working as coordinator is a maximum of SEK 14,000 per month plus on the average 3,900 for shift working, and 500 to 750 for the time actually working as coordinator, depending on the size of the group. The minimum wage for an adult (base pay) is SEK 9,350.

The model of the amines plant (and another pioneering unit, maintenance) diffused during the 1980s. Almost all production teams in the company introduced a system with no formal supervisor but instead a coordinator. You may apply for the coordinator role after being recommended by your teammates and after having reached a sufficient skill level. The production manager decides who should be accepted for training to become a coordinator. Being coordinator means reaching the top pay in the knowledge-based wage system. The youngest coordinator today at the amines plant is 23. To date, according to the production manager, all the coordinators have lived up to the demands of the job. In fact, people "grow" when given the role of being coordinator. Rotation of the coordinator role takes place every five weeks in each of the teams. Each team is very different in character. A distinct culture has developed in each team, reflecting the personalities of the team members.

In the amines plant, the level of complexity in the production process has increased greatly during the 1980s—with no corresponding increase in staffing.

Challenges of the 1990s

In the late 1980s, Statsföretag changed its name to Procordia and also changed its strategy and portfolio of business in the group. Berol Kemi was put up on the transfer list. A series of potential buyers were considered. According to the principles of Berol Kemi, the unions were heavily involved in the choice of new owners. During a period of six months, the unions participated in secret meetings with seven potential buyers. Finally the Nobel Group bought Berol Kemi. The CEO of the Nobel Group, Anders Carlberg, came down to Stenungsund, the Berol Kemi head office, on two occasions and met with the unions to discuss the planned merger with Nobel, which at that time had 400 employees. During a period of about a year, Ralph Edebo stayed on as managing director of the new company, called Berol Nobel. In fall 1989 Christer Andersson joined Berol Nobel to take over the role of managing director. The formal transition of managing director took place in March 1990.

The story of the merger of Berol Kemi and Nobel is interesting from several perspectives. It reveals the unions' strong position and also the mutual trust between the top management (Edebo) and the union leadership in the 1980s.

The story also raises the issue of how a new top management team should approach the need for further development. Andersson saw a need to develop the company's strategy and to create a new vision and business focus. He has also identified a need to develop the middle management and their position in the company. In the old organization, middle managers sometimes felt that their subordinates were better and faster informed about business decisions. The union members, through the unions' participation in the many boards, had quick access to information and a mechanism for sharing it. There were 16 internal boards, which usually met about five times per year, with four union representatives on each board. These included internal boards for regions, staff units, and divisions.

The challenge for the new top management was to develop a new business-oriented and management-led culture that could unite the two merging parts: Berol Kemi and Nobel. That process is well underway.

In the new organization, the managing director, the Management Group, and the Business Coordination Group are the centers of power. The link between the sales units and the division are more direct—the divisions are mirroring the customers rather than the production. Also the relations between the support structure (such as personnel and administrative services) and the line organization are changing. The number and influence of the joint labor–management committees has decreased. The joint committees for each support function have ceased to exist. Instead, the support functions are now seen more as the resource for management and for the line organization. The support specialist may veto a line manager's decisions—but he or she may not take the decision "for" the manager. The link between the divisions and the regional sales organization has become more direct.

The changes in the early 1990s have not been directed toward the principles of the work organization. The amines plant is still built on the basic organizational principles from 1978; the coordinator role rotates among those who have been recommended by their teammates and have passed a test. A person is coordinator for a fairly long period each time—up to five weeks. Table 17–6 and Figure 17–4 present the firm's business and organizational components in the early 1990s.

Table 17–6
Berol Nobel in 1992

- 100 percent of the shares owned by Nobel Industries since 1988.
- 1,100 employees at four facilities: Nacka, the former Nobel head office with 60; Stenungsund, head office and main facilities of Berol Kemi with 530; Sundsvall, a Nobel plant, with 160; and Örnsköldsvik, a Berol Kemi plant with 130. In addition, there are 150 employees abroad in the sales organization.
- Invoiced sales (in 1991) totaled SEK 1,700 million, which was 8 percent of the group's sales.
- Return (in 1991), inclusive of financial items, was SEK 67 million (15 percent of the group's earnings).
- 90 percent of production was exported.
- Union membership was roughly the same as in 1978.

Figure 17–4
Berol Nobel as Organized in April 1991

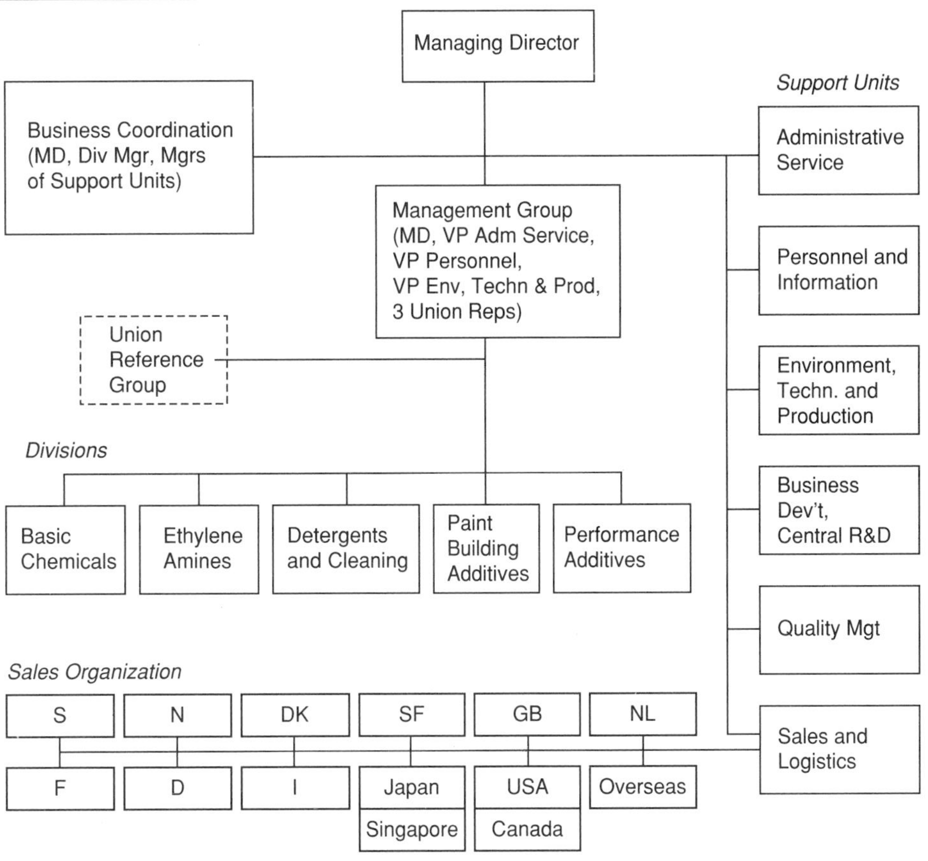

Conclusions and Reflections

One way of summarizing the changes around 1980 and in the 1990s is to see them as strategies to empower the people in the company. In the 1980s, efforts to empower people and to create commitment were directed at the employees in general. In the 1990s, empowerment efforts focus on the line organization, especially middle management. It should be possible to strengthen the power of middle management and the employees simultaneously. But how will the unions' position and influence be affected by the attempt to strengthen the position of middle management? And to what extent can the unions themselves influence their own future position and strength?

The developments in Berol Kemi in the 1980s provide an example of a successful strategy for saving a company in a crisis situation. The series of Lifts were attempts to energize the organization by mobilizing the employees. Does a process, such as the one in Berol Kemi, have a natural ''life line'' where the mobilization is dependent on the existence of a real crisis? What are the possibilities to sustain the mobilization in a longer time perspective?

The organization and culture of Berol Kemi seem to have been well fitted to the personality and values of Ralph Edebo. Is the organizational culture in reality only an expression of the personal style and values of the managing director of the company?

The developments in Berol Kemi during the 1980s and early 1990s are interesting in their own right. They illustrate the power of collaboration in a crisis and the strength of a process where many parties and persons are involved in solving problems and in developing a new philosophy and culture. They also raise important questions about the viability of such a culture and management philosophy.

Assignment

Prepare notes on the following questions:

1. Based on the limited information presented, identify and briefly describe the major characteristics of Berol Kemi under the leadership of Rolf Edebo.
2. Identify and briefly describe the major characteristics of Berol Kemi under the leadership of Andersson.
3. How did the organizational culture change? What caused the change? What effects did the culture change have on human behavior and organizational performance and effectiveness?

Activity 17–2: The Planned Change Program at General Electric: The Work-Out Program

Objective:

To appreciate the complex process and the management of a planned change program.

Task 1 (Homework):

Participants are to read the case that follows and respond to the questions at the end of the case.

Task 2 (Classroom):

a. Individuals are to share their responses to the questions at the end of the case.
b. Teams are to discuss the process of managing change. (For example, What was Welch's approach? How is it different or similar to TQM or STS?)

Task 3:

The instructor will have each team share its perceptions with the entire class.

Task 4:

The class will discuss the relationships between organizational culture, managing change, and its effects on organizational behavior and productivity.

Task 5:

The instructor will give a short lecture on organizational culture, managing change, and the role that the process plays in fostering or hindering effectiveness.

Case Study: The Transformation at General Electric

John Francis Welch Jr. was appointed chairman and chief executive officer of General Electric in April 1981. His tenure in the job has been characterized by constant strategic and organizational change at GE. Among the initiatives that Welch was associated with were

1. *Changing the shape of the business portfolio.* Welch established two sets of criteria for redefining the business portfolio of GE. The first was to declare, "We will only run businesses that are numer one or number two in their global markets—or, in the case of services, that have a substantial position—and are of a scale and potential appropriate to a $50 billion enterprise." Second, Welch defined three broad areas of business for GE: core, high technology, and service businesses. As a result of these criteria, during the 1980s, GE sold or closed businesses accounting for $10 billion in assets and acquired businesses amounting to $18 billion in assets. Divestment included Utah International, housewares and small appliances, consumer electronics, and semiconductors. Additions included RCA, Employers Reinsurance Corp., Kidder Peabody Group, Navistar Financial, several new plastics ventures, Thomson's medical electronics business, and joint ventures with Fanuc (factory automation), Robert Bosch (electric motors), GEC (major appliances and electrical equipment), and Ericsson (mobile communications).

2. *Changing strategic planning.* Welch largely dismantled the highly elaborate strategic planning system that had been built up at GE over the previous decade. Documentation was drastically reduced, and the planning review process was made more informal—the central element was a meeting between Welch, his two vice chairmen, and the top management of each SBU which focused on identifying and discussing a few key themes. By 1984, the 200-strong corporate planning staff had been halved. The broad objective was "to get general managers talking to general managers about strategy rather than planners talking to planners."

3. *Delayering.* The changes in planning were one aspect of a more general change in the role of headquarters staff from being "checker, inquisitor, and authority figure to facilitator, helper, and supporter." This change involved a substantial reduction in reporting and paper generation, and an increase in individual decision-making authority. These changes permitted a substantial widening of spans of control and the removal of several layers of hierarchy. In most of GE, levels of management were reduced from nine to four.

4. *Destaffing.* Divesting pressures, removing management layers, reducing corporate staffs, and increasing productivity resulted in enormous improvements. Between 1980 and 1990, GE's sales more than doubled while its numbers of employees fell from 402,000 to 298,000.

5. *Values.* A persistent theme in Welch's leadership was a commitment to values. Welch continually emphasized the importance of the company's "software" (values, motivation, and commitment) over its "hardware" (businesses and management structure). Welch's philosophy was articulated in 10 key principles and values:

Being number one or two in each business.

Becoming and staying lean and agile.

"Ownership"—individuals taking responsibility for decisions and actions.

"Stewardship"—individuals ensuring that GE's resources were leveraged to the full.

Source: This case was written by R. Grant and A. B. (Rami) Shani for classroom use. The case draws heavily on the following sources: N. M. Tichy and S. Sherman, *Control Your Destiny or Someone Else Will* (New York: Doubleday, 1992); R. Slater, *The New GE: How Jack Welch Revived an American Institution* (Homewood, Ill.: Irwin, 1993); R. N. Ashkenas and T. D. Jick, "From Dialogue to Action in GE Work-Out," in W. A. Pasmore and R. Woodman (eds.), *Research in Organization Change and Development* (Greenwich, Conn.: JAI Press, Vol. 6, pp. 267–87; and "Jack Welch's Lessons for Success," *Fortune,* February 25, 1993, pp. 86–90.

''Entrepreneurship.''

''Excellence''—the highest personal standards.

''Reality.''

''Candor.''

''Open communications''—both internally and externally.

Financial support—earning a return needed to support success.

This emphasis on values was supported by a type of leadership that put a huge emphasis on communicating and disseminating these values throughout the company. Welch devoted a large portion of his time to addressing meetings of employees and management seminars at GE's Crotonville Management Development Institute.

New Culture, New Systems

During his first five years in office, Welch's priorities were strategy and structure. GE's business portfolio was radically transformed, and within its main businesses GE's strategies gave a much greater emphasis to local presence and global success and to the development and application of new technology. In terms of organizational structure, Welch's crusade against excess costs, complacency, and administrative inefficiencies resulted in a drastic pruning of the corporate hierarchy and a much flatter organization.

At the root of the ''new culture'' Welch sought to build at GE was a redefinition of the relational contract between GE and its employees:

> Like many other large companies in the United States, Europe and Japan, GE has had an implicit psychological contract based upon perceived lifetime employment. . . . This produced a paternal, feudal, fuzzy kind of loyalty. You put in your time, worked hard, and the company took care of you for life. That kind of loyalty tends to focus people inward. . . . The psychological contract has to change. People at all levels have to feel the risk-reward tension.
>
> My concept of loyalty is not ''giving time'' to some corporate entity and, in turn, being shielded and protected from the outside world. Loyalty is an affinity among people who want to grapple with the outside world and win. . . . The new psychological contract, if there is such a thing, is that jobs at GE are the best in the world for people who are willing to compete. We have the best training and development resources and an environment committed to providing opportunities for personal and professional growth.[1]

Creating a new attitude requires a shift from an internal focus to an external focus:

> What determines your destiny is not the hand you're dealt, it's how you play your hand. The best way to play your hand is to face reality—see the world as it is and act accordingly. . . . For me, the idea is: to shun the incremental and go for the leap. Most bureaucracies—and ours is no exception—unfortunately still think in incremental terms rather than in terms of fundamental change. They think incrementally because they think internally. Changing the culture—opening it up to quantum change—means constantly asking, not how fast am I going, how well am I doing versus how well I did a year or two before, but rather, how fast and how well am I doing versus the world outside.[2]

Critical to building a new culture and changing the ''old ways'' of GE was not just the bureaucracy itself, but the habits and attitudes that had been engendered by bureaucracy:

> The walls within a big, century-old company don't come down like Jericho's when management makes some organizational changes or gives a speech. There are too many persistent habits propping them up. Parochialism, turf battles, status, ''functionalities'' and, most important, the biggest sin of a bureaucracy, the focus on itself and its inner workings, are always in the background.[3]

The "Work-Out" Program—a Generic View

GE's Work-Out Program was a response to the desire to speed the process of organizational change in GE. The idea of Work-Out was conceived by Welch in September 1988. Welch conducted a session at every class of GE managers attending Management Development Institute at Crotonville, New York. He was impressed by the energy, enthusiasm, and flow of ideas that his open discussion sessions with managers were capable of generating. At the same time he was frustrated by the resilience of many of GE's bureaucratic practices and the difficulty of transferring the ideas that individual managers possessed into action. After a particularly lively session at Crotonville, Welch and GE's education director, James Braughman, got together to discuss how the interaction in these seminars could be replicated throughout the company in a process that would involve all employees and would generate far-reaching changes within GE. In the course of a helicopter ride from Crotonville to GE's Fairfield headquarters, Welch and Braughman sketched out the concept and the framework for the Work-Out process.

A model for GE's Work-Out was a traditional New England town hall meeting where citizens gather to vent their problems, frustrations, and ideas, and people eventually agree on certain civic actions. Welch outlined the goals of Work-Out as follows:

> Work-Out has a practical and an intellectual goal. The practical objective is to get rid of thousands of bad habits accumulated since the creation of General Electric. . . . The second thing we want to achieve, the intellectual part, begins by putting the leaders of each business in front of 100 or so of their people, eight to ten times a year, to let them hear what their people think. Work-Out will expose the leaders to the vibrations of their business opinions, feelings, emotions, resentments, not abstract theories of organization and management.[4]

A generic summary of the Work-Out Program reveals three interrelated purposes: to fuel a process of continuous improvement and change; to foster cultural transformation characterized by trust, empowerment, elimination of unnecessary work, and boundaryless organization; and to improve business performance.

The Structure of the Work-Out Process

The central idea of the Work-Out process was to create a forum where a cross-section of employees in each business could speak their minds about how their business was managed without fear of retribution. Because those doing the work were often the best people to recommend improvements in how their work should be managed, such interaction was seen as a first step in taking actions to remove unnecessary work and improve business processes. In January 1989, Welch announced Work-Out at an annual meeting of GE's 500 top executives. A broad framework was set out, but considerable flexibility was given to each of GE's 14 core businesses in how they went about the program. The key elements of Work-Out were

- *Off-site meetings.* Work-Out was held as a forum and to get away from the company environment. Two-to-three–day Work-Out events were held off-site.
- *Focus on issues and key processes.* There was a strong bias toward action-oriented sessions. The initial Work-Out events tended to focus on removing unnecessary work. This is what Braughman referred to as the "low-hanging fruit." As the programs developed, Work-Out focused more on more complex business processes. For example, in GE Lighting, groupwide sessions were held to accelerate new product development, improve fill rates, and increase integration between component production and assembly. In plastics the priorities were quality improvement, lower cycle times, and increased cross-functional coordination.
- *Cross-sectional participation.* Work-Out sessions normally involved between 50 and 100 employees drawn from all levels and all functions of a business. Critical to the process was the presence of the top management of the particular business.
- *Small groups and town meetings.* Work-Out events normally involved a series of small group meetings which began with a brainstorming session followed by a plenary session (or "town meeting") in which the suggestions developed by the small groups were put to senior managers and then openly debated. At the end of each discussion, the leader was required to make an immediate decision: to adopt, reject, or defer for further study.

- *Follow-up.* A critical element of Work-Out was a follow-up process to ensure that what had been decided was implemented.

The Results of Work-Out

The results from Work-Out were remarkable. During its first four years more than 3,000 Work-Out sessions had been conducted in GE, resulting in thousands of small changes eliminating "junk work" as well as much more complex and further-reaching changes in organizational structure and management processes. The terms *rattlers* and *pythons* were introduced to describe the two types of problem. Rattlers were simple problems that could be "shot" on sight. Pythons were more complex issues that needed unraveling.

As well as tangible structural changes and performance gains, some of the most important effects were changes in organizational culture. In GE Capital, one of the most centralized and bureaucratized of GE's businesses, one employee described the changes as follows: "We've been suppressed around here for a long time. Now that management is finally listening to us, it feels like the Berlin Wall is coming down."[5]

In five years, more than 300,000 employees, customers, and suppliers went through Work-Out sessions. A large variety of impressive and significant performance and efficiency improvements are reported in GE's internal documents, following introduction of the Work-Out processes. For example, the Gas Engine Turbines business unit at Albany, New York, reported an 80 percent decrease in production time to build gas engine turbines; Aircraft Engines at Lynn, Massachusetts, reduced jet engine production time from 30 to 4 weeks. GE's Financial Services Operation reported a reduction in operating costs from $5.10 to $4.55 per invoice, invoices paid per employee were up 34 percent, costs per employee paid fell 19 percent, and employees paid per payroll worker rose 32 percent. The Aerospace plant at Syracuse, New York, reported that as a result of the Work-Out Program, beyond achieving 100 percent compliance with pollution regulations, the production of hazardous waste materials was reduced from 759 tons in 1990 to 275 tons in 1992. Table 17–7 compares Work-Out Programs in four GE businesses.

Managing Work-Out

Work-Out was intended as a bottom-up process where employees throughout each business would be free to challenge their leaders, and where management's role was primarily to perpetuate the program and to ensure that decisions, once made, were implemented. But Work-Out could not be just a populist movement within the corporation. It needed to be directed toward creating the kind of corporation that GE needed to be to survive and prosper in the 1990s. To this extent, Jack Welch saw his role as communicating and disseminating the principles, values, and themes that would permit GE's continued success.

In 1989, Welch crystallized his ideas about GE's management around three themes: speed, simplicity, and self-confidence:

> We found in the 1980s that becoming faster is tied to becoming simpler. Our businesses, with tens of thousands of employees, will not respond to visions that have sub-paragraphs and footnotes. If we're not simple we can't be fast . . . and if we're not fast, we can't win.
>
> Simplicity, to an engineer, means clean, functional, winning designs, no bells and whistles. In marketing it might manifest itself as clear, unencumbered proposals. For manufacturing people it would produce a logical process that makes sense to every individual on the line. And on an individual, interpersonal level it would take the form of plain speaking, directness, honesty.
>
> But as surely as speed flows from simplicity, simplicity is grounded in self-confidence. Self-confidence does not grow in someone who is just another appendage on the bureaucracy; whose authority rests on little more than a title. People who are freed from the confines of their box on the organization chart, whose status rests on real world achievement—those are the people who develop the self-confidence to be simple, to share every bit of information available to them, to listen to those above, below and around them and then move boldly.
>
> But a company cannot distribute self-confidence. What it can do—what we must do—is to give our people an opportunity to win, to contribute, and hence earn self-confidence themselves.

Table 17–7

General Electric Work-Out: A Comparative Summary

GE Businesses	Implementation Process	Cultural Context	Road Blocks	Reported Outcomes
Gas Engine Turbines Albany, New York	■ Standard Work-Out ■ Delayering ■ Employee decision-making initiative ■ Self-directed work teams	■ Structured assembly line atmosphere ■ High level of union influence ■ Distinctive hierarchy	■ Union influence; fostered a skeptical environment among line workers	■ 80% decrease in production time to build gas engine turbine
Lightening Arresters Puerto Rico (products protect power lines from surges)	■ Flattened organization ■ Worker participation in decisions ■ GE offered employees additional money in exchange for participation in Work-Out ■ GE offered extra money to employees who earned degrees (focused on English and business degrees) ■ Production control by employees—they are the experts	■ Spanish-speaking environment ■ Low level of employee education ■ New plant facility	■ Workers did not anticipate roles as decision makers ■ Initial language barrier	■ Increased worker participation ■ Higher employee morale ■ Expected 8% increase in output per employee per year ■ 50% of all employees in specialized positions have since earned degrees ■ Advances as workplace led to model GE plant abroad
Aircraft Engines Lynn, Massachusetts	■ General Work-Out session ■ Employee empowerment. Problem with raw materials from supplier—bad screw bit heads	■ Standard assembly line atmosphere ■ Apathetic management, skeptical employees ■ Managers committed to philosophy of Work-Out (management buy-in)	■ Management nervous about spending money to solve problems ■ "Walking the Talk" requires full commitment	■ Middle manager and line worker chartered plane to headquarters of the supplier ■ Raw materials (screws) now conform 100% to specifications ■ Employee empowerment ■ Additional employee participation has led to other production highs—jet engines produced in 4 weeks, as opposed to 30 weeks
Aerospace Syracuse, New York	■ General Work-Out session ■ Employee participation in enhancing production process ■ Production control by employees—they are the experts	■ Skepticism by employees—just another band-aid ■ Skepticism by middle management	■ Employee attitudes ■ Management's initial resistance	■ 100% compliance to pollution regulations ■ Production of hazardous waste materials fell from 759 tons in 1990 to 275 tons in 1991 ■ Teams committed to getting the word out on the importance of pollution control

They don't get that opportunity, they can't taste winning if they spend their days wandering in the muck of a self-absorbed bureaucracy.

Speed . . . simplicity . . . self-confidence. We have it in increasing measure. We know where it comes from . . . and we have plans to increase it in the 1990s.[6]

Best Practices

One of the Work-Out Program's many impressive outcomes is that it's a catalyst for new improvement programs. One such program, ''Best Practices,'' is aimed at increasing productivity. The GE business development staff focused on 24 credible companies from an initial pool of 200 that had achieved faster productivity growth than GE and sustained it for at least 10 years. From this list, one dozen companies agreed to take part in GE's proposal to send its employees to their companies to learn their secrets to success. In exchange, GE offered to share the results of the study as well as share its success stories with the participating companies. This learning for the Best Practices program involved companies such as Ford, Hewlett-Packard, Xerox, and Chaparral Steel plus three Japanese firms.

GE was less concerned with the actual work done at the companies than with management practices and attitudes of the employees. The difference between Best Practices and traditional benchmarking is that the former does not require a score to be kept. The focus on learning alternative successful management practices and managing processes was identified as the most critical component for long-term productivity improvements. The basic assumption that through multiple exposure to alternative management practices, managers and employees will be stimulated to continuously improve their own practices continues to guide the program. Best Practices has evolved into a formal course taught to at least one dozen employees and managers per month in each of the business units.

Assignment (Written)

1. Based on the limited information presented, describe the overall planned change approach and phases led by John Welch.
2. Identify and briefly describe the major characteristics of the Work-Out Program.
3. Discuss how the organizational culture changed. What caused the change? What effects did the culture change have on human behavior and organizational performance and effectiveness?

Introduction

Managing change is one of the toughest managerial tasks. In the first module of this book, we argued that the study of organizational behavior looks at the organization as an organic system, ever adapting to the external environment and to the internal dynamic interactions of subunits. As such, organizational culture and organizational change are two integral components of the firm's life. Unique cultures and subcultures emerge as a result of the interaction between the different organizational subsystems; dealing with an ever-changing business environment makes change and planned change a way of survival. Furthermore, from an organizational effectiveness point of view, managers' and organizations' abilities to manage the change process were found to be related to some of the basic criteria of effectiveness (for example, performance, success, improvement, and productivity).[7]

In the context of this text we briefly define and examine the evolutionary process of organizational culture, its meaning, and its impact on individual, group, and organizational effectiveness. In our discussion about change, we focus on those changes that are planned—an attempt is made to consciously and deliberately bring about change in the organization's status quo. Two major categorizations of planned change strategies have been articulated. With the first, according to Chin and Benne,[8] planned change can be divided into three basic types of strategies: empirical-rational, normative-reeducative, and power-coercive. The second describes seven "pure" approaches for bringing about change: fellowship, political, economic, academic, engineering, military, and applied behavioral science.[9] In this module we have chosen to focus on the applied behavioral science approach or, more specifically, the organizational development (OD) orientation, to discuss this total-system strategy for improving organizational effectiveness because of its concerns for both macro and micro aspects of change and development.

In this module we define and discuss the nature of organizational culture and the factors that help determine its uniqueness. We discuss the complexity of organizational culture change, define organizational development, categorize and review the variety of OD interventions, and give examples of the OD approaches designed to influence the total organization. Finally, we discuss results from empirical investigations designed to assess OD's effectiveness.

Organizational Culture

The study of organizational culture represents the newest and one of the more controversial schools of thought in the fields of organizational behavior and organization theory. The organizational culture theories are based on assumptions about people and organizations that depart significantly, and in more than one way, from those of the "mainstream" schools. First, they challenge the system and the structural schools about, for example, how organizations make decisions and how and why humans behave as they do.[10] While the system and structural schools argue that individuals' personal preferences are restrained by systems of formal rules, authority, and norms of rational behavior, the cultural school advocates that individual preferences are controlled by cultural norms, values, beliefs, and assumptions.[11] Second, from the organizational culture viewpoint, every organizational culture is different, and what "works" for one organization won't necessarily work for another.[12] Third, the organizational culture school believes that qualitative research methods are the better way to fully understand and predict organizational behavior[13] (rather than quantitative research methods using quasi-experimental designs, control groups, and multivariate analyses).

Defining Organizational Culture

An examination of the **organizational culture** school reveals diverse definitions and elements. For some, organizational culture has something to do with the people and the unique character of the organization; for some, it means shared top-management beliefs about how they should manage themselves and other employees and how they should conduct their business;[14] for some, it is the shared philosophies, ideologies, values, assumptions, expectations, attitudes, and norms that knit a community together;[15] for some, it is an evolutionary process;[16] and for still others, it is a complex pattern of beliefs, expectations, ideas, values, attitudes, and behavior shared by the members of an organization. Furthermore, controversy exists on the role of organizational culture, its effects on organizational life, and the ability to influence and lead corporate culture change.[17]

For our purposes, Schein's recent definition captures the essence and uniqueness of the phenomenon: Organizational culture is

> (a) a pattern of basic assumptions, (b) invented, discovered, or developed by a given group, (c) as it learns to cope with its problems of external adaption and internal integration, (d) that has worked well enough to be considered valid and, therefore, (e) is to be taught to new members as the (f) correct way to perceive, think, and feel in relation to those problems.[18]

Schein argues further that in analyzing the culture of an organization or group, it is important to distinguish among three fundamental levels at which culture manifests itself: (a) observable artifacts such as physical layout, dress code, the way people relate to each other, company records, statement of philosophy, and reports, (b) values, norms, philosophy, and ideology, and (c) basic underlying assumptions about the organization's relationship to its environment, the nature of reality and truth, the nature of human nature, the nature of human activity, and the nature of human relationships. Figure 17–5 provides an example of specific questions that can guide the exploration of the underlying assumptions around which cultural paradigms emerge.

Factors That Affect the Natural Evolution of Organizational Culture

Among the many factors that affect the evolution of group and organizational culture are (1) work group characteristics such as commitment to the group's mission and task, work group size and composition, and work group design and autonomy; (2) managerial and leadership styles such as philosophical process and output orientations;

Figure 17–5 **Some Underlying Dimensions of Organizational Culture**

Dimension	Questions to Be Answered
1. The organization's relationship to its environment	Does the organization perceive itself to be dominant, submissive, harmonizing, or searching out a niche?
2. The nature of human activity	Is the "correct" way for humans to behave to be dominant/proactive, harmonizing, or passive/fatalistic?
3. The nature of reality and truth	How do we define what is true and what is not true; and how is truth ultimately determined in both the physical and social worlds: by pragmatic test, reliance on wisdom, or social consensus?
4. The nature of time	What is our basic orientation in terms of past, present, and future, and what kinds of time units are most relevant for the conduct of daily affairs?
5. The nature of human nature	Are humans basically good, neutral, or evil, and is human nature perfectible or fixed?
6. The nature of human relationships	What is the "correct" way for people to relate to each other and to distribute power and affection? Is life competitive or cooperative? Is the best way to organize society on the basis of individualism or groupism? Is the best authority system autocratic/paternalistic or collegial/participative?
7. Homogeneity versus diversity	Is the group best off if it is highly diverse or if it is highly homogeneous, and should individuals in a group be encouraged to innovate or conform?

Source: Adapted from E. H. Schein, *Organizational Culture and Leadership* (San Francisco: Jossey-Bass, 1985), p. 86. Copyright © 1985 by Jossey-Bass. Adapted with permission.

(3) dynamics between groups and departments such as degree of dependency, communication processes, and cooperation; (4) organizational characteristics such as mission, product and service requirements, size, technology, policies and procedures, reward system, and organization design; and (5) environmental characteristics such as industry, competitive pressures, and social, political, and legal environments. Figure 17–6 presents graphically some key factors that affect the evolution of culture.

Figure 17–6
Some Key Factors Affecting Group and Organizational Behavior

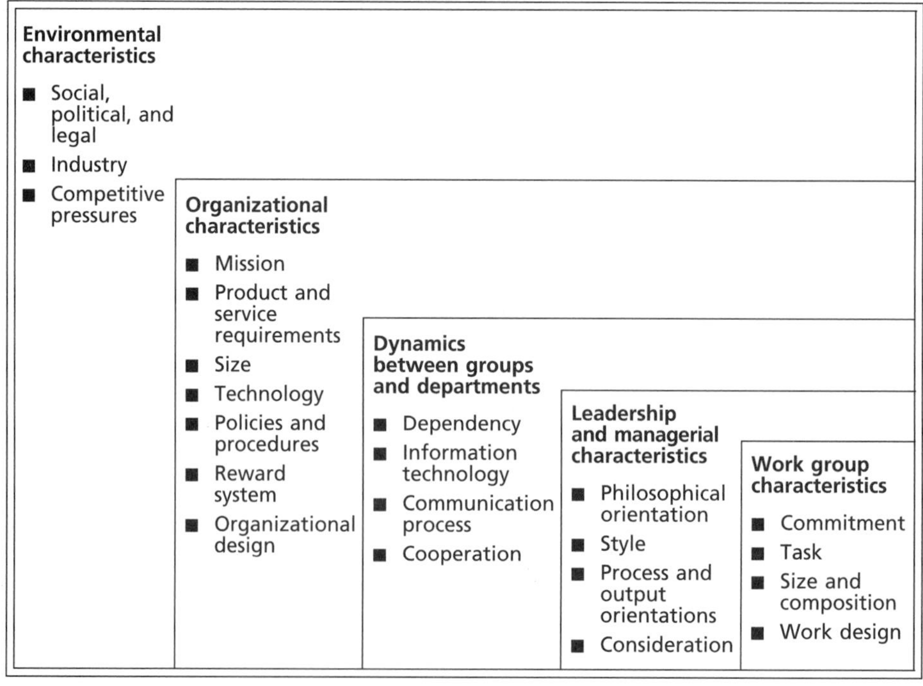

Recently a guiding framework for maintaining and reinforcing a specific organizational culture was proposed. The framework lists the following dimensions: criteria for hiring individuals who fit the organizational culture; criteria for removing employees who consistently or markedly deviate from accepted behaviors and activities; elements that managers and teams pay attention to, measure, and control; behavioral dimensions that compare how managers react to critical incidents and organizational crises; managerial and team role modeling, teaching, and coaching; criteria for recruitment, selection, and promotion; and organizational rites, ceremonies, and stories. Because every group and organization is an open system that exists in multiple work environments, change in the environment is likely to produce pressure inside the group that forces new learning and the adoption of this learning. To some degree there are pressures for any given culture to continuously change and grow. As such, culture can be seen as an ongoing evolutionary process. The difficulty of managing the evolution of organizational culture is complex because of the tendency among individuals and groups to resist changes. Guiding the direction of the evolution in organizational culture is one of the major roles of the management of change and the organizational change and development fields.[19]

Organizational Change and Development (OC&D)

Probably the most widely quoted definition of **organizational development** remains Beckhard's from 1969: Organizational development is

> an effort (1) *planned, (2) organizationwide, and (3) from the top, to (4) increase organizational effectiveness and health through planned interventions in the organization's "processes," using knowledge.*[20]

We also like Burke's definition because organizational culture, which refers in part to values, norms, and roles as we used them in the emergent system, is the focus of change: Organization development can be defined as a *planned process* of cultural change. This process consists of two phases: **organizational diagnosis** and intervention. OD begins with a diagnosis of the current organizational culture (i.e., an identification of the norms, procedures, and general climate of the organization). This identification process becomes more diagnostic as a distinction is made between those standards of behavior, procedures, and so on that seem to facilitate the organization's reaching its objectives (while meeting the needs of its members) from those that do not facilitate the attainment of its goals. Following this diagnostic phase, **interventions** are planned to change those norms seen as barriers to effective individual and organizational functioning.[21]

As OD has been used by professional specialists, it encompasses the following elements:

1. Application of behavioral science knowledge and methods.
2. Improvement or change of interaction patterns (arising from the norms, values, and role expectations) of an ongoing social system.
3. Integration of emotions and feelings into the rational perspective of the formal organization to achieve greater objectivity.
4. A systems focus on affecting individual, team, and organizational interactions concomitantly.
5. Building into the ongoing system the organizational climate and social technology needed to attain both individual and organizational goals.
6. Improvement of the organization design toward an optimal utilization of organizational resources.
7. Integration of organizational strategy and design into a jointly optimized system.
8. A continuing education program for the managerial system.

Organizational development can be better understood by examining what OD specialists do in working with organizations. This starts with a diagnosis and continues with the selection of a strategy to achieve the purpose of OD.

Diagnosis

Before a program for change can be formulated, a study of the problems and needs of a particular system should be made. Frequently consultants start with a "presenting problem"—the one that prompted clients to seek their assistance. This generally turns out to be a symptom rather than a cause, as shown in the data collected through interviews, recordings, observations, meetings, or survey questionnaires. Information is the most basic ingredient of a change program. The technology of information gathering for OD purposes has been developing rapidly. The variety of collection methods and of alternatives for feedback of data to client systems is a current emphasis of OD practitioners.[22]

Selection of Strategies

Basic to all OD strategies is the assumption that management must ultimately define its own problems and change itself. It is not the role of specialists to change the client system; they are only facilitators or change agents. So strategies are chosen that will permit change to take place and will have the greatest potential for coping with the particular pattern of problems in a specific company.

Where, how, and with whom to start the OD effort is a critical decision. Many theorists and consultants insist that real progress in OD can take place only if it starts with top management. Executives must confront the data from the diagnosis and cope with their own behavior and practices to encourage those lower in the hierarchy to do so. When a company's personnel director initiates the use of OD just because other companies are doing it or because the director thinks the company needs it, the diagnosis and strategy are more complicated. Typically the personnel director will want to start with the supervisory or middle-management level as a step to convincing top management of the value of such a program. The consultant has to decide whether such an OD effort would have sufficient effect. Under some conditions it is possible to "optimize," that is, improve one aspect of an organization's functioning and let this improvement spread to other areas.

Types of Interventions

Considerable literature is appearing that describes social and behavioral strategies, methods, and techniques for achieving change. The clustering of OD interventions based on the target group, proposed by French and Bell (see Figure 17–7), has been found to be very useful.[23]

Some Contrasting Approaches to Organizational Change and Development

At the individual and dyads/triads levels of intervention, we have examined the Transactional Analysis approach (Module 5) and career planning and development (Module 18). Team- and group-level interventions were presented in Modules 11 and 12. As for the organizational level, we discussed restructuring in Module 13 and Total Quality Management in Module 14. The improvement of total organization as the target group with the focus on the management of change is represented in this module in two ways. First, we discuss three comprehensive interventions and their paths to organizational effectiveness. Second, we provide a comparative exploration of three structural-based interventions: sociotechnical system, reengineering, and Total Quality Management.

Grid Organization Development

The Managerial Grid of Robert Blake and Jane S. Mouton is a widely known OD approach used in business.[24] It is precisely instrumented in many of its aspects, with each step-by-step progression accompanied by carefully printed instructions, questionnaires, and exercises. This clear design permits managers to learn managerial theory,

Figure 17–7 Typology of OD Interventions Based on Target Groups

Interventions designed to improve the effectiveness of *individuals*	Life- and career-planning activities Coaching and counseling T-group (sensitivity training) Eduction and training to increase skills, knowledge in the areas of technical task needs, relationship skills, process skills, decision making, problem solving, planning, goal-setting skills Grid OD phase 1 Work redesign Gestalt OD Behavior modeling
Interventions designed to improve the effectiveness of *dyads/triads*	Process consultation Third-party peacemaking Role negotiation technique Gestalt OD
Interventions designed to improve the effectiveness of *teams* and *groups*	Team building—Task-directed Process-directed Gestalt OD Grid OD phase 2 Interdependency exercise Appreciative inquiry Responsibility charting Process consultation Role negotiation Role analysis technique "Startup" team-building activities Education in decision making, problem solving, planning, goal setting in group settings Team MBO Appreciations and concerns exercise Sociotechnical systems (STS) Visioning Quality of work life (QWL) programs Quality circles Force-field analysis Self-managed teams
Interventions designed to improve the effectiveness of *intergroup relations*	Intergroup activities—Process-directed Task-directed Organizational mirroring Partnering Process consultation Third-party peacemaking at group level Grid OD phase 3 Survey feedback
Interventions designed to improve the effectiveness of the *total organization*	Sociotechnical systems (STS) Parallel learning structures MBO (participation forms) Cultural analysis Confrontation meetings Visioning Strategic planning/strategic management activities Grid OD phases 4, 5, 6 Interdependency exercise Survey feedback Appreciative inquiry Future search conferences Quality of work life (QWL) programs Total quality management (TQM) Physical settings Large-scale systems change

Source: W. L. French and G. H. Bell, Jr., *Organizational Development,* 5/E, 1995, p. 165. Reprinted by permission of Prentice-Hall, Inc., Englewood Cliffs, New Jersey.

methods, and strategies and to instruct others by leading seminars in their own companies. Managers instructing managers is a means of getting the training into the system.

The conceptual base of the Managerial Grid, represented in Figure 17–8, can be applied to leadership, team, and organizational styles. The horizontal axis of the grid represents the degree of concern for production, while the vertical axis represents the degree of concern for people. Thus a 9,1 style indicates a high degree of concern for production and low concern for people (an autocratic model). These models permit managers and organizations to diagnose their present operating style and contrast it with one that could result in greater effectiveness—usually the 9,9 position.

Figure 17–8
The Managerial Grid

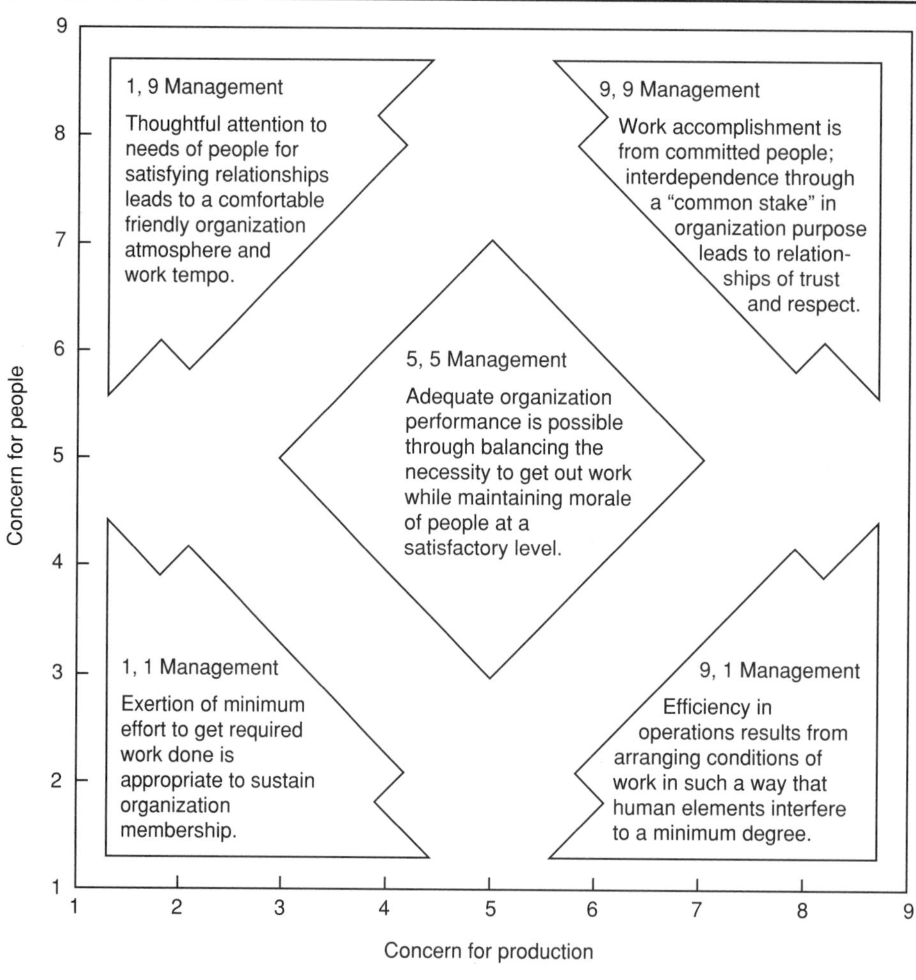

Source: Reprinted with permission from Robert R. Blake, Jane S. Mouton, Louis B. Barnes, and Larry E. Greiner, "Breakthrough in Organization Development," *Harvard Business Review,* November-December 1964, p. 136.

A six-phase educational program is designed for organizations utilizing the grid strategy.[25] Phase 1 is a week-long workshop in which managers learn the grid styles and individual and team skills related to 9,9 effectiveness. A feedback session is included in which the individual has the opportunity to learn what impact his or her leadership behaviors have had on fellow team members. The seminars are made up of strangers so the individual will feel less threatened and more open to exploration and diagnosis of behavior. Phase 2 is an application of Phase 1 back on the job. Ideally a top-management team whose members have all been through Phase 1 completes a series of instrumented activities to incorporate grid personal and team learning into their actual work group. All members of this team will in turn conduct Phase 2 team development activities with their own teams of subordinates until this training has been installed from top to bottom of the management system. Phase 3 is designed to develop intergroup coordination and overcome conflict between different functional elements of the organization to generate win–win instead of win–lose behaviors. This phase is applied only in those areas where problems exist. Phase 4 is an activity for key executives that involves designing an ideal strategy for the organization in such corporate elements as financial objectives, nature of the business, the market, and the organizational structure. Phase 5 involves implementing the ideal strategic model developed in Phase 4. Phase 6 pertains to evaluating, critiquing, and tuning the grid OD as a continuous, ongoing education program.

Through this six-phase educational program, individual, work-team, intergroup, and total organizational effectiveness are examined throughout the management structure. Team skills involving problem diagnosis, problem solving, evaluation of results, critiquing, and goal setting are learned, as are communication skills such as openness, giving and receiving personal feedback, and two-way influence. Various managerial styles are studied so individuals, teams, and organizations can identify their current mode of behavior and decide what they would like it to be ideally to improve results. Top-management planning, implementation, and critiquing of the plans are provided for. Grid OD truly represents a systems approach in that in the process, all of the dynamically interacting aspects of the human organization are being shaped simultaneously. Behavioral science knowledge and technology are being infused into the total system.

From System 1 to System 4

Rensis Likert and his colleagues at the Institute for Social Research at the University of Michigan have conducted intensive research since 1947 that provides the data for a science-based system of management. Relying heavily on survey research, they first studied leadership attitudes of supervisors of high-producing and low-producing sectors of a wide variety of industries, using criteria such as productivity per work hour, turnover, scrap, costs, and job satisfaction.[26]

Patterns of attitudes evolved to differentiate the two groups. Supervisors with the best production records were found to focus their primary attention on the human aspects of their subordinates' problems and were described as employee-centered. They tended to use more group methods in working with their employees and to build effective work groups with high performance standards. They were more apt to keep their people under general supervision and were helpful in problem solving when mistakes occurred. Supervisors of low-producing units tended to be, among other things, more job-centered. They used more one-to-one and fewer group methods in managing people and were often inclined to be punitive about mistakes.

Later phases of this research involved validating the theories of managerial and organizational effectiveness. A questionnaire was constructed to measure managers' supportive attitudes toward employees and the extent to which they believed in using group methods of supervision. These were administered in 31 geographically separated departments of a nationwide company. Their conclusion was "Managers who have a supportive attitude toward their men and endeavor to build them into well-knit groups obtain appreciably higher productivity than managers who have a threatening attitude and rely more on man-to-man patterns of supervision."[27]

Based on extensive research and historical models, Likert developed four systems of management: System 1, exploitative-authoritative; System 2, benevolent-authoritative; System 3, consultative; System 4, participative group.[28] Comparisons can be made on how "operating characteristics" such as leadership processes, motivation, communication, goal setting, and decision making are treated in each of the four systems. For instance, the direction of information flow would be "downward" in System 1, "mostly downward" in System 2, "down and up" in System 3, and "down, up, and with peers" in System 4. From these models, Likert designed questionnaires that can be used by managers to characterize (1) the present management practices of their own units or organizations and (2) where they would like their organizations to be in the future on all the dimensions rated.[29] The profiles compiled from the managers' scores almost always indicate that they would like to see their companies move in the direction of System 4. Thus System 4 is an ideal model to be used in moving toward greater organizational effectiveness. There are three basic concepts of System 4 management that are applied by managers in more effective organizations.[30] Let's look at them now.

The Principle of Supportive Relationships: Likert describes this principle as

> The leadership and other processes of the organization must be such as to ensure a maximum probability that in all interactions and in all relationships within the organization, each member, in light of his background, values, desires, and expectations, will view the experience as supportive and one which builds and maintains his sense of personal worth and importance.[31]

Whether the manager is creating a climate of openness and trust—one that involves both the economic and noneconomic motives of people and encourages personal growth—depends on the subordinate's experience and perception, not the superior's.

Group Decision Making and Group Methods of Supervision: Recognition must be given, of course, to the fact that final accountability for decisions, their execution, and the results remains with the superior.

High Performance Goals for the Organization: The methods of achieving movement toward System 4 in an organization include training managers to develop group membership and group decision-making skills; team use of the linking pin concept; measurement of attitudes and perceptions through questionnaires; and human asset accounting.[32]

The Likert approach, while depending heavily on survey research and data feedback into the human organization, can be regarded as broadly eclectic. Using the System 4 theory and methods, one team of behavioral scientists participated in turning a failing organization into a successful one in just two years.[33] Every social science method that had potential for change was employed in this study, including sensitivity training. The integrated effort among specialists—accountants, engineers, general managers, and behavioral scientists—was lauded by Likert, who points to the contribution quantitative social science research can make in bringing about organizational change.[34]

Parallel Learning Structures

Parallel learning structures (PLS), one of the newest innovations in organizational change and development technology, are supplemental structures created in bureaucratic organizations to aid in problem solving, planning, learning, and change. A growing body of qualitative inquiry on the effects of PLS interventions reports improved productivity, decision-making quality, quality improvements, utilization of innovation, employee satisfaction, and organizational effectiveness.[35]

Parallel learning structure, as a generic label, covers interventions where (a) a "structure" (a specific division and coordination of labor) is created that (b) operates "parallel" (in tandem or side by side) with the formal hierarchy and structure and (c) has the purpose of increasing an organization's "learning" (the creation and/or implementation of new thoughts and behaviors by employees).[36]

At its most basic form, a parallel learning structure consists of a steering commitee that provides the overall direction and authority and a number of small groups with norms and operating procedures that promote a climate conducive to innovation, learning, and group problem solving. Members of the PLS are also members of the formal organization, though within the PLS their relationships are not limited by the formal chain of command. Some PLSs are set up on a temporary basis, whereas others are intended to be permanent. One of the unique features of PLS is that it creates a bounded space and time for thinking, deciding, and acting differently than normally takes place at work. As such, a PLS is likely to create a unique subculture that more often than not influences the subcultures of other groups and the culture of the organization as a whole.

Reengineering

The reengineering approach emerged at the beginning of the 1990s as a practical orientation (1) to combat worsening corporate business results (mainly in the United States) and corporate difficulties and (2) to establish a competitive edge. The basic assumption of reengineering is that incremental improvement of existing processes within organizations does not provide a sufficient answer to the real existing needs.[37] A drastic cognitive and conceptual turning point—a paradigm shift—is required to allow a breakthrough.

Reengineering is defined as ''fundamental rethinking and radical redesign of business processes to achieve dramatic improvements in critical contemporary measures of performance, such as cost, quality, service, and speed.''[38] Radical and dramatic changes are fostered when individuals search for answers to the basic question of, Why are we doing what we are doing?[39] This approach of reengineering ignores existing processes, structures, organizational culture, and human resources, and states that one must begin by pinpointing key organizational processes, which are determined by their conformance to customers' requirements.

Reengineering advocates the design of the required structures and processes based on a customer's requirements. The main structural change necessary is the transfer from organizational structure to process structure.[40] This means breaking down interdepartmental boundaries from ''functional departments'' to ''process teams'' or ''case teams.'' The teams have the responsibility for the entire process. The process-teams—based organization design flattens the organizational hierarchy and significantly reduces existing boundaries. Organizations that implement reengineering can use both centralized and decentralized approaches, and can enjoy their advantages when managing the processes. Information technology, which is the engine of reengineering, permits organizational units to operate autonomously, while the firm as a total entity enjoys the advantages of system centralization. The function of the new process teams is also to influence the creation of a new system of values and beliefs among employees.

The results of a successful application of reengineering are measured by the radical changes in organizational performance. The most common parameters for testing the results are cost, quality, speed, and service. It must be emphasized that impressive results were expected in the short run within various organizations that reported on the application of this approach. Our current knowledge is limited when it comes to the understanding of reengineering's long-term effects.

Total Quality Management

Total Quality Management (TQM) is a managerial approach for improving processes in an organization in order to manufacture products or offer higher-quality services that will satisfy the customer. The approach emphasizes a number of elements: The improvement process is continuous and never-ending; the improvement processes are undertaken by teams, some of which are organic and some of which are task specific and ad hoc; each process has an inherent improvement that must be learned in a systematic manner.[41] The analysis, similar to the solution, needs to rest on solid, tested data. An in-depth discussion of the management of quality as a key organizational process is found in Module 14. In this section we focus on the management of change aspects.

Applying TQM in organizations involves a change of organizational culture and the development of quality awareness from the customers' perspective. Likewise, TQM also encompasses ''empowerment'' which is expressed, on the one hand, in the transfer of responsibility on topics of quality and production to employees, including delegation of authority for decision making in these fields, and on the other hand, in creating workers' commitment to the organization. The approach is applied top-down via a structural mechanism that usually includes a Quality Council and Process Action Teams (PATs). The Quality Council is composed of the executive president or vice president plus additional members who represent the whole system insofar as their functions, influence, and level of responsibility. Its main purpose is to determine the framework of the TQM program and to provide a support system. The mechanism for operating TQM is also called the *parallel hybrid organization.*[42] There are those who see TQM solely as a technique or as an integration of tools and systems designed to improve productivity; some see it as the improvement of a product or service; and others who see TQM as a wider and comprehensive managerial philosophy.[43]

Reports from organizations that adopted TQM indicate that TQM seems to affect customer satisfaction, worker satisfaction, the number of quality or process improvement groups in operation, the percentage of rejected products, the level of exploitation of raw materials, and absenteeism by personnel.[44] Very few firms report radical structural or technological changes resulting from the introduction of TQM. While some argue that TQM affects strategy, little support can be found to confirm this notion.[45]

The Sociotechnical System (STS) Approach

The **sociotechnical system (STS)** theory, originally developed at the Tavistock Institute in England by Eric Trist and his colleagues, contends that organizations are made up of people who produce products or services using some technology.[46] As such, the STS approach attempts to combine the social subsystem (people), the technical subsystem (machines and technology), and the environmental supersystem into a synergistic system.[47] Joint optimization, the ultimate desire in STS, states that an organization will function optimally only if the social and technological subsystems of the organization are designed to fit the demands of each other and the environment.[48] The STS approach emphasizes the need for compatible integration between the organization's social and technical subsystems to ensure organizational effectiveness.[49] An indepth discussion of sociotechnical systems as an organizational framework is found in Modules 4 and 13. In this section we focus on the management of change aspects.

Successful STS design focuses on an "open" interface with the environment the organization faces. This implies that the ability of the organization to effectively match its social and technical subsystems relies on the degree of openness or contact the organization maintains with the environment. Organizational competitiveness necessitates the need for organizations to maintain environmental sensing and scanning mechanisms such that the organization will be able to plan and adapt according to anticipated and unanticipated changes.[50] Changes in any one of the subsystems will disturb the status quo and should result in the realignment of the entire organization.

In the context of organizational development, the STS planned change intervention is based on the action research philosophy. **Action research** is defined as an emergent inquiry process in which behavioral and social science knowledge is integrated with existing organizational knowledge to produce new knowledge, which is generalizable and simultaneously usable.[51] As such, the STS change endeavor is participatory, co-inquiry–based, client- and organization-owned, and scientifically executed. Figure 17–9 shows a flow chart of the STS planned change process.

The first phase of the intervention involves preparation of the organization and its top-level decision makers for conducting the sociotechnical systems analysis and design activities. This phase includes the consultant's entry, scanning, and contracting with the top-level decision makers; formation of a top-level steering committee; analysis of the business situation (that is, macro environment, industry environment, competition environment, and company environment); analysis of business results (in terms of current and desired profit, volume, cost, and operational purpose); and the formulation of a business vision, a total systems strategy, and a vision statement for the redesign effort.

The second phase consists of formation, education, and analysis by the action research system, which is composed of the steering committee, one or more consultants, and one or more groups representing different parts and levels of the organization. The action research system conducts analyses of the technical, social, environment, and design elements of the organization, which lead to recommendations for organization redesign. The recommendations for joint optimization—once they're approved and prioritized by the top-level management of the organization—will be followed by careful planning of experimental implementation.

The third phase consists of the experimental execution of the proposed recommendations. The changes are assessed and modified as necessary to fit the unique organizational characteristics. Overcoming some of the difficulties in the experimental

Figure 17–9
Sociotechnical System Planned Change Process: A Flow Design

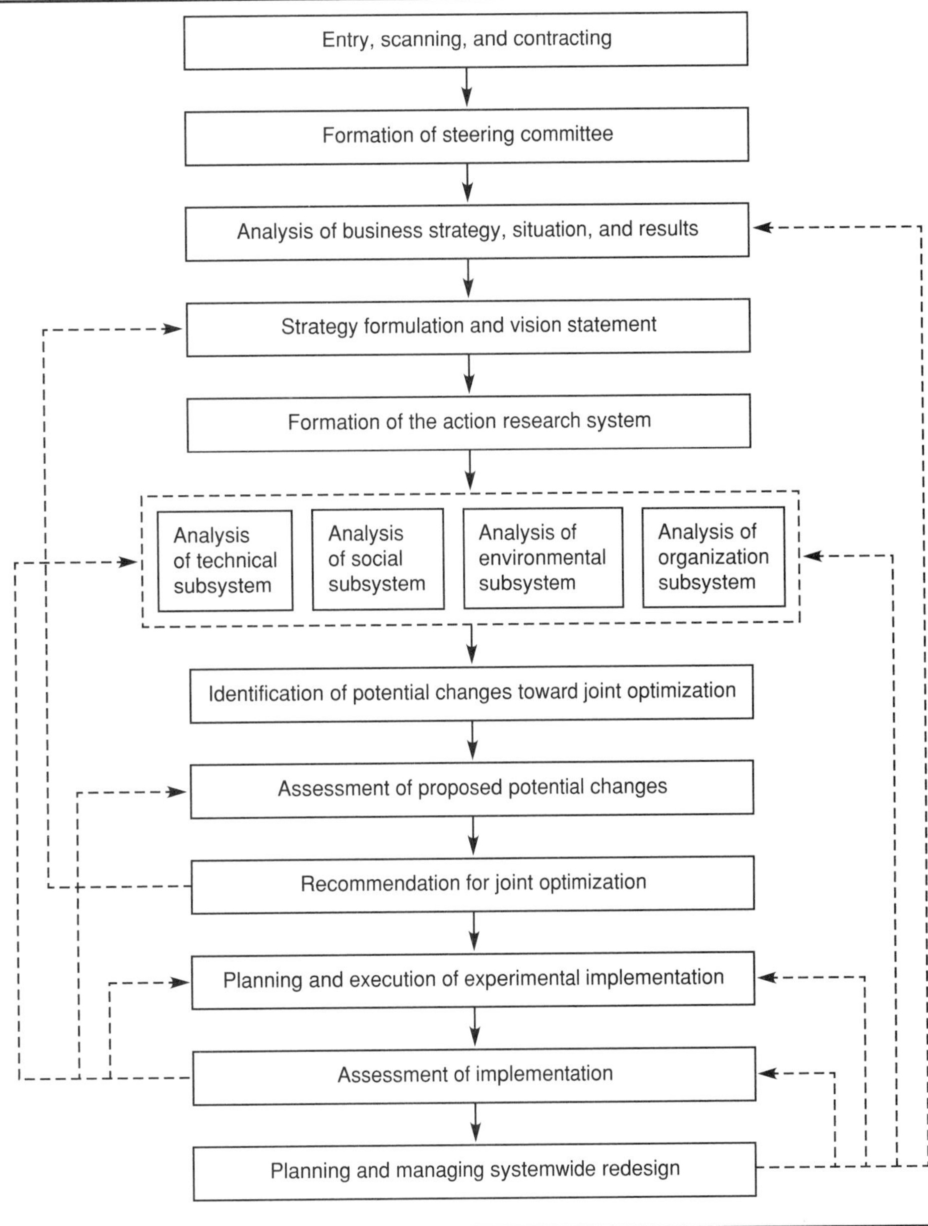

implementation process will aid in the formulation and management of the total organization change process.

Finally, based on learning from the experimental implementation of the recommendations for change, the action research system refines the vision statement, formulates the total systems change strategy, and identifies criteria for effectiveness assessments. The action research system might also be utilized in the management of the implementation process. One of the underlying assumptions of the sociotechnical systems change process is the emphasis on organizational learning as key to organizational success. As such, once the implementation of the new organizational design is done, top-level management will reexamine the business situation and likely continue the process of self-examination and refinement.

A review of 134 recorded STS interventions revealed successful results on eight different organizational effectiveness criteria.[52] The studies were conducted over a period of 30 years and were implemented in a variety of organizations. While 87 percent of the studies reported productivity improvements, 89 percent reported cost savings, 81 percent showed reduced absenteeism, 65 percent had reduced turnover, and 54 percent reflected improved attitudes. A special issue of the *Journal of Applied Behavioral Science* was devoted in its entirety to STS. While the authors represented several different disciplines and theoretical perspectives, all were concerned with the usefulness and effectiveness of the STS approach.[53] In a recent review of two decades of STS interventions in North America, James Taylor illustrates how STS has been expanded to embrace dimensional manufacturing work, service work, nonroutine work, and professional work all within increasingly chaotic environments. Currently there are more than 115 active and successful STS designs or redesigns operating in the United States, of which about a quarter are clearly not continuous process technologies.[54] Continuous process technologies (see Module 14) still predominate in STS applications, but the number and proportion of applications to other work systems are increasing.[55] Although space does not permit elaboration, it is important to note that unique applications of STS can be found in many places around the globe—for example, in Scandinavia,[56] the Netherlands,[57] England, Israel,[58] and Italy.

A Comparative Examination

The preceding overview shows some striking similarities and differences between the last three orientations to organizational change.[59] Table 17–8 summarizes the essence of the three approaches: their theoretical roots and founders; some of the key principles and assumptions; key elements, phases, and mechanisms of the change process; and outcomes. Our purpose in this section is to explore commonalities and differences between the orientations as related to the change process. A comparison between the other dimensions—although intriguing, as can be seen from the table—is beyond the scope of this module.

For the purpose of this module we will examine four distinct similarities between the three orientations. All require a strategic decision that involves major financial and resource investment and commitment. All three orientations focus on the entire system; they follow both customer and improvement focus; organizational learning is an integral part of the change process; and they all require transformation and/or modification of the organizational culture.

The three orientations share the importance of alignment between the change and the overall business strategy. The decision to pursue any one of the change programs is strategic. Managers make their determination based on the perceived congruency between the company's strategic goals and what the change program has to offer. Furthermore, the strategic nature of the **planned change** program needs to be emphasized. The investment in each one of the programs is viewed as strategic due to its perceived importance (i.e., critical value to the firm's overall performance), the substantial resource commitment, the clear time horizon, and the fact that programs are not easily reversible.

Reengineering, Total Quality Management, and sociotechnical systems seem to focus on improvement of organizational functioning in order to better meet changing environmental demands. As such, they take a *holistic system* approach that incorporates all the relevant actors (internal and external customers, supplier, and the like). While some variations seem to exist in terms of initial focus and/or targeted unit for the change program, all take into account the entire organization. Furthermore, at some point in each of the change orientations, the emphasis shifts to the optimal alignment of the different organizational units.

Acquiring new knowledge, skills, and tools seems to be at the heart of each of the orientations. All three acknowledge in various ways the importance of organizational learning. Specific mechanisms that foster organizational learning and organizational dialogue seem to have evolved in each of the orientations. Some form of structural support configuration—with different labels—that houses and guides the organizational learning and the change programs provides the source of energy and continuity.

The last striking similarity among the three orientations is the notion that each transforms or modifies the culture of the firm. The involved nature of the orientations, the

Table 17–8

Partial Comparison between TQM, STS, and Reengineering

Dimension	TQM	STS	Reengineering
I. Theoretical roots	Statistical theory (SPC), system theory	Organization theory, applied social and behavioral sciences, system theory, production engineering	Concurrent engineering, production engineering, practice-driven, system theory
II. Founders	Deming, Crosby, Juran, Imai, Shewhart, Taguchi, Tshikawa	Cherns, Cummings, Davis, Emery, Pasmore, Taylor, Thorsrud, Trist	Champy, Davenport, Hummer
III. Motto	A group of ideas and techniques directed toward enhancing competitive performance through improving the quality of products and processes.	A set of design principles, ideas, and change processes that strive toward best match between organizational, technical, environmental, and social subsystems.	A set of ideas about radical redesign and change in business processes to achieve breakthrough results (major gains in cost, service, or time).
IV. Some basic principles and assumptions	A. *Organizational Goals:* Serving customers' needs to fullest extent possible by supplying goods and/or services of highest quality.	Joint optimization of social, technical, and environmental systems.	Quantum leap in performance by focusing on key processes that really matter, emphasizing strong leadership, technology, and radical change.
	B. *Time Orientation:* Dynamic. Philosophy of incremental and continuous improvement. Short- and long-term perspectives.	Dynamic. Philosophy of innovation, organizational learning, and continuous improvement. Long-term perspective.	Dynamic. Philosophy of radical and rapid changes. Short-term cycle to achieve desired results.
	C. *Coordination and Control:* Coordination through process action groups (cross-functional). Both control and coordination exercised by managers and employees.	Coordination and control through self-managed groups (autonomous work groups). Both control and coordination exercised by managers and employees.	Coordination and control by reengineering teams, process owner, and, steering committee. Both control and coordination exercised mainly by managers.
	D. *Work Design:* System-based optimization guided by specific design principles. Formation of temporary process action teams.	System-based joint optimization guided by specific work design principles. Formation of functional organic teams.	System-based approach guided by key design processes. Formation of process teams.
	E. *Technology:* Technology may be a key factor in quality improvement.	Technology is a fundamental factor in work design.	Information technology is an essential factor in work design.
	F. *Customer and Suppliers Orientation:* Internal and external customers and suppliers are integral parts of the system.	External customers and suppliers are important but are not part of the system.	Processes' customers are an integral part of the system.
	G. *Rewards:* Individual-, team-, and system-based.	Team- and individual-based.	System- and individual-based.
V. Management of Change	A. *Change Orientation:* Led by management and/or Quality Council. The effort is mostly guided by ISO 9000 and/or award evaluation processes and/or some combination of specific guidelines provided by quality experts.	Change process led by design team or parallel learning structure. The effort is guided by a modified action research philosophy.	The change is led by top management and the steering committee. The effort is guided by the process owner and reengineering (processes design) teams.

(*continued*)

Table 17–8

Partial Comparison between TQM, STS, and Reengineering (*concluded*)

	TQM	STS	Reengineering
	B. *Change Phases, Mechanisms, and Processes:* Broadly defined deductive-based phases and basic activities. Team learning and system learning mechanisms.	Clearly defined deductive-based phases, processes, and activities. Team and learning structure mechanisms.	Clearly defined inductive-based phases. Information technology is a key element in team process learning.
	C. *Methods and Tools:* Quality planning (Hoshin planning). Identifying customers and suppliers (both internal and external) and determining needs. SPC. Develop a process that can produce the quality required. Quality-based systemwide diffusion.	Environmental, technical, and social analysis. Variance and deliberation analysis. Experimentation with alternative design configurations. Systemwide diffusion.	Competitive and customers' needs analysis. Identification of processes that require radical improvements based on specific criteria. Broad understanding of current processes. Radical systemwide or subsystem-based diffusion.
	D. *Change Process Performance Measures:* Customers- and suppliers-based orientation. Processes' improvement against benchmarking. Utilization of both "hard" (e.g., defect ratios, customers' complaints) and "soft" (e.g., satisfaction, commitment measures.	Input–throughput–output performance-oriented measures. Utilization of both "hard" (e.g., productivity, profitability) and "soft" (e.g., satisfaction, commitment measures	Measures of improvements in business processes (e.g., profitability, quality of service) and establishment of business competitiveness and superiority.
VI. Outcomes	A. *Continuous Improvements:* Established.	Established.	Unknown.
	B. *Organizational Learning:* Specific to quality-related issues.	Systemwide learning mechanism is established.	Learning mechanism based on key organizational processes.
	C. *Organizational Performance measures:* 1. Customer and supplier satisfaction: Established.	Advocated and at times established.	Advocated.
	2. Quality Standards: Established and extensively improved.	Established.	Established quality standards related to process.
	3. Production Cost Reduction: Advocated.	Established.	Established.
	D. *Organizational Culture:* New quality-based organizational culture.	New system- and innovation-based culture.	New innovation-based organizational culture.

learning that they generate via the ongoing analysis, data collection, and interpretations, and the paradigm shift that they foster set the stage and momentum for organizational culture change.

The preceding similarities among the three orientations are somewhat surprising due to the nature of their evolution and theoretical foundations. As can be seen in Table

17–8, each orientation is rooted in different scientific disciplines. As such, it is relatively easy to identify some of the many differences between them. Now let's discuss some of the differences.

The espoused objectives of each orientation vary. Reengineering focuses on radical changes of key processes; STS focuses on the incremental, gradual, and continuous changes geared toward optimal utilization of organizational resources; and TQM focuses on the continuous quality improvement of products, processes, and services.

As Table 17–8 shows, the three orientations seem to follow somewhat different change processes and phases. STS seems to have a clear analytical road map with specific sequential phases and activities. TQM seems to have broadly defined deductive phases and basic activities. The reengineering change process follows clearly defined inductive-based phases. Furthermore, careful examination of the specific phases and their sequence in each orientation reveals that they vary significantly.

Each of the orientations incorporates the *technological subsystem* differently. The STS redesign process is based on existing technology and/or new technology. (Most STS projects report on the redesign of the organizations without changing the technology.) Reengineering is mostly concerned with the implementation of new technology with special emphasis on information technology. (Some even argue that information technology is at the heart or the engine of reengineering.) TQM focuses on improvements of processes in general.

Finally, the outcomes and measurements seem to vary. The current scientific literature provides support for significant long-term **continous improvements** in both STS and TQM. In reengineering, the expectations are that outcomes can be realized in a short time span. Due to the relative newness, we have yet to learn about the long-term effects of reengineering. Organizational structure seems to change mostly in STS and reengineering in an explicit manner. In TQM only minor structural changes take place. Those are mainly changes in internal and external customer linkages.

Toward an Eclectic Planned Change Approach

As can be seen from the comparative examination of the three orientations, the potential for some kind of combination of the three merits exploration. In practice a natural overlap and multiple combinations of bits and pieces of the three approaches can be found in each planned change implementation. This section provides a brief overview of an **eclectic planned change approach** that pulls together the strengths of each.[60] Table 17–9 summarizes the phases and some key activities in the proposed eclectic framework.

The first phase involves the establishment of the project's foundation. In this phase securing management commitment to the effort is crucial. The scope and purpose of the project is defined by the top-management team/CEO and the basic project strategy is articulated. Top management needs to make a clear decision about the choice of change orientation based on the compatibility between the business strategic objectives and the change orientation. The next set of activities is geared toward developing shared understanding of the need and companywide awareness for making significant changes. The creation of a parallel learning mechanism and its magnitude signal sincere commitment on management's part for change. Overall, the parallel learning mechanism is charged with the responsibility of housing, guiding, and facilitating the learning and change process. The actual criteria and creation process of the parallel learning mechanism is critical. A variety of alternatives are available. Management is required to make the choice that best fits the organization.

The second phase builds on the project initiation phase and moves the focus to the key processes to meet customers' needs. Following the establishment of clarity about the role and mission of the learning mechanism, the project shifts to the identification of the customers (both internal and external), their requirements, needs, and potentials.

Table 17–9
Phases in an Eclectic Planned Change Approach

Phase 1: Project Initiation

- Define scope and purpose.
- Secure management commitment.
- Establish organizational awareness of the need for radical changes.
- Align with business strategy.
- Create a parallel learning mechanism and educate organization members.

Phase 2: Mapping Customers' Key Processes

- Identify customers' requirements, needs, and potentials.
- Determine the key processes.

Phase 3: The Inquiry Process

- Establish benchmarks.
- Conduct business analysis based on sociotechnical system framework:
  Verify key processes.
  Uncover system pathologies.
- Revise company vision based on analysis, strategic opportunities, and enabling technology (i.e., information technology).
- Identify potential improvements to the existing processes.

Phase 4: Design/Redesign to Modify Existing Processes and Organizational Structure

- Formulate specific alternative sociotechnical-based design solutions. (STS-based design includes the optimal integration of key organizational elements such as rewards, control, structure, information, people, and technology.)
- Explore potential impact of proposed solutions.
- Develop joint optimization of key processes.
- Establish learning processes for continuous improvement.

Phase 5: Implementation and Reconstruction of the Key Processes and Organization

- Foster a climate that is conducive to change.
- Create the implementation and support mechanisms.
- Develop training programs.
- Establish learning loops as an integral part of continuous improvement.

Key business processes that have direct impact on customers' requirements, needs, and potentials are identified.

Phase 3 focuses on establishing benchmarks and performing systematic business analysis while verifying the key business processes and major business pathologies plus revisiting the business vision, strategic opportunities, and enabling technologies. The challenge in this phase is the collection and assimilation of the data. The data's complexity requires the utilization of multiple human and technological resources that can be found within and outside the company boundaries. At the end of this phase, ideas for improvement of specific processes begin to surface.

Phase 4 is guided by a set of specific design principles that are derived from sociotechnical system design theory. As such, alternative design solutions that strive toward joint optimization of the different business elements are explored. One key challenge during this phase is to strive toward the development of joint optimization between the key business processes. Beyond the tasks of a careful examination of potential impact of the alternative solutions, the goal is also to develop the learning mechanism for continuous improvement.

Implementation and reconstruction of the organization and its key processes are part of phase 5. Implementation planning is treated as a project. Some planned change models treat this kind of planning as a completely new process.[61] Others see this phase as a natural continuation of the change program and, as such, the implementation will be guided by the parallel learning mechanism. The implementation planning calls for the simultaneous execution of both radical and rapid, as well as gradual and ongoing changes. Key processes can be treated either way. The learning mechanism needs to have the know-how that supports the complexity of this deliberation. Of the many challenges during this phase, the most crucial are the creation of support mechanisms, the development of appropriate training programs, and the establishment of learning loops as an integral part of continuous improvement.

Planned Change and Organizational Effectiveness

The field of OC&D and its growth can be best appreciated by the increased number of books, journals, and articles devoted to OD values, philosophies, intervention methods and techniques, evaluation problems, methods for dealing with these problems, and effectiveness criteria and assessment. Organizational change and development, as a field of theory and practice, can have significant positive effects on the total organization, the individual, and the work group in terms of behavioral, attitudinal, and effectiveness changes.[62] In general, the cumulative results of the published empirical investigations point toward the conclusion that OC&D is a successful strategy of planned change.[63] The 10 volumes that have appeared thus far in the JAI series *Research in Organizational Change and Development* (edited by Pasmore and Woodman) reflect a tradition of provocative scholarly work by many contributors. Coupled with the 30 volumes published thus far in the Addison-Wesley organization development series (edited by Beckhard and Schein) for the organization development and change practitioner and the manager, they demonstrate the vitality of the field.

At the same time, the evaluation of change efforts or interventions is a complex and difficult task. OD was defined as "a planned process of organizationwide change" and as such an empirical research methodology that focuses on assessing the dynamic nature of change processes and their effectiveness had to be developed.[64] Published research on OD evaluation was clustered into three categories: (1) identification of general problems and development of guidelines, (2) demonstrations of methods for evaluating change efforts, and (3) identification and resolution of specific methodological issues.[65]

Furthermore, the documentation of OD results reported that studies of a better quality would permit more rigorous comparative examinations. For example, a survey of the OD literature from 1948 through 1982 identified 65 studies that meet a rigorous set of comparative criteria. These studies made the following recommendations: (1) The goals and expected results of the intervention should be stated clearly; (2) the intervention should be clearly defined and clearly described; (3) the intervention should be demarcated from the outcomes; (4) researchers should note why specific dependent variables were selected and how were they measured; and (5) the experimental design utilized, the sequence of observations, the frequency and time span of measurement, and the beginning and termination of the intervention should be described adequately.[66]

Finally, a massive review of some 800 work improvement efforts by Barry Macy and 3,200 worldwide work improvement efforts by Frans M. Van Eijnatten shows "generally positive conclusions with respect to both performance and worker satisfaction.[67] Taken together, these literature reviews strongly support the conclusion that OC&D programs yield positive improvements at the individual, team, and organizational levels.

Organizational Change and Development in the International Context

The applicability and effectiveness of organizational development and change in different cultural environments are areas of growing interest to managers and practitioners. Reports on OC&D activities on a variety of continents and in many countries (Third World countries, Northern Europe, Poland, Australia, South Africa, Latin America, Egypt, Israel, India, China, R.O.C., Singapore, and Japan to mention a few) have begun to appear in the literature.[68] Although each of the studies examines one aspect of OC&D or an OC&D program or else a specific intervention in the respective continent or country, still comparative empirical studies within a specific country among different interventions, within a specific continent across countries, or across countries on a specific intervention are scarce.

The conceptual and empirical challenges for comparative organizational change and development inquiry and applications are many. First, the underlying values and assumptions of OD, the values and assumptions of the specific interventions, and the values and assumptions of the practitioners need to be analyzed. Second, the cultural elements and intercultural relations at the country, industry, and corporate levels need to be examined. Third, the degree of congruence needs to be explored and the line of inquiry developed.

Recently, guidelines with explicit steps for adopting OC&D in different cultural contexts were proposed:

1. Evaluate the ranking of the dimensions of culture in the given situation.
2. Make a judgment as to which values are most deeply held and unlikely to change.
3. Evaluate the ''problem-appropriate'' interventions ranking on the dimensions of culture.
4. Choose the intervention that would clash least with the most rigidly held values.
5. Incorporate process modifications in the proposed intervention to fit with the given cultural situation.[69]

Summary

The field of organizational development and change emerged in the 1950s with the use of T-groups to improve organizational life. It has gradually expanded to include the total organization. It has focused on influencing human interactions to help organizations guide the direction of their evolution and to enhance the cultural elements that are viewed as critical to maintaining the desired effectiveness and outcomes. Examples of contrasting organizational effectiveness strategies include OD through the managerial grid, Likert's system 1 through System 4, the sociotechnical system approach, the parallel learning structure interventions, Total Quality Management, and reengineering.

Frequently defined as an organizationwide systems approach of planned change, the ongoing strive for empirical research and its complexity remains one of the biggest challenges to the field of culture, managing change, and organization development. Although a significant improvement can be identified in the quality of the reported literature, further advancements are needed. Presently, most organizational change and development specialists are more apt to see themselves as eclectic change agents pursuing an expert or an action research method and applying a broad range of knowledge and skills suited to the nature of the problems identified by their efforts.[70]

Study Questions

1. Discuss the powerful notions inherent in the definition of organizational culture as proposed by Schein.
2. Discuss the relationships between group dynamics, organizational culture, and organizational change and development.
3. Identify and discuss the key elements in the definition of organizational development.
4. What are some of the main objectives of planned change?
5. What are the major phases of an OC&D program?
6. Compare and contrast any two of the planned change interventions described in this module.

7. Describe an organization that you are familiar with that could use an OC&D intervention. What are some roadblocks that the intervention would likely encounter? How would you overcome them? Describe the phases in the intervention process. How would the intervention affect individual, group, and organizational effectiveness?
8. How effective are planned change interventions?
9. What should be the role of the manager in an OC&D intervention?

Endnotes

1. N. M. Tichy and R. Charan, ''Speed, Simplicity, Self-Confidence: An Interview with Jack Welch, *Harvard Business Review,* September-October, 1989, p. 120.

2. Ibid., p. 114.

3. *Fortune,* January 25, 1993, p. 87.

4. Tichy and Charan, ''Speed, Simplicity, Self-Confidence,'' p. 118.

5. R. N. Ashkenas and T. D. Jick, ''From Dialogue to Action in GE Work-Out: Developmental Learning in a Change Process,'' *Research in Organizational Change and Development* 6, (1992), p. 271.

6. Jack Welch, ''Speed, Simplicity and Self-Confidence: Keys to Leading in the 1990s,'' speech at annual shareholders meeting, April 1989.

7. K. S. Cameron and D. A. Whetten, *Organizational Effectiveness* (New York: Academic Press, 1983); and R. E. Quinn and K. S. Cameron, *Paradox and Transformation: Towards a Theory of Change in Organization and Management* (Cambridge, Mass.: Ballinger, 1988).

8. R. Chin and K. D. Benne, ''General Strategies for Effecting Changes in Human System,'' in *The Planning of Change,* eds. W. G. Bennis, K. D. Benne, and R. Chin (New York: Holt, Rinehart & Winston, 1969), pp. 32–59.

9. K. E. Olmosk, ''Seven Pure Strategies of Change,'' in *The 1972 Annual Handbook for Group Facilitators,* eds. J. W. Pfeiffer and J. E. Jones (La Jolla, Calif.: University Associates, 1971), pp. 162–72.

10. J. M. Shafritz and J. S. Ott, *Classics of Organization Theory* (Chicago: Dorsey Press, 1987); and R. M. Cyert and J. G. March, *A Behavioral Theory of the Firm* (Englewood Cliffs, N.J.: Prentice-Hall, 1984).

11. R. H. Kilmann, M. J. Saxton, R. Serpa, and Associates, eds. *Gaining Control of the Corporate Culture* (San Francisco: Jossey-Bass, 1985); G. Hofstede, and M. H. Bond, ''The Confucius Connection: From Cultural Roots to Economic Growth,'' *Organizational Dynamics* 16, no. 4 (1988), pp. 4–21; N. M. Tichy, *Managing Strategic Change: Technical, Political and Culture Dynamics* (New York: John Wiley & Sons, 1983).

12. V. Sathe, *Culture and Related Corporate Realities* (Homewood, Ill.: Richard D. Irwin, 1985); and S. R. Barley, C. W. Meyer, and D. C. Gash, ''Culture of Cultures: Academics, Practitioners, and the Pragmatics of Normative Control,'' *Administrative Science Quarterly* 33 (1988), pp. 24–60.

13. E. H. Schein, *Organizational Culture and Leadership* (San Francisco: Jossey-Bass, 1985).

14. J. W. Lorsch, ''Managing Culture: The Invisible Barrier to Strategic Change,'' *California Management Review* 2, Winter 1986, pp. 95–109.

15. R. H. Kilmann, M. J. Saxton, and R. Serpa, ''Issues in Understanding and Changing Culture,'' *California Management Review* 2, Winter 1986, pp. 87–94.

16. M. R. Louis, ''Organizations as Culture-Bearing Milieux,'' in *Organizational Symbolism,* eds. L. R. Pondy, P. J. Frost, G. Morgan, and T. C. Dandridge (Greenwich, Conn.: JAI Press, 1983), pp. 39–54; M. J. Hatch, ''The Dynamics of Organizational Culture,'' *The Academy of Management Review* 18 (1993), pp. 657–93; and S. A. Sackman, Culture and Subculture: An Analysis of Organizational Knowledge,'' *Administrative Science Quarterly* 37 (1992), pp. 140–61; T. E. Deal, and A. A. Kennedy, *Corporate Cultures: The Rites and Rituals of Corporate Life* (Reading, Mass.: Addison-Wesley, 1982).

17. J. Kerr and J. W. Slocum, Jr., "Managing Corporate Culture through Reward Systems," *Academy of Management Executive* 1, no. 2 (1987), pp. 99–108; and L. K. Trevino, "A Cultural Perspective on Changing and Developing Organizational Ethics," in *Research in Organizational Change & Development,* Vol. 1, eds. W. A. Pasmore and R. W. Woodman (Greenwich, Conn.: JAI Press, 1990), pp. 195–230.

18. E. H. Schein, "Organizational Culture," *American Psychologist* 45, no. 2 (1990), p. 109–19.

19. C. Argyris, R. Putnam, and D. M. Smith, *Action Science* (San Francisco: Jossey-Bass, 1985); R. Beckhard and R. T. Harris, *Organizational Transitions: Managing Complex Change,* 2d ed. (Reading, Mass.: Addison-Wesley, 1987); and D. P. Hanna, *Designing Organizations for High Performance* (Reading, Mass.: Addison-Wesley, 1988).

20. R. Beckhard, *Organization Development: Strategies and Models* (Reading, Mass.: Addison-Wesley, 1969), p. 9.

21. W. Warner Burke, "A Comparison of Management Development and Organization Development," *Journal of Applied Behavioral Science* 7 (1971), pp. 569–79.

22. Excellent sources include D. A. Nadler, *Feedback and Organization Development: Using Data-Based Methods* (Reading, Mass.: Addison-Wesley, 1977); D. G. Bowers and J. L. Franklin, *Survey-Guided Development, I: Data-Based Organizational Change* (La Jolla, Calif.: University Associates, 1977); D. L. Hausser, P. A. Pecorella, and A. L. Wissler, *Survey-Guided Development, II: A Manual for Consultants* (La Jolla, Calif.: University Associates, 1977); and J. L. Franklin, A. L. Wissler, and G. J. Spencer, *Survey-Guided Development, III: A Manual for Concepts Training* (La Jolla, Calif.: University Associates, 1977).

23. W. L. French and C. H. Bell, Jr., *Organizational Development: Behavioral Science Interventions for Organization Improvements,* 5th ed. (Englewood Cliffs, N.J.: Prentice-Hall, 1995); D. Eden, "Creating Expectation Effects in OD: Applying Self-Fulfilling Prophecy." In *Research in Organizational Change and Development,* eds. W. A. Pasmore and R. W. Woodman, Vol. 2 (Greenwich, Conn.: JAI Press, 1990), pp. 235–67; R. T. Golembiewski, and R. J. Hilles, *Toward the Responsive Organization* (Utah: Brighton, 1979).

24. R. R. Blake and J. S. Mouton, *The Managerial Grid* (Houston: Gulf Publishing, 1964). Also see Blake and Mouton, *The Versatile Manager: A Grid Profile* (Homewood, Ill.: Richard D. Irwin, 1981).

25. R. R. Blake and J. S. Mouton, *Grid Organizational Development* (Houston: Gulf Publishing, 1961).

26. R. Likert, *New Patterns of Management* (New York: McGraw-Hill, 1961), Chapter 2.

27. Ibid., Chapter 9, p. 120.

28. R. Likert, *The Human Organization* (New York: McGraw-Hill, 1967), Chapter 2.

29. Ibid., Appendix 2.

30. Ibid., Chapter 4.

31. Ibid., p. 47.

32. Ibid., Chapter 9.

33. A. J. Marrow, D. G. Bowers, and S. E. Seashore, *Management by Participation* (New York: Harper & Row, 1967).

34. Ibid., pp. ix–xi.

35. G. R. Bushe and A. B. (Rami) Shani, "Parallel Learning Structure Interventions in Bureaucratic Organizations," in *Research in Organizational Change & Development,* Vol. 4, pp. 167–94.

36. G. R. Bushe and A. B. (Rami) Shani, *Parallel Learning Structures: Increasing Innovation in Bureaucracies* (Reading, Mass.: Addison-Wesley, 1991), provides a detailed description and analysis of five different PLS implementations in five organizations and a fully developed generic intervention model.

37. G. Hall, J. Rosenthal, and J. Wade, "How to Make Reengineering Really Work," *Harvard Business Review,* November-December 1993, pp. 119–31.

38. M. Hammer and J. Champy, *Reengineering the Corporation* (New York: HarperCollins, 1993).

39. D. L. Schnitt, "Reengineering the Organization Using Information Technology," *Journal of System Management,* January 1993, pp. 14–42.

40. T. Housel, C. Morris, and C. Westland, "Business Process Reengineering at Pacific Bell," *Planning Review,* May-June 1993, pp. 28–34.

41. R. Grant, A. B. (Rami) Shani, and R. Krishnan, "TQM's Challenge to Management Theory & Practice," *Sloan Management Review* 35, no. 2 (1994), pp. 25–35.

42. P. Lillrank and N. Kano, *Continuous Improvement* (Ann Arbor, Mich.: University of Michigan Press, 1989).

43. R. Krishnan, A. B. (Rami) Shani, R. Grant, and R. Baer, "The Search for Quality Improvements: Problems of Design and Implementation," *Academy of Management Executive* 7, no. 4 (1993), pp. 7–20.

44. R. E. Cole, P. Bacdayan, and B. J. White, "Quality, Participation, and Competitiveness," *California Management Review* 35, no. 3 (1993), pp. 68–81.

45. A. B. (Rami) Shani and M. Rogberg, "Quality, Strategy, and Structural Configuration," *Journal of Organizational Change Management* 7, no. 2 (1994), pp. 15–30.

46. E. L. Trist, "The Evolution of Sociotechnical Systems," in *Perspectives on Organization Design and Behavior,* eds. A. H. Van de Ven and W. F. Joyce (New York: John Wiley & Sons, 1982), pp. 19–75.

47. See, for example, W. A. Pasmore, *Designing Effective Organizations* (New York: John Wiley & Sons, 1988).

48. W. A. Pasmore and J. J. Sherwood, eds., *Sociotechnical Systems: A Sourcebook* (La Jolla, Calif.: University Associates, 1978); and E. Emery, *Characteristics of Sociotechnical Systems* (London: Tavistock Institute, 1959); T. G. Cummings, ed. *Systems Theory for Organizational Development,* (Somerset, N.J.: John Wiley & Sons, 1980); T. G. Cummings and S. Srivastva, *Management of Work: A Sociotechnical Systems Approach* (La Jolla, Calif.: University Associates, 1977; W. A. Pasmore, *Creating Strategic Change: Designing the Flexible High-Performing Organizations* (New York: John Wiley & Sons, 1994).

49. A. B. Shani and O. Elliott, "Sociotechnical System Design in Transition," in *The Emerging Practice of Organization Development,* eds. W. Sikes, A. Drexler, and J. Grant (La Jolla, Calif.: University Associates, 1989) pp. 187–98.

50. T. Cummings and S. Srivastva, *Management of Work: A Sociotechnical Systems Approach* (La Jolla, Calif.: University Associates, 1978).

51. A. B. Shani and W. A. Pasmore, "Organization Inquiry: Towards a New Model of the Action Research Process," in *Contemporary Organization Development,* ed. D. D. Warrick (Glenview, Ill.: Scott, Foresman, 1985), pp. 438–49.

52. W. A. Pasmore, C. Francis, J. Heldeman, and A. B. Shani, "Sociotechnical Systems: A North American Reflection on Empirical Studies of the Seventies," *Human Relations* 35, no. 12 (1982), pp. 1179–204.

53. W. Barko and W. A. Pasmore, "Introductory Statement to the Special Issue on Sociotechnical Systems: Innovations in Designing High-Performing Systems," *Journal of Applied Behavioral Science* 22, no. 3 (1986), pp. 195–99.

54. J. C. Taylor, "Two Decades of Sociotechnical Systems in North America," paper presented at the annual meeting of the Academy of Management, San Francisco, August 1990; J. C. Taylor, and D. F. Felten, *Performance by Design: Sociotechnical Systems in North America* (Prentice-Hall: New Jersey, 1993).

55. See, for example, R. Holti, "Sociotechnical Issues in the Software Sector," paper presented at the annual meeting of the Academy of Management, San Francisco, August 1990.

56. See, for example, P. H. Engelstad, "The Evolution of Network Strategies in Action Research Support Sociotechnical Redesign Programs in Scandinavia," paper presented at the annual meeting of the Academy of Management, San Francisco, August 1990.

57. L. U. De Sitter and J. F. Den Hertog, "Simple Organizations, Complex Jobs: The Dutch Sociotechnical Approach" (Maastricht, The Netherlands: MERIT Publications, 1990).

58. Y. Mitki, *Sociotechnical Systems: A Comparative Study of 112 Production Units in the Kibbutz Industries* (Tel Aviv: Tel Aviv University, 1994).

59. This section is based on A. B. (Rami) Shani, Y. Mitki, and R. Krishnan, "Reengineering, TQM and Sociotechnical Systems Approaches to Organizational Change," paper presented at the National Academy of Management Conference, Dallas, August 1994.

60. M. Stebbins and A. B. (Rami) Shani, "Moving Away from the Mafia Model of Organization Design," *Organizational Dynamics,* Winter 1989, pp. 18–30.

61. Ibid.

62. Many recent review-based studies support this argument. See, for example, J. I. Porras, "Organization Development: Theory, Practice, and Research," in *Handbook of Industrial and Organizational Psychology,* eds. M. D. Dunnette and L. M. Hough, 2d ed., Vol. 3 (Palo Alto, Calif.: Consulting Psychological Press, 1992), pp. 719–822; P. J. Robertson, D. R. Roberts, and J. I. Porras, "An Evaluation of a Model of Planned Organizational Change: Evidence from a Meta-Analysis," in *Research in Organizational Change and Development,* eds. W. A. Pasmore and R. W. Woodman, Vol. 7 (Greenwich, Conn.: JAI Press, 1993), pp. 1–39; and B. A. Macy, and H. Izumi, "Organizational Change, Design, and Work Innovations: A Meta-Analysis of 131 North American Field Studies—1961–1991," in *Research in Organizational Change and Development,* Vol. 7, pp. 235–313.

63. W. L. French and C. H. Bell, *Organization Development,* 5th ed. (Englewood Cliffs, N.J.: Prentice-Hall, 1995); T. D. Jick, *Managing Change* (Burr Ridge, Ill.: Irwin, 1993); R. M. Kanter, B. A. Stein, and T. D. Jick, *The Challenge of Organizational Change* (New York: Free Press, 1992).

64. J. I. Porras and S. J. Hoffer, "Common Behavior Changes in Successful Organization Development Efforts," *Journal of Applied Behavioral Science* 22, no. 4 (1986), pp. 477–94.

65. A. A. Armenakis, A. G. Bedian, and S. B. Pond, "Research Issues in OD Evaluation: Past, Present, and Future," *Academy of Management Review* 8, no. 2 (1983), pp. 320–28.

66. J. M. Nicholas and M. Katz, "Research Methods and Reporting Practices in Organization Development: A Review and Some Guidelines," *Academy of Management Review* 10, no. 4 (1985), pp. 737–49.

67. See B. A. Macy, "An Assessment of Improvement and Productivity Efforts: 1970–1985," paper presented at the National Academy of Management, August 1986, Chicago; and F. M. Van Eijnatten, *The Sociotechnical Systems Design Paradigm* (Eindhoven, The Netherlands, 1986).

68. M. N. Kiggundu, "Limitations to the Applications of Sociotechnical Systems in Developing Countries," *Journal of Applied Behavioral Science* 22, no. 3 (1986), pp. 341–54; Z. Chroscicki, "Conceptualization of OD Process Measures in Poland," *Organization Development Journal* 4, no. 3 (1986), pp. 62–67; and M. Rikuta, "Organization Development within Japanese Industry: Facts and Prospects," *Organization Development Journal* 5, no. 2 (1987), pp. 21–32.

69. A. M. Jaeger, "Organization Development and National Culture: Where's the Fit?" *Academy of Management Review* 11, no. 1 (1986), pp. 178–90.

70. A. B. Shani and G. R. Bushe, "Visionary Action Research: A Consultation Process Perspective," *Consultation: An International Journal* 6, no. 1 (1987), pp. 3–19; and M. W. Stebbins and C. C. Snow, "Process and Payoffs of Programmatic Action Research," *Journal of Applied Behavioral Science* 18 (1982), pp. 69–86.

Activity 17–3: Revisiting the Paper Mills Corporation

Objective:

To use the concepts and model of organizational culture, planned change, and the management of change to analyze the Paper Mills Corporation case.

Task 1 (Individual Homework):

Read the Paper Mills Corporation case in Module 14 and answer the following questions:

a. Using Schein's classification scheme, identify the relevant cultural dimensions of the Paper and Carton Product Division.
b. List ways in which the organizational cultural aspects were functional or dysfunctional to the individual, to the group, or to the division.
c. Capture in your own words the TQM planned change process that was implemented at the Paper and Carton Product Division.
d. If Mr. Meiri, the general manager of the division, had chosen to follow the reengineering planned change process (instead of the TQM approach), what would have been the differences in the change process and its management? What other challenges would he have faced?

Task 2:

Individuals are to share their analyses in teams. Teams are to identify common patterns among the analyses described and discuss their impact on individual and group effectiveness.

Task 3:

The class is to discuss cause-and-effect relationships between organizational culture, alternative planned change strategies, and effectiveness.

Activity 17–4: The Management of Change at FoodCo, Inc.

Objective:

To increase the understanding of the concepts of organizational culture, development, and change by applying them to the FoodCo case.

Task 1 (Homework):

Read the FoodCo case that follows and answer the questions at the end of the case.

Task 2:

The instructor will facilitate class analysis and discussion of the case.

Case Study: FoodCo, Inc. (Part A)

FoodCo, Inc., is a national supplier of specialty food products sold through grocery stores. Its headquarters are in Chicago, Illinois; its food-processing plants are spread throughout the country. FoodCo maintains a reputation as a well-managed, profitable company in an extremely competitive industry. As is common in the food products industry, most of FoodCo's top executives have marketing backgrounds.

In January of last year, Tom Hawkins, a consultant specializing in organizational design, received a call from Don Stevens, a top-level staff member in the FoodCo plant in Cleveland, Ohio. Don was interested in talking to Tom about some recent developments at the Cleveland plant. During their brief telephone conversation, Don told Tom that the plant manager, Mr. Williams, had become increasingly uncomfortable with the pressure he was under from corporate management to implement sociotechnical systems changes in the Cleveland facility. Don was anxious to hear Tom's advice on how to deal with the situation since Mr. Williams had made him responsible for preparing a statement on the situation for corporate management.

When they met, Don explained to Tom that FoodCo was organized on a divisional basis around products and that each division was capable of operating as a separate business. However, given the competitive nature of the industry, corporate management felt that it needed to make decisions quickly to maintain an advantage over other firms; this meant that FoodCo's top management became involved in many local decisions. Plant managers throughout the corporation were required to clear even minor changes

Source: This case was contributed by Professor William A. Pasmore, Weatherhead School of Management, Case Western Reserve University, Cleveland, Ohio 44106. We are grateful to him.

in operations with their superiors and were expected to implement changes directed from above.

In the past, rapid changes had created some difficulties at the Cleveland plant. Product life cycles were short (three to five years in many cases); each cycle was accompanied by the hiring and letting go of employees. Shutdowns and retoolings had hit the Cleveland plant more frequently than others, creating dissatisfaction and mistrust on the part of employees. Don described the situation to Tom:

> People come here looking for work and we say, ''Great! We're glad to have you! Welcome to the company!'' Then a couple of years later, we say, ''Sorry–we can't use you for a while.'' That's bad enough; but the trouble is, we never know when the cutbacks will occur, because people in Chicago make those decisions for us based on how well the product is doing in the market, or whether they think another plant could produce it for less, or if they think they have a hotter product for us to make. So we're as much in the dark as anyone—but the employees don't believe us. They think we know, but we just aren't telling them. They say, ''You're management aren't you? If you don't know, who does?'' I understand that these people have families and lives of their own to plan for and that this situation makes it hard for them. It's hard for all of us—but it's just the nature of the business. I can even understand why they voted in a union—I get pretty frustrated myself at times—but the union is only making things worse. Now, in addition to dealing with Corporate, we have to fight the union every step of the way. We can't make any changes around here without someone second-guessing us. If we give in to the union, Corporate screams. But if we follow Corporate's orders, union members become upset—and then it just gets harder to get them to go along the next time.
>
> People at Corporate are market-oriented. They have to be, I guess. But it seems like at times they don't think very much about what impact their decisions will have on people. We're the ones who have to live with these people day after day. Most of the time, we wind up going along with Corporate, since we can't risk losing our jobs or the business for the plant; but we sure would like Corporate to be a little more sensitive to the problems they create for us. This demand to implement sociotechnical systems changes here is just the latest bug of theirs. They really don't appreciate the difficulties we would have in making it work here.

Following the Tampa Example

Don explained to Tom that corporate management had gotten excited about sociotechnical systems design after its success in the corporation's newest plant, located in Tampa, Florida. Here are some of its features.

Autonomous Work Groups: Self-managed production teams were given primary responsibility for major segments of the production process. Each team was composed of multiskilled members who could perform one another's job as well as do most of the maintenance and quality work. The teams were free to decide on their own job assignments, to select new team members, and to discipline members who didn't meet their standards.

Integrated Support Functions: Team members were able to perform most work that would be performed by separate maintenance and quality control departments in a typical plant. The teams were also able to schedule their own production runs, plan product changeovers, determine their own overtime, and even do minor process engineering.

Challenging Job Assignments: Jobs were designed to meet human needs for growth, challenge, and learning. Routine tasks were rotated among all team members.

Job Mobility and Rewards for Learning: Pay increases were given in accordance with the number of tasks employees could perform. All employees were encouraged to learn new jobs throughout the plant.

Facilitative Leadership: The plant operated with a minimum of supervision; those supervisors who were present were chosen on the basis of their ability to work effectively with groups in making decisions and their ability to help team members to develop.

Managerial Information for Employees: Employees were provided with a full range of productivity and cost data that allowed them to make decisions about the effective use of their team resources.

Self-Government for the Plant: No rules were specified in advance; employees were allowed to develop their own rules as they saw fit.

Congruent Physical and Social Context: Status symbols that would separate managers from employees were avoided; common cafeterias and parking lots were used. In addition, rooms were provided for work teams to hold meetings and the plant itself was designed to facilitate discussion among teams that were responsible for interdependent processes.

Learning and Evolution: A commitment was made to continual improvement in the way the organization operated. Employees would have a major influence on changes that would take place.

Plans for the Cleveland Expansion

According to Don, the issue confronting the Cleveland plant was that the corporation wanted the Cleveland plant to follow Tampa's example in designing its new dairy products line. Because Tampa had been successful, corporate management was pressuring the Cleveland plant to adopt the sociotechnical systems approach in managing its operation as well. In fact, the dairy products division manager had already appointed Dick Harold, a manager from the Tampa plant, to head up the new dairy operation in Cleveland. Since the Cleveland plant was part of another division in the company, this move caught Mr. Williams by surprise:

We're not opposed to new ideas here. I've been in this business for 25 years and I've tried a lot of new ideas in my time. In fact, we did a lot here before we ever heard of Dick Harold—our employees keep their own work areas clean—and we even have them rotate jobs in one area. So these ideas aren't really that new to us. Still, I think the corporation is trying to push this thing on us too quickly. Dick Harold was in town buying a house before I even knew he was coming to work here. What's worse, they never told him that he would be working for me. He thought he would have a free hand in the new dairy products unit since it's part of another division. I straightened that out—anything that happens at this plant is under *my* control. I made a phone call to Chicago and my boss made sure that Harold would be working for me.

As I said, I'm not opposed to new ideas. But I think we have a different setup here than Tampa does. They handpicked the best people to work in that plant—we can't do that. They weren't unionized—we are. They didn't have a history of ups and downs that created mistrust—we do. And they built from scratch—we have to make use of our existing building. Besides, we've done all right here using our own way of getting things done. Some of my managers have been with the company for as long as I have, and they don't like the sound of some of Harold's ideas. I've made them hold a tough line in the past and they've held it. They're afraid of what would happen if we turned the place over to the employees to run. They've also heard that Tampa operates with fewer managers than we do and that makes them nervous.

I suppose that with the corporation behind this thing, we don't have much choice but to try it. But I'm pretty sure it won't work here. Maybe when they see that, they'll back off. At least I've gotten them to agree that we should check it out with our people first to see what they think of it. I doubt that they'll go for it—there's been too much change here already—but we'll see.

The Survey

Tom worked with Don Stevens to prepare a survey to be given to employees to find out how they felt about the new management concept. Tom also met with the president and vice president of the local union to discuss the reasons for giving the survey. He explained to them that not all employees would be affected by the proposed changes, but that the survey would be an opportunity for people throughout the plant to comment on how the plant was being run. The union leaders seemed in favor of the proposed changes and agreed that the survey should be given as long as individuals would not be identified with their answers. The results of the survey indicated that attitudes toward management were negative and that communication between management and employees was viewed as practically nonexistent. Although a few employees had written notes on their surveys indicating that the new management concept was a strategy to get more work out of employees for the same pay, overall reactions to the concept by the majority of employees were more positive than Mr. Williams had imagined.

Mr. Williams's Dilemma

Tom discussed the results of the survey with Don Stevens. Don told Tom that Mr. Williams had been surprised by the findings but still was not convinced that employees would really accept the changes associated with the new management concept. What's more, Williams was fairly certain that if the concept was put into practice, it wouldn't work—at least not for long. If Williams went ahead, he would look foolish to the employees, which would make things worse in the future; if he didn't proceed, the corporation would be on his back to explain why, and Williams knew that the people from Chicago weren't good listeners.

Williams decided to put the concept to a vote by the employees. He figured that if they said yes and it didn't work, they would have no one to blame but themselves; if they said no, he might at least have some reason when Corporate asked him why he hadn't gone ahead with its plan. Williams knew that management had the legal right to design work any way it pleased so the corporation would not be bound by the results of the vote. Williams arranged to have the union take the vote at the local union hall quickly since construction on the new unit was being held up by the corporation until the situation at Cleveland was clear. The corporation was anxious to get this work started since it would lose market share if the product didn't go into production soon.

Questions

1. Describe the culture of the corporation.
2. Is the corporation justified in its position regarding the management of the Cleveland plant?
3. How will the vote turn out? What steps should be taken afterward?
4. What advice should Tom give to Mr. Williams?

Activity 17–5: Custom Nests Simulation

Objectives:

a. To help participants become aware of the differences between sociotechnical design principles and traditional bureaucratic principles.
b. To develop participants' appreciation for the sociotechnical systems approach to organizational development and effectiveness.

Task 1 (Homework):

Participants are to read the following organization description of Custom Nests. (Do not read beyond the basic description of the organization.)

Task 2 (In-Class Activities):

a. The instructor will assign roles (Appendix S) with name tags to each participant.
b. The instructor will then assign participants to their workstations and ask them to begin their work as it is described in their role descriptions.
c. Production will be stopped after about 25 minutes and participants will be asked to leave the room for about 10 minutes.
d. The instructor will then lead a brief discussion about the experience of work in the phase just completed. Discussion themes might be
   1. What was it like being a stapler, a supervisor, and so on?
   2. How was this organization like others that you have worked for?
   3. What kind of organizational development strategy would you utilize to improve effectiveness?
   4. How would you go about implementing the change?

Task 3 (In-Class Activities):

Participants will be assigned to new work groups and asked to start production. Production will be stopped after about 25 minutes.

Task 4:

The instructor will lead a class discussion on the following themes:

1. How was the work design in the second phase different/similar to that of the first phase?
2. What would be the implications of the second work design phase to your own experience?
3. Discuss the relationship between the social, technological, and environmental subsystems.
4. What are some challenges for implementing sociotechnical system change in organizations?
5. How would the sociotechnical system intervention be similar/different from the other organizational development approaches discussed in this module?

(*Note to the instructor.* Be sure to read the *Instructor's Manual* before using this exercise.)

Source: This activity was contributed by Dr. Barry Morris. We are grateful to him.

Case Study: Custom Nests Simulation

Organization Description

Custom Nests was founded in 1951 by Mr. Jay Blue. The company began as a small operation consisting of six workers and a manager. Everyone in the company worked as a craftsperson making birdhouses from beginning to end. The explosion in the housing market that followed World War II created massive demand for birdhouses for the displaced birds of this period. As a result Custom Nests grew considerably in a short period of time. Today it continues to be the primary manufacturer of birdhouses, providing the American public with a wide range of quality birdhouses for every occasion and climate. One birdhouse in particular, however, has remained the company's primary and most marketable item and has allowed the business to expand into other birdhouse markets with little risk to overall sales.

The structure of the organization has changed dramatically since its inception. Only the people in research and development actually have the opportunity to build a birdhouse from the bottom up. The majority of the company's products are manufactured in a highly specialized assembly-line–type of process in which few people actually have hands-on opportunities to see how the whole product gets made. Wages for hourly workers are determined based on years with the organization and the complexity of the task. For many years the company had been paying minimum wage wherever possible. In 1969, the company was unionized. Wages are currently slightly less than the standard for similar industrial settings. The relationship between union and management is adversarial. There is a fairly high number of grievances written on a regular basis and neither group has as yet been willing to sit down and iron out their differences in a way that meets both groups' needs. For the most part, decisions in the organization are made by managers while hourly workers are expected to do as they are told.

The company currently employs approximately 175 people. Of these, 140 are hourly employees; the remainder are engineers or managers of one sort or another. The various hourly roles in the organization include cutters, tapers, staplers, and maintenance/supply personnel. The salaried staff includes quality control, supervisors, research and development, and accounting clerks.

The plant's layout has the various specialties spread out and separated from one another in a large single-floor facility. (See the diagram.) Many structural barriers to effective communication between work groups/areas exist. The technology in much of the plant is simple yet antiquated. There is a long history of broken or unuseful tools and inadequate processes for keeping the technology in good working order.

Custom Nest Floorplan

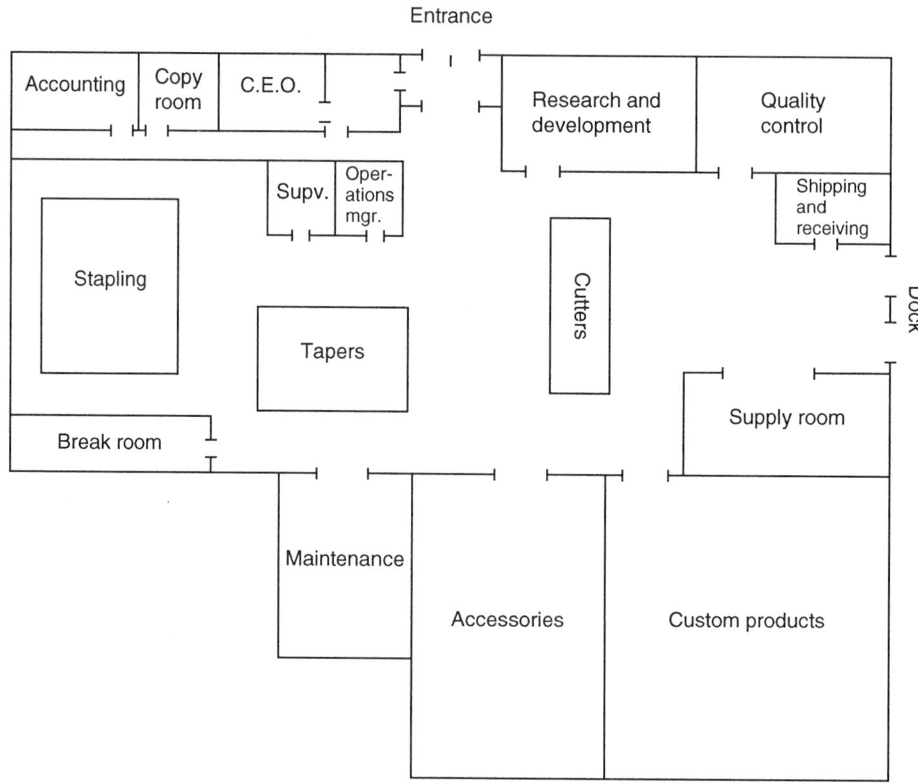

Activity 17–6: Bill (or Bonnie) Dawson's Challenge at Crofts Products Company

Objective:

To use course concepts for (1) analysis of a management situation and (2) planning goals and strategy.

Task 1 (Individual Homework):

a. Study the accompanying Crofts Products Company case. You may find it easier to analyze the case by cutting out the memorandums to be found in Appendix U and spreading them out on the desk just as would be done with an actual in-basket.

b. Scan the text for concepts that would help in problem analysis. (There are many.)

c. Complete the assignment questions at the end of the case study. The instructor will indicate whether this is to be a written examination or notes for class discussion. (*Caution:* Read each memorandum carefully to make sure you understand each paragraph.)

Task 2 (Classroom Activity, First Hour):

a. Teams are to decide on the three most important problems facing Dawson and rank them. The cause of each problem should also be given.
b. A spokesperson for each team will report the team's list of problems, and the instructor will list them on the board.
c. Discussion of similarities and differences follows.

Task 3 (Classroom Activity, Second Hour):

a. Teams are to decide on the three most important goals and list them in order by priority.
b. Teams are to report while the instructor lists goals on the board.
c. The instructor will present a model for systematic analysis of goals.

Task 4 (Classroom Activity, Third Hour):

a. Teams are to decide on Dawson's managerial strategy for handling problems and achieving goals during the week ahead. They also are to sketch out a schedule for using the time available during that week.
b. Teams are to report their decisions.
c. The instructor will comment on team reports.

Case Study: Crofts Products Company—In-Basket Case Study

Crofts Products was one of those companies started in the early 1920s by a few creative men who later prospered by manufacturing their own inventions. Pat Harrison, the present president and one of the original group, had bought out the other shareholders over the years. Last year he looked at the increasing competition, the declining profits, and his advancing years and sold out to Lilliewhite Corporation. The corporation acquired Crofts with the requirements that Pat Harrison remain in his position for another two years and that Alvin Alberts, the executive vice president, remain one year and then retire. It also recruited, from a company manufacturing product lines related to those of Crofts, a young executive named Bill (or Bonnie) Dawson who had a fine track record and great potential. The agreement was for Dawson to understudy Alberts as assistant executive vice president for six months and then to assume full responsibility as executive vice president; Alberts was to stay on as a consultant for his remaining time.

However, Dawson had been on the scene only one week when Alberts had a massive heart attack. Dawson learned that Alberts would not be accessible for several weeks and would not return to work.

You are Bill (or Bonnie) Dawson. You are most anxious to do well with Crofts, particularly since Lilliewhite Corporation offers opportunities for future advancement. So far you have hardly had time to learn the names of your management team. Pat Harrison, however, says you are already an experienced executive, and he decides he wants you to assume responsibility as executive vice president. He assures you that you are in complete control, that he will in no way interfere with your decisions, and that your team will jump in and help you. His role is to work with the corporation and the outside contacts; you are to run the company. This all happens on Thursday, April 14. On Friday morning, you get word to all those reporting directly to you (see the organization chart in Exhibit 1), asking them to write you a memorandum if they have any immediate problems to be discussed with you the following week. By the end of the day your in-basket contains the memorandums to be found in appendix U. You take these home so you can plan your next week's activities.

Exhibit 1
Organization Chart Prior to Alberts's Heart Attack

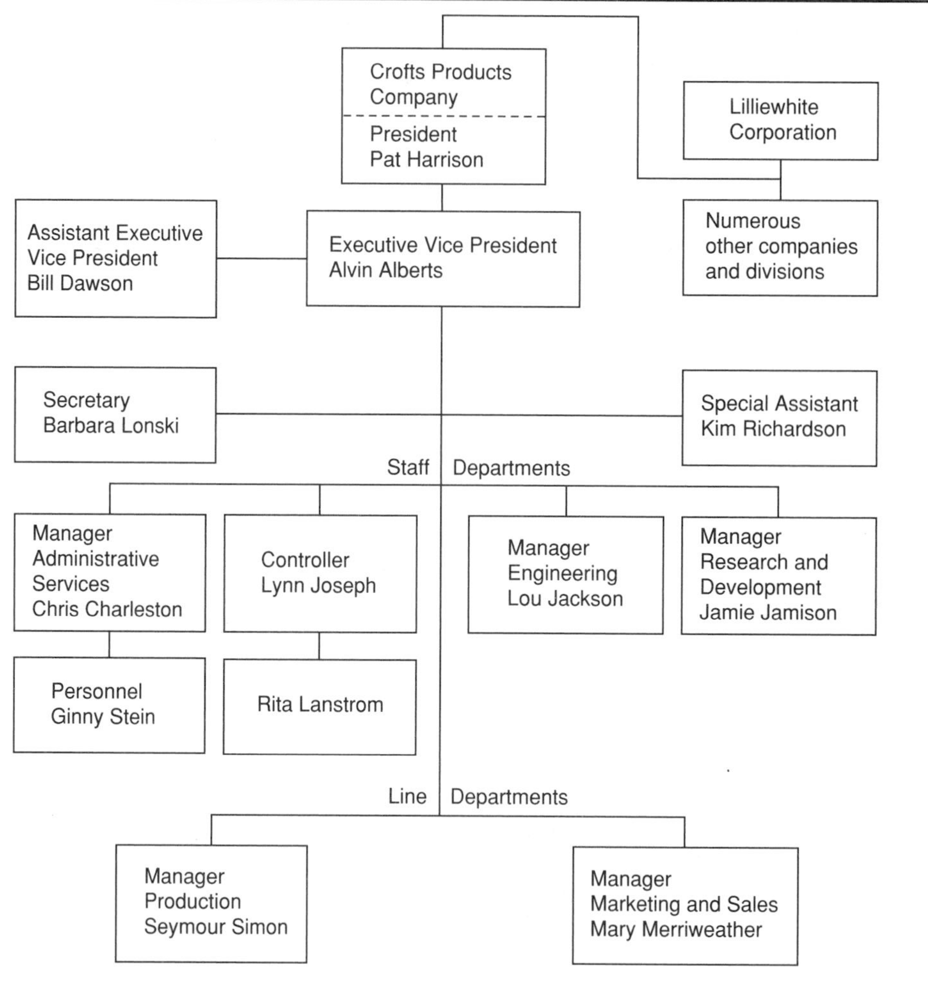

Assignment

Part I

Study the assigned memorandums (Appendix U) carefully and write the answers to the following questions:

1. What are the problems facing you? Make a list. Rank them in order of importance.
2. What are the causes of the problems?
3. Now that you have analyzed the problems, what are the goals you want to accomplish? List these in priority order.
4. What strategy or techniques will you use to work on these problems and goals during the coming week? Make a time schedule showing how you will use the hours of each day of the week. For each entry, state the purpose of the listing, who is to be present (if anyone), what approach you will use, and why. Be specific; don't say, "I am going to solve the problem." Say how you are going to do it.

Part II

How would you handle Rita Lanstrom? Be specific on a step-by-step plan for resolving the situation. Give reasons for your plan. Remember to think in terms of consequences.

(*Note:* This is an opportunity to apply the course concepts in organization behavior to a simulated situation. You will be graded on your ability to use them. Your reports should be typed double-spaced.)

PART 5 MANAGING CHANGE

Review

Managing change seems to absorb a significant amount of time and energy in today's reality of organizations. Some managers argue that their job almost entirely consists of managing change. The complexity, amount, and pace of change have increased significantly during the past decade. Most organizations, employees, and managers are struggling to find the optimal path. The management of change influences organizational behavior and organizational effectiveness.

Part 4 interrelated the four conceptual areas of personality and diversity, motivation, perception, and communication to key organizational processes. The design of work and organizations, the management of quality, the creativity and innovation processes, and the management of technology and information technology foster, as we saw in Part 4, organizational dynamics that result in the emergence of organizational culture. Thus the area that remains to be addressed in detail is the interrelationship of ''effectiveness'' at the individual, team, and organizational levels.

Embedded in organizational efforts to improve effectiveness is continuous improvement or what the Japanese call *Kaizan.* Continuous improvement is a purposeful and explicit set of principles, mechanisms, and activities within an organization designed to achieve positive and continuous change in operating procedures, effectiveness, and systems by the people who actually perform these procedures and work within these systems. *Continuous* means that an improvement activity is explicitly designed and organized for continuity. Improvement projects and episodes should follow each other in the same area or around the same general performance indicators. In this respect, continuous improvement is markedly different from sporadic improvement projects undertaken without a view of continuity, and from suggestions systems, where any kind of improvement suggestions are called for without explicit management of the area, quality, or direction of the suggestions. Usually continuity requires permanent support structure. *Improvement* is a planned change in the state of affairs of an organization that results in positive changes in the organizational effectiveness indicators.[1]

Preview of Part 5

Part 5 will incorporate much of the material already studied into an overall system approach to individual, team, and organizational effectiveness. This part is composed of two integrated modules: ''Managing Organizational Change and Development'' and ''Career Planning and Development.''

In Module 17, managing organizational change and development (OC&D) is described as planned change organizational efforts that attempt to improve effectiveness. The OD approaches initially developed by Robert Blake and Jane Mouton, Rensis Likert, Chris Argyris, and Eric Trist provide contrasting methods of influencing and shaping the human organization. We address six different orientations of managing change. An in-depth comparison of three systemwide change programs—reengineering, Total Quality Management, and sociotechnical systems—provides an insight into the complexity of managing change and development. In concluding the book, we reiterate our view that an integration of important aspects of the traditional and the behavioral models is essential for organizational effectiveness.

The effectiveness of individuals and organizations can be significantly enhanced by fostering career planning and development. This topic is explored in Module 18. Career development includes both individual career planning and organizational career management. Activity 18–1 guides the individual through the first steps of designing a short-range career plan. Whereas the second part of the module deals with the management of career development, the last section discusses specific career issues that individuals and organizations are likely to face during the next decade with specific emphasis on careers in the global environment and managing work force diversity. As such, we have come full circle by concluding with the same topic that was introduced in the first module.

The 12 activities in this part provide for interactive learning in support of the course's learning objectives. As one aspect of team building that supports the theory in Module 11, Activity 18–4 provides a rating form that can be used by the permanent teams to analyze their team climates in preparation for the written reports required by Appendixes A, B, C, and D. This also serves as the basis for each team sharing its learning experience (Activity 18–5) with the entire class in the concluding session of the course. Finally, the FoodCo. Inc. case study (Activity 17–4) and the in-basket case study of the Crofts Products Company (Activity 17–6) can be used for application of the course concepts to a simulated management situation, and ''Custom Nests Simulation'' (Activity 17–5) can be used to integrate most of the course concepts.

Notes

1. For a detailed discussion of continuous improvement, its origin, and current definitions, see P. Lillrank and A. B. (Rami) Shani, ''Continuous Improvement: Beyond a Definition,'' EFI Research Paper (Stockholm, Sweden: Stockholm School of Economics, 1995).

18 Career Planning and Development

Learning Objectives

After completing this module you should be able to

1. Explain the relationship between continuous improvement, managing change, and career planning and development.
2. Explore individual and group differences in career interests, needs, and values.
3. Develop a personal five-year career plan.
4. Gain an understanding of ways organizations can assist individuals in pursuing their career goals.
5. Evaluate the implications of various career management activities for organizational effectiveness.
6. Gain an appreciation of emerging issues in the management of careers.

List of Key Concepts

Assessment center (AC)
Career anchor
Career development
Career path
Career planning
Career plateau
Career-resilient work force
Career stage
Downsizing
Glass ceiling
Human resource information system (HRIS)
Human resource planning (HRP)
Mentoring
Protean or spiral career

This module was contributed by Rebecca Ellis, Professor of Human Resource Management, College of Business, California Polytechnic State University, San Luis Obispo, California 93407. We are grateful to her.

Module Outline

Premodule Preparation

Activity 18–1: Perspectives on Career Development

Objectives:

a. To develop an awareness of the importance and complexity of career development issues.

b. To compare and contrast the perspectives of students and practicing managers regarding the career development process.

Task 1 (Home: Interview with a Manager):

Identify a practicing manager who is willing to be interviewed for 15 to 20 minutes, either in person or over the phone, about career development issues currently facing the manager's organization. Interview the manager, being sure to cover the following suggested questions at a minimum. Probe for additional information; make up your own questions to supplement those given below.

1. What is the most important career development issue facing your organization right now?
2. How important is this issue to organizational effectiveness? What is being done about it?
3. What other career issues do you think your organization will probably face over the next 10 years?
4. Who is responsible for career management in your organization? What programs, activities, and policies does your organization have that facilitate career management?

Task 2 (Homework: Student Interviews):

Interview two or more students on your campus who are pursuing different majors. You are to gather information about the nature and extent of career planning each respondent has engaged in and their ideas about career management activities in organizations. At a minimum, pose the following questions:

1. Why did you select your major field?
2. What do you know about the job opportunities for people graduating with your major? How difficult will it be to find an appropriate entry-level position?
3. What have you done so far to actually explore career opportunities in your field?
4. What sort of career development activities and programs do you think your first employer is likely to make available to employees?

Task 3 (Classroom):

The instructor will lead a classroom discussion integrating the findings of class members. Discussion will focus on (a) major career issues that practicing managers identify as important in the future, (b) student expectations regarding career management assistance from future employers, and (c) the current extent of student career exploration as judged by interview responses.

Introduction

The basic notions of continuous improvement in organizations lend themselves to the need to manage change on an ongoing basis. As we have seen, continuous implies that an improvement activity is explicitly designed, organized, and managed. Integration of the ongoing activity must occur at the individual, team, and organizational levels. Improvement implies planned change in the state of affairs of the firm that results in positive changes at all levels. Career planning and development provides a specific illustration of continuous improvement.

Over time in an organization, most individuals become increasingly interested in their own self-development, that is, the acquisition of new skills and abilities that will lead to continued personal growth and long-term career satisfaction. At the same time, most organizations are interested in strategic human resource development, that is, having people with the right skills in the right place at the right time to ensure long-run organizational effectiveness. Career development can help bring about an integration of these individual and organizational goals. To achieve integration, however, both individuals and organizations must closely examine career development needs, establish realistic goals, and share information. This is not always easy for there are often perceptual barriers to accurate need assessment and there may be communication barriers to effective joint goal setting. This module introduces the core concepts and describes key activities that individuals and organizations need to consider if they are to maximize joint efforts in attaining career development objectives.

In this module, we discuss career planning and career management as well as several important career issues that have emerged in the 1990s. If you read more about career development elsewhere, you will notice that different writers use the terms *career development, career planning,* and *career management* in different ways. Here we define **career development** as the ongoing effort of both individuals and organizations to expand career opportunities and realize career goals. As such, career development includes both individual career planning and organizational career management. When we speak of career planning, we mean the steps an individual goes through to direct his or her own career in ways that will be personally satisfying. This calls for the ability to manage change at the individual, team, and organizational levels. Activity 18–2 will guide you through the many steps of designing a short-range (five-year) career plan for yourself. You may be surprised to find that career planning should begin long before you're ready to search for a permanent job.

The second section of the module deals with career management, which we define as the organization's efforts to manage the flow of individuals through positions over time in ways that will best meet both organizational and individual goals. Here the major issues are associated with the manager's ability to manage change. Activity 18–3 provides the vehicle for examining the existing flow patterns of an automotive parts manufacturer and proposes ways of improving or expanding this organization's career paths.

Finally, along with our discussion of specific career issues that individuals and organizations will face during the next decade, we include a case study of an early retirement program (Activity 18–3). You will be asked to consider how diverse interests and goals can be balanced and managed in such a program to best promote both individual and organizational development and effectiveness.

Individual Career Planning

Career planning is the process through which individuals identify and implement steps to attain their career goals.[1] There are five basic steps in the career planning process: (1) self-assessment, (2) investigating career opportunities, (3) goal setting, (4) action planning, and (5) evaluation.

In the self-assessment phase the individual begins by examining his or her own assets, characteristics, interests, and current level of skill development. Although self-assessment is often done informally, there are also many formal tests and inventories available through school placement offices or career counseling centers. Measures of aptitudes, interests, personality, values, and career maturity can be interpreted by professional counselors and often can prove quite useful in developing a profile for the individual. Two of the most widely used interest inventories are the Strong Vocational Interest Blank and the Kuder Vocational Preference Record.[2] The Kuder, for example, lists sets of activities and asks individuals to pick the activities they most prefer. An individual's interest profile is then compared to the profiles of successful people in a number of different occupations to find those occupations the individual's profile most resembles.

Self-assessment need not be done by a professional counselor. Many questionnaires and checklist inventories are available for the individual to use to evaluate personal characteristics, interests, and skills. Table 18–1 presents one such instrument.

The second phase of career planning involves investigating a range of career opportunities to determine which skills, interests, and abilities they require. Basically, this is an information-gathering step and many sources may be used, including friends, family members, and business associates as well as written sources. Job placement centers often list the qualifications required by potential employers for particular jobs. One may also request job descriptions from companies for jobs that seem interesting. Of course, current employees should investigate opportunities in their own organization as well as those outside.

Goal setting is the process of using what has been learned through self-assessment and the investigation of career opportunities to decide where one wants to go, at least in the short run. Reality checking is important at this stage; be sure to squarely face the facts generated in the preceding two steps. To be most helpful, the goals set should be specific and measurable as well as reasonably attainable within a specified time frame.

Next, the action plan details specific steps required to carry out the goal. An action plan may include seeking additional required training or formal education; developing particular management, interpersonal, or other needed skills either on or off the job; or even seeking an internship or temporary work assignment to gain experience. Whatever is needed to attain the goal must be addressed in the action plan.

Finally, career planning involves ongoing evaluation of progress toward one's career goals. Evaluation keeps planning on track and can also help identify strengths and weaknesses in a career plan.

Career Stages

Self-assessment is important to career planning because individuals differ a great deal from one another in their interests, needs, and values. At the same time, there are likely to be some commonalities in the kinds of career experiences or events that most people go through during their work life. Donald Super (among others) has developed a theory of **career stages** that links certain career-related tasks to the stage in a person's life cycle when these tasks are most likely to be undertaken.[3]

Growth stage: As the child interacts with the home, neighborhood, and school, certain capacities, interests, and values are developed.

Exploratory stage: From adolescence to about the mid-20s, the individual explores various occupational roles through school, leisure activities, and part-time work, thereby further crystallizing his or her interests, aptitudes, and values. Tentative career choices are made and a beginning job is found and tried out as a life work.

Establishment stage: Most people in their mid-20s to mid-40s have found an appropriate career field, and they devote their energies toward making a permanent place in it.

Maintenance stage: At about age 45, most people have made a place in the world of work, and the concern is now to hold it. Little new ground is broken, but there is continuation along established lines.

Decline stage: As physical and mental powers decline (from age 65 onward), work activities decelerate and eventually cease with retirement.

Although this model links career stages to age, it is very likely that "career clocks" begin at different points for different individuals, based on their backgrounds and experiences. There are also likely to be differences in the number of distinct stages through

Table 18–1

Career Anchor Self-Analysis

Circle the correct number in each scale below the following 15 statements to indicate the degree to which you either agree or disagree. Since the purpose of this test instrument is to help you identify important motives that may influence your career decisions, be as honest with yourself as possible, making sure that every response corresponds to your true feelings.

Although some of the statements may seem similar while others are contradictory, respond to each of them independently, without regard to how you may have responded to any others.

	Strongly disagree			Neutral			Strongly agree
1. Success is defined as being the best I can be in my specialty or field.	1	2	3	4	5	6	7
2. I can readily identify significant aspects of a problem and solve it, even when presented with incomplete information and uncertainty.	1	2	3	4	5	6	7
3. Success is defined as long-term job security and financial security.	1	2	3	4	5	6	7
4. Starting my own company or creating my own product or service is important to me.	1	2	3	4	5	6	7
5. Being able to pursue my own life-style without organizational restrictions is important to me.	1	2	3	4	5	6	7
6. Getting each work-related task completed correctly and on schedule is important to me.	1	2	3	4	5	6	7
7. I have the ability to influence others.	1	2	3	4	5	6	7
8. Raising a family and being involved in my community are important to me.	1	2	3	4	5	6	7
9. Success is defined as being associated with a company product, service, or idea that is widely recognized as being mine.	1	2	3	4	5	6	7
10. Having broad discretion in determining what I do and how I do it is important to me.	1	2	3	4	5	6	7
11. Maintaining technical competence in my specialty throughout my career is important to me.	1	2	3	4	5	6	7
12. Success is defined as rising to the top of my organization.	1	2	3	4	5	6	7
13. The organization's interests and goals are my interests and goals.	1	2	3	4	5	6	7
14. I need to get involved with new ventures and products. Stability and routine are boring.	1	2	3	4	5	6	7
15. Success is defined as freedom to make my own decisions, manage my own time, and define my own tasks.	1	2	3	4	5	6	7

Analysis

Write your score numbers for the following combinations of statements in the middle column and the sum of those scores in the third column.

Statements	Scores	Sum of Three Scores
A. 1, 6, 11	________	________
B. 2, 7, 12	________	________
C. 3, 8, 13	________	________
D. 4, 9, 14	________	________
E. 5, 10, 15	________	________

Diagnosis

Groupings A–E correspond to the following career anchors:

A. Technical-functional specialization
B. Managerial competence
C. Security–stability
D. Creativity
E. Independence

The higher your score for a particular anchor, the greater your chance for professional fulfillment if you make compatible career choices.

Source: Adapted with permission from Thomas E. McKee and W. Edward Stead, "Managing the Professional Accountant," *Journal of Accountancy,* July 1988, p. 84.

which different individuals pass.[4] Furthermore, many may find themselves "looping back" through earlier stages whenever major career changes are necessary. The point is that people's career needs are likely to change over their lifetime. Therefore, self-assessment (and career planning) should be a continuous process, not a one-time activity. Organizations also should probably rethink their human resource activities in light of the fact that people in the organization will go through career stages.[5] Figure 18–1 breaks down organizational planning into components that are relevant to individuals at each career stage. The figure also shows the sorts of activities that can help match individual and organizational needs at each stage.

Career Anchors

Although individual needs may change over the career span, Edgar Schein believes that there are also stable aspects to one's career. Schein discusses **career anchors**—distinctive patterns of self-perceived talents, motives, and values—which he believes guide career decision making throughout each person's life. According to Schein, when making career choices, each person will consistently seek to implement his or her own career anchor. Schein identified five distinct anchors, which he claims can probably be found in all occupations: (1) technical/functional competence, (2) managerial competence, (3) security and stability, (4) creativity, and (5) autonomy and independence.[6] The questionnaire in Table 18–1 can be used to identify an individual's career anchor.

Career Plateaus

Another distinctive characteristic of individual careers is the **career plateau,** the point in one's career where the likelihood of further promotion becomes very low.[7] Because there are in fact fewer positions as one moves up the hierarchical pyramid in an organization, one's chances for continued promotion eventually decrease. In today's flatter organizations where promotion opportunities are limited, plateaus may be reached relatively early in one's career. Figure 18–2 shows that some plateauees (people at plateaus) are nonetheless effective (high-performing) individuals or "solid citizens." These individuals are probably the largest group in most organizations and perform the bulk of organizational work. There is often a concern that these individuals will perceive themselves as failures simply because they have ceased to move upward. And it is true that effective plateauees may be neglected by management because they are not performance problems. Solid citizens are generally overlooked for developmental programs, for example.

Protean or Spiral Careers

A number of scholars think there has been a recent shift in young people's career values. Rather than seeking promotions (an indicator of career success from the organization's point of view), many people may be more interested in their own "psychological success," which comes from careers that are self-directed rather than organizationally engineered. In what is called the **protean**[8] or **spiral**[9] **career,** individuals seek their own self-development and follow career paths that meet highly individualistic personal goals. In many cases, these careers bear little resemblance to the traditional linear progression that prevailed in most companies in the past. There may be growth within a single discipline (functional specialization); rotational, lateral movement while remaining at a single location (local generalist); career development within a specific job position (job specialist); or even moves out into the community or to another organization. Many organizations such as Monsanto find that a more individualized approach to career paths fits well in a leaner organization that has slower overall corporate growth.

Organizational Career Management and Development

Career management is the process through which an organization selects, assesses, assigns, and develops employees to provide a pool of qualified people to meet its needs. Responsibility for a career management program is usually assigned to the human resource department (HRD). Establishing a direct link between HRD activities

Figure 18–1
Human Resource Planning and Career Stages

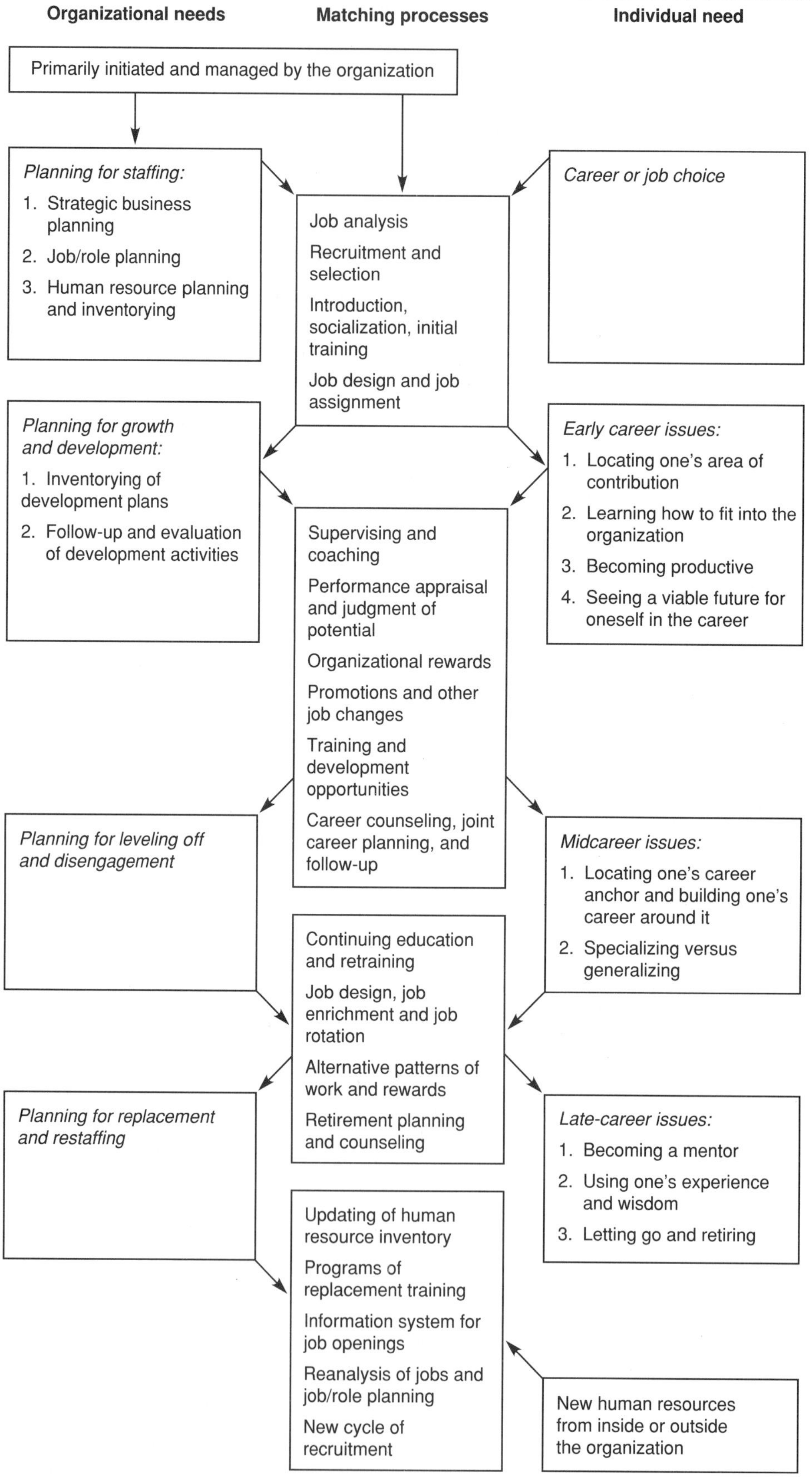

Organizational needs	Matching processes	Individual need
Primarily initiated and managed by the organization		
Planning for staffing: 1. Strategic business planning 2. Job/role planning 3. Human resource planning and inventorying	Job analysis Recruitment and selection Introduction, socialization, initial training Job design and job assignment	*Career or job choice*
Planning for growth and development: 1. Inventorying of development plans 2. Follow-up and evaluation of development activities	Supervising and coaching Performance appraisal and judgment of potential Organizational rewards Promotions and other job changes Training and development opportunities Career counseling, joint career planning, and follow-up	*Early career issues:* 1. Locating one's area of contribution 2. Learning how to fit into the organization 3. Becoming productive 4. Seeing a viable future for oneself in the career
Planning for leveling off and disengagement	Continuing education and retraining Job design, job enrichment and job rotation Alternative patterns of work and rewards Retirement planning and counseling	*Midcareer issues:* 1. Locating one's career anchor and building one's career around it 2. Specializing versus generalizing
Planning for replacement and restaffing	Updating of human resource inventory Programs of replacement training Information system for job openings Reanalysis of jobs and job/role planning New cycle of recruitment	*Late-career issues:* 1. Becoming a mentor 2. Using one's experience and wisdom 3. Letting go and retiring
		New human resources from inside or outside the organization

Source: Adopted with permission from E. H. Schein, *Career Dynamics: Matching Individual and Organizational Needs* (Reading, Mass.: Addison-Wesley Publishing, 1978), p. 201.

Figure 18–2
A Model of Managerial Careers

Current Performance	Likelihood of Future Promotion: Low	Likelihood of Future Promotion: High
High	Solid Citizens (effective plateauees)	Stars
Low	Deadwood (ineffective plateauees)	Learners (comers)

Source: Adapted with permission from Thomas P. Ference, James A. F. Stoner, and E. Kirby Warren, "Managing the Career Plateau," *Academy of Management Review,* October 1977, p. 603.

and the organization's strategic plan is crucial to a successful career management program; it makes little sense to develop careers that no longer fit organizational objectives because business strategy has changed.

Human Resource Planning

Human resource planning (HRP) is the process used by organizations (1) to analyze business plans to establish future human resource needs, (2) to estimate future human resource availabilities, (3) to reconcile needs and availabilities to identify any gaps between the two, and (4) to form action plans (e.g., career management activities) to deal with any such gaps. In essence, HRP is the means of identifying future job openings.

Developing Career Paths

Once an organization has a good idea of the nature of future human resource needs, attention may be directed toward the development of internal career paths. **Career paths** set forth the sequence of job changes that an employee may pursue to attain a given target position. Formalized career paths can communicate to employees the specific types of skills and work experience needed to progress along a given path. They also help employees identify possible role models (or mentors) among persons holding positions on the path. In addition, development of a rational sequence of job assignments can reduce the time necessary to acquire the skills needed on a given target job.[10]

Paths may be developed either descriptively, to reflect the actual routes employees have been pursuing, or normatively, to reflect routes that appear to be desirable from a developmental standpoint. In either case, it is probably wise to begin with a description of existing paths. Often, new and better routes are suggested by the patterns that emerge from a study of historical movements. Transition probability matrixes offer a relatively easy way to summarize historical movement patterns.

Identifying Internal Candidates

There are several ways to identify people in the organization who could fill job vacancies. One way is *job posting.* In this approach, individuals nominate themselves for openings that the organization publicizes—usually by posting a job description in a visible location. The Automobile Club of Southern California uses the job posting method, but has an electronic network that links computer terminals throughout the organization. A current listing of all job vacancies anywhere in the club is sent out to all offices over the network. A nice feature of job posting is that it allows the organization to identify persons who want to make job changes. Thus it can facilitate career planning discussions with those individuals who seem most interested in job movement.

Assessment centers (ACs) are another method used to identify potential managerial candidates early in their careers. Groups of AC participants engage in a variety of individual and group exercises that simulate important aspects of management jobs. Expert observers rate each participant's performance in the AC, and those receiving high scores are typically targeted for "fast-track" career development.

A third method, the **human resource information system (HRIS),** may also be used to identify potential candidates. An HRIS is a computerized database that includes current information about each employee such as skills, abilities, experience, education, previous positions held, training completed, and career interest. The HRIS is used as a cross-matching tool. Whenever job openings occur, job requirements are entered into a program that sorts the data to identify all employees who have the required skills. A presumed advantage of HRIS identification of candidates would be a wider search for candidates throughout the organization. Of course, employee data must be continually updated to remain useful.

Role of the Supervisor in Career Management

In the past, most organizations held individuals primarily responsible for planning and pursuing their own career development. Other than fast-track stars identified through assessment centers or other early-selection devices, employees were often left on their own to figure out suitable action plans for career goal attainment. There were two practical problems with this view. First, organizations tended to control information on the strategic direction of the firm, making it difficult for individuals to know where future job openings might occur. Second, in many cases organizations maintained tight control over the nomination process for job openings (e.g., through AC or HRIS identification of those who would be considered). Thus it was often difficult for individuals to assess the realism of their career plans.

Though these problems have not disappeared, organizations now appear to be assigning increased responsibility to supervisors for the development of their subordinates, perhaps hoping that supervisors can act as mediators between individual and organizational career goals.

Figure 18–3 sets forth a variety of key roles that a supervisor might play in the career development of subordinates, including coach, appraiser, adviser, and referral agent. In some organizations, it is left up to supervisors to decide which roles will be played. In others, subordinate development is an explicit part of the performance appraisal process. Whether responsibility is informally or formally assigned, however, most supervisors themselves need training if they are to play an effective role in career management. And, despite any training they might receive, supervisors will vary in their ability and willingness to provide effective career guidance to subordinates.

Figure 18–3
Possible Roles of Supervisor in Subordinate Career Development

Coach	Appraiser	Adviser	Agent
Listens	Gives feedback	Generates options	Links employee to resources/people
Clarifies	Clarifies standards	Helps set goals	Consults on action plan
Probes	Clarifies job responsibilities	Recommends/advises	
Defines concerns			

Source: Adapted with permission from C. Farren, B. L. Kaye, and Z. B. Liebowitz, *Designing Career Development Systems* (San Francisco: Jossey-Bass, 1986), p. 126.

Mentoring

Another method for employee development and continuous improvement is **mentoring,** which is either formally implemented or informally encouraged by organizations to promote more effective career management. The term *mentor* characterizes a person who advises, counsels, or helps younger individuals within the organization. (In Greek mythology, *mentor* refers to the wise and trusted counselor). The mentor role is typically adopted by midcareer managers who work to develop the talents and skills of either their own subordinates or recognized fast-track candidates elsewhere in the organization. This one-on-one relationship can foster beneficial outcomes for both individuals and organizations.

Recent research into the mentoring relationship has identified nine primary functions of mentoring.[10] These functions are grouped into two clusters of career functions and psychological functions. Career functions emphasize providing developmental experiences on the job whereas psychological functions clarify the employee's self-identity and feelings of competence. The five career functions of mentoring include sponsorship, exposure and visibility, coaching, protection, and ensuring challenging job assignments. The four psychological functions include role modeling, acceptance and confrontation, counseling, and friendship.

Protégés benefit from individual counseling and guidance; they develop deeper insight into company norms, values, and goals; and come to know expanded networks of contacts inside the organization. They experience the influence of a good role model and are likely to be offered advanced developmental opportunities through the mentor. The organization realizes the benefits of on-the-job training without tremendous additional costs and also reinforces its commitment to the career management program. Mentors can benefit from an association with a protégé by enhancing their own skills and expanding their technical knowledge. A mentoring relationship also allows the mentor to demonstrate expertise and knowledge that may have been taken for granted. Thus mentoring can become a developmental program for middle managers and can help keep midcareer solid citizens motivated.

Other Methods of Developing Individuals

Many organizations have on- and off-the-job training programs to assist in the development of work-related skills and encourage personal growth. Kaye categorizes such programs as (1) training and education related to specific topics; (2) experienced-based training, including special projects, job rotation, and other chances for new experiences; and (3) support-guided development that allows for the sharing of experiences among individuals and groups.[12]

There are numerous industry examples of each type of program. Tuition reimbursement is common at many companies such as IBM and Digital Equipment Corporation and at many public agencies as well. Frito-Lay broadens the background of its industrial engineers (IEs) by implementing a "methods improvements program" throughout different functions of the company. In this program, IEs can be assigned (temporarily) to a staff department, sales, or marketing, for example. The IEs gain cross-functional experience and also apply their skills to the functions they visit, often coming up with productivity savings for the company. This is an unusual in-house training program that's working.[13] Hitachi Ltd. has as its general principle of education a defined responsibility of its managers (considered the most important of many responsibilities) to educate, lead, and develop subordinates. The manager is expected to take on the role of mentor.[14]

Managing Career Development and Change: Issues for the 1990s

The past decade has been a period of unprecedented change in labor markets as well as in the economy at large. These changes in turn have led to several new challenges in career development that face individuals and organizations in the 1990s.

Fast-Track Programs for Women and Minorities

As we have seen in Modules 1 and 4, it is now estimated that minorities and women will constitute 92 percent of all new entrants to the labor force by the year 2000. Currently, white males represent only 44 percent of the existing work force.[15] In the past, equal employment opportunity and affirmative action legislation spurred efforts to speed the hiring and development of so-called *protected groups.* Today, labor market realities increasingly dictate the need to draw upon members of these groups, as they have already become the new work force majority. Issues of fairness and equal treatment have given way to concerns about managing diversity. It is now recognized, at least in theory, that different groups probably require different treatment; women and minorities cannot be expected to fit easily into an organization structured primarily around the needs and values of white males. Stresses were already apparent in the 1980s when the *mommy track* was proposed as an alternative career track for women with family responsibilities who wanted to work less than full-time, yet not be relegated to the dead-end jobs and limited careers that are usually associated with part-time employment.

Unfortunately, many old stereotypes persist regarding ''appropriate'' work roles for women and minorities, even among those group members themselves. Perhaps as a result, many efforts to speed their movement into management have been unsuccessful. Some speak of a **glass ceiling** phenomenon whereby women and minorities seem able to move upward just so high in management, plateauing before they reach senior levels. Although the causes of a glass ceiling are not entirely understood, it is becoming clear that training and development for these individuals will have to take their special needs into account.

Dual-Career Couples

A second continuing labor market trend, dual-career families are expected to constitute 75 percent of all families by the year 2000.[16] Dual careers certainly complicate individual career decision making; career plans become codetermined between spouses, limiting the individual's freedom to accept some career opportunities. Organizations also find career management more complex. Geographic transfers, as a way to develop managers, may become a thing of the past. On the other hand, organizations may need to relocate couples rather than individuals and to provide job search assistance for a trailing spouse. An often overlooked impact is the need to consider nepotism policies. Should spouses be allowed to supervise each other? Should any particular job or department assignments (e.g., a position handling sensitive personnel records) be prohibited to couples? Should the organization either encourage or discourage the hiring of spouses? All these questions need to be addressed when managing dual-career couples.

The Aging Labor Force

Mid- and late-career stage issues will arise with increasing frequency as the 20-year cohort of postwar baby boomers gradually moves toward disengagement. Initially there may be concern over midlife crises. Some individuals go through an intense period of questioning their chosen career direction as they begin to sense that time is running out for major career changes. Organizations that wish to help with this problem may prefer to handle it through one-on-one career counseling. A variety of other organizational programs may help relieve midcareer stress, including (1) special career path options that allow individuals to explore new career directions within their existing organization, (2) enlargement or enrichment of the current job, perhaps through the addition of a mentoring role, and (3) sometimes even outplacement assistance if the desire to explore new career options cannot be met internally.

A different set of issues arise in late career as individuals approach retirement. The process of planning for retirement should begin in early career stages although its importance is usually not recognized by young people. Investment counseling, profit sharing, and deferred compensation plans may be offered in the benefits package, for example, but the younger employees' need for income usually does not lend itself to retirement planning. The problem of getting employees to think about retirement before it occurs has become more severe since the abolition of mandatory retirement. Nowadays there is no automatic trigger, such as universal retirement at age 65, to tell employees when it is time to begin planning. Also, individual retiree needs are more variable since the age spectrum for retirement can range all the way from 50 years of age (with early retirement incentives) to 75 years or older. Some companies have instigated preretirement seminars that address the economic, social, and psychological questions associated with this career transition. Companies can help employees through the transition stage by offering flexible work schedules that allow the individual more leisure time to develop other interests while maintaining the link to work. Longer vacation periods associated with years on the job can also allow the employee time to establish outside ties with peers and to reestablish relationships with friends. Innovative preretirement programs that begin well in advance of retirement can increase the satisfaction of retirement for employees and can establish feelings of goodwill toward the organization.

It is also important to recognize that, physiologically, people age at different rates. Counter to common negative stereotypes, many performance areas only reach their height during the later stages of an individual's career. A limited number of physical abilities—such as visual acuity, response time, or stamina—may decline with age and thereby limit certain physically strenuous job assignments. But it is a mistake to assume that older workers are unable to acquire new skills. In fact, most learning difficulties stem from a lack of motivation to learn, not from the lack of ability. Career plateauing may occur because older workers have not been given or offered the necessary training and development opportunities to keep them vital, involved workers late in their careers. An individual's late career development is dependent on good career planning in the early years and a life-long career development perspective.

Recently a number of companies such as Pacific Telephone, Uniroyal, and Chrysler have offered accelerated voluntary retirement programs, sometimes called the *golden handshake.* The purpose of early retirement programs varies. In some cases, they are undertaken to free up blocked career channels for younger workers. In other cases, they are seen as a way to handle a projected labor surplus or as a way to realize labor cost savings. Because such programs are necessarily voluntary, it is also wise to recognize that key players may be lost, and deadwood may decide to stay. Alternatives to early retirement that may better suit particular individual career needs include phased retirement, job sharing, telecommuting, temporary or special project assignments, leaves of absence, and sabbaticals.

At the end of this module, Activity 18–3 (based on a case study, ''Planning for Disengagement'') illustrates many of the issues involved in the final career transition to retirement as well as issues and concerns in effectively managing the careers of older workers and implementing work force reductions.

Downsizing

Another organizational reality of the 1990s is **downsizing,** the term currently in vogue for permanent layoffs and reductions in force (RIF). During the 1980s, an estimated 600,000 managers lost their jobs as a result of organizational restructuring, reengineering, delayering, or economic downtrends. Divestitures and mergers also often result in job loss. A common organizational response to the individual career trauma of such involuntary job losses is some type of outplacement counseling service. These programs offer job search training, skills assessment, résumé writing, and even salary-negotiation services. Perhaps equally important, but often overlooked when a firm downsizes, is clear and frequent communication with employees whom the organization wishes to retain. These individuals need timely and accurate information regarding continued career prospects with the leaner organization.

Downsizing is usually initiated as an organizational response to competitive pressure. In the 90s, many organizations have sought to pare down the size of their permanent (''core'') work force by creating a buffer of contingent (part-time or temporary) workers or even outsourcing some staff functions to specialized consulting firms. As organizations' commitment to permanent employment falls, individuals are increasingly recognizing the need to control their own career destiny. This is leading to what some call the **career-resilient work force,** employees who are continually ready to reinvent themselves to keep pace with change. In this view, workers act more like external vendors than traditional employees, taking complete responsibility for their own career management.

Managing Work Force Diversity: Glass Ceiling Initiatives

Organizational concern over premature career plateaus among women and minorities has gone beyond the desire to more efficiently tap the available labor pool.[17] In many firms, bringing these groups into upper management is seen as a strategic business imperative.[18] As Sara Lee CEO John Bryan sees the problem, many of his company's products are designed specifically for women (Hanes panty hose, for example). Thus, in his view, it makes little sense to have "a bunch of old men sitting around trying to figure out the business."[19]

Various reasons for the glass ceiling have been proposed. Some argue that it is because selection at the top rung of the corporate ladder is so highly subjective; *all* candidates are highly qualified, therefore selection partly becomes a matter of interpersonal fit, or level of trust and comfort, with men at the very top still not too comfortable with people unlike themselves in positions of maximum responsibility. Others claim it is because women and minorities are (perhaps in mistaken benevolence) given less challenging developmental assignments on their way to the top, more often being offered staff positions in public relations or human resources, rather than positions in line productions or start-ups and entrepreneurial ventures. Still others argue that what is lacking is the informal mentoring of the "old boys club" where those "in the loop" share important information about organizational politics or upcoming promotion opportunities that are not generally known until candidates have already been chosen. Finally, the higher voluntary turnover rate of fast-track minority and female candidates can be attributed to subtle messages transmitted by the organization's culture that underrepresented groups in certain firms never truly feel accepted by their white male colleagues (though some minority and female candidates are bid away by competing firms under quota pressures).

Organizations have addressed these problems in a variety of ways. Most try to speed promotion from within by mandating diversity or cultural sensitivity training for all managers, adding the attainment of quantified affirmative action results to supervisors' performance goals, setting up formal mentoring programs, encouraging the formation of within-group support networks, or putting more thought into the career pathing of target candidates. A few organizations such as Burger King and Sara Lee have attempted to jump start their programs with external hiring of minority and female candidates at the highest organizational levels.[20] Unfortunately, the relative effectiveness of these various approaches is as yet unknown.

Careers in a Global Environment

Only a decade ago, managers sent overseas on assignment may have been perceived as having been sent into exile, with their careers on hold—if not in decline. Today, an international assignment is more likely to be viewed as a step on the fast track to the top. This change in perspective can be attributed to the emergence of a clearly global business environment.[21]

The new need to develop highly qualified multinational managers has led to several new principles of international career management: (1) Selection should be made from among currently successful employees whose careers will benefit and who are likely to contribute gained knowledge and experience to the organization. (2) Individuals selected should be developed specifically for international assignment. Predeparture training should focus not only on the technical expertise necessary to complete the assignment, but also on in-depth training for both the employee and family regarding cross-cultural differences addressing social life, political atmosphere, religious differences, and language barriers. (3) Career planning is essential to show how the international route will expand the potential of the employee. Presenting the big picture of where the expatriate cycle will continue beyond the actual assignment is critical to success and can relieve feelings of abandonment. (4) Ongoing communication with expatriates is necessary to keep the individual up-to-date on home country policies, projects, plans, and staffing changes. This keeps the manager in tune with the organization and aids in reentry. (5) Reentry jobs should use the skills and experience the individual has acquired during the assignment. This can be done by assigning previous expatriates as mentors or by providing a forum for sharing the experience. (6) Training for home country managers should be an ongoing function. This training can bring the awareness of the value of international experience and the ways it can be utilized within the organization.[22]

Of course, many of these principles have yet to be implemented by organizations. Perhaps as a consequence, expatriate failure rates of up to 40 percent have been reported.[23] It is therefore recommended that people interested in international experience go through several self-evaluation and planning steps to make sure their international assignment will not harm their overall career objectives. Questions you should ask yourself here include[24]

- Are you flexible?
- Can you adjust to change?
- Do you easily become frustrated by things that aren't done the way you're accustomed to having them done?
- Do you work well with people of other cultures?
- Are your spouse and family supportive of your decision to pursue an international assignment?

Before you commit to any foreign assignment, spend time studying its geographic areas and culture to be sure the area fits your own character and personality.

Summary

This module introduces the topic of career planning and development. We discussed the steps an individual goes through in career planning and the sorts of activities organizations can engage in to assist individuals in attaining their career goals. Several management techniques to manage the flow of individuals through positions in the organization are described, and a number of emerging career development issues are discussed, including anticipated changes in the labor market, competitive pressures to downsize organizations, and efforts to effectively manage a global changing enterprise.

Managing career planning and development enhances individual and organizational effectiveness. The ongoing effort by the individual and the organization to develop human resources is a way to enhance the firm's continuous improvement and competitiveness. Yet, managing the human development process in organizational settings is a complex task that requires multiple resources and managing change know-how. We argued that managers are charged with the facilitation of career planning and development processes. The changing nature of the workplace provides an opportunity to integrate our knowledge of human behavior and the understanding of organizational change and development. As this section and module illustrated, integrating change at the individual, team, and organizational levels is one of the key challenges of this decade. The roadmaps provided in this book are likely to help managers understand better and deal more effectively with the management of change.

Study Questions

1. "Individuals should be primarily responsible for developing their own careers." Do you agree? Why?
2. Describe the five basic steps in the career planning process. Which step do you think is likely to be the most difficult for individuals to implement? Why?

3. Discuss ways that organizations can assist individuals in pursuing career goals. Which of these may also enhance organizational effectiveness? How?
4. Describe the five major career stages that individuals go through, and identify organizational programs that would be important for persons in each stage.
5. What can organizations do to prevent employee obsolescence or ineffective plateauing?
6. Describe several different methods that organizations can use to identify internal candidates for job vacancies. Discuss the advantages and disadvantages of each method, from both individual and organizational points of view.
7. What career management components should an organization have in place before implementing a major downsizing effort?
8. Discuss the five different roles that a supervisor might adopt in career development of subordinates. Are there any conflicts among these roles or between these roles and other roles that supervisors must adopt with subordinates? How might conflict be minimized?
9. Should mentoring be an informal program that is totally voluntary, or should the organization try to formally assign mentors to protégés? Why?
10. Discuss the relationship between managing change, career development, and continuous improvement.

Endnotes

1. G. T. Milkovich and J. W. Boudreau, *Personnel/Human Resource Management,* 5th ed. (Plano, Tex.: Business Publications, 1988).

2. V. G. Zunker, *Career Counseling: Applied Concepts of Life Planning* (Monterey, Calif.: Brooks/Cole, 1990), p. 162; C. Farren, B. Kaye, and Z. Liebowitz, *Designing Career Development Systems* (San Francisco: Jossey-Bass, 1986).

3. D. E. Super, J. Crites, R. Hummel, H. Moser, P. Overstreet, and C. Warnath, *Vocational Development: A Framework for Research* (New York: Teachers College Press, Columbia University, Bureau of Publications, 1957).

4. W. F. Cascio, *Managing Human Resources,* 4th ed. (New York: McGraw-Hill, 1995), p. 310.

5. E. H. Schein, *Career Dynamics: Matching Individual and Organizational Needs* (Reading, Mass.: Addison-Wesley, 1978).

6. Ibid.

7. T. P. Ference, J. A. F. Stoner, and E. K. Warren, ''Managing the Career Plateau,'' *Academy of Management Review,* October 1977, pp. 602–12; D. Feldman, *Managing Careers in Organizations* (Glenview, Ill.: Scott, Foresman, 1988); J. Greenhaus, *Career Management* (Hinsdale, Ill.: CBS College Publishing, Dryden Press, 1987).

8. D. T. Hall and Judith Richter, ''Career Gridlock: Baby Boomers Hit the Wall,'' *Academy of Management Executive* 4, no. 3 (1990), pp. 7–21.

9. Michael J. Driver, ''Career Concepts and Career Management in Organizations,'' in *Behavioral Problems in Organizations,* ed. G. Cooper (Englewood Cliffs, N.J.: Prentice-Hall, 1979), pp. 79–140; E. Burack and N. Mathys, *Career Management in Organizations: A Practical Human Resource Planning Approach.* (New York: Brace–Park Press, 1980).

10. M. London and S. A. Stumpf, *Managing Careers* (Reading, Mass.: Addison-Wesley, 1982), pp. 139–41.

11. K. Kram, *Mentoring at Work: Developmental Relationships in Organizational Life* (Glenview, Ill.: Scott, Foresman, 1985).

12. B. Kaye, ''Career Development Puts Training in Its Place,'' *Personnel Journal* 62, no. 2 (1983), pp. 132–37.

13. B. Paton, ''Managing Your IE Career: IE Careers in Nontraditional Areas at Frito Lay,'' *Industrial Engineering* 20, no. 5 (1988), pp. 20–23.

14. T. Toyoshige, ''Developing Managers in the Hitachi Institute of Management Development,'' *Journal of Management Development* 8, no. 4 (1989), pp. 12–23.

15. *U.S. Department of Labor Statistics, 1988–1989* (Washington, D.C.: U.S. Government Printing Office).

16. R. W. Goddard, ''Work Force 2000,'' *Personnel Journal,* February 1989, pp. 65–71.

17. G. N. Powell, *Women and Men in Management* (Newbury Park, Calif.: Sage, 1993).

18. See, for example, G. N. Powell and D. A. Butterfield, ''Investigating the 'Glass Ceiling' Phenomenon: An Empirical Study of Actual Promotions to Top Management,'' *The Academy of Management Journal* 37, no. 1 (1994), pp. 68–87; Y. Shenhav, ''Entrance of Black Women into Managerial Positions in Scientific and Engineering Occupations,'' *The Academy of Management Journal* 35 (1992), pp. 889–901; and L. K. Stroh, J. M. Brett, and A. H. Reilly, ''All the Right Stuff: A Comparison of Female and Male Managers' Career Progression,'' *Journal of Applied Psychology* 77 (1992), pp. 251–60.

19. R. Sharpe, ''Women Make Strides, but Men Stay Firmly in Top Company Jobs,'' *The Wall Street Journal,* March 29, 1994, pp. A-1, A-8.

20. Ibid., p. A-8.

21. See, for example, K. B. O'Hara, T. A. Beehr, and S. M. Colarelli, ''Organizational Centrality: A Third Dimension of Career Development,'' *Journal of Applied Behavioral Science* 30, no. 2 (1994), pp. 198–216.

22. N. J. Adler, *International Dimensions of Organizational Behavior,* 2d ed. (Boston: PWS–Kent, 1991); J. Callahan, ''Preparing the New Global Manager,'' *Training and Development Journal,* March 1989, p. 29.

23. T. Howard ''Are You Ready for an International Career?'' *The Career Forum* 14, no. 1 (1994), pp. 23–25.

24. Ibid, p. 24.

Activity 18–2: Career Planning

Objectives:

a. To actively engage in self-assessment.
b. To demonstrate the steps in individual career planning.

Task 1 (Homework):

a. Complete the accompanying "Career Planning Questionnaire."
b. Prepare the following questions for classroom discussion.
   1. Why did you choose your major course of study?
   2. How do the five goals you set in Part III of the Career Planning Questionnaire take account of your own personal skills, characteristics, strengths, weaknesses, and values as identified in Part I?
   3. Are there any real-world constraints you know of that might make it difficult for you to reach any of these goals? What are they?

Task 2 (Classroom):

Members are to join their teams. Team members are to take turns presenting their five-year career goals to the rest of the team. Each team member should explain how the goals he or she has set take account of personal skills, values, strengths, and weaknesses.

After each team member explains his or her goals, remaining team members will provide a reality check and feedback on (1) how clear, specific, relevant, and measurable the goals appear to be, (2) how well the goals seem to fit the person, and (3) how likely the goals are to be attained within five years.

Task 3 (Homework):

Following team reality check and feedback, each team member should reexamine and possibly revise his or her career goals.

Each team member should prepare a detailed action plan for each (revised) goal, with a time line, for the next five years. Identify what you need to do each year to ultimately achieve the goal. Indicate which resources can be employed to help in goal attainment. Your plan is due at the beginning of the next class.

Name ______________________________ Date ______________

Career Planning Questionnaire

I. Self-Assessment Inventory

A. Consider the following two lists of skills and personal characteristics. Read them carefully and rate yourself on the extent to which you currently possess each skill or characteristic: (H) to a high degree, (M) to a medium degree, (L) to a low degree.

(1) Transferable skills (those useful in a variety of settings/career roles)

__ Remembering/memory
__ Reading comprehension
__ Writing reports
__ Conducting meetings
__ Listening
__ Group presentations
__ Planning
__ Working with numbers/preparing budgets
__ Solving problems
__ Researching
__ Delegating
__ Managing people

Other unique transferable skills that I possess:

____

____

(2) Management skills/characteristics (those needed in managerial roles)

__ Initiative (a self-starter)
__ Flexibility
__ Interpersonal skills
__ Reliability
__ Enthusiasm
__ Diplomacy
__ Self-confidence
__ Resourcefulness
__ Ability to handle stress
__ Ability to concentrate
__ Assertiveness
__ Ability to work well on teams

Other unique management skills that I possess:

____

____

B. List five personal strengths and five personal weaknesses:

______________________________ ______________________________

______________________________ ______________________________

______________________________ ______________________________

______________________________ ______________________________

______________________________ ______________________________

C. Consider the following list of individual needs or values. How important would it be for you to fulfill each of these needs at work? Rank order the list from most important (1) to least important (11).

__ Leadership—to organize and control others
__ Expertise—to be an authority on a special subject
__ Prestige—to be well known; to receive recognition and awards
__ Service—to bring about the satisfaction of others
__ Wealth—to earn lots of money
__ Independence—to exercise freedom of thought and action
__ Affection—to be well-liked by coworkers, family, and friends
__ Security—to be free from worry about keeping one's job
__ Self-realization—to be able to realize one's full potential
__ Duty—to become dedicated to values, ideas, and principles
__ Pleasure—to be happy and content

D. Briefly list or explain (in writing) any demands you have in terms of salary, geographic location, or any other job or organizational characteristics.

____

____

____

* Questionnaire developed by Frances M. Parrish especially for this volume.

II. Checklist of Career Exploration Activities

1. Can you name at least three fields of employment for which you might be considered? List them.

___

___

___

2. Can you name at least 10 position titles that might be available to someone with your background and skills? List them.

___

___

___

3. Can you name any sources of information that could help you discover potential employers in a particular field or geographical area? List them.

___

___

___

4. Have you talked to people who are employed in your field of interest with the purpose of learning more about what they do? How many people have you talked to?

III. Goal Setting

Consider your responses to sections I and II.

List five goals that you want to achieve in your career or personal life during the next five years. These goals can include the acquisition of specifically needed skills or the additional exploration of career opportunities. They can also include particular job search and job choice objectives.

___

___

___

___

___

___

___

Activity 18–3: Managing the Aging Labor Force

Objectives:

a. To illustrate the wide range of individual differences in the career needs of older workers.

b. To gain an understanding of the organizational consequences of early retirement programs.

Task 1 (Homework):

Read the case "Planning for Disengagement" that follows and prepare answers to these questions for class discussion:

a. Evaluate MI's early retirement program. Which organizational objectives does it serve? What problems might it create?

b. What should Chris say to Will Fiorito? What components of a career management system might have helped MI deal with the loss of valued employees?

c. Speculate on the causes of Bill Collins's performance problem. How should Chris handle this interview?

d. Are there any alternatives to early retirement for Al Cope. What organizational programs might have improved his physical and financial problems?

Case Study: Planning for Disengagement at Motor Industries

What a day! Chris Barger sat back and reflected on the diverse array of career management problems three employees had presented to the human resource department that afternoon. Just two months ago, Motor Industries (MI) had decided to institute an early retirement program as a first step to reduce its work force. The downsizing was deemed necessary in light of MI's declining market share and the general belt tightening going on in the industry. Corporate headquarters had announced the program, which granted all employees aged 50 or over the opportunity to retire with full pension and health care benefits as long as the early retirement option was exercised within 60 days. Now Chris was inundated by employee questions about what the company's offer really meant for them.

The first person to appear was Will Fiorito, 53-year-old head of the design planning unit. Will was an outstanding manager—in fact, the very mainstay of the new design project initiative that MI hoped would restore its place in the product market. But today Will shared a personal dream. He had always wanted to start up his own small design shop, and now he thought he could probably fund it with the retirement incentive MI was offering.

The next appointment had been scheduled weeks ago. Bill Collins, 50 years old, had been a continuing performance problem for his supervisor. A blue-collar worker with 32 years of service to MI, Bill was having trouble adjusting to the company's new emphasis on participative management. He was a major obstacle to progress in quality circle group meetings, continually voicing his conviction that any process changes would lead to "speed-ups" and that all proposed innovations had already been tried but found lacking. Bill's supervisor had practically insisted that he come in and find out about the early retirement program. As Bill saw it, his supervisor was trying to push him out the door. Most of Bill's questions centered not around the early retirement program, but around his legal rights to keep his job. He also seemed interested in finding out what outplacement services MI offered and whether outplacement benefits for early retirees differed from the benefits of those who were laid off or fired.

After Bill's interview, Chris noticed that Al Cope was sitting in the outer office. Al was another 32-year veteran of MI. Al's career had been far from spectacular, but he was a hard-working, loyal employee whose performance had always been acceptable. He's the textbook example of a "solid citizen," thought Chris, who knew that Al was definitely plateaued in his current position as a marketing manager.

When Al sat down in Chris's office and started asking about early retirement, Chris was surprised. Al had always seemed so strongly committed to MI, and he certainly didn't seem ready, at age 54, to head for Sun City and the golf course circuit. But Chris soon learned that Al was having health problems: two minor hearts attacks in the past two years plus an increasing cholesterol count. His doctor was recommending that he make strong efforts to reduce all sources of stress, including pressures at work.

Al's questions revolved around the financial issues—"Do I have enough pension income to retire now? What can I expect from social security? Is my health insurance guaranteed even if there's a takeover?" Chris answered these concerns, but felt certain that there was something else Al needed beyond answers about benefits. Al seemed very unhappy with the idea that he must now sever all day-to-day ties with MI. Wasn't there some way Al could continue to work for MI, even though he had to cut back? The finality of retirement just didn't seem to fit this case.

Activity 18–4: Analyzing the Team Climate

A large block of time is needed for this exercise. This should be the most interesting and important learning experience in the course. One or two evenings could be valuably devoted to it.

Objectives:

a. To apply the team building approach to your own work team.
b. To generate the data for completion of the team term paper on team development required in Task 4, Appendix A. If your team is following Appendix B, this exercise will provide you with information to add to your journal data when you write up your individual report.

Task 1:

a. Each team member, working alone, is to complete the Climate Attribute Scales that follow prior to coming to the team meeting, which is to be held outside of class.
b. Review your journal analysis of how course concepts and team skills have applied to your team's interactions as the team evolved during the course. Be prepared to present your observations at the team meeting.

Task 2:

Team members are to meet. The climate attributes are to be discussed one at a time. Each member will report the rating made prior to the meeting. The differences in ratings will be discussed to determine why members are perceiving the team interactions differently. A group consensus rating will be made for each scale, after thorough discussion. The group consensus rating sheet will be included and discussed in the final team development report as required in Task 4, Appendix A.

The rating sheet given here is only a device to help introduce this session. Now make an analysis of how course concepts and theories applied to your team as it evolved during the course. How did team skills develop? Having reviewed your journals before the meeting, a synergistic exchange should result in added insight into these processes. One approach that might be used is for members to call out in rapid succession all possible topics the group might want to discuss. One member should list these for the group. After members have exhausted ideas for the list, the items can be taken up one at a time for discussion. Conclude this portion of the session by answering the following: If this team were to work together in the future, how could it improve its effectiveness? Be specific.

Feedback Session (an Optional Activity): Teams are to give each member feedback as to what they perceive to be the individual's strengths and the areas where the individual could be stronger in team interactions. If the team members are supportive of one another and an openness-to-learning, concern-for-growth atmosphere exists, this can be a valuable experience. Knowing what impact one is having on others and how one is coming across is important in one's effectiveness. But the atmosphere must be right so that the individuals hear what others say without becoming defensive. As we have seen throughout this course, being able to receive feedback from one's superiors, peers, and subordinates is widely advocated as an area for improved effectiveness for managers. Feedback sessions are one of the best sources of data for your team paper. But remember, the team feedback is optional—only the team can decide if it wishes to complete it. No individual should be pressured. If an individual decides not to participate in this portion of the exercise, he or she should not do so.

Task 3:

Those following Appendix A, Task 4, are to complete the team paper on Team Development and submit it. Those following Appendix B are to complete the Individual Term Paper and submit it. (*Caution:* There is a need for originality in writing individual papers on the application of course concepts to the development of your team. In Task 2, your team synergistically generated considerable data on this subject. Sometimes team members agree to follow the same format in writing their individual papers. This defeats the objective for you to use your own approach in writing your paper, based on all sources of data, your team input being only one source. Since your instructor may read all papers by your team members at one sitting, it would be evident that this process was not followed if all papers were too similar in format and content.)

Task 4:

At a future date your team will have an opportunity to discuss this team building session in class and to hear the other teams discuss theirs. These sessions are best when they are spontaneous and all team members participate, so do not prepare.

Name ______________________________ Date ____________________

Climate Attribute Scales

Climate Attribute	Write an "X" on the scale indicating the degree to which the attribute characterizes your team's activities and members
	To a low degree ... *To a high degree*
Commitment to the task	0 1 2 3 4 5 6 7 8 9
Openness to learning	0 1 2 3 4 5 6 7 8 9
Retired-on-the-job attitudes	0 1 2 3 4 5 6 7 8 9
Candor and forthrightness	0 1 2 3 4 5 6 7 8 9
Attentive listening for understanding	0 1 2 3 4 5 6 7 8 9
Conviction to stand up for honestly held views	0 1 2 3 4 5 6 7 8 9t
Defensiveness or lack of trust	0 1 2 3 4 5 6 7 8 9
Being too polite, too considerate, smoothing over differences	0 1 2 3 4 5 6 7 8 9
Avoidance of conflict	0 1 2 3 4 5 6 7 8 9
Experimental, innovative	0 1 2 3 4 5 6 7 8 9
Attempts to dominate	0 1 2 3 4 5 6 7 8 9
Cutting people off	0 1 2 3 4 5 6 7 8 9
Interest in one another as people	0 1 2 3 4 5 6 7 8 9
Consideration for others	0 1 2 3 4 5 6 7 8 9
Willingness to express feelings, each person "saying where he or she is"	0 1 2 3 4 5 6 7 8 9
Expressing feelings in a way acceptable to others	0 1 2 3 4 5 6 7 8 9
Paraphrasing for better understanding	0 1 2 3 4 5 6 7 8 9
Perceptual checking	0 1 2 3 4 5 6 7 8 9
Willingness to confront differences in ideas	0 1 2 3 4 5 6 7 8 9

Climate Attribute Scales (concluded)

Write in any other attributes that you believe characterize your team:

Climate Attribute	**Write an "X" on the scale indicating the degree to which the attribute characterizes your team's activities and members**
	To a low degree — *To a high degree*
______________________	0 1 2 3 4 5 6 7 8 9
______________________	0 1 2 3 4 5 6 7 8 9
______________________	0 1 2 3 4 5 6 7 8 9

Activity 18–5: Team Feedback Discussion

Objective:

To allow each team to share its learning experience in small group dynamics with the other teams.

Task 1:

The instructor will select one team to sit in a circle in the center of the class. Members of the team will spontaneously discuss, without the benefit of notes, what types of group dynamics learning they gained from the team project exercise. Topics that could be covered include how the group dynamic concepts applied to their team, how conflict was handled, how each member felt about his or her role and the role of others in the group, how the group could be more effective if it were to continue, and anything else that seems important to the group. The team should not be interrupted by outside questions at this time.

Time for questions from the other teams should be provided when the team has completed the discussion.

Each team will have its allotted time in the circle.

Task 2:

The instructor will comment at the end of each team discussion and summarize at the end of the session.

(*Note to instructor:* Be sure to read *Instructor's Manual* before using this exercise.)

Activity 18–6: Feedback on Effectiveness of the Course and the Instructor

Objectives:

a. To reinforce learning by participants sharing what they perceive to be course strengths.

b. To provide the instructor with data for improved effectiveness.

Task 1:

The instructor is to leave the room.

Teams that have met throughout the course are each to appoint a spokesperson who will record the team's answers to the following questions:

1. What are the course's strengths? How could it be improved?
2. In what ways is the instructor effective? How could he or she be more effective?

Any member of the team can give an evaluative comment to the spokesperson. His or her identity will be protected; the spokesperson's report is the anonymous judgments of its team members. However, objectivity is urged. Some teams may conclude on their own that a comment will be included only if the majority of the members agree on its validity.
(Time: 20 minutes)

Task 2:

The instructor is to return to the classroom.

Class participants are to arrange themselves in a giant circle around the room, with team members sitting in adjacent seats. The instructor should take a seat on the circle where he or she is able to make eye contact with all class members.

The instructor calls on each spokesperson to discuss the strengths of the course. On the second round, the spokesperson should discuss how the course should be improved; on the third round, discuss the instructor's effectiveness; and on the last round, discuss how the instructor should improve. After each round, the instructor should ask if anyone other than the spokesperson wishes to comment.

The role of the instructor is to hear what the participants are saying. Periodic paraphrasing of what has been said will help ensure understanding. Avoid trying to justify or explain what has taken place in the course because participants might interpret that as a defensive response.

APPENDIXES

Appendix A Understanding Team Action: Alternative 1

Managers have become increasingly aware of the need for effectiveness in team action. This is due partially to the impact of the rapid and unpredictable change in many aspects of the environment: inflation, scarce natural resources, pollution, and augmented increases in the amount of knowledge and technology available. The future-is-now era we are in makes it increasingly difficult for managers to direct operations by meeting with subordinates and peers one at a time, because the information and methods needed are so complex they can only be shared and understood in team meetings. The coordination of team action and the handling of differences of views becomes ever more important in managing in a "turbulent environment."

In this course two aspects of team effectiveness that a manager can learn well will be studied. One of these is team skills. Management teams can learn skills of members interacting with one another in a sense somewhat similar to that of an athletic team. The skills of the management team, however, are group problem solving, goal setting, decision making, team building, communicating, resolving conflict, and so on.

The other aspect, and the one we will primarily address in this assignment, is understanding small group dynamics. Whenever two or more people come together to accomplish a task or goal, certain predictable processes occur; concepts such as norms, role differentiation, status difference, subgroupings, conflict, and cohesiveness can be used to observe and understand these behaviors, which recur in a patterned manner as the group develops. *Participants can develop and improve their awareness of these ever-changing processes of small groups; this is one objective of the course and the goal of this assignment.* Because understanding group dynamics is essential for the team handler and members who attempt to use team skills, development of these skills will be dealt with as a secondary goal.

Team Task Assignment

This assignment is one of the best means of learning about small group dynamics. Six students will be assigned to a team and given the tasks outlined in the following sections. They will be given no guidance other than what is provided in this appendix and what the instructor might offer in class. They may use any sources available to them, including the library and other professors—but not their own instructor. The team will be self-directing; members must decide what project will be done and how they are to go about it. Under these conditions student teams will make mistakes. These are a part of the learning process and will be allowed for by the instructor when grading the team papers.

Task 1: Completing a Survey

Selection of a Topic

Each team will select a student opinion survey topic that can be completed through team action. This can be on any subject of interest to your team: political opinion, campus issues, and marketing topics have all been found useful. The project should not be too complicated so that it can be kept within the time restraints of the semester or quarter course, allowing time to learn something about survey methods. It is well to *avoid* controversial issues, such as student evaluation of faculty or hot issues on campus, for two reasons: (1) Participants become so involved in the topic that they neglect the group dynamics and skills. (2) It is not possible to do a completely valid, and therefore responsible, survey under these conditions of self-direction. (Mistakes in this context are regarded as an opportunity to learn in a supportive climate.)

It is suggested that each team member generate, before the first team meeting outside of class, ideas for survey topics. At the meeting each individual should have the opportunity to present ideas, and a group decision should be reached as to the topic.

One-Page Summary

Teams are to prepare a one-page summary of the survey topic and how they plan to go about taking the survey and submit it to the instructor before proceeding. (*Note:* Teams may wish to make studies other than the survey suggested here, depending on opportunities available to them. Whatever study is chosen should fulfill the meeting requirement discussed in the next paragraph.)

Pitfalls to Avoid

Team members sometimes find at the end of the course that they do not have sufficient team dynamics data to write the team and individual papers that are required (both to be discussed later). This has been for one of two reasons. First, they become so involved in the task of completing the project that they overlook the primary purposes related to team dynamics and the secondary area of skills development. Second, they do not meet often enough to permit the team processes to occur. It is essential that meetings take place for agreement to be reached on definition of the project objectives, questionnaire development, implementation of the survey, analysis of data, report preparation, and so on. *Meeting times of one-hour blocks should be avoided* because they are not sufficient to allow six people to make good decisions. Participants should not bring guests or family members to outside meetings since they disrupt the group dynamics patterns of the team.

Task 2: Team Term Paper on the Task Project

When each team has completed its student survey, a written report will be turned in to the instructor. The report should include

1. Purpose and objectives of the survey.
2. Rationale for the study, including any relevant literature and related theory on the topic surveyed.
3. Survey and analysis methods used.
4. Findings.
5. Interpretations, implications, and conclusions.
6. If we had to do it over again, what would we do to improve the application of scientific methods to make our survey valid? Outline your procedures, step by step. (*Note:* This can be the most important part of the report. Working under the pressure generated by this self-directed team assignment, it is not possible to do a completely valid survey. When evaluating the papers, the instructor may overlook many of the mistakes made, if this section provides information indicating the team learned how the survey could have been done properly. The instructor will compare the reports of all teams in this regard when grades are assigned.)

All the teams will discuss their surveys with the class at a designated period near the end of the course.

Task 3: Individual Term Paper

Complete this paper after turning in to the instructor the task project write-up of Task 2 and before proceeding with the team development paper of Task 4, which follows. This procedure utilizes the synergistic problem-solving model in which group dynamics are analyzed by individuals working alone first and through interaction second, as is done in the group activities in Module 9. The instructions for keeping a journal and writing the individual paper are given in Appendixes C and D.

Task 4: Team Term Paper on Team Development

After Tasks 2 and 3 have been completed, complete the team building session in Activity 18–4. Teams will then prepare a paper applying small group concepts to their team interactions as they have evolved during the process of completing the survey. The team should develop what goes into this by group problem solving. The paper is to conclude with a discussion of what team skills were developed and what the team would have to do to improve its own effectiveness were it to undertake another project.

Administrative Details

Team Term Papers

Team papers may run up to 25 pages in length to cover the essentials. Length is not important; meaningfulness and completeness are. Your team papers will be compared for quality and effort when evaluated by the instructor.

The due date for the task project paper is at the beginning of class on _______ (date). All team members will receive the same grade, and it will count _______ percent of your course grade. *The due date for the team development paper* is _______ (date). It will count _______ percent of your grade.

Individual Term Papers

These should be completed after the team task project paper (Task 2) but prior to Activity 18–4. The preceding comments on length are relevant here, although individual papers tend to be shorter. *Due date* _______ (date). It will count _______ percent of your grade.

Note: All late papers, team and individual, will be graded down.

Suggested Reading

Textbooks on marketing and social-psychological, sociological, and political science publications are the most available sources for students to consult on how to conduct a survey.

Note on Appendix A: Undergraduates have sometimes been uncomfortable with the self-directedness of this assignment and do not fully realize until late in the course that they share responsibility for team action in achieving the task. Participants may complain late in the course that all team members have not done their share of the work, and yet all are to earn equal credit for the team project. For a team exercise to be successful, all members must attend all team meetings. (*Keep in mind that this and reading the text are the primary homework for the course.*) It is important also that this exercise be self-directing so that members will learn from coping with their own problems.

One solution to these problems came from the students themselves. Two ground rules are suggested. First, a team can ''fire one of its employees'' if that person is not doing his or her share or is being disruptive. All they have to do is tell the instructor when the member is fired. Second, a sign-in sheet is kept at each meeting, and these are attached to the team development term paper (Task 4). (The following ''Team Meeting Sheets'' are for use by teams for this purpose.) When these ground rules are followed, there have been no further problems that the participants cannot handle themselves.

Team Meeting Sheet

Name of Team ____________________ Date ____________________

Team Met from ____________________ Hours to ____________________ Hours.

Those Attending: Sign in, Please.

1. ____________________ 4. ____________________

2. ____________________ 5. ____________________

3. ____________________ 6. ____________________

Please attach these sheets to your team report when it is turned in.

(CUT ALONG LINE)

Team Meeting Sheet

Name of Team ____________________ Date ____________________

Team Met from ____________________ Hours to ____________________ Hours.

Those Attending: Sign in, Please.

1. ____________________ 4. ____________________

2. ____________________ 5. ____________________

3. ____________________ 6. ____________________

Please attach these sheets to your team report when it is turned in.

(CUT ALONG LINE)

Team Meeting Sheet

Name of Team ____________________ Date ____________________

Team Met from ____________________ Hours to ____________________ Hours.

Those Attending: Sign in, Please.

1. ____________________ 4. ____________________

2. ____________________ 5. ____________________

3. ____________________ 6. ____________________

Please attach these sheets to your team report when it is turned in.

Team Meeting Sheet

Name of Team ______________________ Date ______________________

Team Met from ______________________ Hours to ______________________ Hours.

Those Attending: Sign in, Please.

1. ______________________ 4. ______________________

2. ______________________ 5. ______________________

3. ______________________ 6. ______________________

Please attach these sheets to your team report when it is turned in.

(CUT ALONG LINE)

Team Meeting Sheet

Name of Team ______________________ Date ______________________

Team Met from ______________________ Hours to ______________________ Hours.

Those Attending: Sign in, Please.

1. ______________________ 4. ______________________

2. ______________________ 5. ______________________

3. ______________________ 6. ______________________

Please attach these sheets to your team report when it is turned in.

(CUT ALONG LINE)

Team Meeting Sheet

Name of Team ______________________ Date ______________________

Team Met from ______________________ Hours to ______________________ Hours.

Those Attending: Sign in, Please.

1. ______________________ 4. ______________________

2. ______________________ 5. ______________________

3. ______________________ 6. ______________________

Please attach these sheets to your team report when it is turned in.

Team Meeting Sheet

Name of Team ______________________ Date ______________________

Team Met from ______________________ Hours to ______________________ Hours.

Those Attending: Sign in, Please.

1. ______________________ 4. ______________________

2. ______________________ 5. ______________________

3. ______________________ 6. ______________________

Please attach these sheets to your team report when it is turned in.

(CUT ALONG LINE)

Team Meeting Sheet

Name of Team ______________________ Date ______________________

Team Met from ______________________ Hours to ______________________ Hours.

Those Attending: Sign in, Please.

1. ______________________ 4. ______________________

2. ______________________ 5. ______________________

3. ______________________ 6. ______________________

Please attach these sheets to your team report when it is turned in.

(CUT ALONG LINE)

Team Meeting Sheet

Name of Team ______________________ Date ______________________

Team Met from ______________________ Hours to ______________________ Hours.

Those Attending: Sign in, Please.

1. ______________________ 4. ______________________

2. ______________________ 5. ______________________

3. ______________________ 6. ______________________

Please attach these sheets to your team report when it is turned in.

Appendix B Understanding Team Action: Alternative 2

Read Appendix A so you will understand the purpose of the team task assignment for courses that will pursue that activity. For classes that are not able to go that route, an alternative is proposed here.

Participants will be assigned to permanent six-member teams, which will complete all the exercises in the text and four to six outside exercises. Each participant will keep a journal based on the observations of his or her team's interactions in the class and outside of class sessions. Two options are available and will be decided on by the instructor. In *Option 1,* each individual will write a term paper. In *Option 2,* the team will write a team term paper. (Guidance for the journal and the term paper are provided in Appendixes C and D.)

Obviously, the participant will have much more limited data with which to work than would be the case with an outside-of-class team activity. However, many meaningful papers have been written on the group dynamics observations of a team's activities operating under this plan. Participants have rated this activity favorably, as indicated by the anonymous evaluations recorded from seven classes *required* to complete an organizational behavior course during their senior year in business administration.

Question: To what degree did you value the analysis of your team as a learning experience?

		Percentage Responding					
Class	**Number of Students**	**Of Little Value**	**Of Some Value**	**Of Much Value**	**Of Considerable Value**	**No Answer**	**Total**
A..................	36		8%	42%	50%		100%
B..................	33		6	42	49	3%	100
C..................	30		7	56	37		100
D..................	29			49	51		100
E..................	36	2%	14	31	53		100
F..................	39		5	51	44		100
G..................	36		9	39	52		100

If Alternative 2 is followed, there is ample time for additional outside readings and for case study assignments.

Administrative Details

Individual Term Papers: After completion of Activity 18–4, each participant is to write a term paper. (See Appendix C.)

Meeting Attendance and Dropping Members from the Team: Follow the instructions in "Note on Appendix A" and use "Team Meeting Sheets" at the end of Appendix A.

Appendix C Guidance for Keeping a Journal on Team Dynamics and Skills

The primary purpose of the individual and/or team term paper is to apply course learning to the interactions of your team. A secondary purpose is to reinforce the learning of team skills. It is assumed that the participants, through their interactions and the writing of this paper, will enhance their own individual effectiveness in team skills and learn something about coaching others who are attempting to do the same.

Keeping a Journal

Each of you will be a team member, but you will also be a *participant observer* of the interaction dynamics as your group evolves. The first requirement is to keep a journal of your observations on each meeting of the members. Both your class activities and your outside meetings will be good sources. (*Note:* Observation notes should be made from recall by the individual immediately after the meeting is concluded. For members to jot down observations during the meetings would in all likelihood cause discomfort for some and interfere with the natural interactions of the team.)

Your journal will provide the raw data from which you will later make your analysis for your term paper. What observations you make are completely up to you. During your initial meetings you will have studied only a few concepts that you can practice applying; as the course progresses you will have more and more tools with which to work. This is excellent, since starting with the possibly disorganized behaviors of your self-directed team should make you more aware of the need for the tools and skills to shape the group into greater effectiveness and operating proficiency. Here are some suggestions of the learning and concept areas you might use as the basis for observations and journal entries.

1. Your perceptions and feelings about group members and the influence of these perceptions on your behavior. As a first entry in your journal, you might want to describe your initial impressions of each person. What are your expectations of each person and of how she or he will perform? What impact is each having on the team, and what impact is the team having on that person? Later in the course you can see whether your impressions and predictions have proved to be valid.

2. Your effectiveness in the group; your feelings about this; your attempts to develop areas of your effectiveness.

3. How group norms develop. Norms are shared expectations of "how we should, ought, must, or should not, ought not, or must not behave." They develop toward every aspect of the team's interactions as members work together, and they will be very numerous by the end of the course. Many are spontaneous, and you will probably not be aware they are developing. They arise from several sources: the situation, the personality and needs of the members, and the culture, which encompasses values, folkways, mores, and traditions of the society represented by your college or university.

Norms are important because they become determinants of behavior; the group accepts those who conform and rejects those who tend to deviate. They are highly important in this course because *teams can develop and control their own norms* to improve their effectiveness. Norms exist informally in small groups—in fact, members are often not even aware of their existence. As groups increase in size beyond 15 or 20 members, it usually becomes necessary for these informal norms to be stated formally as rules and regulations to control behavior.

4. Development of task, social-emotional, and individual roles.

5. Substructuring in groups: dyads, triads, singletons, and so on. This is often a very subtle process that sometimes goes on beneath the level of awareness. Substructuring *always* exists. For instance, the first time your team meets, you will automatically feel closer to one or more members than to others. This will tend to make you more open to their ideas and possibly more supportive of them. If you observe the interactions in your team, you can become more aware of this process and the influence it is having on the group. These dyads and triads may be enduring or only short-lived and will change throughout the course.

6. Group skills development in such areas as communication, problem solving, and decision making.

7. How course concepts, such as communication, perceptual differences, motivation/frustration, leadership styles (team styles), and groupthink, apply.

8. How leadership *processes* develop in your team.

Some Criteria for the Development of the Papers

First some cautions. Your paper is an analysis of the journal and other observations you consider important. Do not describe every activity; the instructors already are familiar with them. Do not drag out the paper to fill as many pages as possible—a practice that could lower the evaluation.

What we look for is quality such as the following:

1. *Intensive application of course concepts.* For instance, in writing on subgrouping, diagrams can be drawn to show the relationships that occurred. The diagramming may show how subgrouping changed over time. What caused the subgrouping to occur, in your estimation? What was the effect on the group action? If negative, was any effort made to change it?

2. *Illustrations from activities to support your conclusions.* For instance, "During the group problem-solving exercise, the dyad of Mary and John was so strong in insisting on their answers that their views prevailed. Unfortunately, their suggestions proved to be wrong, and our team scored lowest in the class. Two other members of our group had better answers, but their input never was solicited. During the next exercise we made sure we got input from everyone before reaching a decision."

3. *Extensive application.* To what degree did the paper cover a wide range of course concepts? This concerns the thoroughness of the paper.

In addition, we do get an impression as to whether real learning seems to have taken place as we read through the paper. This is a qualitative judgment factor with which instructors are always confronted. Hopefully, everyone will be thinking of her or his own growth in the skills and understanding areas, and this will be reflected in the discussion.

Appendix D Guidance for Writing the Term Paper on Team Dynamics and Skills

The design of the course calls for the instructor to make the decision about an individual paper or team paper.

Individual Paper

Considerable leeway can be used in approaching this paper. Individuals may derive quite different, but overlapping, learning experiences from the team activity. *Your term paper is to show what was most meaningful to you.* The team experience itself and the writing of this paper have been most rewarding for many participants. We have received outstanding papers from people of many backgrounds and experience levels, from university undergraduates to field-grade officers in the Pentagon. Excellent, insightful papers have been produced in these classes from one or more (or all) of the following points of view.

1. *The application of small group theory and concepts to the group.* This analysis can be made very systematically and extensively, with certain selected areas being dealt with more intensively. All writers should keep this viewpoint in mind, although they may wish to weave these applications into a special focus on self, other individuals, or interactions, as discussed as follows.
2. *Focus on self.* How I felt about what was happening in the group. What impact the group had on me. What I learned about my own behavior. What influence I had on the group.
3. *Focus on other individuals.* The impact of each individual on the group and the group on him or her, and how I felt about it.
4. *Focus on interactions.* The interactions and relationships between members of the group, what effect these had on the group, and how I felt about it.

In addition, *all participants are requested to write on the following question:* If this group were to continue, what could I do to improve my own effectiveness? (Be specific.)

Team Paper

Writing a team paper (25 to 30 typewritten pages) on the team experience provides another level of learning for the team as a whole and for each individual. Students told us that, although it was a challenging task and not an easy process to manage and complete, it was one of the most meaningful tasks in the course.

The team is confronted with a few decisions: (1) the focus of the paper, (2) the format of the paper, and (3) how to go about actually writing it. The analytical format that seems to work is to start the process by thinking about a three-part paper. Part 1 is a case study; part 2 the case analyzes, integrating all the relevant OB concepts covered in the course; and part 3 is a reflection about the overall experience. As the students write the case part of the paper, the key issues that deserve to be examined in the analysis part and the final format of the paper seem to emerge. The students must self-manage the process—an activity that serves as another pedagogical way to integrate their course learning.

Appendix E Score Sheet for the Michigan-Based Leadership Questionnaire

Score Sheet

Scoring: Enter your answers for each item by circling the alphabetic choice in the scoring grid. Then enter the corresponding numeric score in the right-hand column.

Item #	1	2	3	4		5	
Leadership Support							
1	a	b	c	d		e	________
6	e	d	c	b		a	________
11	a	b	c	d		e	________
16	a	b	c	d		e	________
					A Total		
					A ÷ 4 =		
Team Facilitation							
3	a	b	c	d		e	________
8	a	b	c	d		e	________
13	a	b	c	d		e	________
18	a	b	c	d		e	________
					B Total		
					B ÷ 4 =		
Work Facilitation							
2	e	d	c	b		a	________
7	a	b	c	d		e	________
12	a	b	c	d		e	________
17	a	b	c	d		e	________
					C Total		
					C ÷ 4 =		
Goal Emphasis							
5	a	b	c	d		e	________
10	a	b	c	d		e	________
15	e	d	c	b		a	________
19	a	b	c	d		e	________
					D Total		
					D ÷ 4 =		
Upward Influence							
4	e	d	c	b		a	________
9	a	b	c	d		e	________
14	e	d	c	b		a	________
					E Total		
					E ÷ 3 =		

Explanation: Total raw scores for each dimension are calculated by summing up scores for individual items. The scoring grid is required because several items are negatively worked. Simply total the raw scores from the right-hand column; then divide by the number of items (four except for ''upward influence'') to produce summary scores for each leadership dimension.

Summary Scores

A	Leadership Support	__________
B	Team Facilitation	__________
C	Work Facilitation	__________
D	Goal Emphasis	__________
E	Upward Influence	__________

Your instructor will provide definitions and discuss the ''upward influence'' dimension.

Appendix F Transcal Petroleum Company, Parts B and C

Part B

As Art McCallum remembered the meeting with Phil Martinez to discuss his request to make direct deposit of paychecks mandatory for all employees, he had been very surprised when, after only about two minutes into his presentation, Martinez had said, "Art, I'm convinced. We don't have to spend any more time on this. Let's go ahead and do it." McCallum had thought the meeting had been scheduled to convince Martinez—he certainly had not expected a decision on the spot.

An announcement saying that effective January 1, direct deposit would be the standard of payroll distribution in the company was prepared for insertion with the September 15 paychecks. This announcement is reproduced as Exhibit 1.

Exhibit 1
Transcal Petroleum Company (B)

MEMORANDUM

FROM: A. V. McCallum

TO: Employees not presently enrolled in direct payroll deposit

SUBJECT: Direct deposit policy

As the level of participation in direct payroll deposit approaches 70%, it has been decided that

> Effective January 1, direct payroll deposit will be the standard method of payroll payment distribution.

This decision was taken to improve overall efficiency and effectiveness for both employees and the company. This policy has been in effect for all new hires for over a year.

Direct payroll deposit has been available in this country for over 25 years. It is well established as a payment distribution method among many employees. You can choose to have your pay deposited to any bank or credit union anywhere in the country. Early vacation paychecks will still be available.

We invite you to enroll by using the enclosed form. We would appreciate your cooperation in returning the completed form at your earliest convenience.

If you have any questions concerning this service, please call

Gloria Reid 432-4170
Karen Simon 432-6782
Art McCallum 432-8563

Thank you.

The day before the checks and the announcement were due to be delivered, McCallum and Martinez scheduled an information session on the new policy with representatives of the refinery union and the clerical employees association. It soon became evident that some employees had heard of the change via the grapevine. There were a few initial questions, which McCallum thought had been satisfactorily answered, but then, as McCallum put it, "All hell broke loose!"

Source: Contributed by Professor David Peach.

One union representative stood up and denounced the direct deposit move in the strongest possible terms. He said that a number of employees were upset by the direct deposit system and wanted no part of it. He said that as a union representative he could not agree to direct deposit being mandatory. A clerical representative, clearly agitated, had then stood up and said that the move to mandatory direct deposit was unconstitutional. Another representative said that the company had no right to "cram this system down employee throats." Another said, "Listen! My bank is in my back pocket and I am never going to let the company get into my pants!"

Martinez replied that the decision had been made and that he was not prepared to revoke it. He said he believed that when those individuals who had not had direct deposit experienced its benefits, their objections would vanish. As they left the room, one clerical representative said to Martinez, "Don't be too sure that you won't be overruled on this."

An hour later, Martinez received a call from the company president. "Phil," he said, "I'm sorry to do this, but I'm going to overrule your decision on direct deposit. I know that rationally your decision was a good one, but some employees are really upset about it, and I don't think we want to operate that way. I hope you understand."

Martinez told the president that he did understand and that he had been surprised at how upset and angry some people had been at the meeting. He certainly had no idea that the decision would be as controversial as it apparently was.

Martinez went to McCallum's office to tell him of the president's decision. McCallum was clearly disappointed. "I really don't know what to do," McCallum said. "I thought we had covered every possible objection."

"Well," said Martinez, "Maybe we'd better try to think of some way to get more people to accept direct payroll deposit voluntarily."

Discussion Questions

1. What errors have Martinez and McCallum made to date in implementing direct deposit.
2. What would you recommend they do now? Why?

Part C

After the company president had overruled Phil Martinez's decision to make direct payroll deposit mandatory, payroll department personnel had to work quickly to remove the memo on direct deposit which had already been inserted into the envelopes with the September 15 employee paychecks.

Martinez and McCallum wrote another memo, had it approved by the president, and placed the new memo in envelopes along with the September 30 paychecks. This memo required employees who did not wish to participate in direct deposit to opt out of the process; it is reproduced as Exhibit 2.

By January, an additional 1,010 employees (87.5% of the work force) had signed up for direct payroll deposit. Of the remaining 470 employees, 245 had neither enrolled in direct deposit nor sent memos stating why they did not wish to enroll. The 225 employees who wrote to say that they did not wish to participate expressed a variety of reasons:

Desire to allocate pay among two or more banks	81 employees
Personal reasons	58
No convenience perceived (still have to go to bank to pay bills, withdraw cash, have passbook updated, transfer money	42
Do not trust computers	18
No bank account	8
Control of their money	7
Infringement of legal rights	4
No reason stated	10

Exhibit 2
Transcal Petroleum Company (C)

MEMORANDUM

FROM: A. V. McCallum

TO: Employees not presently enrolled in direct payroll deposit

SUBJECT: Direct deposit policy

As the level of participation in direct payroll deposit approaches 70%, it has been decided that effective January 1, direct payroll deposit will be the standard method of payroll payment distribution.

This decision was taken to improve overall efficiency and effectiveness for both employees and the company. This policy has been in effect for all new hires for over a year.

Direct payroll deposit has been available in this country for over 25 years. It is well established as a payment distribution method among many employers. You can choose to have your pay deposited to any bank or credit union anywhere in the United States. Early vacation paychecks will still be available.

We invite you to enroll by using the enclosed form and returning it to us at your earliest convenience.

The company recognizes that a few employees not presently enrolled may find enrollment at this time inconvenient. Reasons for not wishing to participate should be expressed **in writing** to the payroll department. Please indicate your name, employee number, and work location.

The inefficiencies of maintaining two payroll distribution methods may make it necessary in the future to introduce direct payroll deposit universally.

In summary, we would appreciate receiving either your enrollment form or a letter specifying your reasons for not enrolling by November 15.

If you have any questions concerning this service, please call

Gloria Reid 432-4170
Karen Simon 432-6782
Art McCallum 432-8563

Thank you.

(The total number of responses was greater than 225 since some employees gave more than one reason for not wishing to participate in direct deposit.)

Martinez had heard from several sources that one major reason for some employees to resist direct deposit was that they did not wish to have their spouse know exactly how much money they made. He assumed that some of these employees had stated, ''personal reasons'' as their rationale for not signing up for direct deposit.

The company had hoped to get over these and other objections by having BankWest agree to set up special accounts for employees into which payroll could be deposited. This account would carry no service charge if the pay amount was withdrawn in cash or by check to another account. Thus employees without a bank account could write a check for cash on payday, while employees who wished to conceal the amount of their earnings could write a check and deposit it to another account. These features had been described to the union and clerical employee association but apparently did not ameliorate the concerns of all employees.

By June 1, an additional 3 percent of employees had signed up for direct payroll deposit, bringing enrollment to 90 percent of employees. Given this number, Phil Martinez wondered whether another attempt might be made to make direct payroll deposit mandatory for all employees.

Appendix G Motivation through Goal Setting

ZEKO Manufacturing Company is installing a Management by Objectives (MBO) system that has two interrelated planning processes: (1) companywide, top-to-bottom determination of organization goals and (2) career development. The latter requires supervisors to conduct goal-setting sessions with each professional employee. It is assumed that these will improve employees' understanding of what is specifically expected of each one. There should also be greater commitment to both job and career goals when employees participate in their formulation. The supervisor then has the opportunity for continuous feedback on progress, which provides reinforcement.

The following procedure was set forth for carrying out the job and personal goal-setting sessions:

1. Each employee receives a list of job goals as the supervisor understands them. Employees are asked to rewrite these in a way that best describes their work. The two lists will be the subject of an interview so that the supervisor and employee can agree on what is to be achieved by the employee over the next six months.

2. Each individual is to submit a statement of personal goals for professional development. These include requests for training both on and off the job, for which the company would pay tuition and expenses. Special work assignments and career assignments desired over the next five years are also to be indicated.

Chris Birch, chief of the Research Design Branch, is responsible for 10 young engineers, all of whom have joined the staff during the past three years. The unit is one in which new professionals learn some of the basics of the business and then are rotated to other assignments. Birch explained this new program to the employees in a meeting 10 days ago and gave them a written statement of the procedures to follow. Each individual was requested to take time to consider this matter and then to make an appointment when he or she felt ready to discuss job and personal goals. This was to be completed anytime within the next 30 days.

Three engineers made appointments immediately, and their interviews were completed the day after the announcement of the program. As the role playing opens, Birch is waiting for Pat King, one of the engineers, to arrive for an appointment.

PAT KING

ROLE OF PAT KING, ENGINEER, RESEARCH DESIGN BRANCH

You have been with the ZEKO company for approximately two years. You have enjoyed the work immensely and carry a full load. You have had good support from your boss. You have two small children and find life in suburbia hectic. Your spouse is most unhappy when you have to work overtime or weekends and feels strongly that you should be more involved with the children.

Ten days ago, Birch, your boss, announced a new goal-setting program. You were given a set of your job goals as the boss saw them for the coming six months and asked to rewrite them as you saw your responsibilities. You are also to write a set of personal goals within the next 30 days.

Today you had lunch with Jan Stage, a young engineer colleague who joined your branch a year and a half ago and has done an excellent job. You regard Jan as the most able of the group in the office, almost as able as you are, but less mature and sometimes in need of closer supervision. Jan likes to jump to a new phase of the work without finishing the last, sometimes causing resentment among the other engineers who are left to clean up the loose ends. Jan is unmarried and enjoys it, playing golf, boating, and dating. Jan is humorous, articulate, and outgoing. At lunch, Jan informed you of the results of a goal-setting session with Birch—Jan had written up goals, although you had not yet had a chance to write yours. Jan has enrolled in a graduate course in systems analysis and has begun to attend sessions already (on company time) and had approval to attend an operations research conference in Miami in the fall. Jan's biggest coup, however, was a new responsibility as branch liaison on the production coordination committee.

You were shocked by this. This is the only liaison committee opportunity your branch has to offer, and you had assumed the assignment would be yours. You have been with the branch six months longer, and your performance has been better. Also, you did not realize the organization would be so generous as to sponsor training courses during working hours or provide funds for attendance at conferences that required a flight across the country.

You have decided to take this matter up with Birch and express your concerns. Immediately after lunch you see Birch's secretary, who says you can see the boss in about 15 minutes.

Take a few minutes and think how you are going to approach Birch on this matter.

CHRIS BIRCH

ROLE OF CHRIS BIRCH, CHIEF, RESEARCH BRANCH

You are highly interested in the new career development system being installed by ZEKO as it is so consistent with the way you see your role. You see yourself as a coach and developer of young professionals. You believe it essential to handle each individual as a unique person. This type of management is a real art in which you are trying to understand performance in terms of each individual's abilities, personality, attitudes, needs, and experience. Growth takes place as the manager gives the individual the experience needed to shape the strengths. Questions you keep asking yourself in regard to each person are, How does the employee see himself or herself in terms of strengths? What are his or her goals, or what does that individual really want? How does he or she feel about the job?

Nine days ago you concluded an interview with Jan Stage. You feel it went very well, a model of what you would hope they would all be. Stage and Pat King are two of the best young professionals you have had in a long time. Stage has outstanding potential, was very definite about goals, and obviously feels good about ZEKO and the supervision here. Stage needs more freedom than the others to express creativity. Among other things, Stage's plan included the following:

1. Attendance at a graduate course in systems analysis at a local university with ZEKO to pay the tuition. It would be necessary to take two hours off every Wednesday afternoon for the class. (This course began two days after Stage's interview with you.)
2. Attendance at an operation research conference in Miami this fall for a three-day period.
3. Assumption of the liaison responsibility on the production coordination committee when its incumbent is replaced in two months. This is a job that you rotate to a different engineer each year.

Stage's plan was well thought out so you gave your full approval.

Your secretary has just informed you that Pat King wants to see you right away and seems a little upset. You assume it is probably for the goal-setting session and are looking forward to it. King is as able as Stage, but they are quite different people. King likes a little more structure in the work environment, and probably is not as creative as Stage, but can be depended on to do a crack job of administering an ongoing program. King is married and has two small children. Stage is single and, from what you hear, enjoys an active social life.

Appendix H Elaine Martin, Part B

Following an unpleasant incident on July 6 involving what Elaine Martin, student intern at the Topanga Valley branch of BancWest, perceived as unwarranted interference and criticism from assistant branch manager Joe Andrews, Elaine made up her mind to take some sort of corrective action. She resolved to tell Joe how she felt about his behavior.

The next day, Elaine summoned up her courage and nervously asked Joe if she could meet with him privately for half an hour or so. Joe's eyebrows shot up quizzically, but he replied that he'd be glad to meet with her as soon as he could find the time.

A week passed before Joe stopped at Elaine's desk and suggested they go to the lunch room for coffee and a talk. Elaine refused the coffee (her stomach was in an uproar!), drew a deep breath as she faced her supervisor across the lunchroom table, and began her carefully rehearsed remarks. Joe listened intently, without comment, as Elaine expressed all of her pent-up thoughts and emotions.

> When I started this summer, you gave me the goal of showing responsibility and leadership, and I can't do that when you're telling me what to do all the time. Nobody can respect me when you obviously don't trust me. So if I'm not doing a good job, take me aside and speak to me. Please don't keep telling me to do this and that in front of people. It's really not fair. And sometimes when you come out of your office and look over and I'm sitting there with people waiting at the counter, it's because those people want only certain employees to handle them. I don't mind doing counter. I want to do my share.
>
> I only got two days' training with Terri on loans this summer, not the two weeks I was supposed to have. So I've been learning how to do the job and do it well, without Terri being around to help or answer questions. I'll do the counter, but I think my job comes first, because that's why I'm here. I've got to learn how to take on different responsibilities and to make decisions. You shouldn't have to rely on me to do the counter, because I'm extra in the branch—and if you can't run the branch without me, there's something wrong.

Joe sat quietly for a few moments and then answered,

> Elaine, I suppose you're right. I have been unfair. I thought you were the same as the other females around here, married women who aren't at all interested in advancing their careers. Maybe I've been unfair to them too. But when I offered Beth a promotion, she turned it down. She certainly has the ability, but she said she wasn't interested, whereas Bob is so eager to get ahead—he's great!
>
> It has been tough trying to get things in shape at this branch, and I'm new at the assistant manager's job. Everybody criticizes me, and I suppose I've followed the path of least resistance. It's easier to ask a trainee to do the dirty jobs than to try to change the habits of regular employees. But enough of that. What can be done to improve things for you?

In September, Elaine was telling a classmate about her summer work experience. She described her interview with Joe and continued,

Source: Contributed by Professor David Peach.

After that talk, things changed drastically! Joe never told me to go to the counter any more. He knew I was good, and he assigned all sorts of other people's work to me. He'd say, "Do you have some extra time? I have something for you to do." He worked it so I got to do some good, interesting jobs, along with the boring stuff. Sometimes he'd ask, "Do you *want* to do this?" And I'd say, "Oh sure, I'll do it for you. But I want you to teach me about this other job." And he would!

He set aside time to do training exercises with me, and one day he even brought in a whole list of questions for me. I got time to study before each set of tests from the head office too. And when the head office wanted to transfer me to another branch, Joe fought to keep me at Topanga!

The counter thing was never a problem. When I went up to the counter a few times on my own, then the others took their turns too. Everyone seemed to get along better. And by the end of July, employees in the bank were actually coming to *me* for answers to their questions. Finally, my staff report was a good one. Joe took two hours at the end of the summer to review my performance with me.

I'm glad I made the decision to speak to my supervisor directly. Things worked out really well.

Appendix I Mountain Survival Task

Your charter flight from Seattle to Banff and Lake Louise (Alberta, Canada) crash-landed in the north Cascades National Park area somewhere near the U.S.–Canadian border and then burst into flames. It is approximately noon in mid-January. The twin-engine, 10-passenger plane containing the bodies of the pilot and one passenger has completely burned. Only the airframe remains. None of the rest of you has been seriously injured. The pilot was unable to notify anyone of your position before the plane crashed in a blinding snowstorm. Just before the crash, you noted that the plane's altimeter registered about 5,000 feet. The crash site is in a rugged, heavily wooded area just below the timberline. You are dressed in medium-weight clothing. Each of you has a topcoat.

After the plane landed and before it caught fire, your group was able to salvage the 15 items listed below. Your task is to rank the 15 items in terms of their importance to your survival. Place the number 1 by the most important item, number 2 by the second most important, and so on through number 15, the least important.

Source: Special permission for reproduction of the Mountain Survival Task is granted by Professors Fremont E. Kast and James E. Rosenzweig. We are grateful to them.

	Step 1: Your individual ranking	Step 2: The group ranking	Step 4: Survival experts' ranking	Step 5: Difference between 1 and 4	Step 6: Difference between 2 and 4
Sectional air map of the area					
Flashlight (four-battery size)					
Four wool blankets					
One rifle with ammunition					
One pair of skis					
Two fifths of liquor					
One cosmetic mirror					
One jackknife					
Four pairs of sunglasses					
Three books of matches					
One metal coffeepot					
First aid kit					
One dozen packages of cocktail nuts					
One clear plastic tarpaulin (9′ × 12′)					
One large, gift-wrapped decorative candle					
			Total (The lower the score the better		
				Your score	Group score

Appendix J Important Days Task

The words below represent important days. You are to write in the approximate date of each item and rank them from 1 to 21, according to the sequence in which they occur during the year. Do this from memory. Guess when you do not know, but assign each a number without using the same number twice.

Item	Approximate Date	Your Ranking 1 to 21	Your Error Points	Key	Team Ranking 1 to 21	Team Error Score
bird						
SOS						
red suit						
Ides						
time						
flag						
election						
St. Patrick						
vernal equinox						
firecrackers						
graveyard						
brides						
work						
Washington						
cats						
hearts						
lilies						
clown						
Santa Maria						
Bastille						
outgo						

Your Total Error Score [ ]

Team's Total Error Score [ ]

Appendix K Task 21

Each of the 21 numbers listed below should suggest to you the idea, fact, word, phrase, quotation, or event that is to be completed to the right of it. For example:

1001 = A.N. (Arabian Nights)
6 = S__ B____ M___. (Six Blind Mice)
7 = S.D. and S.N. (Seven Days and Seven Nights)

Working alone, complete as many items as you can. (Five is about average.) After you have worked for a while, your instructor will ask you to get together with other participants to do a group solution. Don't be threatened. This has nothing to do with your intelligence and is more related to mental flexibility.

	Item No.	Score One Point for Each Right Answer: Your Score		Group Score
(1)	1 = Y____ of O__ L____.		(1)	
(2)	2 = T__ W______ D_ N__ M___ a R_____.		(2)	
(3)	3 = T_____ of a K____.		(3)	
(4)	4 = G____ C_______ W_______.		(4)	
(5)	5 = P_______ on a B___________ T___.		(5)	
(6)	6 = P__________ on the S__________ of D________________.		(6)	
(7)	7 = to be in S________________ H________________.		(7)	
(8)	8 = B______ the E_____ B___.		(8)	
(9)	9 = S_____ in T____ S_____ N____.		(9)	
(10)	10 = H____ T__.		(10)	
(11)	11 = P________________ on a F. T.________________.		(11)	
(12)	12 = B______ D_____.		(12)	
(13)	13 = O_________ S______ in the U.S.		(13)	
(14)	14 = a F_________.		(14)	
(15)	15 = F_____ P_____ in T______.		(15)	
(16)	16 = S_____ S_______.		(16)	
(17)	17 = S__________ Y___ L______.		(17)	
(18)	18 = L_____ A__ to V___.		(18)	
(19)	19 = T______ minus O__.		(19)	
(20)	20 = F.S. and S.Y.A. ____________________.		(20)	
(21)	21 = L.A. to D. ________________.		(21)	
	Total Scores			

Source: The design of this exercise is based on a puzzle titled "Equation Analysis Test," which appeared originally in the May/June 1981 issue of *Games* magazine. We are indebted to *Games* magazine for permission to follow the puzzle concept.

Appendix L Who Gets the Overtime?

Five of you are employees of the Customers' Division of the Mountain Power Company's District Headquarters in Green Valley, Virginia. Your job requires monitoring customer accounts for records, billing, payments, and collection purposes. Answering customer inquiries and opening and closing accounts are a major part of your job. All five of you are considered excellent employees, and the atmosphere in the office is one of congeniality and good morale. One reason for this is that Green Valley is a small town in a beautiful area where few good jobs exist. The small local college is the main activity in the town, and Mountain Power's district office offers one of the few good places to work, even though salaries are modest. Students graduating from the local high schools and colleges move out of the area to find permanent jobs.

All five of you are feeling the squeeze for money. Inflation is a problem, and many of the products sold in Green Valley are higher priced than in big cities because of transportation costs and the limited market. All of you moonlight when you can, but the opportunities are scarce. When overtime work is required, Mountain Power's policy is to rotate employee assignments so all have an equal share on an annual basis; however overtime needs are very low.

Here are some general facts about the employees in your section.

Chris is 22 years of age, has been with the company four years, and has three young children.

Adrian is 27 years of age, has been with the company 10 years, and is the senior person in the office.

Sara is 21 years of age. It is the company's policy to employ two deserving college students half-time and to let them study at the office during times when customer inquiries are low; she is one of these students.

Fran, 25 years of age, is the second half-time student. Fran started work at the same time as Sara two years ago and plans to graduate in one year.

Lynn, 20 years of age, is the newest employee, having decided to make Mountain Power a career after graduating from a two-year college.

Kim is your supervisor. When the instructor gives you the signal to start role playing, the scene is as follows: You have just been called into Kim's office for a discussion. The supervisor will tell you what you are to do. Play your role as if you were in the position described on your role sheet. When facts arise that are not covered by the roles, be creative; make up things that are consistent with the way it might be in a real-life situation.

Note: Return to the instructions of Task 1c, Activity 9–5, before proceeding with the role playing.

Source: This appendix follows the design developed by Norman R. F. Maier's exercise "The New Truck Dilemma," which appears in N. R. F. Maier, A. R. Solem, and Ayesha A. Maier, *Supervisory and Executive Development* (New York: John Wiley & Sons, Inc., 1957). This exercise is printed here with Dr. Maier's permission.

KIM, THE SUPERVISOR

(CUT ON LINE)

FRAN

(CUT ON LINE)

LYNN

KIM THE SUPERVISOR

Your manager has asked you to select one of your employees to work Saturday mornings on a new job in another section of the headquarters office. The manager wants the same person to perform in the job for the next year because it requires technical training in data-processing equipment, and continuous experience will be needed.

Your dilemma is that all five of your people are equally qualified and all need the money. You have recently had a supervision course in which participation of employees in decision making was studied. You decide that this is a case in which they all have an equal interest so you will let them make the decision. You have called them together for this purpose. Tell them what the opportunity is and then tell them to go ahead and decide among themselves who is to get the overtime assignment. Remember, *you are going to let them make the decision.* The team must arrive at a decision.

(CUT ON LINE)

ROLE OF FRAN

You are always pressed for money. You live with your fiancé, also a student, who shares expenses. Your car is old and always requiring repairs. You wish to enter the MBA program at Midwest University next fall; if you can save up for the initial tuition, you might be able to attend classes half-time and work half-time.

(CUT ON LINE)

ROLE OF LYNN

You are married and living with your in-laws so you can save, but you find it most uncomfortable. Your spouse works half-time, having found nothing full-time. The two of you are very frugal because your parents have promised to pay half the down payment on a "starter" house if you can accumulate the other half. You plan no children until this is accomplished. You hope to prove to Mountain Power that your all-around capabilities and two-year community college degree qualify you to work into management. You plan to take a computer course in the near future as part of your personal development program.

CHRIS

(CUT ON LINE)

SARA

(CUT ON LINE)

ADRIAN

ROLE OF CHRIS

You and your spouse have had one child after another so money is tight. Your spouse continually presses you to find extra work, which you do whenever you can. Both of you spend much of your spare time raising chickens and vegetables for the family.

(CUT ON LINE)

ROLE OF SARA

You give part of your earnings to the support of your younger brothers because money is scarce for your mother since your father died. You have been borrowing money for your education. You have been able to carry almost a full load at college in your business administration major and maintain a good average in spite of your work; you are starting your junior year. You like Mountain Power and may want to stay on after you graduate if they will give you a job. You have learned in your business courses that professional women have to be better than their male peers to move ahead in the work world. Your personal effectiveness goal is get "your share of the air time," "to hold your own," or "be assertive in a pleasant way" in discussions with male peers.

(CUT ON LINE)

ROLE OF ADRIAN

You give 10 percent of your salary to the church and are highly regarded for your willingness to help with church responsibilities. For two years you have been building a small house in your spare time. Progress is slow because you have to save up to buy building materials. You are single, but you hope to get married as soon as you find the right person. You feel that your seniority entitles you to first consideration when new opportunities arise.

Appendix M A Card Game Called *Norms*

Card Content

1. Your team agreed to meet at 1 PM Wednesday afternoon for two hours to work on the project. Jane doesn't show up until 1:20.	2. Your team divided up the tasks of the project and decided to have a meeting where each person would report on the progress he or she has made. When it's Fred's turn to present, he says that he didn't have time to complete his part.	3. When decisions need to be made during your team's meetings, Chris often says, "It doesn't matter what we do. Let's just hurry up and get it done and turn it in."
4. Your team members reported on the work each had been doing, but it was clear that Frank had not put much effort into his part.	5. The teams are given the next class period to work on their project. Sandy doesn't show up; she has all of your team's materials.	6. Phil frequently interrupts other team members during meetings.
7. Once Connie has an idea in her head, she won't listen to anyone else's opinions.	8. Bob takes over team meetings. Others rarely get a chance to talk.	9. Sara is a very popular student. It seems that other team members always agree with what she says regardless of the quality of her idea.
10. Tom comes to all your team's meetings but rarely contributes.	11. During your team meetings, Carolyn starts talking about things unrelated to the project, like what's happening in other classes and upcoming parties.	12. Stan and Beth have very different opinions of how your team's work should progress. They seem to be at odds with each other most of the time. They often argue with each other during team meetings.

Agreement Form

1. We have reached consensus on our team's set of norms. The following is the list of the norms:

A. ______________________ H. ______________________

B. ______________________ I. ______________________

C. ______________________ J. ______________________

D. ______________________ K. ______________________

E. ______________________ L. ______________________

F. ______________________ M. ______________________

G. ______________________

2. We agree to abide by these norms.

3. We will bring up for discussion any perceived violation of these norms.

Team Members' Signatures	Date
______________________	__________
______________________	__________
______________________	__________
______________________	__________
______________________	__________

Appendix N Prisoners' Dilemma Round 10 Prediction Sheet and Tally Sheet*

Prisoners' Dilemma Round 10 Prediction Sheet

Predicting team	Predicted choice	
	Red team	Blue team
Red	○	
Blue		○

* Adapted from: J. William Pfeiffer and John E. Jones, eds., *A Handbook of Structural Experiences for Human Relations Training,* vol. 3 (San Diego, Calif.: University Associates, 1974). Used with permission.

Prisoners' Dilemma Tally Sheet*

Instructions: For 10 consecutive rounds, the Red Team will choose either an A or a B, and the Blue Team will choose an X or a Y. The score for each team in a round is determined by the choices of both teams, according to the following payoff schedule.

AX—Both teams win 3 points.
AY—Red Team loses 6 points; Blue Team wins 6 points.
BX—Red Team wins 6 points; Blue Team loses 6 points.
BY—Both teams lose 3 points.

		Scoresheet			
		Choice		*Score*	
Round	*Minutes*	*Red Team*	*Blue Team*	*Red Team*	*Blue Team*
1	3				
2	3				
3	3				
4**	3 (reps)				
	3 (teams)				
5	3				
6	3				
7	3				
8	3				
9†	3 (reps)				
	5 (teams)				
10†	3 (reps)				
	5 (teams)				

Total Score: Red: Blue:

* Adapted from J. William Pfeiffer and John E. Jones, eds., *A Handbook of Structural Experiences for Human Relations Training,* vol. 3 (San Diego, Calif.: University Associates, 1974). Used with permission.

** Payoff points are doubled for this round.

†Payoff points are squared for this round (any minus signs are retained).

Appendix O Team Effectiveness Skills

Now that your teams are well established, it is time to review our learning model and make some midcourse corrections. The design for teams following Appendix A was to put members in a leaderless group, assign a difficult task, and let them struggle to find their way without assistance from the instructor. The assumption is that there is more to be learned from finding your way than from having someone give you instructions. Coping with situations for which there is no definite answer is increasingly a part of our changing environment. However there is also much to be gained from the opposite model, which requires learning, practicing, and then applying skills. To ensure that you can take advantage of this model, a summary is presented here of many of the learning areas from the entire text. Up to this point, teams have been learning new skills as they are gradually introduced. The chapters still to be assigned will provide additional skills. Skills from both the former and latter will be listed at this time.

General Orientation

Before proceeding, orientations for shaping your team's effectiveness will be stated.

1. Teams function as their members make them function. Focusing on and practicing interaction patterns is a valid function of work teams—in athletics and the armed forces there has never been any question about allotting time for this purpose.

2. Teams should concentrate on changing (or developing) norms rather than changing people. Individuals will generally conform to norms that are agreed upon and practiced. The deviant from the norms often is persuaded by the group to conform. If not influenced by the group, the deviant is either rejected or leaves the group of his or her own accord.

Skill Areas

If your teams are taking full advantage of the material available in this text, they will have attended to the following:

1. *Definition of objectives.* Teams frequently have not done this to the extent necessary, or members are not in agreement on what is being attempted.

2. *Planning.* Having a well-formulated plan before implementation usually saves considerable time and results in a higher-quality product. For example, teams are apt to complete a survey and then figure out how they are to analyze the data. An analysis plan must be worked out prior to data collection if costly mistakes are not to be made.

3. *Group problem-solving, decision-making, and goal-setting skills.* These must be practiced to be useful. They not only take advantages of the resources in the team but can stimulate involvement.

Although this appendix is directed toward teams following the plan in Appendix A, it should have considerable value for those involved in the Appendix B activity.

4. *Role differentiation.* Individuals need to be clear on the responsibilities of each member.

5. *Critiquing.* A periodic evaluation of progress against the objectives is needed. Equally important is concern for the means of progress: "Are we practicing the group skills?"

6. *Avoidance of action orientation.* This is an overwhelming problem with managers as well as participants in this course. It results in the skill areas listed being neglected. Teams in work situations move too rapidly into implementation only to encounter barriers that require replanning, a most costly process in terms of both time and money.

7. *Use of time.* Time must be allotted for purposes discussed here, and all members must be present. Research supports the assumption that time spent for planning can result in less time for implementation and completion.

8. *Use of team-style models.* Teams develop styles just as managers do. Models can be used to analyze the character of your present team interactions and contrast it with the model the team feels would maximize its effectiveness.

9. *Development of agreed-upon norms and values.* Activities 4–4, 10–2, and 18–4 provide a list of some of the norms central to team effectiveness.

10. *Use of resources in the team.* Are the resources (abilities etc.) of each individual known and utilized where possible? Heterogeneity of group members is important because of this factor and the differences in perception and motivation it brings to the group.

11. *Communications skills.* These are necessary before any of the preceding factors can be achieved meaningfully. They are a core focus of effectiveness for both the team and the individual. Three major barriers to communication that are often the focus of training in groups are

a. Hidden agendas. Individuals or subgroupings are manipulating others for their own needs at the expense of team needs. Rivalries, distrust, concern for not looking bad, ambitions, and other factors can cause individuals not to say openly how they feel or what they want.

b. Defensive feelings. All of us are subject to these, particularly under pressure.

c. Parental evaluations. Making judgments of what is right and wrong during the process of listening.

The following are approaches for alleviating these barriers:

a. Norms of leveling and confrontation. Team acceptance of the norms and development of skills related to them establish the medium in which conflict can be handled rather than smoothed over or avoided.

b. Dialogue sequence. Includes listening, confrontation, searching, and coping skills; also the radio-receiver model of *nonjudgmental listening, paraphrasing* for understanding.

c. During interpersonal conflict, overcome defensive feelings. The following methods are suggested:

(1) *Don't lay it on the other person.* Attacking the other individual, name calling, and accusations increase defensiveness.

(2) *Deal with the other person's feelings, not your own.* This means controlling your reactions to your own defensive feelings while you concentrate on the other's. Statements such as "You really are feeling very strong about this, aren't you?" help defuse the emotions. (Keep cool!)

(3) *Paraphrase.* This shows the other individual you are listening and hear the message.

(4) *Own your own feelings.* Saying where you are (for example, "I am angry") can be accepted and understood more readily than attacking the other person.

(5) *Deal with the problem rather than focus on the other person.* Say, "The report still needs to include additional material," rather than "You did a lousy job, dummy."

d. Giving and receiving feedback. A means of knowing what impact you are having on others and the work situation.

e. Assertiveness skills. Express feelings in a way acceptable to others.

f. Perceptual checking. Have each person express his or her views on the topic under discussion. This avoids perceptual distortion from group members assuming views expressed by one member are representative of all members. If one member refers to what "we" think, say, "Tell what you think and let others speak for themselves."

Appendix P Building on Strengths

The "Strengths Questionnaire" that follows has the following objectives.

1. To help you become more aware of your own strengths.
2. To continue the coaching process.

After each participant has completed the questionnaire that follows, each team is to divide up into triads. (*Note:* If time and appropriate room space are available, this can be meaningfully accomplished by the entire team working as a unit. This is also meaningful as an outside team exercise.)

One individual will share what attributes he or she has written in the right-hand column, taking them one at a time and giving examples of his or her strengths in that regard. It is not necessary to reveal any person or anything written in the first two columns; only the strengths listed in the "I am better at ______" column are needed. Paraphrasing by the other triad members can be used if and when it appears appropriate.

After an individual has completed discussing his or her strengths, the other members will give feedback of any strengths they have observed in the individual during their association on the team. (This is excellent when done as a team because more data are available for feedback of strengths.) The process is continued until all have had an opportunity.

Name ____________________ Date ____________________

Strengths Questionnaire

Most of us have strengths we are not aware of or do not appreciate in ourselves to the degree others do. For instance, being able to speak openly may be regarded by a person as something he or she would expect of himself or herself and others. Consequently, he or she would undervalue that strength, whereas the person's friends might regard him or her as having accomplished this to a greater degree than many others had.

The purpose here is to help you sort out many of your strengths. This has been found easier to do if you contrast yourself with a number of people you have known or now know. You will not be asked to show this questionnaire to anyone, so feel free to complete it as you desire. You will be asked to discuss only the listings in the third column with your triad.

Person with whom I am contrasting myself	*What that person is better at is . . . . (write in)*	*What I am better at is . . . . (write in)*
Father		
Mother		
Brother		
Sister		
Friend (male)		
Friend (female)		
Boss		

Person with whom I am contrasting myself	*What that person is better at is . . . . (write in)*	*What I am better at is . . . . (write in)*
Fellow worker		
A disliked person (male)		
A disliked person (female)		
Some public figure		
Some historical figure		
Any other persons you can list.		
1.		
2.		
3.		
Etc.		

When you have finished, go back over the list and see if there is more than one thing that you are better at than each of the persons considered. This may increase your strengths lists.

Appendix Q Kate and Jake's Flaky Cakes

Background

As tourists are drawn to the smell of fresh baked cinnamon rolls and blueberry muffins, they discover heaven on earth.

Kate and Jake's Flaky Cakes is nestled in a small seaside California town on the east end of a minimall. The cinder block and glass facility has been the home of this local bakery for 15 years. The original owners, Kathleen and Jackson Kittrell, retired to pursue their first love—sailing. Justin Redo, current owner of Kate and Jake's, bought the bakery four years ago when he was lured by the clean air and luscious green countryside of this small town. However, he has never had any experience in the bakery business.

Justin is ecstatic about the popularity of this bakery. It has a large and fairly complex menu that can be tailored for custom-cake orders. Free menus can be obtained from virtually any news stand in town, resulting in abundant phone orders and deliveries.

In recent times, Justin noticed that inefficient operations caused profits to stagnate despite the continued popularity of Kate and Jake's products. Orders are sometimes misplaced due to the frantic pace of the bakery during peak hours. For example, customer service representatives field both walk-in and phone orders on 3×3 generic paper invoices. These invoices are usually crumpled, smeared, splattered, and speared after traveling through the baking and decorating processes, posing problems for customer service representatives and deliverers. Furthermore, some order slips are lost before the completed cakes are placed in the storage refrigerators. In such cases, customer service representatives must rely on their memory, ask customers to reiterate the inscription of their cake (provided they remember it), or go through the baker's file to find the cake information. This is not an easy task, and the wrong cake can be presented to a customer.

Kate and Jake's recently began supplying local stores with a large number of cakes on a daily basis. This has increased deliveries tremendously. However, bills sent to these customers are often incorrect due to problems such as loss of delivery receipts, improperly invoiced prices, and incorrect line items.

Justin Redo realized that his company faced many problems. He decided to take a walk on the beach to reflect on his business. As he dodged surging tides, he was startled by a high-spirited golden retriever. The retriever nudged and circled Justin playfully. The retriever's owner ran up shortly afterwards and apologized for his canine's intrusion. Justin and the man laughed and introduced themselves. It turned out that the dog's master was a business professor at the local college. The subject of Kate and Jake's difficulties arose during the conversation. After assessing the situation, the professor suggested Justin involve his employees in a creative management approach called self-design. Justin resolved to discuss the idea with his staff the following day.

Key Players

Owner Justin Redo

Mr. Redo purchased Kate and Jake's Flaky Cakes four years ago due to his financial security and love for the area. His lack of bakery expertise explains his hands-off approach to day-to-day operations. He leaves everyday decisions up to his employees, who were trained by the previous owners.

Justin is a very outgoing and personal individual. He enjoys listening to people and discussing their personal concerns. When he is at the bakery, he spends the majority of his day chatting with customers.

(CUT ALONG LINE)

Baker

The baker takes pride in the taste, texture, and aesthetics of his or her creations. He or she is familiar with a variety of recipes, allowing Kate and Jake's to cater to the most refined tastes. The baker's daily duties vary depending on the complexity of orders, which can range from a simple sheet cake to a multitiered wedding cake. He or she receives handwritten sales orders from the customer service representatives. These orders are skewered on a corkboard directly above the baker's station.

To ensure maximum freshness, the baker only processes the next day's orders. This results in fluctuations in productivity. Next-day orders are found by searching through the numerous notes on the board. This is time consuming and often results in overlooked due dates.

Once the baker completes the baking process, he or she places the cake in a traditional pink cake box. The sales order slip is taped to the exterior of the box. This is placed on the "Baked Cakes" rack in the refrigerator for the decorator.

(CUT ALONG LINE)

Decorator

The decorator takes pride in the artistic and creative appearance of his or her work. The decorator's ultimate responsibility is to give the final product the appearance of quality. This forces the decorator to be creative and unique with every cake, especially those that are custom-ordered.

The decorator randomly retrieves the baked cakes from the refrigerator. The sales order slips for standard cakes are easy for the decorator to interpret due to the minimal amount of information on the slip. However, custom-ordered cakes are more difficult to interpret due to the abundant amount of information on the sales slips.

Occasionally, one custom cake can take the decorator's entire shift to complete. In those instances, the decorator must periodically be interrupted to complete other cakes to meet their deadlines.

After cakes are completed, both pickups and delivery cakes are placed on the "Frosted Cake" rack in the refrigerator. Occasionally, due to overcapacity, frosted cakes are placed on the "Baked Cakes" rack, causing confusion for the decorator, customer service representatives, and deliverers.

(CUT ALONG LINE)

Accountant

The accountant takes pride in balancing Kate and Jake's books. The accountant is responsible for billing customers, paying vendors, and creating monthly statements.

The accountant relies on the customer service representatives to provide a copy of the sales slips each day. These sales slips are the sole pieces of information that generate a bill for large-order customers. Customer service representatives often misplace the sales slips or incorrectly complete these slips, causing the accountant to bill a customer incorrectly.

The accountant relies on the purchaser to provide him or her with bills from the vendors. A misplaced bill can cause the relationship between the vendor and Kate and Jake's to deteriorate.

The accountant is responsible for creating monthly statements for Justin Redo. However, inaccuracies in billing of large-order customers and payment of bills to vendors create inaccurate monthly statements for Justin.

(CUT ALONG LINE)

Purchaser

The purchaser is responsible for replenishing inventory as requested by the employees of Kate and Jake's. The baker, decorator, and customer service representatives verbally communicate their inventory needs to the purchaser. This communication only takes place when any of the above personnel find that their supplies are depleted. The baker, decorator, and customer service representatives expect their supplies to be replenished immediately. The purchaser finds this reactive approach to retrieving inventory very stressful.

The purchaser also deals directly with the vendors. He or she obtains bills from the vendors to give to the accountant. Often these bills are misplaced, causing the accountant's records to be inaccurate and bills to be overdue.

(CUT ALONG LINE)

Customer Service Representatives

The customer service representatives are the first line of contact for the customers both on the phone and in person. Therefore they must be both cheery and knowledgeable about Kate and Jake's operations.

Customer service representatives take pride in the aesthetics of Kate and Jake's environment. They are responsible for arranging the cakes and pastries in the display cabinets, stocking drinks in the cooler, and cleaning tables after customers leave.

Customer service representatives take cake orders both by phone and in person. They attempt to place these recorded orders on sales slips in a pile behind the counter throughout the day. At the end of the day, one copy of each order is skewered on a corkboard above the baker's station and another copy is given to the accountant.

Customer service representatives also retrieve cakes from the refrigerator when customers come in to pick up their orders. Many times a cake is difficult to find because the sales slip with the customer's name on it is no longer readable. Often customer service representatives find cakes on the ''Baked Cakes'' rack instead of the ''Frosted Cakes'' rack. Many times customer service representatives must obtain help from the decorator to locate a cake, interrupting the decorator's work. Customer service representatives generally end up asking the customer for the inscription on the cake and then open every cake box until the right cake is found. This process is time consuming and often irritates the customer.

(CUT ALONG LINE)

Drivers

The two drivers are responsible for delivering cakes to residential and business areas each day. Drivers are expected to deliver a cake on time to each customer.

Drivers are not given a delivery schedule each day. Instead, they are expected to go through the cakes in the refrigerator each morning and find the cakes to be delivered that day. They must divide the deliveries among the two of them in the manner they find will work best for them. Drivers are only casually reminded of cakes that must be delivered to big accounts each day.

Drivers must handle any customer complaints that may arise when they deliver a cake. Since they are not the ones who originally take the cake order, they are usually unable to resolve customers' complaints.

Appendix R Paper Plane Assembly

(Note: Read only the instructions for your assigned group.)

After you read the instructions wait for the instructor's signal to start production.

Assembly Plant A—Instructions

The instructor will *randomly* (not according to the worker skill level) devide your group into two equal subgroups and assign an assembly supervisor. Read *your assigned role only.*

QA Team

This group is the quality assurance group responsible for ensuring that all airplanes are produced according to product specifications. Your major concern is product quantity. You are to examine the prototype product and develop product specifications against which you will inspect the quality of each airplane. The inspection process should occur in a sequential (assembly-line) fashion, starting with Inspector 1, and then Inspector 2, Inspector 3, and so on. Keep count as a group for the number of products produced and the number of products that passed the quality assurance inspection.

WB Team/s

This group is made up of worker bees on the production line, who are responsible for making as many paper airplanes as possible in the time allotted. You are *not* concerned with *quality,* but are concerned with *quantity*. Your objective is to produce as many airplanes as possible. The QA group will then inspect each airplane passed to them. The time allotted for this exercise is *ten* minutes. Wait for the instructor to tell you to begin.

Assembly-Line Supervisor

Your role is to monitor the production process. Make sure that assembly workers have enough raw materials. Encourage them to work as fast as they can. Remember your major concern is the number of airplanes produced. Pass every airplane produced to the quality assurance group.

Assembly Plant B—Instructions

The instructor will RANDOMLY (not according to the worker skill level) divide your group into two equal subgroups and assign an assembly supervisor. Read *your assigned role only.*

QA Team

This group is the quality assurance group responsible for ensuring that all airplanes are produced according to product specifications. Your major concern is product *quality.* You are to examine the prototype product and develop product specifications against which you will inspect the quality of each airplane. The inspection process should occur in a sequential (assembly-line) fashion, starting with Inspector 1, and then Inspector 2, Inspector 3, and so forth. Keep count as a group for the number of products produced and the number of products that passed the quality assurance inspection.

WB Team/s

This group is made up of worker bees on the production line, who are responsible for making as many high-quality paper airplanes as possible in the time allotted. Your major concern is *quantity.* Your objective is to produce as many high-quality airplanes as possible. The QA group will then inspect each airplane passed to them. The time allotted for this exercise is *ten* minutes. Wait for the instructor to tell you to begin.

Assembly-Line Supervisor

Your role is to monitor the production process. Make sure that assembly workers have enough raw materials. Encourage them to work as fast as they can. Remember your major concern is the number of airplanes produced. Pass every airplane produced to the quality assurance group.

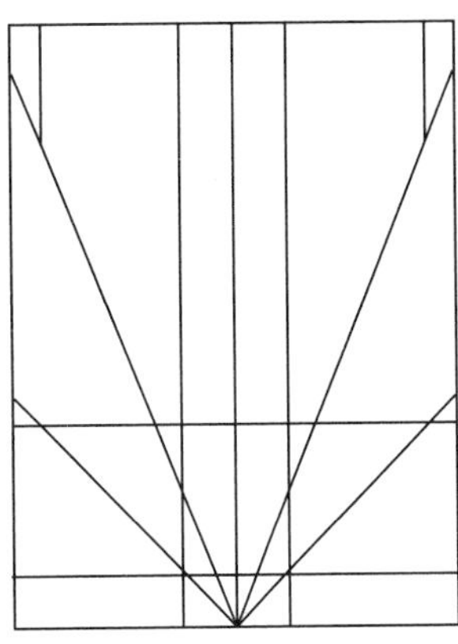

1. Fold along centerline, fold 7, and reopen

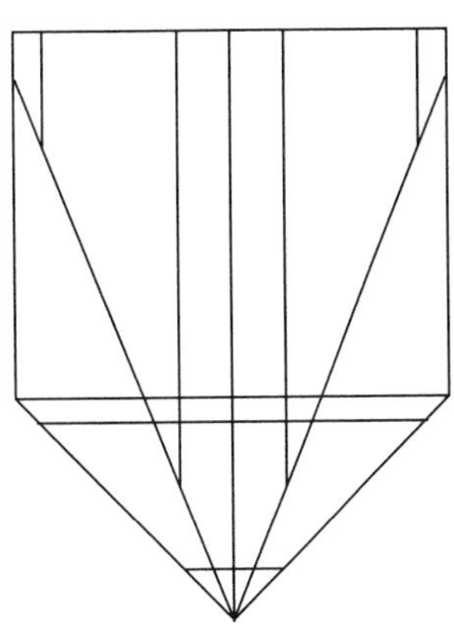

2. Fold along lines 1 and 2.

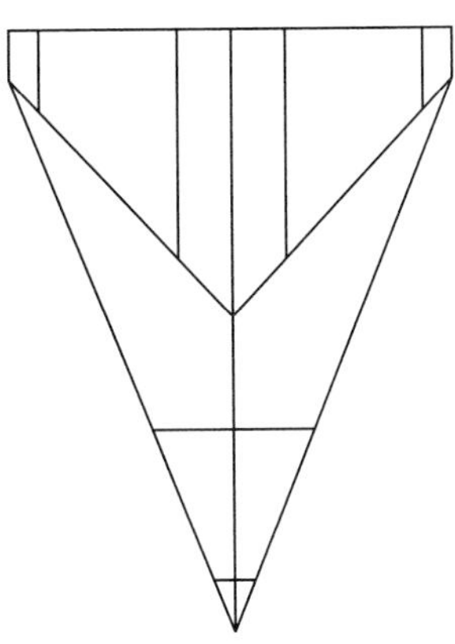

3. Fold along lines 3 and 4.

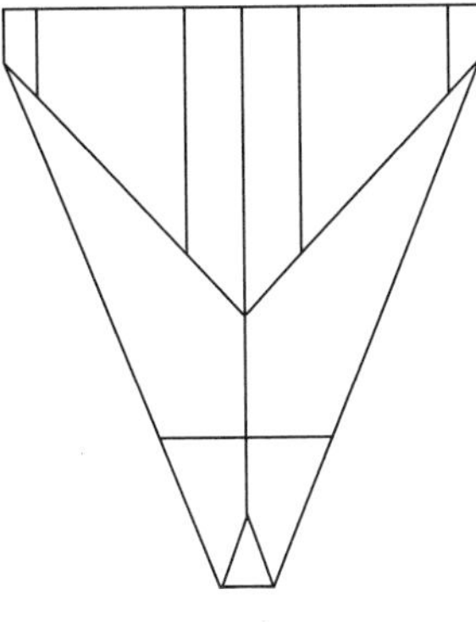

4. Fold nose up on line 5.

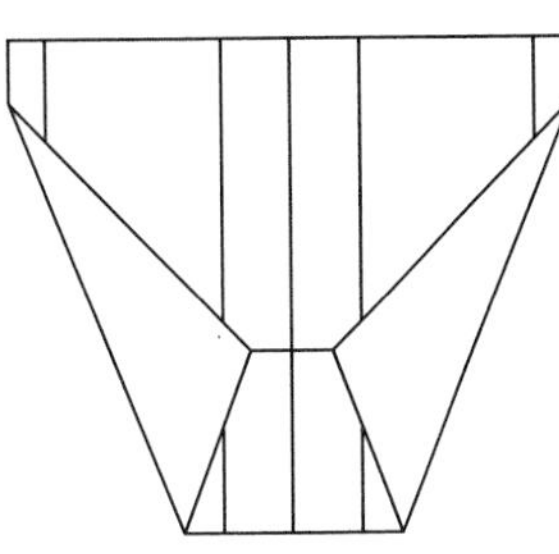

5. Fold nose up on line 6 and tuck under flap.

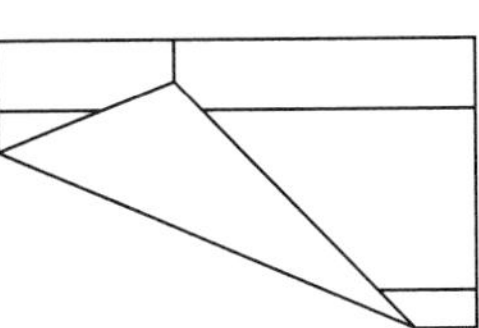

6. Rotate plane and fold in half along its centerline, fold 7.

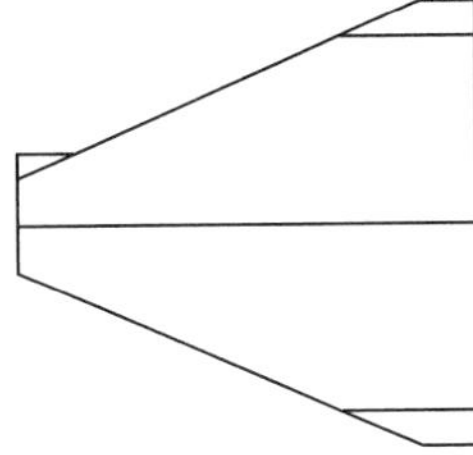

7. Fold wing along line 8.

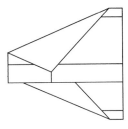

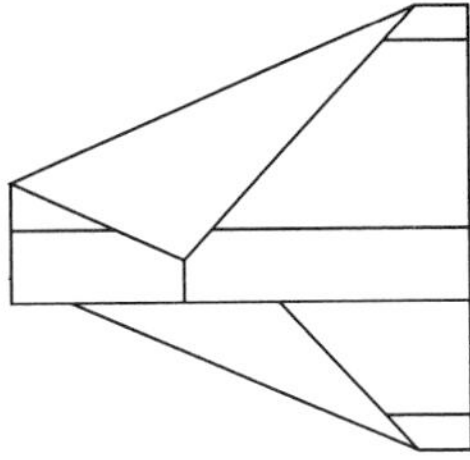

8. Flip plane over.

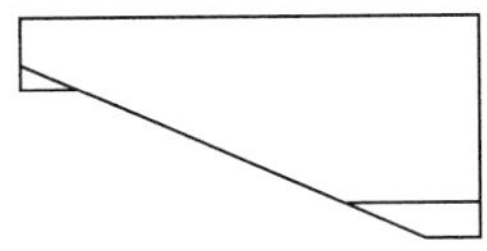

9. Fold wing down along line 9.

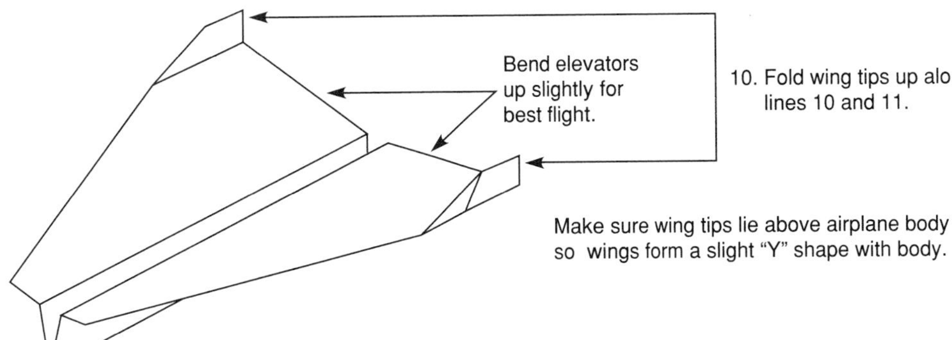

Bend elevators up slightly for best flight.
10. Fold wing tips up along lines 10 and 11.
Make sure wing tips lie above airplane body so wings form a slight "Y" shape with body.

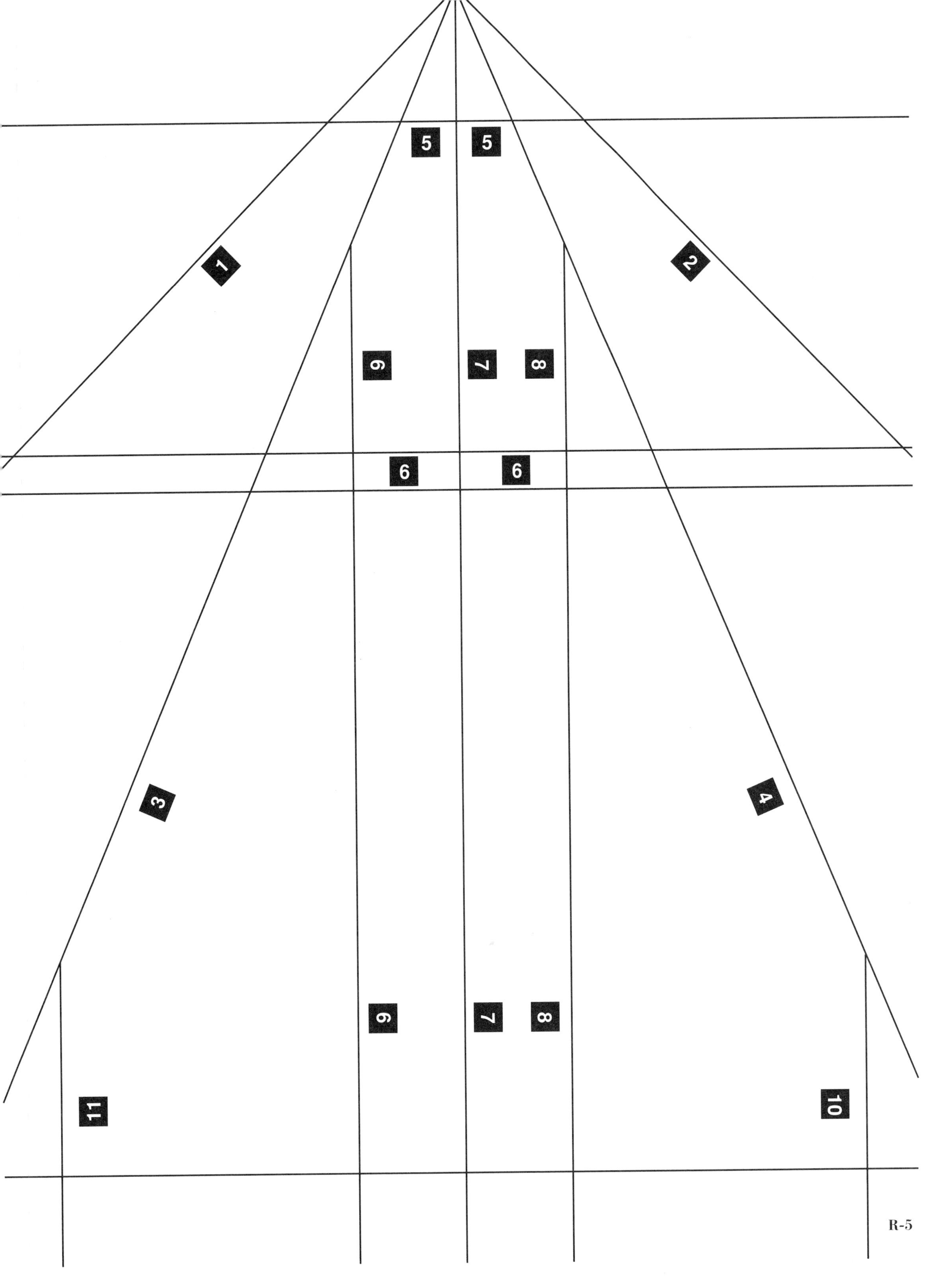
1
2
3
4
5
5
6
6
7
8
9
10
11

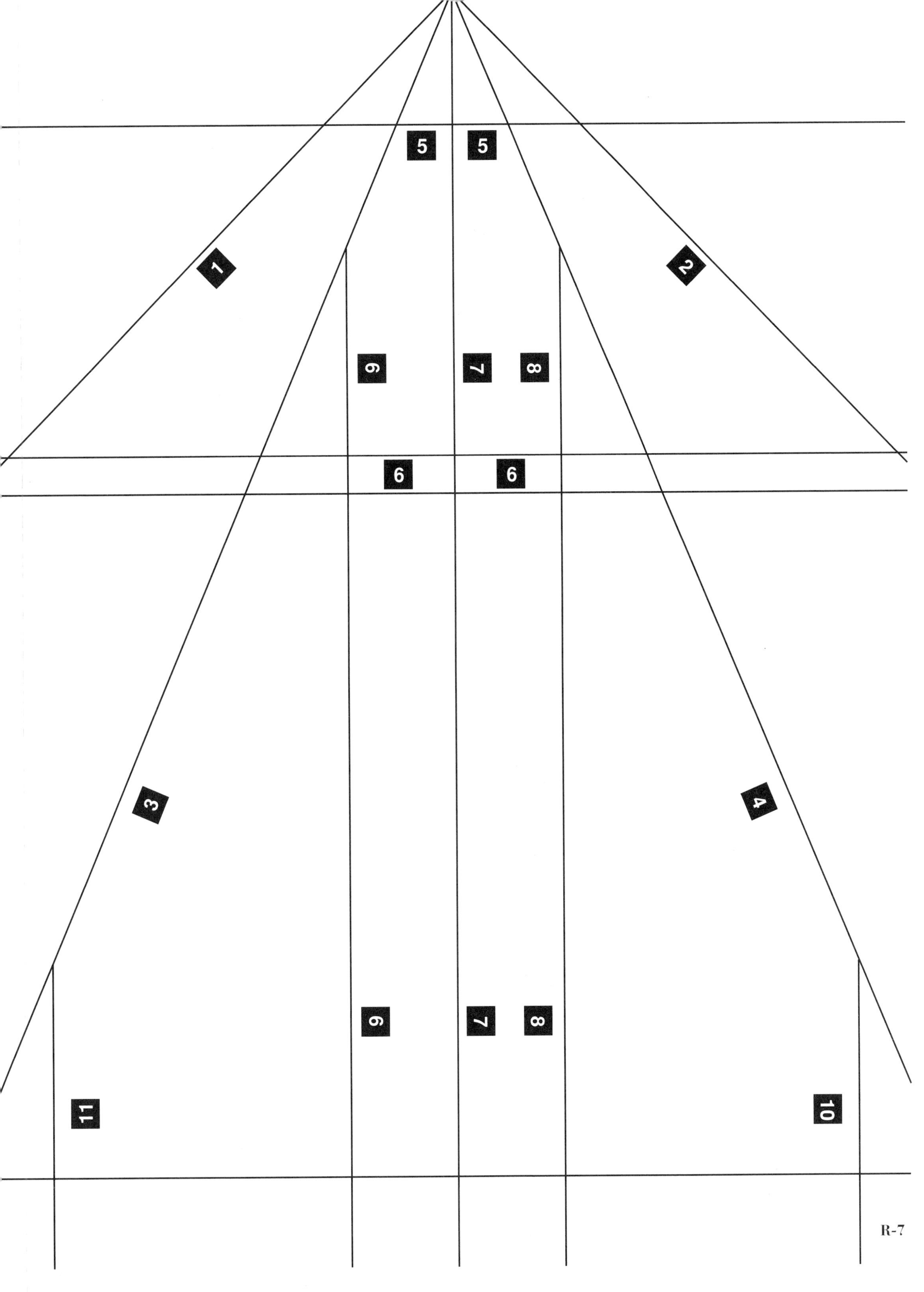
5
5
1
2
9
7
8
6
6
3
4
9
7
8
11
10

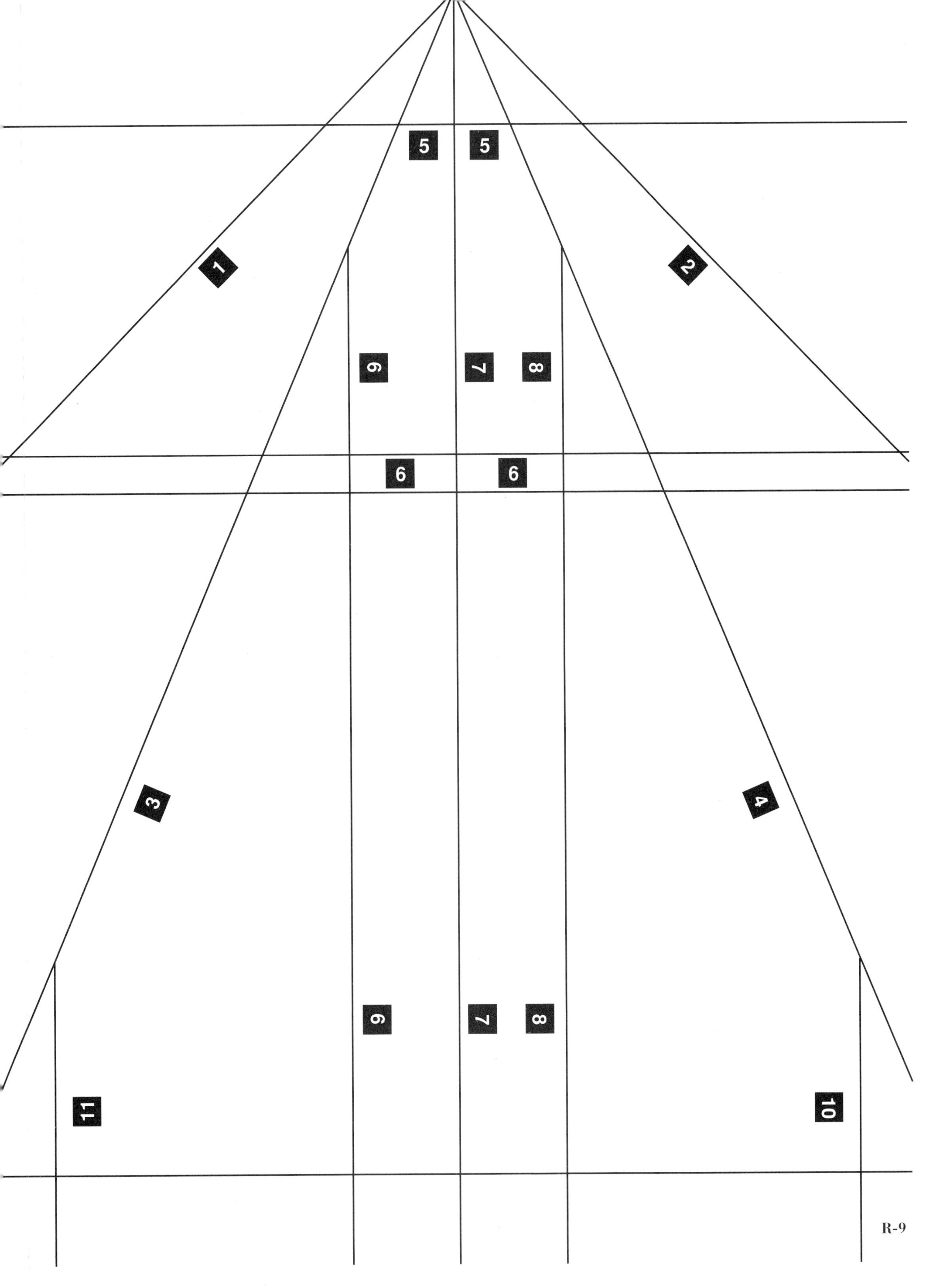
5
5
1
2
9
7
8
6
6
3
4
9
7
8
11
10

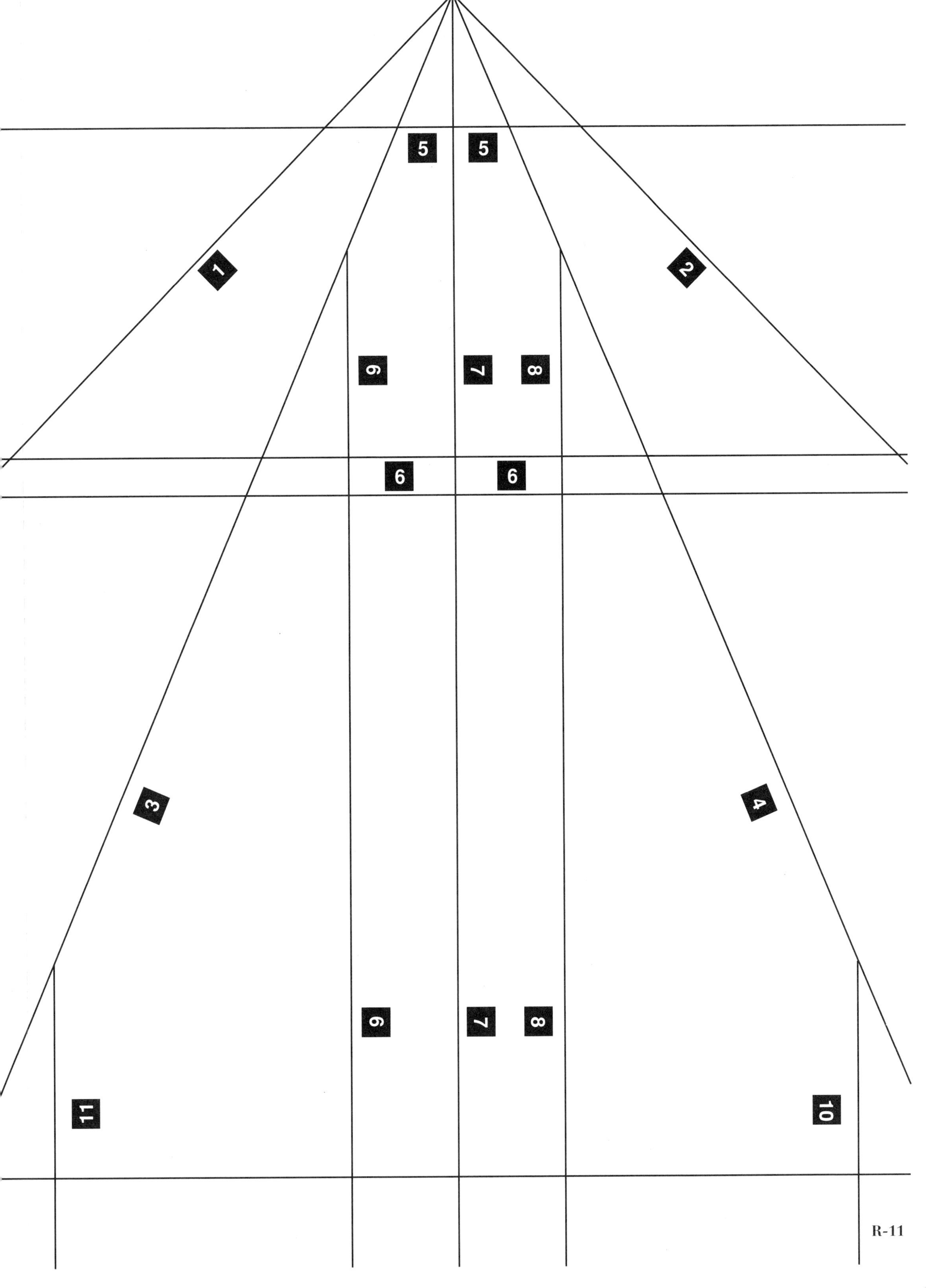

5
5
1
2
9
7
8
6
6
3
4
9
7
8
11
10

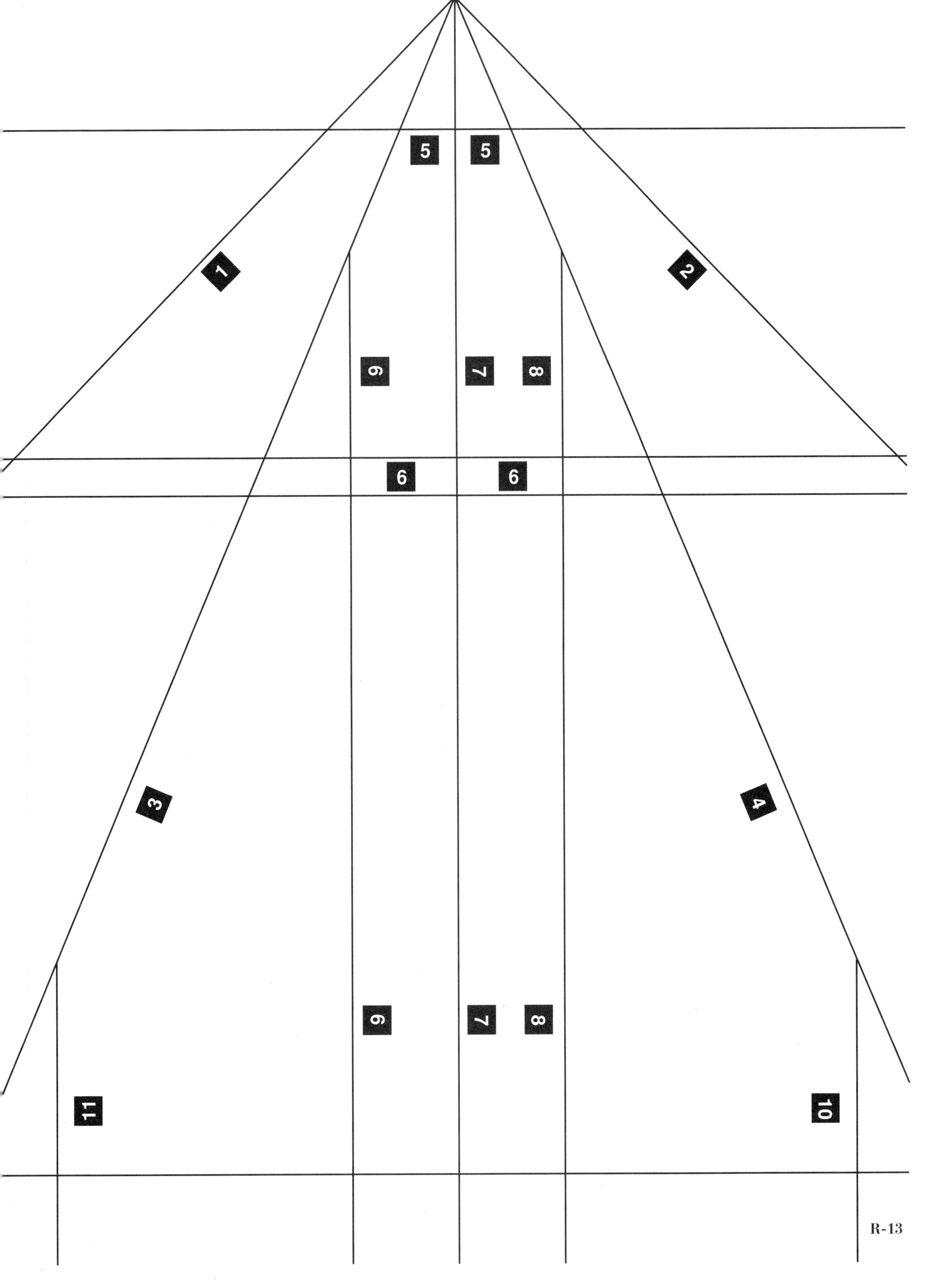
5
5
1
2
9
7
8
6
6
3
4
9
7
8
11
10

Appendix S Custom Nests Simulation: Roles

Supervisor

The supervisor's job at Custom Nests is considered the most important job in the plant. In all, there are three supervisors, but there is little need for interaction among them. The supervisor in this company is considered to be the expert, the conflict manager, the scheduler, the communicator, and the quality control representative, to name a few roles.

You, however, have a very special supervisory role in that you are personally responsible for the production of Custom Nests' standard birdhouse. You are directly responsible for all production and maintenance functions within your product line. Your immediate superior is the only operations manager for all products. Although he recognizes the importance of your product, he prefers to give you total responsibility for operations in your area. This means that from his perspective, when problems arise, you are to blame.

The relationships between you and your direct reports are good for the most part. There are times when you are put in the middle and therefore are thought to be the bad guy, but most people know that you are between a rock and a hard place. You basically do what you have to do to get the job done and to keep your job.

Like all of the other supervisors, you have moved your way up through the system over the years. You know almost all of the jobs from personal experience and got the supervisor's job because of your knowledge of technical processes and your apparent desire to move up in the organization. In addition, you seem to be able to get people to work hard and fast.

Your specific responsibilities include

1. Scheduling, monitoring time cards, and establishing production speeds.
2. Communications from department to department and from management to hourly employees.
3. Supervising maintenance work.
4. Supervising materials handling.
5. Supervising production.
6. Conflict management.
7. Employee counseling and coaching.
8. Handling first-step grievances.
9. Daily and weekly production reports.
10. Managing the absenteeism program.
11. Providing technical skills training.

Source: Contributed by Dr. Barry Morris.

Quality Control

The quality control department was created in the early 1960s when it was impossible for workers and supervisors to build and check the quality of their own work. As the company's products have diversified, the need for a QC department has grown even more essential. Unskilled hourly employees could not possibly understand the importance of quality to the success of the business nor could they keep track of all of the standards and specifications required for each of the company's 33 birdhouse styles, not to mention the accessories.

Finished products are delivered to the quality control department from each product section. The largest group of QC personnel is assigned to Custom Nests' standard birdhouse, which has been the company's primary product since the company was established in 1951 when only six craftsmen built the birdhouses by hand and cared about the results of their labor.

The QC department is located in the back corner of the plant, far removed from the production department. QC personnel tend to have very little contact with any of the workers on the line. They communicate primarily with the manager of operations and occasionally the supervisor, who does a lot of the QC work himself. Under normal circumstances QC does not usually talk to the supervisor, but the manager of operations prefers to let the supervisor from the standard birdhouse production area manage most of his own operations-related issues.

The QC personnel are primarily engineers. They tend to be young and have recently graduated from local colleges. Some of them began with the company as co-op students and, following graduation, continued their work for Custom Nests. The QC engineers responsible for the company's standard birdhouse must examine hundreds of birdhouses a week. They haven't got the time to look at every birdhouse unless there is a production breakdown, which gives them an opportunity to catch up. The work they do is very repetitive and boring. On occasion they get an opportunity to work on technological problems causing consistent quality problems. For the most part, however, their skills are not needed or used since the manager of QC prefers to do any of the really challenging work himself. As a result of boredom and lack of challenging work, there is a lot of turnover in this department. Aside from the manager of QC, the average tenure of QC personnel is three and a half years.

Quality control personnel are responsible for determining the quality of the finished birdhouse based on a set of quality standards listed on the Quality Standards and Specifications List. (See the next section.) They make the final decision to keep a finished birdhouse or to throw it away. In addition, they prepare reports for the operations manager and the accounting department.

Quality Standards and Specifications List

Custom Nests' standard birdhouse quality standards and specifications are

1. No lines are to be on the outside surfaces of the birdhouse.
2. All staples must face the inside of the birdhouse; the flat side of the staple should be on the outside surfaces of the birdhouse.
3. Tape should thoroughly cover the roof's center connection.
4. The stapler's employee number should appear on the bottom of the birdhouse.
5. There should be no gaps in any of the corners and connections.
6. The bottom width of the birdhouse should be as close to 3 1/2 inches as possible.
7. The sides should be between 3 and 3 1/4 inches high.
8. The length of the birdhouse should be between 5 1/2 and 6 inches.
9. The perch should stick out 1 1/2 to 2 inches from the front of the birdhouse.
10. The entry hole on the front panel should be 1 to 1 1/4 inches above the floor of the birdhouse, and it should be centered.
11. The diameter of the entry should be between 2 and 2 1/4 inches.

12. No creases should appear in any of the flat surfaces of the birdhouse.
13. All folds in the front and rear panels should be very close to 1/4 inch.
14. All cuts made to prepare front and rear panels for folding should be as close to 1/4 inch as possible.
15. The finished birdhouse should sit flat on a table.

Research and Development

The research and development department is involved in the design of new products, the improvement of old products, customer relations, and marketing. This department was established in 1976. The housing market was declining and a new line of birdhouses was needed to meet the needs of apartment dwellers. In addition, the traditional Custom Nests product was becoming less effective. More and more home owners and distributors were complaining that the birdhouses were not squirrel-proof. Ways had to be found to keep squirrels from climbing up the birdhouse pole or down from the trees above to steal bird seed from the beaks of hungry baby birds.

Members of the research and development department spend most of their time at the drafting tables or out in the field talking with the customers and distributors of birdhouses. Little if any time is spent in the plant. Any design changes are decided upon by R&D personnel along with management, and these are communicated through the manager of operations, to the supervisor, and so forth. R&D reports directly to the owner, Mr. Jay Blue.

The R&D function is relatively new to the organization and its personnel were hired from the outside. The turnover in the department is high. It seems to be a place where young designers get a chance to learn about the real world just after they have finished their engineering degrees. You therefore have probably been with the company for about two years. The pay is less than you expect to be able to make in the future and the extent to which you are challenged in your work is unsatisfactory. It's just a job and a possible step to a better future.

Accounting

The accounting position was established in 1971 when two major developments occurred: (1) The company had been growing and the owner was no longer able to manage the books and keep up with the growth of the business and (2) you married the boss's younger sister. You are fairly secure in your position since you have been doing it for so long. In addition, your relationship with your brother-in-law is good. He confides in you a great deal since he sees you as his friend and somebody concerned about the business. You must, however, work very hard because you have something to prove to the rest of the employees (that you are not a freeloader). You also know something your brother-in-law doesn't know—your wife is unhappy with your marriage and you are worried about how that might affect your future, even though you know that your brother-in-law likes you better.

You have major responsibility for much of the management work in the plant. In addition to your accounting responsibilities, you must do all of the ordering of materials, while also managing the shipping department. Recently you took over responsibility for employee relations when the employee relations manager was hospitalized for cardiac problems. You expected to have the job for a month or so, but that was five months ago, and the man's health is still uncertain. All you can really handle is some of the administrative trivia required by the union; you have had little time to talk with the employees about their grievances or their benefits.

Some of your specific accounting responsibilities include

a. Purchasing.

b. Supplying raw materials to maintenance/supply personnel.

c. Collecting data gathered by the material/supply department and the quality control department.

d. Analyzing the above collected data in six areas: total number of 4×6 cards distributed; total number of 4×6 cards used; number of birdhouses produced; number of birdhouses accepted; perches distributed and used; and waste.

The data analysis worksheet attached can be used for your analysis.

ACCOUNTING
DATA ANALYSIS WORKSHEET

Raw Materials Data

Total number of 4×6 cards distributed ____________

Total number of 4×6 cards used ____________

Total number of perches distributed ____________

Total number of perches used ____________

Waste ____________

Quality Control Data

Number of birdhouses produced ____________

Number of birdhouses accepted ____________

Waste ____________

Maintenance/Supply

Maintenance and supply personnel are primarily production people who have moved their way up through the system. None of you have any formal training in machine maintenance and repair, though your experience with the company has provided you with the skills to make simple repairs on the equipment used in the plant.

In an effort to cut costs, two years ago the supply function merged with maintenance. You consequently have the responsibility for equipment maintenance, supplying raw materials to all functions in the plant, and the movement of components from one function to another. You move throughout the plant and probably have the best information about the ''goings on'' in the plant. Unfortunately, there is little you can do with all of this information. You must report to and take orders from the supervisor in charge of production.

Your work is anything but boring since you always have plenty to do. The problem is that you are spread too thin and are unable to do any single job to the best of your ability. This bothers you since you have been with the company for a long time and know that product quality and employee morale have been better in the past.

The majority of the maintenance/supply personnel have been with the company for 25 years or more. Many of you are waiting for the opportunity to retire. Your wages and benefits are fair, but not as good as your counterparts in similar industries. Some of you could potentially leave Custom Nests in pursuit of maintenance jobs in other companies, but you know that the skills required here may be inadequate in another organization. Besides, you have been here for a long time and you like the people. As a matter of fact, your ability to see and talk to a lot of people in the plant is one thing that motivates you to come to work.

Maintenance/Supply: Job Description

Your job is (1) to provide raw materials to each function in the plant: 4×6 cards to tapers and cutters, staples and straws to staplers, tape to tapers; (2) to transport finished components of the birdhouse to the next stage in the assembly process: transport front and rear panels from the cutters to the staplers, roofs and side/bottom components from the tapers to the staplers, and finished products from the staplers to quality control; (3) to repair or replace equipment used by cutters, staplers, and tapers; and (4) to maintain records of materials being supplied and components being transported from department to department, and finished birdhouses being transported to quality control.

MAINTENANCE/SUPPLY INVENTORY SHEET

Raw materials:

4×6 cards supplied to tapers ______

4×6 cards supplied to cutters ______

Straws applied to staplers ______

Completed components (record finished sets):

Sets transported from taping to stapling (A set consists of one completed roof and one completed side/bottom panel.) ______

Sets transported from cutting to stapling (A set consists of a front and rear panel cut and folded.) ______

Completed birdhouses:

Number of completed birdhouses transported to quality control. ______

Stapler

In the production area, the stapler position is one of the most complex and highest-rated positions in the company. The majority of workers in this area have been with the company for 20 years or more and have worked in this area for at least nine years. Most of you have worked your way up through the lower-skill positions, and one stapler was one of the original craftsmen with the company in the very beginning. Because of your seniority, it is possible that a few of you will be retiring in a few years. Movement in this position means potential advancement for people in less-skilled positions. The position has the highest pay rate for production workers at Custom Nests, yet your wages are lower than your counterparts in similar industries. As a result, many of you are involved in the union's fight for higher wages. The fact that many of you grew up in the union movement has made you staunch union supporters who believe strongly that the union is the way.

The stapler's job is most dependent on the workmanship of the cutters and tapers who build the pieces of the birdhouse that you must assemble. For the most part, however, you will assemble the parts that you receive, and those you manufacture (perches) regardless of their condition. It is not your job to determine if a part is good enough to use.

The technology that you utilize in the stapling function is rather simple, yet numerous technological problems arise on a regular basis. Parts and maintenance are often hard to find.

Although the work is more complex than other production jobs, you have found that with some experience, the work becomes simple and repetitive, and as a result it is often boring. The fact that you are the final production function means that problems in other areas create work slowdowns or shutdowns for you.

Stapler: Job Description

Your job is (1) to staple the sides and bottom of the birdhouse to the front and rear panels, (2) to staple the roof to the front and rear panels of the birdhouse, and (3) to prepare and attach the perch to the birdhouse door.

Specific instructions and responsibilities are

a. Attach the bottom/side component to the folds in the front and rear panels of the birdhouse.

b. Attach the roof component to the folds in the front and rear panels of the birdhouse.

c. Cut a 2 to 2 1/2-inch piece of straw.

d. Bend and attach the straw to the door of the birdhouse so that the perch extends out from the door 1 1/2 to 2 inches.

e. All staples are to face inward. That is, the flat part of the staples should be on the outside surface of the final product, except for the staples in the bend at the floor. These should face the ground.

f. Each stapler should place his or her employee number on the very bottom of the assembled product.

g. When a birdhouse is complete, it must be transported to quality control.

Employee Number ______

Cutters

The cutters' position is one of the lower-paying hourly positions in the company. The majority of the workers in this area have been with the company for at least 13 years and have been in the cutting area for a minimum of seven years. Over that time most of you have moved up through the organization, learning as you went and bidding on new jobs as they came open.

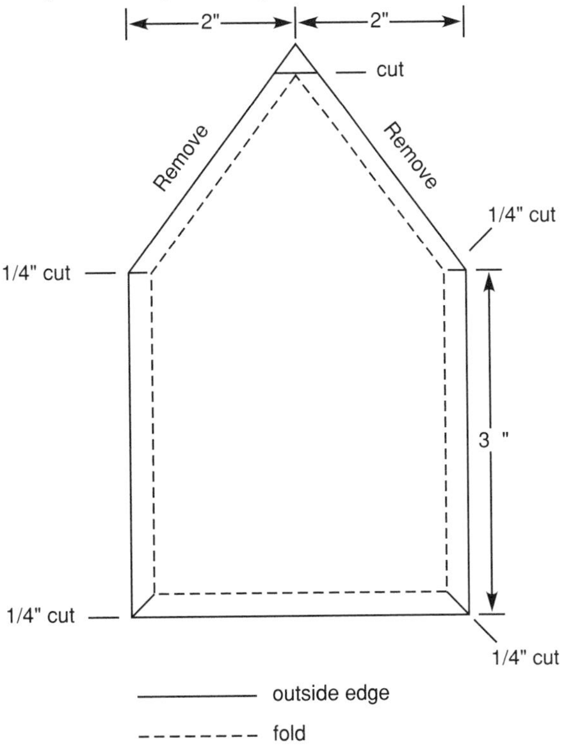

The cutting job tends to be rather boring once you have learned the work. It really takes little thinking for you to do what is expected of you.

Custom Nests pays a little less than other companies in the area. You and your fellow union members have been pushing for the last couple of years to have wages raised to comparable standards. The company just says that the demand for birdhouses is expected to drop as a result of Japanese competition. The only way for you to make more is to move to stapling or maintenance. But these jobs are hard to come by and are bid on by many. The way you see it, cutting is going to be your job for the next few years.

Cutter: Job Description

The job of a cutter is (1) to cut and fold, from 4×6 cards supplied by the maintenance/supply personnel, the front and rear panels of Custom Nests standard birdhouse and (2) to cut the birdhouse door in all front panels.

Specific responsibilities and panel design are included below:

a. Front and rear panels should be made consistent with the above drawing.

b. On all front panels a 2 to 2 1/4-inch hole must be cut 1 to 1 1/4 inches from the bottom of the front panel, and it should be centered.

c. The worker's number must be put on the back of each finished piece.

d. Finished goods (completed front and back panels) must be sent to the stapling department.

e. Panels should be identified as ''front'' or ''back'' on the lined side of the panel.

Employee Number ______

Tapers

The taper's job receives the lowest pay rate in the organization. People in this work area have been with the company for the least amount of time. Like other work areas, your pay rate is lower than most industries in similar markets, and you have been fairly active in the pursuit of higher wages. Unlike some people who have been with the company for several years, you have been fortunate enough to have received a full high school education and some of you have been to college. The job market in the past few years, however, has forced you to take work that underutilizes your abilities.

The perceived stability but no growth position in the birdhouse business means that there is likely to be little advancement for you in this business unless people in higher-ranked jobs either retire or die. As a result you come to work to make a living, to receive your benefits, and to kill time. The work is boring and simple, and it requires little thought.

Taper: Job Description

The job of taper requires that you (1) tape together two 4×6 cards to make the roof of Custom Nests standard birdhouses and (2) tape together and fold three 4×6 cards to make the sides and bottom of the birdhouses.

Job specifications are listed below:

a. Two cards taped together at their longest side make the roof. The tape should be applied so that no water can leak into the birdhouse.

b. The three cards utilized for the sides and bottom must be folded and taped together so that the bottom is 3 1/2 inches wide, and the sides are no more than 3 to 3 1/4 inches tall. Two seams requiring one long strip of tape each are all that are needed based on the original design of the birdhouse. Tape is a most expensive material and must be used with cost in mind.

c. Tapers' numbers should be put on the underside of each roof and floor/side structure produced in your department.

d. Your finished products must be transported to the stapling department.

e. Tapers should identify each part by making it ''roof'' or ''floor.'' All identification markings should be written on the lined side of the 4×6 card.

Employee number ______

Appendix T FoodCo, Inc., Parts B and C

Part B

In February, Tom Hawkins met with Don Stevens to discuss why employees at FoodCo's Cleveland plant had voted against the "new management concept," which would have added more autonomy, decision making, and variety to their work. Tom began by reviewing some comments that employees had written on the recent survey to assess attitudes toward the new management concept. Typical of these remarks were the following:

> You can't trust management at this site. They will tell you one thing and do another.
>
> Why should we listen to this new concept? We have been burned before by listening to management—why should we be burned again?
>
> The new concept is just another way to get more work out of us for the same pay!

Don had regarded these statements as expressions of a few employees who were bitter toward the company because of past layoffs. Don knew that some of the layoffs had been poorly managed; in one instance, employees were hired at the beginning of December and then laid off just before Christmas when the product they were supposed to produce turned out to be a market failure. But now, it was clear that the comments reflected the feelings of a much larger group of employees. The new management concept, despite its potential benefits, was voted down by a margin of 2 to 1 by the employees who showed up for the vote. This caught Don and Tom by surprise since the survey given a short time earlier had indicated widespread support for the concept by a majority of the employees.

Tom decided to meet with the union board to discuss employees' reasons for refusing to support the proposed change. During the meeting, the union president and vice president were silent; one member of the board, Charley White, did most of the talking.

TOM: Needless to say, I was quite surprised by the employees' decision to reject the new management concept. A short time ago, the majority of employees seemed to be in favor of the idea; now it seems that they're against it. What caused them to change their minds?

CHARLEY: It's about time that management recognized that we have a union here! We've had enough changes shoved down our throats. They don't have any respect for us. They think people are stupid. It's obvious that this was just another way for them to get more work out of us for the same pay. They'll screw you every chance they get! You can tell them I said that, because I've said the same thing to their faces!

TOM: What makes you think they don't respect you? And what makes you think that there was something hidden in their proposal that they didn't tell you about?

CHARLEY: Let me tell you about them. They used to think that they could get away with anything. Then we went on strike after the big layoff three years ago. That didn't

Source: Contributed by Professor William A. Pasmore.

make them look very good. One of them passed me while I was on the picket line and started yelling at me about how union people are a bunch of ignorant farmers—I knew they would be out to get even. Since then, they try to stick it to us every chance they get. You can't trust them—they've proved that over and over again!

It was obvious that the union regarded the vote against the new management concept as a major victory in its struggle against management. It hardly seemed like the time to be thinking about raising the issue again. However, Mr. Williams was under increasing pressure from the corporation to put the new concept into practice. Construction of the new dairy products unit was already behind schedule, which meant that the product would be late getting to market—and that precious market share would be lost.

To get a better sense of how employees were feeling, Tom held a meeting with the foremen. He learned that not all employees participated in the vote against the concept. In fact, only about 80 of the plant's 200 employees voted. Still, most foremen felt strongly that it was time to abandon the new concept.

TOM: What do you think the vote really means? And what makes you think that the new concept won't work?

HAL SIMON (a foreman with 20 years of service): Every time we just get things settled down around here, Chicago comes along with another idea to get things stirred up again. What we really need is a chance to let things cool off for a while. It's obvious that the people don't want this new concept, so why don't we just let it die a peaceful death? We're not Tampa—what they did down there just doesn't sit well with people here. We're used to doing things our way—and even though things aren't perfect here, they aren't bad. Why fix it if it's not broken?

When Tom met with Don Stevens, he reviewed the options available to Mr. Williams:

1. He could exercise the company's legal right to design the new unit as it saw fit. There could be some serious labor problems in the short run if this strategy was followed, but it would be one way to get things moving again.

2. He could try to convince corporate management to abandon its demand to implement the new concept. He could explain that people in the plant had voted against it, and that it would be faster to build and operate the plant according to traditional principles.

3. He could approach the union and request that the concept be reconsidered by the employees, despite their overwhelming vote against it.

None of the options appeared attractive, but something had to be done. Don had heard rumors that the corporation might decide to locate the unit elsewhere if Cleveland's problems couldn't be resolved soon.

Part C

About a year later, Tom Hawkins met with Don Stevens to discuss the successful start-up of the new dairy products operation in the Cleveland plant. Both were pleased that things had turned out so well. The new operation had exceeded its first-year production goals by more than a third; at the same time, costs were lower than had been projected for the *original* level of production. (See Exhibit 1.) The new unit operated with fewer employees than the traditional method would have called for, which resulted in an additional fixed-cost savings of over $250,000 per year. Employee attitudes had improved significantly. By all accounts, the start-up had been one of the smoothest and most successful in the corporation's history.

Don reflected on the events that made the success possible:

If we hadn't been willing to go back to the union and ask for their input, who knows where we would have been today. That was tough for Williams. He didn't like the idea of asking for the union's help in making this thing work. I'm not sure that he believed then that it really would—but I guess he didn't have much choice. Chicago was getting pretty upset. Williams knew he

Exhibit 1
Product T Planned versus Actual Start-up Volumes and Costs

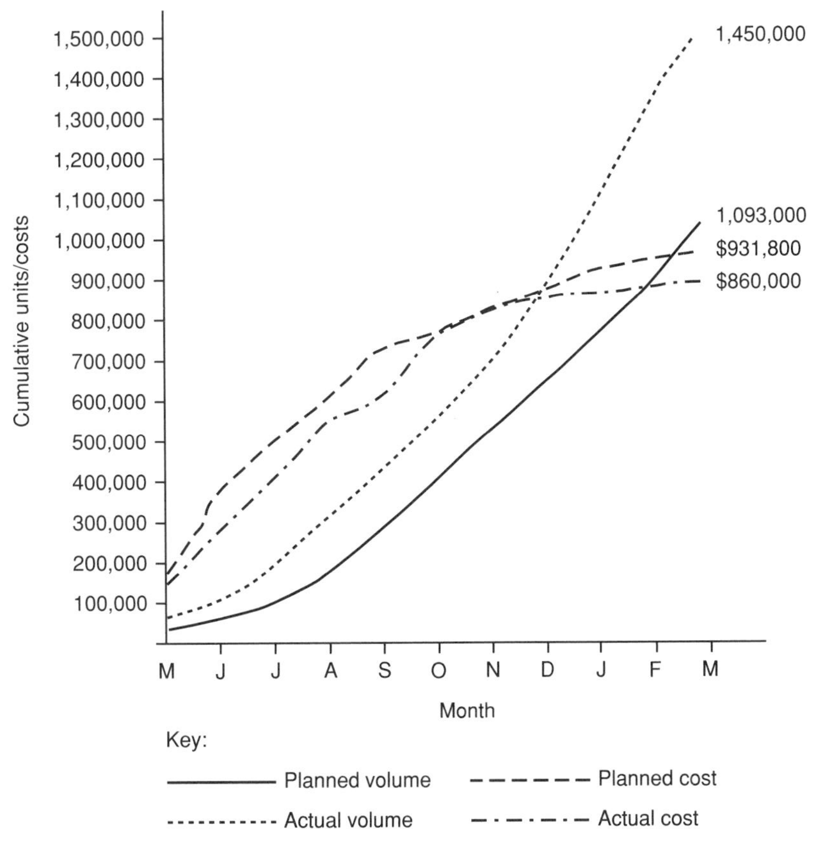

would have to make some concessions to get the union to buy in, and he was right. But they were actually pretty reasonable when you think about it. Sure, they wanted to eliminate the idea of rotating shifts and managed to make sure that moving to the new unit would be voluntary. They even got Williams to agree to their idea that people who worked in the new unit should get more pay than the average person in the existing operations. All that was easy—what was hard was getting Williams to agree to rename the "new management concept" the "union concept." At first he felt like he was giving away the store, but then he realized that the union leadership needed some way to look good if they were going to go back to the membership and ask them to reconsider the vote. This way, they looked like heroes. Williams did too—when he got over being angry and saw how well things were going, he even began to spread the idea to the rest of the plant. We have a long way to go, but we're getting there.

The new operation *was* impressive, Tom thought to himself. Dick Harold had done an outstanding job of selecting a group of people to act as supervisors in the new unit. He had purposely chosen people with a wide variety of backgrounds; but they all had one thing in common, that is, wanting to learn how to work effectively with people instead of just giving orders. Dick had each of them go through extensive interpersonal training in addition to learning about the new technology. Then he had them conduct a sociotechnical systems analysis of their parts of the operation so that they would understand what kinds of problems might arise and what people would have to do to prevent those problems from occurring.

The teams had exceeded everyone's expectations; they learned faster and assumed more responsibility for the operation in the first year than employees ever had in the rest of the plant. In that short time, each team was already handling its own quality control and a good portion of its own maintenance work. Team members were teaching each other how to perform all of the jobs in the teams, and team members used the production information they received from management to make most of their own decisions concerning the scheduling of production and ordering of raw materials. The plant had been designed to make it easy for the teams to meet and discuss problems or do planning; meeting rooms were provided and buffer inventories were installed between team areas to allow teams to meet without disrupting the work of other teams. Some supervisors in the new unit accomplished their ultimate objective—working themselves out of a job. Their teams had assumed enough responsibility to operate effectively without them so they moved to other jobs in the corporation.

Don Stevens received a promotion when Mr. Williams retired. Yes, Tom thought, things had turned out well. But he couldn't help thinking that there should have been a better way. He admitted to himself that they had been lucky—things could easily have turned out differently. How would he do it the next time?

Appendix U Crofts Products Company: In-Basket Memorandums

Office Memorandum

To: Mr./Ms. Dawson, Executive V.P. Date: April 15
From: Barbara
Subject: Your correspondence

These are all the memos that have come in today. The most important is Mr. Harrison's, which is on top.

Note I already have scheduled you for the following times next week:

Monday, April 18, 1:00 PM–5:00 PM	Corporation meeting
Tuesday, April 19, 11:30 AM–1:30 PM	Retirement lunch
Wednesday, April 20, 8:00 AM–9:00 AM	Your weekly staff meeting
Thursday, April 21, 10:00 AM–12:00 PM	Meeting with Pat Harrison and the corporation. (Note: You are to make presentation.)

The following agenda items were already scheduled by Mr. Alberts for your Wednesday staff meeting, which is attended by all managers reporting directly to you:

1. Energy conservation discussion.
   a. Turning out lights in buildings.
   b. Lowering room temperatures.
   c. Employee car pools.
   d. Gasoline supplies on hand.
2. Paper shortage problems.
3. Change in retirement benefits. (Chris Charleston needs 30 minutes for this.)
4. Expanding opportunities for women and minorities. (Ginny Stein, Personnel, to make presentation.)

Have a good weekend!

——————————————————————(CUT ON LINE)——————————————————————

Office Memorandum

To: Mr./Ms. Dawson, Executive V.P. Date: April 15
From: Pat Harrison
Subject: Attendance at meetings

1. In meetings prior to your arrival on the scene, we decided to accelerate the expansion of our hardline products. We have not been making appropriate progress with plans for new hardline developments, and decisions must be made soon for allotting funds and workers to this area. I would like you to present new ideas for hardline products when you and I meet with the corporation representatives from 10:00 AM to 12:00 PM, Thursday, April 21.

2. One thing I am specifically unhappy about is the development of our latest hardline item, the PQS machine, since I have not received the latest monthly report, which was due a week ago. Please have this completed and bring it to my office for the Thursday meeting.

3. I am supposed to attend the monthly corporation meeting in their downtown office on Monday, April 18, from 1:00 to 5:00 PM, but will be out of town until late Tuesday afternoon. Alberts usually sat in for me when I could not be present. I would appreciate your attendance since it will be a good chance for you to meet some of their executives. The meeting agenda does not pertain specifically to Crofts so no preparation is necessary. Just listen for your own information. The corporation will send me a copy of the meeting summary.

Office Memorandum

To: Mr./Ms. Dawson, Executive V.P. Date: April 15
From: Rita Lanstrom
Subject: Request for Appointment

1. If you have an open door policy, I would appreciate an opportunity to speak with you before I make an important career decision.

2. I have been employed here for six months in the controller's office. Today I completed my first appraisal interview with Lynn Joseph. It may be difficult for you to understand when I express great dissatisfaction for receiving a fitness report that was just about perfect. For me, however, the report described the stereotype of the bright, effective, but conforming young professional that this organization would like me to be. The report has little reality for me in terms of how I see my own capabilities or how I feel about my job. My specific complaint is that my attempts to use my analytical abilities and training have been greatly frustrated. I am allowed considerable leeway as to how to do my work, and I am encouraged to write and say anything I want, but my ideas are having no influence on what is happening here. Also, I do not see the controller's office controlling anything at Crofts. Most of the departments do about as they please regardless of requirements. How can I be effective when my role does not permit it?

3. Although by background, education, and interest I feel exceptionally well suited for this organization, I have concerns about working under the present type of management system. I hope you will want to hear more of my views on this matter.

(Note from Barbara)
Mr./Ms. Dawson: This just came is as I was about to leave the office. Rita is one of five MBAs Crofts has recruited over the past two years. She seemed upset when she brought this memo in, and she wanted me to put her down for an appointment. For some reason she does not want anyone to know she is trying to see you. When do you want to see her?

——————————————————(CUT ON LINE)——————————————————

Office Memorandum

To: Mr./Ms. Dawson, Executive V.P. Date: April 15
From: Jamie Jamison, Manager, R&D
Subject: Need for funds

1. You will probably hear we are having problems with the PQS machine, but I wish to assure you everything is proceeding normally and we expect to have the final report out next month. There is something more pressing on which I need your support.

2. Al Alberts promised me we could get $200,000 immediately to start on new developments. Some of our guys have unique and original ideas that could have big payoffs, and they are already starting work on them. Could you arrange to have Lynn Joseph spring loose the $200,000? If we go through all the administrative nonsense of writing formal plans for review and approval of the money, we will not only lose valuable time but may interfere with the "inventive process." Remember, Crofts Products is here today because a few creative guys had some ideas. They never would have made it if they had spent half their time on paper project proposals.

Office Memorandum

To: Mr./Ms. Dawson, Executive V.P. Date: April 15
From: Kim Richardson, Special Assistant to the Executive V.P.
Subject: Monthly Reporting on the PQS Machine

1. There is one item I am handling that does require your immediate attention. Al Alberts made me special assistant for coordinating the monthly report on the development of the PQS machine when it was initiated six months ago. At that time, I got together with Chris Charleston, manager for administrative services, and Lynn Joseph, controller, and we worked out the company's reporting plan for this project. It was designed to control personnel and funding allotments and to ensure that Al was kept informed on the progress of every aspect of the machine.

2. The only way our system can work is for the departments to coordinate activities closely and to follow the procedures set forth in the monthly reporting requirements. The departments are not taking this project seriously, no matter how much fuss we raise. R&D is following its usual ''do-your-own-thing'' approach. Instead of a monthly report, I received Jamie Jamison's note saying, ''All these reporting procedures are overemphasizing the PQS machine. Problems are not too great, and we expect the final report next month.'' Seymour Simon in Production merely sent a memorandum saying, ''Seasonal pressures have prevented us from completing production estimates for the PQS machine.'' The other departments have a similar attitude but have not even bothered to meet my request for their overdue monthly reports. I am only a staff coordinator and cannot enforce compliance.

3. Lynn Joseph and Chris Charleston have read this memorandum and agree that the above accurately describes the situation on the PQS machine. In summary, we do not know the present status and cannot prepare an overall report until all departments provide us complete information.

4. This is only one of my activities, but most of my responsibilities involve similar problems. I would like to discuss these with you.

————————————————————(CUT ON LINE)————————————————————

Office Memorandum

To: Mr./Ms. Dawson, Executive V.P. Date: April 15
From: Seymour Simon, Manager, Production
Subject: Inventory Needs

1. One matter I must discuss with you soonest is the inventory problem. At this time of the year, we are getting many small orders for seasonal items. Each order requires considerable expense for set-up time. Sometimes we complete a small order and two days later receive another small order for the same item. This means two set-up times for a small-volume product. We should at least be making estimates for orders for the entire season and building up an inventory from which orders can be filled.

2. Lynn Joseph tells me he cannot let me have the money to build up the inventory. I took this up a week ago with Al Alberts, who agreed with me; I have been awaiting his response. We really can't let this go any longer.

Office Memorandum

To: Mr./Ms. Dawson, Executive V.P. Date: April 15
From: Lou Jackson, Manager, Engineering
Subject: Engineering Activities

1. Our shop is in excellent shape so we have no immediate problems to take up with you. We are prepared to brief you on our ideas, activities, and plans whenever you can work it into your schedule.

2. You will probably hear something about the PQS machine developments. Although there is no immediate urgency in this regard, we cannot proceed with redesign until we get the latest final report from R&D. They tell us we already have received from them all the data we need, and their final report confirming this is only a formality. My men say they do not have all the data required. I discussed this with Al Alberts a couple of weeks ago and he was going to take it up with Jamison.

————————————————————(CUT ON LINE)————————————————————

Office Memorandum

To: Mr./Ms. Dawson, Executive V.P. Date: April 15
From: Chris Charleston, Manager, Administrative Services
Subject: Retirement Luncheon

1. Sam Frank, one of our oldest production employees, will retire this month; a noon banquet has been scheduled in the Hotel Intown's Beef and Bourbon Room for Tuesday, April 19, from 11:30 AM to 1:30 PM.

2. Al Alberts was to make the farewell talk and present the company gift, since he felt this was an important occasion to show the company's intense interest in the fine quality of those working here at Crofts. I have asked Seymour Simon to fill in for Al, but I was sure you would want to be with the rest of the management team to salute Sam's farewell, so I asked Barbara to put it on your calendar.

————————————————————(CUT ON LINE)————————————————————

Office Memorandum

To: Mr./Ms. Dawson, Executive V.P. Date: April 15
From: Mary Merriweather, Manager, Marketing and Sales
Subject: PQS Machine

I would appreciate an early opportunity to brief you on our needs and planning which are based on the most recent information from our field representatives. The most urgent pending matter is the PQS machine. This should go on the market immediately, priced at least as low as our competitors, or it could start affecting our well-established products. Although it is not a major item in itself, it is timely in the sense that businesspeople want to experiment with it. Alvin Alberts assured me that I was right on this and that I had his complete support for the earliest date of completion. The pressures on our representatives in the field are great, and they have been telling their customers that we will have the PQS on the market by May 15. We can't let them down.

Glossary

A

360-degree leadership feedback psychometric instruments designed to measure on-the-job development; individuals are rated by themselves, their peers, bosses and employees on theory based leadership skills.

accommodating orientation a conflict handling where one group attempts to satisfy the concerns of the other by neglecting its own concerns or goals.

achievement oriented leadership a path-goal leadership style where the leader is preoccupied with setting challenging goals for the work group.

action orientation a focus on doing or acting as opposed to planning.

action research an emergent inquiry process in which behavioral and social science knowledge is integrated with existing organizational knowledge to produce new, usable knowledge.

actors employees or the human organization

adaptation-innovation model a creativity approach that identifies two types of people in organizations—adaptors and innovators. Adaptors prefer structured situations and seek answers to the problems at hand. Innovators appreciate unstructured work environments and seek to answer questions that have not yet been asked.

adaptors of IT developers and users who have already made information technology an essential element of their value-based planning.

administrative innovation innovations that pertain to daily organizational activities, for example, incentive systems, and communication networks.

administrative school a classical management approach led by Henry Fayol; focused on the five basic functions of management-planning, organizing, commanding, coordinating, and controlling.

adoptors of IT those who purchase "off the shelf" products and apply them in a routine fashion for either short-term survival or catching up with competitors.

adult learner individuals beyond adolescence engaged in learning.

age diversity a broad age distribution in organizations.

assertiveness the degree to which the group wants to satisfy its own concerns

assessment center (AC) a method of evaluating employees—usually managers—by conducting job simulations to observe the job-related behaviors of candidates.

attribution process a perceptual process whereby the perceived causes of events, not the actual events, influence individual behavior.

avoidance orientation a conflict-handling approach in which both groups neglect the concerns involved by sidestepping issues or postponing conflict by choosing not to deal with it.

B

behavioral leadership theory an approach that attempts to identify what good leaders do.

behavior modification an attempt to change behavior by operant conditioning, that is, voluntary behavior is rewarded and incorrect behavior is ignored or punished.

behavioral science school a neoclassical management approach that was an outgrowth of the human relations school; focused on individual behavior within work groups.

big five personality theory theory postulating that there are five factors of personality-extraversion, agreeableness, conscientiousness, emotional stability and openness to experience-that can serve as a meaningful taxonomy for classifying personality attributes.

brainstorming a group thought-generation process that revolves around the spontaneous, uncontained expression of ideas.

C

career anchor distinctive pattern of self-perceived talents, motives, and values that guide career decision-making throughout a person's life.

career development an ongoing effort of both individuals and organizations to expand career opportunities and realize career goals.

career path a sequence of job changes that an employee may pursue in order to attain a given target position.

career planning a combined effort between an organization and an individual to meet organizational and individual goals by managing the flow of individuals through positions over time.

career plateaus the points in one's career where the likelihood of further promotion is low.

career-resilient work force

career stage the five steps most people go through in their careers: growth, exploratory, establishment, maintenance and decline.

cell system an advanced manufacturing system consisting of equipment and materials for the production of parts.

charismatic leader individuals who, by sheer strength of their personality, effect strong influence over others.

classical conditioning a basic form of learning involving reflex training.

classical era period of management thought from 1880s to 1930s; early studies centered on the search for alternative ways to organize and structure the industrial organization and the ways to motivate people who work within the emerging organizational structures.

client/server technology a tool that enables the transfer and access of information from computer systems located within a company, its customers or suppliers, and its competition.

cognitive dissonance perceived inconsistency between beliefs and knowledge or between a belief and a behavioral tendency.

cognitive theories learning approaches that emphasize the internal mental processes involved in gaining new insights.

collaborating orientation a conflict-handling code that attempts to satisfy the concerns of both groups.

common enemy an organization's closest competitor which can often inspire teams that are in conflict to work together.

communication the transfer of information from one person to another.

communication dialoguing open exchange of views, beliefs, and, when appropriate, feelings, between individuals or groups; it implies hearing each other out and listening for understanding.

communication media the means by which messages are conveyed, such as conversation, computers, and body language.

communication network the flow, pattern, and pathway of signals or codes between two or more individuals.

competitive orientation a conflict-handling mode in which the groups attempt to achieve their own goals at the expense of the other through argument, authority, threat, or even physical force.

compromising orientation a conflict-handling mode that involves give-and-take from both groups.

computer-integrated manufacturing (CIM) the use of computer-aided design and computer-aided manufacturing to sequence and optimize a number of production processes.

computer networks the software, hardware, logistics, and connection between computers that allow and facilitate the conveyance of information (electronic impulses) between them.

conflict opposing thoughts, actions, or feelings.

conflict prevention through change programs managerial practices that take a preventive and coping strategy to increasing team effectiveness and eliminating conflict.

conflict handling mode methods of resolving or eliminating opposing thoughts, actions, or feelings.

consensus process a group process in which the ideas of all individuals are contributed and evaluated fully in arriving at a decision.

consideration a leadership behavior that creates mutual respect by focusing on group members' needs and desires.

content learning learning based on knowledge, facts, and theory, which serve as the database for analysis and reasoning.

content theories of motivation a cluster of theories that emphasize understanding reasons for motivated behavior or the specific factors that cause it.

contingency school decisions made or actions taken after considering all of the most relevant factors in a situation; in other words, management is situational.

continuous quality improvement (CQI) team see quality control circles

continuous improvement a non-stop effort and commitment to producing quality products.

cooperativeness the degree to which the group wants to satisfy the concerns of the other group.

craft technology technology characterized by limited task variety that is difficult to analyze.

creative process the development of anything new and currently nonexistent.

creativity an individual's ability to take bits and pieces of seemingly unrelated information and synthesize the pieces into new understanding or useful ideas.

creativity-relevant skills the abilities of an individual to break out of old ways of thinking.

cultural diversity individual differences in behavior, values, beliefs, and motivation based on cultural heritage.

cultural values personal beliefts (about such things as morality, worthiness, or beauty) that have been reinforced through lifelong learning.

culture a pattern of basic assumptions proved valid over time and taught to new group members as correct reacitons to certain problems and opportunities.

D

decoding the interpretation of encoded information once communicated and received.

demographic diversity individual differenecs based on characteristics such as gender, age, marital status, number of dependents, and tenure with a firm.

denial a defense mechanism in which the individual is not aware of his or her own needs or concerns and denies they exist.

design dimensions the elements that are considered in configuring an organization including information processing requirements, the roles and mechanisms that integrate the work, and management systems.

deviant an individual who refuses to conform to the group norms and is consequently rejected by members.

differentiation an aspect of the organization's internal environment created by job specialization and the division of labor.

directive leadership characterized by a leader who informs subordinates of what is expected of them, gives specific guidance as to what should be done, and shows how to do it.

dissatisfiers factors that Herzberg says psychologically do not necessarily motivate workers but cause dissatisfaction when not adequate.

distortion the misrepresentation of the meaning of a fact, feeling, or experience.

diversity individual differences in demographic and lifestyle characteristics, such as religion, age, disability status, military experience, sexual orientation, economic class, education, gender, race ethnicity and nationality.

domain-relevant skills abilities in the area that an individual must bring to the situation, such as specific academic discipline.

downsizing the planned elimination of positions or jobs.

dual ladders a career planning system in which a high-performing individual may choose to climb the managerial or technical ladder, depending on his or her own personal preferences and goals.

E

eclectic planned change approach an orientation to organizational change that pulls together the strengths of total quality management, (TOM), sociotechnical systems (STS), and reengineering.

effectiveness the ability to define goals and objectives then accomplish them. Efficiency, in contrast, pertains to the ratio of output to input.

emergent role system the activities, interactions, and attitudes that spontaneously develop as individuals strive to follow the organization script but also satisfy their own needs.

employee involvement the participation of employees in interactions with managers, in decision making, and problem solving.

employee stock ownership plans a type of profit-sharing plan wherein employees acquire company stock with the benefit of company subsidization.

encoding the forming of information to be communicated into codes or symbols that are meaningful to the sender, and, ideally, to the receiver.

engineering technology technology characterized by a wide variety of tasks that are relatively easy to analyze.

equifinality a principle that states there are many avenues to the same outcome, and not just one best way.

equity the premise that individuals want their efforts and performance to be judged fairly relative to other individuals.

expectancy a person's perceived probability that the level of the effort will lead to a desired level of performance.

expectancy effects the results or consequences of beliefs about one's abilities or performance.

expectation a judgment of the likely consequence that a behavior will produce.

experiential learning learning based on or from experience, such as interaction, involvement, or process learning.

F

fair conditioning system a continuous and open flow of communication in which fairness is an essential ingredient.

family group an intact, ongoing work team.

flexible work schedule work schedules that give employees the latitude and freedom to determine their own work hours.

form of structure the method of grouping employees together into work units, departments, and the total organization.

formal organization a script which includes the purpose and functional roles of the employees, the coordination of the interactions between the employees' roles and the nature of the different types of work to be performed, and the status accorded to the different work roles by the employees or public.

four life positions of personality development four perspectives on life that adults develop as a result of the treatment they received from the parents: 1) I'm not ok-you're ok; 2) I'm not ok-you're not ok; 3) I'm ok-you're not ok; and 4) I'm, ok-you're ok.

fractal organization an organizational form that has similar patterns of structure and characteristics at the top and bottom of the organization

frustration a psychological state arising when a barrier interferes with goal achievement.

fully integrated system an advanced manufacturing system which links the entire manufacturing function and all of its interfaces through extensive information networks.

G

GE's Work-Out Program conceived by GE CEO, Jack Welch; an open forum, typically helf off-site where employees vent problems, frustrations and ideas and eventually agree on actions. Purpose is to fuel a process of continuous improvement, to foster cultural transformation, and to improve business performances.

gender diversity a mixture of both men and women in organizations.

glass ceiling an invisible barrier that makes it difficult for certain groups, such as minorities and women, to move beyond a certain level in the organizational hierarchy.

grid organization development a six-phase model of change involving the entire organization.

group a set of three or more individuals that can identify itself and be identified by others in the organization as a entity.

group cohesiveness the attractiveness of the group to its members; the degree to which members desire to stay in the group.

group development the process by which a group adapts to internal and environmental forces.

group dynamics the patterns of behaviors of interacting members as a group develops and achieves goals.

group maturity a developmental state of a group that is inclusive of several attitudes and skills, such as the acceptance of individual differences, development of interpersonal relationships, and others, that indicate a highly functional group with wisdom about the group-decision process.

group problem-solving process the phases a group goes through in solving problems (can be either rational and/or intuitive).

group structure reference to certain psychologically shared properties of the group that result from the interaction of its members.

groupthink the mode of thinking when pressure toward conformity (concurrence seeking) becomes so dominant in a group that members override realistic appraisal of alternative courses of action.

groupware computer programs that allow for sharing information via computer networks.

H

hierarchy of needs Maslow's theory that psychological needs have a hierarchical interrelationship; those lower in the hierarchy (physiological needs) have to be satisfied before those in higher categories (safety, social, self-esteem, and self-actualization) become activated.

hidden agenda a purpose that the individual or group does not wish to reveal; the intent is to manipulate others so this purpose can be achieved.

high LPC relationship-oriented individuals who obtain satisfaction from working with others.

horizontal organization a type of design that is organized around processes and adoption of information technology.

human organization employees or "actors."

human relations school a classical management approach that viewed organizations as cooperative systems and not the product of mechanical engineering; early studies illustrated the importance of workers' attitudes and feelings.

human resource information system (HRIS) computerized databases comprised of detailed information about employees, which can be searched, and which cross-match when job openings occur.

hygiene factors characteristics of the workplace, such as company policies, working conditions, pay, and supervision that make a job more satisfying.

I

incremental innovation relatively gradual innovation as compared to radical innovation.

individual diversity differenes based on behavior, demographics, cultural background, personality, and ability or skills.

initiating structure a task-related leadership dimension covering a wide variety of behaviors including role definition and the guidance of subordinates toward attainment of work group goals.

information processing design approach a decisions-making process that includes choices about goals, tasks to be accomplished, technology to be adopted, ways to organize, and ways to integrate individuals into the organization.

information technology technologies dealing with computers, communications, user interfaces, storage, software, artificial intelligence, robotics, and manufacturing.

innovation a change in technology; a departure from the old way of doing things.

innovation process the implementation process of an idea new to the firm.

integration the degree to which differentiated work units work together and coordinate their efforts.

intergroup communication message transmission within a group.

internal background factors elements that relate to designing the formal organization such as 1) ownership, 2) acquisition and layout of physical facilities, 3) finances, 4) technology, 5) work design, and 6) work flow.

interpersonal communication message transmission between individuals.

interpersonal skills human or people skills; the ability to lead, motivate, and communicate effectively with others.

interteam/intergroup conflict opposing thoughts, feelings or actions between work units.

intervention method or technique for achieving change, which is targeted at the individual, group, or organizational level.

intragroup communication message transmissioin within a group.

intragroup conflict opposing thought, actions, or feelings between group members.

inventor of IT technology creators who seek opportunity through scientific breakthroughs and innovative use of state-of-the-art technology.

involvement learning see experimental learning.

J

job characteristics approach a work design approach combining management practice and psychological theory and moderated by the employee's need for growth. Describes a flow between job dimension, psychological states, and work outcomes.

job engineering a term synonymous with scientific management. Seeks one best way of performing a job, scientific methods of work performance, production, standards, rigid time frames, and motivation by monetary reward.

job enlargement increasing the variety of activities in a job to stimulate interest and reduce fatigue and monotony.

job rotation rotating among jobs to stimulate interest and reduce fatigue and monotony.

job sharing dividing a job between two or more employees.

Jung's theory of personality theory postulating that individuals have four basic preferences in the way they approach life: 1) introversion or extroversion; 2) intuition or sensory; 3) thinking or feeling; and 4) judging or perceiving.

K

kinesic behavior body motion, such as gestures, facial expression, eye behavior, and touching.

L

leadership the behavior of an individual when he or she is directing the activities of a group toward a shared goal.

leadership style an individual's expectation about how to use a leadership position to involve himself or herself and other people in the achievement of results.

lean production system an operation that strives to achieve the highest possible productivity and total quality cost effectively, by eliminating unnecessary steps in the production process and continually striving for improvement.

learning the process whereby new skills, knowledge, ability, and attitudes are created through the transformation of experience.

learning community classroom interactions shaped to create norms, values, and roles conducive to a supportive and stimulating learning climate.

least preferred co-worker description of an individual with whom a manager has worked least well.

left-brain mode of functioning processes of the left hemisphere of the brain which are logical, rational, and based upon analytical reasoning and causal relationships.

linked island system an advanced manufacturing system in which some cell systems are linked together to form production islands.

local area network (LAN) connections that allow the transmission of data or information among a group of machines and systems within a building or among buildings within a limited geographical area.

low LPC task-oriented individuals who obtain satisfaction from accomplishing tasks and generally enjoy achievement for its own sake.

M

macro organization design model an outgrowth of information processing theory where all design choices are driven by information technology and cultural variables.

management the process of working with people and resources to accomplish organizational goals.

management involvement the participation of managers in interactions with employees, decision-making and problem solving.

management science school a classical management approach that applied scientific methods to analyze and determine the "one best way" to complete production tasks.

managerial role the skills and knowledge necessary for a manager to accomplish duties and relate ito superiors, peers and subordinates.

managing diversity managing a culturally diverse work force by recognizing the characteristics common to specific groups of employees while dealing with such employees as individuals and supporting, nurturing, and utilizing their differences to the organization's advantage.

maintenance role a functional role that develops spontaneously and allows a group to develop constructive interpersonal relationships.

manufacturing technology an organizational level technology which includes traditional manufacturing processes and advanced manufacturing systems.

mentoring a formal or informal, one-to-one relationship that develops usually between an older and more experienced employee and a younger less experienced one in order to advise counsel or help the younger employee.

message what is communicated

modern era the current period of management thought; views organizations as systems composed of interrelated and interdependent components that function within an environmental context.

motivation psychological energy directed toward goals.

motivational potential score (MPS) a way of measuring the degree that the five core job dimensions—skill variety, task identity, task significance, automony, and feedback—are perceived in the work itself.

N

n achievement need for achievement; a need characterized by a strong orientation toward accomplishment and a high focus on success and goal attainment.

n power need for power; a need characterized by a desire to influence or control other people.

negative entropy the conscious changing of purpose, goals and practices to match emerging environmental demands.

neoclassical era a period of management from the 1930s to 1960s that posed a direct challenge to the classical schools; focused on the dimension of human interaction with the setting and other individuals in a group.

network organization an organizational form that blends traditional management concepts such as the value or management planning and controls with market concepts such as exchange agreement.

new product development teams (NPDT) small groups of workers that collectively have the knowledge and skills needed to facilitate the introduction of new products from conception to production.

nominal group technique a structured group problem-solving process in which individuals first write their ideas independently, discuss them for clarification, vote on them, discuss them again, and finally vote on them silently (nominal in the sense of being little more than a group by name alone).

nonroutine technology technology characterized by high task variety with a conversion process that is difficult to analyze.

nonverbal communication message transmission without the exchange of words, such as body language.

norms expectations shared by group members of how they ought to behave under a given set of circumstances.

O

organizational behavior (OB) 1) the study of the interactions of people as they carry out functional activities in organizations, 2) tools of analysis, applications, and skills development, including theories, concepts, models, and technologies. OB involves the application of the behavioral sciences (for example, sociology, social psychology, and social anthropology) to organizational activities. A "micro" approach starts with the focus on the individual and expands to interactions, groups, intergroup activities, and so on. A "macro" approach begins at the organizational level—or even the interorganizational, industrial, or institutional level—to improve understanding and the ability to predict and influence behavior. The emphasis is on improved effectiveness of individual, group, intergroup, and organizational activities.

off-line team work groups that do not operate on a daily basis, but take "time out" to periodically address workplace issues.

open system a perspective that expands the study of management to include the interaction between the organization and its environment.

operational research school a modern management approach that applies quantitative techniques, methods, and technologies to organizations and management issues.

operant conditioning an extension of classical conditioning that focuses on the process by which individuals learn voluntary behavior.

organization design work design at the organizational level; a decision process.

organizational change and development (OC&D) a program or organization diagnosis and intervention that addresses the norms seen as barriers to effective individual and organizational functioning.

organizational culture the pattern of basic assumptions that a given group has invented, discovered, or developed in learning to cope with problems of external adaptation and internal integration.

organizational development (OD) an effort planned, organization-wide, and managed from top down, to increase organizational effectiveness and health through planned interventions in the organization's processes using behavioral science knowledge.

organizational diagnosis an identification of the norms, procedures, and general climate of the organization.

P

PAC theory of personality theory in which the multiple nature of the human is perceived as ego states—parent, adult, child—that interact to direct the person's life and relationships with others.

P-L (Porter-Lawler) model an individual approach model of motivation that relates effort to performance.

paralanguage a type of nonverbal communication consisting of voice quality, volume, speech rate, pitch, nonfluencies (e.g., yaa, um, and ah), and laughing.

parallel learning structure a specific division and coordination of labor that operates in tandem with the formal hierarchy and structure and has the purpose of increasing the organization's learning.

part-time, temporary, and leased employees employees who work only part-time or on a non-permanent basis allowing managers to staff the workplace according to peaks and valleys in work demands, while driving down wage and benefit costs.

participative management an employee's involvement in decisions relevant to his or her work.

participative leadership a path-goal leadership style which emphasizes consultation with subordinates before decisions are made.

path-goal theory a theory that concerns how leaders influence subordinates' perceptions of their work goals and the paths they follow toward attainment of those goals.

perception patterns of meaning that come to the individual through the five senses.

perceptual process mental and cognitive processes that enable people to interpret and understand their surroundings.

personal growth the process of understanding personality and its influence in the interpersonal communications process, establishing personal goals, and developing the thinking and behavioral skills needed to achieve those goals.

personality the compilation of emotions, thoughts, background, and behavior that give a person his or her identity.

person-oriented creativity a perspective on creativity that studies patterns of personality traits and characteristics observed in individuals who exhibit creative behavior.

planned change an attempt to consciously and deliberately bring about change in the organization's status quo.

premature closure forming impressions on limited data, such as in stereotyping.

prescientific era period of management thought before the 1880s characterized by trial and error and includes practices of ancient Chinese, Greeks and Romans.

procedure-oriented IT technology systems that are used for repetitive tasks and processes such as ordering and billing.

process learning learning that arises from interacting or thinking; see experiential learning.

process-oriented creativity a perspective on creativity that examines the development of a new and valuable idea or product through the unique interaction of the individual with the available resources, settings, people, and situations.

process theories of motivation theories that attempt to understand and explain the elements that foster individual choices of behavior patterns and the forces that increase the likelihood the behaviors will repeat.

product innovation changes that affect the methods of producing output.

product-oriented approach a perspective on creativity that focuses on the production of novel and useful ideas by an individual or a small group of individuals working together.

profit-sharing plans benefit programs that link employee compensation with organization profits.

projection defense mechanism of interpreting the world or actions of others in terms of one's own needs and concerns; unawareness of one's needs is implied.

protean/spiral career self-directed employment in which employees focus on highly individualistic goals that are typically nontraditional.

proxemics a type of nonverbal communication comprised of the ways people use and perceive space (e.g., seating arrangements and conversational distance).

psychological contract the understanding between the worker and the organization in which each is aware of the other's expectations concerning important issues such as rights, privileges, obligations, etc.

pygmalion effect self-fulfilling beliefs that influence a favorable change in behavior.

Q

quality the set of processes supporting structural configurations and production method either in a manufacturing or service environment that economically produces goods or services that meet the customers' requirements.

quality control the means by which an individual, group, or organization verifies that it is producing goods and services commensurate with its goals.

quality control circles (QCC) a group of employees who meet periodically to study and solve job-related problems.

quality-circle see quality control circle.

quality improvement an effort and commitment to increasing the level of quality in goods and/or services.

quality planning a managerial process whose purpose is to provide the operating forces with the means of producing products that can meet customer's needs, such as invoices and sales contracts.

R

radical innovation innovation that leads to considerable change.

rational problem solving a methodical, systematic approach to a solution (described by some as left-hemisphere focus).

rationality based on logic and reason; contrast with irrationality, which emphasizes feelings, faith, emotions, impulses, and intuitions.

rationalization finding a good reason rather than the real reason for your action.

reengineering the fundamental rethinking and radical redesign of business processes to achieve dramatic improvements in critical contemporary measures of performance such as cost, quality, service, and speed.

reinforcement theories of motivation an approach that concentrates on behavior (rather than needs, for example) and the ability to change behavior by reward, avoidance, or punishment.

relationship behavior actions whereby a leader engages in two-way or multiway communication.

required system the behavioral requirements of the role an individual plays when performing the tasks of a specific work position, it can refer to the entire network of interacting roles that make up the total formal organization, but is frequently used synonymously with required a role system.

required role system the interlocking of the role behaviors of a specific position with those of one or more other roles in the basic work group to form a system.

right-brain mode of functioning processes of the right hemisphere of the brain which are intuitive and insightful, and holistic.

role behavior pattern of behavior an individual learns in order to perform tasks and relate to people while fulfilling the responsibilities of a given position.

role differentiation patterns of behavior that develop for individual group members, and are repeated as the activities of the group progress.

routine technology technology characterized by little task variety that is highly analyzable.

S

scientific management school an innovative concept of the early 1900s that emphasized developing efficiency through specialized and standardized work tasks.

script a set of requirements the individual must perform to complete tasks and interact with others.

self-design approach an approach to job design that encourages managers to plan and to implement their own strategy/structure and change programs.

self-efficacy a judgment of one's capability to accomplish a certain level of performance in a situation.

self-fulfilling prophecy beliefs that influence the direction of the outcome.

self-learning competency the capability to learn actively in a variety of situations.

self-managing teams see autonomous work teams

semantics word meanings; particularly various meanings for the same word

service quality quality within the service industry—with the goal being that of meeting or exceeding what the customer expects.

service technology an organizational level technology which includes such services as law firms, consulting firms, schools, airlines, hospitals, hotels, and amusement parks.

small group leadership an emergent role within groups that may include monitoring, taking action, and could be task- or maintenance- oriented.

social loafing an effect where total effort expended by a group is less than the sum of individual efforts.

situational leadership management whose direction is guided by its response to the existing conditions.

social intervention approaches workshops methods that are used to reduce conflict and promote collaboration between groups.

social learning learning new behavior by watching others in social situations and imitating their behavior.

social learning theories learning theories that integrate the behaviorist and cognitive approaches with the idea of imitating behaviors. Learning occurs when the individual tries the observed behavior and experiences a favorable result.

sociotechnical school a modern management approach that considers every organization to be made up of a social subsystem (the people) using tools, techniques, and knowledge (the technical subsystem) to produce a product or a service valued by the environmental subsystem.

sociotechnical system (STS) organizations are comprised of a social subsystem (people) and technical subsystems (machines, technology) and the environmental suprasystem. The goal is to optimize the "fit" among the systems to ensure organizational effectiveness.

sociotechnical systems design approach an approach to job design that attempts to redesign tasks to optimize operation of a new technology while preserving employee's interpersonal relationships and other human aspects of the work.

sociotechnical systems (STS) team autonomous work groups that integrate the requirements of social and technical systems.

special groups work groups that have a limited life span, such as start-up teams, special project teams and task forces.

stand-alone system an advanced manufacturing system typically consisting of robots and/or numeric control machine tools.

statistical process control (SPC) the application of sampling theory to production processes in order to detect malfunctions faster than is possible with final inspection.

strategic intention what a group attempts to accomplish in satisfying their own and others' goals.

structuralist school a classical management approach led by Max Weber; focused on the basic tenets of the ideal type of organization, the bureaucratic model, as the most effective way to organize and manage organizations.

structural support configuration a multi-layered structuee that functions parallel to the formal organization.

steady state maintaining the operations of a system within the limits of tolerance related to its targets.

stereotypes beliefs assumed to apply to a particular group.

strategic organization design a decision-making process that focuses on customers, changing market needs, and desired outcomes.

superordinate goals primary goals of an organization or competing groups that exceed those of individuals or subgroups.

synergy a group solution or decision in which the total effect is greater than the sum of the individual inputs, or 2 + 2 = 5.

system a regularly interacting or interdependent group of activities or objects that forms a whole. Dynamics are involved in that a change in one aspect an effect change in other aspects.

system boundary a physical, temporal, social or psychological border that separates one system from another.

system-maintaining innovation (SMI) new ideas that enhance or improve some aspect of the business without changing the overall nature of how the organization operates.

systems 1 to 4 an electric organization development approach that relies on survey information gathering and stresses the importance of management's support of the individual.

systems school a modern management approach anchored in general system theory, views the organization as a system composed of subsystems or subunits that are mutually dependent on one another and that continuously interact.

system-transforming innovation (STI) new ideas that affect the fundamental aspects of the organization.

T

task behavior actions whereby a leader engages in spelling out duties and responsibilities of an individual or group.

task motivation an individual's natural inclination either toward or away from a task.

task role a functional role assumed spontaneously that helps a group to define, clarify, and pursue a common goal.

team a small number of people with complementary skills who are committed to a common purpose, set of performance goals, and approach for which they hold themselves mutually accountable.

team building a process for helping a team diagnose its problems and become a more effective working unit.

team effectiveness the performance and viability of a work team. Performance is the acceptability of output to customer within and outside the organization. Viability refers to team members' satisfaction and continued willingness to contribute.

team management a style of management in which each person in the nonsupervisory structure must be a member of an effective work group and must be skilled in both leadership and membership functions and roles.

team style a method of operation that a work group develops over time.

technological complexity the extent of mechanization of the manufacturing process.

technology the tools, techniques, methods, devices, configurations, knowledge, procedures, and actions used by organizational members to acquire inputs, to transform inputs into outputs, and to provide outputs in terms of products or services to customers.

tool-oriented IT system a technology system designed to help people communicate and make decisions at all levels of the firm comprised of end user software products ranging from spreadsheets word processing, and e-mail etc.

total quality control an effective system for integrating the quality development, quality maintenance, and quality improvement efforts of various groups in an organization so as to enable production and service at ten most economic levels which allow for full customer satisfaction.

Total Quality Management (TQM) an integrative approach to management that supports the attainment of customer satisfaction through a wide variety of tools and techniques that result in high quality goods and services.

total quality management (TQM) team supplemental groups that coexist alongside the formal organization and draw on organizational resources, skills, and knowledge to make improvements.

traits and skills theory an approach that focuses on individual leaders and attempts to determine the personal characteristics and abilities that great leaders share.

transactional analysis the use of the PAC concepts and the four life positions to describe and analyze transactions or exchanges between people.

transformation process the conversion of materials and energy from the environment into outputs.

transformational leadership the process of influencing major changes in the attitudes and assumptions of the organization's members and building commitment for the organization's mission or objectives.

Z

zero defects a goal of achieving no manufacturing flaws.

Index

D

H

N

Q